BUSINESS STUDIES

John Birchall • Graham Morris

Nelson

Thomas Nelson and Sons Ltd
Nelson House Mayfield Road
Walton-on-Thames Surrey
KT12 5PL UK

Nelson Blackie
Wester Cleddens Road
Bishopbriggs
Glasgow
G64 2NZ

Thomas Nelson Australia
102 Dodds Street
South Melbourne
Victoria 3205 Australia

Nelson Canada
1120 Birchmont Road
Scarborough Ontario
MIK 5G4 Canada

First published by Thomas Nelson and Sons Ltd 1995
I(T)P Thomas Nelson is an International Thomson Publishing Company
I(T)P is used under licence

ISBN 0-17-448219-1
NPN 9 8 7 6 5 4 3 2 1

Printed in Spain

Preface

We hope that this textbook helps you understand the complexities of Business Studies. Like many books this one began life as a reaction to our inability to find a suitable text for our own students. Alas, all we could recommend were 'Revision Guides', or books that gave insufficient attention to important areas of the syllabus.

What has emerged is the first real attempt to provide a text that illustrates the level to which Business Studies has now risen. It is no longer the new subject on the curriculum, but is now firmly established in most schools, colleges and universities.

We have deliberately concentrated on providing in-depth coverage of all the syllabus items that students find testing. As such the text covers all the current syllabuses available for A-levels and Advanced GNVQ Business. Those studying for a degree or HND will find the questions, activities, and case studies of considerable assistance in their studies.

To help readers appreciate the integrated and complex nature of Business Studies we have traced the development of a 'high-tech' company. This should enable readers to appreciate how the theory and the reality of the commercial world relate.

We would like to thank Matthew Tyler, our publishers, editors and advisers, and all members of our respective families for their patience and understanding as a book of this length and complexity evolved.

Dedicated to Sue, Patricia, Sally, Clare, Jeremy, Timothy, Anya and our parents.

John Birchall
Graham Morris

Acknowledgements

The authors and publishers wish to thank the following for permission to reproduce photographs:

Page 20: Tony Stone (bottom left, bottom centre, bottom right)
Page 23: Tony Stone (top right); Barnaby's (right centre); Greg Evans (bottom right)
Page 47: Greg Evans (top)
Page 49: Barnaby's (bottom)
Page 71: Greg Evans (bottom left)
Page 105: Greg Evans (top left)
Page 238: Greg Evans (bottom)
Page 252: J Allan Cash (top left, left centre, bottom left)
Page 260: Tony Stone (bottom)
Page 270: J Allan Cash (bottom right)
Page 274: Greg Evans (top left)
Page 275: Tony Stone (right centre)
Page 359: Greg Evans (top right)
Page 433: Tony Stone (bottom left)

The authors and publishers are grateful to the following for permission to reproduce copyright material:

The Associated Examining Board for examination questions on pages 27–28, 41–42, 67–68, 87, 95, 118, 151, 153, 163–64, 194, 212, 224, 235–36, 266, 276, 306, 353;
The Times for material on page 7;
The Daily Telegraph for material on page 19;
Fortune magazine for material on page 22;
PT Barito Pacific Timber for material on page 58;
UBS Limited for material on page 59;
The Horsham Corporation and Société Quebecoise d'assainissement des eaux for material on page 60;
Lloyd's Bank International Factors for material on page 64;
The Independent for material on pages 163 and 235;
The Quarterly Review of Marketing for material on page 236;
Longman UK for an extract from *Organisational Behaviour* by J.G. Duncan, 1981, on page 288;
The British Psychological Society for an extract from the *Bulletin of the British Psychological Society*, 1983, on page 364.

If any acknowledgement has been inadvertently omitted, this will be rectified at the earliest possible opportunity.

Contents

Part 3   The Management of the Product

A. Marketing

1
What is business?

Preview

▽ In this first chapter, a comprehensive definition of a business will be developed, and a selection of important business terms introduced and explained. The range of inter-relating groups, both internal and external to the company, which make up the business world will be discussed. Special emphasis will be placed on the interplay of the government with business.

Definitions of a business

What is a business? What does it do and why does it do it? These are common questions which are difficult to answer. Read on, and you will develop the skills to enable you to give your own answers.

Businesses are organisations dedicated to the provision of goods and services. They operate among other organisations, sometimes in association with them and sometimes in competition. All require customers to buy the goods or services produced. Businesses must relate to their environments at local, national and international levels. All organisations have to make decisions, and a major theme of Business Studies is the development of the skills needed to make sensible, successful decisions – *fast*!

A first definition of a business:

A business is a decision-making organisation dedicated to the production and sale of goods or services.

What does a business do? In its simplest form it takes resources, blends them together to produce a product and then sells it. This product may be a good, like a CD player, or a service, like the insurance policy which covers the player. The resources used, the *factors of production*, can be summarised as *land*, *labour*, *capital* and *enterprise*.

Land

This input can be considered as *natural resources*.

Natural resources include the land itself, but also the seas and oceans. They cover all the raw materials available from the air, land and water surfaces, and from beneath these surfaces.

The reward for land being used is called *rent*, and is expressed as a sum of money per unit space per unit time. Rents change with time and reflect changes in demand for land and the supply of it.

Natural resources are sold by quantity.

Labour

Most businesses *employ* people to work for them. This work may be physical, as in the case of a building labourer, or mental, as in the case of an accountant. Most occupations require a mixture of both.

Employees may be paid a wage, a salary or a fee for their work (see Chapter 34).

Wages are paid for each hour worked, and workers are usually employed by the week. Overtime is paid at premium rates for working extra approved hours. One or perhaps two weeks' notice is all that is necessary to end the employment of wage earners.

Salaries are paid monthly. Salaried staff are usually employed by the month, and may have to be given three months' notice to terminate their employment. Overtime is rarely paid, even though hours are often irregular and long. The salaried employee has greater job security than an hourly-paid worker.

Some professional people, like architects and solicitors, are paid a *fee* when they undertake a specific job, the size of the fee reflecting the time and expertise required in its completion.

In today's very competitive and cost-conscious world many previously salaried 'permanent' jobs have been 'contracted out' and replaced by fee earning, or contract staff.

Some examples of the differences between wages and salaries for different occupations in the UK are shown in Figure 1.1.

How basic salaries vary across the UK

REGION	HIGHER MANAGERS £ a year	MIDDLE MANAGEMENT		JUNIOR MANAGERS £ a year	SENIOR STAFF £ a year
		UPPER £ a year	LOWER £ a year		
London	38,390	31.827	25,296	20,525	16,030
Scotland	36,050	28,400	22,715	18,642	14,321
South-East	33.207	26,897	21,930	18,289	14,762
South-West	30,276	24,823	21,100	16,961	14,062
West Midlands	31,302	24,394	20,492	16,343	13,000
North-West	29,200	25,250	20,004	16,877	13,284
N. Ireland	31,120	23,575	19,309	16,755	13,853
East England	29,863	24,720	19,870	16,500	13,334
North-East	29,945	24,223	19,778	16,478	13,545
UK overall	32,055	26,000	21,378	17,500	14,063

Figure 1.1 How basic salaries vary across the UK and by occupational level

Capital

Capital is the money invested by the owners to set up and run the business. It is used to buy land and labour, as well as to pay bills for any materials bought. Capital is also needed to cover the business until the final product is sold and cash brought in. There are different types of capital used in firms, but these will be discussed later (see Chapter 5).

The cost of capital is *interest*. If a firm borrows money it has to pay interest to the lender. If it spends money it has in the bank it will lose the interest it was being paid. This is the *opportunity cost* of spending the money, and is the 'next best alternative' to actually spending it. Firms need to know how best to exercise their choices, since every choice has an opportunity cost.

Enterprise

All businesses need more than money, labour and land to succeed. They have to be started using someone's *ideas,* and somebody has to take a *risk* with his

or her personal capital. This person is known as the *entrepreneur.* The entrepreneur sees an opportunity, develops it, and turns it into a thriving business. The reward for the entrepreneur is *profit.*

The proportion of factors used in a business depends on what the business does, and how it chooses to do it. For example, a firm may decide to use modern computer-controlled machines operated by a few highly qualified people, or employ a large work force to do the job 'by hand'. The decision will depend on the availability of skilled labour, the amount of capital available, and the intentions of the owner. Some trades are *labour intensive*, like the garment industry, and others are *capital intensive*, like the automotive and aerospace industries. This has implications for the operation of the business – but more of this later (see Chapter 6).

Thus the definition of a business can be expanded:

A business is a decision-making organisation that uses a blend of land, labour, capital and enterprise to produce and sell goods or services.

Why do firms and businesses exist at all? What are they for? What are their objectives?

Businesses may have different objectives. For many, particularly those privately-owned, profit seems to be most important. For others, particularly those owned by the government, the provision of a service at prices that the user can afford is the objective, e.g. subsidised council housing, or the National Health Service. Some businesses, regardless of ownership, may provide employment. Sometimes the objective may be personal, particularly where the owner is a private individual. In other instances the objective is to provide aid in situations of real disaster or need. This is the objective of charities.

A picture should be developing now of a unit consisting of firms, customers and government working together. This unit is called an *economy*, and is usually viewed in the context of a particular state or country. The role of government is critical. Its fundamental functions are to make laws and regulations to control businesses and individuals, and to protect the consumers from exploitation. It also has to provide some goods and services which private firms could not or would not provide. Examples include defence, fire services, street lighting and the police. The government also provides other services at low prices or free of charge, such as education and public transport. In addition, the government tries to provide favourable conditions for business and industry to operate in, and attempts to promote a fair distribution of wealth through taxes. Finally, the government is responsible for relations with other countries.

Governments have another role within an economy, which has a direct bearing on business and industry. They are customers in their own right. They buy the products from businesses in a whole range of industries. They are virtually the sole cus-

tomer for some industries and businesses. In the UK, for instance, some shipyards once specialised solely in the construction of warships for national use. Firms that supply schools might also fall into this category: about 93% of all schools in England are owned by the state. Look at Case Study 1.1.

CASE STUDY 1.1

The government as customer and employer

It is generally believed that the UK, particularly under a Conservative government, favours private companies, *a free market*, and the minimum of State control and intervention. One would expect government spending to be low, and at least a small proportion of the total expenditure. (We call this total expenditure, or income for a country the *national expenditure*, or more frequently the *gross domestic product*, or GDP.) Is this so?

At a *Budget* presentation by the Chancellor of the Exchequer, the government's spending proposals for the year were described. He presented the following forecasts:

UK government expenditure proposals (£ billions) (1985 Prices)	
Health	14.4
Social Security	35.9
Defence	14.0
Education and science	4.2
Local government	13.1
Home Office	3.2
Transport	3.0
Local authority spending	9.4
Employment	2.4
Housing	4.4
Others	24.1
SUB-TOTAL	128.1
Gross debt interest	11.2
Adjustment	2.4
TOTAL	141.7
Capital expenditure	5.5

The total seems a very large sum of money!

At the same time, forecasts were made of the total spending that would be made over the same period by all the various groups in the economy, private as well as state. This amounted to £ 336.3 billions.

Analysis of forecast national spending expressed as part of gross domestic product, or GDP, units – £ billions, 1985 prices	
Consumers' expenditure	255.7
General government expenditure (revenue)	76.6
Gross investment - state and private	74.2
Stock change	1.9
Exports of goods and services	111.2
Imports of goods and services	126.9
Expenditure taxes, less subsidies	56.4
GDP at factor cost	336.3

(GDP is simply a measure of the size of an economy for a particular period. There will be more on this, and other measures for the same thing later.)

Analysis of the government's plans reveals that its major item of expenditure, overall, is '*wages and salaries*'. It is the largest employer of people in the UK! (Just think of who owns and employs the defence forces, the police and the staff of the National Health Service.) In parts of London the government is virtually the only employer of staff, i.e. Whitehall. There have been steps to take some government activity out of London in an attempt to *decentralise* employment potential to the regions, e.g. Driving and Motor Vehicle

Licences to South Wales, part of the Inland Revenue to Scotland, and Social Security to Newcastle, with the Department for Education.' Some data is given below.

Structure of employment: Britain, 1990
(% of employees)

Public administration and defence	7
Education and health services	15
SUB TOTAL	22
Manufacturing	23
Other	55
TOTAL	100

Total number employed 22.8 million.

Questions and activities

1. Define the terms in italics in the case study.
2. Approximately what percentage of GDP is generated, or accounted for by the government.
3. What might happen to the level of GDP, the amount of unemployment, and the level of activity in private businesses if the government was to reduce its total spending by a uniform 20%?
4. What might be the immediate effects of the cutback in defence spending after the end of the Cold War on (a) the finances of the government and (b) the economy as a whole? Is there anything that can be done about this effect?

It should now be clear that Business Studies involves the study of various interacting groups, some internal to a business and others external to it. Four groups have been encountered – *firms, customers, employees* and *government*. An action by one group will inevitably affect, and interact with at least one other group. There will often be conflicts of interest between the different groups. The most important groups both internal and external to the firm are now listed.

The internal groups

Shareholders

Shareholders own the firm. Each share represents a portion of the business. The owner is entitled to a share of the future profits of the business concerned. The shareholder receives an annual fee, or *dividend*, for investing this money. Dividends are rather like interest, and increase and decrease with the profitability of the firm. Many shareholders own shares purely to get this annual income. Others, particularly those with large holdings of shares, may want to attempt to control the operation of the business.

Shares in many firms are bought and sold on the London Stock Exchange. These are second-hand shares, i.e. ones already sold by the firms themselves and now owned by individuals or other companies. The money paid for these shares does not go to the business, only to the previous owner of the shares. Prices of shares change very often, and are published each day in such papers as the *Financial Times*. It is also highlighted on the radio and TV, with regular broadcasting of the *FT-SE 100 index*, the price index for the 100 representative firms monitored by the *Financial Times* and the London Stock Exchange.

Share prices are very volatile (see Chapter 15). Examine Case Study 1.2. Note how the method of presentation can have a marked effect on the impact of the data.

CASE STUDY 1.2

Share price movements

The prices of shares change very often or, in financial language, are very volatile. Weekly comparisons can be quite revealing. Examine the two reports shown on the next page, reproduced from consecutive weeks of *The Sunday Times*, then tackle the questions and tasks that follow.

THE SUNDAY TIMES
30 APRIL 1995

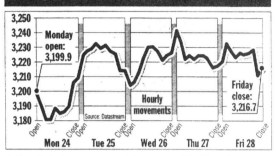

FT-SE 100 index

Monday open: 3,199.9

Friday close: 3,216.7

Hourly movements

Source: Datastream

Mon 24   Tue 25   Wed 26   Thu 27   Fri 28

- New York: Dow Jones ended the week at 4321.27, up 51.18
- Tokyo: Nikkei ended the week at 16,806.75, down 161.49

Major share movements

RISERS	Friday close	Change on week %	1995 high	1995 low	Reason for change
National Express	365	+15%	365	289	Completes bus deal
DFS Furniture	280	+14%	280	238	30% advance in profits
HTV Group	188½	+12%	188½	132	Cross-media ownership
Body Shop	180	+11%	194	155	Ahead of figures
Amstrad	199	+8%	199	127½	Expected new orders
Fisons	188	+5%	188	103	Zeneca bid hopes
FALLERS					
Cray Electronics	73	−53%	170	71	Profit warning
Bespak	255	−16%	333	238	Profit warning
Betterware	42½	−11%	52	38½	Slump in profits
Delian Lloyd's	79	−6%	98	78	Lloyd's fall-out
Carpetright	255	−6%	278	235	Profit-taking
Chesterton	64	−5%	88	64	Sector gloom

Top 100 companies

	Stock	Price	Change on wk	1995 high	1995 low	Yield	P/E	Mkt cap (£m)
1	Glaxo	734½	+ 18½	741	587	4.8	16.8	25,501
2	BP	447½	− 3½	459	392	2.9	15.9	24,688
3	Shell Transport	736½	+ 7½	750	687	4.6	*	24,415
4	BT	388½	− 5½	411½	364½	5.5	16.1	24,223
5	HSBC	732½	− 17½	756½	589	4.6	9.2	18,790
6	BAT Industries	469	+ 13	478	405	5.8	14.1	14,464
7	British Gas	301½	− 6	317½	280½	6.2	32.2	13,175
8	SmithKline Beecham	491½	− ½	532	444	3.4	14.5	13,015
9	Hanson	236¼	+ ¾	248½	228	6.3	14.7	12,235

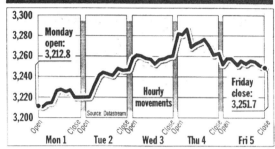

THE SUNDAY TIMES
7 MAY 1995

FT-SE 100 index

Monday open: 3,212.8

Friday close: 3,251.7

Hourly movements

Source: Datastream

Mon 1   Tue 2   Wed 3   Thu 4   Fri 5

- New York: Dow Jones ended the week at 4,343.40, up 22.13
- Tokyo: Nikkei ended the week at 17,088.66, up 281.91

Major share movements

RISERS	Friday close	Change on week %	1995 high	1995 low	Reason for change
Henlys Group	391	+20%	391	258	Coach acquisition
The Sage Group	945	+14%	945	662	Bumper results
WEW Group	34	+13%	34	24	Analysts' visit
Angerstein	85	+10%	91	76	Speculative buying
Asprey	84	+8%	140	65	Cost cuts
British Airways	419	+5%	423	348	Broker's profit upgrade
FALLERS					
Tibbett & Britten	518	−21%	713	500	Profit warning
Body Shop	149	−17%	194	144	Growth prospects few
Automated Security	50	−15%	74	43	Institutional selling
RJB Mining	404	−5%	431	317	Broker's sell note
Rugby Group	115	−4%	123	104	Downgrades work load
Badgerline Group	144	−3%	155	130	Profit-taking

Top 100 companies

	Stock	Price	Change on wk	1995 high	1995 low	Yield	P/E	Mkt cap (£m)
1	Glaxo Wellcome	732	− 2½	749	587	4.8	16.8	25,415
2	BP	455½	+ 8	461½	392	2.9	16.1	25,129
3	Shell Transport	758	+ 21½	758	687	4.5	16.9	25,127
4	BT	399	+ 10½	411½	364½	5.4	16.5	25,017
5	HSBC	747	+ 14½	756½	589	4.5	9.4	19,186
6	BAT Industries	474	+ 5	487	405	5.8	14.2	14,622
7	British Gas	303½	+ 2	317½	280½	6.1	32.4	13,263
8	SmithKline Beecham	502	+ 10½	532	444	3.3	14.8	13,199
9	Hanson	237	+ ¾	248½	228	6.3	14.8	12,274

Questions and activities

1. The presentation of data is an important aspect of Business Studies. In the business world the selection of the correct, or most appropriate method to support the case being put forward is critical. As a first exercise, look at the two graphs showing the FT-SE 100 index changing with time, and try to draw some conclusions. Then plot the data for the two weeks on a single set of axes. Does this change your conclusions? What might have happened over the weekend when the Stock Exchange in London is closed?

2. Examine the table called 'Major share movements'. Is there any pattern in the 'reason for change' for both the 'risers' and the 'fallers'?

3. Examine the tables of the 'Top 100' companies. Take the top six companies and work out for each the percentage difference between their highest and lowest share prices in 1995. Can you draw any conclusions from this analysis? Would you consider that it is the market change as a whole which is the major force, or events happening in the company itself?

Shareholders normally fall into three groups:

1. *Institutional shareholders* These are usually companies which have bought shares for an income. They are often banks or pension funds and, because of their share holding, often have a *director* on the Board. They can influence, therefore, the workings of the firm.

2. *Private shareholders* Shares are owned by individuals, not companies. They have no direct representation on the board. They have little or no say in day-to-day operations of the company. They are relatively powerless.

3. *Worker shareholders* Worker shareholders are a recent development, at least in this country. The aim of such holdings is to improve communications between the groups, and avoid potential conflict. This introduces another key aspect of Business Studies, namely *communication*, of which much will be said later (see Chapter 39).

All these groups are shareholders, but a difference in real power is evident. Conflicts of interest can easily develop. For example, a pensioner with say £100 in shares has virtually no power in relation to an insurance company which may have £10 million invested in shares of the same company. The company is run 'democratically' – one share, one vote.

Directors

Directors are employed by the shareholders to direct the firm's operation and look after their interests. A group of directors is called a *Board*, and it is controlled by the Chairman. They are paid fees for their services. Some directors are also employees of the firm, and receive a salary for this work, in addition to the director's fees.

The main function of the Board of Directors, is to ensure the survival and success of the company. They must ensure that all legal requirements are complied with. In addition they appoint the senior managers of the company, decide on the raising and spending of capital, and the distribution of profit. It is the latter decisions that often get publicity, e.g.: Company Y cannot pay an interim dividend. Company Z is pleased to inform shareholders of a record dividend of 25p per share.

A firm's most senior director and manager is the Managing Director, or its Chief Executive Officer. (CEO).

The other directors fall into two groups.

Executive directors

Executive directors sit on the Board as representatives of the owners, but are also employed to work within the firm and act as managers. The Board of Directors as a whole will decide on policy and will set the direction in which the firm is planned to go. The Executive Directors now in their management role, have the responsibility for turning this strategy into tactical plans, and issue the necessary instructions. They will also be expected to report on progress towards the firm's goals. They will be very senior managers and paid employees of the firm, and they will be involved in both the making and execution of policy. They are in a position, potentially, to 'mark their own homework', with all the risks that this involves.

A further complication often arises. Directors of firms often have shares in the company. They are then both representatives of the owners, part owners of the same firm, and in a position to influence its progress and performance – another clear situation where there is a danger of conflict of interests.

Non-executive directors

Non-executive directors are advisors only and not employees of the firm. They may have been put there, however, by a major shareholder with the objective of protecting the interests of that particular power group. Sometimes they are selected for their contacts. Moreover, non-executive directors often sit on the Boards of more than one company, so confidentiality may be a problem.

Workers

Anyone working for a firm, other than the directors, is a worker.

Managers

Managers are often considered as being between the workers and the directors. They are charged with taking the strategic instructions from the Board and converting them into detailed, tactical orders. They have to ensure that the orders are followed, and the desired progress made.

These internal groups are responsible for developing the product or service of the company. They may be directly involved in the provision of this, or may provide a service. This leads to two further subdivisions of the internal groups.

Line (functional) groups

Line, or functional groups are those directly involved with the 'product' of the company. Traditionally, they include production, sales, marketing, engineering, etc. They are employed in work directly related to the products or services of the company.

Staff groups

Staff groups are essentially the support or checking operatives. Typically, you would find personnel, accounts, planning, finance, etc., here.

The organisation of groups is illustrated in Figure 1.2. A conflict of interest may arise between a worker who owns shares and his desire to have a certain level of wages. Directors are often shareholders of the

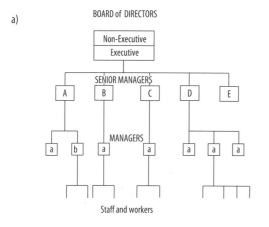

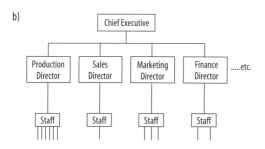

Figure 1.2 *Examples of types of organisation*

company that employs them.

The definition of a business can be refined once again:

A business is a decision-making organisation , made up of groups of workers, managers, directors and shareholders, that uses a blend of land, labour, capital and enterprise to produce and sell goods or services.

Businesses do not exist in isolation. They have to interact with a number of external groups in order to survive.

The external groups

Customers

Customers are those people or firms who buy the products or services concerned. They may use, or consume the product, or resell it to other customers. Thus the customers of a supermarket will be the general public. The corner shop is the customer of a wholesaler. The wholesaler is the customer of the manufacturer of the goods.

Suppliers

Firms need many goods and services from many other companies in order to produce their own products. They buy raw materials, packing materials, spare parts for machinery, lubricants, stationery, from suppliers.

They also need services. These might include transport, architects, solicitors and barristers, consultants, secretarial agencies, and catering services.

Competitors

Firms that supply similar goods and services are in competition with each other. These businesses may be within the country of the firm or may be overseas. The market for goods or services is effectively shared with the competition, but each firm will usually aim to get as large a share as it possibly can.

Note, if firms start to work together in a market, or *collude* as it is called, they are acting illegally.

The locality where the firm operates

A firm is part of the environment in which it operates. It is part of the local community, and has responsibilities to the people, the environment, and to the local authority. The local authority, in turn, has a responsibility to the firms in its area. It should, for example, provide good roads, street lighting and make public health provisions.

The government

Firms have to operate in an economy, which is regulated by a government. They have to obey the laws, particularly those related to businesses, health and safety at work, consumer protection, and taxation.

The nature of the government can also have a profound effect on the type of firm to be found in an economy. The majority of countries nowadays operate with a mix of private companies, state enterprise and government control. This is called a *mixed economy*. Two other forms of economy exist – at least in theory: *command* and *free market* economies.

In a command economy, all significant output and production decisions are made by the state through a central planning organisation. There are no workings of the market, as prices are fixed by the state, and no competition as only one version of a product is provided. Marketing in this type of economy is reduced to distribution of the goods. Profit is not a motive for business, as all businesses are owned by the state.

In a free market economy the government does no more than set and administer the basic laws and regulations. The force of the market rules, and it becomes the survival of the fittest. Little is done by the government to help the sick or the poor, all services needed being provided by private firms or the family.

The environment as a whole

Firms have a responsibility not to pollute the air, water or ground. They are now being forced into looking much further forward when they make decisions.

External groups are illustrated in Figure 1.3, which shows the interrelated nature of an economy.

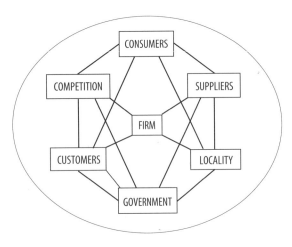

Figure 1.3 The firm in its environment

The definition of a business can be refined once more:

A business is a decision-making organisation, which exists in association with customers, suppliers, competitors, the environment, and the government, and is made up of groups of workers, managers, directors and shareholders, that uses a blend of land, labour, capital and enterprise, to produce and sell goods or services.

Internal and external groups exist independently and are sometimes isolated from each other. They do, however, have to work together. The interactions are either internal to the firm, or external.

Internal interactions

Workers look to the managers and directors for leadership. They also expect planning to be done to ensure the survival and growth of the firm. They expect continuing employment, fair and reasonable reward for the work done, and an improvement in their living standards. They also want to be consulted and listened to, as they are part of the whole organisation. Some want to be part of the decision-making process and become worker directors.

At the other extreme shareholders expect the company to be run profitably and with their interests in mind. They have appointed the directors to do just this.

However, high dividends to shareholders usually mean low salaries and wages for employees.

Consider the following familiar types of newspaper headlines, and the problems that they may cause:

- 'Utilities bosses give themselves 100% pay rises,'
- 'Managers' salaries rise at a rate of 12%, but wages rise by only 4%,'
- 'Company X, after making a loss of £12 million last year, is to shut its Northern factory and make 2,000 workers redundant. Final dividend of 15p agreed.'

Managers and directors tend to be caught in the middle, for they cannot satisfy everyone's interests, and not for all of the time! As shown earlier, directors can be in a very dangerous position, with the potential for conflict in all directions. The shareholders have different objectives from those of the workers and other groups. Consider the example of the takeover of Rover by BMW. Rover is British but

BMW is German. Will BMW look after the interests of **all** the internal groups?

External links and dependencies

The firm needs customers. It draws its workers from the local community. The local authority has to raise revenue from these people to pay for the services expected – schools, police, fire service, refuse collection, sports centres and swimming pools. If the local people do not have jobs, then there are fewer people to tax. This is another example of interdependency. It is thus in the interest of the local authorities for firms in their areas to be successful. Consider the advantages that the local authorities in Sunderland, Swindon and Derby were able to offer to Nissan, Honda and Toyota, and the benefits to all parties in these areas.

Examine and work through Case Study 1.3.

CASE STUDY 1.3

The government and international industry

There has been a steady flow recently of Japanese firms coming to the UK to set up factories. Nissan have a large factory operating in Newcastle, Toyota and Honda are soon to open their car plants in Derby and Swindon respectively. Sony and Hitachi already assemble TVs, videos and other audio-visual equipment in Wales. Unlike the earlier *assembly operations*, when virtually all parts were made overseas, these new ventures are using large quantities of *locally sourced materials*. Some European firms are being attracted to these booming industrial centres by this demand for components, e.g. Bosch from Germany. Others are forming *joint ventures* with domestic UK firms.

These Japanese firms came to Europe because they had to! The 1992 developments of the *Single European Market,* where all barriers to free trade within the European Union (EU) countries – Germany, France, Italy, Belgium, Luxemburg, the Netherlands, the United Kingdom, Ireland, Denmark, Greece, Spain and Portugal – were being removed, but expensive, common import taxes, or *tariffs* were being imposed. This means that the traditionally imported cars and TVs, etc., would become far too expensive for UK consumers. Inside the tariff barriers, these firms become as European as Rover, Mercedes, Phillips and Siemens – at least as far as their products are concerned.

Why come to the UK, rather than any other country? The UK had a ready supply of skilled engineering labour due to the decline of its traditional industries – steel-making, shipbuilding and, ironically, car-building. The land was also available, or was made available by the local authorities, some of which took positive action to attract these large businesses to their areas. The necessary planning approvals went through very quickly. On balance, there resulted a good investment for both the new companies and the UK economy.

Questions and activities

1. Define the terms and expressions in italics above.
2. Carry out a survey in your home of all the electrical goods you have. Identify, as far as possible, where they were made. Prepare a report, and be prepared to present it to your class.
3. Examine the case study and consider how the groups you have studied so far stand to gain or lose from the entry of these Japanese firms into the UK.

Firms need materials and services to operate, and the companies which provide these will tend to develop locally. As the firm becomes successful it will want to expand. It may need land as well as new or expanded buildings. The authority can help by granting the necessary licences and approvals speedily and efficiently. The workers and managers require shops, restaurants, cinemas, clubs, etc. as well as schools, clinics and libraries. Again the local authority will be involved. Obviously their collective success depends on the level of activity of the firms. The benefit that the firms bring is 'multiplied' throughout the whole local area.

On a larger scale, the government of the country needs the firms, the employees, the shareholders and customers to pay tax to fund all the services provided by central government as opposed to the local council. These include defence, public transport such as British Rail, universities, hospitals and the whole of the National Health Service. The major taxes paid by companies and individuals include the following.

Income tax

Income tax is levied on earned income. It is also charged on dividends and interest received. Income tax is a progressive tax in most countries. The amount to be paid is proportional to the income earned. The tax structure in the UK for 1994/95 is shown in Table 1.1.

Table 1.1
UK Income Tax Rates – 1994/95

Taxable income	Rate	Cumulative tax
£1 - £3,200	20%	£600
£3,201 - £24,300	25%	£5,775
£24,300 upwards	40%	

Notes: 1. Personal allowances (under 65): single individual, £3,545; married couple £1,720.

2. Employees are taxed on company cars and other 'benefits in kind' such as health insurance. Employees may get relief on interest payments for houses, but these are strictly limited. Pension payments (private schemes) are also tax free, subject to limits.

Corporation tax

This is charged by the government on the profits made by companies.

Value added tax

Value added tax – VAT – is charged on the sale of goods and services, at all the stages of production. In the publishing business, tax is paid on the sale of wood to the paper mill, paper to the printer, books to the retailer and finally when the customer buys the book. In the UK, VAT is not charged on food, children's clothes nor newspapers, but is charged on other essential services such as fuel.

VAT is charged at 17.5% on most qualifying goods and services in the UK at the moment. This means that a seller has to add 17.5% to the 'before tax' price to determine the actual selling price. The buyer, therefore, does not pay 17.5% of the price actually paid. An example: an electrical retailer wishes to sell a TV set for £350, before tax. VAT is charged at 17.5%, so the retailer has to add £61.25 to the £350 to set the selling price. The price to the customer is £411.25, and the customer pays £61.25/£411.25% VAT, or 14.9%. Be careful when dealing with calculations; it is a danger area.

Be aware of the small print. Look at any advertisement carefully. Advertisements for computers in newspapers need close study. Look at the example in Figure 1.4. Note the prominence given to the before VAT price, with the retail price only in small letters.

There are two other VAT rates in the UK. A few of these are 'zero rated' and, since late 1994, domestic fuel is charged at only 8%.

Figure 1.4 The treatment of VAT on advertisements

Excise duty

This is a special tax charged on petrol, diesel fuel, alcohol and tobacco. (Note: these products carry VAT as well, so the government taxes these products twice.) For example, a litre bottle of whiskey costs £2.50 in 'Somewhere Land'. The government there applies VAT at a rate of 20%, and also excise duty on alcohol at a rate of 120%. What will a bottle cost a customer?

Basic price, £2.50 + 120% = £2.50 + £3.00 = duty paid price of £5.50.
VAT now has to be added.
Price to consumers = £5.50 + 20% = £6.60.

VAT and excise duty are both collected by Customs and Excise in the UK.

Social Security contributions

This is really a form of payroll tax. Everybody in work has to pay this, and it is charged as a percentage of gross income. Like income tax it is deducted by the employer before the worker is paid. The employer also has to pay the tax, again a percentage of the employee's income. Thus Social Security charges in the UK have two components, the employee's and the employer's contributions. The rates applicable in UK in early 1994/95 are shown in Table 1.2.

Table 1.2
UK National Insurance contributions 1995/96

Class 1. Persons in employment

	Not contracted out		Contracted out	
Employees charges				
Earnings	On first	On excess	On first	On excess
per week	£59pw	to £440pw	£59pw	to £446pw
£0 - £56.99	-	-	-	-
£57 - £430	2%	10%	2%	8.2%
Over £430	£38.44 pw		£31.72pw	

Employers charges	
Earnings	Rate applied to
per week	all earnings
£0 - £58.99	-
£59 - £104.99	3%
£105 - £149.99	5%
£150 - £204.99	7%
£205 - £440.00	10%
Over £440	10%

Class 2 (Self - Employed)	
Small earnings exception (annual)	£3,310
Weekly rate	£5.85

Class 3 (Voluntary contributions)	
Weekly rate	£5.75

Class 4 (Self - employed)	
Lower limit of profit or gains	£6,640
Upper limit of profit or gains	£22,880
Rate 7.3%	

In addition, most people and all businesses pay a local tax. This used to be the *rates*, a tax based on property values. This was replaced by the Conservative government led by Margret Thatcher with the *Community Charge* for individuals and the *Uniform Business Rate* for firms. These have now been replaced by another property tax for residential property, keeping the Uniform Business Rate for business properties.

The significance of these taxes in the financing of the government is illustrated in Table 1.3.

Table 1.3
Government receipts (£ billions, 1985 values)

Taxes on incomes (Incomes and Profits Tax)	51.6
Taxes on expenditure (VAT and Excise Duty)	56.7
Social Security contributions	24.1
Rents, dividends, intrest	11.8
Taxes on capital (capital gains tax, death duty etc.)	2.4
Other	2.8
TOTAL	149.5

This can be represented by the *circular flow model* (Figure 1.5) which represents the financial interaction between firms, customers and the government.

This shows the cyclical nature of an economy. Workers are employed by firms to make goods. They are paid for this, and use this income to buy goods and services from other firms. This is the basic loop: money goes from firms to potential consumers and back again. Unfortunately, the government takes its share of income in the form of tax. The consumer also saves some, and buys goods made overseas. On the other side, the government puts money back through its spending, even if only as pensions, sick pay and unemployment benefit. Some firms export goods, and others invest in future productive operations.

Imports seem to flow out, and exports into the economy, because the model is in terms of money flows. When someone buys a Japanese TV at least part of the payment has to go back to Japan. Some money will have to be converted into Yen at some time. Conversely, when a firm exports it is paid in

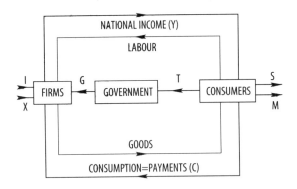

Figure 1.5 *The circular flow of money: model of an economy*

Sterling. If imports are more than exports, then the country will have a *balance of payments* deficit (see Chapter 4.3). If it is the other way round, with exports greater than imports, then the economy will have a balance of payments surplus. Look at Figure 1.6.

Domestic customer buys Japanese CD player

Customer buys player in sterling

↓ £ flow

Retailer buys player in sterling from importer

↓ £ flow

Importer buys Yen from UK bank

so as to buy CD player from Japan

↓ £ flow   ↑ Yen

bank

Japanese manufacturer

Figure 1.6 *Money flow from Import Transaction*

If the government plans to spend more money than it intends to raise by taxes, it will have to borrow to fill the gap. It will have a *public sector borrowing*

requirement or *PBSR*. In the rare event of income exceeding expenditure it will be able to clear some of its old debt. It will then have a *public sector debt repayment – PSDR*.

The interaction between a firm and its consumers is known as the *market*. It is represented by the classic *supply and demand* diagram illustrated in Figure 1.7. As price rises there will usually be less demand for the product, but a more ready supply. When supply and demand match, there will be no gluts or shortages, and no pressure for the price to change.

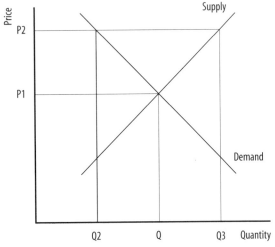

Figure 1.7 *The basic supply and demand diagram (e.g. butter in Europe)*

In response to pressure from farmers, the government sets a minimum price of P2, and guarantees to buy any surplus butter supplied to the market. They will have to! Demand will fall to Q2, but supply will rise to Q3. Soon there will be a 'butter mountain', and increased taxes to pay for it! The Common Agricultural Policy of Europe?

SUMMARY

Having studied this chapter you will be able to:

▼ Define the factors of production, namely:

– Land
– Labour
– Capital
– Enterprise

▼ Understand the complex structure of a business, and be able to supply a reasonable definition of one.

▼ Explain the key role of government in running the economy, and its impact on the operation of businesses.

▼ Identify the various groups that make up the business world, and be able to describe their significance, namely:

– *Internal elements:* shareholders, directors, managers and workers
– *External elements:* suppliers, customers, competitors, government, the environment

Questions and activities

Course work

This is the first example of this regular section at the end of each chapter. With the exception of the first exercise, the methods of reinforcing learning are well known, and are suitable as examination practice and revision. The section on technical terms and glossary replaces the conventional glossary often found at the end of a book. In this case the student is recommended to prepare his or her own glossary, using a computer if one is available, and thus reinforce learning. It is recommended that this section is worked through carefully, and not replaced by the purchase of a Business Studies dictionary. If the student prepares his or her own, there is a good chance that much of it will be learnt and hopefully understood.

Technical terms and glossary

In the sections below you are given a series of technical terms and their meanings. They have been scrambled. You must match up the business term with its definition. When you have got them correctly paired, transfer them to an alphabetical vocabulary book or glossary book.

You are also advised to transfer the definitions obtained during the exercises in the case studies into this glossary book.

Technical terms

1. Gross debt interest
2. Factors of production
3. Salaries
4. Opportunity cost
5. Line functions
6. VAT
7. Social Security contributions
8. Institutional shareholdings
9. Capital gain
10. Staff functions
11. A business
12. Dividend
13. FT-SE index
14. Executive director
15. Mixed economy
16. PSBR
17. PSDR
18. Share option

Definitions

A. Large blocks of shares held by pension funds, insurance companies and investment companies.
B. The total amount of interest due on outstanding loans, before any allowance for any interest earned, or for any tax reliefs that may be due.
C. A decision-making organisation, which exists in association with customers, suppliers, competitors, the local and national environment, and the government, and is made up of groups of workers, managers, directors and shareholders, that uses a blend of land, labour, capital and enterprise to produce and sell goods or services.
D. Positions within a business directly related to production, or the product.
E. Payment system where labour is paid per month, and where the employee does not claim overtime, but has a generally secure position.
F. Those positions within a firm that are support roles, and assist or monitor the productive activity of it.
G. The cost, or benefit of the next best alternative to the one selected. As a consequence of the

decision to do the first activity, the next best cannot be done.

H. A tax applied at a percentage rate to goods and services at the point of sale. Part of this tax is paid to the EU (European Union, or EEC as it was once known).

I. A share of the profits made by a company which is paid to the holders of shares. Each share gets an equal payment.

J. The amount by which a government's spending plan exceeds its planned income. Results in the need for government borrowing.

K. Land, labour, capital and enterprise. A summary of the 'materials' used by a firm in its operations.

L. The positive difference between the purchase price for something and the amount obtained when it is sold. Often applied to share dealings.

M. A tax on income. A percentage is deducted to pay for state-provided services and allowances, such as sick pay, unemployment benefit, old age pension.

N. An economy where the government and the market interact to make decisions.

O. A director of a company who is also an employee of it. Will usually work in the firm on a full-time basis.

P. An agreement where a director has a right to buy shares of his company in the future at a predetermined price.

Q. The amount by which a government's revenue raising will exceed its spending plans. Government can then reduce its debt.

R An index number showing the relative movements of the prices of a selection of 100 shares.

Short answer questions

1. Distinguish between 'line' and 'staff' relationships in a company.
2. Name two pressure groups whose activities may affect business decisions.
3. Define a business.
4. List three external groups to which a firm has responsibilities.
5. Who is the largest employer of labour in the UK?
6. Explain the differences between a wage and a salary.
7. Explain the difference between an Executive and a Non-executive director.
8. Who are the external groups which a company must consider in its decision making?
9. What is a market?
10. What is a pressure group?

Case studies

Interdependency and interrelationships

British Aerospace to close its Hatfield factory

On 23rd September 1992, British Aerospace, who employs over 100,000 people in UK and is one of Britain's largest exporters, announced the closure of its aircraft factory at Hatfield. This was part of a package of measures announced by the company in response to its reported loss of £129 million in the first six months of this *financial year*. The company also reported losses in its Vehicles (Rover Cars) and Property Divisions.

Profit data for BAe

Cost centre	Profit/loss (£ millions)
Defence	+ 296
Commercial aircraft	- 286
Rover cars	- 43
Property	- 6

The Hatfield airfield and factory, originally the de Havilland Aircraft Company base, had been used for the BAe range of Commercial Aircraft based on the 146, the 'Whisper Jet', its Feeder Jet, and the 125, its executive aircraft. Both products are in a *highly competitive market*, and demand for both products has fallen steeply in the recession. In particular, sales of the 146 have slumped, and BAe have only sold some 200 in its ten-year life. The model is a little aged, and needs a redesign and refit to make it competitive again. This would require a large input of cash to pay for the necessary research and development (R&D).

BAe is closing the factory, making some 2,000 people *redundant*, and transferring production of the 146 to Scotland. At the same time it announced the signing of an Agreement in Principal with a firm in Taiwan, Taiwan Aerospace, over the future joint production and development of Feeder Aircraft for the Far East.

Adult unemployment in Hatfield, where BAe has been easily the largest private employer, running at 18%. The new shopping centre, only recently opened, has been put into the hands of the receivers.

Shares of BAe, which once stood at some £5 each, fell 86p on the news of the closure to 113p. This was a drop of 43% in one day.

It is estimated that BAe employees contribute some £12 million per year to local spending. The jobs of up to 1500 workers in the area whose livelihood is directly related to the Hatfield factory are also at risk.'

Questions and activities

1. Define all the terms in italics.
2. Using the case study as the subject, explain the groupings that exist within and outside of business, and show how they are dependent upon one another.
3. What might the government or the local authority have done to prevent this happening?
4. Examine the profit table in the above case study. Experiment with ways of presenting this data in pictorial or graphical form. (Consider bar charts, pie charts and ordinary graphs. If you have access to a computer, please use it.)

Business calculations – VAT

Some calculations always cause problems with some students. The object of this occasional work section is to give the reader practise in doing these calculations.

1. A firm has to add 25% to its price to determine the consumer's, or ticket price. The firm's price is £350. What will the ticket price be?
2. A customer buys another product from the same firm, with VAT still set at 25%, for £550. How much VAT did the customer pay, in money terms and as a percentage of the total price paid?
3. The VAT rate is increased at the budget to 30%. What will the ticket price have to change to in (1) if the seller wishes to keep the same seller's price?
4. The seller in (2) does not change his price. How much VAT is now paid, and how much will the seller receive now?
5. A firm has to include 35% in its selling price as VAT. It sells a stereo TV for £600, including VAT. The government reduces VAT on TVs to only 18.5%. What will the ticket price become if the firm wishes to get the same revenue before VAT?
6. Prepare a graph showing the relationship between the VAT rate (%) added by the seller, and that rate (%) actually paid by the customer.
7. A product carries excise duty and VAT. Excise duty is added first, then VAT is charged on the new price now including excise duty. Initially the excise duty was set at £2.00 per bottle, with VAT at 20%. In an attempt to reduce consumption, excise duty was increased to £4.00 per bottle, and VAT to 35%. If the initial price before duty and VAT was changed from £3.50 per bottle, by how much did the consumers price rise?
8. VAT is applied at all stages of production. A product is made in a factory, then sold to wholesalers, who then sell it on to retailers, who sell it to the final customers. The mark-ups used by the firms to set their selling prices are as follows:

Manufacturers 20%
Wholesalers 30%
Retailers 50%

The common VAT rate is 25%.

Two firms are in direct competition making and selling transistor radios. Firm A has a production cost of £50, and Firm B a production cost of £55. By how much do the retail selling prices differ?

2
The classification of business and products

Preview

▼ Businesses come in many different forms so have to be classified. The important methods of classification based on *function*, *ownership*, *legal structure* and *size* will be explained.

▼ The products and services available from businesses are even more diverse than the businesses producing them, so a method of codifying products and services will also be introduced.

▼ Finally, the conditions necessary for the formation of firms will be examined.

Businesses come in many different forms, are of many different sizes, and are involved in a whole range of activities. They are owned, organised and operated in many different ways. This can cause confusion so firms have to be classified. How? There are a number of accepted methods.

Classification by function

Some firms make things, others sell them or provide a service. Some companies are involved in the production of raw materials or the growing of crops. Others do a number of these things and some even do all of them. Companies can be divided into three common types based on activity. Look at Figure 2.1.

Primary industries

Primary industries consist of firms involved in the production of basic materials, or the provision of basic services. Examples include farming, fishing, mining and the production of basic utilities such as power and water.

There are some very large firms in this sector which operate on an international scale. Good examples of firms in this sector are RTZ (Rio Tinto Zinc), British Coal, British Gas, Thames Water and Southern Water.

Secondary industries

Secondary industries take materials from primary

industries and convert them into manufactured items and products which are sold to other firms or consumers. This group is also known as the *manufacturing sector*, and is considered by some as the power house of any economy. This sector is shrinking and declining in Britain today, and has been since the start of this century.

Typical examples of manufacturing companies are

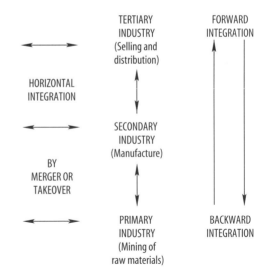

Figure 2.1 *Structure of business classification by type based on function (horizontal and vertical integration added)*

British Aerospace, TI (Tube Investments), Reckitt and Colman and Proctor and Gamble.

Tertiary industries

Tertiary industries can be summarised as the service industries. They are involved in the sale of goods and/or the provision and sale of services. It has been a growth sector in the UK over the last 25 years. The City of London has been a major world supplier of financial services for decades. There are numerous examples of service industries:

- *Services* Banks, insurance companies, travel and estate agencies, theatres, cinemas, air lines, shipping companies and many more.
- *Selling* Retail stores and supermarkets, departmental stores, wholesale outlets, cash-and-carry warehouses.
- *Professional services* Accountants, recruitment consultants, merchant banks, transport companies, marketing agencies, public relations companies, publishers, doctors, dentists and veterinary surgeons.

The stock market also classifies the shares it sells by what the firms make or do. Look at a report on prices in *The Daily Telegraph*, and see the headings used. Look at Figure 2.2 and observe the groupings of buildings, insurance, media and retailers.

Classification by ownership

The first major difference is between those businesses owned by the government, and those owned by private individuals. Be very careful with these names and definitions as they are easily confused.

Government-owned organisations

In the UK both central and local government control directly or indirectly many businesses, e.g. the Post Office, the National Health Service and British Rail (see Chapter 43). But they are not operated the same way. They may be:

Public corporations

Public Corporations include the Post Office, or that part which handles letters. The BBC is another example, as is the Bank of England. The government provides the finance and there are no private shareholders.

Nationalised industries

Nationalised industries comprise those companies owned by the government. There are no private shareholders, as all shares are owned by the government.

The government specifies exactly what the business can do, and appoints the Chief Executive who is expected to report directly to the Minister responsible for the particular industry. The government may provide financial help.

Privately-owned organisations

Privately-owned firms are those owned by private individuals, or groups of individuals. They are often referred to as public companies. Do not confuse them with public corporations.

- Public companies are owned by private individuals, or groups of individuals, or other private companies.

BUT

- Public corporations are owned by the government.

Private firms can also be classified according to how they are legally set up.

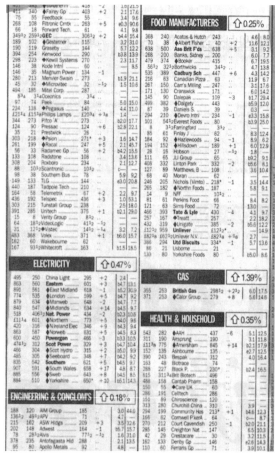

***Figure 2.2** Classification of firms according to* The Daily Telegraph

Classification of private businesses by legal structure

Many private as opposed to state owned firms exist in the UK. These vary from the simplest form, the sole trader, through partnerships and private limited companies, to the most complex form of the public limited company, the plc. The main legal difference that can be drawn is between incorporated and unincorporated firms.

Unincorporated businesses

Unincorporated firms are those where the law draws no distinction between the firm and its owners. The owner is the firm, makes all the contracts, and is personally responsible for all the firm's debts. There is no limit to this liability, and in some circumstances the owner may lose all his or her assets, including the family house and furniture. The two forms of unincorporated business are *sole traders* and *partnerships* (see Chapter 3).

Incorporated businesses

Under certain circumstances firms may register as either *private limited companies* or *public limited companies*. They will put Ltd or Plc after their name, as appropriate. Incorporated firms and their owners are separate legal entities. The financial liability of directors and shareholders is limited, and they will not automatically lose anything if their firm fails.

There are strict controls on the formation of incorporated firms (see Chapter 3).

Cooperatives

A cooperative may seem like a partnership. This is true to some extent, but not when it comes to unlimited liability. They are a special form of incorporated company and it is the shareholding that is different. In a cooperative the shares are owned by the workers, or the customers in the case of a retail cooperative.

Producer or worker cooperatives

The workers in a factory or farming community cooperate in production and share the workload. They take decisions together, and share the profits made. A fundamental principle of cooperatives is 'one worker, one vote'. Some whole communities have become cooperatives, probably the most famous being the Mondragon cooperative in Spain. This is a full village community.

In the farming community, groups of farmers often join together, form a partnership, to sell their products collectively. They share the costs and the profits and, by operating collectively, get better prices for their products. Many marketing boards are cooperatives.

Examples of primary, secondary and tertiary industries

Retail cooperatives

Retail cooperatives exist today, but is not as strong a force as they were earlier this century. They work on the basis that the profits from the business will be shared equally with the members. Members are customers, and the profits, in the form of a coop dividend, are shared out in proportion to the value of purchases made in the period. Members are thus able to buy goods at prices much nearer the wholesale price than normal.

Franchise businesses

A final form of business which may be a sole trader, a partnership, or even a private limited company is the franchise. This is not really a legal identity, as such, but is a growing and important way of operating a business.

New businesses face serious problems, especially at the early stage. They often lack business skills, particularly in the areas of financial planning and marketing. Later, when they become successful, the firm will face problems with raising finance. The franchise arrangement is a way of solving both problems to the benefit of both parties.

The firm with the product or service, the franchiser, has a successful business, usually with an established name in the marketplace, and a reputation. Instead of expanding by buying new sites or shops, etc., the franchiser licences other firms to sell its product, but under its name. It also provides national marketing, professional advice on the running of the business, and sometimes a purchasing service for the key raw materials.

The firm buying the service, the franchisee, pays a fee to the franchiser. In return it gets all the help it requires, and the permission to use the key name, or sell the product.

Some well-known businesses are franchise businesses. The McDonald's chain is usually a set of franchises in most countries, as is Coca Cola. In this country most of the retail printing firms, like Prontaprint, are franchises, as are Pizza Hut, many Benetton shops, and Sketchley dry cleaners.

Consider your high street again, and try to count and name the franchises you identify.

Do franchises have advantages? The franchiser gets the benefits of expansion, additional sales and profits, without the need to invest large amounts of capital. The risk element for the franchiser is considerably reduced. On the other hand, the franchisee gets help and assistance, plus the benefit of selling an established product, right at the beginning of the firm's operation. The risk is considerably reduced here also. The franchisee will make less profit than if it achieved the same level of success on its own, but would be much less likely to be successful without the benefit of the franchiser.

Both the franchiser and franchisee businesses can, theoretically, be in any of the legal forms. It is much more likely that the franchiser will be a plc or a private limited company. The franchisees will usually be sole traders, or private limited companies. The range of business types is shown diagrammatically in Figure 2.3.

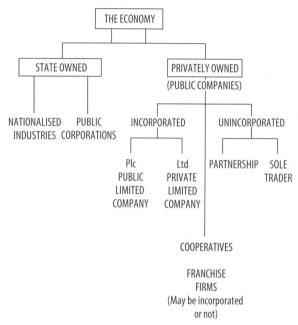

Figure 2.3 *Types of business*

Classification by size

A further, and temptingly simple classification is by size, but what is size? It varies from country to country. What is large in Switzerland or Luxemburg may be considered very small in the USA.

Common measures of size are:

1. *Turnover* The amount of money that a firm earns through selling its products or services.
2. *Number of employees* Notice how part-time and casual workers are dealt with. Also, the definition of what is large or small is relative.
3. *Profit* This is a much more difficult concept than it seems. By definition, it is the difference between the value of a sale, and all the costs associated in producing it.
4. *Assets* refers to the value of saleable items used

in a business. It would include the value of land, buildings, plant and equipment, cars, furniture and fittings, computers and the like. There are great problems here with the methods of valuation. (Much more of this in Chapter 11.)

5. *Share value* This really only applies to plcs. It is simply the number of shares issued multiplied by the share price at the time concerned. It is only a notional value, as any attempt to buy shares would change the price.

6. *Market share* The amount of a market, in terms of sales value, held by a firm. It is mathematically simply the turnover of the firm expressed as a percentage of the total market value, i.e. a firm has £20 million sales per year from a market

worth £80 million in total. The firm has a market share of 25%. It puts sales in perspective, and relates them to an absolute.

All the above are perfectly good measures of size, but deciding which is the best or correct one to use depends on what you are looking at, what you are trying to show.

A firm with a market share of 70% of its industry will be a large firm in that industry regardless of any of the other measures. Be careful, though, because national difference can also be important. A firm with 1,000 employees in the UK is considered large; in the USA it would be seen as small: it is all relative. Examine this further by working through Case Study 2.1.

CASE STUDY 2.1

Analysis of businesses by size

Fortune Magazine produces regular league tables of firms by industry, activity and various measures. A part of a page of the 1993 'Largest Industrial Corporations' is reproduced below.

THE FORTUNE 500

LARGEST U.S. INDUSTRIAL CORPORATIONS

RANK 1992	1991	COMPANY	SALES $ millions	% change from 1991	PROFITS $ millions	Rank	% change from 1991	ASSETS $ millions	Rank	TOTAL STOCKHOLDERS' EQUITY $ millions	Rank
1	1	GENERAL MOTORS Detroit	132,774.9	7.3	(23,496.3)†	500	—	191,012.8	2	6,225.6	22
2	2	EXXON Irving, Texas	103,547.0¹	0.3	4,770.0	2	(14.8)	85,030.0	5	33,776.0	1
3	3	FORD MOTOR Dearborn, Mich.	100,785.6	13.3	(7,385.0)†	476	—	180,545.2	3	14,752.9	5
4	4	INTL. BUSINESS MACHINES Armonk, N.Y.	65,096.0	(0.5)	(4,965.0)†	475	—	86,705.0	4	27,624.0	2
5	5	GENERAL ELECTRIC Fairfield, Conn.	62,202.0	3.3	4,725.0	3	79.2	192,876.0	1	23,459.0	3
6	6	MOBIL Fairfax, Va.	57,389.0¹	0.8	862.0†	17	(55.1)	40,561.0	8	16,540.0	4
7	7	PHILIP MORRIS New York	50,157.0	4.3	4,939.0	1	64.3	50,014.0	6	12,563.0	9
8	8	E.I. DU PONT DE NEMOURS Wilmington, Del.	37,643.0	(3.1)	(3,927.0)†	474	(379.9)	38,870.0	9	11,765.0	10
9	10	CHEVRON San Francisco	37,464.0¹	1.8	1,569.0†	8	21.3	33,970.0	11	13,728.0	7
10	9	TEXACO White Plains, N.Y.	37,130.0¹	(1.1)	712.0†	24	(45.0)	25,992.0	15	9,973.0	11
11	11	CHRYSLER Highland Park, Mich.	36,897.0	25.6	723.0†	22	—	40,653.0	7	7,538.0	17
12	12	BOEING Seattle	30,184.0	3.0	552.0†	31	(64.8)	18,147.0	24	8,056.0	16
13	13	PROCTER & GAMBLE Cincinnati¹	29,890.0	9.1	1,872.0	6	5.6	24,025.0	18	9,071.0	12
14	14	AMOCO Chicago	25,543.0¹	(0.2)	(74.0)†	380	(105.0)	28,453.0	13	12,960.0	8
15	17	PEPSICO Purchase, N.Y.	22,083.7	11.7	374.3†	47	(65.3)	20,951.2	20	5,355.7	27
16	16	UNITED TECHNOLOGIES Hartford	22,032.0	3.6	(287.0)†	440	—	15,928.0	30	3,370.0	51
17	15	SHELL OIL Houston²	21,702.0¹	(2.2)	(190.0)†	427	(1,050.0)	26,970.0	14	14,608.0	6
18	19	CONAGRA Omaha³	21,219.0	8.8	372.4	48	19.7	9,758.7	52	2,232.3	71
19	18	EASTMAN KODAK Rochester, N.Y.	20,577.0	4.7	1,146.0†	12	6,641.2	23,138.0	19	6,557.0	21
20	20	DOW CHEMICAL Midland, Mich.	19,177.0	(0.7)	(489.0)†	457	(151.9)	25,360.0	16	8,074.0	15

Questions and activities

Examine the table above, and answer the following questions.

1. Which industries seem naturally to be big? (Use as many measures as you can.)
2. Are they employers of people or users of capital to achieve this size?

3. It will not take long to identify two industries that dominate the Top 20 – automobiles with seven firms and petroleum, with four. In fact, 20 out of the largest 50 firms, based on sales revenue fall into this grouping.

Note the interdependence here; there is no oil industry and no automobile industry as we know it. Now, as a group exercise, consider these industries and try to identify what it is that might account for this dominance.

This concludes the analysis of firms as such and the ways of classifying them. Chapter 3 will look at how they start and then operate, and what skills are needed to do this successfully. First, though, a look at the products themselves.

Classification of products

An examination of products reveals that they can be split into two primary groups: those for the final consumer to use, and those for factory use in the manufacture of other products to sell. Each of these two primary groups can be subdivided into goods that are used at once, and those that last.

Consumer goods

Consumer goods are those purchased, usually from a retail outlet, for the use, or consumption of the buyer or his/her family. The retail outlet is usually a shop, store, mail order company, market stall, etc., that sells to the general public who will not usually resell the product again. It is for the buyers own direct use. These goods can be divided into two very different groups.

FMCGs – fast moving consumer goods

FMCGs are goods bought by the consumer for virtually immediate consumption. They are bought frequently, and are generally low in price – low ticket items, in business jargon. They are sold in large quantities – 'volume lines' – usually from supermarkets, grocers, newsagents, and, in increasing numbers, from the modern petrol station shops. Typical products are sweets, cigarettes, soaps and detergents, bread, petrol, etc. Once bought they have no value; in fact some today even carry a 'sell by' date. This is a highly profitable business for the efficient company. The key is to have a strong range of brands to offer, e.g. Persil, Lux, Shell, Hovis, Mr Kipling, etc. – the list is long.

Consumer durables

Consumer durables are goods bought by the consumer, but with the intention of keeping them and using them for a considerable period of time.

Types of goods: (top) consumer durable; (middle) fast moving consumer goods; (bottom) capital plant.

23

They will have a value, even when they have been slightly used. They are durable. Many examples are to be found in and around the home.

- White goods. Those found in the kitchen and includes things like washing machines, refrigerators, microwaves, and cookers. (They were traditionally made of white enamel.)
- Brown goods. Radios, TVs, hi fis and the like used to be made out of brown Bakelite.
- Other goods. In the house these would include all furniture and fittings, including carpets and curtains. Outside one would find cars, motor cycles, lawn mowers, as well as clothes, etc. Most sporting equipment will fall into the category.

Industrial goods

Industrial goods are those made by firms and sold to others who will use them to make consumer products. These also can be divided into two subgroups:

Capital goods

Capital goods are goods, like process plants, computers, cars, electrical switchboards, transformers, etc., that will be used to establish or expand a factory. The goods have a life, and a value. Money spent on these items would be considered as capital expenditure. Major firms who supply such goods would include, in the UK APV, NEI, in Europe Siemens, Bobst, and Lurgi, and in Japan, Hitachi.

In their own special way, these products are branded. Certain firms and suppliers have a reputation. A firm may well not require simply a generator for electricity; it may want a Caterpillar generator, or a Rolls Royce –Petbow unit. Firms in this area tend not to be household names, but they are very significant businesses in an economy. Other firms, which you think you know all about, are not what they seem! What does Hitachi sell? Look at Case Study 2.2.

CASE STUDY 2.2

Hitachi – Known or not?

Everybody knows the name Hitachi in this country, and must know it as the Japanese company that produces quality *consumer electronics* such as video recorders and TVs. It has not become the number 12 firm in the world sales league on the backs of products like these, though. These products are only a small portion of this giant corporation's business.

Hitachi analysis of 1991 sales
(sales value – £36.5 billion)

	%
TVs, VCRs, etc.	12
Wire, special steels, ceramics	25
Power plants, steel mills, trains, robots	29
Chips, computers, telephones	34

Hitachi is a rather low-profile *high-technology industrial company*. In many ways its most popular, if not most used products are the 'bullet trains' in Japan itself. Even here, though, the success of its integrated electronic control systems are under-publicised.

Hitachi is a highly *decentralised* technical business. It operates through divisions which are encouraged to make their own decisions. They are subject to the minimum of controls from the centre, or headquarters.

It owns 28 factories, 800 subsidiaries, and employs 320,000 people. In itself it accounts for 2% of Japan's GNP (*gross national product*), and each year spends some £2.3 billion on research and development (R&D). It is a 'scientific' company, employing some 1,200 engineers. Most of the divisional heads are engineers, and the company president is a nuclear engineer.

Hitachi has come through the present recession quite well so far. It has been prepared to work to *low margins* (4.5% on sales value) and has cut or frozen salaries and wages. Even the President, has cut his earnings to £180,000. It has not cut its R&D expenditure at all, though. This it considers as its *seed corn for the future*. It does have the advantage of being '*cash rich*', with £7 billion in the accounts, and no significant loans outstanding. Hitachi is not the diverse business it seems to be. All divisions and activities have a common link, a common technology, or a *core activity*.

(Based on an article in *International Business Week* November 1992)

Questions and activities

1. Define the terms in italics above.
2. Convert the sales percentage to sales value, then present the data so generated in the form of a pie chart, and a bar graph.
3. How can the presence of so many subsidiaries be used to support the secrecy of the company?
4. Explain the sentence: 'This it considers as its seed corn for the future.'
5. What is the 'core activity' for Hitachi?

Industrial consumables

Industrial consumables are the industrial equivalent of the FMCGs. They include the raw materials that businesses use and other items that are essentially for 'direct use'. Examples include paper, pens, forms, lubricants, chemicals, etc. They are often considered as commodities, with no brand being evident. Examples would be wheat and soya oil. Generally these products have no value once purchased, and definitely none once packets have been opened.

SUMMARY

Having studied this chapter you will be able to:

▽ Explain the classification of firms according to:

  – 'Activity': primary, secondary and tertiary
  – Legal structure: unincorporated business (sole trader, partnership); incorporated business (limited company, plc)

▽ Discuss the advantages of being a *cooperative* or a *franchise*.

▽ Discuss the merits and problems associated with classifications based on size. How do you measure it? What does 'big' mean?

  – turnover
  – number of employees
  – value of assets
  – share value
  – market share

▽ Classify products into consumer or industrial goods, capital or consumption products. Further, you will be able to differentiate between:

  – FMCGs
  – consumer durables
  – industrial consumables
  – capital goods

Questions and activities

Technical terms and glossary

In the sections below you are given a series of technical terms and their meanings. They have been scrambled, though. You must match up the business term and its definition. When you have got them correctly paired, transfer them to an alphabetical vocabulary or glossary book.

You are also advised to transfer any definitions obtained during the exercises in the case studies into this glossary book.

Technical terms

1. Public corporation
2. Assembly operations
3. Public company
4. Retail operations
5. Incorporated business
6. Primary industries
7. Unincorporated business
8. Franchise business
9. Tertiary firms
10. Turnover
11. FMCGs
12. Secondary industries
13. Market share
14. Consumer goods
15. Consumer durables
16. Cooperative

Definitions

A. Those firms involved in the extraction of raw materials, mining or fishing. Those firms involved in the provision of the basic services such as water, electricity, or gas.

B. That part of a market, expressed in terms of the percentage total sales value held by a firm, calculated as Firms Sales/Total Market Sales x 100%.

C. The service sector, including general and professional services such as the cinema, and architects.

D. Those goods produced for and bought by the general public. They may be consumables, when they are considered as FMCGs, or durables. The latter are capital goods that have a life.

E. A business where all of its shares are owned by the government. The chief executive reports to a government minister. Shares cannot be bought by the general public.

F. A production process where parts made elsewhere are assembled to form the final product. Typical products made this way are popular motor vehicles, domestic white and brown goods, and even modern aircraft.

G. Operations involving the selling of goods or services to the general public for their own use. Goods and services are not expected to be resold.

H. An incorporated business with its shares traded on the Stock Exchange. It is owned by its shareholders, institutional or otherwise, which are part of the private as opposed to the state sector.

I. Firms involved in the manufacture of goods from materials produced in the primary sector.

J. A business owned by its customers or its workers. The owners or workers are entitled to share all the profit of the business between them, or decide democratically how it should be spent.

K. That category of good that is bought and used by the final consumer, but the good will be expected to have a life and a value at some point in time. Examples would be washing machines, TVs and video recorders.

L. A business which operates under licence from another, who supplies the product/brand, selling and business advice, and national advertising support. The holder of the licence pays a fee to the granter of the licence usually based on turnover, and may have to buy all raw materials from it. Examples are McDonald's, many Benetton shops, most Sock Shops and Tie Rack.

M. Forms of business which do not have limited liability, and where the firm and the owners are inseparable in the eye of the law.

N. A business registered with Companies House which has a legal identity separate from its owners and directors. It will have limited liability and it will have shareholders, but shares may not necessarily be sold on the Stock Exchange.

O. The total value of the sales of a business over a period expressed in money terms. It is the sum of the sales revenue over a period, say a month or a year.

P. Goods produced for the retail market. It is expected they will be used by the purchaser, not resold by way of trade or business.

Short answer questions

1. List three firms from each of the classifications primary, secondary and tertiary, which were privatised by Margaret Thatcher's government.
2. Distinguish between vertical and horizontal integration.
3. Why might the directors of a business wish to retain private limited company status rather than seek public limited company status?

4. List three advantages of a company taking a franchise on a particular service.

5. What advantages does a firm get by franchising its product or service to other businesses?

6. Distinguish between a public company and a public corporation.

7. Which two documents must be provided by the promoters of a new company before it can be registered? What are the main differences between them?

8. Describe how all goods can be put into one of four categories.

9. Describe four ways that the size of a company can be measured.

1. State three methods of comparing the size of firms in the same industry, other than by 'number of employees'.

2. Explain why 'number of employees' on its own right might be a misleading indication of the size of firms.

3. Explain two reasons why small firms tend to be less capital intensive that large ones.

4. Explain four different methods governments have employed in an attempt to encourage the small firm sector.

5. Outline two reasons why the small firm sector is considered to be important to the UK economy.

(Associated Examining Board, Business Studies (A), Paper 1, 1988)

Data response questions

1. Read the following extract and answer the questions below:

> 'The Bolton Committee (1971) suggested that the three main characteristics of a small firm were that it had a relatively small share of the market; that it was managed in a personalised way by its owners who took all the principal decisions and exercised the principal management functions; and that it was independent in the sense that it did not form part of a larger enterprise.
>
> These characteristics provide an economic definition of a small firm, but in censuses and surveys, firm size is determined by means of statistical measures such as employment or sales, and in terms of employment, for example, the latest size of firm which will typically conform to the Bolton characteristics varies with industry. In some manufacturing industries firms with 500 employees will often conform, whilst in retailing a firm with 200 employees will be relatively large, and in the world of finance firms with fewer than 50 employees will typically not conform. Since similar remarks also apply to any other statistical measure of size, considerable care needs to be taken when using such measures to define a small firm. However, provided account is taken of industry, they do give at least a rough guide. In the manufacturing industry, for example, nearly all firms with less than 200 employees will also be small according to the economic definition.'

Source: R. Allard, 'The important position of small firms', *The Economic Review*, 1, 2, 1983.

2. Study the information and answer the questions that follow.

The Universe of Franchising

The franchising business has mushroomed during the past decade. Not only have numbers of franchisers multiplied, the number of franchisees per franchise has also increased.

A clear indication of the health of franchising compared to the generality of small businesses appears in a survey undertaken for the **Financial Times** in 1986. Within a five-year period, 80% of all new small businesses had ceased trading for one reason or another. By contrast, well over 80% of franchised businesses were still trading after a five-year period. However, the more recent Power Report also notes an increase in the failure rate of both franchised systems and of franchised outlets, although these come out at a modest 14% and 10% respectively. Problems, it observes, stem not only from the franchises themselves, but from failures of other kinds, in selling and basic business and marketing skills.

Scale and growth potential franchising

Year	Annual sales from franchised units	Numbers of units operated	Jobs attributable to franchising
1992 projected	£7.7 bn		
1987	£3.1 bn	15,000	169,000
1986	£2.2 bn	12,500	149,000
1984	£1.0 bn	8,300	71,000

Source: Adapted from an article by Derek Ayling, *Management Today*, April 1988.

(a) Explain the term franchising.
(b) (i) Calculate the percentage change between 1986 and 1987 of sales from franchised units, units operated and jobs attributable to franchising.
(ii) What do your figures suggest about developments in franchising between 1986 and 1987?
(c) (i) Explain the advantages to a business of selling franchises.
(ii) Explain the advantages of starting a business by buying a franchise.

(Associated Examining Board, Business (A), Paper 1, November 1990)

3
How do businesses form and grow?

Preview

▼ You know now what a business is, and how complicated it may be. You are able to classify businesses in a number of ways.

▼ Now you will examine the formation of firms. In particular, the requirements for unincorporated and incorporated businesses will be described in detail.

▼ Businesses grow or die. Some grow and become multinationals, others become conglomerates. These two important business forms will be examined.

How do businesses start, and what do they need to maximise the chance of success? There are three essential requirements:

1. The financial resources necessary to support the business.
2. A product or service that is wanted outside the business, and can be sold and exploited by it.
3. People to run and work for the business.

First, though, we will look at the establishment of companies and then at how they grow.

The formation of businesses

When a business is formed the owners can choose to be one of any of the legal forms outlined in Chapter 2. They will be limited by their resources, however. What will be the situation if the business starts as a sole trader? Why is this form of business so popular?

Sole traders

The sole trader business is the easiest to set up and start. The advantages of being a sole trader are:

- There are no legal formalities to follow, the person just starts trading, hopefully after preparing a proper business plan, assessing the risk involved, and raising enough capital both to start the firm, and to run it for a sufficient period. (This is often where sole traders go wrong and eventually fail.)
- There are no requirements for the preparation of

formal audited accounts, or their submission to Companies House. The sole trader will have to satisfy the Inland Revenue that the records are fair and the profits truly stated. The IR are experts at judging this!

- All profits belong to the sole trader.
- The sole trader can run the business as he or she wishes. A sole trader business does not have to be a 'one man band' and other personnel may be employed. The important aspect is that the owner is in complete command, and responsible financially.

However, there are a number of potential problems, namely,

- Sole traders find it difficult to raise capital. Banks will require security, and beyond a house, a sole trader will rarely have any. The only real source of capital is profits being ploughed back into the firm.
- The sole trader has to do many different jobs within the firm, and may not be properly qualified or experienced. The paper work might suffer, to the annoyance, usually, of the Inland Revenue.
- The owner has to put in long hours to make the business work, especially initially. Sickness can be a real problem because of the lack of cover staff.

Many businesses are sole traders, in spite of the problems. Typically they are taxi firms, plumbers, decorators, window cleaners and the like.

The common characteristic is that low capital input is required, and they can be operated by one person for long hours.

The partnership

In its simplest form, a partnership is a sole trader firm owned and managed by more than one person. The partners share the responsibilities and the money raising.

Partnerships are governed by the Partnership Act of 1890. Unless there is an agreement to the contrary, all partnerships are assumed to be governed by this law. All partners will be equally and severally responsible for all debts, unless there is a specific Deed of Partnership in existence. This means that if, in a partnership of two people, one puts in the money and the other the work, both are liable for any debts. If one partner could not be found, then the other would have to settle all the debts. On the other hand, the partners are entitled to equal shares of any profits.

The partnership has several advantages over the simple sole trader business. The main ones are:

- A partnership can raise more capital, and it will often be looked on more favourably by the banks.
- Partners share the expenses of the business, and the work. By recruiting partners with different skills, a fairer and more efficient division of labour can result.
- A partnership still does not have to publish detailed, audited accounts. But the profits are considered as income and are liable for income tax.

Partnerships come in two forms, ordinary and limited.

Ordinary partnerships

In an ordinary partnership, there are between two and 20 partners. Each is personally responsible for all the firm's debts. The Deed of Partnership, if one exists, will define:

- How much capital each partner will put into the firm.
- How any profits will be shared, i.e. proportionally to the capital inputs.
- Rules for how new partners will be brought in, how any decisions will be voted on, and how the partnership may be ended.

Partnerships have a limited ability to raise capital, when compared with incorporated companies, described below.

Limited partnerships

These are a special form of partnership where one or more partners have limited liability. These will normally be partners who put money into a partnership, but take no further action. They are really investors, and are called 'sleeping partners'. At least one partner must have unlimited liability.

Because partnerships are relatively complicated to set up, and require a great deal of trust to be operated efficiently, they are relatively rare. They have a specialised niche now amongst the professions. Many solicitors and barristers are partnerships, as are many group practices operated by doctors and dentists.

A partnership may become incorporated.

Incorporated companies

The law relating to this form of company is enshrined in the Companies Acts. The most recent, important changes were made in 1985.

Incorporated firms, or joint stock companies, are the most common form of business organisation in the UK. Two types of limited company are found in the UK: private limited companies and public limited companies. A limited company, either private or public, is a legally separate body from its owners, the shareholders and the directors. The company can make contracts and agreements, and can be held responsible and sued in its own name. Under certain circumstances directors may also be sued, as in the case of negligence, but the important aspect here is that they are sued *as well as* the company. The shareholders are not liable for the debts of the company beyond the value of their shares. In other words, their financial responsibility is limited. The value here is the original price, or the original investment, not the value based on the current price of the share on the stock market. The company has a life of its own and can exist beyond the life of its original owners.

Limited companies have to be registered with Companies House, and a strict procedure has to be followed if registration is to be granted. In particular, two key documents have to be prepared and lodged with the Registrar of Companies, namely:

1. *Memorandum of Association*
2. *Articles of Association*

Memorandum of Association

This has to describe the general objectives of the company, and what the business is. It will give the name of the firm, its registered address, its objectives and its initial capital. It is a document relating to the outside of the company, for an outsider.

Articles of Association

This describes the rules that govern the operation of the company. It is an internal document in many ways, and states how the business will be run. It must include a description of the rights of the shareholders, election of directors, conduct of meetings, and details of the keeping of financial accounts.

When accepted, and after the payment of the correct fee, the Registrar will issue a *Certificate of Incorporation*. After registration the firm may sell shares and start to trade. Each year thereafter it will have to report to the Registrar by submitting as well as a director's report, a set of accounts which will normally consist of a *Balance Sheet*, a *Profit and Loss Account*, a *Cash Flow Statement*, a set of detailed explanatory notes, and a report from the company's auditors.

This process takes some time. Some businesses are registered in advance, and in suitably vague terms, so that they may be sold to people who want a registered company quickly. These are known as 'shell companies'.

It is simpler to become a limited company, so why do some firms become plcs? Like so much of Business Studies, the answer is 'it all depends' on what is wanted. There are specific rules governing the qualification of limited companies or plcs. Examine Tables 3.1 and 3.2 which shows the requirements for, and differences between, plc's and limited companies.

Private limited companies tend to be regional firms, rather than national, and are often family businesses. Senior managers, directors and shareholders tend to be very close, sometimes they are one and the same. They tend not to be household names, unless they happen to be subsidiaries of plcs. There are some significant exceptions, however, and JCB, the building machinery manufacturer, is a good example.

Table 3.1
Legal differences between private and public limited companies

	Private limited company (Ltd)	Public limited company (plc)
Memorandum of Association		Must state that the company is a public company
Name	Must end with the words Limited or Ltd.	Must end with the words 'public limited company' or plc
Minimum authorised capital	None	£50,000
Minimum membership	2	2
Minimum number of directors	1	2
Retirement of directors	No age set, unless firm is a subsidiary of plc when director must retire at 70	Must retire at 70 unless otherwise resolved
Issue of shares to the public	No advertising to the public, sale by private agreement only	May do so on the Stock Exchange, by means of a prospectus
Company Secretary	Anyone	Must be qualified as such
Accounts	Small and medium companies may submit modified accounts (see Table 3.2)	Must file, unless a small or medium company: a Balance Sheet, a Profit and Loss Account, group accounts where applicable and Auditors' and Directors' Reports.
Meetings	A proxy may address the meeting	A proxy cannot speak at a the public meeting

Note: A *proxy* is someone authorised to act on behalf of another. Here the proxy may vote.

Table 3.2
Some size definitions (Companies Act, 1981)

Basis of measure	Small company	Medium-sized company
Turnover	Less than £2 million	Less than £8 million
Capital employed	£975,000	£3,900,000
Employees	Less than 50	Less than 250

Public limited companies (plcs) often find it easier to borrow money from banks, and tend to be much larger organisations than limited companies. They seem to inspire greater confidence, but there is no solid reason why they should. The plcs tend to be the large companies in a country. Thus there are far more limited companies in the UK than plcs, but the majority of the total capital invested is with plcs.

Some large companies that operate through a range of different firms often organise themselves as holding companies.

Holding company

A holding company is a joint stock company that controls one or more other companies.

The holding company publishes one set of consolidated accounts, reports only a combined level of profits, etc., and can keep the dealings of its subsidiary and associated companies secret.

Two new terms:

1. *Subsidiary companies If a firm has a controlling interest in another firm, i.e. it owns 51% of its shares, then the firm concerned is a subsidiary of it. The shareholding firm makes all the policy decisions for the other. It can vote itself all the profits if it so wishes.*

2. *Associate companies If a firm has a shareholding in a firm, but less than 50% of the total number of shares, then it has an investment in an associate company. It has an influence in the running of the associate, this influence rises as the share holding rises. At 25%, say, it can have effective control.*

The company 'holds' the shares of its component firms. It has its own Memorandum and Articles of Association, and is registered as a separate company.

The main disadvantage, and some would say the only disadvantage, of being limited rather than plc is regarding the raising of capital – more difficult in the case of limited companies – and being unable to sell shares on the Stock Exchange.

Companies are dynamic and many grow. They can grow in a number of different ways. They can merge with another company, or they can take another company over. Two more definitions to learn:

1. *A takeover: the purchase of one firm by another. One firm buys the shares of another, and takes control. It may be by agreement, but it may also be a hostile takeover. In this case the firm will try to defend itself. BTR's takeover of Hawker Siddeley in 1992 is a good example of a hostile takeover. In other words, a firm is bought without its agreement.*

2. *A merger: the joining together of two firms to become one. (for example, the Halifax and Leeds Building Societies). They become partners, in effect, but one will normally assume control. The shares of one will be exchanged for those of the other firm.*

Takeovers or mergers may be forwards or backwards. Consider a firm that manufactures products. This will make it a secondary concern. If it sets out and buys firms which produces its major raw material, it will have performed a backward integration takeover. If it then agrees to join with a multiple retail company which sells the product, this will be a merger, a forward integration merger. The resulting group will now be fully integrated vertically as it is made up of firms in all three sectors, primary, secondary and tertiary. Look at Table 2.1 again.

Some companies, especially large *multinational corporations*, become very complicated, making many different products in many different countries. Examine Case Study 3.1.

Remember, there has to be a product link for the expansion to be horizontal or vertical integration. If a firm grows by taking over unrelated concerns, then the firm is developing into a *conglomerate*.

A good example of a fully integrated concern is Unilever. Examples of conglomerates are BTR (British Tyre and Rubber), and The Hanson Trust. Integrated businesses can operate in one single country, so are called nationals, or they may operate and trade in many countries, and are known as multinationals. Thus Unilever and IBM are multinationals, and are also integrated businesses. Conglomerates can also be multinationals. The terms 'conglomerate' and 'multinational' are unpopular today, at least in the eyes of the media. Why might this be so?

CASE STUDY 3.1

Unilever plc

Unilever plc is one half of the Anglo-Dutch multinational which ranks 21st in the world sales league. Its activities can be divided into the following product groups:

Analysis of Unilever sales and profits by product group

	Sales (£m)	Profits (£m)
Margarine, edible fats and oils, dairy products (Stork, Flora, Elmlea, Country Crock)	4,617	361
Frozen foods and ice cream (Birds Eye, Walls)	2,645	233
Food and drinks (Bachelors, John West, Ragu, Lipton)	3,499	378
Detergents	4,589	336
Personal products (Faberge, Timotee, Elizabeth Arden, Rimmel)	2,310	246
Specialty chemicals	1,798	238
Agribusiness (PBI, salmon farming, BOCM, tea estates, plantations)	671	29
Others	1,392	157
Total	**21,521**	**1,978**

R&D spending – £395 million

Geographically, it operates and trades as follows:

Analysis of Unilever sales and profits by region units (£ millions)

	Sales	Profits
Europe	12,900	1,070
North America	4,641	463
Rest of world	3,980	445

Unilever today consists of two joint *holding companies* in UK and Holland – Unilever plc and Unilever NV respectively. These control at least 186 companies worldwide.

Unilever: Number of principle group companies

Europe	123
North America	17
Rest of world	46

It also has significant but not *controlling interests* in some 14 other companies, including Lever Brothers Nigeria Ltd.

Historically, the company grew from the *merger* of Lever Brothers, the soap maker in UK, and the Margarine Union in the Netherlands. Rather than fight for common raw materials – nut oils – they merged and shared them. Lever Brothers itself had grown by *taking over* a whole range of smaller soap firms in UK.

At one time it owned and operated companies in all three sectors of the economy, e.g.:

- Primary – Tea estates and plantations for oil seeds, oil extraction plants, power station at Bromborough, near Port Sunlight.
- Secondary – Thames Board Mills.
- Tertiary – McFisheries Food Stores, Palm Line (Ships), SPD (Road deliveries).
  (Some of these have been sold.)

It also practised an amount of horizontal integration, absorbing competition and suppliers alike. This process seems to have been reversed, particularly in the UK, with the disposal of some of these non-core businesses, including the named ones above.

(Based on the Company's Annual Report)

Questions and activities

1. Define the terms in italics.
2. Which region, and which product group are the most profitable? (Express profit as a percentage of sales revenue, or turnover.)
3. Prepare a graph showing the variation of profit/sales (%) with the different product groups.
4. Discuss in groups the possible reasons for:
   a) Unilever's actions in horizontal and vertical integration, and
   b) its divesting itself later of some of these.

Be prepared to present your findings to the class as a whole.

Conglomerate businesses

All businesses have an objective. For all it is first survival, followed by making money. For many businesses the first objective seems obvious, but there may be a more complex interpretation. Consider a supermarket chain. Its objective is to sell groceries at a 'fair' price. Or is it? Is its objective 'to make money', or 'profit'? The supermarket chain's objective is probably 'through the marketing of groceries at a fair price, to make a profit'. Who gains by the firm's success, or its growth?

- *Shareholders* – They will receive an increased dividend.
- *Employees* – There will be more jobs in the supermarkets. The workers may well get better pay and conditions.
- *Customers* – They should get the benefit of lower prices and more choice. They may even get better quality goods.
- *Government* – It will receive more tax revenue.
- *Suppliers* – They will receive more orders for goods, more employment, and increased profit. Their internal groups will all gain from this, and the government will get another slice.

As the firm expands and becomes more successful, the gains seem to increase. The effect is multiplied through the economy. Imagine that the supermarket takes over other shops, and also expands into manufacturing of some of the products sold. Prices should be even lower now, and the supermarket should become even more competitive. Who loses out, though?

- *Other stores* – because of the competition, they may have to close. There will be unemployment but there may be some re-employment of staff by the expanding supermarket chain itself.
- *HQ or staff personnel* – As one firm absorbs another it is this group who will face dismissal. The 'buying' firm will tend to replace the directors and senior managers of the 'bought' firm.

This form of growth, towards a fully integrated company, even a multinational one, is generally acceptable up to a point. This point is usually where the firm has become so big that it has monopoly powers, i.e. it is in a position to be able to prevent any opposition being successful, and can dictate the price of any goods or services it provides. (More of this later in Part 5.) There are problems, but, on balance and considering the community as a whole the process is tolerated.

The conglomerate firm is different from the multinational in that its objective differs. Its aim is to make money, both a return on its investment and, if possible, a capital gain. Its method of growth is different. It grows by purchase, not always of willing businesses. It seems to act like a predator.

Two more definitions:
1. *Return on investment: the profit made by the firm expressed as a percentage of the capital employed.*
2. *Capital gain: a firm buys a share for £1 today, but sells it tomorrow for £2. It has made a capital gain of £1. Or, it buys a firm for £500 million, splits it up and sells it again for a total of £600 million. It has made a capital gain of £100 million.*

Conglomerates grow by buying and selling other companies. They research the business world and look for poorly run firms, or those holding valuable hidden assets. They will then try to buy them and reorganise them, and often resell all or part of them for more than they have paid for them.

Badly run firms
Badly run firms, when reorganised and managed properly, will earn a good return. The usual mix of actions will be to remove at least some of the senior management, reorganise production, put in new processes, and lay off some workers and staff. For a firm operating happily and contentedly the way it wants, this is unwelcome attention. If the firm is a plc there is little it can do to stop the process. It can try to defend itself, but the final decision will be made by the shareholders. If the price offered for their shares is attractive they will probably sell. The result:

- The firm becomes more efficient – higher returns for the conglomerate.
- There will be redundancies – unpopular, even when jobs are easy to get.

Hidden assets
Conglomerates will research the assets of companies and find out what they are worth, i.e. what they will generate if sold. They will not do this looking at the business as a whole, but will value assets individually. They will look at sites rather than land as a whole, they will consider the products, or brands of the firm one by one, not as a group.

The firm under review thinks of itself as a whole; the potential buyer thinks of it as a set of parts that it can sell. The firm under review may not be aware of this difference of value for its assets depending on the point of view. So the conglomerate buys the business 'cheap', splits it up and sells off the parts at a profit. This is known as 'asset stripping'. The buyer, or predator, makes a capital gain, but who are the losers?

The losers are the staff of the firm bought by the conglomerate. Many jobs will probably be lost.

Individual products could be sold to a competitor and be absorbed into its factories with no extra jobs.

Often these actions and aims are combined. The conglomerate retains some parts and sells off others. The actions of conglomerates are seen as threats by managers and workers alike. Examine Case Study 3.2.

CASE STUDY 3.2

Conglomerate activity

'Hanson Launches £780 million Bid For Rank Hovis McDougal'

On Monday 5th October 1992, Hanson, the Anglo-American conglomerate, launched a £780 million cash bid for RHM. Let us look at the two 'contestants' in the battle, or dual.

RHM is a well-established baking and grocery group. It has large interests in flour milling and baking of bread and cakes, and has *diversified* into foods and food services. It has some overseas interests. Baking and flour now account for some 40% of turnover only.

Product group	Sales (£m)	Profit (£m)
Milling and bread baking	667	60
(Including Mothers Pride and Hovis)		
Grocery products	281	35
(Including Paxo, Robertson's and Sharwoods)		
Cakes	176	18
(Including Mr Kipling and Cadbury's Mini Rolls)		
Food services	207	17
(Including Chesswoods and Rombouts)		
US activities	187	14
Others	15	5
TOTAL	1,533	149

Milling and baking is a *highly competitive market* in the UK, and is dominated by the major supermarket buyers. It owns some very well-known *brands* in the grocery lines, i.e. Sharwoods, Paxo, Bisto and Mr Kipling.

RHM is no stranger to takeover bids, having fought off raids from the Australian firm Goodman Fielder Wattie, and a consortium of investors headed by Sir James Goldsmith.

RHM's performance has been slipping over the last few years. Shareholders have seen the price of their shares fall from about 450p to today's price of 175p. The bid from Hanson, equivalent to a price of 220p caused the market price to rise to 241p, though.

The RHM Group, if broken up, could be worth around £1.1 billion, with the grocery products division being worth about £430m and the food services business about £200m. *Large investors* are reported to be willing to accept an offer of about 240p.

Hanson, the Anglo-American conglomerate, has interests in many fields. Its sales and profits for 1991 were as follows:

	Profit (£m)	Sales (£m)
Coal mining	170	1099
Chemicals	136	563
Materials handling	49	276
Gold mining	38	98
Tobacco	240	2670
Aggregates	69	573
Forest products	44	178
Others	229	2234
Profit on disposal of assets	17	
Net Interest Income	188	
Expenses	(34)	
TOTAL	1,319	7,691
Taxation	(284)	
Profit after Tax	1,035	

The Hanson Group own many well known firms and brand names, e.g. Grove Cranes, Imperial Tobacco, Seven seas, Ever Ready, ARC, London Brick, and the

Volex range of electrical fittings.

Food products and brands are noticeable by their absence! They do have interest, with less than 50% shareholdings, in a US restaurant chain and a shrimp and tuna packing company. Earlier food businesses were rapidly sold by Hanson, i.e. the food businesses of Imperial (Tobacco) and SCM in America. How will RHM fit in? Is Hanson likely to dispose of the assets, or aim to turn it into an efficient, profitable business? Recent announcements by Hanson would indicate that perhaps they are now aiming for 'organic growth of existing businesses'.

(Adapted from Articles in *Financial Times*, Hanson's 1991 *Annual Report* and *The Observer*)

Questions and activities

1. Define the terms marked in italics.
2. Present the sales and profit data from the above case in the form of bar and pie charts. Which form of presentation is best if you wish to compare and contrast the performance of the two companies? What other presentation methods are there?
3. Using the information contained in the case above, what action do you think Hanson might take after it has taken over RHM? Attempt to quantify your answers.

Some companies grow from being purely national and become international.

Multinational companies

Multinational companies are defined as those companies which operate from a headquarters in one country, but manufacture and trade in other countries through subsidiary companies.

Multinationals are a topic of debate and are unpopular in many parts of the world, and with much of the media these days. The description 'multinational firm' itself is better replaced with a fairer, less emotive title such as 'international company'. Multinationals are an old phenomenon, the first having been established by Prussia in 1815.

A multinational company operates factories and other facilities in many parts of the world, and has total control over them. The governments in these countries may have little say in how they are run, or how dividends are allocated. Many multinationals are household names, e.g. Ford, General Motors, Shell, Unilever, Cadbury Schweppes, Siemens, BAT (British America Tobacco), RTZ, and Volkswagen. Certain industries are dominated by multinationals – the motor industry, the oil industry, soaps and detergents. First, a little history of multinationals. Multinationals developed initially to get round import restrictions, and to secure supplies of materials.

Trade based multinationals

Initially, when all manufacture was small scale, firms tended to manufacture in the same country. When modern mass production methods made high output and low costs possible, exports started to occur. A country which was good at the process would develop a distinct advantage in this export trade, and soon thrived. Naturally, and in particularly in the 1930s and the time of the Great Depression, countries started to put barriers in the way of imports. The exporting countries then built factories overseas, and one type of multinational was born. Find out when and why the US Ford Motor Company came to the UK. The first wave of this type of multinational development came from US firms. Later, in the 1950s, the main drive came from British and European companies. Now, the trend is for Japanese companies to expand their manufacturing worldwide, but particularly in Europe following new restrictions of imports into Europe under the '1992' legislation. Look at the development of Honda, Toyota, Hitachi and Nissan in the UK, since new restrictions of imports into Europe under the '1992' legislation.

Material based multinationals

Manufacturing companies need raw materials. Many of these are mined, grown or produced overseas. Some companies set up farming, mining or refining operations in these countries to secure their raw materials. They thus became multinationals as they established subsidiaries overseas. Tea companies established plantations in India and Sri Lanka, coffee firms in Brazil and Kenya, soap companies developed plantations in the Far East and so on. The best example, must be the oil industry. Here the crude oil, tends to be found in undeveloped areas of the world, but the markets for the products are in the highly developed countries of the western world.

The oil firms secured their crude oil through arrangements with the source economies. This worked well at first, but problems soon developed, sometimes getting close to war. For example, the oil industry in Iran was developed by the Anglo Iranian Oil Company. It was a British multinational, which was to become BP eventually. It was run by the British and, as seen inside Iran, for the British. In July 1951 the company was effectively nationalised by Iran's Prime Minister, Mohammad Mossadegh, and all expatriates were expelled from the refinery complex at Abadan. The diplomatic fall-out nearly led to war between the two countries, and Britain sent a cruiser to the head waters of the Gulf. Later, the British were asked to return, but now in the role of managers of the business for its Iranian owners.

However they develop, multinationals are all international firms. There are advantages and disadvantages for this type of firm. The key points of view concerned are that of the 'host' nation, and that of the nation where the multinational is based. Study Table 3.3, which summarises the advantages and disadvantages. Some important points will be looked at in more depth after this.

Table 3.3
The advantages and disadvantages of multinationals

	Advantages	Disadvantages
For the host nation	They bring in foreign exchange	They can interfere in the politics of the country
	They provide high quality training and education	They can destroy local culture
	They widen the tax base of the host nation	They can remove the country's foreign exchange
	The host economy gains employment	They make development harder for local businesses
For the donor nation	They destroy jobs	They have no real alternative as they would have to close down as they can export no longer
	They export special skills and knowledge	

Multinationals destroy local jobs

Multinationals do destroy local jobs, but these are usually in the 'home' country. Most multinationals end up by transferring manual jobs from the home country to the host. What is lost at home is gained overseas. Labour here is often cheaper, so it makes economic sense. The multinational may also avoid trade union power, and gain even more financially. Here are two examples to illustrate this point.

1. *Example 1. Nissan Sunderland* In 1994 Nissan put its new factory in Sunderland on full production. The cars, which are being sold in UK and mainland Europe, would otherwise have come from Japan. So jobs in Japan have been lost, but replaced by different ones in the UK.

   It is not really as simple as that. Nissan will now sell more cars than they would have been allowed to import into the EU. They would have been subject to a high import tariff, a special tax on imported goods, or (worse) a tight quota, i.e. a limit on the number of cars which can be imported. So the number of new jobs created in the UK will exceed the number lost in Japan. Some of these will still be employed making car parts for use in the UK factory. Also, some new, higher skilled jobs will be created in Japan monitoring the performance of the new subsidiary company, and accounting for its profits.

2. *Example 2. Switching jobs from UK or USA* to, say, China where much cheaper labour is available. Labour in Asia is also far less protected by trade unions, so terms and conditions may be easier and cheaper for the company. It is all about productivity, or the output/unit of labour expressed in terms of money, i.e. value of production/unit labour cost.

Multinationals deprive the host country of foreign exchange

This can be and has been a real problem. Multinationals have the ability to move capital and profits around the world and avoid tax and exchange control regulations through its policy on inter-company pricing. An example will explain.

A firm, part of a multinational concern, makes a product in country X. It imports a part from the home country Y at a cost to it of £10. As a result of the business in country X, the firm makes a profit of £10 in country X. It cannot remit profits from X to Y, and will have to pay 50% tax to the government of country X. It avoids this by fixing the price of the part, which it is effectively selling to itself, at £20.

The home country Y now makes the profit, and the overseas firm now just breaks even. The host government loses profits, and also has to part with more foreign exchange than it should have. This is illustrated by Figure 3.1.

In fact, a multinational that trades with itself can make its profit exactly where it wants. Governments have developed methods of trying to control this, but with only partial success. For example, some governments use independent agencies to check invoices and agree that they represent a fair value for what is being bought or sold. They will also certify the actual transfer of the goods. Without these clearances the foreign exchange will not be released. In addition some governments have tight inter-country taxation regulations. This can result in tax being due on profits made overseas.

Now, some good points regarding multinationals.

Modern skills and training are brought to the host nations by multinationals

Multinationals do bring in skills and training, and many set up first-class training schools in the host nation. A good multinational training is a qualification in many countries. One question arises: is the technology right for the country? Perhaps it would be better off with more manual processes— the reality is that they have no choice. Multinationals also give professional and management training to some local staff, and the more forward-thinking multinational will give them positions of real responsibility.

Multinationals, then, present us with a very tricky situation, with a clear balance of pros and cons – the typical Business Studies dilemma. They are unpopular, but are probably getting a worse reputation than they deserve.

The recent tendency of firms to diversify, expand into an unrelated product area to reduce the risk of having 'all ones eggs in one basket', has resulted in many complex firms. An example would be BAT, British American Tobacco, where it has interests in insurance and financial services as well as the original tobacco based industries. This type of firm can be a national or multinational conglomerate.

As firms grow they tend to become more complex. The management of the firm will be put under more and more pressure, and control of the firm may become lax. At this point the firm will have to reorganise if it is to continue to grow satisfactorily. This is true if the firm has grown by merger or takeover, and particularly if it has diversified, i.e. expanded into different product groups. At this point the firm may decide to adopt a policy of *centralisation* or *decentralisation*.

Centralisation

Centralisation is where control is gathered to the top, or heart of the firm. Reports and requests will flow in, and decisions will eventually flow out.

Assumption. The host nation forbids the parent company to transfer profits or dividends to country in foreign exchange. It does allow payment for approved imported machinery, and encourages the export of materials and other products.

Donor country	Host country
Parent company	Subsidiary company

Case 1. The donor company, the parent, sells machinery to the subsidiary company.

Secondhand machines are refurbished and exported at a price of £100,000. Book value to parent is £30,000 ⟶ Subsidiary accepts the item, gets approval to pay, and remits all the £100,000 to the parent.

Parent company now has £70,000 in foreign exchange from its subsidiary. ⟵

Case 2. The subsidiary company exports commodities to the parent at below world market price.

Subsidiary produces a basic commodity with a value of £1,000 per tonne, but sells it to the parent for £500 per tonne.

Parent sells the commodity on the open market, or uses it itself. It profits by £500 per tonne. If the subsidiary sells 1,000 tonnes the parent will gain a profit of £500,000. ⟵

Figure 3.1 *How multinationals may extract foreign exchange from the host nation*

The structure of the firm will resemble a triangle. Decision makers are at the point, and the operational units at the foot. In between will be layers of staff.

This type of organisation will tend to be associated with a lack of trust at the top. The business will have a high proportion of fixed costs, or overheads. Decision making will be slow.

Decentralisation

Decentralisation is the reverse of centralisation. Decisions are devolved down to the operating units. The minimum of reports and requests flow up and down. The staff roles, now not needed, are redundant. The firm will reduce costs, act and respond faster, and be a fitter, leaner organisation. This type of organisation is associated with trust.

In diagrammatic terms, the firm now resembles a drawing pin – a wide base with a thin path leading to the top.

This tends to become an ongoing situation. A firm grows, then begins to falter. It reorganises, and may decide to decentralise. It grows again, then falters as it outgrows the organisation. It will reorganise again, perhaps centralising this time. If this is successful growth will begin again.

Now, an introduction to College Dynamics (CD) plc. This is the fictional company that will be followed throughout this book. Study Case Study 3.3 carefully and, applying the knowledge gained from this chapter, trace how the company has grown and developed.

CASE STUDY 3.3

College Dynamics plc

College Dynamics (CD) plc is an advanced consumer electronics company in UK. It manufactures a range of high quality audio equipment, but also imports a range of cheaper mass produced equipment from Japan. It markets 'software' for its range of compact discs and tapes, and owns its own music publishing business. It exports compact discs and tapes, as well as very high quality speakers, expensive TVs and high fidelity equipment, all of which it makes in its factory in Warrington.

CD plc was founded by two University friends who had read Management Science together. The business started as a simple import exercise, bringing tapes and CDs from Germany to sell in the UK. As the firm prospered they added audio equipment from Japan to their list of products. Later they bought a factory and business in Warrington where quality equipment was made. Using the success of their original firm they were able to expand rapidly this declining business, and turn it into a good profit and cash generator.

The music and software side of the business was favoured by one of the founders who expanded it by the merger of the company with a recording studio and musical publishing firm in London. They now both publish and promote music and artists for other companies, and retain quality performers for themselves. They now own a compact disc production

company in Taiwan where their 'own label' CDs are made.

Future plans include the diversification into video tapes, the purchase of a small plastics factory, and a specialist firm in the Midlands that specialises in quality electromagnets, the key part of a speaker.

Questions and activities

1. Trace the development of CD plc through the various sectors of industry.
2. Illustrate the growth of the company on a diagram.
3. Identify specific examples of vertical and horizontal integration, mergers and takeovers.
4. What might the firm get out of its proposed diversification and expansion?

SUMMARY

Having studied this chapter you will be able to:

▽ Explain clearly the differences between unincorporated and incorporated companies.

▽ Describe the requirements of:

– *Sole traders*
– *Partnerships*
– *Private limited companies (Ltd)*
– *Public limited companies (plc)*

▽ Understand the legal differences between Ltd and plcs.

▽ Outline what conglomerates are, and describe their motives and the way they grow.

▽ Examine critically the pros and cons of multinational corporations.

▽ Briefly explain the cyclical nature of organisations, and describe the processes of

– *Centralisation*
– *Decentralisation*

You will also have learnt the meanings of the terms:

– *Articles and Memorandum of Association*
– *Takeovers and mergers*
– *Subsidiary and associate companies*

Questions and activities

Technical terms and glossary

In the sections below you are given a series of technical terms and their meanings. They have been scrambled, though. You must match up the business term and its definition. When you have got them correctly paired, transfer them to an alphabetical vocabulary or glossary book.

You are also advised to transfer any definitions obtained during the exercises in the case studies into this glossary book.

Technical terms

1. Sole trader
2. Assembly operations
3. Partnership
4. Retail operations
5. Memorandum of Association
6. Articles of Association
7. Multinational business
8. Public limited company
9. Takeover
10. Merger
11. Subsidiary company
12. Associate company
13. Private limited company
14. Holding company
15. Conglomerate concern

Definitions

A. A form of business where a group of people act together. They share the risk and the profit equally or severally.

B. One company purchases another by buying its shares, often without the agreement of the company concerned. The purchase would then be considered as hostile.

C. The simplest form of business. The owner is the business, as far as the law is concerned, and carries the full financial responsibility.

D. Two companies becoming one by agreement.

E. The legal document which governs the internal relationship between the company and its shareholders. It defines the rights and duties of the membership, i.e. the powers of directors, the conduct of meetings, etc.

F. A company where a controlling interest in its shares is held by another firm, i.e. 50% of its shares, plus 1, are owned by another company.

G. A joint stock company which controls others.

H. The legal document which governs the external relationship between the company and third parties. Must include the name of the company, its objectives, the amount and division of the share capital, etc.

I. A production process where parts made elsewhere are assembled to form the final product. Typical products made this way are popular motor vehicles, domestic white and brown goods, and even modern aircraft.

J. A firm where a significant, but not a controlling interest is held by another firm (between 20% and 50% of the shares)

K. An incorporated business but its shares are not traded on the Stock Exchange. It is owned by its shareholders. Shares cannot be advertised for sale, so can only be sold by private arrangement.

L. Operations involving the selling of goods or services to the general public for their own use. Goods and services are not expected to be resold.

M. A form of business which grows by purchasing others. The only thing in common between them is their ability to make money. This is usually done by splitting the firm and selling the parts separately.

N. An incorporated business with its shares traded on the Stock Exchange. It is owned by its shareholders, institutional or otherwise, which are part of the private as opposed to the state sector.

O. A business with subsidiaries all over the world, but has its headquarters in one country.

Short answer questions

1. Why might the directors of a business wish to retain private limited company status rather than seek public limited company status?

2. Distinguish between a public company and a public corporation.

3. Which two documents must be provided by the promoters of a new company before it can be registered? What are the main differences between them?

4. What is a conglomerate? How does it make its money?

5. What is a multinational company? What advantages does it give to the donor and recipient countries?

6. List five differences between the legal requirements of public and private limited companies.

Data response questions

1. The following extract is part of a document sent to Trafalgar House shareholders informing them, among other things, of a proposed acquisition. Read the article and answer the questions which follow.

Trafalgar House and its activities

Trafalgar House was incorporated in England on 22nd December, 1965 as a private limited company under the Companies Act 1948 with registered number 867281 and was re-registered on 20th January, 1982 as a public limited company pursuant to the Companies Act 1980. The Company now operates under the Companies Act 1985. The registered office of the Company which is also its principal place of business is at 1 Berkeley Street, London W1A 1BY. The principal objects of Trafalgar House, as set out in clause 4 of its Memorandum of Association, are to act as a holding company and to invest in and develop property and to enter into financial and commercial transactions of all kinds.

Trafalgar House is the holding company of a group whose principal activities include property and investment, construction and engineering, shipping, aviation and hotels, and oil and gas.

(a) What distinguishes a public limited company from a private limited company?

(b) Explain the main purpose of the Memorandum of Association.

(c) List *two* pieces of information, other than the Memorandum of Association, required by the Registrar of Companies when forming a public limited company.

(d) Explain the term 'holding company'.

(e) Suggest and explain *three* factors that might be considered by Trafalgar House when assessing whether to go ahead with any acquisition.

(Associated Examining Board, Business Studies (A), Paper 1, June 1989)

2. The following passage is adapted from 'Business Brief' (*The Economist*, 29/10/83). Read the passage carefully and answer the questions which follow.

The recent decision of Nissan's chairman to drop his opposition to building cars in Britain means that a formal announcement of the controversial investment is only weeks away. Arriving at that decision took three years of indecision. This was caused by anxieties over:

1. The duration of the recession in the United Kingdom economy.

2. The amount of UK manufactured components to be used in Nissan cars.

3. Whether or not Britain would continue to be a member of the Common Market.

4. The number of unions the Nissan Company would have to deal with. It would prefer to work with only one negotiating body.

Note: Nissan is a multinational company which manufactures cars.

(a) Define the term 'multinational company'.

(b) State and explain
(i) *two* reasons why a multinational might be welcomed by the host country;
(ii) *two* reasons why a country might be suspicious of a multinational's wish to invest in it.

(c) Explain why the four anxieties of Nissan listed in the passage made the company reluctant to invest in the UK.

(Associated Examining Board, Business Studies (A) Paper 1, June 1985)

4

The importance of money

Preview

▼ This chapter establishes the importance of the management and control of money.

▼ The important technical terms of profit, cash, stock, capital, capital expenditure, revenue, revenue expenditure, cash flow and working capital will be introduced and defined, and then the much misunderstood difference between profit and cash flow will be studied in depth.

▼ The concept of a firm's liquidity will be developed and the importance of credit, both given and taken, and its management will be studied.

Why are we starting with the management of money, rather than products or people? Any successful business requires a first-class combination of a product for which there is a strong demand, an efficient management and adequate cash. Since it is the lack of cash which will force a firm into liquidation, money is considered first. A firm without a good product will, in the end, fail, but only when it runs out of cash. Failure in the area of management skills will probably also result in the closure or sale of the business even if it has a good product. Good financial management will not guarantee success, but may well mask the poor product quality or the bad management skills for some time. Poor performance in the area of financial management will virtually guarantee failure, though, thus showing the importance of money and its management today.

The earliest businesses were based on the exchange of goods and services, or *barter trade* as it is called (also known as *counter trade*). This was a complicated and slow process. Bartering is very restrictive, and the medium of money was invented very quickly. Now all businesses run on money, and in many countries the reward of workers by other than money is illegal. Its management is now vital to the operation of businesses, and in some cases it is the business itself. (Look at the modern money markets.) Nowadays the objective of private businesses seems to be to make money, or a profit,

through the provision of goods or services. The importance of money to businesses should be coming clear.

A firm operates by combining the *factors of production* to produce its goods or services. It has to pay for these factors, so needs money (see Chapter 1).

Money, therefore, can be considered as the 'life blood' of a company, and a lack of it will clearly jeopardise a firm's future. The efficient and effective raising, use and control of money is the route to survival and success. As this part of the book develops, some basic questions will be posed and answered. A series of money control 'tools' will be developed, and their value in decision making described.

A business has to carefully balance the inflow of cash from sales with the outflow of cash from payments being made. The most important terms to consider are: capital, capital expenditure, revenue, revenue expenditure, profit, working capital, cash, cash flow, and liquidity.

Capital

Capital is a much used term, with more than one meaning. In the financial sense, it is simply another word for money. If you start a business with £100 of your own money, the business has £100 capital available to it. If you sell shares to friends, say 100 shares at £1 each, you have generated another £100 of capital for the concern. It is a measure of wealth.

A suitable business definition is:

Capital is the funds invested in a business in order to acquire the assets which the firm needs to operate.

Capital expenditure

Capital expenditure is the spending of money on plant and equipment for use in the business over a period.

It is usually spent to provide productive facilities for the business. Examples would be buildings, land, plant and equipment, furniture and fittings, cars and computers. All these items have a useful, or productive life, from a few years in the case of cars, to 40 years or more in the case of factory buildings. Domestically, it is the purchase of furniture, TVs, CD players, cars and other *consumer durables*. They wear out with time, and need replacing eventually.

Revenue

Revenue is the money coming into a firm from sales of goods and services.

It is calculated by multiplying the sales volume (number of items sold) by the price. An example: a firm sells 100 tape decks a day at a price of £17.50 each. It has a sales revenue of £1,750 per day. When this money actually comes into a firm depends on the credit terms given.

Revenue expenditure

Revenue expenditure is the spending of money on goods and services that are used at once, and have no value in later periods.

Examples are spending on raw materials, packaging and packing materials, paper, fuels, salaries and wages. Domestically, it is the spending on food, drink and petrol.

Profit

Just what is profit? The answer is less simple than might be supposed. An example: a firm buys in a tape deck for £50 and sells it for £150. All transactions are made in cash. The firm has made a profit of £100. If this was the only dealing made in the period, there would be an increase in the cash of £100.

There is a small change. If the firm was to sell the deck on 60 days credit, it would not expect the money for 60 days. It would have spent £50 to buy it. By definition the firm has still made £100 profit on the sale, even though the firm will not have the £150 in cash until the 60 days are over.

Another version: if the firm was to buy the deck on 90 days credit, and sell on 60 days credit, it will still, by definition, make £100 profit on the sale of each deck, but would now maximise its holding of cash, i.e. it would make £100 profit at time of sale. It would get £150 in cash in 60 days. It would then hold all of this for 30 days until it pays out £50 to the supplier.

The giving and taking of credit has no effect on profit. A sale is made when ownership is transferred, and profit is earned at that point. The government usually taxes profits, and the firm is liable for this when a good is sold. It can be seen that in some cases of credit transactions, the firm may have to pay tax on profits when the actual cash has not been received. Remember that a profitable company may not have any cash, and, equally, a cash rich firm may not be a profitable one.

Profit is one of the most misunderstood terms used in business. It is an accounting concept and is strictly defined. It is rarely the increase in money in the till at the end of the day, nor is it likely to be the increase in the firm's bank balance at the end of the month.

The full definition of profit is thus:

Profit is an accounting concept, and is the difference between the price paid for a good or service, and all the costs associated with its production and sale, irrespective of any credit terms given or taken.

Profit is recorded in a firm's Profit and Loss Account. An examination of the Profit and Loss Account for CD plc for 1992 shown as Figure 4.1, reveals that there are many types of profit (see Chapter 4).

Gross profit

Gross profit is the value of sales less the direct cost of those sales.

Consider CD plc. It buys in products and components, assembles them, and finally sells them. The gross profit is the sales value from all their sales, less the cost to CD plc of all the bought in components. It does not allow for the selling costs they incur, e.g. head office expenses, research, sales assistants, managers, rental of stores, purchase of land, and rates.

Net profit

Net profit is gross profit less the selling, marketing and administration costs.

Examine Figure 4.1 again.

This is the amount of profit left after all selling and marketing expenses have been deducted. This is also called the profit before tax.

	1992	1991
	£m	£m
Sales	1,500	1,200
Cost of sales	(750)	(600)
Gross profit	750	600
Distribution costs, including marketing	(350)	(300)
Administration expenses	(150)	(100)
Other expenses	(70)	(50)
	(570)	(450)
Trading profit	180	150
Net interest paid	(10)	(10)
Profit on ordinary activities before tax	170	140
Profit/Corporation taxes	(40)	(35)
Profit on ording activities after tax	130	105
Extraordinary items	(0)	5
Profit attributable to shareholders	130	110
Dividends	(80)	(45)
Profit retained for year	50	75

Figure 4.1 *College Dynamic plc Profit and Loss Account for year ended 31st December 1992, i.e. forecast profit after 1 year's trading*

It is now generally accepted in accounting circles to calculate net profit as follows:
Gross profit *less*
Selling and distribution expenses *less*
Administration expenses *less*
Financial expenses *equals*
NET PROFIT

Profit after tax

Businesses are liable for tax in many areas. For instance they will have to pay corporation tax on any profits made. This tax is a first call on profits, and takes precedence over all other calls on it. The remainder, the 'profit after tax' is the amount of profit made by the firm that 'belongs' to the owners, the shareholders. It is up to them to decide what is done with it.

Be very careful when looking at profit and be sure that the correct one, gross or net, is being considered. A statement about 'a good year' or '12% profit this year' is only of value if the reader knows which profit is being referred to.

Net profit, therefore, will be distributed to tax, to shareholders as dividends, or retained in the business for the purchase of stock, assets or as reserves. This is known as the appropriation of profits, or the *Appropriation Account.*

Working capital

The money, or rather cash, that a firm needs to enable it to operate on a day-to-day basis is called working capital. It will cover the purchase of materials, etc., the financing of stocks and of sales made on credit. It will also be needed to pay for items and expenses that are not related to sales as such, but are costs of running the business itself. Examples would be insurance, rent, Unified Business Rates for the premises, and salaries of employees.

Accountants look at this in a more formal way. They refer to it as ' Net Current Assets' or the difference between 'Current Assets and Current Liabilities'. (See Chapter 11.)

Cash

Money in a 'liquid' form is called cash (see Chapter 11) and is easily accessible. It may be literally cash in the till or it may be bank accounts that are in credit. It is money that can be spent.

Cash flow

The movement of money into and out of a business is called the cash flow. Positive cash flow is a critical management target. It is one of the key *performance indicators.*

Liquidity

Liquidity is the ability of a business to pay its bills, or to be able to meet its liabilities.

A 'liquid' firm will have adequate cash to pay its bills. When a firm is forced into bankruptcy, it is not liquid, it is out of cash. As shall be seen, it may be profitable, and may have many assets, but it has no cash.

An important point here is the difference between *bankruptcy* and *insolvency.* Individuals and unincorporated firms can be declared bankrupt. Incorporated companies can declare themselves insolvent. They cannot be declared bankrupt, but can be forced into insolvency.

To see how these all interlink, where the problems come from, and how a good company will manage these, you will trace the history of a firm first starting up, then expanding and finally thriving in a competitive market. You will identify its requirements for money, how its profitability and liquidity will change with time and size, and develop a set of methods, or tools, that can be used to assist in assessing and managing problems as they occur, so making decisions on courses of action easier. Finally, you will examine means of reporting, in financial terms, both within a firm, and externally, the results of a firm's trading. First, though, it is important to ensure that the differences between money, profit and liquidity are really understood.

Profit or cash?

One of the critical distinctions in business is between profit and cash, or rather cash flow. It is the difference between the profitability of a firm (the amount of profit it is earning, expressed as a percentage of sales value, or of the money invested in the business) and its liquidity (its ability to pay its bills).

As stated earlier, profit is defined as an accounting concept and is the difference between the money brought in from the sale of a good or service, and all the costs incurred in producing it, regardless of the credit terms given or taken.

Credit terms

Profit is earned when a good is sold 'legally', i.e. when its ownership is transferred. The fact that it is a credit sale, or that you may not actually have paid for the materials used in its manufacture is ignored in calculating profit.

One month's credit is virtually a cash sale for most businesses, and others expect much more, up to 120 days. Other buyers pay late, and need a lot of pressure before they will part with their valuable cash. So a business may be owed money for sales made and where the goods have been delivered. It will have many debtors, or people who owe it money. They are an asset of a business, provided that they are seen as able to pay the debt eventually. Effectively the seller is lending money to its customers free of charge.

Every manufacturer and seller is also a buyer. Firms do not always pay their bills on receipt of the materials or services bought. So a firm conserves cash by holding on to it. It has a list of creditors, i.e. firms it owes money to. Until it pays them, it is taking a free loan from its suppliers.

A basic rule for businesses is to get your sales revenue in fast, but do not pay your bills until you are forced to. All firms try to do this, but the larger the firm the greater the success there is likely to be in following the rule. A large firm has buying power: its order would not be given up lightly. Equally, it can pressurise its smaller customers.

Stock

Firms often make or buy products in batches, or groups. Since profit is made when an item is sold, it does not affect profit whether the item sold was the first or last of a batch. More so, the quantity of unsold stock has no effect on profit. Stock ties up money and influences liquidity, but does not change profit.

Here is a simple example to illustrate the critical differences between profit and cash, and between liquidity and bankruptcy. CD plc, in its early days, bought and sold video cassettes. It bought them for £3 each, and sold them for £6. Thus it made a profit of £3 on each one it sold. This is the basic cost structure for CD's early business. What actually happened? Its liquidity and cash position will depend on the terms of trade, and the credits given and taken. Work through the following situations.

Scenario 1
In week 1 CD sold 400 tapes. It made £1,200 profit. CD is profitable. Is it liquid? It all depends on what the full situation is. Consider this scenario.

CD got the cheapest price for its tapes by buying them in batches of 1,000. It had to borrow the money for this, so it has a loan of £3,000 outstanding to the bank. CD's total revenue after selling 400 tapes is only £2,400. CD still owes the bank £600. If it had to pay the loan back right now it could not do so. CD does have 600 tapes in stock, though. It has profit of £1,200, but no cash. CD is technically not liquid. If pressed it could not pay the bank, so would be declared bankrupt. But CD has made a profit, so where is it? It is tied up in stock, i.e. CD's stock of 600 unsold tapes. CD has no money, so it is not liquid. But it may well survive if it has secured a line of credit with the bank.

Lack of cash does not mean lack of profit. Profit, however, is no guarantee of liquidity.

Here is another situation for CD:

Scenario 2
During the second week CD sells 1,000 tapes. Price and costs are the same, so the firm now makes £3,000 profit.

The situation now is that CD bought the tapes on credit and will not have to pay for them for two weeks. All the sales are for cash. CD was able to bank

Dealers in a modern trading room

£6,000. The business is profitable, and liquid. It can meet its bills. Note, though, that £3,000 of the cash should be reserved to pay the supplier eventually. It is liquid now, but careless spending could mean that it will not be able to pay the supplier in the future. It has time, but it has to be careful.

The presence of cash means survival in the short run. But this cash has to be managed carefully.

An additional situation:

Scenario 3

In week 3 CD sells another 2,000 tapes at the same costs and prices. It now buys for cash, otherwise it would have had to pay £3.50 each, but sold them all on five days credit. CD paid its supplier by cheque.

CD has made a profit of £6,000, but has received no cash in at all yet. It has given a cheque for £6,000 to the supplier. If the bank will not honour this, CD is bankrupt. If the bank waits for five days, there should be £12,000 in the account, and all would be satisfactory. It is these five days that are critical.

High profitably is no guarantee of liquidity, in fact there seems to be an inverse relationship, i.e. a lack of cash seems more likely.

In all three examples, CD was profitable. The point of these examples is to show how a firm may be profitable, but may or may not be liquid. Cash flow was different in all three cases. It also demonstrates that the growth of money in a firm's bank balance is not a valid indication of profitability.

A final example to illustrate this point:

Scenario 4

Return to the first example, but now CD also sold for cash a computer for £800 cash. It still has a profit of £1,200, but has a cash balance of £200. It is both profitable and liquid. It is only keeping itself liquid, or solvent, by selling some of its assets.

Cash rich is no indication of profitability.

Now, you will examine the practical applications of the above in the context of College Dynamics. It set up a small office in Bath and employed two members of staff to do the clerical work and administration involved with importing from the Far East. The partners would do the marketing, selling and accounting themselves. They arranged an overdraft of £50,000 with the bank and put in £10,000 of their own cash. After the first two months, when they sold nothing but built up many contacts, their current account fell to £1,250. They started selling well in the next two months. All began to look good.

At a meeting after seven weeks the partners were happy. Imagine this scene.

'Profits are now up to £20,000, we will soon be able to get those 8 Series BMWs', said Bob. At this moment his secretary put her head round the door.

'Bob, ring the bank manager. She is worried about our overdraft. She claims it now stands at

£52,000 and wants to know we why have not contacted her. If you don't get in contact in three days she will call in the overdraft!'

Somebody must be wrong. Who is it?

Examine the entries in the financial records of CD for the period (Table 4.1). Note that not all of the firm's bills have been paid, and it was also owed cash by some of its customers. It has been selling, but has not been getting money in. Has it got its credit under control? Does it know how much money of its own it is absorbing in giving credit to its buyers? It is very

Table 4.1

CD Ltd: record book for two-month period

Rent for offices	£1,000 per month. all paid
Rent for furniture	£500 per month, only one month paid for
Rent for office equipment	£700 per month.,all paid
Rent for cars	£700 per month, only one month paid
Payments for business rates	£300 per month, both paid
Insurance payments	£250 per month, both paid
Pension contributions	£500 per month, both paid
Tax and VAT collected (net)	£500 outstanding, none paid
Gas	£50 paid
Electricity	£100 paid
Water	£30 to pay
Postage	£200 all paid
Telephone	£350 to pay
Materials and supplies	£150 paid cash
Petty cash	£150 paid
Salaries for staff	£3000 per month all paid
Salaries for owners	£5000 per month one month paid
Travelling expenses	£400 all paid
Sales:	Order 1 £12,000 paid for, i.e. cash received by the bank
	Order 2 £24,000 paid for
	Order 3 £24,000 half the cash received
	Order 4 £36,000 no payment received
	Order 5 £72,000 no payment received
Purchases	Batch 1 £6,000
	Batch 2 £12,000
	Batch 3 £12,000
	Batch 4 £54,000 all these invoices have been paid by CD Ltd

tempting to go for sales, if the business can afford it.

Now tabulate the costs, and analyse them between paid, received, outstanding or due. The

Table 4.2

CD Ltd: analysis of debtors and creditors

Item	Paid	Received	Outstanding	Due
Offices	2,000	0	0	0
Furniture	500	0	500	0
Equipment	1,400	0	0	0
Cars	700	0	700	0
Rates	600	0	0	0
Insurance	500	0	0	0
Pensions	1,000	0	0	0
VAT	0	0	500	0
Gas	50	0	0	0
Electricity	100	0	0	0
Water	0	0	30	0
Postage	200	0	0	0
Telephone	0	0	350	0
Materials	150	0	0	0
Petty Cash	150	0	0	0
Salaries (1)	6,000	0	0	0
(2)	5,000	0	5000	0
Expenses	400	0	0	0
Sales (1)	0	12,000	0	0
(2)	0	24,000	0	0
(3)	0	12,000	0	12,000
(4)	0	0	0	36,000
(5)	0	0	0	72,000
Purchases (1)	6,000	0	0	0
(2)	12,000	0	0	0
(3)	12,000	0	0	0
(4)	54,000	0	0	0
TOTALS	101,850	48,000	7,080	120,000

CD has issued cheques for £101,850 but has received only £48,000. This represents a net withdrawal from their account of £53,850. Their account at the bank would have stood at (£52,600), £2,600 over their agreed overdraft limit. No wonder the bank manager got in contact.

When all the cash comes in, the firm will be liquid again. The account should stand at £60,320. Note that the business has generated £59,070 if and when it gets all its money in, and pays all its outstanding accounts.

Now, the profit forecast. CD have been able to operate with a mark-up of 100% to fix their price. This has come through hard negotiating, and an agreement to pay cash with order. So:

Sales for period:	*£168,000*
Cost of sales	*(£84,000)*
Gross profit	*£84,000*
Expenses for period	*(£24,930)*
Net profit	*£59,070*

If CD had not given or taken any credit, it would have generated £59,070 in cash, the same as its net profit. The importance of allowing for credit terms can be plainly seen.

The profit is very satisfactory, but look at the cash position. The firm's money is tied up in the debtors that the firm has. These, at £120,000, should be reduced. (The cash position would have been even worse if the partners had bought compact discs for stock, but luckily they did not do so). Perhaps they should not have paid cash for the items. One month's credit would have kept them clear of their overdraft limit.

They now have a problem. Since the cash position was so easy to keep track of, they are building a reputation as poor businessmen. The bank may be more difficult in future, may not be so ready to agree new overdraft limits, or advance loans. They may even start to charge higher rates of interest since they now consider the firm to be a greater risk because its management seems poor. This is a high price for some overactive selling, and a slip in the accounting department. Perhaps CD should employ an accounts clerk as soon as possible?

Let us recapitulate. Money flows into a firm when its goods or services are actually paid for. Money flows out when the firm pays its bills, or pays its staff. This will not be when the goods were legally bought or sold, however, so will not be related directly to the earning of profit. The balance between these two flows, and the control of them, is critical to the operation of a business. Examine two extreme cases:

A supermarket chain

This is a cash business, and very few goods are sold on credit. It is a powerful firm, however, so can negotiate favourable terms from its suppliers. If it buys on 60 days credit, which would not be impossible, it will probably be 'cash rich'. It will have the cash to pay the suppliers long before it has to pay them. It can even lend this money, using the *overnight market*, i.e. that part of the money market where firms can lend or borrow large sums of money for a very short period and make even more. This type of business collects its money early, but pays late. If it is slack it will be unlikely to go into liquidation; it will just lose a little of its profit.

The airline industry is highly capital-intensive.

A shipbuilder

This, on paper at least, is just the opposite to the supermarket chain. The ship can take three years to build. The buyer would like to pay for it after it has been built and delivered, but the materials suppliers will have to be paid long before that. The firm will be 'cash lean', and will have to be especially careful. It could easily go bankrupt if it lets itself become insolvent. There will be little opportunity to exploit the overnight market here. The firm will arrange *stage payments*, i.e. it will get some money paid at stages throughout the construction based on work done to date, but not any profit element. This is a very precarious business to be in.

The control of cash is an important operation for all firms, and is done using a cash flow forecast. In this, the firm calculates and estimates its demand and supply positions for cash. As will be revealed, the problem of cash flow increases as a firm grows. In fact, the faster the rate of growth of a firm, particularly a manufacturing firm, the greater the problem is likely to be. Why? Generally a firm has to spend well before the item made is sold. If this sale is on credit, then the time gap can be many months.

Overtrading

A firm is overtrading when it produces and sells its product at a rate such that it exceeds its available working capital.

It will experience liquidity problems, and may eventually be forced into bankruptcy. Look at Case Study 4.1.

Examine the way money flows into and out of a business.

Money inflows come from sales. CD plc sells on two month's credit, so the money will be received in two month's time. Equally, money received today will be for sales made two months ago.

Money outflow is related to production. Ignoring any costs involved with the factory itself, CD plc has to pay production labour and for materials. Labour is paid for in cash each week. Materials are bought and paid for one month before use. Tapes are made one month in advance of sales. Examine Figure 4.2.

Consider tapes sold today. The revenue will not be received for two months. The labour involved in the manufacture of them was paid last month, and the materials a full month before that. There is a delay of five months between the first payment out and the receipt of the corresponding revenue. In an expanding market, at any point in time, money goes out at a rate related to greater sales than that coming in. The greater the rate of expansion of a market, the greater the potential problem.

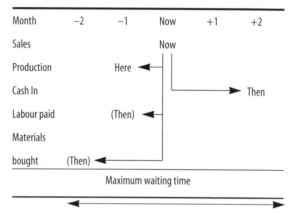

Figure 4.2 *Relationship between expenditure and receipts for CD and the production of video tapes*

Now look at Case Study 4.2, and see the effect on actual cash. What is the problem? Do some calculations yourself before you look at the tables that follow.

Examine Figure 4.2, where the first forecast has been converted into a cash flow chart. It concentrates on the middle months of the year.

CD plc and its proposal to manufacture video tapes

CD plc imports video tapes from a manufacturer in Japan. Sales are very high and expanding fast. One Director of CD plc proposes to set up a manufacturing facility in the UK, the other, the Financial Director, is against this. He states: 'It will consume far too much cash, stretch the working capital to the limit and put us in danger of overtrading.'

CASE STUDY 4.2

CD plc and the video production proposal – Part 2

The projects department has now supplied costs and sales forecasts to support the production proposal. The key data is as follows:

Selling price : £1.50 per unit
Labour cost : £0.20 per unit
Materials cost : £0.80 per unit

The marketing director thinks these are an understatement of the market. His forecast are as follows:

Sales forecast: 1st year's sales (thousands)

Month	1	2	3	4	5	6	7	8	9	10	11	12
Sales	10	11	12	13	14	15	16	17	18	19	20	21

Month	1	2	3	4	5	6	7	8	9	10	11	12
Sales	10	12	14	16	18	20	24	28	34	40	50	65

Month	2	3	4	5	6	7	8	9
Sales	11	12	13	14	15	16	17	18
Cash Inflow								
Ad. sales	9	10	11	12	13	14	15	16
Revenue	13.5	15	16.5	18	19.5	21	22.5	24
Costs								
Ad.sales	12	13	14	15	16	17	18	19
Labour	2.4	2.6	2.8	3	3.2	3.4	3.6	3.8
Ad.sales	13	14	15	16	17	18	19	20
Materials	10.4	11.2	12	12.8	13.6	14.4	15.2	16
Total costs	12.8	13.8	14.8	15.8	16.8	17.8	18.8	19.8
Net cash flow	0.7	1.2	1.7	2.2	2.7	3.2	3.7	4.2
Cumulative cash flow	0.7	1.9	3.6	5.8	8.5	11.7	15.4	19.6

Figure 4.3 *Cash flow chart for project figures*

Month	4	5	6	7	8	9
Sales	16	18	20	24	28	34
Cash Inflow						
Ad. sales	12	14	16	18	20	24
Revenue	18	21	24	27	30	33
Costs						
Ad. sales	18	20	24	28	34	40
Labour	3.6	4	4.4	5.6	6.8	8
Ad. sales	20	24	28	34	40	50
Materials	16	19.2	22.4	27.2	32	40
Total costs	19.6	23.2	26.8	32.8	38.8	48
Net cash flow	-1.6	-2.2	-2.8	-5.8	-8.8	-15
Cumulative cash flow	-1.6	-3.8	-6.6	-12.4	-20.8	-35.8

Figure 4.4 *Cash flow chart for marketing director's figures*

There has been a very slow build up of cash.

Rapidly expanding sales means that expenses build up faster than revenues. The firm may face liquidity problems. It may even go bankrupt due to overtrading. Knowing where a business stands is a vital piece of business information. It is a key management indicator, but is kept confidential for obvious reasons.

Work through the questions and tasks that follow, and confirm your understanding.

SUMMARY

Having studied this chapter, you should be able to:

▽ Explain why money and cash are so important to a business.

▽ Define the important terms:-

– *Capital and capital expenditure*
– *Revenue and revenue expenditure*
– *Profit in its many forms*
– *Cash and cash flow*
– *Working capital*
– *Liquidity*

▽ Clearly explain the difference between profit and cash flow, and outline why a profitable firm may go bankrupt, but a loss making one may be cash rich.

▽ Perform profit and cash calculations.

▽ Demonstrate the meaning of the term overtrading.

Questions and activities

Technical terms and glossary

In the section below you are given a series of technical terms and their meanings. They have been scrambled, though. You must match up the terms and the definitions. When you have them correctly paired, transfer them to your alphabetical vocabulary or glossary book.

You are also advised to transfer any definitions obtained during the exercises in the case studies into this glossary book.

Technical terms
1. Profit
2. Factors of production
3. Working capital
4. Cash flow
5. Capital
6. Revenue
7. Liquidity
8. Stock
9. Debtors
10. Creditors
11. Overtrading
12. Barter trade

Definitions

A. The ability of a business to meet its liabilities, or to be able to pay its bills.

B. The people or firms that a business owes money to because they have supplied goods or services for which they have not yet been paid. Purchase may have been made on credit, or the firm may be deliberately holding back on payment to preserve its cash position.

C. The difference between the revenue obtained from the sale of a good or service and the sum of all the costs incurred in its preparation. Any credit terms given or taken are ignored.

D. A summary of the basic elements used by businesses. They are: land, labour, capital and entrepreneurship.

E. Sometimes known as counter trade. One person, firm or country exchanges goods and services with another. No money is needed, nor does it change hands.

F. The people or firms that owe money to the business, because they have taken goods or services but have yet to pay for them. Sales may well have been made on extended credit terms, or the debtors may be delaying payment.

G. Another term for cash. It is the day-to-day expenditure on materials or labour, and the receipt of monies from the sale of goods or services.

H. Expanding production and sales without making sufficient provision for the extra funds needed to finance the extra working capital needed.

I. The amount of money or credit facilities that a firm needs to operate on a day-to-day basis. It is the balance of cash receipts, and the sum of all the firm's spending.

J. The materials, or their value, held by a firm in the form of raw materials, packing materials, finished goods, even work-in-progress.

K. The funds invested in a business that are used to purchase land, buildings, plant and equipment, etc.

L. The movement of money into and out of a business.

Short answer questions

1. Explain how a firm can be profitable, yet be declared bankrupt because it cannot pay its bills.
2. What is meant by 'the four factors of production'?
3. What is 'work-in-progress'?
4. What is a firm's sole source of regular income?
5. What is the difference between capital and revenue expenditure?
6. Why should a business aim for cash payments for all its sales, but delay payment of all its bills for as long as possible?

7. Why should a firm aim to keep its stock levels as low as possible, subject to giving a good level of customer service?
8. 'Money is the life blood of a business today'. Discuss.
9. What is 'capital'?
10. How can a firm which is making a loss have no cash flow problems, and seem to have a ready supply of cash?

Data response questions

1. Maze Green Builders

You are the *Financial Director* of the above company, which is developing a site near the Motorway. Costs and sales data is as follows:

Costs per house:	Materials	£25,000
	Labour	£15,000
	Land	£20,000
		(Paid two years ago)
Overheads:		£10,000 per month
Selling price:		£100,000 per house

It is now mid-January. Houses are timber framed, system built and take one month to complete. Two houses per month are built. Materials are paid for one month after construction, labour in the month it carries out the work. At the start of the financial year there is a stock of six unsold houses. The firm also has an overdraft of £330,000 with the bank. No houses were built in December last year.

Forecast sales are as follows:

Month	1	2	3	4	5	6	7	8	9	10	11	12
Sales	1	1	1	3	3	4	4	3	3	2	2	1

The money from the sale of a house is obtained in the month of the sale.

The firms financial year runs from January to December.

Prepare the following:

1. Profit forecast for the year to come.
2. Cash flow projection for the coming year.

The economy had overheated, and inflation rose. The government raised interest rates, and confidence collapsed. House sales fell significantly, giving revised sales as follows:

Month	7	8	9	10	11	12
Sales	2	2	1	1	1	1

3. What effect does this loss of sales have on profit and cash?
4. Why is the change in profit so different to the change in the cash position?
5. What might the firm do to try to improve the cash position it finds itself in?

2. The main chance

A firm is facing a steady increase in sales. The forecast produced by its marketing department is as follows:

Month	J	F	M	A	M	J
Sales	100	120	140	160	180	200
Month	J	A	S	0	N	D
Sales	220	240	260	280	300	320

On 1st April it has £10,000 in the Bank. Its costs and price structure is as follows:

Price: £100 per unit. Cash received 3 months after sales.
Costs: Fixed costs – £5,000 per month – Paid one month in advance.
        Variable costs – £40/unit – paid 2 months before the good is sold.

a) Is the firm profitable over the period April to September? Fully quantify your answer.
b) What will happen to their bank balance over the period?

A major competitor goes bankrupt, and the demand grows even more. The revised sales plan is as follows:

Month	J	J	A	S	0	N	D
Sales	200	240	280	320	360	400	440

c) How will this increase in demand effect the profitability and the cash position of the firm?
d) What might the firm do to improve its cash position?

3. Diplomatic cash flow

You are the *Financial Director* of CD plc. It is 1st July 1992 and you have to make the following payments in the near future:

VAT (Net of Claims) September 1992: £120,000
Corporation Tax December 1992:   £200,000

You are concerned about this, and have put an item on the *agenda* for the next Board meeting. You propose that special arrangements be made at once with the bank for a special *overdraft*.
        Your Chairman has had a word with you, in advance, as he is against your proposal. Why? We will be making more than enough profit between now and then. You are being far too cautious, as usual!
        You both had the same information to work with, and your very different conclusions have been drawn from this.

Cash balance on 1.07 92	£10,000
Stock level at 1.07.92	100 units
Selling price (until 1.01.93)	£1,000 per unit
Labour cost	£200 per unit, paid in the month of production.
Materials cost	£300 per unit, paid one month after production.
Overheads	£50,000 per month. 50% paid one month after production, the balance two months after.

In the business concerned, all sales are made on three month's free credit.

Sales and production forecasts and plans (units)									
	Apr	May	Jun	Jul	Aug	Sept	Oct	Nov	Dec
Sales	100	100	150	200	200	250	300	250	200
Production	150	200	250	250	350	250	250	150	150

Questions and activities

1. Define and explain the terms in italics above.
2. Prepare a monthly profit forecast for the period July to December 1992.
3. Prepare a detailed cash flow forecast for the period July to December 1992.
4. Draft a report to be submitted to the Board supporting your proposal.

CD plc and its accounts

It is 1st July 1992. You are the junior cost accountant with CD plc and are working on the budgets for the firm for the next year. You are looking at the accounts for vinyl records, which are produced in a separate factory at Harlow. The following information is available:

1. Cash balance at bank £6,000 (1.7.92)
2. Sales forecast (thousands of records)

Apr	May	June	July	Aug	Sept
200	250	300	350	400	500
Oct	Nov	Dec	Jan	Feb	Mar
500	450	400	400	350	300

3. Production plan (thousands of records)

Apr	May	June	July	Aug	Sept
250	250	350	400	450	500
Oct	Nov	Dec	Jan	Feb	Mar
500	600	600	450	450	450

4. Sales are paid for three months after sale.
5. Records sell for £12 per unit, wholesale.
6. Costs of records are made up as follows:

Labour:	£1.50 per unit, payable in the same month as production.
Materials:	£ 3.50 per unit, paid two months after production.
Semi-variable costs:	£3.50 per unit, over the range of production for the year (generally paid in the month of production).
Overheads:	£600 per month, half paid in the month of operation and the remainder one month later.

7. CD have to pay a royalty payment of £10,000 in November 1992.

Draw up a Cash Budget for the firm for the period 1st July 1992 to 31st March 1993.

5
The sources of capital

Preview

▼ This chapter identifies and evaluates the major sources of capital that are available to the different forms and types of business, and then discusses their suitability and availability for the various forms of business organisation.

▼ The methods of raising money will be classified between being suitable for short, medium or long-term requirements, and their different costs, both in strict financial terms and in terms of business control, will be examined.

You saw in Chapter 4 that businesses need money to fund working and fixed capital. They will have to raise money at a moment's notice, and for short periods of time, as well as on a planned basis, for a long period of time.

There are many ways of obtaining money, but not all are open to all types of business. The cost of finance raised varies with the type of company raising it, the length of time the loan is needed for, and the financial state of the company. The cost, i.e. the rate of interest charged, is also influenced by the state of the economy and the policy of the government at the time – yet another example of interdependence.

In general, it is the small unincorporated company, the sole trader or the partnership, that has the least choice and has to pay the most for its capital, and it is the larger incorporated firm, the private limited company and the public limited company, that have the most opportunities and get the lowest prices – yet another example the effect of size on business matters.

Capital is usually borrowed for short, medium or long periods of time and these periods are generally understood to be 'under one year', 'one to three years, and 'over three years' respectively. It is usual for a business to borrow 'long' for expenditure on fixed assets such as land, buildings and plant and machinery, and 'short' for working capital spending and to cover short-term cash shortages. As is usual there is a middle ground where special finance can be used.

Sources of long-term finance

Long-term money is usually borrowed for a minimum of three years. This comes from the owners of the business, the banks, or other 'investment sources'.

The owner's own capital

The form the owner's capital takes will vary with the legal form of the company, since this dictates who the owners are.

Unincorporated businesses

Unincorporated firms are owned by the individual concerned, or by the partners. They are clearly able to put their own money into the business, i.e. their own savings. This will be limited, particularly for the small sole trader who is just starting up, and for the business set up with a low skills base. A professional partnership, solicitors or dentists for example, may be better placed. In all cases it is literally personal wealth that is used, and personal property may be provided as security for any loan given.

A good example of this form of capital injection are the 'Names' at Lloyds. Here the name, or investor, underwrites the policies drawn up by the syndicate of which they are members. If it makes a profit, they get a share of it in the form of an annual dividend. If, however, it loses money, then the members have to make up the difference. Things came to a head in 1992 when, for the first time for many years, members were called on to meet their obligations, and some had to sell their houses to be able to do so. They have unlimited liability.

Incorporated businesses

Incorporated firms are owned by their shareholders. These put their money into the businesses through buying shares. (As will be remembered, unincorporated firms are not allowed to sell shares in their business.) There are a range of ways that this can be done, particularly in the situation where an unincorporated firm is 'going public'.

Shares earn a dividend if a profit is made, but the business has no legal obligation to pay one. The decision to do so is taken by the shareholders through a majority vote at the Annual General Meeting. If you own 50% + 1 of the shares, you have control, and can decide the dividend – a position of power. Companies sell ordinary shares, which carry a vote, and other non-voting shares in an attempt to keep control.

Ordinary shares

Any incorporated company may sell shares, but only plcs may sell them to the general public. Shares are sold when a firm first goes public, and also at stages through the life of the business when conditions are right. It is often said that the Stock Exchange exists to finance industry. In fact the exchange in a country or region only provides a market for the buying and selling of issued, or 'used' shares. Businesses raise their finance outside of the Stock Exchange, but the state of the market influences the ease with which this can be done. To be a 'listed company' and to be able to have their shares sold on the market eventually they have to meet the requirements of the Stock Exchange. These are set out in the 'Admission of Securities for Listing Rules of the Stock Exchange'. The main requirement for a full listing are:

- minimum capitalisation of £700,000
- at least 25% of shares must be offered to the public
- full trading accounts must be published for five years or more.

Alternative markets are available, with easier entry requirements. These are called the *unlisted securities market*, and the *third market* on the London Stock Exchange.

The shares will be sold 'new' directly to the public, independently of the stock exchange.

New issues

When a firm wishes to raise money, it arranges with a merchant bank to offer new issues for sale. It will issue a *prospectus*, which will tell the potential investor all about the business, and the likely profits that will be made, and will set the price. The format and contents of this document is detailed in Parts IV and V of the 1986 Financial Services Act. A firm may aim to sell 1 million shares, with a face value of 50 pence each, at a price of 60 pence each. If the offer is successful the business will have raised £600,000. This premium over face, or nominal value, will be possible if the profit projection for the firm is very good. There is no guarantee of a dividend, though.

A prospectus is a document prepared by a Joint Stock Company as an invitation to the public to subscribe to shares in the company. It gives details of the firm's past trading record, current capital structure and borrowings.

What does the buyer get having bought ordinary shares?

The purchaser buys a future right to a share of the profits of the business, and also a right to vote at *general meetings* of the company. The shareholders appoint the directors, who will manage the firm for them. A dividend is paid each year out of the firm's profits. Some plcs even pay a dividend to their ordinary shareholders when they are making a loss! In theory the individual shareholder is party to the decision on the size of a dividend, but in reality this power only falls to the large institutional shareholders, and those individuals with large individual holdings. Their attraction to the buyer is that the dividend grows with the success of the firm, but the investment does not change. The share itself should increase in value and then can be sold for a price higher than was paid for it. A *capital gain* is made.

If a shareholder wishes to sell shares they will be put up for sale on the Stock Exchange. Thus the Stock Exchange sells only 'second hand' shares; it cannot sell newly issued shares. It is a market, and the price will change with supply and demand. If a firm is doing well, its shares will be in demand and the price will rise. If the whole economy is in trouble, then share prices will probably fall as well. Every time a share is sold the change of ownership is recorded by the Registrar's Department of the business. The dividend will be paid to the *registered owner* at the appropriate time.

Ordinary shares are the most common form of share issued and traded. When new shares are sold the company places them through a *merchant bank*, and an announcement or advertisement is placed in the financial press. An example is shown as Figure 5.1.

All of these shares having been sold, this announcement appears as a matter of record only

PT BARITO PACIFIC TIMBER

Rp. 612,000,000,000.00
(Six Hundred and Twelve Billion Rupiah)

Public Offer of 85,000,000.00 shares

INTEGRATED MANUFACTURER OF PLYWOOD
AND WOOD-BASED PRODUCTS

Lead Managing Underwriter
International Coordinator

P.T. MAKINDO

Underwriters

PT Bapindo Bumi Sekuritas	PT Danareksa Sekuritas	PT Bumi Daya Sekuritas
PT Danamon Securities	PT Indovest Securities	PT Pentasena Arthasentosa
PT Nikko Securities Indonesia	PT Asjaya Indosurya Securities	PT Astra Securities
PT Buanamas Investindo	PT Daiwa Indonesia Securities	PT Deemte Arthadharma Sekuritas
PT Jardine Fleming Nusantara	PT PDFCI Securities	PT Gadjah Tunggal DBS Securities
PT Donatama Makmur	PT Ficor Sekuritas Indonesia	PT Ichiyoshi Alfa Securities
PT KLS Sinar Mas Securities	PT Nomura Indonesia	PT Panin Sekuritasindo
PT Sanyo Primarindo Securities	PT Sinarmas Ekagraha	PT WI Carr Indonesia
PT Asian Development Securities	PT Aspac Uppindo Sekuritas	PT CEF Andromeda Securities
PT Credit Lyonnais Capital Indonesia	PT GK Goh Ometraco	PT Mashill Jaya Securities
PT Merincorp Securities Indonesia	PT Milcor Sekuritas	PT Morgan Grenfell Asia Indonesia
PT Multicor Securities	PT OCBC Sikap Securities	PT Piranti Ciptadhana Amerta Securities
PT Putra Saridaya Persada Sekuritas	PT Sigma Batara	PT Standard Chartered Securities
PT Sun Hung Kai Securities Indonesia	PT Tifa Securities Company	PT Wardley James Capel Indonesia

Figure 5.1 *Example of share offer.* (Source: *The Economist*)

If the firm closes down, or goes bankrupt, the shareholders are the last group of creditors who will receive any compensation. In theory they receive the balance of any assets left after all debts have been paid, but in most cases their investment is lost. If there was to be any money left after all the debts had been paid it would be shared between the shareholders. They cannot be called upon for any more money though; their liability is limited to the value of their initial investment. This is the basis for the 'Limited' in their name – it is short for 'Limited Liability'. The company is limited to the value of its initial capital; the shareholders to the face value of their shares.

Subsequent issues

A business may have two opportunities for raising more money from share sales after the initial launch. If it does not sell all the approved shares initially it can sell the balance later, e.g. a firm has authorised share capital of £10 million, but only sells £6 million initially. It can then offer the remainder for sale at any time when it thinks that the market conditions are suitable. It can also prepare a *rights issue*.

Rights issue

A rights issue is an offer of ordinary shares to existing shareholders. The offer is usually made in terms of one new share for a given number of existing shares, e.g. one for one, or one for three. Price is made attractive, and existing shareholders may buy the shares on offer, sell their rights to the shares on the Stock Market, or refuse to do anything. Examine the article presented as Figure 5.2.

A company has issued 1,000 shares at £1 each. They now trade on the Stock Market at a price of £2. The business has a value on the market of £2,000.

If the firm was to issue another 1,000 shares free of charge, the price on the market is likely to fall back to £1. The value of the firm will not have changed, but there are now 2,000 shares. Share price can be expected to fall to £1 each. The owner of the original shares will now have twice as many as before, but will receive exactly the same total amount of dividend.

Sometimes firms do give away shares like this, and such an issue is called a *scrip issue*. The firm will have lowered the price of its shares, making them easier to buy. It will also have doubled the number of shares in the company, making it harder for the firm to be taken over against its will. This procedure is rare, though, as no money is gained by the firm.

In a rights issue the shares are sold to existing shareholders. Now go back to the earlier example. Assume that the new shares were offered for 50p each. The firm would receive £500, and the buyers a share worth £1. In theory the buyer can sell the shares for £1 at once and make a profit of 50p per share. The firm would be offering the shares at a discount of 50% over their theoretical ex-rights (after the rights issue) price.

Every successful rights issue requires handling with care.

Five major corporates: but by no means five similar issuers. For British Airways and Saatchi, UBS Limited acted as joint broker and underwriter to both issues which were SEC registered to enable US shareholders to subscribe. For CRH we acted as joint broker and underwriter to raise funds in Ireland and the UK. As joint broker to Trafalgar House and United Newspapers, the emphasis was predominantly on the UK. Each one was successful.

In large international transactions, UBS has the proven skills to ensure a successful outcome.

Figure 5.2 *Examples of real rights issues.*

In 1994, Stakis, a hotels and casinos group, aimed to raise £28 million this way, and ASDA a massive £347 million. Stakis offered one new share for every three already held, and ASDA a complicated 'three for ten' deal. Both companies must have been confident that their shareholders would pay. If they all tried to sell together the market would be flooded, and the share price would tumble. A simple exercise in supply and demand again. If only a few people sell the price would only fall a little. If the increase in supply is large there will be a serious loss.

Remember, an ordinary shareholder is an owner of the business, and is one of the internal groups to which a firm has responsibility. This is not the case for the next type of share.

Preference shares

The owner of a preference share has no ownership of the company at all, and so has no vote. The shareholder is guaranteed a dividend, though which is usually fixed in advance, and has to be paid in preference to, or before, the ordinary shareholders dividends. A 6% preference share would guarantee a dividend of 6% of its face value, each year, irrespective of the profits earned by the business.

Some preference shares are cumulative, which means that if any dividend is passed, i.e. not paid in any year, then the back payment has to be paid out of future profits ahead of the ordinary shareholders again.

The preference shareholder is repaid, in preference, if the business closes. But it is not paid in preference to the Inland Revenue.

Preference shareholders are external to the company, and are one of the external groups to which a business has responsibility. They are low risk investments, usually, so why buy ordinary shares with their risk? The earnings of preference shares are fixed, but there is the opportunity of gaining much more from ordinary shares.

Debentures

A debenture is a loan made to a company, usually to finance a fixed asset, that will be repaid at a set date, usually 10 to 15 years. Interest may be paid, but it is often paid 'in kind'. It is commonly used by sports clubs, when membership or tickets can be the payment. The All England Lawn Tennis Club at Wimbledon financed its expansion by a debenture, and debenture holders receive Centre Court tickets in return. The Arsenal Football Club financed its new stand, being built through the 1992/93 season by a debenture scheme where the interest payment was in the form of special rights to buy tickets.

Debenture and bond holders have no voting rights.

Bonds are sold by many large companies, as well as governments. Look at Figure 5.3.

Non-voting ordinary shares

Non-voting ordinary shares are rare. They are ordinary shares, with no guarantee of a dividend, and no voting right either. They are very attractive to the firm selling them, but not so good for the buyer, at least in theory. They may be attractive to a small shareholder, though. Here the value of the vote is marginal, so if the non-voting share is cheaper it may be a better buy. It all depends on the guarantee of the dividend. The risk is not really as big as it seems, as the firm would not want to get a bad reputation. The firm sells these shares because it wants to raise share capital without losing control of the company itself. It wants individual shareholders, not institutional ones. The non-voting arrangement guarantees them their control. These are also traded on the Stock Exchange.

The banks

Banks are usually prepared to lend money to businesses. This they do through overdrafts and term loans.

Term loans

With a term loan the bank lends the firm a specific sum of money for a set period of time, and charges interest. It may or may not require some form of security to 'guarantee' the sum borrowed. The term of the loan can be for a short term, less than one year, or long term, more than one year. The interest rate may be fixed or variable over the period of the loan. Fixed interest loans are more likely for very short-term loans. Variable interest is virtually the norm for long-term loans. Capital may have to be repaid either in equal instalments during the period of the loan, or as a lump sum at the end of the loan period.

Again the larger, established incorporated firm will have advantages over the small, newly established sole trader or partnership. Interest, which again is charged on the basis of 'base rate + x%', is likely to be higher for the smaller, newer firm. The requirements for security will also often be harder, and the small firm will also have greater problems in finding the security in the first place. A bank will accept property, some works of art, share certificates and other types of fixed asset. Almost by definition, the small firm will find these harder to arrange. The sole trader will often have to put his or her own house up as security, as this is usually the largest asset that the sole trader can raise.

Venture capital

Strictly speaking venture capital is not a loan at all. A firm with a good proposal, but a lack of capital, gets an advance from a venture capitalist in return for a share of the future profits of the firm, and a share holding. It may well obtain or demand a controlling interest of more than 50% of the shares.

A major provider of venture capital in the UK is the 'Investor In Industry' or 'three's company'. This is owned by a consortium of banks, and puts in funds if the proposal can be justified. The supply of such capital is small in UK but is very common in Japan.

Figure 5.3 *Example of a bond.*

Figure 5.4 *Another example of a bond.*

Here most banks finance firms this way, and have a director on the Board as a result.

Insurance companies

Insurance companies collect a large sum of money from their customers, and need to invest this to earn an income and to generate a profit on their activities. Sometimes they do this simply by buying shares, on other occasions they will lend it to companies. They do this by buying *bonds*, or '*commercial paper*' as it is called. This is very similar to government stock and is traded, but is a very specialist market. Such company 'paper' will usually carry fixed interest and, like government stocks, will be dated. Examine Figure 5.4.

Pension funds

Pension companies, like insurance firms, amass large sums of money which they need to invest. They, too, are potential customers for business 'paper'.

A company will need to be well established and reliable to be able to raise money this way. It is a common source of funds for local authorities and councils in the UK. These loans are often 'short-dated', however, i.e. two years or less.

How companies actually raise funds, particularly initially, depends on their choice and objectives. Do they want low cost, but with a loss of control, or do they wish to keep the maximum of decision making power to themselves? Examine Case Study 5.1.

CASE STUDY 5.1

CD plc and its funding balance (1994)

After many years of trading as a *partnership*, then as a *private limited company*, CD decided to '*go public*', in other words, to become a *public limited company* and have its shares listed on the *London Stock Exchange*.

The partners had employed a merchant bank to advise them, and also to organise the **flotatation** for them. The first decision was to agree the number of shares to be issued in total, what proportion of these would be offered for sale, and what other forms of capital raising should be used.

The following proposal has been discussed.

Authorised share capital	£4 million
Sold to public	45%
Retained by partners	55%
Long-term loans	£3 million
Debentures (10 years – 8%)	£2 million
Preference share issue	£2 million
(Undated – 9%)	

CD's properties forecast 'profits after tax' of £1.2 million in the year of issue, rising to £2.2 million in five years. Bank interest rate is 6% at present, and is forecast to rise to 9% in the same five-year period.

Questions and activities

1. Define all the terms in italics above.
2. Comment on the implications for (a) the firm and (b) the shareholders of the above cost structure.

Sources of medium-term finance

Medium-term finance is wanted for between one and three years. It is often used to finance the purchase of fixed assets with relatively short lives, i.e. motor vehicles, or those likely to be overtaken by rapid advances in technology, i.e. computers and other IT equipment. It also has become common for some very expensive items such as commercial airliners. The following sources are available:

Hire purchase and leasing

Hire purchase, strictly speaking, means that the firm buys the equipment in instalments. At the end of the period, say three years, the item becomes the property of the firm that has been paying for it and using it. Leasing means hiring. The firm get the use of the item, but not ownership.

With hire purchase firms essentially rent the asset. It is widely used for company cars and delivery vehicles. Modern agreements means that the firm pays a monthly fee, which usually includes licensing and maintenance, in return for which it gets full use of the vehicle. To all intents and purposes the car or vehicle belongs to the firm. At the end of the hire period the business can either buy it at a predetermined price or return it. A new vehicle would be supplied against a new hire agreement.

Leasing is a common means of financing aircraft. A 'dry' lease means the aircraft only, a 'wet' lease includes the crew and operating cost. The aircraft is supplied in the appropriate colours, the only clue to its actual ownership being the registration number on the tail. A major supplier in this business is GA, the Irish company that attempted to go public in 1992 but withdrew at the last minute. The operating airline is saved the huge sums of capital required for modern airliners – a new Boeing 747 could easily cost £50 million, with spares!

Sell and lease back

This is a common way of dealing with land and buildings purchased, particularly where the business does not want to build up a portfolio of property. It wants to concentrate its capital in the area it is expert in. Consider a major supermarket chain. It is expert in retailing consumer goods, but needs many expensive sites and buildings. The company will buy land, and sometimes it will even finance the construction of the supermarket. To finance further expansion it sells the developed site to a property developer, and agrees to lease it back for a period, retaining the first option on using it.

An example: A supermarket owns a site in a high value area and has a large hypermarket on it. It sells it to a property company for £100 million, but contracts to lease it back at a rent of £8 million per year. The property company gets a return of 8%, and the supermarket gets £100 million in cash to invest in new sites. Consider Case Study 3.3, and see how it was advantageous for College Dynamics to make such an arrangement early in its life.

Merchant banks

Merchant banks will invest money directly in suitable businesses. They may well consider slightly less well-known firms than the high street banks, and definitely more risky projects (for which they will demand a higher rate of interest).

Clearing banks

Mid-term money may be available from the clearing banks, but loans will be subject to the qualifications mentioned above.

Sources of short-term money

Short-term money is that lent to the business for less than one year.

Trade creditors

When a business orders materials or services from another company it forms a legally binding contract. One firm contracts to buy, the other to supply. The contract will include the terms of payment for the order which will have been negotiated by the two purchasing departments. It may be a cash arrangement, say 'Net Cash 28 Days' (the firm has contracted to pay the full account as cash within 28 days), or a credit arrangement, i.e. payment in 90 days. By delaying payment of a bill a company is taking a loan from this company, which will be recorded in the accounts of the firm as a creditor. No security is normally given for this form of loan. The creditor company also tries to attract cash in. It may offer a discount for prompt payments, i.e. 2.5% discount if the account is paid within five days. Cash on receipt is a very rare arrangement for business, and would usually indicate that the purchasing firm has a bad record, or is known to be in a liquidity problem.

The more powerful the buyer, the better payment terms it will be able to negotiate. If a firm sells all its output to a single buyer, it will be very vulnerable during payment negotiations. Sixty, 90 and even 120 days are possible, and are accepted, if reluctantly. The small firm will often have to take the terms offered, even if it means cash payments, or a charge for credit. Firms will try to get a range of customers, with a range of order sizes in an attempt to reduce the risk here.

This is a valuable source of funds for many companies. Examine a company's Balance Sheet shown as Figure 5.5 and see that this shows that in 1989 they apparently raised £815.5 million from this source. (See also Figure 5.6.)

	Note	**Group** 1989 £m	1988 £m
Fixed assets			
Tangible assets	1	2,338.1	1,742.5
Investments	2	31.5	67.7
		2,369.6	1,810.2
Current assets			
Stocks		286.1	239.6
Debtors	5	97.3	31.8
ACT recoverable	6	25.2	14.7
Cash at bank and in hand		90.0	68.8
		498.6	354.9
Creditors: due within one year	7	(1,314.1)	(913.0)
Net current liabilities		(815.5)	(558.1)
Total assets less current liabilities		1,554.1	1,252.1
Creditors: due after one year	7	(377.1)	(212.4)
Deferred income	9	–	(3.3)
Deferred tax	10	(2.1)	(5.2)
Minority interest		(7.3)	(6.8)
		1,167.6	1,024.4
Capital and reserves			
Called up share capital	11	375.6	373.4
Share premium account	12	179.1	165.9
Revaluation reserve	13	24.9	40.3
Profit and Loss Account	14	588.0	44.8
		1,167.6	1,024.4

Figure 5.5 *Balance sheet, 18 March 1989*

Overdrafts

Overdrafts are a facility, not a loan as such. The business is allowed to write cheques for more than it has in its account, up to an agreed limit, the overdraft limit. The firm pays interest, usually expressed as 'base rate plus a percentage' on any

	£(k)
1. Fixed assets	800
2. Current assets	
Stock	100
Debtors	100
Cash	50
	250
3. Current liabilities	
(Amounts falling due within one year)	
Creditors	(150)
Borrowings	(50)
	(200)
4. Net current assets	50
5. Long-term liabilities	
Bank loans	(250)
6. Net capital employed	600
7. Financed by	
Share capital	400
Retained profits	200
	600

Figure 5.6 *Balance Sheet for College Dynamics plc, as at 31 December 1991*

amount that has been borrowed this way. The firm has to pay a fee to set up an overdraft, and will have to negotiate renewals at regular intervals, often every six months. Overdrafts do not usually need security, in other words, the borrower does not have to give the bank any asset to cover the loan. In theory the bank can call in an overdraft at any time, but is unlikely to do this if the firm keeps to the terms set out when the overdraft was agreed.

The interest charged by the bank will depend on three things:
1. The banks own base rate. This is influenced by the government, through the actions of the Bank of England. Economic conditions, both domestically and worldwide, and the basic policies of the government of the day will affect this.
2. The size of the business.
3. The reputation of the business with the bank.

Thus a small, new business that is growing may well have to pay 'base rate + 5%', but a large, well-established plc only 'base rate + 2%'.

Debt factoring and bill discounting

Debt factoring and bill discounting is a means of raising money against accounts owed to the firm, or against its debtors. A debt can arise for two reasons:

1. The item ordered has not been delivered or paid for yet.
2. An account has been passed over for some reason.

The firm can get the money, for a fee, if it wants cash at short notice. In the former case the bill will be discounted, in the latter it will be factored.

Bill discounting

A firm has agreed to deliver a machine to a customer overseas. It will take 12 weeks to make and another six for delivery. The firm will then expect to be paid in another two weeks, i.e. in 20 weeks' time. The account is for £250,000.

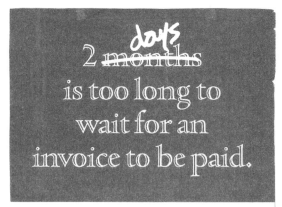

There's no need for a 60 day payment delay on your invoices. Not even a 2 day wait. International Factors can pay up to 85% of your approved invoices the next working day. Cut the coupon for **International Factors** details or call us on 0800 521371. Why wait?

My turnover is over £250,000. Please send me details ☐ Please call me ☐

Name _____ Company _____

Address _____   DES 5

Telephone _____ Nature of Business _____ Annual Turnover _____

Send to: David Richardson, International Factors Limited, Freepost (BR 1490), Brighton BN1 1ZX. Or fax (0273) 207651.

Figure 5.7 International factors.
(Source: Evening Standard, 26 October 1993.)

The firm can go to a discount house and effectively sell this bill. The house will advance a proportion of the value of the bill to the firm, and will charge interest on the money until the money is received from the customer. There is relatively little risk, so the interest is low and the amount of the advance, as a percentage, is often high. If the customer does not pay, the debt falls back on the supplier, as does the ownership of the good supplied.

Discount houses are very old established firms, like Lloyds of London based on the old City coffee houses. They were in great demand in the days of sea transport when journey times were long. Some very well-known names are involved. Examine Figure 5.7.

Debt factoring

Companies often build up a list of customers who have exceeded their credit terms, but they still cannot or will not pay. The company can apply pressure, but it may well not work. The alternative is to sell the debt to a company that specialises in debt collection. This firm will pay for the debt, a percentage of the outstanding amount, in cash and will keep the full payment when it collects it. The discount will depend on the perceived risk involved by the debt collection company. The larger the risk, the lower the percentage that will be advanced.

The firm factoring the debt gets a certain proportion of the debt at once; the factor gains when it recovers the full debt, or at least more than it advanced. Its debt collection methods can be more 'positive' than those of the original 'owner' of the debt.

This market also operates on an international basis, and it is possible to purchase Under Developed and Developing Country debt at a considerable discount. This is a sophisticated, high risk market.

Banks

Banks will make short-term loans to firms, especially where they think that this will ease their cash flow and make the eventual pay-back less risky.

A summary of the various sources of finance is shown as Figure 5.8.

Short-term finance (1 to 3 years)	Medium-term finance (3 to 10 years)	Long-term finance (Over 10 years)
For temporary working capital, bridging finance, capital to meet seasonal finance for short-lived assets.	Finance for assets with a medium-term life, e.g. plant and machinery, general working capital, etc.	Finance for long-life assets, e.g. buildings, permanent working capital, business aquisitions, etc.
Clearing banks Accepting houses Finance houses Discount houses Factoring companies Invoice discounting companies Clearing and other banks Leasing companies	Clearing banks Merchant banks Leasing companies Finance houses Specialist organisations Clearing and other banks	Insurance companies Pension funds Specialist organisations Clearing and other banks

Sources available to incorporated companies only

Preference shares, Debentures, Company 'Paper' (Remember, ordinary shares are not loans but money invested in the firm for a dividend.)

Figure 5.8 Summary of the sources of funds available to firms, depending on the term required

SUMMARY

Having studied this chapter you will be able to:

▽ Describe and define the various forms of capital used by firms, with particular reference to investment and working capital.

▽ Discuss and describe the various types of shares and bonds that a firm may sell, namely:

– *ordinary and preference shares*
– *non-voting ordinary shares*
– *debentures*
– *commercial paper (bonds)*

(continued)

▼ Explain how the rights issue works for both the firm and the buyer.

▼ Identify and evaluate the various forms of capital available to businesses.

▼ Discuss the suitability of the different forms of capital for the various business forms and structures, i.e. be able to compare and contrast the sources of finance open to sole traders, partnerships, limited companies and plcs.

▼ Determine short, medium and long-term sources of finance.

▼ Evaluate the costs of the various types of capital to the borrower/raiser, and to consider their advantages and disadvantages.

Questions and activities

Technical terms and glossary

In the section below you are given a series of technical terms and their meanings. They have been scrambled, though. You must match up the terms and the definitions. When you have them correctly paired, transfer them to your alphabetical vocabulary or glossary book.

You are also advised to transfer any defintiions obtained during the exercises in the case studies into this glossary book.

Technical terms

1. Working capital
2. Fixed capital
3. Depreciation
4. Ordinary shares
5. Unlisted securities market
6. Prospectus
7. Share option
8. Preference shares
9. Debentures
10. Non-voting ordinary shares
11. Hire purchase
12. Leasing
13. Merchant bank
14. Clearing bank
15. Trade creditors
16. Overdraft
17. Debt factoring
18. Bill discounting
19. Venture capital
20. Balance Sheet

Definitions

A. A facility granted by a bank on request, and the payment of a fee. The firm or individual may spend more money than is in the current account without further request, up to an agreed limit. This loan may be called in by the bank on request, though. It is the cheapest form of 'loan' that a firm may have. You only pay interest on the amount borrowed at any moment in time.

B. The most common form of share sold by an incorporated company. The shareholder is entitled to a vote at an Annual General Meeting, and also to a share of the profits in the form of a dividend. This does not have to be paid, however, and may be passed for a good reason.

C. A method of obtaining a capital item which does not require the expenditure of capital. The item is purchased through the payment of instalments for an agreed period. At the end of this period, ownership passes to the purchaser on the payment of a nominal fee.

D. A statement at a point in time of the assets of a company, where they are distributed, and where the capital behind them has come from, i.e. it states what capital is being used, where it has come from and what it is being used for.

E. The items that the company owns which have an ongoing value, such as buildings, land and plant and equipment. These assets are tangible, in other words they can be seen and measured.

F. An investment into a company that does not carry an interest charge. The investment gets its reward in the long run through the shareholding it acquires, usually a controlling interest.

G. (a) Money necessary for the day-to-day operation of a business.

(b) The net current assets of a firm (current assets minus current liabilities).

H. The selling of an invoice to a financier before it is due, and for a sum below its face value. It is a means for a company to obtain sales revenue before it is strictly due.

I. An accounting allowance, set against the Balance Sheet, that reduces the value of fixed assets to allow for wear and tear, etc. It can also be set against profits, and therefore against tax.

J. The business name for renting. An item is not bought, but used for as period after the payment of a monthly fee.

K. The sale of a debt to another company for a fee below its face value. The debt will be overdue already, and the discount given will be based on the likelihood of the debt being eventually recovered.

L. An arrangement where an individual, usually a director, is given the right to buy shares at a set price at any time up to an agreed date in the future.

M. A bank, originally set up to finance trade, that now specialises in financing businesses and acting for commercial clients.

N. A non-voting share where the holder is guaranteed a predetermined dividend which will be paid before any dividends are paid to other shareholders. It may have a redemption date.

O. A special part of the London Stock Exchange where selected non-plc shares may be traded. Companies must qualify for a listing, but the requirements are more lenient than for full public limited companies.

P. One of the major retail banks in the UK which is one of the operators of the central cheque clearing system. Many of the new, ex-building society banks, are not members of this system.

Q. People and/or firms which are owed money by another business. Money is due to be paid in a short period of time. Money is effectively a free loan to the company which owes the money.

R. Shares in a company which do not carry a fixed dividend, can be passed if the firm wishes, but which give the holders no say in the operation of the business.

S. Fixed interest loans to a company. Interest may be a service or a privilege (tickets for Wimbledon, for example) rather than a money payment.

T. A document prepared by a company when it offers new shares for sale. Its form and content is set down within company law.

Short answer questions

1. What is an ordinary share?
2. What is a debenture?
3. What is traded on the London Stock Exchange?
4. Who sells the shares of a company that 'goes public'?
5. Differentiate between merchant banks and clearing banks.
6. Why is a rights issue an 'offer you cannot refuse'?
7. What advantages does the firm gain from selling non-voting ordinary shares?
8. Compare and contrast commercial 'paper' with government stock.
9. What are the advantages to a firm of operating a sell and lease back scheme for its retail outlets?
10. Why are trade creditors an attractive but short-term method of raising cash for a company?
11. What is an overdraft?
12. What are the advantages and disadvantages of raising money by taking bank loans or selling ordinary shares?
13. Give **two** reasons why businesses may sell a debt to a factor. (Associated Examining Board, Business Studies, Paper 1 1987)
14. Why might a company decide to revalue its fixed assets? (Associated Examining Board, Business Studies (A), Paper 1, 1987)
15. A company wishes to install a new machine. Give **four** methods of financing the purchase.

(Associated Examining Board, Business Studies (A), Paper 1, November 1987)

Case study

Read the article and answer the questions which follow.

Prime Movers

Stocklin Limited is the wholly owned UK subsidiary of the Swiss materials handling specialist company, Walter Stocklin AG. It is one of a number of European based organisations that has been chosen to locate its UK operation at Aston Science Park, Birmingham.

Two years ago, under the direction of Bill Strickland, Stocklin Limited was formed. The company has installed materials handling systems across a wide range of manufacturing, distributive and service industries including numerous companies such as Nationwide Building Society, Walkers Crisps, and Proctor and Gamble.

Stocklin Limited works in close collaboration with another Swiss company which also has its UK headquarters in Aston Science Park. In fact, Bill Strickland reports that the decision to start up from Aston was largely influenced by the presence of Sprecher & Schuh Automation Limited – specialists in complementary computer control and software for warehouse applications.

'There were also a number of other factors that we considered important to Stocklin', explains Bill Strickland. 'We appreciate the range of facilities offered by Aston – and the big city environment with its tradition of engineering means that we can draw on a specialist engineering labour pool.'

Through its two divisions, Stocklin Limited covers all aspects of factory and warehousing materials handling – conveyors, cranes, lift trucks, trailers – equipment for moving anything from pallets through granules to bulk carrying containers.

The company specialises in designing complete warehousing systems. However, all Stocklin equipment will interface with that of other suppliers – and conforms to European and UK standards.

Increasingly Stocklin Limited is being commissioned to install systems in banks and building societies, to store property deeds, stocks and share certificates and wills for clients. 'Many such institutions are centralising their deed stores – which can amount to some 6 million items under one roof. Such facilities need to be fully automated – and that means total accuracy. Without that assurance you could end up with complete chaos!' Bill Strickland points out.

(Adapted form Aston Science Park, *Venture*, 2, 6. Autumn 1990)

Questions

(a) What is meant by the term 'a wholly owned subsidiary'? (2 marks)

(c) Consider three reasons why Walter Stocklin AG decided to locate its UK operation at Aston Science park. (9 marks)

(c) Why is it important to the success of Stocklin Ltd that its equipment 'conforms to European and UK standards'? (7 marks)

(d) Explain two advantages and two disadvantages to 'companies such as nationwide Building Society ...' of centralising and automating their document stores. (8 marks)

(Associated Examining Board Business Studies (A), Paper 1, June 1993)

6

The costs and revenues of a firm – break-even analysis

Preview

▽ This chapter will look at the costs, expenses and revenues of a firm, and will study their interaction in theory.

▽ It will look at how costs can be classified into *fixed*, *variable* and *total* costs, and see how the distribution of these determine the cost structure of the firm.

▽ It will examine the effect of the cost structure of a business on its operational policy.

▽ It will then go on to develop the method of analysis known as *break even*, i.e. 'at what point in sales will the costs just match the income?'

All firms worry about the costs and revenues arising from their business. If revenues do not cover costs, the firm would seem to be in trouble. All businesses are concerned, therefore, with the answers to two key questions.

1. What has the product or service cost to make or provide?
2. Is the selling price for the good or service adequate?

Without a knowledge of costs, a business cannot assess its profit. Remember the following simple formulae:

$$Cost + Profit = Price \text{ ....} (1)$$

$$or$$

$$Price - Cost = Profit \text{ (or Loss).......... } (2)$$

The second equation is more realistic. As will be seen later in this chapter, the price that a particular product sells for is decided by the consumer. The firm sets the price, the customer then decides to buy it or not. (If the price is too high the customer will ignore it. If it is too low the consumer might view the product with suspicion. This introduces the concept

of a 'right price' for an item.) The supplier, however, is in complete control of the costs. Profit, therefore, is a 'joint effort' or the result of the decisions of both the seller and the buyer. Thus costs and prices are critical to business.

Since a business faces far more costs than prices, and has control over them in many ways, they will be examined first. Initially, though, here is a challenging statement:

Any firm which makes and sells more than one product does not know precisely what each one costs to make, and cannot do so!

It may be hard to believe, but it is true.

Costs are of different types and characteristics. Return to the Case Study about College Dynamic's (CD's) first two months of selling, when it had problems with profit and cash flow. Look at the chart of costs and incomes in the previous chapter.

Some of these costs will vary with the number of items ordered – freight, import taxes, as well as the order values themselves. These are known as direct costs. The others are independent of sales but are fixed for a period of time. These are known as indirect costs. Over a period of time all costs can change. All costs, fixed or variable in the short run, can be increased by their supplier. Rents and taxes can go up, raw materials or telephone charges can go down. Thus the concept of fixed and variable costs apply to a set point in time.

This time aspect is important, and gives a way of picturing the difference between these costs. Most indirect costs are fees to operate. CD needed offices and equipment before it could start to trade. Thus these rentals had to be agreed and at least one payment made in advance. So indirect costs can be considered as the costs that have to be paid before a firm can operate. They buy a firm time. This time, the time between payments of indirect costs, is considered as the 'short run'. So, indirect costs tend to be expressed as money per unit of time, e.g. rent for the offices of £1,000 per month, insurance fees of £3,000 per year. In the period known as the short run the firm has to generate enough money to be able to pay the next instalment of indirect costs.

In the case of CD, its costs can be classified so far as follows:

Indirect	*Direct*
Insurance	*Purchase of compact*
Rentals for offices,	*discs and disks*
furniture, cars and	*Freight charges*
equipment	*Import taxes*
Business rates	

So, *direct costs* and *indirect costs* have been identified.

Direct Costs (also known as variable or prime costs) are those which are a consequence of production or sale, and vary directly with them.

Direct costs can be expressed as a sum of money per item made or sold. The sum spent varies directly with the quantity sold. The more business a firm does, the more direct costs it will incur. The amount spent per unit sold will remain fixed, however. Examine Figure 6.1 which illustrates this relationship.

Indirect costs (also known as fixed costs or overheads) are those which relate to the existence of the business. The amount spent does not change with output or sales made.

Examine Figure 6.2.

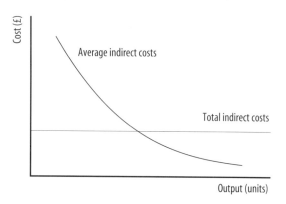

Figure 6.2 *Diagrammatic representation of indirect costs*

It is important to note that the more that is sold of a product, the cheaper the fixed cost per unit, or the average fixed cost becomes.

There is a useful check question. Ask 'If production was to stop, would the cost stop or disappear?' If the answer is Yes then the cost is *variable*. If the answer is No, then it is an *overhead* or *fixed* cost. In some cases the answer may be Yes, but not entirely. (More on these later.)

Total costs of production are simply the result of the addition of the fixed and variable costs involved. Look at Figure 6.3. This clearly shows that the fixed costs of operation is the cost of producing 'output zero', or is the 'fee' that has to be paid to be able to operate at all.

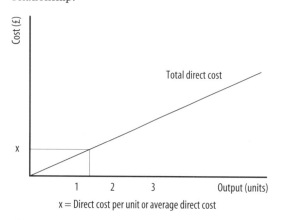

x = Direct cost per unit or average direct cost

Figure 6.1 *Diagrammatic representation of direct costs*

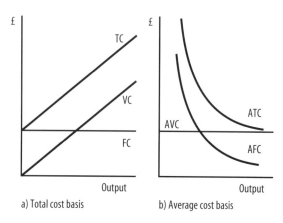

a) Total cost basis b) Average cost basis

Figure 6.3 *Diagrammatic representation of a firm's total costs*

Consider the average values for the costs, or the cost per unit of output, and the other classic diagram is produced. Look carefully at Figure 6.3 again. Average total cost (ATC) will fall as output increases, but at an ever decreasing rate.

The above analysis should have revealed the basic cost equations for a business, namely:

$$TC = FC + VC \dots\dots\dots\dots\dots\dots (3)$$
$$ATC = AFC + AVC = AC \dots\dots\dots (4)$$

(Note: average total cost is usually shortened to average cost, or AC.)

So, the more players and tapes that CD sells, the lower will be its average costs. The magnitude of the reduction will depend on the cost structure of the firm.

Cost structure

Cost structure is defined as the relative proportion of fixed and variable costs within the firm.

Consider the two extreme cases of all fixed costs and all variable costs. For a firm with all fixed costs its average costs will decrease regularly and significantly with production. Each doubling of capacity will halve the average cost. Average cost will be very sensitive to sales volume, therefore. Planned sales will have to be achieved or the firm will be in serious trouble, e.g. assume a fixed cost of £100,000 and sales of 10, 20, 40, 80, 160, and 320 Average fixed costs will be £10,000, £5,000, £2,500,

Street market at Southall, in West London. An example of a labour intensive industry.

£1,250, £625 and £312.5, respectively. Plot this data, and note that at a theoretical output of infinity the firm would have average costs of zero.

Equally, a firm with only variable costs will have constant average costs regardless of volume made. Its actual cost, therefore, will depend on the actual level of variable costs obtained, not on the number sold or produced. It will be the buying of materials that will be critical, rather than the level of sales.

These two examples are at the extreme and are unrealistic. A firm will combine fixed and variable costs, but the proportions will vary widely from firm to firm. This constitutes the cost structure for the concern.

A firm with a high proportion of fixed costs would be considered as being very capital intensive, where one with predominantly variable costs would be considered as labour intensive. Remember that the variable cost concerned may not be labour, but any variable cost. In fact labour has not been mentioned with reference to costs yet, and there is a very good reason for this. First, two new definitions to be learnt.

Capital intensive company

A company where the majority of its costs are fixed costs, rather than variable cost, is a capital intensive company.

These will be firms that use a large amount of capital equipment, spend much on research and development, and often own much land and many factories. Good examples are the steel industry, aerospace companies and pharmaceutical companies. Transport companies can also be capital intensive. Consider British Airways. As a scheduled airline which has to fly regardless of the passenger load, virtually its only variable cost is fuel used, not all the fuel, though, only the extra amount that is burnt as a result of the weight of the passengers. A capital intensive firm is very concerned that it meets its sales targets, but far less worried by increases in direct costs. The business will have set its prices based on its knowledge of costs and will have predicted a certain level of sales. BA must achieve the load factor it has based its budget on. Consider the fictional example shown in Case Study 6.1.

Labour intensive company

A business where the majority of its costs are variable is a labour intensive company.

CASE STUDY 6.1

Domestic Aircraft plc

Domestic Aircraft plc manufactures and sells an executive jet. Its main product is a twin engined, nine-seater aircraft with full trans-Atlantic range. In 1992 it forecast sales of ten aircraft, after fixing its selling price at £5 million per aircraft. Costs were forecast as follows:

Variable costs – £2 million per aircraft.

Overheads – £20 million per year, including research costs.

The profit plan was as follows:

Sales revenue – 10 x £5 million		£50 million.	
Less:	Fixed costs –	£20 million	
	Variable costs – 10 x £2 million -	£20 million	
	Total costs –	£40 million	(£40 million)
	Planned profit –		£10 million.

This would represent a profit of £1 million per aircraft, or a net margin of 20%. This seems both reasonable and secure against changes.

In the event, sales and production only reached seven planes because of a lack of orders. The effect on profit was severe as it fell to only £1 million overall. How?

Sales revenue – 7 x £5 million		£35 million	
Less:	Fixed costs –	£20 million	
	Variable costs – 7 x £2 million –	£14 million	
	Total costs –	£34 million	(£34 million)
Actual profit –			£1 million

A 30% drop in sales has caused a 90% drop in profits.

Now consider what would have happened if the variable costs had risen by 30%, but the price and sales stayed the same.

Sales revenue – 10 x £5 million		£50 million	
Less: Fixed costs –		£20 million	
	Variable costs – 10 x £2.6 million –	£26 million	
	Total costs	£46 million	(£46 million)
	Profit		£4 million

The 30% rise invariable costs has reduced the level of profit by 60%, less than the effect of a loss of sales of the same 30%.

A rise in prices of 30% in a year is unlikely. However, a loss in demand of 30% in a year is very possible. It has and does happen in the aircraft industry. Look at the changes in the sales of Boeing, British Aerospace and Airbus Industries in the early 1990s. Under these circumstances the firm may well offer to cut prices, or offer other 'inducements' to purchasers to encourage them to sign the order.

Activity

Calculate the effect on profits of a 10% price cut for Domestic Aircraft. This reduction is sufficient to keep sales at the planned ten in the year.

Examples would be market stalls, small retail outlets, particularly where they rent the property, and high labour clothing production companies. Consider the worked example in Case Study 6.2.

In the original analysis of CD's costs, a number were ignored and have not been classified. Examples are stationery, postage and salaries. Perhaps the most surprising and startling are the charges for people. First, the salaries for CD and all labour costs in general.

CASE STUDY 6.2

College Dynamics (Retail) Ltd

CD has considered setting up a direct retail division, CD (Retail) Ltd which would sell tapes and other audio software to the general public. The cost structure for the typical small shop to be set up in the provinces is as follows:

Rental of shop	£1,000 per month	Insurances, etc.	£200 per month
Rental of fittings	£300 per month	Staff costs, etc.	£2,000 per month
Rates	£500 per month	Total costs	£4,000 per month

Sales were predicted at 10,000 units per month at a price of £8 each. Costs to CD were known to be £3 per unit.

Profit forecast

Sales revenue 10,000 x £8		£80,000
Costs: Fixed costs – £4,000		
Variable costs – 10,000 x £3 –	£30,000	(£34,000)
Profit forecast		£46,000

Shops were planned to earn £46,000 profit per month, a margin of 57.5% on the value of the sales – a very satisfactory margin, it would seem.

Examine the effect of a loss of sales of 10% or an increase in price to CD also of 10%.

a) Sales fall by 10%

Sales revenue 9,000 x £8		£72,000
Costs: Fixed costs –	£4000	
Variable costs – 9,000 x £3 –	£27,000	(£31,000)
Profit forecast		£41,000

There would be a loss of profit of £5,000. The margin would still be about 57%, a marginal decrease.

b) Variable costs increase by 10%

Sales revenue 10,000 x £8		£80,000
Costs: Fixed costs –	£4,000	
Variable costs – 10,000 x £3.3 –	£33,000	(£37,000)
Profit forecast		£43,000

Now there would be a loss of profit of £3,000.

Labour is one of the most difficult costs to classify. Mention is often made of the 'direct labour costs', which means that the costs of labour will vary directly with production. Can this be the case? Consider two different employees of a business, the managing director and a production worker.

The managing director is clearly a fixed cost. He or she is paid a salary, often a very large one, which is not related to output or sales (see Chapter 1). (If sales double, the salary does not double, nor does the firm employ a second MD!) So this salary is a fixed cost. Or is it? There is a growing trend these days towards paying a productivity bonus, especially to senior managers and directors. This is directly related to profits, so brings a variable element into this 'total renumeration package'.

Production workers can be paid on the basis of piece work, i.e. where they are paid according to how much they do. A packer may get so much per case packed, a riveter so much per rivet set. This is clearly a variable cost, but this method of payment is not common or popular. Rates are difficult to set, and there are arguments over quality. Also, only a few jobs in a factory can be treated this way. If the pace of work is machine or line set, then the method will not be acceptable. Car assembly workers would not accept this method of payment unless they could control the speed of the line, and even then there would be much discussion over who should set it. So workers tend to be paid on a time basis. Wages can be by hour, day or week. Once employed a worker usually has to be given notice. In this sense labour is a fixed cost – it is fixed for the duration of the notice period.

So labour costs can be fixed or variable, or combine the characteristics of both. Be careful, and do not use it as an example of fixed or variable costs. It, like others, is best described as semi-variable, or even semi-fixed.

Semi-variable costs (or semi-fixed) are those costs which have some of the characteristics of both fixed and variable costs. They vary with output, but not proportionately.

Additional examples would be supervisory staff, quality control, personnel, repair costs, and marketing expenses. They are related, in part, to output, but are not direct relationships. Examine the situation with quality control. Quality control only exists because of production, so has some variable element. However, the increase in costs will relate to the workload of the staff. This will not be directly related to output, but will increase in a series of steps. Examine Figure 6.4.

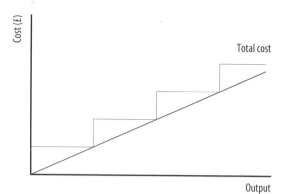

Figure 6.4 *Relationship between output and costs for quality control function*

There is a minimum level of spending on quality control – that corresponding to one analyst and a small laboratory. This can then only increase in steps corresponding to an increase in staff and their additional equipment.

These strange costs are usually expressed in terms of output, over a limited range, like the variable costs; they are added to the normal variable costs. This means that over a short range of outputs at least, the costs of a firm can be expressed as either fixed or variable, and the cost curves as described in Figure 6.3 apply.

One result of this cost analysis, and the presence of fixed and variable costs, is that one of the most difficult questions to answer in business is 'How much will the product cost?' This question cannot be answered unless the quantity required is known. It is another one of those common 'it all depends' answers that are peculiar to Business Studies.

It is now possible to apply a revenue curve and to start to look at both costs and income, and potential profit situations. The point where a firm will be able to break even will be revealed.

Sales revenue is simply the money received from the sale of the goods or services concerned. If only one product is concerned it is simply the product of the number of units sold and their price. Assuming that price does not change with the amount sold, then revenue is given by the equation:

Sales revenue (R) = Price (P) x Quantity Sold (Q) .... (5)

This is illustrated in Figure 6.5.

When this is combined with the corresponding cost curves the break-even chart for the firm results. A firm will break even when the costs of production exactly balance the revenue produced. Examine Figure 6.6 very carefully.

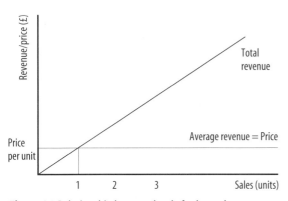

Figure 6.5 *Relationship between level of sales and revenue received*

plenty of additional opportunities to practice this skill when the questions at the end of this chapter are answered.)

P represents the break-even point. Q represents the break-even volume or quantity for the operation, and R represents the break-even revenue. In a real business production would be more concerned with the quantity being sold. They would look at their production rates and the quantities of goods in their stores and warehouses. Marketing, on the other hand, would be more likely to be monitoring sales revenue.

When sales exceed the break-even level the firm will go into profit. Profit is represented on the graph by the area between the TC and TR (total revenue) curves. This is illustrated in Figure 6.7, commonly called the *profit/volume* graph.

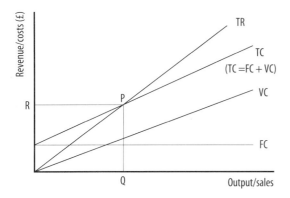

Figure 6.6 *Illustration of a basic break-even chart*

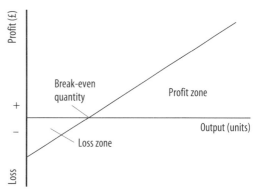

Figure 6.7 *Relationship between output and profit (the volume/profit graph)*

This diagram can be constructed in a number of ways. A variation on the above is not to draw the line FC (fixed costs) at all. Instead the VC (variable costs) line is started at the point on the Y axis that corresponds to the fixed costs. This way TC (total costs) is produced directly.

Notice, also, that provided a product is sold at a price that exceeds its variable costs of production, then it will make a *contribution* to the firm.

The contribution is the difference between the price of a good or service and the variable cost of producing and selling it. It will go towards paying the fixed costs, or overheads and any excess is profit.

If the contributions from all the products sold in a period exceed the fixed costs of the firm, it makes a profit. If it does not, then the firm is in trouble when the overheads have to be paid again. The firm may not have cash to do so, and may be forced out of business.

Now go back to Case Study 6.1 and draw a break-even chart for Domestic Aircraft plc. (There will be

Break-even point is the level of sales where the revenue obtained from the sale of the item just balances the cost of producing that quantity. So, another definition:

The break-even point is that level of sales and output where the cost of production and selling exactly equals the revenue derived from their sales.

Every product has a unit variable cost (VC) and a price (P). The difference between its variable cost and its price is the contribution that product makes towards paying the fixed costs. So:

Price – Variable cost = Unit contribution

To find the number of units we need to sell to break even we simply divide the total fixed costs by the unit contribution. So:

Break-even level of output = Total fixed costs / Unit contribution

Another term has to be understood, and that is the margin of safety.

The margin of safety is the difference between the planned or actual level of sales and production, and the break-even output.

This is illustrated in Figure 6.8. Imagine a firm knows it has a break-even output of 10,000 units and that it expects to actually sell 15,000 in the same time period. It has a margin of safety of 5,000 units, or 50% of its break-even output.

The margin of safety is expressed as a number, but it is useful to also express this difference as a percentage of the break-even quantity. An example to illustrate the point and purpose of this technique is provided in Case Study 6.3.

This is a typical 'it all depends' type of question.

Again, for the high price strategy, the following should be found.

CD and its pricing strategy

CD plc is considering making and selling its own brand of CDs instead of importing them from Japan. It has analysed both the market and the production process, and has produced the following cost/price information:

    Fixed costs of production £300,000 per annum

    Variable costs of production £4 per unit

    (including all semi-variables)

    Estimated market size at price of £10 per CD 100,000

However, if it lowers its price to £7 per unit, well below the existing market standard, sales are predicted to rise to 130,000. Which strategy is recommended?

The solution

1. Draw break-even charts for the two situations described in Case Study 6.3.

The following method is recommended. The high price situation is used to illustrate it.

- Calculate the break-even point. This is found by solving the following equation:

300,000 + 4X = 10X
6X = 300,000 so X = 50,000 i.e. break-even quantity is 50,000 CDs.

- Set and scale the X and Y axis:

X axis – Units of Sales/Production – 0 to 100,000 the level of forecast sales.
Y axis – Costs/Revenue. Revenue is usually the largest value at forecast sales.
Forecast Revenue £10 × 100,000 – £1 million. So axis units must go from 0 to £1 million.

- Add Fixed and Variable costs, Total costs and the Break-even point. Draw the Revenue line, and check that it passes through the break-even point.

This routine should ensure that break-even charts are drawn accurately and quickly, and that drafting errors do not result in strange break-even quantities.

2. Determine the break-even quantity for each situation, and then calculate the margin of safety. Calculate the level of profit that will be achieved if the forecast sales are obtained.

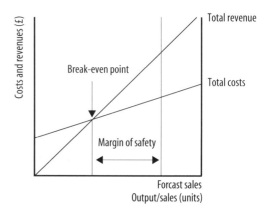

Figure 6.8 Diagram showing the margin of safety

Break-even quantity – 50,000
Margin of safety – 100,000 – 50,000 = 50,000, or 100% of the break-even quantity
Profit at forecast sales – £300,000 per annum.
(Check calculation: Costs £300,000 + 100,000
                                        (£4) or £700,000
                       Revenue 100,000 x £10 =
                       £1,000,000)

Sales forecasts would have to be very inaccurate to cause a loss situation to result. Remember, though, sales forecasts tend to be optimistic and high, and cost estimates, or forecasts, optimistic and low. Their combination can result in a disaster!

3.   Draw a contribution diagram for the company.
4.   Compare the two sets of results and make a recommendation. Remember there are more than one objective for the firm – maximising profit, sales etc or minimising risk of losses; recommend accordingly. The margin of safety, as a percentage should be used here.

Break-even analysis is the first business tool, or decision aid, encountered. It is a simple and easy procedure, and requires only a limited amount of data. It is a valuable calculation, but has its limitations. These are important, and must be understood and remembered. The major errors and inaccuracies are:

- The chart is only as accurate as the data used in its construction. Any optimism or pessimism here will be reflected in the final result. (This is a criticism that can be levelled at all calculations, in fact.)
- The chart assumes that all the elements of it are independently variable. This is not usually the case.
- The model totally ignores stocks of materials. The placing of items into stock, or the use of existing stocks is ignored. In fact it assumes that all items are manufactured and then sold. This is rarely the case and can influence cash and profit/liquidity forecasts.
- The model is basically a static one. A dynamic one would be more realistic.
- It concentrates solely on profit, and makes no attempt to look at the cash position. It does not look at the actual receipt of money, nor its expenditure. It assumes, in effect, that no credit is given or taken.
- The chart assumes only straight line relationships. Whilst this is sometimes true over narrow ranges of output, it does not hold true over the full range.

SUMMARY

Having studied this chapter carefully, you should understand fully the difficulty associated with answering the question 'what has a product cost to make ?' In detail, you will:

▽ understand the differences between fixed, variable and semi-variable costs.

▽ know why labour costs today are really semi-variable.

▽ be able to demonstrate how capital structure effects the costs and decision making ability of firms.

▽ be able to construct a break-even chart, to derive the profit position and the margin of safety, but be fully aware of the limitations of this decision-making tool.

You will now be aware of the need to be able to rate the profit potential of an operation against its costs.

7

The costs and revenues of a firm – real cost curves, and economies and diseconomies of scale

Preview

▼ You saw theoretical cost curves in the last chapter, and learnt all about break-even analysis. This chapter will concentrate on developing *real cost curves*.

▼ It will develop the critical 'size-cost' relationships for businesses of different types, through an examination of the concepts of *economies and diseconomies of scale*.

▼ Finally, it will introduce you to the concept of *marginal costs*.

In the last chapter you saw the theoretical curves, and were introduced to some of the problems of break-even analysis. What shape are real cost curves?

Costs and revenue do not change in a straight line manner other than within a narrow range of outputs. A straight line revenue curve supposes a constant price. In fact it is normal to have to drop the price to achieve high sales levels. Thus the real revenue curve is downward sloping, away from the diagonal. This is shown in Figure 7.1.

Equally, costs do not behave as the theory predicts. No mention has been made of the capacity

of a plant or factory to produce; in fact, it is assumed to be unlimited. In reality this is not so, and all units have a design capacity. This leads to the existence of real as opposed to theoretical cost curves.

Real cost curves

Theory predicts that the average costs of production for a firm will always fall with increasing output. In the real world this is not so. Costs do decrease, initially, but they reach a minimum then rise again. Costs also seem nearly always to be higher than theory predicts. This is illustrated in Figure 7.2.

This divergence between theory and practice happens because:

• Production plants do not have an infinite capacity. Plants have been designed to produce a certain output, the 'design capacity'. Consider, for example, a bakery. The supermarket, its customer, wants 100 loaves per hour so the owners of the bakery have invested in a plant with a maximum capacity of 120 loaves per hour, (point (b) on Figure 7.2) and an economic output of 100 loaves per hour, the production requirement (point (a) on the diagram). So both

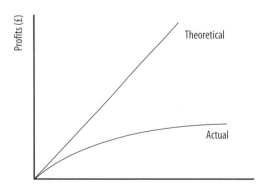

Figure 7.1 *Relationship between theoretical and actual profit*

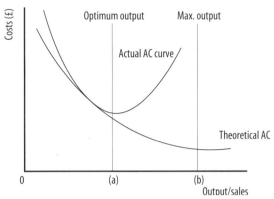

Figure 7.2 *Relationship between real and theoretical cost curves*

the theoretical and the actual average costs curves cannot exist beyond output Ob because such outputs are not possible. Costs rise between outputs (a) and (b) for the following reasons:

• The higher rates mean that the plant has to be pushed towards its limit. Maintenance costs increase, as does the amount of wastage, or poor quality product that is produced. The breakdown rate increases, so materials are wasted and overtime has to be worked to catch up.

Costs rise as output is lowered below output (a) at a greater rate than theory predicts for the following primary reasons:

Waste of materials

Theory assumes no difference in wastage with output, but practise shows that this is not true. Slow rates of production will mean that raw materials are used at a slower rate and there is a greater chance of these materials deteriorating before they can be used. For the bakers, open flour bags may get contaminated, salt may get wet, and yeast may start to ferment too early. This increases costs as the materials have to be paid for. The alternative, to buy materials in smaller units, also results in increased costs.

The waste of materials when the plant is shut down and cleaned will also not change with output, and will become a larger and larger proportion of total cost as the output is reduced. Imagine the mixing bowl at home after a chocolate cake has been made. The mix left is 'waste'. The amount of waste depends on the size of the mixing bowl, not on the number of cakes made. The same applies to the bakery. This waste is a fixed cost, and grows in importance as output falls. At one loaf per hour it could be more than the variable cost of the loaf itself.

Waste of energy

It takes energy to start up a plant, to preheat an oven. It takes the same amount of energy to heat the oven before baking one loaf or 100. The costs are increased. The same logic applies to cleaning and shutting down costs.

This analysis suggest that most costs are semi-variable, rather than fixed or variable. This is the case, other than over very narrow ranges of outputs. This must be remembered when doing break-even analysis, and making decisions based on its results. It is a simplification and must be treated with caution.

Now combine actual total cost with actual revenue, and see that a 'profit envelope' results. Look at Figure 7.3 below.

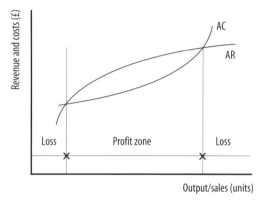

Figure 7.3 *The 'actual' cost envelope for a company*

It should also be clear now what a difficult question 'How much will it cost to make?' is. You must know the number required, and the size and cost structure of the plant to be used. As was said at the start of the chapter, most firms do not know what it costs to make an individual product in its range.

Costs vary as the capacity of a factory changes, in the same way as the fuel consumption of a car increases with the speed maintained. Costs also vary as the basic size of the plant is changed. This leads to the important topic of economies and diseconomies of scale.

Economies and diseconomies of scale

It has already been shown how the costs for a particular size of production unit, or factory, change with output, and are minimised at the design capacity of the plant. What happens if the size of the plant is changed?

Go back to the example of the bakery. The supermarket increases its order from 100 to 200 loaves per hour. The bakery now has two choices, buy another identical line or scrap the first and buy one of double the capacity. In fact it has a third option, the one that is always available. It could opt to ignore the order and stay as it is. Taking the 'no risk' option, but also the 'no growth' and 'no future' option. It is an attractive option to those people who dislike making a decision, though. (Another example of the interaction between people and business.) The bakery selects the second option, and finds that the optimum cost of production is reduced. Examine Figure 7.4. Observe that the two cost curves cross, and that at outputs below Ox the bread from the larger plant will cost more than that from the first.

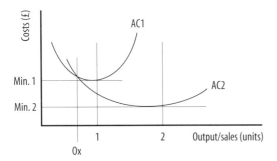

Figure 7.4 *Effect of increasing capacity on the cost curves for an operation*

The bakery owner gets even more orders, and so orders an even larger plant, expecting even lower costs. There is some concern when actual costs, as opposed to those calculated in support of the expansion project, are shown to have risen. The full cost curve is illustrated on Figure 7.5.

It is generally accepted that costs have fallen over the output range O to Od as a result of economies of scale, but have risen from outputs Od as a result of diseconomies of scale. What is it that actually causes the costs to change?

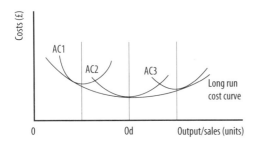

Figure 7.5 *Diagram showing the full effect of size of a factory on production costs*

Economies of scale

As a business grows in size it gains a whole range of advantages. These are considered to be the various economies of scale. They fall into two major groups – internal and external. Internal economies of scale fall to the business itself, but external economies accrue to the industry that the individual firm is part of. In the example followed so far the internal economies fall to the individual bakery, while any external economies will accrue by the growth, or concentration together of the baking industry as a whole.

The major groupings of the internal economies of scale are:

Technical

The technical side is a major source of savings, and covers many areas. Consider the following:

Increased specialisation

The larger a business the greater the opportunity for the employment and use of specialist staff and machinery. Workers are more efficient at their job, so costs are reduced. Specialist staff, such as accountants, electronic engineers and buyers can be fully utilised and can generate maximum savings.

Increased dimensions

Large process plants and factories do not cost as much per unit as small ones. Consider a simple example of a fence around a factory site. Double the size of the site and twice the amount of fence does not have to be erected. Examine Figure 7.6, which illustrates two different sites.

Site 1: 10 x 10 m = 100 sq. m:
Site 2: 20 x 20 = 400 sq. m
Area has increased by a factor of 4.
Fence length 1: 4(10) = 40 m
Fence length 2: 4(20) = 80 m

Length of fence has increased by a factor of 2.

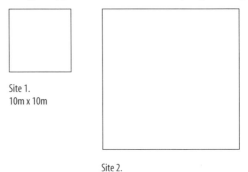

Figure 7.6 *Illustration of two alternative factory sites*

It is cheaper per square metre of site to fence the large one rather than the small one. This ignores any effects of the fence itself being cheaper per metre when a long length of fence is purchased.

This 'rule' seems to apply to most plants, processes and equipment, and is known as the 'Root Two' Rule. Double the size or capacity, and the cost rises by a factor of 1.4, or $\sqrt{2}$.

1. Cost of LPG storage vessels

Holding Capacity (K Cu.Ft)	Capital Cost (£k)	Capital Cost (£k/Cu.Ft.)
10	6	600
100	20	200
500	50	100
2,500	197	90
5,000	350	70

2. Costs of US car advertising

Company	Total ($m)	Per Car Sold ($)
General Motors	80.7	22.56
Ford	49.0	27.22
Chrysler	47.0	47.76
Studebaker-Packard	7.3	64.04
American Motors	6.6	57.89

Figure 7.7 *Examples of plant and materials costs*

Examine Figure 7.7 which shows a range of materials and plant costs which illustrate this rule.

Minimum size

All plant and equipment comes in a range of sizes, but there is usually a minimum size that can be purchased, e.g. a stamping machine produces 50 pressings per minute, minimum, or a packing machine fills 25 cartons per minute. If a firm wants 25 pressings per minute, or to pack at 12 cartons per minute, it has to purchase the minimum size machine and to bear the extra cost.

This factor also applies to some key departments within a firm. The vital functions of quality control and research and development have a minimum effective size and cost. This may be beyond the means of the smaller firms, who may thereby fall behind in the market.

The use of chains of machines

Most production operations require the use of more than one machine, with operations being carried out in a sequence. Since each machine will be subject to a minimum size, the small firm will already have incurred a cost penalty. Now examine the effect on a sequential operation. Work through Case Study 7.1 which follows. You should produce the following answers:

Output (units/min)	10	20	30	50
Capital cost (£k)	82	112	150	232
Cost / unit (£k/u)	8.2	5.6	5.0	4.6

CASE STUDY 7.1

CD plc and the production of tape head cleaning fluid

CD plc manufacture a high quality range of audio tape equipment, and wishes to add to this a range of head cleaning fluids. The necessary plant and equipment to do this with its costs and capacities are shown in the table.

What is the total capital cost, and the capital cost per unit, of purchasing lines to produce 10, 20, 30 and 50 units per minute?

		Capacity (units/minute)	Cost (£)
Injection moulder	– bottles	10	20,000
	– caps	50	20,000
Bottle filler/capper		20	5,000
Labeller		30	4,000
Cartoner		20	8,000
Over-wrapper		10	10,000
Shrink wrapper (dozens)		10	15,000

Marketing

Marketing covers the economies of buying and selling.

The most obvious economy here is the effect of bulk buying. The more that is bought at a time the lower the unit cost to the purchaser. As a large customer it can not only demand a better price, it can also demand favourable payment terms. This can reduce its cash flow problems, and reduce its cost of borrowing.

Selling costs are also reduced for large firms. Many marketing and selling expenses are semi-variable, and decrease as a cost per unit as the size of the operation increases. Advertising is paid for by 'time' or by 'page', and is also able to be purchased in bulk. Thus a large firm gets its advertising media cheaper than a small advertiser, over and above its initial unit cost advantage.

Marketing and sales staff are also a semi-variable cost, and can handle large outputs better than small.

Financial

The financial grouping covers sources of finance, interest rates charged, and confidence. As was seen earlier, many more sources of finance are available to the larger firm, particularly if it is incorporated. It can sell 'paper', and deal with the larger financial institutions. The larger firms have greater access to the cheaper sources of money.

Larger firms often have better reputations than the smaller ones. They are seen as a better risk, and may well have a far better credit rating. They will have borrowed capital before and will have repaid it and kept to the terms of the loans. They will, as a result, be charged a lower rate of interest.

The result is that large firms have lower financing costs than small ones, and many fewer problems in arranging finance.

Risk-bearing ability

Large firms are generally in a better position to cope with the risks of business life. There are a number of reasons for this.

Large firms do not usually depend on one product, so can handle the decline of a market easier than the small, single-product firm that sees its market decline by 25% in a year, say. They are able to diversify into other markets, and so spread their risk. Their working capital is usually a smaller proportion of turnover than for a small firm, so they can absorb changes easier without incurring cash flow problems.

Small firms are generally much more sensitive to changes in the economy and the market than large ones. They usually can start up quickly and easily, but shut down equally rapidly. Just consider the effect of the recession of the early 1990s on UK business.

Large, single-product firms are at risk, though. Consider the defence industry in general, and the building of nuclear submarines in the UK in particular.

All these internal factors give large advantages to large companies, particularly if they are involved in the process industries, i.e. are in the secondary sector, and are involved in research-based mass production. In addition, a firm might be able to benefit from external economies of scale, or those which accrue to the concentration of firms within an industry.

External economies of scale

If firms that are in the same industry, even though they may compete with each other, group together in a suitable location, they are able to achieve some cost savings. These will be in the areas of:

Labour

The labour in such an area will tend to be trained and skilled for the particular trade concerned. Thus steel workers are likely to be found in the Sheffield area and skilled electronics operators in the M4 corridor. Schools, colleges and universities will tend to specialise in the technologies of the region, leading to the availability of suitably qualified staff.

Services

Repair and service companies will develop in the area and will be readily available. They will be attracted by the concentration, and will thereby benefit the region as a whole. Thus there might be many light engineering and hydraulics service firms around the aerospace district of Bristol. Aluminium casting, and high quality and reliability testing may also be a relatively available service here.

Cooperation

In some industries firms will cooperate in areas of non-competitive research and development and trade associations, e.g. industry research companies funded jointly, and the Association of Motor Manufacturers and Traders.

Specialised commercial services

Specialised banking or insurance services may develop in areas of high need, making such services cheaper for the users. Export shippers will be found near concentrations of export orientated companies. Specialised horse transport services are found near Newmarket.

All these factors combine and result in the general tendency for costs to decrease with increasing output. The rate of reduction reduces, though, as size increases greatly. This is illustrated in Figure 7.8.

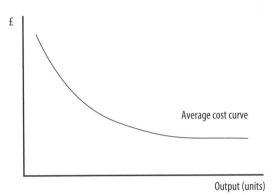

Figure 7.8 Diagrammatical representation of the full effects of economies of scale on the costs of a firm

While these economies are essentially technical and available to all, they do have to be both understood and taken advantage of. It will fall to the senior managers of firms to ensure that this is done. Some companies will do better than others in this respect.

Diseconomies of scale

These may also be either internal or external. The major effects are likely to be the result of internal diseconomies.

As has been shown, the internal economies of scale are of a technical or material nature, while the diseconomies will soon be seen to be people related. The major internal diseconomies are:

Slow decision making

A small business, specially if it is a sole trader, can make decisions rapidly as the owner, the decision maker, is also running the business. As a firm grows, and its organisation structure changes, more people are involved, and the power to make decisions is usually reduced. There are more managers now, and the owner is remote. Decisions may require Board action, which may not always be possible. As the decision-making process slows, the opportunity to take advantages of possibilities as they arise is reduced. Eventually the firm starts to lose out to its smaller, more responsive competitors.

This is clearly not an automatic process, and many firms take positive action to reduce this effect of expansion. Others, depending on the management style of the directors and senior managers, seem to encourage its onset.

Increased growth of bureaucracy

Small firms tend to run with the minimum of paperwork and formal procedures. All staff are involved in the performance of the firm, all are 'line workers'. As businesses grow there is an increasing tendency for paperwork to develop. Firms tend to be bound by systems, and the number of 'staff roles' proliferate. Costs grow, with no corresponding increase in output or productivity.

Again the actual effect of this problem, which is really a matter of trust, or the lack of it, varies with the management style of the firm, and also with the type of firm concerned. It is very prevalent in nationalised industries and government departments in the UK. Is there a link with the profit motive here? The profit motive must be a powerful inducement to reduce costs.

Slow and inefficient communications

A business can only operate efficiently when all parts of it know what is going on, and are able to take the decisions that they have to in full view of all the relevant facts. As a business grows the chances of this happening decrease, and wrong decisions will increase. An efficient system of coordination is necessary, but this will only be cost effective if it avoids the dangers of bureaucracy, creating more interdependence and linkages!

Poor morale

As firms grow they tend to become impersonal. As morale drops mistakes will be made, the pace of work will slow, and costs will rise. It can be a considerable problem with large firms, and it is one of the major jobs of management to prevent it. Good relations between workers and management must be maintained. Management structure and style must be set to keep the feeling of an individual's involvement high.

The diseconomies of scale can set in at any time after the size of a company exceeds one person!

They tend to be minimal in effect initially, though. Their effect is largely the responsibility of the senior managers, its management style and its objectives. (This is covered fully in Part 4. Note the interdependence here; man management and costs.)

External diseconomies result from the over-concentration of firms in a particular region. The availability of labour, materials and energy, for example, may be overstretched resulting in increased costs.

The effects of the diseconomies of scale can be summarised diagrammatically. Examine Figure 7.9. Note that the increase in costs starts at almost zero output.

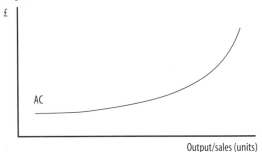

Figure 7.9 *Diagrammatical representation of the effects of diseconomies of scale on the average costs of a firm*

A scale cannot be put on the output axis, not even for a particular business or industry. As has been shown above, much is dependent on the senior managers of the firms. Some firms 'suffer' diseconomies of scale more than others.

So it can now be seen that both economies and diseconomies of scale produce individual cost curves that start at the origin, i.e. at 'output zero'. The well-known average cost curve is the result of the summation of these two curves. Look at Figure 7.10. This shows that the economies and diseconomies are continuous and additive, and combine to give the usual 'U' shaped average cost curve.

Initially, the economies of scale dominate, producing the downward sloping section. Eventually the diseconomies cancel these out, and then themselves dominate. This produces the upwards sloping final part. The objective of management must be to maximise the effects of the economies of scale on its business, and reduce and delay the effect of the diseconomies. Businesses differ widely in their ability to do this.

So, costs of production are even harder to predict. The size of the plant and the efficiency of the management of the plant and the company is now relevant.

Some industries are dominated by a few large

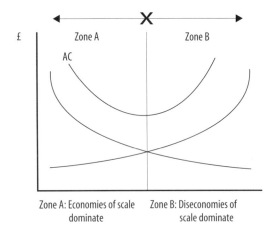

Figure 7.10 *The effect of economies and diseconomies of scale on the average costs of a firm*

firms and others consist of many small units. This is the result of the relative importance of economies and diseconomies of scale to the particular industry. Consider two extremes, the oil industry and the retail greengrocery industry.

The petrochemical industry is capital intensive, employs relatively few people, and is organised on a global or multinational basis. It is subject to massive economies of scale, and is able to suppress the diseconomies. The optimum size of plant is very large. A few large refineries can easily supply a country as the product is very easy to distribute. It is also non-perishable.

Greengrocers, on the other hand, only supply a small area because of the perishability of the product. There are few economies of scale available, but some opportunity for diseconomies to set in. The result is an industry with many small businesses.

The nature of an industry is measured through the concentration ratio for it. This is defined as follows:

Three-firm concentration ratio
The amount of a market controlled by the three largest firms in that industry. Market share is usually measured in terms of sales.

Refer back to the extract from the 'Fortune 500' given in Chapter 1 and observe the dominance of firms in the petrochemical and motor industries. These have high concentration ratios on a world basis. Look at the supermarket business in the UK. The three-firm ratio here must be about 40%.

There is one more cost that must be mentioned – the marginal cost. This is a cost much loved by economists, but not so well understood or used within business. It is simply defined as the cost of producing one more item, or the extra cost of producing the last item.

Marginal cost

Marginal cost, the cost of producing one more, will be made up essentially of variable costs.

It is not just variable cost, though, and it is definitely not a proportionate relationship. Consider the set of

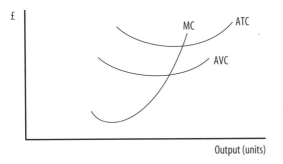

Figure 7.11 *Relationship between marginal and average costs*

actual cost curves that were identified earlier. Look at Figure 7.11, which illustrates the relationship between marginal and average costs of a firm.

If the average cost is rising, then the marginal cost must be rising even faster. The marginal cost must also be greater than the average cost. Equally, when the average cost is falling, the marginal cost must be below the average cost. Marginal cost and average cost will be the same where the average cost is a minimum. At this point average cost is neither rising nor falling, so must equal the marginal cost.

A short summary

Break-even analysis gives a business a quick though approximate way of deciding if a product is worth selling, and if the combination of price and market size is likely to be profitable. But the technique requires a full knowledge of the costs of production, and this is very difficult to find out accurately. *It gives no information about the wisdom of spending the capital that will be necessary to produce the product.* In other words, it gives no indication of the real value of the product.

SUMMARY

Having studied this chapter carefully, you should understand even more fully the difficulty associated with answering the question 'what has a product cost to make ?' In detail you will:

▼ Be able to illustrate and explain the difference between theoretical and actual cost curves.

▼ Understand the differences between economies and diseconomies of scale and be able to use them to explain the differences in the size of firms in different industries.

▼ Be able to define, use and interpret the concept of concentration ratio.

▼ Be able to describe the concept of the marginal cost of production.

You will now be aware of the need to be able to rate the profit potential of an operation against its costs.

Questions and activities

Technical terms and glossary

In the section below you are given a series of technical terms and their meanings. They have been scrambled, though. You must match up the terms

and the definitions. When you have them correctly paired, transfer them to your vocabulary or glossary book.

You are also advised to transfer any definitions obtained during the exercises in the case studies into this glossary book.

Technical terms
1. Direct costs
2. Indirect costs
3. Cost structure
4. Capital intensive company
5. Labour intensive company
6. Semi-variable costs
7. Contribution
8. Bankruptcy
9. Insolvency
10. Break-even quantity
11. Break-even revenue
12. Margin of safety
13. Technical economies of scale
14. Economies of scale
15. Marginal cost
16. Concentration ratio
17. Depreciation
18. Diseconomies of scale
19. Profit/volume graph
20. Bureaucracy

Definitions
A. An allowance made by accountants to reflect the fact that assets such as buildings, plant and motor vehicles wear out with time and lose their value.
B. A business which has a high proportion of direct costs compared with its indirect costs.
C. Office work. Usually meant to imply an excess of paper work and administration, at the expense of efficiency.
D. A diagram, based on a break-even chart, which shows how the profit earning potential of a firm changes with output and sales.
E. The proportion of a market held by a predetermined number of firms. For '3', it would be the total of the market share of the three largest businesses in the industry.
F. Those costs incurred by a business which vary directly with the quantity made or sold.
G. Those influences on the costs and efficiency of a firm which result in an increase in average costs as output increases.
H. The situation an incorporated company applies for when it cannot meet its financial responsibilities, i.e. it cannot pay its bills.
I. The cost of making one more unit, or the cost of the last unit made. In the short run, this will be the same as the variable cost.
J. The difference in output between the break-even quantity and the amount sold or planned to be sold.
K. Those influences on the costs and efficiency of a business which result in a reduction in average costs as output is increased.

L. The relative proportion of fixed and variable costs within a firm.
M. A firm with a cost structure that includes a high proportion of high fixed costs when compared with variables.
N. Those costs which have characteristics of both direct and indirect costs. The costs vary with output, but only disproportionately.
O. Those engineering and scientific influences which work on the costs of a firm and cause its average costs of production to fall as production increases.
P. Those costs incurred by a business which are fixed for a period of time, and do not change with production level.
Q. That level of sales revenue that, when achieved, shows that costs have just been recovered.
R. That level of output for a company so that the revenue received from sales exactly equals the total costs of manufacturing them.
S. The situation an individual, sole trader or partnership is in when it cannot meet its financial liability, i.e. is unable to pay its bills.
T. The difference between the revenue received from the sale of a product or service, and the direct costs of producing it.

Short answer questions
1. Why is it so difficult to classify labour as a fixed or a variable cost?
2. What is a capital intensive company? Why will its management worry less about increases in materials costs than about poor sales figures?
3. What does 'labour' mean in the expression 'a labour intensive company'?
4. Describe the concept of break even.
5. Describe the weaknesses of break even as a decision-making tool.
6. Can a plc be declared bankrupt?
7. Explain why the actual average cost curve for a firm is so different from that predicted by theory.
8. Outline the differences between internal and external economies of scale.
9. What does the 'three-firm concentration ratio' tell you about an industry?
10. What is marginal cost?

Data response questions and break-even problems
1. A company makes video tapes with a selling price of £10 per unit. variable costs of production are £6 per unit, and the firm has fixed costs amounting to £20,000 per month.
   (a) Draw a break-even chart for the above, and

determine the break-even output per month. Confirm this by calculation.

(b) How many will the firm need to make and sell to achieve a profit of £4,000 per month.

2. A firm makes cheap alarm clocks which it sells for £12 each. It has variable costs of £7 each, and fixed costs of £50,000 per quarter. The factory has a maximum capacity of 20,000 clocks per quarter. It plans to sell 15,000 units each quarter.

(a) Draw up a break-even chart for the above factory. What is the firm's break-even quantity and revenue?

(b) The firm manages to sell only 11,000 clocks. What will be the level of profit earned?

(c) Prepare a Profit/Volume chart for the above company.

3. A firm making and selling TV sets has a maximum capacity of 20,000 sets per week. It is actually working at a rate of 15,000 sets each week. The Accounts Department report the following costs and revenues at that rate of operation:

Revenue	£750,000
Raw materials	£100,000
Direct labour	£150,000
Packaging	£50,000
Overheads	£300,000

(a) Draw up a break-even chart for the above firm.

(b) What is the firm's present level of profit, and its margin of safety?

(c) Sales fall to 8,000 sets per week, but, after a recent productivity deal, the labour cannot be reduced. What is the level of profits now. What is the new break-even quantity now?

4. A firm manufactures camera bodies, which it retails for £250 each. It can produce 100 per week, but only makes and sells 50 per week at the present time. Its design and cost structure is such that its variable costs are £150 per camera, and it incurs indirect costs of £4,000 per week.

(a) Prepare the break-even chart for the above factory and determine its break-even point.

(b) How much profit is earned, and what is the margin of safety at the moment?

Case studies

1. The following information relates to a company which produces a single product.

Direct labour per unit	£11
Direct materials per unit	£6
Variable overheads per unit	£3

Fixed costs	£200,000
Selling price per unit	£30

(a) Explain the term 'break even'. (2 marks)

(b) Using these figures, produce a chart to show the minimum number of units which must be sold for the company to break even. (9 marks)

(c) Market research has indicated potential sales for the coming period of 30,000 units at the current price, or 37,500 units if the selling price were lowered to £28 per unit. Which strategy would you advise the company to adopt and why? (10 marks)

(d) Outline the factors which *any* business should take into consideration before using break-even analysis as a basis for decision making. (9 marks)

(Associated Examining Board, Business Studies (A) November 1987, Paper 1)

2. A local authority, whose area includes a holiday resort situated on the east coast, operates, for 30 weeks each year, a holiday home which is let to visiting parties of children in care from other authorities. The children are accompanied by their own house mothers who supervise them throughout the holiday. From six to 15 guests are accepted on terms of £100 per person per week. No differential charges exist for adults and children.

Weekly costs incurred by the host authority are:

	£ per guest
Food	25
Electricity	3
Domestic expenses	5
Use of minibus	10

Seasonal staff supervise and carry out the necessary duties at the home at a cost of £11,000 for the 30-week period. This provides staffing sufficient for six to 10 guests a per week but if 11 or more guests are to be accommodated, additional staff at a total cost of £200 per week are engaged for the whole of the 30-week period.

Rent, including rates for the property, is £4,000 per annum and the garden of the home is maintained by the council's recreation department which charges a nominal fee of £1,000 per annum.

(a) Tabulate the appropriate figures in such a way as to show the break-even point point(s) and to comment on your figures.

(b) Draw a chart to illustrate your answer to (a) above.

(Chartered Institute of Management Accountants, May 1987)

8

Investment appraisal – or 'Is it worth spending the money?'

Preview

▼ You will now examine the various numerical methods available for the evaluation of a project or investment.

▼ The methods known as *payback period, average rate of return, net present value* and *internal rate of return* will be studied and evaluated.

▼ The concept of the time value of money will be explored in detail.

▼ The importance of factors other than purely financial ones will be established and stressed.

In the last chapter you saw how to assess, through break-even analysis, if a product could be sold profitably (see Chapter 7). It gave no clue, however, towards the desirability of spending capital on it. What capital?

When a new product is produced capital has to be spent to produce it. This will include research and development (R & D) costs, both for the product and its market, the costs of the land, buildings and plant and equipment necessary to make it. All these capital costs, most of which will add to the asset value of the firm, have to be paid for. Firms have to decide if it is worth spending such capital or not. There is always a choice: make product A or product B, or make product A or stay as it is. The firm has to consider the *opportunity cost* of its spending decision.

Investment decisions involve trying to answer the following question:

If the capital is spent on a project, will it bring in enough money to make it worthwhile?

This is not a simple question to answer, and different firms will arrive at different answers for the same proposal. It will depend on the objectives of the business, its financial state and its market, as well as

the economic state of the country concerned. In particular, it will depend on the rate of interest being charged for money by the banks. Since this varies with the size and reputation of a firm, the complexity of the problem becomes apparent.

There are many ways of answering this question, and the ones that will be studied here are:

- payback period
- average rate of return
- net present value
- internal rate of return

Payback period

Payback period is the length of time necessary for the profit from the proposal, or rather its net cash inflow, to just recover the initial investment.

An example: a firm makes nuts and bolts for industry. It wishes to modernise its production, and has identified two machines that will enable it to do this. The capital costs for the two machines are known, as are the two patterns of subsequent spending and income. This data is summarised as follows.

Machine	A	B
Capital cost (Year 0)	(£25,000)	(£40,000)
Net cash flow		
Year 1	£10,000	£10,000
Year 2	£8,000	£10,000
Year 3	£5,000	£15,000
Year 4	£5,000	£15,000
Year 5	£5,000	£15,000
Year 6	Zero	£10,000

Machine	A		C	
Capital cost (Year 0)	(£25,000)		(£25,000)	
Net cash flow		Cumulative		Cumulative
Year 1	£24,999	£24,999	£1	£1
Year 2	£0	£24,999	£0	£1
Year 3	£0	£24,999	£0	£1
Year 4	£1	£25,000	£24,999	£25,000
Year 5	£0	£25,000	£50,000	£75,000

To work out the payback period follow this procedure.

1. Produce columns showing cumulative net cash flow.
2. Identify the zone where cumulative cash flow equals the initial investment.
3. Estimate the payback period, assuming equal cash flow within a year.

This is done below for the initial example.

Machine	A		B	
Capital cost (Year 0)	(£25,000)		(£40,000)	
Net cash flow		Cumulative		Cumulative
Year 1	£10,000	£10,000	£10,000	£10,000
Year 2	£8,000	£18,000	£10,000	£20,000
Year 3	£5,000	£23,000	£15,000	£35,000
Year 4	£5,000	£28,000	£15,000	£50,000
Year 5	£5,000	£33,000	£15,000	£65,000
Year 6	Zero	£33,000	£10,000	£75,000

Payback time for Machine A = 3 years + 2/5 years = 3.4 years, i.e. at the start of year 4, £2,000 is needed to achieve payback, but the full year will yield £5,000.

Payback time for Machine B = 3 years + 5/15 years = 3.33 years.

There is very little difference between the two, but Machine B is mathematically the best. It will pay back its initial investment marginally quicker than Machine A. Machine B costs more but, on the other hand, it seems to bring in much more money in the end – another problem with payback.

Examine different alternatives, and their net cash flows in the next table.

Both machines show identical payback periods of four years. But are the two investments identical?

The patterns of cash flow both before and after the payback point are very different. Depending on the objective of the firm one might select either machine. Why, then, is payback period important?

- For some companies, especially those operating in a potentially unstable country, it is important because they cannot see much beyond a certain time, e.g. if the reliable, or viable future is seen to be no more than three years, a firm would want to see payback periods well below this.
- The future is always uncertain, and the sooner any investment is recovered the smaller the risk of losing it.
- At times of fast technological change, investments which repay themselves fast are preferred. The firm concerned can then make rapid changes and keep at the forefront of technology – provided it has the will to do so.
- It concentrates on cash and cash flows which are of immediate importance to a firm, rather than profits, which are not.
- It is easy to calculate, and is apparently easy to understand.

Payback period is a very limited measure however. It tells the firm the payback period and no more. It totally ignores the following factors:

- any money earned after the point of payback
- the pattern of cash flows up to the payback point.

So, it a dangerous rule to apply on its own, unless there are very special circumstance applying at the time.

Some of the problems are overcome if another measure is taken of a proposal.

Average rate of return

The value of a project as a percentage return based on the value of the initial investment is known as the average rate of return.

It is comparable, in some way, with the rate of interest charged on or earned by money.

Numerically, it is the average net cash flow per year for a project, expressed as a percentage of the investment value.

An example is the same example used for payback. The cash flow table is reproduced below. The method for the calculation that should be followed is:

1. Add up all the net cash flow figures.
2. Subtract the initial investment from this.
3. Divide by the number of years that the project or machine will last.
4. Express this as a percentage by dividing this number by the value of the initial investment and multiplying by 100.

The resulting percentage is defined as the average rate of return for the proposition. Examine this table:

Machine	A	B
Capital cost (Year 0)	(£25,000)	(£40,000)
Net cash flow		
Year 1	£10,000	£10,000
Year 2	£8,000	£10,000
Year 3	£5,000	£15,000
Year 4	£5,000	£15,000
Year 5	£5,000	£15,000
Year 6	Zero	£10,000
Total cash flow	£33,000	£75,000
Project life	5 years	6 years
Cash flow - investment	£8,000	£35,000
Av./year	£1,600	£5,833
Average rate of return	£1,600 x 100	£5,833 x 100
	£25,000	£40,000
	6.4%	23.3%

Machine B has the highest average rate of return, and is thus the favoured machine based on this measure. Again there are problems with this method. Look again at the second example used before, but with a slight modification.

Machine	A		C	
Capital cost (Year 0)	(£25,000)		(£25,000)	
Net cash flow		Cumulative		Cumulative
Year 1	£24,999	£24,999	£1	£1
Year 2	£0	£24,999	£0	£1
Year 3	£0	£24,999	£0	£1
Year 4	£1	£25,000	£24,999	£25,000
Year 5	£25,000	£50,000	£25,000	£50,000

Both machines show a return of 20% ([£50,000 – £25,000]/5, all divided by £25,000 then multiplied by 100), and on the basis of this test, are identical. They clearly are not the same, though, as the pattern of the cash flows are markedly different, and favour Machine A.

This method of assessment also ignores the pattern of cash flows. Both methods ignore what is known as the time value of money. They both assume that a pound today has the same value as one in say five years time. This clearly is not the case. Imagine if the pound was borrowed. The one paid back in five years would have incurred interest, so would be of less value. Also, today's pound can be spent again tomorrow, but the one received in five years is 'frozen' until then. The remaining methods take this into account, and are more accurate. Why, then, use these two inaccurate methods?

- they are easily calculated and understood
- they are cheap to produce
- they are very good 'filters' through which a project or proposal has to pass before it is more rigorously and expensively examined.

CASE STUDY 8.1

CD plc and its initial selection of record making machines

CD plc had been making and selling compact discs for some time, but it saw the opportunity of producing the old style vinyl records as there had been a resurgence in their popularity and it was now fashionable again to own and play them. They had maintained their market for high quality turntables and speakers so records were a logical extension of their product range. Their factory had plenty of space so the investment was really only in the machines necessary to produce the plastics. (They also had the rights to produce records for the titles they already handled as CDs, luckily!) The marketing and production directors were strongly in favour of the proposal, but the financial director was more sceptical. The financial director had laid down the following rule for any new project for CD plc.

'Before proceeding to detailed investment appraisal a project must better the following performance criteria:

- Payback period – 2.5 years or less

- Average rate of return – Bank rate + 4%, or better.'

At the time of this proposal the bank rate stood at 8.25%.

An example to illustrate the method is given in Case Study 8.1. Work through it *before* you read on.

Two processes were under review, and the production department had produced the following figures. These were based upon their calculations and investigations, and estimates of market potential and price produced by the marketing department.

Process		X			Y
Capital cost		(£150,000)			(£250,000)
Net cash flow					
Year 1	£50,000	£50,000	£150,000	£150,000	
Year 2	70,000	120,000	150,000	300,000	
Year 3	50,000	170,000	100,000	400,000	
Year 4	50,000	220,000	50,000	450,000	
Year 5	30,000	250,000	50,000	500,000	
Year 6	20,000	270,000	50,000	550,000	
Payback period		2.6 years			1.66 years
Average rate of return		(270 - 150)/6 = 20			(550 - 250)/6 = 50
		20/150 = 13.3%			50/250 = 20%

Action standards: 2.5 years, maximum Payback. 12.25% minimum Average Rate of Return.

Check:

	Payback		
Payback	Fail, just	Pass	
Average rate of return	Pass	Pass	

Process Y has passed through the two screening tests, so may go on to the more detailed and costly evaluation procedures that follow. Process X has only failed the payback test by a very small amount, so may also be given the go ahead. It has the big advantage of being cheaper than the alternative process.

The more detailed methods of investment appraisal are grouped under the heading of discounted cash flow methods and recognise that money received today is worth more than money received tomorrow.

Consider that a pound is held in a bank today, and the bank pays 10% interest on it. The pound grows steadily as shown in Table 8.1.

Equally, if a firm has the option of a pound today or one three years later, the early one is best. It can then earn interest, and grow. The money lost at an interest rate is found by taking the reciprocal of the growth value, i.e. if £1 held for five years at 10% is worth £1.611, then £1 received in five years is worth £1/1.611 today, or £0.621. Examine the Table 8.2.

These tables, known as discount tables, are published for a full rate of interest rates. A table of net present values for various rates of interest is given as Appendix 1.

Two methods of project appraisal based on discounted cash flow methods are commonly used in business.

Table 8.1

Growth of £1 at an annual interest rate of 10%

Years held		2	3	4	5	6	7	8	9	10
Value	1.100	1.210	1.331	1.464	1.611	1.772	1.949	2.144	2.358	2.594

Table 8.2

Value of a £ received in the future in terms of today's £ - 10% interest

Years delay	1	2	3	4	5	6	7	8	9	10
Present value	0.909	0.826	0.751	0.685	0.621	0.564	0.513	0.466	0.424	0.386

Discounted cash flow methods of project appraisal

Net present value

Here the net cash inflows are adjusted to today's values, so are directly comparable to the cash outflow, or the initial investment. An interest rate, known as the firm's action standard, is selected by the firm concerned that it considers as its minimum requirement. It will be based on the interest rate ruling at the time, an adjustment for its likely change over the life of the project, an adjustment for risk, and any other premium it decides to add. If the adjusted net cash flow is then still positive, the project will be worth more than the interest rate selected, it will have reached the firm's 'action standard'. The positive value means that the annual cash flows are being generated at a higher rate than would be needed at the specified rate of interest. In the situation where a firm is selecting between projects, the favoured one is the project with the greatest net present value. Another worked example to illustrate the procedure is given in Case Study 8.2.

Process. Multiply net cash flow by appropriate factor and add the results together.

Year	£ Factor
1	150,000 x 0.870 = 130,500
2	250,000 x 0.756 = 189,000
3	250,000 x 0.658 = 164,500
4	500,000 x 0.572 = 286,000
5	500,000 x 0.497 = 248,500
6	600,000 x 0.432 = 259,200
7	500,000 x 0.376 = 188,000
8	500,000 x 0.327 = 163,500
9	300,000 x 0.283 = 84,900
10	200,000 x 0.247 = 49,400
Total	3,750,000 1,763,500
Initial investment	1,200,000
Net present value	563,500

CASE STUDY 8.2

CD and its investment in CD manufacture (Project Alpha)

CD are proposing to build a new factory for the production of compact discs. It is estimated that the factory will cost £1,200,000 to build, but will produce the following cash inflows over the 10-year life of the project. The firm has an action standard of 15%.

Statement of net cash inflows	
Year	£
1	150,000
2	250,000
3	250,000
4	500,000
5	500,000
6	600,000
7	500,000
8	500,000
9	300,000
10	200,000
Total	3,750,000

Discount factors for 15%

Year	1	2	3	4	5	6	7	8	9	10
Factor	0.870	0.756	0.658	0.572	0.497	0.432	0.376	0.327	0.283	0.247

The project is said to have a net present value of £1,763,500 - £1,200,000, or £563,500 at a discount rate of 15%. In other words, the project exceeds the firm's action standard significantly, i.e. it would earn more than 15%.

Internal rate of return (IRR)

This method uses the same principles as the net present value method, but now the aim is to find which discount rate will produce a net present value of 0%. Thus it will express the value of the project in terms of a percentage.

It is a trial and error method, as rates have to be tried in turn until the zero result is straddled. The actual rate can then be found graphically.

The internal rate of return is between 20 and 25%. A more accurate estimate can be made if the above data is plotted as a graph. Examine Figure 8.1.

The internal rate of return seems to be about 24%. This is considerably better than the requirement of 15%. If two projects are being compared, then the one with the highest internal rate of return would be favoured.

It must be remembered that all these methods only evaluate the options in terms of their financial considerations. There are many more factors to take into account before a fully evaluated decision can be made.

Now it is your turn. Work carefully through the examples and questions that follow.

Discount rate	15%		25%		20%	
Year £	Factor		Factor		Factor	
1	150,000 x 0.870 = 130,500.	x 0.800 = 120,000.	x 0.833 = 124,950
2	250,000 x 0.756 = 189,000.	x 0.640 = 160,000.	x 0.694 = 173,500
3	250,000 x 0.658 = 164,500.	x 0.512 = 128,000.	x 0.579 = 144,750
4	500,000 x 0.572 = 286,000.	x 0.407 = 203,500.	x 0.482 = 241,000
5	500,000 x 0.497 = 248,500.	x 0.328 = 164,000.	x 0.402 = 201,000
6	600,000 x 0.432 = 259,200.	x 0.262 = 157,200.	x 0.335 = 201,000
7	500,000 x 0.376 = 188,000.	x 0.210 = 105,000.	x 0.279 = 139,500
8	500,000 x 0.327 = 163,500.	x 0.168 = 84,000.	x 0.233 = 69,900
9	300,000 x 0.283 = 84,900.	x 0.132 = 39,600.	x 0.194 = 58,200
10	200,000 x 0.247 = 49,400.	x 0.107 = 21,400.	x 0.162 = 32,400

TOTAL

| 3,750,000 | 1,763,500 | 1,182,700 | 1,386,200 |

Initial Investment

| | 1,200,000 | 1,200,000 | 1,200,000 |

Net present value

| | 563,500 | (17,300) | 186,200 |

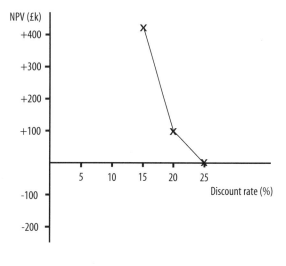

Figure 8.1 *Graphical method of calculating the internal rate of return*

SUMMARY

Having read this chapter, you will have a clear understanding of four investment appraisal tools, namely:

– *Payback period*
– *Average rate of return*
– *Net present value*
– *Internal rate of return*

and you will be capable of doing all the necessary calculations.

(continued)

▼ You will also be able to explain the time value of money.

▼ You will be fully aware, however, that financial methods give only part of the picture. They are an aid to decision making, but a full range of non-financial considerations have to be allowed for.

Questions and activities

Technical terms and glossary

In the section below you are given a series of technical terms and their meanings. They have been scrambled, though. You must match up the terms and the definitions. When you have them correctly paired, transfer them to your vocabulary or glossary book.

You are also advised to transfer any definitions obtained during the exercises in the case studies into this glossary book.

Technical terms

1. Opportunity cost
2. Investment appraisal
3. Payback period
4. Average rate of return
5. Time value of money
6. Discounted cash flow methods
7. Net Present Value
8. Internal rate of return
9. Action standard
10. Bank rate

Definitions

A. A discounted method of analysing a project. It is the difference between the costs of the project, and all its revenues, or earnings, after these have been adjusted for the various delays in receiving them.

B. The minimum discounted rate that a project or product must give before a firm will agree to its introduction.

C. The base rate for interest payments. All interest rates are set with reference to this rate, which is 'set' by the Bank of England.

D. The next best alternative. The next best project that the firm can not do as it has decided to do another.

E. A discounted cash flow method of investment appraisal. It is the value of the discount factor that will give the project a net present value of zero.

F. The principle that money decreases in value the longer you have to wait to get it. You lose the opportunity to gain interest, in other words.

G. Investment appraisal methods which recognise the time value of money.

H. The process by which an expenditure on a project or product is evaluated and compared with others and a base standard.

I. The average earnings of a project, in simple terms, expressed as a percentage of the initial investment.

J. The time a project will take to recover its initial investment, in simple terms, through increased revenues.

Essay questions

1. Describe the principle of opportunity cost to a business.
2. Why are the simple, undiscounted methods of investment appraisal considered as inaccurate?
3. How might a firm establish its action standard?
4. What is meant by 'the time value of money'?
5. Compare and contrast the net present value and internal rate of return methods of investment appraisal.
6. Do numerical appraisal methods give a management a complete picture against which to make decisions?

Case study

Read the information and answer the questions which follow.

White Hart Fabrication Ltd is faced with the problem of deciding between two investment projects. The first involves expansion of the plant by the purchase of premises which have become available next door. The other involves the automation of their present manufacturing system. Both projects have advantages, but since the market for their product is constantly expanding, they need to make a quick decision.

Some thought has been given to possible costs and returns over the next six years, the information being provided is as follows:

Expansion				Automation
£250,000	Cash Outflow	Yr 0		£200,000
–	Cash Inflow	Yr1		£ 60,000
–	Cash Inflow	Yr 2		£ 50,000
£150,000	Cash Inflow	Yr 3		£ 90,000
£100,000	Cash Inflow	Yr 4		£ 90,000
£160,000	Cash Inflow	Yr 5		£ 90,000
£116,000	Cash Inflow	Yr 6		£ 90,000

Present value of £1 receivable at the end of a number of years at 10%

After	1 yr	2 yrs	3 yrs	4 yrs	5 yrs	6 yrs
Present value of £1	£0.91	£0.83	£0.75	£0.68	£0.62	£0.56

Question and activities

(a) For each project, calculate:
   (i) the payback period (2 marks)
   (ii) the average rate of return and (6 marks)
   (iii) the net present value (use a discount factor of 10%, relevant data provided in the table). (10 marks)

(b) Taking into account only your calculations in (a), which project would you choose and why? (3 marks)

(c) Discuss *three* other factors that might have a bearing on this investment decision. (9 marks)

(Associated Examining Board, Business Studies (A) Paper 1, June 1991)

9
Costing and pricing methods

Preview

▼ This chapter introduces the concept of demand for a product, and examines how this is influenced by: *price, price of other goods, income, fashion, season* and *market size*.

▼ The concept of *elasticity*, or the sensitivity of demand to changes in these determinants, will be investigated. In particular, the sensitivity of demand to changes in price, income and the price of other goods will be studied.

▼ The chapter will then review the ways that the price of a product may be set, and the effect that this might have on sales, revenue and profit. The particular methods known as *cost plus, skimming, penetrating, competitive* and *value pricing* are introduced.

▼ It is vital that the costs and price of a product are compatible. The chapter ends, therefore, with a study of various costing methods commonly used, namely: *full costing, absorption costing* and *contribution costing* (sometimes known as *marginal costing*). This includes an assessment of their various advantages and disadvantages.

Most businesses have to make a profit to survive and for many firms profit making is their only objective. It is vital, therefore, that they set a price for their product that will exceed their costs of production. The price, however, has to be acceptable to the consumer – potential conflict, again.

As has been demonstrated earlier, the costs of a product are decided by the choice of manufacturing method used and the efficiency that is achieved by the manufacturer (see Chapter 4). The price may be set by the manufacturer, but the quantity actually bought, or the demand for the product, depends on the attitude of the buyer. It is important, therefore, to understand how demand works and what influences it. Only rarely can a firm sell the quantity it wants at the price it also wants, it will have to choose one or the other. There usually has to be a compromise somewhere.

First, an examination of demand and price, and their vital interrelationship.

Product demand

Demand has a precise meaning in business. Demand is the quantity of a good or service that would be bought at each and every price. It combines the desire for a good with the ability to pay for it. This is important to understand. An example to illustrate the definition: consider the Jaguar XJ 220 sports car that entered the market in 1992.

Jaguar Motors are making only a few of these sports cars which retail for nearly £400,000 each. Ask a group of young drivers the question 'Would you like a Jaguar XJ 220', and the answer is likely to be 'Yes'. The supply would soon be exhausted as this 'demand' would exceed the supply available. Rephrase the question to be 'Are you prepared, willing and able to pay £400,000 for the car?', and the majority answer will now be 'No'. Demand for the car has been determined. The desire to own has been linked with the ability to pay.

Units of demand should always be qualified with a price and a location. Considering the Jaguar example again, the manufacturer hopes that the demand for the XJ 220 will be about 300 cars throughout the world in the year of manufacture. The demand in the UK only will be a lot less. If it is greater than this then a shortage will develop, and probably a 'black market' for the car will form. If it is lower Jaguar will find that they cannot sell all the cars they have made and stocks will build up. Might Jaguar deliberately undersupply the market, create a deliberate shortage and so generate publicity for the car and the firm? This is a marketing question, and will be looked at in Part 3. It is another illustration of the integrated nature of business, and shows the link or dependency between finance and marketing.

The demand for a good depends on a number of factors, namely:

The price of the goods

The price of the goods is a very powerful determinant of demand. This should be clear, from experience. The price of strawberries fall, and more of them are bought and eaten. However, when their price rises at Christmas, as they have to be air-freighted from the Far East, sales fall. Thus there is almost universally an inverse relationship between price and demand. This leads to the normal downward sloping demand curve illustrated in Figure 9.1.

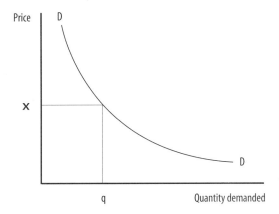

Figure 9.1 *The downward sloping demand curve*

Quantity q is sold at price X. Put the price up, and demand will fall (contract). Cut it, and it will increase (expand).

The price of other goods

Goods can be linked with others, and can be either substitutes or complements. Price changes of one product can affect demand for other products and services. As the price of beef rises the demand for it, and hence sales of it are likely to fall, as are the sales of mustard and horseradish sauce. However, lamb and pork sales are likely to rise, as also are sales of mint and apple sauce. Pork, beef and lamb are substitutes, but lamb and mint sauce, and beef and horseradish are complementary goods.

Another example: Ford put up the prices of all their cars and vans, but Rover keep their prices unchanged. Sales of Fords can be expected to fall, while the demand for Rovers should rise. A Ford and a Rover can be considered as substitute goods, but there is another explanation.

Consider the market for toilet soap in the UK. There are four major suppliers, Lever Brothers, Proctor and Gamble, Colgate Palmolive and Cussons, but many more actual brands, e.g. Lux, Lifebuoy, Imperial Leather, Dove, Pearl, Fairy, Palmolive, Rexona. Imagine that the price of Lux is increased by 5%, but at the same time all the other brands rise in price by 7%, demand for Lux will rise. This is not because its demand is 'odd' but because it has become *relatively* cheaper than the competition.

Some goods are in joint supply, or production. Think of the meat example again. If customers want steak the butcher has to get it from a full carcass. The butcher has to sell all the animal or there will be no profit. So the butcher has to adjust all prices for all the cuts so that the whole carcass is sold. This may well mean that the popular cuts have to be made very expensive to reduce the demand for them.

The income of the buyers

For most goods, the greater the income a potential customer has, the more goods likely to be bought. However, there will often be a movement towards higher quality products. Boutique sales may well rise, while the chain stores may not gain so much. Rover may sell more at the top end of their range. Overall, though, increasing income will normally increase sales.

Some goods, known as inferior goods, will lose sales. Less cheap quality products will be bought.

Fashion or taste of the buyers

Sales increase as goods become more popular or more fashionable. An excellent example is the rubic cube. Sales soared as they became a craze. Sales fell away as rapidly, as their popularity collapsed almost overnight.

Firms attempt to influence the popularity of their products through advertising. They aim to tell the consumer that the good or service on offer has no substitute, and that it is the 'in thing'.

Season

This is obvious for some goods, but firms aim to make their products as insensitive to season as possible. This is not always possible, and it is tried frequently. Look how ice cream manufacturers promote their products as a desert, and how hot cross buns now appear in the shops in January.

Population, or size of the market

Obviously the bigger the market the larger sales are likely to be. One would expect to sell more ice cream in USA than on the Isle of Wight!

Demand is summarised by the following equation:

$$Demand = \int \begin{array}{l} (Price, price\ of\ other\ goods, \\ income, fashion, season, \\ population) \end{array}$$

This cannot be drawn because there are too many variables, so it is normal to consider that demand is a function of price only, with all the other determinants being considered constant. This produces a single downward sloping demand curve. Change one of the 'other things' and a new quantity/price relationship, or demand curve, is produced. The demand curve is shifted as a whole. This is illustrated as Figure 9.2.

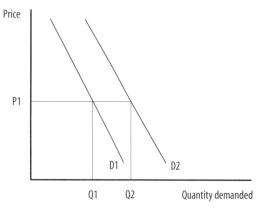

Figure 9.2 *Illustration of how advertising may shift a demand curve*

The firm was initially operating with demand curve D1. At its price P1 it sold Q1 units of its product. It then mounted a successful advertising campaign, increased demand to D2, and sold quantity Q2 at the same price P1.

Firms usually face one simple fact with pricing. If they set a high price they will sell less than if they set

a low price but how much less? Firms need to know the shape of their product's demand curve, or at least its pattern of demand, how sensitive their sales are to price, and the other main determinants of demand. This 'sensitivity' is measured through determination of the product's elasticity. Note that a firm has absolute control over the price at which the good or service is offered, some control through advertising and other marketing activities on consumer taste, but no influence at all on any of the other determinants of demand. It just has to predict what might happen, predict how the economy might develop, watch what the competition is doing, and act accordingly.

Now, look at a means of quantifying the effect of changes in the determinants on demand. It will give an indication how sensitive demand will be to changes.

Price elasticity of demand

Price elasticity of demand is the sensitivity of the quantity demanded of a product to changes in its price. In other words, it tells you how much demand for something will be changed by alterations in its price.

It is calculated as follows:

% Change in quantity demanded ÷ % Change in price.

or

%Δ Q ÷ % Δ P in the conventional shorthand.

This produces numbers from 0 to infinity, or rather 0 to minus infinity. The normal downward sloping demand curve, where demand is inversely proportional to price, results in the price elasticity being negative. It is conventional, though, to quote price elasticities as positive numbers and remember that they are actually negative. Remember that, normally, a rise in price will result in a fall in demand.

Price elasticity can be determined by observation of sales at different prices. An example is given in Case Study 9.1.

Work out the two percentage changes. This calculation is made easy if a grid is set up showing the two prices and the two corresponding demands.

	Before	After
Quantity demanded	Q1	Q2
Price	P1	P2

Price elasticity of demand can then be worked out by inserting the relevant numbers into the following equation:

$$\frac{Q1 - Q2}{Q1} \times \frac{P1}{P1 - P2}$$

CASE STUDY 9.1

CD plc and the market for video tapes

CD plc sold video tapes for £8 per pack of three. At this price they sold 75,000 units per month. They raised their price to £9 and sales fell to 70,000 units per month. What is the price elasticity of demand?

Add the relevant quantities from the above case material.

	Before	After
Quantity	75,000	70,000
Price	£8	£9

Change in price: P1 - P2/ P1 = £8 - £9 ÷ £8 = − 1/8 = - 12.5%

Change in demand:Q1 − Q2 / Q1 = 75,000 − 70,000 ÷ 75,000 = 5,000/75,000 = 6.66%

Price elasticity of demand = %Δ Demand ÷ %Δ P
= 6.66/ − 12.5
= − 0.53.

Demand for CD's tapes is *inelastic*. It would be quoted as 0.53, the negative sign being ignored usually. If it had worked out to be a number over 1, then it would have been named as *elastic*.

Elastic demand: A product with a price elasticity of demand greater than 1.

Inelastic demand: A product with a price elasticity of demand less than 1.

Necessities, and goods which have no real alternatives, tend to be inelastic in terms of demand. Because they are needed they tend to be insensitive to price. The consumer will try to buy cheaper products, but overall demand will be relatively insensitive to price. Basic food is an obvious example of such a product group, and a modern example is petrol, as the consumer becomes dependent on the car. Note, however, that the demand for petrol as a whole will be inelastic, but that for any specific brand will be less inelastic. Consumers will switch between Shell and BP, for example, if one is cheaper than the other, but they still need petrol.

Habit-forming products also fall into this group, where examples are cigarettes and other tobacco products, and alcoholic drinks.

As price changes, demand for a good or service will change. A firm sells products to get a revenue and to make a profit. What is the link between elasticity and sales revenue? Examine an example set within CD plc (Case Study 9.2). The increase in price will depress demand, and the elasticity is negative.

CASE STUDY 9.2

CD plc and the revenue from tapes

CD plc knows that the price elasticity of demand for its tapes is 0.5. It sells 100,000 tapes per week at present at a price of £2.50 each. It plans to increase its price to £3.00. What effect will this have on sales and revenue?

Price change proposed = increase of £0.5 on a base price of £2.50, or 20%.
Price elasticity of demand is given by the equation:

$$\frac{\% \text{ Change in demand}}{\% \text{ Change in price}}$$

It is known that this is equal to −0.5 for this product, so:

$$\frac{\% \text{ Change in demand}}{\% \text{ Change in price}} = -0.5$$

But the change in price proposed is +20%, so:

$$\frac{\%\Delta \text{ Demand}}{20\%} = -0.5$$

Cross-multiply, and it will be deduced that demand will fall by 10%.

Revenue, which is the product of price and quantity demanded, will change. It was £250,000 but will change to 90,000 x £3, or £270,000. Note that it has increased.

Demand will go down, as will the level of sales. The revenue from these decreased sales will be greater than the original. So, for products where the demand is inelastic, increases in price will result in increases in sales revenue. Conversely, a price reduction will produce a greater sales volume but a lower revenue.

A firm facing an elastic demand for its product will see the total reverse of this. If it raises its price it will both sell less and receive less revenue. However, if it lowers its price it will not only get a greater volume of sales but also an increased revenue. Elastic demand is associated with luxury goods and ones where there are many alternatives, or much competition. A worked example will help to further illustrate the use of elasticity information to a business (see Case Study 9.3).

CASE STUDY 9.3

CD plc and the market for portable CD players

CD plc has been in the market for consumer entertainment equipment and software for some 10 years. Their research and development department has developed and tested a new portable CD player, and it is expected that this will be particularly popular with the youth market. The marketing department of the company has carried out detailed market research and has published the following predicted demand information. The marketing director considers that the product should be put on the market at a price of £70 per unit.

Price (£ per unit)	80	50	10
Demand (units per week)	1,000	5,000	10,000

They also attempted to study the effect of price on demand, and found that if the price of a player was decreased from £70 to £60, demand would increase by 50%.

Questions and activities
1. Draw the demand curve for portable CD players.
2. Assess how price elasticity changes as the potential price for portable CD players is reduced. (*Hint:* Pick a price, say £10, then read off the demand conditions at prices £9 and £11. Work out an estimate of price elasticity. Repeat the calculations for different prices, say separated by £10.)
3. If CD plc were to sell its portable players at £60 instead of £70 what would be the effect on their sales revenue?
4. What other factors, other than elasticity, might CD plc take into account before deciding the price for its new product?

The answers, and the necessary calculations:

1. The demand curve. Examine Figure 9.3.
2. Select £75, £45 and £15 as the prices to be investigated. Set up the calculation grid.

	Before	After	Before	After	Before	After
Price	80	70	50	40	20	10
Quantity	1,000	2,300	5,000	6,300	8,700	10,000

Work through, using the Q1 – Q2/Q1 ÷ P1 – P2/P1 formula, and the following elasticities should result.

Price	£75	£45	£15
Elasticity	– 10.4	–1.3	– 0.3

The elasticity varies along the demand curve. Sales become less sensitive to price as the demand increases and the price falls. Try plotting this data yourself.

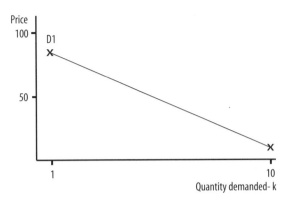

Figure 9.3 *Demand curve for CD plc and its tape sales*

Observe what this means. The elasticity of demand varies along the demand curve, the higher the demand the lower the elasticity. This generally means that the lower the price the lower the elasticity of demand. This can have important implications for a government. Consider the taxation of cigarettes. If they are taxed to raise revenue, then as price rises, demand falls, and elasticity rises. Tax revenue is not as high as expected. However, if the objective is to reduce the consumption of cigarettes, it will be very effective. The truth is probably that the government aims to do both, so has to compromise. Another example of conflict.

3. A table will help the calculation, and the important presentation aspect of business calculations.

Price	£60	£70
Demand (units per week)	3,600	2,300
Revenue (Sales x price)	£216,000	£161,000

The price could be lowered to get more revenue, but this will only be possible for CD if the costs are right.

With a relationship such as this the ability to produce cheaply and efficiently is critical.

4. Consider such things as the price of other portable CD players on the market.

Firms prefer to trade in goods or services where their demand is inelastic. Marketing in general, and advertising in particular aim to make their products seem to be necessities, to seem to have no ready substitutes or alternatives and, in the process, make the demand inelastic.

It can also be useful to know two other elasticities, to know how demand changes with changes in consumers incomes and the prices of other relevant goods.

Income elasticity of demand

The income elasticity of demand is the sensitivity of the quantity demanded of a good or service to the level of real income of its consumers.

This relates changes in the incomes of the buyers to subsequent changes in demand. If the result is positive, i.e. demand increases with income, the good or service is said to be normal. If the result is negative the good or service is said to be inferior.

$$\text{Income elasticity of demand} = \frac{\%\Delta \text{ Demand}}{\%\Delta \text{ Real income}}$$

Real income is the income of a consumer, adjusted for inflation, or the effect of rising prices. If money income, or the salary or wage actually received, and prices rise by 5% there is no change in real income. If income rises by 5% but prices by only 2% then the change in real income is about 3%. An example is given in Case Study 9.4.

The effect of income changes on demand for CD's equipment

The demand for CD players is 20,000 per month at a price of £130. It is known that the demand is income elastic, and has a value of + 2.5. It is expected, due to the continued expansion of the economy, that real incomes will rise by 4% during the next year. How will demand for CD players change?

1. The formula: %Δ Demand ÷ %Δ Real income = + 2.5
2. Insert the known income increase:

   %Δ Demand = 4% x 2.5 = +10%

Sales of CD players should increase by 10%, to a total of 22,000 units per month.

Any goods, when compared with each other, may be normal, or one normal and the other inferior.

The one considered the best will be the normal one. Two goods cannot both be inferior, one must be less inferior, or less unpopular than the other.

This factor is unimportant in times where salaries and wages change little. This is not the case nowadays. When it is considered that the standard of living of an economy is rising in real terms it may be an important factor to a business, depending on what is being sold.

Changes in incomes have another peculiar effect in the UK. The UK consumer has a strong tendency to buy imported goods, or has a 'high propensity to buy imported goods' as it is called technically. This tendency, or propensity is also sensitive to income. In times of prosperity, when real incomes rise, the UK consumer tends to purchase even more imported goods. Good for an importer and seller of imported goods, but not so healthy for an all-UK firm.

Cross-price elasticity of demand

Cross-price elasticity of demand is the sensitivity of the quantity demanded of a product to changes in prices of other related goods or services.

Firms rarely sell in a market with no competition, alternative or choice for the consumer. It is important, therefore, to know how the demand for a product is influenced by the price for others. Thus, the cross-price elasticity is studied.

Cross-price elasticity relates the price of one good with the demand for another. Some goods compete for purchasers, like beef and lamb, apples and pears, records and CDs, pens or biros. These are substitute goods, or substitutes. Others, like lamb and mint sauce, cars and petrol, tape decks and tapes, tend to be bought together. These are complements, or complementary goods.

$$\text{Cross-price elasticity} = \frac{\%\Delta \text{ Demand for X}}{\%\Delta \text{ Price for Y}}$$

If the result is negative then the two goods are complements, if positive they are substitutes. The higher the value of this elasticity measure the stronger the relationship. An example is given in Case Study 9.5.

CASE STUDY 9.5

CD plc and the sale of discs and audio tapes

CD plc sells both CD discs and pre-recorded audio tapes. The present situation is as follows:

Product	CD discs	Audio tapes
Sales (units/month)	10,000	30,000
Price (£)	12	7.50

The cross-price elasticity of the demand for discs against the price of audio tapes is known to be +1.5. The competition is known to be planning a price reduction for audio tapes, which CD will have to follow, of 10%. What will happen to the sales of CD discs?

1. Formula: %Δ Demand for CDs ÷ %Δ Price of tapes = X Price elasticity.
2. Insert the known data.

    %Δ Demand for CDs / − 10% = + 1.5

    %Δ Demand for CDs = − 15%

    i.e. CD will loose 15% of their sales of CDs.

Demand for CDs can be expected to fall to 8,500. CD can drop the price of CDs if they wish to keep the level of sales the same.

The value of the cross-price elasticity for a pair of goods will not be the same for both 'directions' of the relationship. Consider cameras and film. These are clearly complementary goods, but the change in price of cameras will have a greater effect on film sales than the other way round. Equally, the demand for cars will not increase significantly when the price of petrol falls by 5 pence per litre.

Some complex situations can be modelled if all three elasticities are known, but this is beyond A Levels.

Elasticity tends to be a theoretical concept within business. The exact numerical data may not be measured, and it is not easy to do so in a real business environment, but the concepts are clearly understood and applied.

Through an analysis of demand and elasticity a firm has an understanding of how the demand for its product, or range of products and services, behaves, particularly in relation to its price. The importance of price to a firm should now be obvious. How can a firm now decide the best price to charge for its products or services? What is the 'best' price, anyway? A definition might be:

The 'best' price is that price which enables a firm to sell the quantity it wants, so that it then meets its objectives.

Remember, firms have many different objectives. Consider the problem of pricing against that background.

Demand, elasticity and business

The concept of the demand curve for a product, and all its associated elasticities, is clearly understood. However, it is a very theoretical concept. Consider the following:

Demand is a function of price, *all other things being held equal.*

This last statement is rarely true in the real world. Firms are competing against each other, so determinants are rarely constant for any significant period of time. The determination of a demand curve for a product is a difficult task, and rarely attempted in practice. It was done by Kelloggs for Rice Krispies, but then only as part of a marketing competition.

Elasticity is even more rarely considered. Firms are aware of price elasticity, etc., but will not specifically use elasticity calculations to plan any marketing action.

In summary – elasticity is an important concept but of limited practical use.

Product pricing

A firm appears to have total freedom to set whatever price it wishes for its product. It must consider a number of factors first, though, and remember the objective of the firm at the time (see Chapter 17).

An important factor to consider is whether there is any serious competition for the product. If it is a new product on the market then no price image has been established. The firm then has a great degree of choice. If it will be facing established competition, then a price pattern will already have been established. Diverting from this price can be difficult.

The basic pricing methods, or policies are as follows:

Cost plus

Cost plus is a method widely used in business, particularly by retailers. Retailers buy in the goods from manufacturers or wholesalers, add on a fixed percentage to cover their costs and a profit, and sell at that price. Firms can compete by varying the percentage added, or all follow an industry 'norm'. The danger of this method is that the seller tends to forget that the price/volume relationship is determined by the consumer, not the seller.

Until a few years ago all retailers were compelled to charge a price set by the manufacturer of the good. This was enforced through *retail price maintenance* which is now largely illegal. It is still in force in the area of newspapers, and in book selling, though it is beginning to crumble here.

It is also a popular method for pricing industrial goods, particularly specialised process plant and 'one offs'. These are orders for a single, usually unique product. The supplier costs it, adds a percentage and sets that as the price. There are no '*price points*' so the buyer has nothing to judge it against.

It has also been a common and popular method for government contracts, especially in the defence area. There was often only one supplier to place the order with. These orders often include a large research and development element and the product is not really known, other than as a performance specification, until this work has been done. Consider, as examples, the orders for Trident submarines, new advanced fighter aircraft, weapons systems and vehicles. Costing will obviously be difficult at best. Cost plus meant that work was paid for as it was done, including a profit element. The danger was that there was no motivation for a firm to be quick or efficient; in fact it works in exactly the opposite way. In the very cost conscious world of today this type of contract is rare.

Skimming

This is one of the pricing policies often adopted when a firm is faced with the opportunity of launching a new product, especially one where it is expected that the consumer will assume 'status', from owning it. The producer deliberately sets a high price initially and 'skims the profit' from the market. Consumers who 'must have it' will buy at this high price. When this market is exhausted the price is reduced, and the level of sales allowed to grow. Consider the launch of CD players, video cameras and even portable tape players. They have become much cheaper with time, sometimes even under the same brand name. The price fall cannot all be explained by the workings of economies of scale.

This method is aimed at maximising profit for the firm, at the expense of the level of sales and total revenue. It is a method much used in the area of consumer durables, especially domestic electronic goods.

Penetrative pricing

Penetrative pricing is another of the new product pricing policies. Price is now set low so as to get the market initially. Profit is sacrificed in an attempt to secure customers. Once they are secure then price can be eased upwards. This makes it hard for competition to come into the market initially, so gives advantages to large well-financed businesses. It is a method much used with FMCGs.

Competitive pricing

This method is used when a firm is entering a market that is already established. The existing products have established a price level, so any new product has to conform to this pattern. Any higher price than the norm has to be supported by some product advantage. Equally, a lower priced variant will have to fight the assumption that 'cheap' means 'inferior'.

This method is used in all sectors of the economy and for all types of goods.

Value pricing

This is a method used by the developers and suppliers of special or potentially 'one off' items. The supplier bases the price on the estimated value, or the savings potential of the item or service to the purchasers, e.g. a computer software supplier will estimate the value of a programme to the user, and base the price on that. It will be based on project appraisal methods, now used to set prices. It will be used to answer questions like 'Will the firm be likely to pay that for this solution to its problem?' (See Case Study 9.6.)

CD plc would set a price for the tester at about £66,000. This may be considerably more than a price set by the cost plus method used by many businesses in this situation. How is this price arrived at?

£10,000 is 15% of what capital sum? Work it out – £66,666. Any price less than this will mean that the savings to the buyer is worth more than its action standard of 15%.

This method maximises prices to the supplier, but also prevents them presenting unreasonably high prices. This is very much an industrial goods pricing method. The key to it is knowing what firm's action standards are. (If all else fails they can be based on the rates of interest charged by banks.)

Thus there are many ways of setting a price for a firms product. Price can only be set properly if the firm has full knowledge of both the market for its product, and the costs it will incur in its production and sale. The cost side of the equation will now be examined very carefully.

Costing problems and methods

It is relatively easy to work out what a product has cost after it as been made, but this information is of little value to a firm. It has spent or committed the money, so it is too late to do anything about it if the costs are too much, and even exceed the agreed or proposed selling price. A firm has to devise methods for working out, or estimating costs in advance, and then to check that these forecasts are met. Thus:

CASE STUDY 9.6

CD plc and a special order for an electronic tester

A firm orders a special testing device from CD plc. It is expected that use of this device will save the buyer £10,000 per year. Market rates for money are running at about 10%, and the customer seems to expect about 15% from its investments. There is no alternative supplier as the unit is to be specially made by CD. What price should CD set if it was to follow value pricing? (CD will make the unit at a direct cost of £14,500.)

The cost of distributing a firm's products must be costed into the overhead.

Product costing is first a forecasting exercise, then a checking procedure. It is designed in an attempt to ensure that the business makes a profit, and helps with its control of cash.

This is the way that the firm, or rather a group consisting of production, marketing and accounts staff, can be sure that its costs and prices are compatible, and that it will trade profitably. This is a much harder task than it may seem.

Costing demands that a product or service has to be designed and specified fully, and all the items and components needed to produce it have to be quantified in advance. This should include not only the obvious materials items, but also requirements for labour, services, space, etc.

The cost structure of a product follows, and then a more detailed look at the cost elements included. Each element will then be examined in turn, first in the context of a single product firm, then the more likely multi-product situation.

Costs can be variable, semi-variable or fixed, i.e. they may vary directly and proportionally with production or sales, they may vary with output but not in a proportional manner, or they are unrelated to production.

The single product firm

A single product is quite rare for the developed, large business, but is very common for the small, new firm. They are vulnerable, until they get established – another example of the effect of size.

Direct materials

These may seem the easiest, and in some ways they are, but there may be many snags and pitfalls in the way. Consider as an example a video tape made by CD plc. It needs the following materials:

- plastic A for the outer case
- paper label for case
- plastic B for the inner case, the video itself
- plastic C for the tape wheels
- length of video tape
- paper labels for the video

The prices of these? Consult a trade catalogue, or telephone a supplier, and read it off. Three problems are immediately apparent:

1. *How much is to be bought?* There will be buying economies of scale to take advantage of, so which price will be used?
2. *Should the full advantages of economies of scale be taken?* Should a firm have a single supplier at a low price, or the safer situation of multiple suppliers but at a higher price? This is a policy decision made by the directors of a firm.
3. *When is the purchase to be made?* Prices change with time, usually upwards nowadays. This process, known as inflation, means that costs will be changing all the time. At this stage a 'best estimate' has to be made, based on timings, quantities and prices obtained from marketing for the product and suppliers for the materials. There is clearly a potential, or margin for error here but this is minimised by the employment of specialist purchasing staff. Large firms will have an advantage here.

They are direct or variable costs, clearly, but the actual unit price is also variable.

Direct labour

Is there such a thing? Most labour today is a semi-variable cost at best, if not fixed for at least a week. The rate of pay is also liable to fluctuate. In general, though, if actual production exceeds the forecast, then labour costs per unit will fall, but if production falls short of the plan then the unit cost will rise. In both cases, over a reasonable range of outputs, the actual labour bill will be the same. It behaves as a fixed cost, but is generally considered as a variable, or direct one. This can lead to many cost mistakes.

Direct expenses

There may not be any of these, but they include items such as special testing materials or tools purchased for a special, specific product. This is a danger area, though. Small tools and low cost items are no problem. They are assumed to be 'used' when they are issued to production, and included immediately into costs. Examples would be saw blades, drill bits, special spanners or sockets and cleaning materials. Consider, though, the case of CD and its video production line. They need injection moulding 'tools' which are very expensive, but last a long time if looked after. They cannot be costed directly to production, but have to be treated as capital expenditure and spread over many years' production through the operation of depreciation.

A picture of cost is developing, but remember that it is an estimate, and therefore likely to be wrong. At this point the firm has an estimate of its likely prime cost of production.

Production overheads

Production overheads are costs arising from the provision of the factory and the like. They are associated with the factory space, and include such items as rent, business rates and insurance. They also include the plant and equipment itself. If the plant is owned it will include the capital cost of this also. This raises the question of how to include capital cost in this product cost. The items purchased have a life, and this must be allowed for.

Capital costs are included through the operation of depreciation. This is a notional or artificial cost that is included which allows the capital costs to be recovered over their lifetime. A simple example is illustrated by Case Study 9.7. (More of this in Chapter 11 on Accounts.)

Any monies spent on repairs and maintenance of buildings and plant and equipment will be treated as semi-variables, and will be included in costs as they occur.

CASE STUDY 9.7

CD plc and a building project

CD plc erects a building for the production of video tapes at a cost of £100,000. It has a life expectancy of 20 years. A depreciation allowance of £5,000 will be made and added to the cost. Note, however, the following points carefully:

- CD has paid out £100,000 for the building before it makes any tapes.
- CD does not actually pay £5,000 per year towards the building or product, but simply adds a nominal sum to the costs of the product. This will reduce the profit apparently made when the product is sold.

- CD's liability for tax on its profits will be reduced.
- CD's cash flow is not affected by the notional charge of depreciation to costs.

Sales and distribution overheads

These are the costs arising from selling the goods and services, and include all marketing and selling costs, including advertising. They also cover the costs of distribution, or getting the goods from the factory to the customer, and will include transport costs. They are usually subject to the advantages of economies of scale.

The costs in this group will include both direct and indirect elements; they are one of the classic semi-variable costs. As will be seen they are one of the major problem areas when it comes to multi-product costing.

Administration overheads

These are the costs incurred in the basic provision and existence of the business. They will include the costs of the Board and all the administrative support functions, such as security, finance, gardeners and corporate planning. This area of cost has a habit of growing as the size of the firm and the number of its products and operating units grows. The magnitude of this growth will depend on the structure and management style of the company – another example of a money/people interaction.

For a new business starting out with a single product all these costs can be estimated, and a cost profile built up. It matters little if any of the distinctions between overheads is wrong as there is only one product, one revenue earner, to support and pay for them. It may 'hide' excessive overheads costs, though, and give a warped picture of the efficiency of a business.

Now the different situation for a multi-product business.

Multi-product businesses

Multi-product businesses are very common, and also give rise to the maximum number of costing problems. The major difficulty, though, is the handling of overheads and other indirect costs. First, an overview.

Overheads, which are costs not related to products but to the business itself, cannot be attributed to individual products. (If they could they would be direct costs anyway!) Overheads can only be allocated, and then rather arbitrarily, to products. This will inevitably produce a set of arbitrary and potentially inaccurate, misleading costs. An example is illustrated by Case Study 9.8.

CASE STUDY 9.8

CD plc and the effect of its expansion on its costs

CD plc was successfully selling video tapes as its sole product. After some very successful years it expanded into the audio tape market. This was achieved without any increase in administration overheads. The cost and revenue position of the firm before and after audio tapes were introduced is reproduced below.

Before video tapes	Sales revenue	£1,000,000
	Direct costs	£300,000
	Indirect costs	£200,000
After audio tapes	Sales revenue	£1,500,000
	Direct costs	£600,000
	Indirect costs	£200,000

With video tapes only, the product clearly cost £500,000. But what is their costs after the introduction of audio tapes? The following cost position is known: (Units £s)

	Video	Audio	Total
Revenue	1,000,000	500,000	1,500,000
DCs	300,000	300,000	600,000
Overheads	?	?	200,000
		Profit	700,000

The overheads due to the video or audio tapes cannot be known, and cannot be allocated in any accurate or logical way. If an attempt is made, and an arbitrary allocation made, then a picture can be produced. Depending on this allocation a range of supposed costs are possible. Examine the figures below.

		Video	Audio
All to the video	Costs	500,000	300,000
	Profit	500,000	200,000
All to the audio	Costs	300,000	500,000
	Profit	700,000	zero

They cannot both be correct. The confusion comes because a cost which has no relevance to the products has been forced upon the products. A dangerous practice.

CD plc and the effect of bulk buying on unit costs

CD plc were buying 10 tonnes per year of a material it needed in the production of video tapes at a price of £200 per tonne. As a result of the introduction of records its consumption rose to 14 tonnes per year, but the price fell to £180 per tonne.

Buying costs before records were made – 10 x £200 = £2,000 per year.
Buying costs with records being made – 14 x £180 = £2,520 per year.

By introducing the records the unit cost of the compound for videos has fallen, but how is the change incorporated into the costs? Another 'it all depends' answer.

Either Videos £2,000 (as it was without records)

Records £520 (the extra cost of the compound as a result of the records)

or Videos 10 x £180 – £1,800
Records 4 x £180 – £720

Now some of the problems in detail before some of the solutions are examined.

Direct materials

Often the same material is used for more than one product. This causes the unit price for the materials to drop due to even larger bulk orders and contracts forcing down the price. Do all the products gain from this price reduction? The firm clearly does benefit, but what about the individual products? As seen already, there are a number of ways of handling the situation. Examine the example of Case Study 9.9.

Both seem to be valid and accurate ways of costing the materials. Depending on the choice made the firm will calculate different rates of profit for the products. No extra profit will be made whichever method is used, but some wrong and bad decisions may be taken as a result of the distorted picture that may be produced.

An acceptance that a firm does not know what its products cost to make must be beginning to form now.

Direct labour

Direct labour is a problem for a single product firm, and the same problem is carried forward. There are new ones, though. A problem can arise with two or more products made on a single plant. Utilisation will rise, and unit costs will fall, in the same way as was seen for shared materials costs.

Production and other overheads

If production overheads are really overheads and not semi-variable costs, then they cannot be allocated in any reasonable way to a product. This is the nub of the problem of over-pricing, and cannot be avoided. The important thing is to examine all costs carefully to see if they are variable, semi-variable or fixed, then distribute them to products or company overheads as appropriate. All costs then have to be controlled and kept to a minimum.

The various costing methods will now be described.

Costing methods

There are three costing methods that will be examined. Which one is used depends on a number of factors, and include the wishes and policy of the owners or directors, the nature of the products and production and the management style. A firm attempts to cost its operations for two reasons, to be able to check the suitability of its proposed prices and also so as to be able to control its actions thereafter.

Marginal costing

Marginal costing (also known as contribution costing) is a method that makes no attempt to allocate overheads to products. It examines costs carefully and divides them into those which are product related and those which are not. It applies the 'test question', and groups the unallocated costs into indirect or overhead costs. It then subtracts the direct costs identified from the revenue the product brings in, and calls this difference the contribution made by the product. It is the contribution to overheads and profit. This is what was done, virtually, in the example that introduced the problems of the multi-product costing. Examine it again, with its new headings in Case Study 9.10.

The business is making a profit, and its two products are both making a contribution towards overheads and profit. The position is healthy. The firm does not know exactly how much profit each product has contributed, but it is not important. The level of contribution is the key 'profitability' indicator for a business working on this method of costings. If a product is making a contribution it is of value to the business. It is better off with it than without it, provided all other factors stay the same.

CASE STUDY 9.10

CD plc and its multi-product expansion (contribution costing basis)

Contribution costing statement for CD plc's production of tapes

	Video	Audio	Total
Total			
Revenue	1,000,000	500,000	1,500,000
Direct costs	300,000	300,000	600,000
Contribution	700,000	200,000	900,000
Overheads			200,000
Profit			700,000

This is a very simple and logical method of costing. It is particularly useful in a number of situations usually involving decision making. These are:

- The setting of selling price, especially when introducing a new product, or when competition or an economic depression force a company to reduce prices.
- Deciding if something should be made by a firm or whether it should be bought in. (Break-even analysis can also be used here.)
- Deciding whether to close a plant or not.
- Deciding if special orders should be accepted or not.
- Comparison of different methods of production, or the revision of the firms product range.

Ranking of products

Businesses operate in an organic, dynamic environment. New products are developed, consumer tastes decline and develop. It means that the product range of a company has to be reviewed periodically. Some products become out of date, others become part of a highly competitive market. Firms will only be successful over time if they produce and sell what the market requires. New products have to be developed, tested, then considered for inclusion into the product range. One way of doing this is by producing a full contribution statement, placing the products in rank order, and then inserting the new products' contribution estimate. Then the firm can identify its large contribution earners and also highlight its poor products. It can then plan its product portfolio. Work through Case Study 9.11, which gives an opportunity to test this procedure.

A refinement of this method enables the priority use of a scarce material to be decided, at least on a contribution maximising basis. Imagine that a firm uses a particular chemical in all its products, but that the supply of this material is limited. The firm should use this in the most economical way, and get the maximum profit from it for the quantity available. It has to ensure that it gets the maximum contribution per unit used from it, i.e. if it is a chemical, and it has only 5 tonnes for a year, it has to maximise the contribution per tonne it obtains from this supply.

CASE STUDY 9.11

CD plc and its annual product performance review

CD plc has been operating and trading for some five years now. It has developed and launched a range of six products, and its research and development team has produced a range of four more for consideration at the annual Product Performance Review.

The company aims to maximise contribution, and hence profit. It is a company policy to have no more than eight products in the range at any one time.

You are the marketing manager for CD plc. Prepare a report for the meeting making your recommendations for the product range. You have the following data to help you in your preparation.

1. Present products

Name	Sales	Direct costs
	£m per year	£m per year
Audio tapes	1,000,000	600,000
CD players	1,500,000	500,000
CDs	6,000,000	1,000,000
Head cleaners	500,000	400,000
Portable CD players	3,000,000	2,000,000
Speakers (pairs)	600,000	500,000

2. New Products

Name	Forecast Sales	Direct Costs
	£m per year	£m per year
Radio alarms	1,000,000	800,000
Car CD players	2,000,000	1,600,000
Language CDs	500,000	100,000
Computer games	600,000	450,000

This can be done using contribution statements. The firm has to get its accountants to produce contribution details for its products, but to also identify the quantity of the scare chemical used in each product. The product range can then be ranked in terms of contribution/unit used, and its use optimised. A worked example to illustrate the procedure is given in Case Study 9.12.

CASE STUDY 9.12

CD plc and its shortage of a special polymer

CD plc use a special polymer in its range of products. As a result of an accident at the factory where it is made, this polymer is in very short supply and will remain so for two years. Supply is strictly rationed and CD plc can obtain no more than 35 tonnes each year. As a result of an instruction given by the Board, the accounts department have produced the following information, which is on an annual basis.

Product	Video tapes	Audio tapes	Records	Computer floppy discs
Sales (units)	10,000	50,000	50,000	100,000
Price (£)	8	3	3	1
Direct cost (£/unit)	5	1	1	0.5
Polymer content (kg/1,000 units)	100	200	50	400

STEP 1. Calculate the Sales Value (Sales x price)

Revenue (£)

80,000	150,000	150,000	100,000

STEP 2. Calculate the Total Direct Costs of the Sales (Sales Volume x Direct Cost), then determine the Contribution (Revenue - Total Direct Cost).

Direct Costs (£)

50,000	50,000	50,000	50,000

Contribution. (£)

30,000	100,000	100,000	50,000

STEP 3. Calculate the quantity of the polymer used per line (kg/1000 x Sales Volume in thousands. Remember that 1000 kg is 1 tonne), then the Contribution per tonne of polymer for each product (Contribution / Usage)

Polymer use (tonnes)

1	10	2.5	40

Contribution / tonne (£)

30,000	10,000	40,000	1,250

STEP 4. Allocate the material so that the high Contribution per tonne products get priority use of the valuable chemical

Priority order

2	3	1	4

Production (%)

100	100	100	54

Cumulative Use (t)

3.5	13.5	2.5	35

Students may check that this will give the maximum contribution and hence profit for the firm. Try calculating contribution for a range of possible production schedules.

Shutting down an activity

To shut down an activity is never an easy or popular decision to take within a firm. Tradition and sentiment are strong forces, and many business people are born optimists. Probably more firms have gone bankrupt as a result of holding on too long to loss-making products than dropping one too soon.

This is really a modification of the methods shown above. The decision to shut would be taken if it is found that a product or production unit is producing a negative contribution, i.e. its sales revenue does not cover its direct costs of production. An example to illustrate the point is found in Case Study 9.13.

Now go ahead and write the report! What other non-financial considerations will have to be considered before making a final decision?

This last point must be stressed. This chapter is about financial analysis as an *aid* to decision making. This is particularly true for operate or close decisions. It must be remembered that there are clear and equally important social and economic implications of all such decisions. To close a factory in an area of high unemployment generates a great deal of bad publicity and may create a national alienation of the product. Is Timex watches an example of this?

CASE STUDY 9.13

CD plc and the possible sale of a factory

CD plc has developed its product base over the years, and has also acquired others as a result of takeovers and mergers. It has now been decided that it must rationalise its production, and concentrate its activities on no more than three sites.

You are the production director, and have to prepare a report for the next Board meeting. It is the policy of CD plc to base all appropriate evaluations on contribution methods. You have the following data to help you in the preparation of the report (units: £000s)

Site	Sales value	Direct costs	Site overheads
1 Dover	5,000	3,000	1,000
2 Portsmouth	4,000	2,000	1,000
3 West Ham	7,000	3,000	2,000
4 Cardiff	2,000	500	500
5 Warrington	9,000	6,000	4,000
6 Leeds	6,000	4,000	1,000
7 Glasgow	2,000	1,000	1,000

Site overheads are eliminated if the site is closed. Sales values and direct costs are transferable.

All sites are large enough to accommodate the work of the smaller sites themselves.

Acceptance of a special order

This is a common decision for a firm to have to make, especially an established one. It is made harder if the decision makers do not have a full understanding of the costing process, and especially if they have come to think of total costs which include a notional allowance for company overheads.

Consider the situation where a firm is in business making, say, televisions for the UK market. It has its price, and also its costs and its overheads. A customer comes along and offers to buy sets for overseas, say, but at a reduced price. These sales will be in addition to the firm's plan, and will increase the number of sets made and sold. Such an order is worth taking, on a financial basis, provided the actual price exceeds the direct costs, i.e. provided the special order brings in a positive contribution to the seller.

This is financially sound, but there are major implications for the business. How will the existing customers view such 'special terms'? Might they be lost in the long run? Will the firm establish a price precedent for future sales? It is a complex decision, but an easy one to assess on a financial basis. This is often the case, and there is more behind most decisions than just money. Another worked example to illustrate the point is given in Case Study 9.14.

CASE STUDY 9.14

CD plc and its market for video recorders

CD plc produces video players in the UK. The plans for the current year include the sale of 100,000 units in the UK, but the firm has the capacity to actually make 150,000. They are considering expanding their selling to include export markets, and are currently examining the potential in Europe and South Africa. The financial plan for video recorders by CD plc is as follows:

Sales	100,000 units
Price	£350 each
Sales Revenue	£35,000,000 per year
Production Costs	
Materials	£150 per set
Labour	£75 per set
Manufacturing semi-directs	£25 per set
Overheads (share of total overhead)	£50 per set
(£5,000,000 spread over 100,000 sets)	
Profit	£50 per set
	£5,000,000 per year

It is eight months into the year, and sales have reached 45,000 units. Equal monthly sales are forecast as TVs are seen as a non-seasonal product.

An enquiry has been received from a retailer in East Europe. This potential buyer wishes to buy 40,000 sets, but demands a special price of £280 per set.

Should the order be accepted or not?

Approach this through contribution. CD are making a contribution of £100 per set on their normal sales.

$(£350 - (£150 + £75 + £25)) = £350 - £250 = £100$. The TV's direct costs are £250 per set.

The East European order, at £280 per set, will make a contribution of £30 per set. Since the contribution is positive the order is worth taking, financially.

Other reasons for accepting it are:

1. The firm is operating below plan domestically, so this order will help overall.

	Domestic	Special	Total	Capacity
Sales (units)	45,000	40,000	85,000	150,000
Price (£)	350	280		
Revenue (£)	15,750,000	11,200,000	26,950,000	
Direct Costs (£)	11,250,000	10,000,000	21,250,000	
Contribution (£)	4,500,000	1,200,000	5,700,000	
Overheads (£)	5,000,000		or 5,000,000	
Profit/Loss (£)	(500,000)		700,000	

In fact, without it the firm will probably operate at a loss.

2. The order will get CD into an export market.

There are dangers. What will the UK customers think? Is East Europe really a market for CD? Will after-sales service be good enough, and will the reputation of CD be protected?

Financially, if the order will generate a positive contribution it is worth taking.

Make or buy in a component or product
The decision about buying or making a product, particularly a component, is a very common one for a manufacturing firm. If it is a new product, where the firm will have to install plant and equipment to make it, the decision is best aided by a break-even analysis. However, if the firm can make a component without incurring any extra capital costs, and provided it has spare capacity and can continue with all its existing production, then a contribution statement is useful. Basically, if the direct costs of producing the item 'in house' is less than the purchase price it is worth doing financially. An example to work through is given as Case Study 9.15.

CASE STUDY 9.15

CD plc and the manufacture in-house of audio tape covers
CD plc, now a major supplier of audio tapes both pre-recorded and empty, has just started producing its own plastic tape cases in its recently established Injection moulding facility. The decision was not an easy one, and the proposal had been rejected once before.

1. The rejection
The proposal some five years ago was to set up a new factory for the covers alone. Sales were estimated at 500,000 per year and CD plc could buy them in at a price of 20p each. If they set up their own plant, it would require a fixed cost of £200,000 per year, and they would incur variable costs of 5p per case.

Task A: Draw a break-even chart to confirm the validity of the decision to go on buying in then.

2. The acceptance
CD plc have now set up a plastics department to make

a whole range of injection, blow and vacuum forming machines for all its components. They have considerable spare capacity on their injection moulding equipment.

Cases now cost them 22p to buy in, but the direct cost of manufacture will be 7p per case for materials, plus 3p per case for semi-variables. There will be no additions to fixed costs. Sales are now running at 1,000,000 tapes per year.

Task B: Should they do it? Will they get a contribution, and how much? Will there be an increase in profits? But what about the opportunity cost of the decision?

Marginal costing is a very useful and flexible method of dealing with the costing problem, but it is not the only one. Some firms prefer the apparent precision of methods where overheads are included in product costs. There are two methods commonly used, and both involve allocating overheads to products in some way. Remember, any allocation of true overheads to a product must, by definition, be arbitrary and inaccurate. In some situations it can be positively dangerous.

Full costing
Overheads are allocated to products in proportion to another easily calculated cost or unit of production.

It can be as a percentage of direct costs, material costs, or even direct labour used. (Remember the problem of identification here.) An example to illustrate the method is shown in Table 9.1.

Table 9.1
Sales and cost forecast for CD plc, 1993

	Video		Audio		Total
Revenue	1,000,000		500,000		1,500,000
Material costs	200,000	150,000		350,000	
Labour costs	100,000	150,000		250,000	
Direct costs	300,000		300,000		600,000
Overheads	?		?		200,000
				Profit	700,000

Overheads, at £200,000 can be expressed as 33.3% of direct costs, 57.1% of material costs or 80.0% of direct labour costs. Assume that the firm decides to base its total costing on material costs, it will then allocate overheads to the products on the basis of its materials cost. Examine the Table 9.2.

Table 9.2

Sales and cost forecast for CD plc, 1993

(total cost basis)

	Video	Audio	Total
Revenue	1,000,000	500,000	1,500,000
Material costs 200,000	150,000	350,000	
Labour Costs 100,000	150,000	250,000	
Direct costs	300,000	300,000	600,000
Overheads			
57.1 % of materials	114,200	85,800	200,000
TOTAL COST	414,200	385,800	800,000
Profit	585,800	114,200	700,000

Profit and direct costs are the same, but the total costs of the products are given a value. It seems very precise and accurate. Examine another example (Table 9.3), where the labour cost is used as a basis for the allocation of overheads.

Table 9.3

Sales and cost forecast for CD plc, 1993 (Revised)

(total cost basis)

	Video	Audio	Total
Revenue	1,000,000	500,000	1,500,000
Material costs 200,000	150,000	350,000	
Labour costs 100,000	150,000	250,000	
Direct costs	300,000	300,000	600,000
Overheads			
80 % of Labour	80,000	120,000	200,000
TOTAL COST	380,000	420,000	800,000
Profit	620,000	80,000	700,000

This is exactly the same situation, the same costs, but videos now seem to be much more profitable. This cannot be a true position, or at least no more true than the one base of materials. This illustrates the danger of the method; it seems to give precision but in fact gives arbitrary values. Why try to allocate that which cannot reasonably be allocated?

A real problem with this method comes to light when there are changes between the forecast situation and

the actual. Imagine in the example above that sales of videos actually reaches 1,500,000 units instead of the planned 1,000,000. When this happened, due to an upsurge in the market and a very effective marketing campaign by CD plc, no additional overheads were incurred. Examine the revised costing shown in Table 9.4.

Table 9.4

Sales and cost forecast for CD plc, 1993 (revised)

(total cost basis); (increased sales)

	Video	Audio	Total
Revenue	1,500,000	500,000	2,000,000
Material costs 300,000	150,000	450,000	
Labour costs 150,000	150,000	300,000	
Direct costs	450,000	300,000	750,000
Overheads			
80 % of Labour	120,000	120,000	240,000
TOTAL COST	570,000	420,000	990,000
Profit	930,000	80,000	1,010,000

The profit will have increased, but by more than shown in the table. The profit has been understated by £40,000, the amount by which the overheads did not rise. A measure of 'real' profit would have been obtained from a marginal costing approach. Examine the alternative Table 9.5.

Table 9.5

Contribution costing statement for CD plc's production of tapes

	Video	Audio	Total
Revenue	1,500,000	500,000	2 000,000
Direct costs	450,000	300,000	750,000
Contribution	1,050,000	200,000	1,250,000
		Overheads	200,000
		Profit	1,050,000

It must be remembered that the ratios used in total costing will change with every change of sales and the associated direct costs.

It is sometimes argued that this method, and its related absorption costing, gives a firm greater control over its costs. It means that the overheads are allocated to a cost centre, in this case the products, and so can be monitored. This is a fallacy as in marginal costing overheads are simply considered as a cost centre called 'Overheads' and are measured and controlled. They are not hidden within an alien cost centre, so are under more direct exposure in marginal costing.

A new definition:

Cost centres are a way of dividing a factory or business into groups of machines, departments or products where costs can be ascertained and used for purposes of cost control.

CD plc can divide itself into operating divisions such as storage, production, dispatch, marketing and sales, as well as head office and staff departments. It can also consider itself as a set of product divisions and an overhead division. It is both of these, and a firm will divide its costs both ways, and then use the two results for different control purposes.

Cost control is a matter of will and procedure, not of the costing method used. Marginal costing is simpler than total costing, so why adopt procedures more difficult than necessary. Some people like the apparent precision, however, of seeming to know the full costs of a product. (More on cost control in Chapter 10.)

Absorption costing

This is a more 'refined' way of allocating costs than *total costing*. In this method all the components of overheads are considered individually and allocated to the products or the cost centres in as appropriate a way as possible. Note, however, that if an apparent overhead element can be allocated reasonably to a product it is a semi-variable cost anyway. If it cannot then the firm is still trying to allocate what it should not be. The method is complicated, involves much time and effort, but suffers from all the disadvantages of total costing. In effect, for a good business, the *absorption method* and the *contribution method* are the same up to the point where absorption costing forces the staff concerned to allocate the overheads to some cost centre.

Consider the following examples of overheads within the costs of a business, and ways that they may be allocated:

- Salaries of personnel staff – according to the size of the payroll, or the number of staff.
- Stores – turnover?
- Rent – allocate according to the floor area occupied by the production line or the department.
- Insurance – allocate according to the capital value of plant, equipment and materials used.
- Depreciation – allocate according to the capital cost of buildings, plant and machines used. Remember, it is an allowance, though, not a cost as such.
- Directors and their staff – a difficult area. Sales value of products? Might an inverse relationship with profits be best, i.e. most cost to the poorest profit earner? Absolute or percentage profit?
- Company Secretary and Registrar – No relation at all. Probably allocated according to sales value.

Nevertheless, they are all fixed costs so cannot, by definition, be allocated to a product. The work necessary to produce an answer does tend to endow the method with a level of perceived accuracy.

Thus it is perfectly reasonable to say that a firm, or any of its employees, will not and can not know how much any particular product actually costs the firm to produce. Component costs change, though, and a good firm will know exactly how these changes alter the costs of the individual products. The contribution that each product makes should be known accurately.

It should be clear by now that costing is a very difficult problem. In the multi-product situation exact costs can never be known, and the most realistic costing method is to use contribution costing, or marginal costing. Other methods suggest a precision that is not there as they are based on allocating unrelated overheads to products. If it were possible, the costs would not be overheads, anyway!

SUMMARY

Having studied this chapter carefully, you will have a good understanding of the problems of pricing and costing for a product and a company. In particular you will:

▼ be able to describe and explain the concept of demand, and its determinants for a product or service

(continued)

▽ be able to explain the concept of elasticity of demand, i.e. the sensitivity of demand to changes in its determinants

▽ be able to perform simple elasticity calculations, and be able to interpret the results

▽ understand that the customer ultimately decides the level of sales that will be achieved by a firm at the price that the firm sets

▽ be able to describe and explain the use of various pricing methods, namely:

– *Skimming*	– *Competitive pricing*
– *Cost plus*	– *Value pricing*
– *Penetrative pricing*	

The real difficulty involved with attempts to cost the production of a good or service, particularly in the case of a multi-product firm, will finally be accepted. In particular, you will:

▽ have a sound understanding of the elements of cost – *fixed*, *variable* and *semi-variable*

▽ realise that all costs can vary with the quantity handled, and with time

▽ be able to describe and handle simple calculations involving *contribution costing* and be fully aware of its uses and limitations

▽ be able to describe and handle simple calculations involving *absorption* and *full costing*, and be familiar with both their advantages and disadvantages.

Questions and activities

Technical terms and glossary

In the section below you are given a series of technical terms and their meanings. They have been scrambled, though. You must match up the terms and the definitions. When you have them correctly paired, transfer them to your vocabulary or glossary book.

You are also advised to transfer any definitions obtained during the exercises in the case studies into this glossary book.

Technical terms

1. Demand
2. Determinants of demand
3. Price elasticity of demand
4. Complementary products
5. Substitute products
6. Elastic demand
7. Cost plus pricing
8. Penetrative pricing
9. Value pricing
10. Production overheads
11. Marginal cost
12. Cost centre
13. Inelastic demand
14. Full costing
15. Income elasticity of demand
16. Cross price elasticity of demand
17. Absorption costing
18. Skimming
19. Pricing policy
20. Overheads

Definitions

A. A division of a company where costs can be collected together, and controlled.

B. A measure of the sensitivity of demand for a product to changes in prices of other goods. The 'sign' of this elasticity indicates if the products are substitutes, complements or totally unrelated.

C. Another name for indirect costs, or fixed costs. Those costs of a business which do not vary with output. They usually have to be paid per period of time, often in advance of production.

D. The situation where a set percentage price change brings about a lower percentage change in demand. Price elasticity will be less than one, or between 0 and −1.

E. The desire for a product, combined with the ability to pay. It is the quantity that will be demanded, or required, at each and every price.

F. The decisions taken by a firm that determines how its prices will be set.

G. Products, like beef and lamb, or butter and margarine where one may be substituted for another depending on the relative prices.

H. The sensitivity of the demand for a product to changes in the real incomes of buyers.

I. Those factors which affect the demand for a product.

J. The setting of the initial price of a product very low so as to obtain a large share of the market. Sales volume will be more important than profit at this time.

K. The sensitivity of the demand for a product to changes in its own price. The relationship is usually negative, i.e. a price rise will result in a loss in demand and sales.

L. The cost of producing one more. Over a small range of outputs, this may be the same as the variable costs of production.

M. A policy of setting the launch price of a product high, initially, to obtain those customers who will pay a high price for a product. They 'skim the cream' from the market.

N. Goods, like lamb and mint sauce or tea and milk, which tend to be used together. If the demand for one rises, the demand for the other will do likewise.

O. A demand situation where a small percentage change in price results in a larger percentage change in demand, i.e. a 5% price increase causes a 10% decrease in sales.

P. A costing system where overheads are spread 'as accurately as they can be' to all products. (Remember, they are overheads simply because they cannot be allocated or identified with a particular product.)

Q. A pricing method where the price is set on the basis of the value of an item or service to its purchaser.

R. Those costs which are dependent on production but do not change in direct proportion to the level of production or sales.

S. A costing system where all overheads are allocated proportionally to individual products.

T. A costing method where all the costs of production

or sale are calculated, then a set amount added to this to determine the selling price.

Short answer questions and essay topics

1. 'Nine out of ten 6th formers would like to own a BMW.' Does this mean that the demand for BMWs is huge?
2. What are the determinants of demand?
3. (*Essay*) Explain how effective advertising reduces the price elasticity of demand for a product.
4. (*Essay*) 'All products are substitutes for others, at least very weakly.' Explain this statement.
5. When can 'cost plus' pricing be used relatively safely?
6. (*Essay*) Why is it so hard to determine the cost of producing a single product in the situation of a multi-product business?
7. Are production overheads fixed or variable costs?
8. (*Essay*) Why are full costing and absorption costing methods bound to produce inaccurate results?
9. Explain the uses of 'marginal costing'.
10. (*Essay*) What is contribution? How can it be of use to a firm when planning a product portfolio?

Case studies and data response questions

The marketing department of CD plc have been studying the market and the demand conditions for its CDs, audio tapes, video tapes and video recorders. It has identified the following relationships:

(a) When real incomes for its customers rose by 10%, sales of video recorders rose by 5%.
1. What is the income elasticity of demand for video recorders sold by CD plc?
(b) CD has been selling 20,000 CD players per week at a price of £250 each. They increased the price to £300 each and sales fell to 18,000 units per week.
2. What is the price elasticity of demand for the CD players?
(c) Sales of CD players ran at 15,000 units per week when the Company spent £1m per year on advertising. It raised its advertising expenditure to £1.25m per year and sales rose to 16,000 units per week.
3. What is the advertising elasticity of demand for CD players?
(d) The cross-price elasticity of demand between CD players and CDs is known to be − 0.75.

The original situation was as follows:

117

	CD Players	CDs
Price	£250 each	£12 each
Q	14,000 per month	150,000 per month

CD raised the price of CD players by £25.

4.   What affect will this have on the sales of CDs?

5.   Hot Air Products Ltd makes a wide range of industrial and domestic dryers, including a very successful domestic hair dryer. Read the following memos and answer the questions which follow.

HOT AIR PRODUCTS LTD INTERNAL MEMORANDUM

To: Marketing Manager   Date: 19.9.91

From: Managing Director   Ref: RL/PS/7/1

Subject: Market Share Targets 1992/93

To exploit our competitive advantage in the domestic hair dryer market, the Board is considering ways of increasing our market share. Please prepare relevant research data for the Board Meeting of 30th November.

HOT AIR PRODUCTS LTD INTERNAL MEMORANDUM

To Managing Director   Date: 29.9.91

From: Marketing Manager   Ref: JA/LM/3/1

Subject: Your Memo dated 19.9.91 (RL/PS/7/1)

Data on domestic hair dryers indicates the following:

i) The total annual market in the UK is 800,000 units and this is likely to remain static for a number of years;

ii) We have a 10% share of the total market at retail price of £20 per unit. We are among the market leaders;

iii) This product is likely to show a price elasticity of -4;

iv) The estimated advertising elasticity is 0.8. Our present advertising expenditure is £80,000 per year;

v) Our output of domestic hair dryers can be increased by 20% without increases in plant or manpower;

vi) Variable costs per unit will remain unchanged.

(a)   Prepare information for the managing director to present to the Board. She has asked you to calculate the following:

Show all your workings.

   (i)   The number of hair dryers the company will produce at full capacity.   (4 marks)
   (ii)   Their percentage share of the market, if all these units are sold.   (2 marks)
   (iii)   The retail price of hair dryers considered likely to capture this share of the market.   (3 marks)

   (iv)   The estimated advertising expenditure to attract this increased market share.   (3 marks)
   (v)   The increase or decrease in sales revenue that would result from selling all the units produced at full capacity, at the new retail price.   (3 marks)
(b)   Outline three additional pieces of information that would assist the Board in deciding whether to attempt to expand their market share for hair dryers.   (6 marks)
(c)   Discuss the value of the concept of elasticity in determining pricing policy.   (6 marks)

(Associated Examining Board, Business Studies (A) Paper 1, November 1992)

6.   Study the information and answer the questions which follow.

Watcher Ltd is a small firm that manufactures high quality pillow cases, duvet covers, and fitted sheets. Solely on the basis of the following figures, the Board of Directors has decided to discontinue producing duvet covers and not to replace them with any other product. This will leave production capacity unused, and fixed costs unaltered.

	Pillow Cases	Duvet Covers	Fitted Sheets	Total
INCOME				
Sales Income	100,000	120,000	70,000	290,000
DIRECT COSTS				
Direct materials	30,000	40,000	20,000	90,000
Direct labour	35,000	50,000	25,000	110,000
OVERHEADS				
Variable overheads	10,000	12,000	7,500	29,500
Fixed overheads	15,000	21,400	10,700	47,100
Total cost	90,000	123,400	63,200	276,600
Profit (loss)	10,000	(3,400)	6,800	13,400

Show any appropriate calculations.

(a)   Explain to the Board the implications of its decision to discontinue the production of duvet covers:
   (i)   in the short term   (6 marks)
   (ii)   in the long term   (4 marks)
(b)   The directors decide not to discontinue duvet covers production. Outline two other options that may be available to them.   (6 marks)
(c)   One of the directors suggests that there should be a more structured decision making process. What might be the key elements of such a process?   (6 marks)

(Associated Examining Board, Business Studies (A) Paper 1, June 1993)

Preview

▽ This chapter introduces the operation known as *planning*, and examines the *planning cycle*.

▽ It then looks briefly at the methods and processes for setting up *budgets*, the means of controlling them.

▽ Two types of budget will be examined, the *capital budget* for a firm, and its *revenue budget*.

▽ The second part of the chapter looks at budget control through the *variance analysis*, where 'actual' performance is compared with the 'forecast' of the budget. It also shows how it can be extended to all types of budget – sales, profits, manpower, plant utilisation, for example.

All businesses are concerned with the answers to four basic questions. These questions and answers constitute the *planning process* and cycle that firms have to carry out. The fundamental questions are:

1. Where is the business now?
2. Where is it going?
3. How is it progressing towards this target?
4. Has the business reached its goal?

When the answer to the last question is 'yes', then the process starts again.

This process is very similar to any navigation process, and fits particularly well with aviation. Consider a flight from London to New York. The first stage is the pre-flight briefing of the crew at Heathrow, the second the detailed route planning. The flight then has to pass through a set of check points and report at various times, then finally arrives at John F. Kennedy Airport. After landing the crew has to go through the whole process again to plan and execute the return journey.

Businesses tend to do their 'navigation' in terms of money. They use Balance Sheets, Trading and Profit and Loss Accounts, financial budgets, and financial reports and variance reports to perform the process. They consider the future through two plans:

- *five-year plan*: An outline plan covering each of the next five years. No great detail is expected, but any major changes should be included.
- *two-year plan:* A detailed analysis of operations for the next two years.

This process produces an annual budget, which is a forecast for the 'present year'.

These are rolling plans, and the process is continuous. The result of this is that each 'Year' will have been reviewed five times before it actually 'happens'. It can and will be revised and refined during this process. This is illustrated in Table 10.1.

Table 10.1
The planning timetable

Year	2 Year				5 Year
	1	2	3	4	5
1	93	94	95	96	(97)
2	94	95	96	(97)	98
3	95	96	(97)	98	99
4	96	(97)	98	99	00
5	(97)	98	99	00	01

Note how 1997 would be reviewed regularly if the timetable above was followed.

The plans for each year will include detailed plans, or forecasts, of capital expenditure, and profit (or capital generation). The profit plans are summarised from all the firms plans for revenue generation and use or, in other words, sales revenues and costs. First, though, the capital budgets will be studied. If you do not have the productive capacity, you can not have products to sell!

Capital budgets

In Chapter 3 the various methods of evaluating capital expenditure on projects was introduced. No attempt was made to see how the proposed expenditure was calculated. Many of the case studies have included statements such as:

- The plant will cost £1.2 million to purchase and install.
- The new factory will cost £4.5 million to design and build.
- The new product will require capital expenditure of £400,000.

Behind each such statement lies a capital budget. This can be an extensive document, and can take a considerable amount of time and money to draw up. Just consider the cost estimates made by Boeing for the 747 facility in the USA. This not only involved the factory in making the aircraft, and the R&D costs to develop it, but a complete airport to enable the product to be delivered – a long and expensive process.

The budget has to be built up in steps, with each step having to be completed and approved before the next one can commence. The basic steps are:

- feasibility study
- full design and costing.

As was stated earlier, capital budgeting can be time consuming and expensive. Let us return to the aircraft example. An aircraft builder would have to know all of the following before it could undertake such a budget.

- The market forecast giving sales forecasts and price expectations covering the expected life of the product.
- The cost estimate of the aircraft, including design costs. This will probably require extensive R&D and product testing for this type of product. It will also require cost information from subcontractors and suppliers. Areas such as engines and

electronics could also face extensive costs in preparing the information required.
- The cost estimate for the production facility.

These interlock – production need the sales forecasts to be able to size and design the factory, marketing need the cost estimate to be able to check their market size and price assumptions. The directors want all the information before they make the final decision to go ahead or not.

In order to save time and prevent the waste of money, costings are done in steps with ever increasing accuracy. Only as a product 'passes' the first hurdle will it advance to the next.

Feasibility study

This, as its name implies, is a preliminary estimate, or a screening exercise. Estimates of costs and sales are made to an accuracy of say + or - 20%. Small teams of experts from marketing, production, finance and development produce this quick estimate. They will use as much past information as they can, and produce trends. This feasibility study will be considered by the Board, and if approved will be passed for full evaluation. Only after this approval will expenditure on specific research and development be allowed.

Full design and costing

A detailed exercise, and great accuracy is expected – at least + or – 5%. The sum produced from this exercise will be the one submitted to investment appraisal. Only after the successful completion of this will the project become part of a firm's capital expenditure budget.

How might the project have been costed? How can you cost an extensive petrochemical plant, a new factory, or even an office extension? Divide the project up into units you can recognise. Divide it up into accounting units, also. Get estimates of the capital requirements for land, buildings, building services, roads, power and steam distribution, plant and machinery, instrumentation, and even furniture and fittings. The final capital budget document might look like Figure 10.1.

Contingencies are allowances for unforeseen items, and changes that could not reasonably be allowed for. Note how the headings conform, at least in outline, to the asset entries on a Balance Sheet. The document can be understood by engineer and accountant alike.

The final total will only be as accurate as the work put into it. Complete accuracy is neither possible nor

Cost centre	Budget actual variance
Section 1. Buildings and related services	
Land	XXX
Buildings	XXX
Related services	XX
Roads	XXX
SUB-TOTAL	XXXX
Section 2. Plant and equipment	
Plant and equipment	XX
Piping, cocks and valves	XX
Utilities	XX
Instrumentation	X
Mechanical service	XX
Electrical services	XXX
Furniture and fittings	X
SUB-TOTAL	XXXX
Section 3. Installation and commissioning	
Contractors	XX
Commissioning engineers	XX
Travel and hotels	X
SUB-TOTAL	XXX
TOTAL	XXXX
Contingencies	X
APPROVAL TOTAL	XXXXX

Figure 10.1 Example of capital budget summary sheet

necessary. Each 1% extra accuracy after 5% demands more and more work and costs, and eventually becomes self-defeating.

This is a snapshot of capital budgeting. Now we turn to the revenue budgets.

Revenue budgets

A firm will need to forecast its profits for a year to come. It will have to plan both sales and costs to do this. Thus revenue budgets, which may well be prepared by the accounts department, will involve considerable input from both marketing and production departments, not forgetting engineering and research and development. It will also need to consider the overheads, or fixed cost areas of the business, such as personnel, quality control, finance and accounts. They are not revenue earning cost

centres, but are clear spenders, and need to plan and control their costs. Obviously, however, the personnel department cannot really plan until it has got all the manpower budgets from the other cost centres. It will have to account for its fixed costs required to pay for its core, corporate work, and its semi-variables where it is working for its 'home' clients. Another good example of the integrated nature of business.

Thus a good system for revenue budgeting is to split the company completely into cost centres (see Figure 10.2.). Each cost centre prepares its budget to meet the requirements from the master plan. It is a cyclic process, but where does it start?

The starting point for any profit forecast has to be

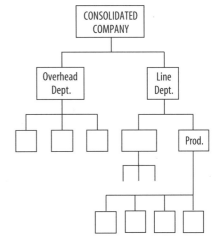

Figure 10.2 Cost centre structure of CD plc (outline form only)

the sales budget. This has to give the forecast sales for all products, including any new launches, and forecasts of all advertising expenditure. This will be prepared by the marketing department, who should also prepare a manpower budget.

The production department has to prepare its production plan, but cannot do this until it has the sales plan, in units, from the marketing department. It can then work out its costs, having worked out its manpower and plant utilisation budgets, and a purchasing/stock holding plan.

Accounts will then take all the plans, and consolidate them into a master plan.

At this point the capital and revenue budgets come together and finance department can prepare 'forecast' Profit and Loss Accounts and Balance Sheets for the year under consideration. These then become the master plan for the whole consolidated business. This will be reviewed by the Board, and then either approved, or returned to the appropriate department for alteration. (If the latter happens, the process starts all over again.) Budget time is a very worrying one for staff. This is another example of interaction, and not a pleasant one.

We have described a cyclical process, which is summarised and illustrated in Figures 10.3 and 10.4 below.

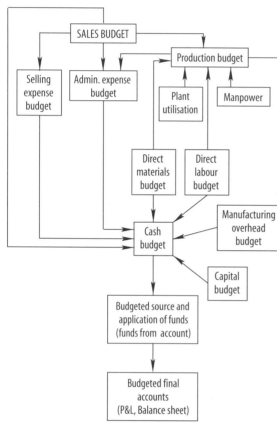

Figure 10.3 *Types of budget*

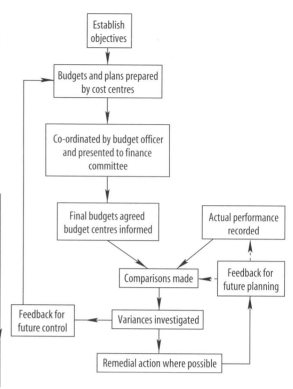

Figure 10.4 *The budget procedure*

Budget control through variance analysis

Budgets are only forecasts, so have to be monitored, and corrective action taken if necessary. This is done using a process known as variance analysis. The difference between the 'plan' of a budget and the 'actual' is defined as the variance. Consider the following situation for CD plc. Budget sales for CDs was 25,000 in April 1994, but actual sales were recorded as 23,000. There was a negative sales variance of – 2,000 units.

Variance analysis is used to monitor and control both capital and revenue budgets.

Capital budget control

When a firm buys anything it will be against a budget. The amount paid will be compared to this. Thus a variance will be determined. The variances from all purchased items can be added up, and a forecast made of the actual outcome. Look at Case Study 10.1. It is rather early to do it as the project is so young. What does the table show, though? At 30th September 1995 the project had consumed £180,000 against approved budgets of £163,000. The project is £17,000 or 8.5% overspent. If the project continues in this way it will be closed out at about £365,000 (8.5% added to the budget before contingencies). There will need to be a lot of management if it is not to go overspent. One claim against contingencies could be a real problem.

Variance has been used to 'measure' the present and 'predict' the future. These are two classic planning operations.

Revenue budget control

Exactly the same method is applied here. 'Actual' incomes and expenditures are compared with the 'planned' figures and the variances determined. These also can be used as measures of 'now', and as indicators for the 'future'. An example is given in Case Study 10.2.

The whole operation has been examined, so action can be taken to help the area which is in biggest trouble. Look at the case study.

Here sales and price are below forecast.

Control of budget for expansion of Rye factory

CD plc have an approved budget to expand their factory at Rye. You are the project manager and have to make a report to your manager on the state of the budget today. Your project accountant has produced the following variance analysis report.

Capital variance report (Units: £000s)

Project 7/123		Date: 30th September 1995	
Item	Budget	Actual	Variance
Building Mods	115	140	(25)
Roads	8	10	(2)
Plant and equipment	40	30	10
Utilities	40		
Instrumentation	50		
F&F	4		
PCVs	4		
Electrical services	45		
Commissioning	20		
Contingencies	35		
TOTAL	371	180	(17)

CD plc and the sales of CDs

CD plc had forecast the sales of compact discs as £250,000 for April 1995. This was based on a level of unit sales of 25,000 and a price of £10 each. The budget report, issued in May 1995, contained the following information:

Sales report – April 1995
CD sales department

Sales	23,000 units
Average price	£9 each

Marketing department produced the following variance chart.

CD plc
Variance Report on CD Sales
April 1994

	Plan	Actual	Variance	%
Sales revenue (£)	250,000	207,000	−43,000	−17.2
Sales units	25,000	23,000	−2,000	−8
Selling price	10	9	1	−10

Competition must have been severe, or the original forecasts were optimistic. Other analysis is necessary to find which one is true.

Variance analysis is a simple process which can give very valuable results. The regular flow of such information from the management accountants is important if a firm is to be run as successfully as it can be.

SUMMARY

Having studied this rather advanced chapter, you will be able to:

▼ Describe the principles of the planning process and cycle.

▼ Outline methods for preparing revenue and capital budgets.

▼ Show how variance analysis can be used to monitor and control budgets.

▼ Use variances to make forecasts of the future.

Questions and activities

Technical terms and glossary

In the section below you are given a series of technical terms and their meanings. They have been scrambled, though. You must match up the terms and the definitions. When you have them correctly paired, transfer them to your vocabulary or glossary book.

You are also advised to transfer any definitions obtained during the exercises in the case studies into this glossary book.

Technical terms

1. Planning cycle
2. Cost centre
3. Five Year Plan
4. Capital budget
5. Revenue budget
6. Feasibility study
7. Variance analysis
8. Contingencies
9. Production plan
10. Investment appraisal

Definitions

A. A method of assessing the accuracy of a forecast. The actual result is compared with the forecast and the difference computed. The reasons for the difference can then be examined.

B. The timespan against which plans are made and reviewed against actual performance. It enables a company to 'keep itself on course'.

C. A division of a company against which costs can be allocated and controlled.

D. Plan or forecast of the investment expenditure to be made by a company for a period.

E. Methods for evaluating and comparing alternative capital expenditure strategies for a firm against themselves and the firm's absolute standards.

F. Financial plan for a company which covers the next five years operation. Inevitably it will not be detailed or accurate.

G. An allowance in a budget for items or expenses that were not and could not be foreseen at the time of the preparation of the budget.

H. Plan in terms of output and cost of how the manufacturing department of a firm will meet the requirements of the sales and marketing plan.

I. A preliminary estimate of the cost of a project. It is prepared to a low level of accuracy, but quickly and cheaply. The 'budget' must be approved before any further work is done.

J. Plan or forecast of the revenue expenditure of a firm for a period.

Short answer questions

1. Why might a firm produce a feasibility study for a project?

2. Why is the planning process continuous?
3. What are the four key questions the planning and control system sets out to answer?
4. 'Variance analysis prevents a manager hiding errors.' Comment on the validity of this statement.

Data response question

CD plc is expanding its factory at Warrington by the introduction of an injection moulding facility. The budget for the project was approved some 15 months ago. The following report was tabled at the recent project review meeting.

Project: 04/007	Warrington Injection Moulder		
Approved: 01/94			Review: 04/94

Part 1. Completed Activities (Units; £000s)

Cost Centre	Budget	Actual	Variance
Section 1. Buildings and related services			
Buildings	15	18	
Related services	25	22	
SUB-TOTAL	40		
Section 2 Plant and equipment			
Plant	250	260	
PCVs	10	8	
Utilities	50	60	
Instrumentation	30	25	
Mechanical services	50	60	
Electectrical services	70		
SUB-TOTAL	460		
Section 3 Installation and Commissioning			
Contractors	50		
Company engineers	10		
Travel and hotels	5		
SUB-TOTAL	65		
Total	565		
Contingencies	35		
GRAND TOTAL	600		

Part 2 Incomplete activities

	Budget used	Actual	variance
Electrical services	40	50	
Contractors	30	50	

Questions and activities

1. (a) Complete the variance column in the report. (An overspend is to be recorded as a plus.)
   (b) Forecast the eventual outrun cost for this project.
2. The sales department of CD plc has produced the following sales report for its audio tapes in April 1995.

11
Financial accounting and reporting

Preview

▼ This chapter describes the three basic financial reports that businesses produce: the *Balance Sheet, Profit and Loss Account* and the *Cash Flow Statement*.

▼ It shows how they are constructed and read, but introduces the dangers that may be encountered with financial reports, particularly the problems of valuation. A mention will be given to the more modern problem of accounting for inflation.

Business Studies students are not normally required to be able to construct accounts, nor are they required to be bookkeepers. They are expected to be able to read and interpret a set of accounts, and to be aware of their limitations. It is important to examine their construction, however, and this will involve some work on double-entry systems.

Most well-organised, and successful firms have one thing in common. Namely, they have available to them a steady supply of accurate and useful records and other reports. These will include reports on stock levels, sales, dispatches and receipts into the warehouses as well as those prepared by the accounts department. The latter reports or records are prepared in terms of money, and are called accounts. Companies produce two forms of accounts – company or financial accounts, and management accounts.

profit forecasts and investment appraisal calculations, i.e. calculations to show if an investment is worth making when compared with alternatives. They are not the responsibility of accountants alone, but involve the whole management team in data collection, preparation, interpretation, planning and action. They have largely been covered already in the earlier chapters in the money component of this book.

It is often said that a firm will have two sets of books, or two sets of financial records. As far as the above is concerned, this is true. However, this is another example of interdependency as the company accounts depend on the management accounts as they are prepared from them. Company accounts, or financial accounts as they are more commonly called, will now be examined in more detail.

Management accounts

Management accounts are records and reports prepared for use within the firm and they are issued so that the managers can make decisions based on up-to-date and accurate information. Such documents would include budgets, i.e. forecasts, in money terms, of the future for the company, variance reports, i.e. those that compare what has happened as opposed to what the firm planned or forecast would happen, cash flow forecasts, product costings,

Financial accounts

Financial accounts are records produced primarily for external use. They are to be read by shareholders, investors and other interested parties, as well as the Inland Revenue. These documents include the Balance Sheet, the Profit and Loss Account, and the Cash Flow Statement. They will be accompanied by a set of notes explaining entries in the reports in more detail, and a statement of the accounting methods or conventions used in their preparation. Finally, there will be a report, or certificate from a firm of auditors which guarantees the accuracy of the reports. If the firm is an incorporated company, then these documents, at least in a basic form, are required by law, and are public information, i.e. they are available to be studied by anybody who asks to see them. These documents are also used as an aid to decision making, but now by persons, organisations and groups external to the firm itself, i.e. shareholders and potential investors, investment advisers, business analysts accountants and the tax and excise duty authorities.

Anyone reading financial accounts is probably trying to answer two very basic questions about a business:

1. How has the concern managed its affairs over a period of time?
2. What is its current financial situation?

These public domain documents give an outsider a record, or picture of the progress of a firm. They can be used to compare one company with another, one industry with another, or one year with another. What are these documents?

The Balance Sheet

A 'still' picture at a set point in time. It shows, basically, how much money, or funds the firm is using (the capital employed), where it came from, and where it has been put to work. It does not tell a reader how well it has been used or worked.

The Trading and Profit and Loss Account

A record of how the business has operated during the year in question. It shows the sales and expenses of the firm, and how much profit has been made. It will also show what has been done with this profit, at least in very general terms. (It might be better or more accurate to call it a Profit or Loss Account, as a firm will be making one or another.)

The Cash Flow Statement

The cash flow statement is a report which shows where a firm got its funds, or cash from during the year, what it did with it, and records the effects of these actions on the firm's main accounts. In particular, it shows how the firms borrowings, i.e. its loans, have changed.

These reports are of little value on their own. A reader needs at least the first two documents to get any sort of view of a firm. For a reasonably accurate picture, the reader will need all three documents. If a really full and accurate picture is required then the reports for a series of years are needed, ideally with sets of similar documentation for other firms in the same business, i.e. the company accounts from the major competition. With all this data the student will be able to carry out a full range of ratio analysis, but more of this later.

A copy of the three reports are sent each year to Companies House.

These documents are written and published in a set way. This has to be familiar, and readily understood. Attempts to 'converse' without understanding the language of accounts will lead to real problems and dangerous misunderstandings.

Company accounts all conform to one of two basic layouts, though the actual format in detail may vary from firm to firm at their choice. There have been horizontal and vertical formats, but the modern convention calls for a vertical presentation. This fits better with computers, and onto a spreadsheet. The Companies Act of 1985 laid down standards, and gives forms of presentation that conform to EEC (European Economic Community, now the Economic Union) Regulations. These are not as yet compulsory, but are simply recommendations. The content, essentially, is the same regardless of layout.

These formal accounts will become clear as the chapter progresses. It will help to remember why they are prepared. Think how and why firms are set up. They are established to make a profit, usually through the production and sale of a good or service. They do this using money, or capital, provided by owners, partners or shareholders. Now think why these reports may be prepared.

- to account for the use of the money, or funds as it is often called, that has been provided by the shareholders.

   The ordinary shareholder is entitled to know where his or her money is going, and to judge if this is what he or she wishes to support. There is a question of ethics here; with the rise in environmentalism some products are becoming unpopular. Other firms, with operations overseas and in sensitive countries may be avoided, as may those involved in the manufacture and sale of tobacco products, or alcohol.

- to account for the profits made using these funds, and thus justify the dividends paid out to shareholders.

   If this is not satisfactory to the share-holder/investor, then the shareholder may remove the funds, i.e. sell the shares and reinvest the money elsewhere.

- to satisfy the 'tax man' that the correct level of taxation has been paid.

The Inland Revenue will not just take a firm's word. It will expect that the reports are audited, i.e. checked and passed by a firm of qualified, independent accountants.

Because they are so important, they are all drawn up following an agreed set of principles, or policies. These are known as the principles of accounting. These are summarised as:

Going concern

It is assumed when preparing the accounts that the business is, and will continue to operate and trade in the future. This is particularly important when considering the value of things the firm owns, i.e. its assets. Values have a habit of falling when it is known that they have to be sold!

Accruals

This means that items of income and cost will be included in the accounts as they become due, not when they are actually received or paid. In other words credit terms are ignored. Thus revenues and profits are matched with the relevant expenses incurred in earning them.

Consistency

All information from one year to another shall be consistent, and reports prepared the same way so that they are comparable. Any change should be well highlighted to avoid any confusion. Dealing with depreciation, which is an allowance to reflect the fact that some items wear out and lose value during their life, is a key area here, but more of this later in the chapter.

Prudence

Accounts should be based on reasonably reliable information. Income should not be anticipated, nor should very optimistic valuations be included. Again, more of this is discussed later.

Materiality

Minor items may be left out of accounts. Obviously the definition of 'minor' is critical.

Objectivity

Personal opinion, particularly over valuations should be avoided. Because of this accountants use a set of conventions, which have to be published with the accounts. Again, more of this can be found later in the chapter.

The effect these have on accounts will be seen as the various accounts are developed.

Now, a detailed examination of each of the three reports in turn is done.

The Balance Sheet

As stated earlier, this gives a picture, at a particular point in time, usually at the end of the firm's financial year, i.e. that period of 12 months that the business selects as its own personal year. (The government's financial year runs from 5th April of one year to 4th April of the next.) of a firms 'value', and where it has got this value from. It is concerned with assets, liabilities and sources of capital. What are the assets of a company? These are classified as Tangible or Intangible assets.

Tangible assets

Tangible assets are assets that have a physical identity. Examples would be: land, buildings, stocks of materials and finished goods, cars, furniture, plant and machinery, computers and a whole range of spare parts and lubricants. Do not forget all the office equipment and stationery. They have a value which is usually accepted and recognised by all parties. The value will change with time.

Intangible assets

Intangible assets are those that do not have a physical form. Examples would be: ownership of a trademark (McDonald's), licensed design (the Coke bottle), customer base, or the skills of particular employees (the creative staff in advertising agencies). The value of these assets is a problem, as there is really no basis or standard against which to judge it.

The former tend to present far fewer valuation problems than the latter. The valuation of intangibles presents firms with ethical problems as well. This topic will be reexamined later when the problems associated with using or reading Balance Sheets are considered in detail. Intangible assets will not be used in any of the examples in this chapter.

How is a Balance Sheet prepared? How does a Balance Sheet work? Consider the examples that follow very carefully. They will all be set in the environment of CD plc.

STAGE 1. CD aimed to start and run a business buying and selling prerecorded tapes. It needed some money to start. It had £10,000 of its own, which the owners contributed in return for shares in the company, and raised another £10,000 from its external shareholders. CD thus had £20,000 to spend. The first Balance Sheet, drawn up before the firm started trading would be like that illustrated in Figure 11.1.

ASSETS	
Cash	£20,000
LIABILITIES	
Loan	
NET ASSETS	£20,000
CAPITAL AND RESERVES	
Shares	£20,000

Figure 11.1 Balance Sheet for CD plc as at 30th September 1991

CD has £20,000 in cash, raised through the investment of the owners and the taking of the investments from the shareholders.

Note three things about this simple Balance Sheet:

1. The Balance Sheet has a date. It must do otherwise it has no reference point. It is a snapshot of the firm taken 'as at' or 'on' the date concerned.
2. Net assets and the capital and reserves (employed in the business) balance. This must be so, by definition. It is a Balance Sheet, remember.
3. Everything is in the account twice. This is the principle of double-entry accounting, or bookkeeping. This will be briefly explained.

Double-entry accounting

Double-entry accounting is really very simple and logical. Every action within a firm, in financial terms, requires two actions to record it fully, accurately and safely. Just take a simple personal example: a student has £20 in her purse. She buys an LP record for £8. She keeps a cash book and a personal assets register. The two entries. are:

Cash book: **Opening balance**   *£20*
            Purchase of record   *£8*
            Closing balance   *£12*
Asset register – Purchase of record – value £8

Eight pounds has moved from 'pocket' to record. One asset, cash, has been converted into a fixed asset, the record.

It gets a little bit more complicated when credit transactions are handled. Be careful, and apply a little logic and there will be no problems. Consider these examples:

CD buys tapes on credit

It gains an asset, the tapes. Its cash is unchanged, but it now has a bill. There is now an increase in

creditors, effectively to balance the cash still in the firm which is really already allocated.

CD sells an item, say a car, for cash

A fixed asset has been disposed of, to be replaced by another asset, cash. If the items sold were products from stock, then a current asset has been reduced now, to still be replaced by the asset called cash.

CD sells CD players on credit

A current asset has been disposed of, and the value of current assets decreased. There is no increase in cash, but the firm is now owed the sum of money concerned. Debtors must increase by the amount due. Debtors are an asset, and must balance the value of the goods sold.

Now, return to the developing Balance Sheet for CD plc.

STAGE 2: The firm buys a small, old store for £5,000 to keep its stock in. This changes the Balance Sheet. The firm now has a fixed asset, the store, but has reduced its cash. Again, there will be two changes in the account. The balance sheet will change, so examine Figure 11. 2 carefully.

ASSETS	
Store	£5,000
Cash	£15,000
	£20,000
LIABILITIES	
Loan	
NET ASSETS	£20,000
CAPITAL AND RESERVES	
Shares	£20,000

Figure 11.2 Balance sheet for CD plc as at 1st January 1992

The cash has been reduced, the firm has become less liquid.

So far the firm has been spending capital. If it continues this way it will soon run out of cash, and will not be able to buy anything or to pay its bills. It will need new capital. Where might this come from?

- a loan from a bank or other firm which makes loans to businesses
- the profits of the company.

A loan is clear. If the business is a success and the firm has serviced any earlier loans properly, i.e. it pays the bank the agreed amounts of interest, and repays the loan itself as agreed initially, the bank may be willing to advance more.

STAGE 3: Balance Sheet adjusted for the new loans and the retention of profits. Assume the bank grants CD a loan of £10,000.

The firm has made a profit as it has been trading. Assume that this amounted to £20,000 and that the dividends paid to the shareholders amounted to £5,000. Tax took another £5,000 and the balance of £10,000 was reinvested, or ploughed back into the business. The Balance Sheet now looks like that shown in Figure 11.3.

ASSETS	
Store	£5,000
Cash	£35,000
	£40,000
LIABILITIES	
Loan	£10,000
NET ASSETS	£30,000
CAPITAL AND RESERVES	
Shares	£20,000
Retained profits	£10,000
	£30,000

Figure 11.3 Balance Sheet for CD plc as at 12th May 1992

CD is now in a much better position. It has some cash, but must not forget it has to service its loans. Observe again that 'Capital and Reserves' balance the 'Net Assets' being used in the business.

Some more detailed examples follow. In a full Balance Sheet for an operating business the assets are divided between fixed and current assets.

Fixed assets (fixed capital)

Fixed assets that have been bought for a long-term use are valuable items in a firm, and are not consumed in the trading process. Examples of fixed assets include: land, buildings, plant and machinery, furniture and fittings, vehicles, electrical and other services distribution equipment and even computers. As shall be seen later, they wear out with use, and their value is reduced slowly, or depreciated, through the process known as depreciation.

Current assets (working capital)

Current assets are assets used in a firm's day-to-day trading activities. They include: cash, stocks of raw materials, finished goods and even partly finished goods, and debtors, i.e. the money owed to the company by firms or retail customers who have not paid their accounts with the business. Another example of a Balance Sheet follows.

STAGE 4: CD has now spent £5,000 on vehicles, £1,000 on furniture and fittings, and has £5,000's worth of tapes in stock. It is also owed £1,000 as the result of a credit sale, .ie. it sold some tapes on the understanding that they would be paid for in three months' time. One month's credit, or 28 days, is considered absolutely normal in business and hardly rates as credit. However, the firm itself owes £500 to its garage for service and fuel which it purchases on a credit account. (With this type of account the business takes fuel and has work done as it needs it, but only gets a single account, or bill, each month. This will normally be paid in 28 days, so CD will have, on average, 1.5 months credit on these items.) The revised, up to date Balance Sheet is shown on Figure 11.4.

FIXED ASSETS	
Store	£5,000
Furniture and fittings	£1,000
Vehicles	£5,000
	£11,000
CURRENT ASSETS	
Stocks	£5,000
Debtors	£1,000
Cash	£23,500
	£29,500
TOTAL ASSETS	£40,500
LIABILITIES	
Loan	£10,000
Creditors	£500
	£10,500
NET ASSETS	£30,000
CAPITAL AND RESERVES	
Shares	£20,000
Retained Profits	£10,000
	£30,000

Figure 11.4 Balance Sheet for CD plc as at 23rd October 1992

The cash has been reduced by the purchase of the assets. Liabilities have increased by £500 as this bill will have to be paid eventually. Cash is further reduced by £1,000 being the amount of money owed to the business. CD has, effectively used its own money to fund this purchase. When the account is paid the cash entry will rise by £1,000, but the debt will be cancelled. Again, this is a double entry.

Why is the cash balance £23,500 not £23,000? It is the £500 that appears in Liabilities as Creditors. £500's worth of Stocks have not been paid for. CD still has this cash in its bank, or cash box. Not too difficult to follow provided each change is analysed carefully, and the account prepared slowly and

methodically. Remember the principle of double-entry-bookeeping.

The Balance Sheet is all about assets and liabilities, about cash, about credits and debits, about retained profits and shareholdings. This is very simple, in principle, but there are dangers ahead if one is not careful. Work through Case Study 11.1.

CASE STUDY 11.1

College Dynamics goes public

Extract from *Financial Telegraph* of 25 May 1989

After 10 years successful trading CD Ltd has decided to *go public*. It is to become a plc and is offering shares to the general public to finance a major expansion of its *manufacturing base* in the UK. Shares will be on sale on 15th July 1989, and the public may apply for shares using the application forms in the *Prospectus*. CD Ltd hopes to raise £300 million this way. Examination of the accounts and forecasts in the prospectus indicates that the offer price of 30p, which represents an initial premium of 10p, is very favourable, and a level of *over-application* is probable.

CD Ltd needed money for the purchase of fixed assets – some land in a *development area* in South Wales, its investment there, including a factory and office buildings, the plant and equipment within them, warehouses, roads and services, the purchase of stocks of all types, cars and vans, and furniture and fittings.

CD list the following purchases in the prospectus:

Land £5 million, Vehicles £3 million, Work in progress £20 million, Plant and equipment £180 million,

Raw materials £50 million, Furniture and fittings £5 million, Finished goods £100 million,

Packing materials £30 million, Buildings £75 million, Services £25 million.

They also predict a level of creditors of £7 million, and a level of debtors of £300 million. Cash is predicted at £10 million.

Questions and activities

1. Explain the term in *italics*.
2. Prepare a schedule of assets, dividing them clearly between fixed and current assets.
3. What additional information would you need to be able to complete the Balance Sheet for the date in question?

Examine the full Balance Sheet reproduced as Figure 11.5.

This is how they look in the Annual Reports of most UK companies. Get hold of some yourself; they are free! Just write to the Registrar's Department at the Head Office of the Plc of your choice and ask for a copy of their most recent annual report and accounts. An analysis of the accounts of many well-known firms will reveal a new term. They will talk about consolidated accounts.

Consolidated accounts

Many businesses are made up of a series of subsidiary companies, all owned by a common parent.

This parent, or holding company as it is called, presents a report that is the result of adding together, or consolidating all the individual reports from its subsidiaries. The consolidated report, or group report, then represents the activity of the company as a whole. When the accounts of the Unilever Group is examined it is the sum of many individual subsidiary reports. There may be a problem sometimes when subsidiaries operate in many countries. The individual accounts now have to be converted to a common currency. This problem is beyond A-Level, though.

'Current assets less Current liabilities', or 'Net current assets' is the firm's working capital. This is a very important sum for a company, and a lack of

	1992	1991
	£m	£m
FIXED ASSETS		
Tangible	293	300
Investments	7	0
CURRENT ASSETS	300	300
Stocks	200	80
Debtors	300	260
Investments	50	50
Cash	10	10
	560	400
CREDITORS: AMOUNT FALLING DUE		
WITHIN ONE YEAR. (Current Liabilities)		
Borrowing	(150)	(150)
Trade creditors	(50)	(50)
	(200)	(200)
NET CURRENT ASSETS	360	200
TOTAL ASSETS LESS CURRENT LIABILITIES	660	500
CREDITORS: AMOUNTS FALLING DUE		
AFTER MORE THAN 1 YEAR		
Borrowings	(100)	(90)
PROVISIONS FOR LIABILITIES AND CHARGES	(10)	(10)
	(110)	(100)
	550	400
CAPITAL AND RESERVES		
Called up share capital	300	200
Share premium account	100	100
Profit & Loss Account	150	100
	550	400

Figure 11.5 College Dynamic plcs, Balance Sheet as at 31st December 1992, i.e. the forecast balance sheet after one year's trading

working capital will cause really serious problems for a business. This was examined in the section on cash flow. Do you remember what overtrading is, and how it can force a firm into closure? (See Chapter 4.)

A real Balance Sheet will always give two 'pictures' of the company. It will give two Balance Sheets separated by one year so that a comparison can be made. In this case it is for 1991 and 1992, or rather 'as at 31st December' for both years.

There is an entry under 'Fixed assets' for 'Investments', and another in 'Current assets'. The difference between the two is the length, or likely duration of the investment. Many firms do not just trade, but also buy small quantities of shares of other firms. (less than 50%, otherwise they would have bought the company. Remember the fuss when Hanson bought a stake in ICI). This is done as an investment, with the objective of earning money from it. Other investments may be bank deposits which earn interest. Government bonds might also be purchased. The firm may also buy a plot of land, with the objective of selling it much later at a profit. These all go into the Balance Sheet as fixed assets if they are considered as long-term investments, e.g. a land purchase, the purchase of a valuable painting, or as current assets if they are short-term investments. A bank account with money available when required, or 'on call', would be an example.

In the liabilities section, the loans or borrowings are now shown in two parts, those which are short-term and will have to be repaid within a year, and those which are long-term and will not be repaid within 12 months. Remember, when a firm delays paying its bills, the firm or person who is owed this money is, effectively, lending the business money. Some loans in the section may be really long term, and not require repayment for say 10 years. Long-term loans may become part of the capital employed in the business. Where will CD have got all this capital from?

Basically it will come from three sources: the shareholders, organised long-term loans, and 'loans' from the suppliers to the firm. The latter is money that CD will owe to its suppliers, it will be credit negotiated and taken from them, often at no interest. The firm will 'pay in 90 days' means that it will have a free loan for that period of time. Knowing this, the supplier may have adjusted the price, however, so watch purchasing terms and price carefully. There is a clear interdependency again here.

Capital is split into two categories, therefore.

Equity capital

Equity is the capital belonging to the ordinary and preference shareholders. It includes issued share capital, reserves and profit retained in the company. The shareholders will be rewarded with a payment called a dividend, based on the profit the firm makes.

Loan capital

Finance that has been borrowed and not obtained from shareholders, is loan capital. The firm has to pay interest, regardless of how it performs.

One difference may have sprung to mind already. Equity capital has to be rewarded with a dividend only when a profit is made, and the dividend is related to the profit, i.e. the greater the profit made by the firm, the larger the dividend the shareholders might expect. Loan capital, however, has to be paid for each year through the payment of interest. There is no link to profit, however. If a firm makes no profit it has to pay the interest due somehow. Failure to do so could result in the business going bankrupt. Maximising the amount of share capital might be a good objective, therefore. Let us look at the structure of CD's capital, or its capital structure. A firm will publish a set of notes with its Balance Sheet that gives these details. The appropriate note for CD plc to accompany the Balance Sheet for 31st December 1992 is reproduced as Figure 11.6.

EQUITY CAPITAL
Share Capital:

Ordinary Shares (1,000 million shares at 20p/share)	£200 million
Preference Shares (500 million shares at 20p/share. 8%)	£100 million
Share Premium Account (1,000 million shares at 10p/share)	£100 million
Retained Profits (from P&L Account)	£150 million
LOAN CAPITAL	
Bank loans: Secured against Mortgages	£100 million
Unsecured	£120 million
Bank overdrafts	£20 million

Figure 11.6 *Extract from notes of CD plc's accounts. Note 10: capital structure as at 31st December 1992*

Equity capital is the money raised by the firm from its shareholders. This includes the money directly invested by the shareholders in return for the shares, and also the profits retained in the business over the years. Since the profits of a business really belong to the shareholders they have to be shown as a part of equity capital. The CD plc note shows ordinary shares, preference shares and a share premium account. What does this mean?

Ordinary shares

As the name implies ordinary shares are the most common shares of the company. Each share carries a vote, so the owner is part of the executive of the firm. Dividends are paid on the shares, but the amount is variable. In a profitable year the dividend may be expected to be high, but may be non-existent in a very bad year.

Preference shares

Special shares that carry a fixed rate of interest, or a fixed dividend. This will be a percentage of the face value, in this case 8% of 20p, so each shareholder must be paid a dividend of 1.6p each year, regardless

of profits. They are called preference shares because the owner has to be paid the dividend before any ordinary shares are paid a dividend, and also has to repay the face value of the share if the firm goes bankrupt in preference to ordinary shares after all other debts have been paid. Thus, there is less risk for the owner. The price paid for reducing the risk is the fact that the shares carry no voting rights. Preference shareholders are not part of the executive at all, simply money providers.

Share premium account

CD plc is a going concern and has a history for all to see. It has been profitable, and is predicting that it will continue to be and will probably improve. The ordinary shares are seen by the market as a good investment, so CD plc predicts that investors will pay more for them than their face value. This difference is known as the share premium. Why pay it? Consider the alternative: to invest, say, in a bank. If the interest paid here is 10%, and the forecast dividend to be paid by CD represents say 15% on the price actually paid, then the premium is justified. An example to clarify this: CD plc shares have a face value of 10p but are being offered at 20p, i.e. twice their nominal or face value. Current interest rate available from the bank for equivalent investments is 10%. The CD prospectus predicts dividends of 3p per share.

Price per share = 20p, Dividend per share = 3p, Equivalent rate of interest = 3/20 = 15%, which is better than the bank rate. A good buy.

Long-term loans

Long-term loans are defined as those of one year or more.

A bank loan is a sum of money advanced to the borrower, in this case CD, for a fixed period, at an agreed rate of interest. It is often paid back on a monthly basis, but, equally, may not have to be repaid until the period is up. If the terms of the loan are followed, the bank cannot ask for it to be repaid early.

Loans will normally be for a set period and will carry interest. This interest may be fixed or variable. An example: £10,000 over five years at 12%. Interest paid monthly.

The firm has borrowed the sum for five years, and must pay interest monthly at a rate of 12%. Since no capital will be repaid until the five years is up, it knows it will have to pay £100 per month to the lender. Example: £100,000 over 10 years at 2% over bank rate.

The government effectively sets the minimum rate of interest in the country by setting the bank rate. This is the rate that banks charge between themselves, and is set by the Bank of England. This loan is set at 2% above this, so if the bank, or base rate was 10% the firm would pay 12%. If the rate rose to 20% then the firm would have to pay 22% now. The firm knows when it will have to repay the loan, but not how much interest it will have to pay, therefore.

Loans may be secured or unsecured. If a loan is secured, then the firm will have put up some security, i.e. will have to lodge with the lender some item of value that will be given up if the terms of the loan are broken. An example of a secured loan is a mortgage on the firm's property, where its assets, or, in some cases, the private property (houses) of the directors would be the security needed. In this case the ownership of the property flows to the lender. (If a house owner fails to keep paying a mortgage loan, the building society will take possession of the house and evict the old owner.) Remember the problems of being a sole trader or a member of a partnership? Other forms of security could be shares, or works of art. Firms prefer unsecured loans, but banks want security. The relative amounts of secured and unsecured loans advanced to a company is an indication of its standing, or credit worthiness.

Short-term loans

Short-term loans are loans of less than one year, and also overdrafts. Short-term loans may be of a similar nature – secured or unsecured, fixed or floating interest rate – but the overdraft is the preferred method for short-term lending.

An overdraft is a *facility*, not a loan as such. The firm may draw money against its accounts, and go 'into the red' to a sum equal to the agreed overdraft limit. An overdraft is cheap, the bank just charges a fee, then interest on the money actually 'borrowed'. The rate of interest will usually be lower than a fixed term loan. It has a time limit, though, and the bank can call it in at any time without notice. It can be risky. Consider the following examples: £10,000 overdraft, 12% interest. Valid for six months.

Any overdraft, or money borrowed from the bank, has to be repaid at the end of the six months, i.e. the account has to be back in credit. At the end of the time the firm is still £3,000 overdrawn. It has to renegotiate another overdraft, or get a loan from somewhere. Here is another example: A firm has an overdraft limit of £5,000 and has drawn its account down to £3,000.

The Bank of England put a squeeze on the banks, so the bank asks the firm to reduce its overdraft to £1,500 at once. The firm has to do this, presenting it with a real problem. Since it has an overdraft it is unlikely to have the cash available. It will have to sell an asset fast, or raise the money another way.

There are other ways of raising finance for a business than borrowing from a bank. Types and sources of capital will be examined in more detail elsewhere in the book.

Here is a summary, and definition:

A Balance Sheet is an accounting statement showing the net assets (the items of value) held by a firm, and the sources of its finances at a point in time. It shows the financial position of the business at this point in time.

It has little value on its own, however, and one needs the remaining documents, at least, before any real conclusions can be drawn about the business concerned. So the Balance Sheet gives a partial answer to the first question that is being asked.

The Trading and Profit and Loss Account

A Profit and Loss Account is a report on the profitability of a business over a period of time. This period is usually the firm's financial year, but may be some other period. Thus it differs from a Balance Sheet, which you will remember is a report 'at a point in time'. A Profit and Loss Account should always state 'For period from x to y' or 'For year ended z', where x, y and z are dates. The Profit and Loss Account examines how a business has used its capital employed to generate sales and sales revenue, and compares this with the costs involved in their production and sales, to produce the firm's profit for the period. Capital employed is covered in the Balance Sheet, but there are some other key words in this sentence which must be clearly understood:

Profit

Profit is probably one of the most misunderstood words in common use in business. It is an accounting concept, and can be defined as:

Profit is the difference between the proceeds from the sale of a good or service, and all the costs incurred in producing that good or service.

This simple definition ignores the effect of the timing of the receipt of the money from the sale, or the paying of any of the costs incurred in making the item or service that is sold. This is absolutely correct, since profit ignores any credit given or taken. What does this mean? Examine the following simple examples (Case Studies 11.2–11.6).

CASE STUDY 11.2

CD, when it first started, bought compact discs for £5 and sold them to the public for £12 each. On a particular day it bought and sold 100 tapes for cash.

Sales revenue = 100 x £12 = £1,200

Cost of sales = 100 x £5 = £500

Profit = £(1,200 - 500) = £700.

Cash, or money in the till = £700 at the end of the day. This is then put into the bank.

CASE STUDY 11.3

Next day, CD sells the same number of tapes for cash, but manages to buy them on credit. It will pay for them the next day.

Sales Revenue = 100 x £12 = £1,200

Cost of Sales = £500, but the bill is not paid, i.e. No cash actually paid out.

Profit, which ignores any credit arrangements = £700

Cash in till = £1,200

CASE STUDY 11.4

On the third day CD still sells 100 tapes, but this time on credit. The buyers will pay for them the next day.

Sales Revenue = £1,200, but payment will not be made until tomorrow, i.e. No revenue actually received.

Cost of Sales = £500. Cash actually paid = £1,000 since the account from yesterday is to be cleared.

Profit = £700

Cash in till = (£1,000). The accountant for CD will have had to go to the bank to get cash!

CASE STUDY 11.5

The fourth day. No sales are made, but the buyers from yesterday pay their bills.

Sales Revenue = £0, but £1,200 is received from old customers.

Cost of Sales = £0

Profit = £0

Cash in Till = £1,200

CASE STUDY 11.6

The Accounts for the four days work.

Sales = 300 CDs = 300 x £12 = £3,600

Purchases = 300 CDs

Cost of Sales = £5 x 300 = £1,500

Profit = £3,600 – £1,500 = £2,100

No bills to be paid to or by the firm.

Cash in Till = £2,100

The important point to observe is that cash in a business does not mean profit, and that cash flow and profit are totally different concepts. As shown above, a firm can have profit, but no cash, or a good cash position but no profit. Thus a better definition of profit is:

Profit is the difference between the income received from the sale of a good or service, and all the costs associated in its production and sale, assuming that all accounts have been paid.

The difference between profit and cash flow has been covered earlier in this book, but is worth repeating. It is the lack of cash that forces firms into bankruptcy, not usually a lack of profit. As is illustrated in the cases above, CD was cash rich on Day 4, but if the bank would not let the accountant have £1,000 on Day 3 the firm would have had to close down then and would never have reached Day 4. However, CD was profitable, according to the definition, for all four days.

Sales revenue

It should now be clear what sales revenue is. It is the money earned by a business when it sells its goods or services. For a single product it is simply the product of the number of units sold in a period multiplied by its price. For the more common multi-product business, then, the product of sales x price must be worked out for each product, and then the whole series added up, e.g. CD sells 10,000 CDs for £15 each in a week, as well as 15,000 prerecorded tapes at £8 each and 20,000 at £3 each blank tapes. Its weekly sales revenue is:

CDs 10,000 x £15 = £150,000
Prerecorded tapes = 15,000 x 8 = £120,000
Blank tapes = 20,000 x £3 = £60,000
Total sales revenue = £330,000 per week

So, sales revenue can be defined as:

Sales revenue is the total value of the sales of a business, in money terms, for a given period.

Note that this will be the same as consumers' expenditure, this being the amount of money spent by the consumers on a particular company's products.

The profit will be found by first adding up all the sales made. Then all the costs will be added up, and subtracted from the sales revenue to give the profit or loss. Remember, if costs exceed revenue, a loss will be made. This calculation is standardised in the

SALES	XXX
Cost of sales	–XXX
GROSS PROFIT	= XXX
Other costs of the business	–XXX
TRADING PROFIT	= XXX
Other income	+ XXX
PROFIT ON ORDINARY ACTIVITIES BEFORE TAX	= XXX
Profit/Corporation tax	– XXX
PROFIT ON ORDINARY EXPENSES AFTER TAX	= XXX
Extraordinary items	+ or – XXX
PROFIT ATTRIBUTABLE TO SHAREHOLDERS (1)	= XXX
Dividends	– XXX
PROFIT RETAINED FOR YEAR	= XXX

Figure 11.7 Layout for a Profit and Loss Account

layout of the Profit and Loss Account. This has to conform to a set layout (see Figure 11.7).

Some further definitions before the construction of a Trading and Profit and Loss Account is investigated.

Cost of sales

'Cost of sales' can be rewritten as the 'Cost of the goods that have been sold'. Only the product that is actually sold is included. Materials held in stock, for any reason, will not be included here at all. Stocks absorb the cash of a business, and may cause cash flow problems, but have no effect on the profit made, nor the profitability of the concern.

Subject to the qualification above, this is the costs incurred in producing the product. If the business is a selling company, such as Sainsbury's, then the cost of sales is the total amount of money J. Sainbury pays to its suppliers for the goods it will resell, e.g. it is the sum of all the monies paid to Heinz, Lever Brothers, Cadbury's, Kelloggs, Nestlé, etc., for all the goods it buys.

If the company actually makes something itself, like Heinz, then its cost of sales is the money it spends to make the product. It does not include the selling costs, nor the firms administration expenses. For this type of business, the cost of sales is virtually the same as the firm's direct cost of production. (If the semi-directs are included then the match is even better.)

Other costs

The 'Other costs' include distribution costs, marketing expenditure, administration and a general category known as 'other expenses'. For a firm like Sainsbury's this is the costs it incurs over and above the cost of buying the goods that are sold, i.e. it is the cost of running all the stores, plus all the money spent on advertising, etc. For a manufacturing firm it is the costs to the firm for marketing and selling the product.

Separating these cost may not be strictly necessary, but it does give an analysis, or other interested party, a way of seeing how well a firm actually operates. A very efficient firm will be able to show a high level of both gross and trading profit.

Other income

Businesses earn money from various sources other than trading. It may have money in the bank that earns interest, or it may be able to invest its sales revenue on the 'Overnight market', i.e. a part of the money market in London where a firm can lend a large sum of money literally overnight. This would not be considered as part of the firms 'normal business', so should not be part of trading profit.

What 'Other income' is depends on the firm concerned. For a manufacturing company it would be investment operations, but for a bank it would be any selling of items they did.

Extraordinary items

Occasionally firms have to do things on an emergency basis, or take actions on a 'one off', basis. These are separated from the normal activities of the business. Some examples follow:

Example 1. Because of a depression in the economy as a whole, CD has to make 10% of its labour force redundant. It offers very generous terms. The costs here are considered as 'extraordinary' and should not be allowed to disguise the firm's trading performance. Separate them, and this can be done. In this case the profit of the company would not be lowered artificially, i.e. CD has a trading profit of £1,000,000, but has paid out £800,000 in the form of a 'one off' redundancy payment to staff. The records show the trading profit as £1 million, show the extraordinary item of (£800,000) and a final profit of £200,000.

Example 2. CD sells a piece of land it does not want to a property developer. It gets £1 million for the plot in a year when it makes only £100,000 trading profit. The firm is not a land development business, so the account will show a 'Trading profit' of £100,000, an 'Extraordinary item' of £1 million,

and a final 'Profit attributable to shareholders' of £1.1 million.

The method of accounting is aimed at giving the shareholder, buyer, or any interested person a true, undistorted picture of the efficiency of a business. The distorting effect of extraordinary items is eliminated by having to declare them.

How does a Profit and Loss Account develop? Follow the examples in the next series of cases.

Example 3. The first month's operation is over. This week is all expenditure. (A business usually has to spend before it can get any revenue, let alone profit.) It buys some product, £10,000 worth, and spends another £10,000 on administration and selling. The resulting Profit and Loss Account is recorded as Figure 11.8.

SALES	0
Cost of sales	0
GROSS PROFIT	= 0
Other Costs of the business	10
TRADING PROFIT	= –10
PROFIT ON ORDINARY ACTIVITIES BEFORE TAX	= –10
Profit/Corporation tax	0
PROFIT ON ORDINARY EXPENSES AFTER TAX	= –10
Extraordinary items	+ or – 0
PROFIT ATTRIBUTABLE TO SHAREHOLDERS (1)	= –10
Dividends	0
PROFIT RETAINED FOR YEAR	= –10

Figure 11.8 *College Dynamics plc, Profit and Loss Account, week ended 1st August 1992 (units – £000s)*

Since CD has made no sales it cannot have any 'Cost of sales' either. The £10,000 of stock just does not show on the Profit and Loss Account. It will have reduced its Cash Account, but more of this very soon. (This is why there are three accounts to consider, these two and the Cash Flow Statement.) So far so good. CD has made a loss of £10,000. No tax to pay yet, it is not the end of the financial year. Earnings per share, if they were calculated, would be negative – not good news for the shareholders.

Example 4. The second month's operation. CD plc now sell £30,000 of CDs, so there now is some 'Cost of sales'. They purchase another £10,000 of stock, though, and spend another £5,000 on selling and administration. They are also able to sell some old equipment that was left in the offices they rent. This is a 'one off' exceptional item, and raises £50,000.

It buys CDs for £5 and sell them for £15 each. The account now for the two-week period is recorded as Figure 11.9.

So CD has made a profit of £55,000 in the period. It is clear, though, that this largely comes from the 'Extraordinary item', so this cannot be taken as a normal period. It explains nothing about the amount of money the firm is using, as it ignores the money spent on stocks.

SALES	30
Cost of sales	−10
GROSS PROFIT	20
Other costs of the business	−15
TRADING PROFIT	5
Other Income	0
PROFIT ON ORDINARY ACTIVITIES BEFORE TAX	5
Profit/corporation tax	−0
PROFIT ON ORDINARY EXPENSES AFTER TAX	5
Extraordinary items	50
PROFIT ATTRIBUTABLE TO SHAREHOLDERS (1)	55
Dividends	0
PROFIT RETAINED FOR YEAR	55

Figure 11.9 College Dynamics plc, Profit and Loss Account, week ended 1st August 1992 (units – £000s)

Now consider a Profit and Loss Account for CD plc for a full year. First, though, here is another warning about the report, and another area where costs have to be calculated carefully.

Annual profit is the difference between the revenue from the sales of items sold during the year, and all the costs associated with the manufacture and sale of these goods only. One does not include the cost of things bought for use next year, nor any money received from sales made last year. Watch, therefore, the flow of credit payments by the firm and its customers. Materials bought on credit by the firm must be included if they have been used in products that have been sold, even though the cash has not been paid out. Equally, money coming into the firm for products or services sold in the previous year must be excluded. Watch items like rentals, also. Firms rent space, plant and equipment, and some services. The Profit and Loss Account for a year must include only the sums for the period under consideration. Here is an example:

Example 5. CD rents, or leases as it is sometimes called, a warehouse in Felixstow, the port through which it receives most of its imports. The rental is charged on a quarterly basis, is paid in advance, and is subject to regular review. The rates for the last five quarters are as follows:

Quarter   *1 2 3 4 5*
Rental (£000s) *10 12 12 12 16*

CD's financial year is such that a years extends from mid-quarter 1 to mid-quarter 5.

Rental paid in the financial year = £(12 + 12 + 12 + 16) = £52,000
Rental charged to the Profit and Loss Account for the financial year = £(0.5)(10) + 12 + 12 + 12 + (0.5)(15) = £49,000

A reminder: the Profit and Loss Account simply follows a natural process for working out profit. It starts with sales, deducts all the costs associated with its production and sale to get profit. It then deducts tax and arrives at the profit belonging to the owners, the shareholders. The firm decides what it will do with this, and states this at the end of the report. The report for CD plc published in its Prospectus was as shown in Figure 11.10.

	1992	1991
	£m	£m
SALES	1,500	1,200
Cost of sales	(750)	(600)
GROSS PROFIT	750	600
Distribution costs, including marketing	(350)	(300)
Administration expenses	(150)	(100)
Other expenses	(70)	(50)
	(570)	(450)
TRADING PROFIT	180	150
Net interest paid	(10)	(10)
PROFIT ON ORDINARY ACTIVITIES BEFORE TAX	170	140
Profit/corporation tax	(40)	(35)
PROFIT ON ORDINARY EXPENSES AFTER TAX	130	105
Extraordinary items	(0)	5
PROFIT ATTRIBUTABLE TO SHAREHOLDERS	130	110
Dividends	(80)	(45)
PROFIT RETAINED FOR YEAR	50	75

Figure 11.10 College Dynamics plc, Profit and Loss Account, week ended 31st December 1992, i.e. forecast profit after one year's trading

Notice a new convention that has been used here. All inflows of money are shown without brackets, but all outflows are shown in brackets. If the firm had made a loss in the year concerned, then its 'Profit' would have been shown in brackets also.

As the report covers a year, tax has been deducted. These will vary from time to time, but are the firms equivalent to an individuals income tax. CD is proposing to pay out £60 million in dividends to ordinary shareholders, and is to retain only £70 million in the business that year.

The Profit and Loss Account is obviously about profits, while the Balance Sheet is about capital employed in a business and its sources. Do these two reports link together at all? There is one entry which is common to both, and only one, 'Retained profits'. The 'Profit retained for year' above, £70 million should be reflected in the Balance Sheet. Since the Balance Sheet is a 'snapshot' at a point of time, the increase between the value of retained profits at the two points in time should be the same as the retained profits in the Profit and Loss Account. Check to see that it is.

This looks very simple, and deceptively easy. Again there are potential dangers, often associated with valuations once more. Things might not be what they seem!

It is now possible to say more about the company. It is possible to see the trading profit, and get some idea how efficiently it is being operated. Its financial strength is indicated in the Balance Sheet, so it is possible to start to see how well the funds invested are being used. It is still very difficult to see what is happening to the cash position. (An analyst could examine carefully the details about interest paid, but any conclusions would be very approximate.) It has been necessary to have both the Balance Sheet and the Profit and Loss Account to be able to come to this situation. The potential shareholders are now able to make some decisions, but still need the third report to be able to make reliable decisions.

The Cash Flow Statement

The importance of cash flow to a business was clearly demonstrated earlier in the book. Since it is so critical, shareholders are entitled to a report about the cash position of the business. The key 'in house' document produced is the Cash Flow Forecast, and is used for forward planning. Its equivalent report for public use is the Funds Flow Statement, but this is a 'historic' document, and looks backwards. It reports on the way that the firm has generated and used its funds, how prudent but at the same time how efficient it has been. The statement answers three basic questions.

1. Where did the firm get money from during the financial year in question?
2. Where did the money go to during this year? (How was it used, or spent?)
3. What was the overall effect of all these transactions on the firm's balance sheet and financial health? (What has happened to the firm's borrowings? Is the firm in a satisfactory state of liquidity?)

The Funds Flow Statement attempts to answer these questions, and refers to changes over a year. It reports on a whole year, like the Profit and Loss Account. It is not a 'snapshot' picture, as the Balance Sheet is. A Funds Flow Statement must include 'for period from x to y', where x and y are dates.

The main sources of money for a firm during a year are:

Sales

This is a source of funds only if the goods or services are actually paid for. Supermarkets get virtually all their income from sales at once as cash or near cash (cheques or credit cards). A manufacturing company will often have to wait for its cash. Sixty or even ninety days is not an unusual time to wait, especially if the money is due from a large, important customer. This is one of the problems of size. The small firm will have no power, so will have to pay quickly. It will find it impossible to put pressure on large customers, so will have to wait, or not get the sale at all. The major supermarket chains, and store chains are very powerful here, and can effectively write their own terms.

Debtors

They owe the firm money, and it becomes a source of funds when they actually pay up. Take the two sources together and one can see a picture where the sales, in Profit and Loss Account form, bear little relation to the picture shown by the Cash Flow Statement. One can imagine a position where there are physical sales in one year, on a year's credit, so no actual money is received. In the next year, where there are no new sales, for instance, but there is a strong inflow of money from (previous) sales. This could be the situation, or nearly so, with say an aircraft manufacturer who experiences a sudden downturn in sales.

Shareholders

Shareholders can be asked to put in more cash. They can be offered new shares at an attractive price.

This would be a Rights Issue, and would only be used occasionally. Remember, the firm gets no income when shares are sold on the stock markets of the world. These markets deal in second-hand shares only. The company only gets the income when new shares are sold.

Selling assets

A business would be wise to sell any assets it no longer requires, or are becoming too expensive to maintain. It is common for firms to sell redundant fixed assets such as old plant, unused buildings, etc., as well as motor vehicles. It is sometimes better to sell a plant and replace it by a more efficient one, or one which is cheaper to operate. This income would be irregular, and not relevant to trading profit.

Loans

These may be either long or short term. It is a very common way of raising funds, until the 'credit' of a firm runs out.

Creditors

By not paying bills a business is keeping money in its books, and it is available to be spent on other things. It is a source of funds. Note the problems illustrated under Debtors. The businesses which are most likely to need money, young expanding ones with exciting new products, are the very ones unlikely to be allowed such 'credit.'

Selling from stock

If the item sold is already made and in a store or warehouse, it will cost nothing more to make. When sold the money tied up in such stocks will be released. These are sales generated without the need to pay for their manufacture. These goods are prepaid, in effect. Refer back to the section on the Profit and Loss Account. These are the purchases that were not recorded in that document because they were not sold.

This is clearest in the case of a shop. If it sells something from its shelves, then it gets the full retail value in the till, and has to pay nothing. If it has to order the item, then it may still get the sales revenue, but will now have to pay the supplier the wholesale price.

Depreciation

Depreciation is a difficult concept and needs to be studied very carefully.

A Balance Sheet records all the assets a firm has.

Its fixed assets have a life and are not directly consumed in production or operation. Some of these assets lose value with time, and this is accounted for through depreciation. The first thing to remember is that depreciation is an accounting concept, and is an allowance, not a bill or a charge.

How does it give rise to a positive flow of money to a firm? Start with the Balance Sheet. If some of the Fixed Assets lose value over a year, then this loss will have to be balanced by a loss or reduction in the supporting funds. Look at the example for CD in the section on Balance Sheets. Consider the effect of allowing for depreciation of some of the fixed assets that amounts to £20 million. There are no other changes. Look at Figure 11.11.

	1992	1991
	£m	£m
FIXED ASSETS		
Tangible	293	300
Investments	7	0
	300	300
CURRENT ASSETS		
Stocks	200	80
Debtors	300	260
Investments	50	50
Cash	10	10
	560	400
CREDITORS: AMOUNT FALLING DUE WITHINE ONE YEAR. (Current Liabilities)		
Borrowing	(150)	(150)
Trade creditors	(50)	(50)
	(200)	(200)
NET CURRENT ASSETS	360	200
TOTAL ASSETS LESS CURRENT LIABILITIES	660	500
CREDITORS: AMOUNTS FALLING DUE AFTER MORE THAN ONE YEAR		
Borrowings	(100)	(90)
PROVISIONS FOR LIABILITIES AND CHARGES	(10)	(10)
	(110)	(100)
	550	400
CAPITAL AND RESERVES		
Called up share capital	300	200
Share premium account	100	100
Profit & Loss Account	150	100
	550	400

Figure 11.11 *College Dynamics plc, Balance Sheet as at 31st December 1992, i.e. forecast Balance Sheet one year's trading*

The value of the 'Tangible fixed assets' must be reduced by £20 million to £273 million. Since there are no other changes, the 'Total assets less current liabilities' falls to £640 million. Since the 'Loans' and 'Provisions' have not changed, this must be balanced by a reduction in 'Capital and reserves'. Since the share capital and the share premium account cannot change unless the share issue is changed, this loss has to be absorbed out of 'Profit and Loss account'. In this case the transfer of profit will have to be reduced by £20 million. Now, examine the corresponding Profit and Loss Account.

If this has now got to show a profit reduced by £20 million, then the £20 million of depreciation has to be added as a cost. Unless it is shown separately, it will be included in 'Other expenses'. Remember, though, it is not an expense as such. The assets were bought some time ago, and CD does not get a bill for depreciation. It is a notional, or imaginary cost. Examine Figure 11.12 carefully.

	1992	1991
		(+ Depreciation)
	£m	£m
SALES	1,500	1,200
Cost of sales	(750)	(750)
GROSS PROFIT	750	750
Distribution costs, including marketing	(350)	(350)
Administration expenses	(150)	(150)
Other expenses	(70)	(90)
	(570)	(590)
TRADING PROFIT	180	160
Net interest paid	(10)	(10)
PROFIT ON ORDINARY ACTIVITIES BEFORE TAX	170	150
Profit/corporation tax	(40)	(40)
PROFIT ON ORDINARY EXPENSES AFTER TAX	130	110
Extraordinary items	(0)	(0)
PROFIT ATTRIBUTABLE TO SHAREHOLDERS	130	110
Dividends	(80)	(80)
PROFIT RETAINED FOR YEAR	50	30

Note: In fact tax would be reduced, but this is ignored at this stage.

Figure 11.12 College Dynamics plc, Profit and Loss Account, year ended 31st December 1992, i.e. forecast profit after one year's trading

Profit retained for the year is now reduced by the £20 million, the same as the amount of depreciation. The accountant is able to ignore effectively £20 million of its sales value. (Note that this has exactly the same effect on Retained Profits.) As a result CD has a source of £20 million. This is why depreciation

appears on the Funds Flow Statement, and is a source of funds.

The use of depreciation gives firms a source of cash, and reduces the amount of tax paid. Thus the Inland Revenue has an interest in depreciation and has to agree how a firm calculates it. CD cannot decide how it will calculate its own depreciation.

How is depreciation calculated? Which assets are considered to depreciate?

The calculation of depreciation

Consider a motor car, purchase price £12,000. After four years it is sold for £3,000. The car has lost value, £9,000, over the four years. It has depreciated by £9,000.

How it has lost this value, month by month, year by year, is a matter of debate. Accountants usually use one of two standard methods, straight line depreciation and reducing balance depreciation.

Straight line method

Value is assumed to be lost regularly and uniformly, the same amount each year. In the case of the car it would be equal to £9,000/4 or £2,250 per year. Plot this on a graph, and the 'straight line' is obvious. Look at Figure 11.13. It is very simple to work out, but it may not be realistic. Cars, for example, are known to lose value very rapidly at first. This is the reason behind the alternative method.

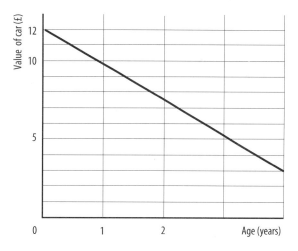

Figure 11.13 Straight line depreciation chart

Reducing balance method

A fixed percentage of the value of the car would be deducted each year. If 30% was deducted each year one arrives at almost the same residual value, e.g.:

Price new – £12,000. 1st year's depreciation charge = £12,000 x 0.3 = £3,600.

Value at start of 2nd year = £12,000 – £3,600 = £8,400. 2nd year's depreciation = £8,400 x 0.3 = £2,520.

Value at start of 3rd year = £8,400 – £2,520 = £5,880. 3rd year's depreciation = £5,880 x 0.3 = £1,764.

Value at start of 4th year = £5,880 – £1,764 = £4,116. 4th year's depreciation = £4,116 x 0.3 = £1,235.

Value at end of 4th year = £4,116 – £1,235 = £2,881.

A comparison is made in Table 11.1.

Table 11.1

Comparison of annual depreciation charges based on straight line and reducing balance methods

(Basis: Car value £12k reducing to £3k in 4 years) Units £s				
Year	1	2	3	4
Straight line method	2,250	2,250	2,250	2,250
Reducing balance method	3,600	2,520	1,764	1,235

The reducing balance method gives a greater deduction earlier. This means that a firm will get the maximum benefit from depreciation earlier. Whichever it selects, the firm must follow the Principle of consistency, and stick with it, and declare it in the Notes to the Accounts.

Thus there are two ways of calculating depreciation, straight line and reducing balance. Which items are depreciated in the accounts of a firm? They all are to be found in 'Fixed assets'.

Buildings
It is usually accepted that industrial buildings have a life of 40 years, and are depreciated over this period. Straight line methods are usually used, so are reduced in value by 2.5% per year. However, many industrial buildings are over 40 years old, but that does not matter.

Plant and machinery
This clearly wears out. Parts have to be replaced and, eventually, the entire equipment scrapped. Plant and machinery in this country is usually depreciated over 10 years using straight line methods. Other countries allow this equipment to be depreciated faster. This has the advantage that firms will be more ready to replace equipment with more modern and more efficient versions. Long life tends to encourage retention of old equipment. Couple this with the ability, if not desire, to keep old equipment going and one has the conditions for the generation of an outdated industrial base.

Motor vehicles
Four years' life is common for motor vehicles.

Furniture and fittings
This is very variable, but five years would not be unreasonable.

Depreciation was calculated per year in the above examples. It can be calculated per month, per day or even per machine hour if it is wanted. If an asset is purchased part way through a financial year, then depreciation will be included into the accounts for a part year initially.

A summary:

Depreciation is a charge, or allowance included in the accounts to reflect the fact that some fixed assets wear out with time and lose value. The effect of its inclusion is to increase the cash available to a firm in any given year.

Cash balances
Most firms will have cash in the bank and available to spend. While this is normally quite a small amount, and is of a working nature, sometimes large balances do build up. These are clearly available to the business at any time. Holding cash is not normally an objective of a company, though banks and building societies have, by law, to keep a set proportion of their funds as cash, or liquid reserves as they are called. Cash reserves are both good and bad news for a firm.

Thus it might be considered that there are nine sources of money, or cash, for a business during a year. Some of these are the direct result of the firms operation, and result directly from the firm's efficiency. Others may be considered as being of a non-trading nature. The split:

1. *Trading related sources:*
   - Sales
   - Debtors
   - Creditors
   - Selling from stock
   - Selling (unwanted) assets
   - Depreciation
2. *Non-trade related sources:*
   - Shareholders
   - Loans
   - Existing cash balances

The Funds Flow Statement follows this pattern. More of this a little later.

Funds tend to flow out of firms with even greater ease than they flow in. It is the responsibility of management to control this, and keep the business liquid. The major areas of spending are:

Operating expenses

Operating expenses are the spending on materials, services and people. In service industries, or labour intensive firms the wage bill can be a large majority of all expenses. This is largely the cost of the goods sold, particularly if the costs of stocks are shown separately.

Stock building

Stock building relates to the money spent making goods to go into store. Sometimes this is deliberate, other times it results from optimistic sales and production plans, or from the economy going into a decline unexpectedly. In the early 1990s the world economies all declined, and the UK economy was particularly slow in coming out of it. Stock building, at least initially, was an inevitable consequence of this.

Buying assets

The purchase of assets is a firm's spending on capital items like plant, cars, etc. This is known as capital expenditure. These assets may be for immediate business use, or may be as investments.

Buying a new business

Buying a new business is a special example of the purchase of assets. It is an area which is separated from this, though, because of its importance. Such purchases may be of a willing or unwilling partner. The firms would then have joined together either by agreed merger or hostile takeover.

Repayment of a loan

Repayment of a loan has to be done when the terms of the loan calls for it. It will consume cash, but the firm may extend the loan, or take out a new one to cover the first. The government frequently does this when its stocks reach maturity, it just issues a new bond.

Paying creditors

Creditors have to be paid sometimes! The effect on a business can be influenced by the speed at which they are paid.

Interest payments

Interest payments depend on both the size of the loans, and the rate of interest the lenders charge. They are therefore an unpredictable item. When interest rates rise this charge can rise to become a very large proportion of a company's expenditure. Since high interest rates normally indicate some economic problems, which will hit sales potential usually, a firm finds the effects of interest rates magnified – another example of interdependence.

Taxation

Taxation is an item of very high priority. Remember that a firm also acts as a tax collector for both the Inland Revenue and Customs and Excise, and will be holding Income Tax paid by its employees, National Insurance contributions as well as VAT included in its prices. These groups will not wait for their money, and failure to pay by the due date may lead to a firm's closure.

Dividend payments

These are paid at least annually. Some firms make quarterly or half yearly payments, i.e. they make interim payments and a final payment.

These also can be divided between normal business, trade related and non-trade related activities.

1. *Trade related:*
   - Operating expenses
   - Buying assets
   - Taxation
   - Stock building
   - Paying creditors
2. *Non-trade related:*
   - Buying new businesses
   - Dividend payments
   - Repayment of loans
   - Interest payments.

This largely answers the second key question asked of business. Put the two analyses together and derive a Funds Flow Statement, and there is an answer to the third question. This is illustrated below with a Funds Flow Statement for CD plc.

The statement follows a set format. It first identifies the sources, then analyses the uses of funds. Look at the report from CD that is reproduced in Figure 11.14. See how it is linked and related to the other two public accounts; another example of interdependence.

Thus, this report shows how College Dynamics plc has generated cash of £200 million during the year. This has not been enough, however, to fund the range of purchases and payments made during the same year, including the dividend of £60 million. The firm had to borrow a further £10 million to finance this. In effect, CD plc borrowed the money to pay part of the dividend.

	£m
SOURCE OF FUNDS	
Profit before Tax	180
Depreciation	20
USE OF FUNDS	
Increase/(Reduction) in working capital	(20)
Investment	(40)
Tax paid	(0)
Capital expenditure	
Dividends paid	
Reorganisation and other costs	(7)
	(67)
NET INFLOW/(OUTFLOW) FROM OPERATIONS	
Acquisition of businesses	100
	(33)
NET INFLOW/(OUTFLOW) OF FUNDS	
APPLIED TO/(FUNDED BY)	
Issue of shares	(60)
Short-term deposits and cash	(110)
Borrowings	(10)

Figure 11.14 *College Dynamics plc, Funds Flow Statement for year ended 31st December 1991*

An investor or shareholder can also examine the results of the firm's attempts to control stocks, creditors and debtors. Thus an answer to the third key question has been developed.

The interested party now has three reports available which give an indication of the efficiency and health of a business. These are the Balance Sheet, the Profit and Loss Account and the Funds Flow Statement. Why are there three documents? They all look at a company, but from a very different point of view. They tell the interested party different things. Their real value comes when they are considered together, or rather items from different reports are taken and combined as a ratio. Consider the profit made by a firm. Compare the profit with the value of sales value, or capital employed, and there is more information now, particularly suitable for inter-firm comparisons. This is ratio analysis, but more of this soon. Just how reliable are these documents? Each document has to be examined and discussed separately.

The accuracy of financial reports

The Balance Sheet
The Balance Sheet can be a very misleading document, and it has to be read very carefully, along with the notes attached to the account. The main problems occur over valuation of assets, and the inclusion of intangibles. Each will be looked at in turn.

Tangible assets
Accountants have attempted to reduce the problem, and have laid down some accounting principles that affect valuation policy in particular. These principles, or rules, are known as SSAPs – statements of standard accounting practice. These were met at the start of this chapter, but the most important ones are repeated below:

1. *Going concern.* It must be assumed that the business is a 'going concern', i.e. that it is and will go on trading.
2. *Consistency.* Accounts must be prepared using the same system of valuation each year.
3. *Prudence.* Do not assume sales, and value at the lower of any alternative. The meaning of this is best understood through an example.

A firm wants a car for its Chairman. The purchasing department buys a 'special edition' Jaguar at a price of £45,000. On the day of purchase it has an accounts value of £45,000. It is to be kept and used. However, if the firm was to close, and the car had to be sold, it would fetch much less: (a) because it is now second-hand, and (b) because the purchaser would know that the firm was in trouble.

The first SSAP states that it is valued at £45,000 as the business is a 'going concern'. It will lose value due to depreciation, an allowance for wear and tear,

	1992	1991
	£m	£m
FIXED ASSETS		
Tangible	**293**	300
Investments	**7**	0
	300	300
CURRENT ASSETS		
Stock	**200**	80
Debtors	**300**	260
Investments	**50**	50
Cash	**10**	10
	560	400
CREDITORS: AMOUNT FALLING DUE		
WITHIN ONE YEAR. (Current Liabilities)		
Borrowing	**(150)**	(150)
Trade creditors	**(50)**	(50)
	(200)	(200)
NET CURRENT ASSETS	**360**	200
TOTAL ASSETS LESS CURRENT LIABILITIES	**660**	500
CREDITORS: AMOUNTS FALLING DUE		
AFTER MORE THAN 1 YEAR		
Borrowings	**(100)**	(90)
PROVISIONS FOR LIABILITIES AND CHARGES	**(10)**	(10)
	(110)	(100)
	550	400
CAPITAL AND RESERVES		
Called up share capital	**300**	200
Share premium account	**100**	100
Profit & Loss Account	**150**	100
	550	400

Figure 11.15 College Dynamics plc, Balance Sheet as at 31st December 1992, i.e. the forecast Balance Sheet after one year's trading

furniture, etc. Many of these cause no valuation problems – they are taken into the account at their purchase price and then are depreciated on a regular, uniform basis. However, look again at land and buildings. Businesses may well own these for many years, and their value will change. Consider a plot of land upon which a firm has a factory. Land does not depreciate as such, so there is no entry under depreciation for it. Its value will rise and fall, though, but will tend to rise on a long-term basis. If it rises, should a firm revalue its assets? Just think about it. The Balance Sheet is supposed to show the worth of a business. If the land it has is undervalued, then so will the firm be. It may be likely to be bought then and its assets acquired at a low price. A firm may then sell the land and make a profit. (Remember the activities of conglomerates discussed in the Introduction. This is just what some firms look for.) So, revalue the assets when their values change significantly, adjust the Balance Sheet accordingly, and state that a revaluation exercise has been done in the Notes to the Accounts. How is this done, and what effect will it have?

Consider the Balance Sheet for CD plc again, now reproduced as Figure 11.15. Assume that CD has not revalued its assets for some time. It employs a firm of chartered surveyors to value its properties and they produce the summary that is published as Table 11.2. Thus CD would seem to be entitled to increase the value of its fixed assets by £60 million. In other words, it should raise its entry in the above account from £300m to £360m. It will then be able to charge itself more depreciation, at least on the buildings, and save some tax. First, though, the Balance Sheet. It does not balance now! A new entry has to be made, 'revaluation reserves'. This goes with the group 'Capital and reserves', and is illustrated as Figure 11.16.

Table 11.2

Report of CD's property portfolio as at 22nd June 1993 (basis: £ million)

	Present book value	Today's valuation
Land	10	30
Buildings	30	70
Total	40	100

The Balance Sheet is now back in balance. A new reserve has had to be created since there has been no changes in the shares, nor in the profit of the company. The Balance Sheet looks better, though, the company would be considered to have a 'stronger Balance Sheet'. It might be able to get bigger bank

but might also rise due to its uniqueness. The second SSAP says value it at the lower depreciated value. Be prudent and only use a higher value if it has actually been sold for this price. So the firm now only has to decide how it is going to depreciate the car over its life, and then publish its decision and stick to it.

A firm has to state in its report and accounts what accounting principles it has used in their preparation.

Any firm has a range of fixed assets that it uses as part of its normal business activities. These include land, buildings, plant and machinery, vehicles,

	1992	1992
	£m	£m
FIXED ASSETS		
Tangible	**353**	293
Investments	**7**	7
	360	300
CURRENT ASSETS		
Stock	**200**	200
Debtors	**300**	300
Investments	**50**	50
Cash	**10**	10
	560	560
CREDITORS: AMOUNT FALLING DUE		
WITHIN ONE YEAR. (Current Liabilities)		
Borrowing	**(150)**	(150)
Trade creditors	**(50)**	(50)
	(200)	(200)
NET CURRENT ASSETS	**360**	360
TOTAL ASSETS LESS CURRENT LIABILITIES	**720**	660
CREDITORS: AMOUNTS FALLING DUE		
AFTER MORE THAN 1 YEAR		
Borrowings	**(100)**	(100)
PROVISIONS FOR LIABILITIES AND CHARGES	**(10)**	(10)
	(110)	(110)
	610	550
CAPITAL AND RESERVES		
Called up share capital	**300**	300
Share premium account	**100**	100
Profit & Loss Account	**150**	150
Revaluation Reserve	**60**	0
	610	550

Figure 11.16 College Dynamics plc, Balance Sheet as at 31st December 1993, i.e. the forecast balance sheet after two year's trading and including the effects of an asset revaluation

loans on the strength of this, and thus put more cash into the business.

As was mentioned, this exercise has tax implications, so values and revaluations have to be approved by the authorities. Firms also do not want to revalue too often, but must not delay it too long lest they expose themselves to hostile takeover. When examining a Balance Sheet the basis and time of the valuation of assets should be noted.

Stocks of goods and materials also produce valuation problems, but these will be examined under Profit and Loss Accounts.

Intangible assets

Another major and growing problem area in Balance Sheets is the handling of intangibles. Two areas in particular give rise to trouble – goodwill and brand names.

Goodwill

When a business is bought, an element in the price represents goodwill. This is a sum of money added to the asset value of the business to cover things like its reputation, its strong customer base, its ability to make profits. Consider somebody selling a freehold pub. It has value as a property itself, then there is the value of the furniture and fittings, and the stock. It seems reasonable, though, to add something to reflect the takings that it is making. (You would expect to pay more for a busy pub, and definitely for a very profitable pub.) It is this premium over the tangible asset value that is called goodwill. Where can it go in the Balance Sheet, though? It is not a fixed asset, since it does not have a physical identity, so it must be an intangible. How is it valued? There is no formal method. The owner of the pub wants as much as can be got, the buyer wants to pay as little as possible. It will depend on the state of the market for pubs at the time, and also on the efficiency of the negotiations. It is like the value of a picture in many ways. It is worth whatever somebody will pay for it! Revert to the pub example. You pay the goodwill for the custom, then find all the customers follow the old owner to his new establishment. The goodwill has been lost. It was paid, though, so how should it be recorded?

In the UK, the concept of prudence has meant that goodwill, if paid, was usually written off (against retained profit and cash, or other reserve) in the year the asset was bought. There is a growing tendency, however, to include it as an intangible asset, and write it off slowly over the next few years. The former method, whilst being prudent, will weaken the Balance Sheet. The latter method may be accused of inflating the Balance Sheet and giving a false picture of the strength of the firm.

Look for the notes in a report; the policy on goodwill must be shown. Watch for any change in policy from one year to another. An example: during 1994 College Dynamics purchased a business that makes and sells specialist, high quality CD players. This example of *vertical integration* will strengthen CD plc's place in the compact disc market overall. The purchase price is agreed at £50 million, £10 million of which represents goodwill. (A 25% premium, in fact.) The premium was asked for by the firm, and negotiated and agreed by CD. It is the maximum value that CD put on the gains to be obtained from the merger.

College Dynamics plc
Balance Sheet as at end 1994

	Before Takeover	After Takeover	
		Writing off Goodwill	Capitalising Goodwill
FIXED ASSETS			
Tangible	600	640	640
Investments	10	10	10
Intangibles	0	0	10
	610	650	660
CURRENT ASSETS			
Cash	20	10	10
Others	720	720	720
	740	730	730
CREDITORS: SHORT TERM	(450)	(450)	(450)
NET CURRENT ASSETS	290	280	280
NET CURRENT ASSETS LESS			
CURRENT LIABILITIES	900	930	940
CREDITORS: LONG TERM	(170)	(210)	(210)
CAPITAL EMPLOYED	730	720	720
CAPITAL AND RESERVES			
Shares	300	300	300
Reserves (ex Profit & Loss Account)	430	420	430
	730	720	730

Figure 11.17 College Dynamics plc, Balance Sheet as at end 1994

What effect will it have if CD adopt the policy of capitalising goodwill rather than writing it off in the year of purchase? Examine the three Balance Sheets of CD plc reproduced in Figure 11.17.

CD plc is proposing to pay for the firm by using £10 million of its cash, and taking out further loans amounting to £40 million. When the £10 million has to be written off, an asset (cash) has been used without providing a compensating asset. To balance the accounts, an equivalent amount has to be removed from the Reserves.

Only a small change but a significant one. The lower figure generated by writing off the goodwill element is probably a truer picture of the value of CD plc now. The goodwill has been paid by CD plc, but would anybody else? It is prudent to write it off at once, and less misleading.

Brand names

Brand names, trade marks, patents, registered designs, etc., are obviously of value to the firm that owns them. If you wanted to sell hamburgers you would obviously gain a considerable advantage by calling your firm McDonald's. Since the name 'sells' burgers the name must be an asset, and have value.

True, but isn't the value already in the accounts – in the Profit and Loss account to be precise, under the entry entitled 'Sales'? Doesn't the name McDonald's sell burgers anyway? Recording it in the Balance Sheet as well as an asset seems dangerous and misleading. It looks like an example of 'double entry' in quite the wrong sense.

In spite of this, there is a growing tendency for firms to add such items to their Balance Sheets as Intangible Assets. Look carefully at the notes. The basis for the valuation is pure opinion, and insider opinion at that. It cannot be an unbiased estimate of the value. One would only really know its value if the firm owning it put it up for sale, with a guarantee of exclusivity, and saw what it actually sold for!

What happens if a firm decides to do this? What would happen if CD plc decided that its brand names had a value as intangible assets of £100 million? It would transform the Balance Sheet at a stroke. Assets would rise, but with no corresponding change in the liabilities. (Unlike goodwill, no money has actually changed hands over this, it is purely a book transaction.) Thus, since the capital employed will have risen by the £100 million, then the reserves must be increased accordingly. The firm will look stronger, it will have a better Balance Sheet, but nothing has really changed. Is this ethical? On the strength of the change, CD might find it easier to get further loans. A dangerous policy for the company, and eventually for the investors and shareholders. An example: CD plc decides to include its brand names in its accounts from the end of the 1993 financial year. How will the Balance Sheet change? CD assess the value of their brand names at £50 million. Examine Figure 11.18 very carefully to see the effect that this has.

This is an active topic within the business world in general, and accounting circles in particular. The basic convention of Prudence suggests that such items are excluded from the accounts. However, a growing number of companies are now including them as intangibles.

A deceptively simple document is becoming a little more difficult to read and understand. So far only reasonable adjustments have been made. The problem of Balance Sheets that have been deliberately adjusted is a totally different matter, and beyond the scope of A Level studies.

	1993	1993
	£m	£m
FIXED ASSETS		
Tangible	353	293
Investments	7	7
Intangibles	50	0
	410	300
CURRENT ASSETS		
Stock	200	200
Debtors	300	300
Investments	50	50
Cash	10	10
	560	560
CREDITORS: AMOUNT FALLING DUE		
WITHIN ONE YEAR. (Current Liabilities)		
Borrowing	(150)	(150)
Trade creditors	(50)	(50)
	(200)	(200)
NET CURRENT ASSETS	360	360
TOTAL ASSETS LESS CURRENT LIABILITIES	770	660
CREDITORS: AMOUNTS FALLING DUE		
AFTER MORE THAN 1 YEAR		
Borrowings	(100)	(100)
PROVISIONS FOR LIABILITIES AND CHARGES	(10)	(10)
	(110)	(100)
	610	550
CAPITAL AND RESERVES		
Called up share capital	300	300
Share premium account	100	100
Profit & Loss Account	150	150
Revaluation Reserve	110	0
	660	550

Figure 11.18 College Dynamics plc, Balance Sheet as at 31st December, i.e. the forecast Balance Sheet after two year's trading and including the effects of an asset revaluation and the effect of valuing brand names

The Trading and Profit and Loss Account

This document again looks deceptively simple, but is also full of potential dangers. The main one, again, centres on valuation, particularly of stocks. The sales revenue, and most of the costs, particularly the charges for labour, marketing, distribution and administration, are matters of fact. The problem lies in the second item in the report, 'Cost of sales'. How

might these be estimated?

The firm starts a year with a known stock of goods and materials. During the year more are purchased, and all the invoices are available. At the end of the year the stock is again counted and valued. The 'Cost of goods sold' is given by the equation:

Value of opening stock + purchase for the year – closing stock = Cost of goods sold.

It seems simple enough, but what are stocks worth? With inflation, things rise in price on a regular basis. Should items be valued at their purchase price or at their replacement value? For example, CD buys tapes for £3 each in 1990. In 1991 they go up to £4 each. Should any stock be valued at £3 or £4? No more can be purchased at the old price. If one wants to maximise profits in the account, one must minimise the cost of goods sold. This can be achieved by over-valuing the stock, i.e. take it all at the replacement value. This will increase the tax paid, though. How do firms deal with this problem?

To see the picture, the method of stock valuation must be known. Two methods are available for use, FIFO and LIFO. FIFO, or 'first in, first out', assumes that the firm uses the oldest items first, i.e. the cheapest. Stock values will be high, cost of goods low, and profits and tax increased. LIFO, or 'last in, last out', on the other hand, assumes the opposite, and has the opposite effect. Whichever one is used, again, has to be published in the Notes to the Accounts, and is covered by one of the accounting conventions. The Inland Revenue, however, only accept accounts prepared on the basis of replacement costs, or FIFO. Thus the stock is always assumed to be the newest and the most expensive. This way the amount of corporation tax that firms pay is maximised. (More of this in Chapter 24.)

The general message: read the reports very carefully, and study the notes and the statement of conventions used most carefully. Be aware of changes – yet another reason for not relying on a single set of accounts.

A further problem of accounts today is the distorting effects of inflation.

Accounting for inflation

One of the major difficulties when examining a series of accounts is inflation. Inflation is 'the persistent rising of prices' and has many causes which will be examined later. It affects companies in many ways, but it will result in both prices and costs increasing. It can distort accounts so it is necessary to be aware of the rate of inflation over the period being considered, and to attempt to strip this out from the figures. If a firm has increased sales revenue by 4% in a period when inflation was running at 8%, it would not be doing very well. It could have lost sales, in volume terms, in spite of the numerical increase in revenue. (Remember, as always in Business Studies, there is an alternative possibility. The firm may be doing a lot better than its competition. If the competition had only managed to keep their sales revenue at a constant level regardless of inflation, a 4% increase in money turnover would be impressive. Beware of the apparently simple answer!)

In an attempt to remove this problem there is a trend in accounting circles to prepare 'Current cost accounts'. Some firms publish these already, as well as the 'legal three'. Adjustments have to be made to both the Balance Sheet and the Profit and Loss Account, as inflation affects the value of assets, including stocks and investments, and creditors, as well as selling prices and the cost of sales, especially salaries and wages.

This is a complex subject, but the point to remember is that inflation can distort the picture given by a firm in its annual accounts. How? Consider a few examples.

Example 1. CD plc buys a wrapping machine for £4,000. It is assessed that it will need replacing in four years, so the accountants put by £1,000 each year to allow for its deterioration in value, and to provide for its replacement. When the time comes to buy a new machine, CD finds that its price has risen to £4,850, an increase of about 5% per year, compound. The £850 is due to inflation, probably. Where will the extra money come from? The money 'put to one side' could be in the bank, so the interest earned will help. If it is simply 'in the books' as depreciation, CD will have a problem.

Perhaps a fairer way is to revalue the machine each year by the rate of inflation (this is published by the government), and adjust the value and the rate of depreciation accordingly (refer back earlier in this chapter), though this will involve a regular series of changes and is to be avoided. Preparing a parallel set of accounts 'Adjusted for Inflation' is the answer.

Example 2. CD plc buys a seasonal raw material and converts it into part of its product range. It expects prices to rise, so buys three years' requirements at once. Over the next three years the price rises by 100%. How should profit be calculated in the third

	Year 1	Year 2
	£m	£m
Turnover	40	50
Less costs	20	25
	20	25
Depreciation	5	5
Trading profit	15	20
Assets	100	95
Less depreciation	5	5
Book value of assets	95	90
Profitability (Profit/BV of assets)	15.8	22.2

Figure 11.19 College Dynamics plc – Profit and Loss Accounts

year? Sales will be Year 3 values, but the materials in 'Year 1' values. This will inflate profits, so one argument suggests that revenues and costs should always be comparable. The higher replacement value, therefore, should be taken – although the Inland Revenue will not be impressed.

Now examine a pair of accounts that come from an operating division of CD plc. They are published as Figure 11.19.

These records might be misleading. Inflation could have caused the rise in sales revenue and costs, so there might be no change in volume. The increase in profit, therefore, might not be real. Equally, the asset value would have been changed by the effects of inflation, and could well be understated in Year 2. Thus, in Year 2, by following 'conventional' accounting, profit may have been overstated, and the asset base understated. The measure of profitability might well have been overstated significantly, compared with inflation adjusted accounting.

One way of tackling this problem is to adopt 'Current cost accounting' methods. This system, covered by SSAP 16, defines how a firm should make certain basic adjustments. These are made in the following areas:

• depreciation
• cost of sales
• monetary working capital
• gearing (more of this in Chapter 12)

Inflation accounting is a very 'fluid' issue, and is still the subject of much debate in the accounting world. The reason, and perhaps the need for it is clear, but the potential for confusion, particularly with the 'ordinary' investor rather than the financial professional, is high.

SUMMARY

Having studied this chapter very carefully, you should be able to:

▽ Explain the differences between financial and management accounts.

▽ List and describe the major concepts of accounting and the setting of the basic 'rules', namely:

– *going concern, accruals, consistency, prudence,*
– *materiality, objectivity*
– *SSAPs*

▽ Construct, describe and use the three major accounts, namely:

– *Balance Sheet*
– *Trading and Profit and Loss Account*
– *Cash Flow Statement*

▽ Outline and demonstrate alternative ways of dealing with depreciation, namely:

– *straight line method*
– *reducing balance method*

▽ Discuss the likely accuracy of financial reports

▽ Explain the problems associated with handling of:

– *intangible assets*
– *inflation*

Questions and activities

Technical terms and glossary

In the section below you are given a series of technical terms and their meanings. They have been scrambled, though. You must match up the terms and the definitions. When you have them correctly paired, transfer them to your 'vocabulary or glossary book'.

You are also advised to transfer any definitions obtained during exercises in the case studies into this glossary book.

Technical terms
1. Financial accounts
2. Management accounts
3. Balance Sheet
4. Trading and Profit and Loss Account
5. Cash Flow Statement
6. Going concern
7. Accounts
8. Prudence
9. Tangible assets
10. Intangible assets
11. Loan capital
12. Equity capital

13. Profit
14. Extraordinary item
15. Creditors
16. Financial Reporting Statements (FRSs)
17. Straight line method
18. Reducing balance method
19. SSAPs
20. Inflation

Definitions

A. An accounting principle, or concept. Accounts are prepared on the basis that the business is operating, and is not likely to close or go into liquidation in the near future.

B. Finance put into a firm by its shareholders. This will be the money obtained from the sale of shares, plus any retained profits.

C. Records prepared for external use. They are public domain documents and usually consist of a Balance Sheet, Profit and Loss Account and a Cash Flow Statement, plus notes and conventions followed.

D. A persistent rise in prices.

E. An asset that does not have a physical appearance (e.g. goodwill) or have no means of valuation in isolation (e.g. patent, trade mark).

F. Replacing some SSAPs providing rules in accounting.

G. A method of accounting for depreciation where a fixed sum is deducted each year from the asset value.

H. A statement at a point in time of the amount of capital in use by a firm, where it is using it, and where it has been raised from.

I. Finance put into a firm through loans from, banks, etc. Loans may carry fixed or variable interest, and have to be repaid after a predetermined period. Interest cannot be passed by the firm.

J. An event or decision which is not a normal part of trading but which will affect the financial results of a company. An example would be a reduction in the work force which will incur redundancy costs.

K. An accounting report which states where a firm got money from during a period, where the money has gone, and what was the overall affect of this on the firm's financial position.

L. An accounting concept. All valuations should be treated cautiously, not optimistically. For example, stock must be valued at cost or net realisable value, whichever is the lower.

M. Statements of standard accounting practice. The 'rules' of accounting.

N. People or firms which are owed money by another.

O. An accounting concept. It is the difference between the revenue received from the sale of something and all the costs incurred in its manufacture and sale, irrespective of any credit terms given or taken.

P. Financial records prepared for internal use only.

Q. A set of financial records which formally set out the health of a firm at a point in time.

R. A method of accounting for inflation where a set percentage of the value of an asset is deducted from its value each year.

S. Assets which can be physically detected, are of a lasting nature, and have a real value. Examples are land, buildings and plant.

T. Statement of the profit (or loss) made by a firm over a period, and how this profit has been spent, or appropriated.

Short answer questions and essays

1. Which of the following are direct costs in a company manufacturing a range of furniture?
   (a) depreciation of production machinery
   (b) royalty paid to the designer for each unit made
   (c) rent on the factory building
   (d) wages paid to the production workers
   (e) salary paid to the production manager
   (f) fabric for covering three-piece suites.

2. List *three* current assets which might appear on a Balance Sheet.

3. In a limited company who decides the amount of money paid to shareholders as dividends?

4. (*Essay*) 'Accounting is a creative art form rather than an exact science.'
   (a) Using examples wherever possible, state what you think this quotation means.
   (8 marks)
   (b) How far do you think the quotation is true? Explain your answer.
   (17 marks)

5. (*Essay*)
   (a) Explain, to someone with no knowledge of business studies, the difference between cash flow and profit.
   (8 marks)
   (b) Evaluate the importance of each of these terms to a firm's survival.
   (17 marks)

6. (*Essay*) Explain the differences between a Profit and Loss Account, a Balance Sheet and a Cash Flow Statement.
   (9 marks)
   Why are they all needed in order to give a clearer picture of a company's performance? (16 marks)
   (Associated Examining Board, Business Studies (A) Paper 2, June 1991)

7. Why are SSAPs and their newer versions so important to accountants and investors alike?
8. Why does inflation have a distorting effect on company accounts?
9. What is 'goodwill'? What alternatives does the accountant have for recording it in the books of the company?
10. Is depreciation a cost?

Case studies and data response questions

Questions involving the preparation of accounts are rare in Business Studies papers since it is not required in the syllabus. A question from an A Level Accounting paper has been included for completion. Try it; it will not be as difficult as you think.

1. The information below is available from the books of Abbingdon Ltd for the financial year ended 31st October 1993.

Trading and Profit and Loss Account for year ended 31st October 1993

	£000		£000
Cost of goods sold	910	Sales	1,300
Gross profit	390		
	1,300		1,300
Administration costs	70	Gross profit	390
Selling and distribution costs	40		
Financial charges	10		
Depreciation of fixed assets	30		
Net profit	240		
	390		390

Balance Sheet as at 31st October 1993

	£000	£000	£000		£000	£000
Fixed assets				Issued capital		
at cost			1,100	50p ordinary shares,		
less aggregate				fully paid		400
depreciation			230	11% £1 preference shares,		
				fully paid		50
			870			450
				Share premium		200
				Retained earnings		700
Current assets				Current liabilities		
Stock		120		Trade creditors	100	
Trade debtors	100			Accrued expenses	20	120
less provision for						
doubtful debts	10	90				
Balance at bank		390	600			
			1,470			1,470

The newly appointed managing director decided that in order to increase profits it is absolutely necessary to control costs. Thus he decided to introduce budgetary control.

The following forecast information is available for the year ending 31st October 1994.

1. The sales are forecast to increase to £1.6 million for the year.

2. A more efficient buying programme is expected to increase the gross profit/sales ratio to 32%.

3. In order to finance further expansion as the recession recedes, a rights issue of one new ordinary share for each two shares currently held is to be made on 1st August 1994. It is expected that the issue will be fully subscribed and the issue will also be underwritten. The issue price is 65p per share, fully paid.

4. Despite heavy inflationary pressures the managing director is determined to reduce costs. The forecast level of costs is: Administration costs will be 5% of forecast sales. Selling and distribution costs will be 3.5% of the forecast sales. There will be no change in financial charges as compared to 1992/3.

5. Owing to the recession bad debts are expected to rise substantially and thus the provision for doubtful debtors is to be increased to 15% of trade debtors. Forecast trade debtors as at 31 October 1994 are £150,000.

6. A general reserve will be created on 31 December 1994 of £300,000.

7. Land and buildings which cost £350,000 (nil depreciation as at 31st October 1993) are to be written down to £200,000 due to the falling prices in the property market.

8. Dividends during 1993/94 will be restricted to paying:
   (i) The preference dividend for the year.
   (ii) A final ordinary dividend of 3p per share, but only on the shares issued before 1 August 1994.
   The dividends would be paid on 1st January 1995.

9. All fixed assets other than land and buildings will be depreciated at 10% per annum based on the cost of assets held at the end of the financial year. There are to be no additions or disposals of fixed assets during 1993/94.

10. Other forecast balances as at 31st October 1994

	£000
Expense creditors	17.0
Trade creditors	97.0
Stock	290.0
Balance at bank	760.5

Required:

(a) A budgeted Trading, Profit and Loss Account for the year ending 31st October 1994. (18 marks)

(b) A budgeted Balance Sheet as at 31st October 1994 (16 marks)

(c) Identify ways in which profits could be increased by making better use of forecast current assets. (16 marks)

(Associated Examining Board, Accounting A. Paper 2, 1993)

2. Balance Sheet Exercise
Prepare a set of Balance Sheets that account for the transactions listed below. Each change requires a new Balance Sheet.

(a) Three brothers start a new limited Company. They put in £100,000 of their own capital each, in return for shares in the new company.

(b) The firm buys a small factory for £100,000, and buys £20,000 of raw and packing materials on credit. The factory is valued at Land – £20,000, Buildings – £30,000, and Plant and Machinery – £50,000.

(c) The company converts the materials into finished goods which it sells for £40,000, also on credit. Thus it made a profit, which is returned in the business, of £20,000. It has not paid for the materials yet.

(d) The firm pays for the materials, but still awaits receipt of the sales revenue.

(e) The firm receives the outstanding revenue. It now buys a delivery van for £20,000, financing it through a medium term loan from the bank for £40,000.

(f) At the end of the first year of trading the firm has made £60,000 profit. It pays tax of £10,000 on this, pays a dividend of £30,000 and retains the balance in the business for expansion purposes.

(g) The brothers raise more capital by selling a Debenture for £30,000, new shares for £20,000 in close relatives, and by taking a long term loan of £50,000 from the bank. They pay off the medium term loan early as the rate of interest is too high.

(h) The firm buys another plot of land for £30,000 and invests another £30,000 in shares of a major supplier to enable it, the supplier, to improve its efficiency and quality.

(i) At the close of the next year's trading the company makes another profit, and retains £30,000 of this in the business. However, the accounts revalue the buildings at £35,000 and the land at £55,000. The bank loan is reduced to £35,000.

(j) The auditors insist that depreciation be allowed for at the following rates:

Buildings – 2.5%
Plant – 10%
Vehicles – 20%

All depreciation is calculated by the straight line methods. Work to whole numbers only.

(k) Another year has gone by. During this period the firm spent £50,000 on new plant and equipment, £15,000 on vehicles and £10,000 on further investments in its suppliers. At the year end it owed it suppliers some £25,000 but was owed £35,000 by its customers. It has increased its bank borrowing by £50,000 and has sold a further £15,000 of shares to relatives. It has made a profit again. It retained £35,000 in the business, and paid out £50,000 in dividends. Depreciation was allowed for according to the rates in (j). After this had been done, a change in planning regulations in the area where the factory was located resulted in the land holdings of the company being revalued by +20%.

(l) Stock taking reveals the following quantities and values:

Raw Materials – 20 tonnes at £1,500 per tonne
Packing Materials – 10 tonnes at £4,000 per tonne
Finished Goods – 15 tonnes at £6,000 per tonne
Tools, Spares etc. – Valued at £5,000

They were recorded previously as Cash.

(m) The auditors consider that 25% of all stocks must be considered as unusable, so must be fully written down in the accounts.

2.5 (b) Calculate the Gearing Ratio where appropriate. Comment on trends revealed by this exercise.

2.5 (c) Calculate the firms Current and Acid test Ratios. Again, comment on trends revealed.

2.5 (d) Assess the value of the company's shares with time. Express the dividends received by the shareholders as a percentage of the share capital invested. If the bank had been paying 8% on long term investments during the period, was the investment in the business worthwhile? Discuss and justify your answer fully.

3.6 Incomplete accounts
The following is the print-out from the computer, and is incomplete. Fill in all the gaps.

XYZ plc
Balance Sheet
as at 1 May 1995

Current assets		
Land	150	
Buildings	200	
P&E	500	
Vehicles	200	
P&P	?	
Investments	150	
Total	1400	1400
Current assets		
Cash	?	
Stock	300	
Debtors	250	
Total	600	600
Current liabilities		
Creditors	200	
Unpaid tax	50	
Unpaid dividends	150	
Overdrafts	?	
Short term loans	50	
Total	?	?
Long term liabilities	500	
Net capital employed	700	
Financed by		
Share capital	?	
Share premium account	50	
Revaluation reserve	50	
Retained profits	400	
Total	700	

12
Ratio analysis of company accounts

Preview

▽ The use of ratios as a means of evaluating the performance of firms will be developed, and the more important ratios examined in detail. In particular, ratios will be introduced in operating groups terms discussed including: *growth ratios, profitability, stock market performance, financial strength, assets, operational ratios.*

▽ The chapter ends with a discussion of the limitations of ratio analysis in particular, and accounts in general.

Accounts are very useful documents. They are studied and read by a whole range of interested parties, and it is useful for them to have some short, quick methods of summarising the accounts and making comparisons. This method is known as *ratio analysis*.

Ratio analysis

By examining sets of accounts for various years, and for similar companies in the same industry over the same period, it is possible to check on the growth, profitability, financial strength, assets, borrowings and the operational efficiency of a business, both in isolation and relative to its competition. This analysis is made by calculating various ratios. There are sets of key ratios that need to be learnt.

WARNING: When making ratio analysis, and coming to conclusions, ensure that you are aware of any differences in the systems and conventions used in the reports, particularly when analysing different companies. Try to compare 'like with like'! This is why the consistency concept is so important.

The various groups of ratios will now be developed and examined. Remember, though, that the ratios are only as accurate as the data upon which they are based. Accounts can be misleading, as well as inaccurate. Treat ratios with some reservation, therefore.

Growth ratios

Growth is the increase in size of the firm. Size in this area is usually confined to sales.

These are the only group of ratios that need two year's data to calculate, and where more than one pair of years is necessary. Since it is growth, or a change, that is being examined, then there must be at least two reference points to get a measure. Equally, one year's growth can be an exception, so the reviewer must see a trend. Conventionally, one looks at the growth in sales, both in money terms and in volume terms, if the data is available. Consider CD plc for the years 1994 and 1993. Only sales value is available, and has increased from £588m to £610m, an increase of £22m, or, more importantly, 3.7%. Data is converted to percentage so that comparisons can be made with other companies. Is this growth rate reasonable? As in most Business Studies questions, it all depends on the rate of inflation in the economy concerned, the business itself, the industry the firm is in, and so on. One would hope that a firm at least kept up with inflation, though.

Is this performance good? It all depends. The investor will need more than one 'bit' of growth data, as well as competitive firms' data, and a knowledge of the economic conditions – interdependence, again. This shows a clear need to analyse and evaluate, before making a recommendation. Here is an example to work through. Examine Case Study 12.1 in detail.

CD plc and its growth in the electronics sector

A potential investor in CD plc is considering investing money in the electrical sector of the UK stock market, and is proposing to buy shares in CD plc. He has been studying the market and has identified the following information:

Year	1990	1991	1992
Sales – CD plc	£1.00m	£1.20m	£1.50m
– Main Competitor	£2.00m	£2.10m	£2.20m
Inflation	5%	3%	2%

How has CD plc performed? How impressive is its growth?
It is useful to turn the data into Index Numbers.

Year	1990	1991	1992
Sales			
CD plc	100	120	150
Competition	100	105	110
Inflation	105	108	110

Profitability ratios

Profitability ratios are the ratios that link the profit made by a firm with the various 'investments' made by different parties. They measure profitability as a percentage. They also appear to relate to the rate of interest charged by the banks. Profit, as a sum of money is fine, and there must be some at least in the long run. The measures of profitability show how efficient the firm has been in earning profit. It shows how well the firm has been using the resources put at its disposal.

These ratios are calculated as 'profit' / 'investment'. The 'profit' being considered can be the operating profit, total earnings, or dividends paid. The 'investments' being used, or managed, by the firm can be assets employed, equity capital, or number of shares issued. Note that two documents are needed to be able to make these calculations,

the Balance Sheet for the investments and the Profit and Loss Account for the profit itself.

The most common ratios are return on capital employed and return on equity.

Return on capital employed – ROCE

Operating profit/capital employed

Capital employed here is all the capital employed, share capital, retained capital, reserves, etc. It is the capital being used by the firm. Here is an example from CD plc:

	1994	1993
Operating (or Trading) Profit	*£200m*	*£195m*
Capital Employed	*£730m*	*£668m*
ROA (%)	*27.4*	*29.2*

This gives a picture of what CD plc is doing with all the capital invested in it.

It seems high, and looks very satisfactory, but you need the equivalent from at least one competitor to be sure. The pair of ratios also raises more questions. Why has ROCE fallen over the last year? What have they earned before? How does this fit into the pattern of ROCE for CD over a longer period, and what is the trend?

Return on equity – ROE

Operating profit/equity capital employed

Remember, equity capital is that put in by the shareholders. It includes retained profits as this belongs to the shareholders. Again, for CD plc note that both the Balance Sheet and the Profit and Loss Account are needed:

	1994	1993
Operating profit	*£200m*	*£195m*
Equity capital (share capital)	*£300m*	*£300m*
ROE (%)	*66.6*	*65*

This gives a picture of how well CD plc is using the money the shareholders have invested in the company. Again it seems very high, and in this case it is improving. The same reservations and qualifications apply.

Earnings per share

Earning per share is the net profit of the firm, after the payment of tax, and after deducting profit that minority interest and preference shareholders are entitled to, divided by the number of shares in the company.

The ratio is calculated by dividing the 'earnings' by the number of ordinary shares issued at the date of the Balance Sheet. The number of shares issued by a company are recorded in the Notes that accompany the accounts. Again, here are some examples based on CD's accounts:

	1994	1993
Qualifying profit	*£120m*	*£145m*
No. of shares (m)	*1,000*	*1,000*
Earnings per share (p)	*12*	*14.5*

The shareholder, however, is likely to be interested, first, in the dividend ratio.

Dividend cover

Earnings per share/dividend per share

This tells the shareholder how much of the earnings are paid out to the shareholder. The dividend per share is published, but be sure you use the full dividend, as they are often paid in instalments.

	1994	1993
Earnings per share (p)	*12*	*14.5*
Dividend per share (p)	*6.2*	*9.5*
Dividend cover	*1.9*	*1.5*

CD plc would seem to have paid out more of its earnings to maintain a dividend level. Why? Will this affect future liquidity? How high have the borrowings gone? Consult the Cash Flow Statement; it may help to provide the answers.

These ratios give a picture of how the firm is earning money from the capital it is using. Note, they all seem to ask as many questions as they answer, and all need other, comparative, information to be of real use. In particular, observe that both the Balance Sheet and the Profit and Loss Account have to be available to calculate these ratios, along with the important set of Notes.

Investors and shareholders will be concerned with ratios relating profit to the price actually paid for the shares, as opposed to their face value. These are known as *stock market performance indicators*. Since they all use the price of the shares 'today' and compare it with earnings made 'yesterday', they are variable. Also, since the price of shares depends on other things than just the performance of the firm, (for example, the state of the economy both here and overseas) these ratios are another example of interdependence. They can be compared with those of competitors, provided they were calculated on the same day. The most common ratios are shown below. The price of CD plc's shares are assumed to be 58p and 110p at the end of 1994 and 1993 respectively.

Stock market performance indicators

Dividend yield

Dividend per share/market price per share

You now need the market prices as well as the accounts. These are available in most good newspapers. The ratio shows what the investment is earning today, assuming that the share was bought today. Actual shareholders may have to work out the ratio based on the price actually paid in the past.

	1994	1993
Dividend per share (p)	*6.2*	*9.5*
Market price (p)	*58*	*110*
Dividend yield (%)	*10.7*	*8.6*

To be able to assess the meaning of this the interested party needs to know what rate of interest you can get from a bank – another example of interdependence.

Price-earnings ratio (P/E ratio)

This is often quoted in the financial press. It is calculated as:

Market price per share/earnings per share

	1994	1993
Market price (p)	*58*	*110*
Earnings per share (p)	*12*	*14.5*
P/E ratio	*4.8*	*7.6*

What does it mean? Generally a popular share will have a 'high' P/E ratio. CD plc must have become less popular over the year.

Firms consider these ratios when deciding on dividends. A firm has a problem with its targets over these ratios. It has to juggle the interests of different groups, while, at the same time, looking to the future of the business itself. It has to try to:

- Give an adequate reward to shareholders who have invested their money in CD plc. (High dividend.)
- Provide funds for the development and growth of the firm. (Low dividend.)
- Provide security for the employees, lenders and suppliers of the firm. (Maximise growth. Retain profit. Low Dividend.)
- Attract new funds and investments from outside the firm. (High yield required, high dividends.)
- Be able to cope with inflation without eating into reserves. (Retain as much money in the firm as possible.)
- Compare reasonably with the banks' deposit rates.

It is most unlikely that all these tasks can be achieved at the same time. Another example to be studied. Perform the tasks required in Case Study 12.

CASE STUDY 12.2

CD plc and its rating on the London Stock Exchange

The potential investor is still interested in CD plc, and has been seeking information and support from his investment adviser. They have supplied him with the following raw data.

Years	1990	1991	1992	1993
Market price (p/share)	120	110	100	130
Dividend/share (p)	18	18	16	20
Earnings/share (p)	24	26	24	22
Bank interest	10	12	14	8
Rate (% per year)				

Work out dividend yield and P/E ratio for CD plc and comment on your results.

Financial strength (or liquidity) ratios

The financial strength of a company indicates how well it might cope with problems. If it is strong it will be able to meet its liabilities (or pay its bills) easily and reliably. Thus, financial strength is really about liquidity. There are some very 'popular' ratios here!

The current ratio

The current ratio is also known as the working capital ratio. It compares current assets with current liabilities. Again, using CD plc's Balance Sheet:

	1994	1993
Current assets	£740m	£739m
Current liabilities	£450m	£400m
Current ratio	1.6	1.8

CD has its current liabilities covered by its current assets. It should be able to pay its current liabilities relatively easily. What is a good ratio? It is generally believed it should be approximately 2:1, but it really depends on the industry. What are the ratios for CD's competitors?

The acid-test ratio

The acid-test ratio is a modification of the current ratio. Some of the assets included in the current ratio may not be easy to sell, particularly quickly. This ratio, therefore relates liquid assets only, i.e. those near to cash, to current liabilities, those bills that have to be paid soon. Liquid assets are considered to be cash + debtors + short-term investments, but stocks are left out. These are not often easy to sell quickly, otherwise the firm will have sold them anyway!

	1994	1993
Liquid assets	£520m	£514m
Current liabilities	£450m	£400m
Acid-test ratio	1.15	1.29

These are satisfactory ratios, by any standards. A 1:1 ratio is considered acceptable, but it again depends on the industry in question. The decline with time would need investigation. Was it peculiar to CD, or is it a general industrial trend?

Interest cover

How easy will the firm find it to pay the interest it owes? It indicates the sensitivity of the company's finances to changes in interest rates. A useful ratio. It is defined as:

Total profit/Interest paid

Back to CD plc!

	1994	1993
Total profit	£200m	£195m
Interest charges	£30m	£20m
Interest cover (times)	6.6	9.8

There are no problems here. Either the interest rates are very low, or CD plc does not have many loans. They would have to rise a great deal, though, before payment of interest would become a problem. Equally, the firm could cope with a large fall in profits without getting into problems. Remember this ratio when gearing arises.

Loan cover

Loan cover is a measure of the 'backing' potential for the firm with respect to long-term loans. It is measured as:

Fixed assets/loans over one year.

	1994	1993
Fixed assets	£610m	£588m
Long-term loans	£150m	£250m
Loan cover (times)	4.0	2.3

This is a big improvement over the year – CD plc has reduced its long-term debt during 1994. A ratio of two or less would start to be worrying.

There are some very 'popular' ratios here. Again, both the Balance Sheet and the Profit and Loss Account are needed. And again, to be of real value, a fuller set of accounts is needed, plus the vital competitors' information.

Now examine Case Study 12.3.

CASE STUDY 12.3

CD plc and its financial strength

Just how solid a business is CD plc? Does it look to be in any financial risk position? Again, the potential investor has the following data available.

Year	1990	1991	1992	1993
Profit (£m)	5	5.5	6.5	5.0
CAs (£m)	0.15	0.20	0.23	0.30
CLs (£m)	0.10	0.15	0.20	0.25

Asset ratios

These ratios examine how a firm is using its capital, where it is using it, and if it is working it hard enough. Look at these relationships.

Asset turnover or sales to assets

Asses turnover looks at the rate at which a firm's assets are 'converted' into sales. This is a measure of the productivity of a firm's assets. This is calculated as the firm's Net assets/Sales x 365.

	1994	1993
Net assets	£739m	£668m
Sales	£2,000m	£1,800m
Asset turnover (days)	135	135

This is a very fast asset turnover. One would suspect that the firm was in the retailing of consumer goods if one only saw that ratio.

Debtors

This is a measure of how well a firm is controlling its debtors, or how much credit it is giving. It is measured as: Debtors / Sales x 365

	1994	1993
Debtors	£400m	£390m
Sales	£2,000m	£1,800m
Debt turnover (days)	73	79

It isn't bad, and it is moving in the right direction. Compare it with the next ratio.

Stock turnover

Stock turnover looks at the speed with which a firm turns over, or sells, its stock. It is calculated as Stock Values/Sales x 365

	1994	1993
Stocks	£220m	£225m
Sales	£2,000m	£1,800m
Stock turnover (days)	40	46

Stock turnover is very fast! CD plc is behaving far more like a supermarket than a manufacturer. Just how large and important is its retailing arm? Again, look for questions and clues.

Financial structure ratios

Financial structure ratios form a very important group of ratios that look at the financial structure of a firm. They show how the firm is formed, and where the capital has come from. The critical ratio is the gearing ratio.

Gearing ratio

The gearing ratio examines the relationship between the equity capital of a firm and its loan capital. A high level of loan capital means a high level of interest to pay, irrespective of profits and earnings. The ratio is calculated as:

Loan capital (long term)/total capital employed

	1994	1993
Loan capital	£150m	£250m
Capital employed	£730m	£668m
Gearing (%)	20	37

What is a good gearing ratio depends on the state of the business, and its rate of growth.

The higher the gearing, the greater the amount of interest a firm has to pay out of its profits. If sales are poor, and profit down, the firm will still have to pay this interest. However, if the firm is very profitable, and there is a high degree of loan capital, there will be a large amount of profit left for distribution to the shareholders, resulting in a large dividend. So, link this ratio with the Interest Cover. If this is high, then a high gearing can be accommodated. High gearing and low interest cover is a danger sign!

High gearing is good for the shareholders in times of a high level of business and expansion, but is bad when business is in decline or in a depression.

Operational ratios

This last group of ratios looks at the performance of the firm in relation to sales. We know the profitability in relation to capital, we now examine the relationship to sales.

Profit to sales

The profit to sales ratio – also known as the profit margin – is the common ratio, particularly for shopkeepers. CD plc's data once again.

	1994	1993
Profit	£200m	£195m
Sales	£2,000m	£1,800m
Ratio (%)	10	11

This ratio is more important for a business where sales revenue is very much higher than the capital employed. Do you see why it is the shopkeepers' ratio?

Limitations of ratio analysis

This chapter has listed and discussed a whole range of ratios. It has also highlighted their interrelationship, and identified many of their limitations. They seem to ask as many questions as they answer. The particular limitations on their valuation and use are:

- They are often based on insufficient data, especially for large, multi-product firms.
- The valuations often vary from firm to firm, making inter-company comparison risky.
- All is based on past events. The most up-to-date public account can be three months or more old. Different companies have different years, which also makes comparisons difficult.
- Accounts report past events, and do not attempt to predict into the future. (There may be an element of this in the report, but usually unquantified.)
- Accounts are all about money. They ignore the key asset of a firm, its employees.

A single ratio from a single firm has virtually no value. An analyst, or potential investor needs a full range of ratios for the firm in question, and a range of its competitors. Some idea of the firm's objectives is necessary, as is an understanding of the underlying economic conditions in the country concerned. With all of this, we will still only have a hazy picture, at

best. Ratios are easy to calculate, but do not be over-optimistic about their value. Ratios vary tremendously from industry to industry between firms of equal standing and reputation. This is illustrated in Table 12.1, which is based on real companies, and their results published between 1988 and 1990.

Observe the wide variations for each ratio, and between ratios. Think of the cost structure and form of the businesses involved, i.e. supermarkets buy and sell goods, but do not manufacture anything. Most sales are for cash. By the prudent 'rule of one' for the current ratio they should be in trouble, but are they?

Examine the industries and see if they are capital or labour intensive. Why should stock turnover be so long, or is it poor, in the aerospace industry? Lastly, think about the banks. They deal in money, directly, so examine how their accounts are unusual.

This all reinforces the fact that:

- You must treat ratios with great care, and respect.
- You need much information about a number of years, and a number of firms, to get any reasonable picture.
- You need to read annual reports and accounts with great care. Check that they are all prepared using the same conventions and assumptions.
- Inflation can confuse everything.
- You must know what you are doing, and be aware of the possible weaknesses of the analysis before you make any real decisions.

Table 12.1
Some selected accounting ratio's for different types of companies. (all firms are UK registered and based)

| Company | Multiple retailer | Multinational manufacturer FMCGs(1) | Multinational manufacturer FMCGs(2) | Bank | Industrials | | | |
| | | | | | Textiles | Metals | Chem. | Aero. |
Ratio								
ROCE (%)	33	22	38	12	22	31	30	21
Profit margin (%)	7	8	14	13	6	13	10	05
Asset turnover (days)	72	136	136	389	101	154	120	91
Stock turnover (days)	18	55	46	N/A	83	47	60	124
Debtors ratio (days)	6	53	62	N/A	63	71	70	73
Gearing (%)	32	14	14	N/A	29	23	9	27
Current ratio (%)	38	150	150	100	170	200	170	140
Acid test (%)	16	90	100	100	80	140	100	80
Interest cover (times)	40	7	9	N/A	5	15	29	12
Loan cover (times)	6	7	6	N/A	3	4	7	3
Dividend cover (times)	3.3	2.8	3.4	2.5	0.7	4.3	2.1	3.4

SUMMARY

Having studied this chapter, you should be able to:

⬇ Describe the principles and processes of ratio analysis when applied to company accounts

⬇ Calculate, use and comment on the following groups of ratios:

– *Growth ratios:* size, ROCE, ROE, earnings per share, dividend cover
– *Stock market indicators*: dividend yield, P/E ratio
– *Financial strength*: acid test, current ratio, interest cover, loan cover
– *Asset ratios*: sales/assets, debtors, stock turnover, gearing
– *Operational ratios*: profit/sales

⬇ Discuss the limitations of ratio analysis.

Questions and activities

Technical terms and glossary

In the section below you are given a series of technical terms and their meanings. They have been scrambled, though. The student must match up the terms and the definitions. When you have them correctly paired, transfer them to your Vocabulary or glossary book.

Students are also advised to transfer any definitions obtained during the exercises in the case studies into this glossary book.

Technical terms

1. Ratio analysis
2. ROCE
3. Gearing
4. ROE
5. P/E ratio
6. Earnings per share
7. Acid test
8. Dividend cover
9. Debtors ratio
10. Stock turnover
11. Stock market performance indicators
12. Interest cover

Definitions

A. A growth ratio. The net profit of the firm, after tax, divided by the number of ordinary shares issued.

B. A financial structure ratio. The ratio of interest bearing loan capital to share capital in the financial structure of a firm.

C. A financial strength ratio. The number of times the interest payable by a company could have been paid using the net profit after tax.

D. The calculation and use of accounting ratios to analyse the performance, liquidity and financial security of a company over a period of time.

E. A stock market performance indicator. The ratio of the price of a share on the stock market divided by the earnings per share. Thus, it relates price to profitability.

F. A growth ratio. The operating profit of the business expressed as a percentage of the capital employed in the firm at the time.

G. An assets ratio. The debtors of the company, expressed as a percentage of the sales of the company. Usually expressed in 'days'.

H. A profitability ratio. The operating profit of the company expressed as a percentage of the equity capital employed.

I. A financial strength ratio. The liquid assets (current assets less stocks) of the company expressed as a proportion of the current liabilities.

J. Ratios that are of particular use to investors in a company.

K. An assets ratio. The number of time the stock of a company is sold, or turned over, per year.

L. A profitability ratio. The number of time the

dividend could have been paid out of the profits. Calculated as earnings per share divided by the dividend per share.

Short answer questions and essays

1. Explain the meaning of the expression 'A highly geared company' (Associated Examination Board, 1987/1).
2. Discuss the limitations of ratio analysis as a means of measuring the performance of a company.
3. Why should interest cover be considered alongside the gearing ratio?
4. What are the stock market performance ratios?
5. Of what value is one Balance Sheet to a company analyst?
6. Why is the history of the earnings per share of use to an investor, as well as the price and dividend history?
7. What are the growth ratios?
8. Compare and contrast the profitability ratios from a supermarket operating company and the manufacturer of defence systems.
9. Why is profit measured against sales as well as capital employed?
10. What ratios would be used to assess the liquidity of a business?

Data response questions and case studies

1. Read the article and answer the questions which follow.

Reorganisation pays off for FKI

The electrical engineering firm, FKI, began to see the fruits of its new business strategy when it announced a big jump in half year profits and an increase in its interim dividend to shareholders. Pre-tax profits rose by 18.5% to £16m in the six months to 30 September on sales that were 10.5% down at £332.2m.

Since last year, the business has been reorganised into five divisions. Each division has been streamlined to eliminate unnecessary costs and to make it more efficient.

The 12,500 workforce has been cut by 516 during the half-year at a cost of £2m. There will be similar cuts in the second half of the year, at similar cost.

Prices have been increased by 0.75% over inflation to create more revenue in real terms.

Further changes are planned. Some companies owned by FKI will be sold and the money used to make acquisitions. In particular, FKI is looking to strengthen its automotive division by acquiring an automotive business in North America.

Partly as a result of these changes, and partly because the recession is lessening, four of the five divisions have increased their operating profits. Only one division showed an operating profit lower than the previous year and plans are in hand to improve its performance.

FKI shares finished up 6p at 88p. Earnings per share rose from 2.2p to 2.65p.

(Adapted from *The Independent*, 13 November 1992)

(a) (i) Calculate the pre-tax profit for the previous six months to 31 March. (3 marks)
    (ii) Calculate the sales for the same period. (2 marks)
    (iii) Calculate and comment upon the sales ratios for the periods ending 31 March and 30 September. (6 marks)

(b) (i) Identify from the article three elements of FKI's new business strategy. (3 marks)
    (ii) Explain how each of these contributed to achieving increased operating profits. (6 marks)

(c) Explain two ways in which a knowledge of the earnings per share ratio might be of use to an investor in FKI. (4 marks)

(Associated Examining Board, Business Studies (A) Paper 1, June 1994)

2. Study this extract from the balance sheet of Heads and Toes Ltd, a manufacturer of fine, specialist scissors for hairdressers and manicurists, and answer the questions which follow.

	1989	1990	1991	1992
Current assets	£	£	£	£
Raw materials	1,500	2,100	2,700	4,100
Work in progress	900	1,800	2,400	4,300
Finished goods	3,000	3,900	6,000	12,900
Debtors	4,500	6,300	8,000	8,000
Pre-payments	240	–	–	–
Cash in hand/bank	3,000	1,380	100	1,480
Current liabilities				
Trade creditors	2,100	2,400	3,600	4,800
Short–term borrowings	1,080	1,380	2,580	4,000
Provision for tax	240	1,500	2,040	920
Current ratio	3.8:1	2.9:1		
Acid-test ratio	2.3:1	1.5:1		

(a) Explain why both current and acid test ratios are necessary to measure a company's liquidity. (4 marks)

(b) (i) Calculate the current ratio for the years 1991 and 1992. (3 marks)

   (ii) Calculate the acid-test ratio (quick ratio) for the years 1991 and 1992. (3 marks)

Show all your workings.

(c) What do these ratios tell you about Heads and Toes liquidity over the four-year period? (6 marks)

(d) A new managing director joined Heads and Toes Ltd in January 1993.
Discuss the additional information she would need to examine *before* taking action to correct the position shown in (c). (8 marks)

(Associated Examining Board, Business Studies (A) Paper 1, June 1992)

3. Read the information and answer the questions that follow.

Time-Wise, a subsidiary of a major computer manufacturer, makes only one product – an electronic, pocket sized, personal planner. This product is distinctive and is enjoying rapid sales growth with little competition at present. However, competition is expected to increase during the next year. The parent company sets one overriding objective for its subsidiary – a net profit to sales ratio of 10% or better. The next stage in the growth of Time-Wise is under consideration. The following statement has been prepared by Time-Wise Ltd for the year 1st June 1991 to 31st May 1992

	£	£
Sales revenue (80,000 units @ £20 each)		1,600,000
Direct costs	800,000	
Production overheads	300,000	1,100,000
Gross profit		500,000
Marketing & sales overheads:		
Sales persons salaries	80,000	
Sales administration	40,000	
Advertising & sales promotion	80,000	
Marketing research	20,000	
	220,000	
Administration overheads	100,000	320,000
Net profit		180,000
Net profit to sales ratio = 11.25%		

For the year 1st June to 31st May 1993 a 20% increase in sales volume is planned. The following decisions have been taken by the Board:

(i) because competitors are entering the market the sales price will be lowered to £19 per unit. Production overheads will remain unchanged.

(ii) advertising and sales promotion expenditure will be increased by 20%.

(iii) an additional sales person will be employed: salary costs will increase by £14,000 per annum.

(iv) an assistant sales administration manager will be employed at an additional cost of £14,000 per annum.

(v) the level of administration costs will be kept at the same proportion of gross profit as before.

(a) What is meant by the term 'overheads'? (2 marks)

(b) Calculate the net profit to sales ratio for the planned sales period 1st June 1992 to 31st May 1993. *Show all your workings.* (12 marks)

(c) Discuss whether the Board's decisions are appropriate at this stage in their product's life cycle. (11 marks)

(Associated Examining Board, Business Studies (A) Paper 1, June 1992)

13
The legal aspects of money and businesses

Preview

▼ This chapter outlines the laws that govern the start-up, operation and closing down of a business.

Each part of this book will close with a short chapter on the legal aspects of, and implications relating to the topics covered, except for this chapter which covers two parts, both Part 1: Introduction and Part 2: The Management of Money.

The objective of these chapters is to identify the major Acts and Laws that relate to the topic and to identify areas of contention that may exist. It is not intended to give a crash course in business law; that is far beyond the scope of this book.

Laws change frequently, often with little publicity, at least as far as the general public and the Business Studies student is concerned. This chapter, and the others of its kind in the book, may not be fully up to date, therefore. They may only give a recent legal history.

UK law is divided between civil, for which damages can be claimed, and criminal, for which punishment is given. Businesses are exposed to both. Also, for incorporated firms, the firm and the directors/employees may, in some circumstances, both be liable in the eyes of the law.

First, the law relating to the operation of a business: start up, operation and termination.

Business organisation

Companies Act 1989

The Companies Act 1989 is the major one concerned with the legal structure of businesses. It sets out the requirement for the Memorandum and Articles of Association. It is concerned with Incorporated companies. Any person who complies with the provisions of the Act can form a registered company.

This is done by submitting the necessary papers to the Registrar of Companies at Companies House.

Partnership Acts

The 1890 (yes, 1890) Partnership Act set the limit on partners at 20. An amendment in 1967 altered this for selected professions, namely solicitors and accountants.

Bankruptcy Act
Insolvency Act

Note that incorporated companies cannot be made bankrupt, they can only go into liquidation.

Operation of a business

The basic law applying to the operation of a business is the Law of Tort, or Negligence. An area of law in itself, and beyond the scope of this book.

The Companies Act 1989

The Companies Act, 1989 still applies. It gives protection to minority shareholders, and sets standards for accounting and recording. Certain sets of books have to be kept, namely:

- Register of members
- Register of debenture holders
- Register of charges
- Minute books
- Register of directors' interests
- Register of directors' service contracts
- Register of substantial individual interests.

It is here that laws relating to competition apply.

Consider, too the following:

The Food and Drugs Act 1955, 1981 and 1982

These control the quality of food displayed. An inspection system is administered by a series of Inspectors.

The Dangerous Drugs Act, 1975

This controls the sale and use of certain dangerous drugs.

Fair Trading Act, 1973

This is a very wide ranging Act, and is discussed later in the chapter on marketing law. As far as operation is concerned, the Act looks carefully at monopolies and mergers, potential as well as existing, so influencing the expansion plans of firms. It is a very powerful Act.

SUMMARY

Having studied this chapter, you should be able to:

Explain the laws regulating the start-up of businesses, namely:

– *Partnership Act, Companies Act*

Outline regulations that influence the operation of firms, namely:

– *The Companies Act*
– *Food and Drugs Acts*
– *The Dangerous Drugs Act*
– *Fair Trading Act*

and

Be aware of the laws regulating the closure of businesses, namely:

– *Bankruptcy Act and Insolvency Act*

14
Introduction to product marketing and the product life cycle

Preview

▼ Products do not sell themselves, they have to be marketed. Products do not last for ever, and have to be nourished and nurtured through their life. Products can also have their life extended through the correct use of extension strategies, if they are managed properly.

▼ The key concept of a product's life cycle will be developed, and the determinants of its length will be studied. Three different cycles will be examined, those based on sales volume (or revenue), profit and cash flow. The prime importance of the management of cash flow will be reinforced again.

▼ The role and function of marketing within a firm will be examined, and its major activities will be identified and introduced. These functions will be examined against the product life cycle, and the type of product being made and sold.

▼ The important 'tools' or 'weapons' of marketing will be introduced. These can be summarised as 'the four Ps', namely: *product, price, place, promotion.*

▼ The important link between marketing and production will be clearly established.

The marketing function is responsible for a series of key activities. These may be summarised as follows:

- to identify the present and future needs of the customers of the firm
- to communicate these needs to the company
- to coordinate the development of new products
- to manage the selling process for the goods and services that the business provides today.

The marketing department has to work closely with the production department, research and development and finance. It also contributes to the work load of the personnel department.

Marketing's main activity, from the point of view of the consumer, is advertising. It should be obvious by now, however, that this is only a small part of the marketing department's work.

The role of marketing is summed up well by Tinniswood in his 1981 book *Marketing Decisions*.

'Marketing is an all-embracing function which assesses future market needs, coordinates the other functional areas of the firm (finance, production, research and development) to meet these needs, and promotes and distributes the goods or services at a price giving maximum satisfaction to the customer, and profitability to the firm.'

Marketing has a role in all companies, regardless of the goods or services they produce. It is more obvious in some companies than others, though. Remember, marketing is far more than just advertising.

Good marketing cannot help a poor product for very long, but bad marketing can seriously damage the prospects of even a good one extremely quickly.

Marketing is all about product management, so it is necessary to look at products first. Products do not last for ever. Some come and go rapidly while others seem to last for ever. They all have one thing in common, though, a life cycle. Like the human life cycle, the length of it depends on how it is brought up, how it is nurtured and nourished, and the environment or market in which it 'lives'.

Product life cycle

Product life cycle is a representation of the life of a product, splitting it up into a series of different behavioural stages.

Life cycles are commonly prepared in terms of the sales of the product against time. Imagine a new product, like a novel packaged food product. It will pass through four or five stages:

Stage 1: Introduction and launch

Sales commence after the product is launched. It is introduced to potential customers, who buy it. It will be receiving support from the marketing department, heavy advertising and other inducements to buy. The company will have set a target for its sales in this period, and when this is met it passes to the next stage of its life.

A product that fails to reach this initial target may well be withdrawn from the market. It will have 'died'.

The launch of a space satellite is a good analogy for this process. Stage 1 is the firing of the first stage rocket. A vast amount of energy is expended in getting the rocket off the ground, and moving it only relatively slowly. If it fails, though, there is a crash. Hopefully the second stage rocket will fire well!

Stage 2: Growth

The product now starts to sell well. Consumers know of it, some start to buy it a second and then third time. It starts to build a group of loyal consumers. It has developed *brand loyalty*. A new definition:

Brand loyalty is the strength with which consumers buy a particular brand of a good rather than a similar brand.

The product will be sold in more and more outlets, and there will be demand from potential

sellers to be able to stock it and sell it. Eventually the rate of growth of sales declines. The product has moved out of the growth stage and has entered the next stage of its life.

To return to the rocket anology, speed has built up, and the successful satellite has now been established in a stable orbit. All seems well, but the future depends on the height of the orbit.

Stage 3 (A): Maturity and saturation

The product now sells well to an established market of loyal consumers. It needs little marketing support, other than occasional bursts of 'reminder' advertising. Competition may well be building up, and eventually sales will begin to fall. The market will be saturated and the product will have become rather old fashioned. It will have entered the final stage of its life.

The maturity stage for products have widely different lengths. Some products decline almost as soon as they reach the peak, but others seem to stay on the plateau for ever.

Returning to the space analogy, the orbit has decayed. Short bursts of energy have to be put in to keep the orbit stable. Eventually the fuel runs out. Unless something is done about it the satellite will fall back towards earth and burn up.

Stage 3 (B): Extension strategies

Marketing personnel have a set of tools that they may use in an attempt to extend the maturity stage of a products life cycle. These are called extension strategies. The most widely used methods are:

- develop more frequent use of the product
- develop new uses for the product
- develop major styling or design changes
- develop new markets for the product
- develop a wider range of products.

Consider the turkey. In Britain in the not too distant past the turkey was an expensive seasonal food eaten at Christmas. It was bought as a huge, whole bird, and it was served up in various disguises for a considerable time after the main celebration. Examine the situation today, and think how the marketing of turkey has been developed:

- It is available all the year round.
- It is available in many forms – joints, breasts only, legs, wings, burgers, escallops, etc.
- It is sold as an everyday product.
- It, or rather that part of it considered unsuitable for human consumption, is added to pet foods.

This is a good example of the effective use of extension strategies.

In the rocket analogy, the satellite has been refuelled in orbit. Not an easy task, but it is not easy to find effective extension strategies all the time.

Stage 4: Decline

Sales fall away, and eventually the product will be withdrawn.

The four stages combine to give the typical illustration of the life cycle which is reproduced in Figure 14.1.

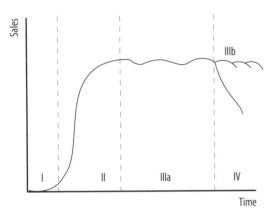

Figure 14.1 *Typical product life cycle based on sales – units or reserve*

Examine the shelves and cupboards at home, and try to place some of the products you see into their correct place in their life cycles. Fill in Figure 14.2, where some suggestions have been included to start you off.

Businesses want a product that will pass quickly and successfully through the first two stages of its

Life cycle stage	Products
I	DAT recording systems
II	
IIIa	Instant coffee
IIIb	Soap powder
IV	Shoe polish

Key			
I	= Introduction	IIIb	= Extension strategy
II	= Development	IV	= Decline
IIIa	= Maturity		
Note: Transition from IIIa to IV sometimes call 'Saturation'			

Figure 14.2 *Product life cycles band on net cash flow*

life, then have a long, if not permanent maturity stage. Marketing sets out to do this, so one of the major functions of the marketing department is to manage the life cycle of their products.

Marketing is responsible for managing the life cycles of the company's portfolio of products.

The life cycle has a time scale, but no time is shown. It will vary from product to product, and with the efficiency of the business in general and its marketing in particular. It will also vary from time to time depending on the state of the economy. Consider a few examples:

- Fashion items, like the Filofax. A rapid growth market in its day, with a high level of sales in its short maturity period. The product declined quickly and quietly.
- Fashion items, like the mobile telephone. Its launch in what turned out to be a time of recession has resulted in low growth. Imagine if it had been available earlier and could have been launched with the Filofax.
- Luxury items like Jaguar cars. The consumer needs a sound income to be able to buy them, and no fear of redundancy. (Most, in fact, are bought by companies.) They sold well in the mid-1980s, but the market collapsed in the early 1990s. Positive marketing in the USA in 1993 has boosted sales significantly.
- Persil detergent. This is a well-managed domestic consumer product. Wide and successful use of extension strategies, especially major 'redesigns' to meet changing washing conditions and demands. Highly successful exploitation of the brand name. Whatever happened to Oxidol, or even Omo? Omo used 'to add brightness to even perfect whiteness' and was a household name in the UK.

Life cycles can be drawn against other units than sales or revenue. Sales volumes in themselves are no reliable indication of success. It is essential to monitor profit and cash flow during the life of a product. First, though, it is necessary to consider how a product gets to the market ready for its launch. Every product has a 'pre-launch stage', in fact.

In the pre-launch stage

This stage starts when the company decides to commence work on the product. Research and development will be done, both on the product itself and its manufacture, and on how to market it most efficiently.

Products will need to be tested, plant and equipment purchased and installed, advertising developed and tested, products made and sent to the shops, advertising booked and paid for. Sales staff will have to be briefed, and the new product introduced to the trade. All of this will be done before any of the new product is sold. Money flows out but nothing flows in. The firm experiences negative cash flow. Only when the product is launched on the market and sales start to be obtained will cash start to flow in, but only slowly. When the product is actually launched the firm will have made a significant investment in the new product. It will have invested capital in buildings, plant and equipment, etc., and revenue in the form of spending on stocks of materials, advertising materials, sales forces, etc., Obviously the firm has made no profit at this point, in fact it is in a loss position.

The length of the pre-launch stage varies from product type to product type, as well as from company to company. The more efficient a firm the shorter the pre-launch stage usually. Consider the following products:

Pharmaceuticals

New drugs are the result of extensive research. This is costly, and can take many years. They have to be tested to ensure that they are effective, safe and free of side effects. They have to meet costly government regulations and have to be registered. The product then has to be manufactured in production quantities, and the resulting pharmaceuticals sold. This is an expensive, slow process which can be handled by only a few concerns. Economies of scale dictate that the world is dominated by a few large international pharmaceutical companies.

Pharmaceuticals need to be expensive to recover this investment in money and manpower, and to recoup the costs of research programmes that fail. A successful new drug can earn the inventing company a lot of money, especially after it is protected by a patent. Consider the history of Beechams and its invention of synthetic penicillin, of Glaxo and its drug Xantac, and ICI and its heart drugs.

Aircraft

Another product area characterised by a long and extremely expensive pre-launch stage is the aircraft. This can take many years, and requires a huge investment in both money and skilled people. Boeing had to build a new airport when they developed the 747. Costs are so high today that only a few companies can contemplate developing new aircraft.

The very costs of R&D are a barrier to entry into the industry for all but the very brave. The resulting lack of real competition may push up prices to the consumer. The future seems to lie in joint, international developments. Consider the European company Airbus Industries, and also the possible joint venture between Boeing and Airbus for the possible new super jumbo.

This type of limited competition is quite common for capital intensive industries, and may be examples of oligopoly – 'control by the few'. This type of industry is characterised by 'sticky' prices, and little or no price competition. They may even seem to work together as a cartel to fix prices. It is almost impossible to check if they do or do not. Just consider the oil supply position in the UK.

Here is a summary of the position so far:

At the start of the launch stage a product will already have gone through a pre-launch stage. It will already be in a debt position, the cost of this pre-launch work. Cash flow is negative, and it starts its life in debt. Since there are no sales, the accountant can see no profit (or loss) either.

In the launch stage

As sales increase the cash and profit position may still grow worse. Output will be so low that the product sells at a loss. A point will be reached, eventually, where the product breaks even. Cash earned will just balance the cost, and the product will start to earn an accounting profit. This maximum loss position will probably occur near the end of the introductory phase, but will be delayed well into development or even maturity for some products with costly and long pre-launch phases.

The cash cycle will lag behind profit. The cash outflow will be at its worst when the rate of growth of sales is the highest. The magnitude of the problem will depend on the credit terms given and taken by the firm. In these early life situations firms usually give good credit if they can, so cash is stretched to the limit frequently. At the end of the introductory phase the cash position is often negative and still falling.

In the development stage

Profit should be increasing in this stage, and cash flow should turn positive at last. Cash flow and the demands of working capital should ease as the rate of increase of sales eases off.

In maturity

Profit and cash flow will reach their maximum here. They will both plateau in this stage of the life cycle. Both cash flow and profit will take small dips as the firms increase advertising regularly to remind the customer of the product, and also make small design changes to 'modernise' the products image.

In the extension strategy stage

These can be costly, so will drag both profit and cash flow down. The cash position will suffer much more, though, especially if capital expenditure is required.

In decline

Since growth is now negative, both profit and cash flow will fall. Profit is likely to decline more rapidly than the cash position since the credit terms are now in favour of the firm.

So, there are three life cycles, at least. They are all illustrated in Figures 14.3 and 14.4.

Observe the importance of cash management again. A firm can easily go bankrupt in the process of successfully developing a product's sales, particularly when high rates of sales growth are being achieved.

Marketing activities

Marketing operates in a number of different ways when managing a product. They exploit the marketing mix, or the 'four Ps' as it is conveniently shortened to. The 'four Ps' are *product, price, place* and *promotion*. When the marketing research, after sales service and selling functions are added to this, they summarise all the major variables that can be used and adjusted by marketing. In all cases marketing has to make a decision, or a series of decisions on how to use or set these variables.

Now, an explanation and development of the 'four Ps' follows:

1. Product

With regards to the product the marketing staff, in collaboration with production and the board, have to decide on quality, performance, versatility, design, capacity, size, accessories, service provisions and guarantee. Note that not all these decisions can be made freely. A decision to produce a high quality product, for example, will dictate the requirements for performance, service and guarantee. CD plc was faced with these decisions when it decided to launch its CD players. It wanted them to be seen as quality products, of modern design. This dictated that the

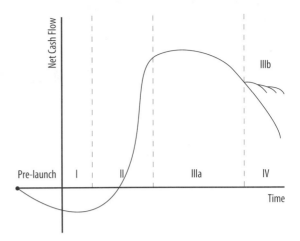

Figure 14.3 *Product cycle based on net cash flow*

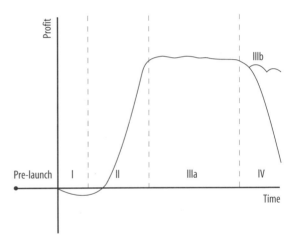

Figure 14.4 *A product cycle band on profit assumption: no profit can be made until sales start*

performance of the units should be high, and better than the competition's. As quality products they should be supported by a long, good guarantee, and a reliable service support.

Consider how the major car manufacturers evaluate their products, and how they view quality, performance, design, etc. Ford take a very different position than BMW and Porsche. Morgan Cars consider that their design, with its wooden chassis, and their manual production methods are critical to their image.

Decisions taken here will often determine the firm's image and reputation with the buying public, provided the other marketing variables are managed successfully.

2. Price

Price covers the whole range of price and near price options. Decisions have to be made on the 'list price' for the goods, arrangements for trade-ins and credit, discounts, payment methods and periods. Examine the windows in the high street. Examine all the price offers. Sales and reductions are common, along with 'buy now, pay later' deals. The 'list price' seems to exist only as a basis for the discounts and reductions.

A firm can choose any price policy it likes. However, decisions made over the product will influence the price decision. CD's quality product will have to be sold at a quality price, but it could offer generous trade-ins to attract customers. This is a common way of influencing price actually paid in the motor trade. Firms with 'no discounts' policies can get round this by offering 'very low mileage' second-hand cars. 150 miles on the clock is not unknown, with a healthy discount because the car is 'used'.

3. Place

The place where the good or service will be sold includes shops, supermarkets, warehouses, department stores, supermarkets and hypermarkets, and even mail order. This is largely a matter of tradition, but new ground is often being broken.

If decisions are being made in the 'four Ps' order there will be only very limited room for manoeuvre by now over place. CD plc will probably have to sell through exclusive shops, and a few high reputation department stores to support the quality image. Quality and wide availability in many different outlets is unusual, but Marks and Spencer seem to have found the secret!

4. Promotion

The area that is often prominent and obvious to the buyer is regarding the product's promotion. Decisions will cover advertising, sales promotion, publicity and PR, packaging, selling, sales force and merchandising. It is often thought that advertising is the only weapon, but that is far from the case.

Advertising is widely used. It is best known on TV these days, but also occurs in the press, on hoardings, public transport, at sports and theatrical events, etc. It is now a very developed, sophisticated and potentially expensive means of promotion. Often there is no guarantee that the advertisement will reach the potential buyer.

Sales promotion covers all the non-advertising options such as competitions, coupons, free gifts, 'buy one, get one free' offers, money off offers, trading stamps, 20% free, link purchases, and free samples. Promotion can be targeted at the final customer and/or the retail outlet. Manufacturers will offer inducements to outlets to stock their new products. These can be gifts, money off, and even holidays.

Publicity and PR (public relations) involves sponsorship of sports and the arts, entertaining at sports and theatre events, lobbying and the planting of newspaper and magazine articles. It is often used as a way of saying thank you to trade customers.

Packing is designed to protect the product in transit, and to give the handlers essential stacking information. Packaging is designed to enclose and promote the product. Packaging is important for many products. It is the means of identity for many, and supports the product image set earlier. Just consider the cosmetics industry and the quality and complexity of its packaging.

Selling

Merchandising is the art of sales maximisation at the point of sale.

It is concerned with the design of stores and the shelves. It is the design and provision of advertising materials and display systems on the counter or shelf. It is no accident that most supermarkets draw you in via fruit and vegetables and then circulate you clockwise. Shelf layout is planned in detail. Sweet boxes which open to form a high impact display unit have been designed and extensively tested.

These will support all the other marketing decisions. CD players will need advertising, but not in the press. Sales are unlikely to justify TV advertising, but the product will need support. It will need to be sold to the outlets, so a sales force may well be necessary. High quality material for display at the shops will be important. Remember, promotion is essentially a support function, supporting and reinforcing the decisions made about the first three of the 'four Ps'.

Product and place tend to be strategic decisions, and are taken at the start of the product's life. Changes in these factors are costly and major and are not undertaken lightly. Price and promotion are much more tactical in nature, and are varied frequently during all stages of the life of a product. This will be examined in detail in later chapters.

After-sales service

After-sales service, which includes guarantees and maintenance contracts, is critical for some products.

It is vital for cars, where 'two years *free* service' can be an excellent 'promotion', but not for toothpaste. Even here, though, the customer is provided with an 'agony aunt' to which they may complain!

There is a clear size effect here. The larger and more expensive the product, the more likely that after-sales service can be a real marketing 'tool'.

The weight given to the individual components of the marketing mix will vary with the type of product concerned. Remember the groupings that products are put into:

* *Consumer goods* – FMCGs and consumer durables
* *Industrial goods* – consumables and capital goods.

There are few advertisements for oil refineries on TV or in the press. Equally, there is little sales engineer support for cornflakes or toothpaste! (See Chapter 19.)

The full list of these variables in marketing operations, or the marketing tools, is as follows:

* Marketing research
* Product planning and development
* Pricing policy
* Distribution policy
* Marketing communications
* After-sales service

Note also that there are six possible variables, but these cannot all be varied independently. When the first is decided marketing had an absolutely free choice. After five have been set, the sixth is decided already. In statistical terms, there are six variables but only five degrees of freedom.

These key operations will be examined in subsequent chapters which will show how their application and use varies with the age of the product concerned or its position in its life cycle.

SUMMARY

Having studied this chapter, you should be able to:

▼ Define marketing and explain its function within a firm.

▼ Describe the concept of the product life cycle in terms of sales, profit and net cash flow.

▼ Define the marketing operation in terms of 'the four Ps', or the marketing mix as it is sometimes called, namely:

– *Product*

– *Price*

– *Place*

– *Promotion*

▼ Realise that this simple list is incomplete, and that marketing research, selling and after-sales service need to be added to give the full range of tools or weapons.

▼ Be able to explain the different life cycles of various products, and show how these influence the operation and working of the marketing mix.

Questions and activities

Technical terms and glossary

In the section below you are given a series of technical terms and their meanings. They have been scrambled, though. You must match up the terms and the definitions. When you have them correctly paired, transfer them to your vocabulary or glossary book.

You are also advised to transfer the definitions obtained during the exercises in the studies into this glossary book.

Technical terms

1. Marketing
2. Product life cycle
3. Extension strategy
4. Brand loyalty
5. Pre-launch stage
6. The 'four Ps'
7. Marketing mix
8. Merchandising
9. FMCGs
10. Decline stage

Definitions

A. A series of measures a firm may take to extend the life of a product through significantly lengthening its maturity stage.
B. An all-embracing function which assesses future market needs, coordinates the other functional areas of the firm to meet these needs, and promotes and distributes the goods or services at a price giving maximum satisfaction to the customer, and profitability to the firm.
C. A simplification of the list of marketing tools available to a firm. These are summarised under the major headings of product, price, place and promotion.
D. The blend of marketing weapons used by a company in the promotion and marketing of the company.
E. The last and terminal stage of a product's life where it is allowed to fade away and die.
F. A diagrammatical representation of the stages that a product goes through from birth to death.
G. That stage in the life of a product that occurs before it appears on the market. This 'gestation' period is usually expensive!
H. Goods bought regularly by the public which have no value once purchased. They tend to be consumed rapidly and often.
I. The promotion of a product at the point of sale. This includes shelf design, layout and display design, etc.
J. The strength with which consumers buy a particular brand of a good rather than a similar brand.

Short answer questions and essays

1. (*Essay*) Discuss the use of extension strategies using the turkey as an example.
2. What is the 'marketing mix'?
3. (*Essay*) Explain the concept of the product life cycle.
4. Why is the pre-launch stage of a product's life cycle so critical for a firm like Boeing?
5. Should a firm advertise its products that are in the decline stage of their life cycle?
6. (*Essay*) Compare and contrast how Fords and Jaguar exploit the 'four Ps' in their marketing strategy.
7. What additions to the 'four Ps' complete the marketing 'weapons'?

15
Market research

Preview

▼ This chapter will introduce the world of marketing research. After a short description of the areas where research is done, the differences between field and desk research will be established, as will be their relative advantages and costs.

▼ Market research is essentially an information gathering operation, using interviews, questionnaires, telephone surveys, consumer panels and discussion groups. This requires a knowledge of the design of questionnaires, the preparation of consumer profiles, and the statistical process of sampling. The processes of random, systematic, quota, and stratified sampling will be described, and their advantages and disadvantages outlined.

▼ The statistics used in analysing market research data will be introduced. First, the differences between the mode, median, and the arithmetic mean will be established. Then the basis of using standard deviations and variances to assess the spread of data will be outlined. A means of testing if any differences found are significant will be described.

▼ Market research is concerned with forecasting performance in a market as a whole based on sample data. Some simple forecasting techniques will then be described, namely the Delphi technique and time series analysis (i.e. index numbers).

▼ The chapter ends with a brief section on the presentation of data. In particular it discusses tables and a range of diagrammatical presentations, pie charts, graphs, bar charts and histograms.

Marketing research is one of the main arms of any marketing department. It is concerned with all aspects of marketing. It studies the market, the consumer, the competition, the effectiveness of all the relevant forms of advertising and sales promotion. It will investigate the effectiveness of sales forces, and will attempt to explain and develop means of influencing consumer behaviour.

Marketing research is concerned with the collection, analysis and interpretation of information. It examines the past and the present and attempts to predict the future.

The British Institute of Management (BIM) defines marketing research as:

'The objective gathering, recording and analysing of all the facts about problems relating to the transfer and sale of goods and services from producer to consumer or user.'

It is usually concerned with providing answers to five basic questions: Who? What? When? Where? and How? The question 'Why?' is far too difficult to answer.

The research findings are of use to many sections within the marketing department and other departments of the firm. Market researchers have to be skilled in the presentation of results and forecasts, as well as their interpretation.

Marketing research will examine questions in the area of the market, the product, selling, advertising as well as economic and business trends. It will provide answers to questions similar to the ones that follow:

- What is the size and nature of a particular market?
- What is the nature of the customers for a particular product?
- What are the market shares of competitors?
- Is the new product acceptable?
- How effective will the new advertisement be?
- How effective is the sales force?
- Where can new markets or uses be found for a product?
- What is the economic forecast.

Market research has its own professional society, the Market Research Society.

Market research, like any other research activity, is best run according to a set plan or procedure. A suggested plan is:

- Prepare a statement of objectives of the research.
- Prepare a design of the experimental or survey work to be done.
- Collect the data.
- Tabulate and analyse the data, and draw up conclusions and recommendations.
- Publish or present report of findings.
- Obtain feedback from 'customers'.

Marketing research can be done within a firm, or by one of the many specialist companies that exist. Advertising agencies have a research department within them which will establish the likely efficiency of any campaigns that it suggests to its clients. Marketing or market research is done in one or both of two different ways.

Desk research

Here the researcher makes use of existing or published data. This is known a secondary data. Information may be available within the firm, or may be available from outside sources. An important definition to remember is:

Secondary data is data or information already available inside or outside a firm. Data that was collected originally for a different piece of research, or a completely different purpose.

Researchers can obtain information from within a firm from purchasing, production, personnel, marketing, sales and finance departments. Much of this information will be in the form of raw data and will need to be processed and analysed within the research department.

External sources are vast. The main sources of data are the government, universities and other research organisations, trade associations, professional journals and commercial research organisations. The government, in particular, publishes a vast amount of economic data both monthly and annually. A particularly useful and interesting publication is *Social Trends*. A list of just some of the more international sources is given below:

Central Statistical Office publications
UN Yearbook of Labour Statistics
DOE Gazette
Retail Price Index
Economic Trends

Subscription services are available from Nielsen which markets its inventory audit of retail sales. This monitors sales and stock levels at a full range of retail outlets for the product groups foods, drugs and pharmaceuticals. Television Consumer Audit also sells data covering consumer expenditure, market share, product penetration, special offers and prices by region and by product group. Other significant sources of information are the Attwood Consumer Panel and the British Market Research Bureau's Target Panel.

Much information is now available through electronic database programmes. These commercial packages give the user access to data on a worldwide basis. University libraries operate a similar service, and operate international specialist databases.

This form of research should always be done first. It can provide the answers to complex questions, and has the advantage of being relatively cheap. It will not always cope, though. Then, and only then, the firm should switch to the other form of research.

Field research

Here the researcher performs original work. Procedures are designed and used to provide special data, known as primary data, to enable answers to be found to specific questions. Another definition to remember is:

Primary data is new data collected to answer a specific research question. It is data that is original to the investigation in hand.

This work is costly and potentially slow. It can provide detailed, fresh information and the most up-to-date solution. It is almost always used to answer questions about the effectiveness of new advertising, the acceptability of new products and their packaging, and studies into consumer behaviour.

Data, both primary and secondary, may be qualitative or quantitative. Statements such as 'the liquid was hot' are qualitative. Make the statement more specific, such as 'the liquid was heated to 27°C' and it becomes a quantitative statement. 'Most people prefer product X' is qualitative. 'Product X was preferred by 80% of the test consumers' is quantitative. Quantitative data is easy to process, particularly on a computer.

Sampling, the survey and various forms of interviews and questionnaires are the tools of field research. The choice of which is used can be critical to the validity of any eventual findings. Let us examine some of these methods and assess their use. This will be set in the area product development, and will involve potential consumers.

When a researcher wishes to investigate the potential for a new product, and decides that a consumer survey is the correct method of investigating the problem, then two major decisions have to be taken, relating to the questions:

- How will the questions be asked?
- How many people will be asked, and how will they be selected?

Information gathering

Information can be gathered in a number of different ways. These include unstructured or structured interviews, questionnaires, telephone surveys, consumer panels and discussion groups. Each have advantages and disadvantages, but cost effectiveness must never be overlooked. Let us now take a brief look at each of these.

Interviews

In an unstructured interview the discussion is allowed to develop as it comes. Data is obtained on almost a random basis. This is a slow and expensive process, but it can produce some high quality data. It is only used in special circumstances. This type of interview is very informal, and the interviewee comes under the minimum of pressure. Recording such an interview can be difficult. Today they can be taped, but this is expensive. Later analysis is also very difficult.

The structured interview, the situation where the interviewer follows a 'script', are more common. They are more formal than unstructured ones, and are much easier to record. The quality of data may not be as high as from the unstructured interview, though.

Interviews are slow and expensive. There is also the danger that they can be manipulated, particularly in the case of the structured interview. Leading questions must be avoided. At the end of an interview data has to be assembled and processed. The records of interviews are likely to be notes, so may not be suitable for data processing.

Thus, there is a need for a cheaper, quicker process of gathering data.

Questionnaires

Questionnaires are prepared sets of questions, specific questions, designed to get certain data. A great number of people can be asked the same questions, in the same form.

Questionnaires can be completed face to face with the interviewer, or may be completed at home and either collected or sent in by post. Collection has its advantages as it gives an opportunity for checking, but it is the more expensive route. However, collection tends to obtain a higher completion and return rate.

Questionnaires are cheap to operate, especially postal ones. There is a danger, though, as there is no real guarantee of who has actually completed the questionnaire. (Questionnaire design is an important topic and is discussed below.)

Telephone surveys

The telephone survey is becoming more popular, and can be less intimidating than a face-to-face interview. Information can be obtained quickly, especially if the panel composition is flexible. The wide availability of telephones today mean that this type of survey is now far less biased than it used to be. It obviously has real potential if the views of the users of telephone services are sought. There is growing risk for the researcher today, that the call may be confused with telephone selling. Telephone selling can be very intrusive and can make telephone surveys difficult.

Consumer panels

A consumer panel is a group of consumers which is used to test and report on a product. The test can be done at home, in which case the consumers never meet, or it can be done at a central location. In both cases the consumer, or tester, will complete a report. The design of this report is critical, and follows the guidelines described for questionnaires above.

Panels are usually controlled by a 'host' researcher, particularly if they are being carried out at the premises of a market research business. The panel may be watched and filmed in action here, not always with their knowledge.

Discussion groups

A discussion group is a form of group interview. A number of consumers can be brought together and shown a new product or a new advertisement and then encouraged to discuss it. Meetings can take place anywhere, hence their popular name of 'Town Hall' tests. They can be better managed, though, if they are held in suitably designed premises. It is a structured situation, at least in part, but the discussion can be far reaching. Recordings can be made and the group can even be secretly observed. It is widely used by advertising agencies. Interactions within the group can also be observed.

Panel selection is important. Some researchers use a set panel which it brings together from time to time. In other cases groups are brought together on a 'once off' basis.

If a questionnaire is to be used, then the design of this document is critical. How is this done?

Design of questionnaires

The first part of the document, before even the identity questions, must be the title and introduction. Tell the respondent what the aim of the survey is, and stress the importance of the answers. Respondents have to be persuaded to give up their time. This is particularly important with postal surveys. Recent research has indicated that the number of refusals to answer a questionnaire may introduce bias into the eventual conclusions.

Design is vitally important to the accuracy and value of any information gathered. It will be the prompt during the interview, if there is one, or will be the sole contact with the interviewee if it is a postal survey. The document, which will also be the report and the source of raw data, must contain two pieces of information. It must 'identify' the respondent, and must record the answers to the questions.

Identity information

Many questionnaires are confidential, and in most cases the name and address of the respondent is not required. Generalised data about the respondent may be important, i.e. sex, age group, income, occupation, marital status, car owner, and residential status may be important and may be asked. It is not normal to ask the exact age of respondent. More of this when the question of a 'representative sample' is examined. Now for the questions themselves.

Only ask for information which is relevant. Do not say the survey is confidential and then ask for the respondent's name and address. Remember, long and involved questionnaires are daunting and may put the respondent off. Do not 'waste' questions and the respondent's goodwill on these identity questions.

The body of the questionnaire

The questions themselves must be drafted with the purpose of the survey being kept in mind. Individual questions must:

- Be precise and unambiguous.
- Be easy to understand (avoid technical jargon).
- Be inoffensive.
- Not lead the respondent towards a particular answer (this would be a leading question).
- Avoid asking the respondent to perform calculations.
- Be capable of simple answers: give 'yes/ no/ don't know' options, or ask for an evaluation on a scale. Five- or seven-point scales are ideal. An example of a question with its answer scale follows is shown in Figure 15.1.

'Question 1' Spice Level. Did you consider that the strength of the curry was: (Circle one box only)

Excessively hot	Too hot	Hot	Satisfactory	Mild	Too mild	Completely bland
1	2	3	4	5	6	7

Figure 15.1 *A typical MR question and answer structure*

This question might have been used in a survey about a new variety of prepared food, or convenience foods.

The respondent has answered 'Mild'. This can be entered on the computer as '5' and then all answers analyses numerically and compared. Only ask one question at a time, but related questions may be set together in groups. Remember, the data will probably be processed by computer so digital responses are required. The questionnaire should be designed to make the subsequent computer entry easy.

A final point: provide a stamped, addressed envelope with any postal survey. It is unreasonable to expect the respondent to have to provide these and so pay part of the costs of the survey.

Who should the questionnaire be sent to? This is the problem of sampling.

Sample selection

It is impossible to interview everybody, so a sample has to be used. This sample has to be big enough so that the results will be significant, and representative of the potential users of the product in question.

Sample size is a matter of statistics. A sample of about 1,000 is usually more than adequate, provided the correct people are questioned. (Public opinion polls for the whole country are based on samples of about this size.) It is a problem of cost and accuracy. Costs tend to be directly related to the sample size, while the accuracy increases in a squared relationship, i.e. for double the potential accuracy the sample size has to be increased by a factor of 4.

The sample has to be representative. What does this mean?

A representative sample

Most products and services are used by only a portion of the general population. Some split clearly between male and female consumers, others are aimed at the young while others are targeted at the pensioner. If a firm wishes to carry out a survey about a particular product or service then the sample must be representative of the users or buyers. The firm must be aware of the 'user profile', and must then ensure that the sample used reflects this known profile. Note that the 'user profile' will probably have been found out by a market researcher. Consumers or buyers will have been interviewed and their key data determined.

A consumer profile for a product will contain the following information:

- sex
- age – this will usually be specified in terms of broad ranges, i.e. under 18 years, 18 to 30 years, 30 to 40 years, over 65 years
- socioeconomic grouping
- working or non-working
- income group.

It may sometimes be necessary to classify according to ethnic grouping or even religion, but do not probe here unless it is absolutely vital to the survey.

Socioeconomic grouping

This is an attempt to get a measure of the income, or class of the respondent into the sample profile.

One of the most common groupings is that produced by the Joint Industry Committee for National Readership Surveys (JICNARS). This classifies on the basis of the occupation of the head of the household, and splits people into social grades A to E. This is illustrated in Figure 15.2.

Group	Description	Head of Household's Occupation
A	Upper middle class	Higher managerial, administrative or professional
B	Middle class	Intermediate, administrative, or professional
C1	Lower middle class	Supervisory or clerical and junior managerial, administrative or professional
C2	Skilled working class	Skilled manual workers
D	Working class	Semi-skilled and unskilled manual workers
E	Those at lowest level of subsistence	State pensioners or widows (no other earner), casual or lower grade workers

Figure 15.2 The classification of consumers into socioeconomic groupings (Basis – JICNARS)

Thus middle managers and their families are in Group B. A new engineering graduate would start work as a supervisor or a junior management position, so would be classified into Group C1. As his or her career develops grading will change first to B and with luck and ability to A. There are other classifications available but the JICNARS groupings are very widely used.

A business needs to know its consumer profile, and will find this out by doing market research. It may survey actual buyers, and if it uses a questionnaire as part of the guarantee documentation, will get a sample of nearly 100% of its purchasers. The results of such a survey of the buyers of high quality CD players by CD plc might give the information shown in Table 15.1.

In this profile the income of the buyer has not been identified separately. There is assumed to be a relationship between income and social grouping. CD plc also did not consider it necessary to probe the ethnic basis of its customers.

Table 15.1
Consumer profile for quality CD players sold by CD plc

Data collected over a 10 week period in UK during January, February and March 1992. 85% of purchasers responded.

1. Sex: Male 75%   Female 25%

2. Employment Status:

	Working males	85% of male buyers
	Working females	55% of female buyers

3. Age: (%)

	Under 20	3
	20 - 30	27
	30 - 40	40
	40 - 60	20
	Over 60	10

4. Social group: (%)

	A	13
	B	25
	C1	45
	C2	15
	D	2
	E	0

5. Purchase region (GB only): CD plc's sales regions
(Units. % of total sales)

South East	30	South	15
South West	8	Midlands	20
North East	10	North West	8
Scotland	5	Wales	3
Northern Ireland	1		

This information, which needs to be reviewed regularly, is vital for planning other research activities, and later when planning advertising campaigns and other marketing operations. This consumer profile will be used again later.

The researcher now knows who should be interviewed. How should they be selected? This is the problem of drawing a sample.

Drawing a sample

There are five common ways of drawing a sample. Which one is used depends on the type of survey being planned, the location and the budget available.

1. *Random sample.* People are chosen in such a way so that each and every person has exactly the same chance of being selected. It is not widely used within market research, at least not as a method of selecting a complete sample. A random sample presupposes a product that is used by everyone. Premium Bond prizewinners are chosen at random, but the respondents in a political opinion poll are not. Here people under 18 need to be eliminated at the very least since they cannot vote yet. Their opinion and voting potential is therefore irrelevant.

2. *Systematic sample.* This is a modified form of random sampling. People are selected according to a predetermined pattern, i.e. every tenth person. It is used in some situations in a population census. Rather than question the residents in each house in the country, every tenth one may be sent a questionnaire.

3. *Quota sample.* When the population being studied is very dispersed, say deep in the country, it may be more economic to interview everyone in a particular village. Equally in high density housing estates it may be more economic to confine interviews to the residents of a single block of flats.

None of these methods will produce a representative sample other than in very special circumstances. The last two methods do produce a fully representative sample.

4. *Stratified sample.* The researcher knows the consumer profile for the product being studied. The sample size is also known so a sample plan can be prepared. Thus the interviewer will be given a set of instructions to interview specific people. An example is given in Case Study 15.1.

- **Step 1:** *Establish the consumer profile (see Table 15.1).*

CASE STUDY 15.1

New product reception

CDs Survey of Potential CD Buyers in the South East

CD plc has developed a new CD player for the quality end of the market. It wishes to carry out a survey of potential customers, and wishes to confine the survey to the Southern Region.

How should it plan the interviews? Remember, CD plc has a consumer profile available to it.

- **Step 2:** *Design the questionnaire.*

- **Step 3:** *Establish the sample size (1,000 was recommended by the Statistics Department).*

- **Step 4:** *Prepare an interviewing plan. This will be done using the consumer profile. It is a matter of numbers and percentages. Since there are to be 1,000 interviews, and 75% of customers have been shown to be male, CD should plan to interview 750 males overall. How are the subdivisions planned? Examine the following examples.*

Example 1. Under 20 age group.
The profile indicates 30 interviews should fall into this gross grouping. However:

Under 20 males, socioeconomic group A
   $30 \times 0.75 \times 0.13 = 3$

Under 20 males, socioeconomic group C1
   $30 \times 0.75 \times 0.45 = 10$

Example 2. Age group 30 to 40.
The profile indicates that 400 interviews should fall into this group. However:

30 to 40 females, socioeconomic group B
   $400 \times 0.25 \times 0.25 = 25$

30 to 40 females, socioeconomic group C2
   $400 \times 0.25 \times 0.15 = 15$

So the interview planning section is developing a sampling profile. At this stage it will see that it needs to identify:

25 females in the age group 30 to 40, in socioeconomic group B

15 females in the age group 30 to 40, in socioeconomic group C2

10 males under 20, in socioeconomic group C1
3 males under 20, in socioeconomic group A

Fifty-three interviews are planned so far; only another 957 to go!

Now it is your turn. Confirm that the following numbers and types of people will be needed to satisfy the test plan and the consumer profile.

Female: 40 to 60, Group B	*12 or 13*
Male: Over 60, Group D	*1 or 2*
Female: 20 to 30, Group C2	*10*
Male: 40 to 60, Group B	*37 or 38*

- **Step 5:** *Identify persons to be interviewed who meet the specification required. Issue instructions to interviewers, and possibly book interview times. If an agency or consultantcy firm is used, a contract and fee must also be negotiated.*

Actually naming and finding people can be difficult. Names may be chosen at random from records held by the company, but these detailed records must be available. How can the process go on if actual names cannot be found?

5. *Quota sampling.* This is very similar to stratified sampling, but the interviewer is left to pick actual respondents. Thus, the schedule may require that ten people are interviewed – five male, five female; age group 20 to 30; social group C. The interviewer can then select people who meet the specification. This can cause problems, also, and lead to interviewers having to work unsocial hours. Working people are not likely to be found in residential areas during the day. Equally they do not easily give up their lunch break to the interview, nor do employers readily accept interviews in the office during working hours.

The sample has been prepared, the interviews completed. Now the information collected has to be processed and analysed. This analysis is based on statistical methods. (The rest of this chapter is quite demanding, mathematically, and much of it is beyond the scope of some A-Level boards.)

Analysis of research data

Much of market research is about forecasting, or predicting what will happen in the future. Market research staff are expected to be able to forecast the likely sales of the firm, and assess the effects of the marketing variables on this. It will also be expected to be able to analyse and forecast the influences of economic factors such as the cost of living, or the level of real incomes on the operations of the firm. It follows, therefore, that marketing staff are much concerned with data collection, analysis and presentation. They rely heavily on statistical techniques in this part of their work. The most widely used techniques involve measures of the 'average', measures of spread and accuracy, sampling and forecasting.

Three measures of the 'average' are commonly used, the median, the mode and the arithmetic mean. (The latter measure is the one commonly known as 'the average'.) These are attempts to summarise a group of data by a single number, or to develop a measure of its central tendency. The definitions of these measures of central tendency are as follows:

The mode is the most frequently occurring value in the sample or group.

The median is the middle value of a group of data when all the results are put into ascending or descending order.

The arithmetic mean is the result obtained when all the individual results are added together and then divided by the number of values in the sample.

This important set of definitions is summarised in Table 15.2.

**Table 15.2
Summary of the different 'means'
used in research.**

Average	Meaning
Mode	Most frequently occurring
Median	Mid-point or middle answer
Arithmetic	Sum of all answers
mean	divided by the number of answers

Consider the following situation, which involves CD plc and the use of its products. See Case Study 15.2.

CASE STUDY 15.2

CD plc and use of its records

CD plc wished to know how often its popular 'Top Ten' recordings were played by the buyers each week. A small survey was taken amongst 25 buyers, who were asked the following question:

Having just purchased a 'Top Ten' Record, how many times do you expect to play it in the next week?

The answers are summarised in the table below.

**Table 15.3
Results of the survey by CD plc
into the playing of its 'Top Ten' records
(collection order)
(left to right, top to bottom.)**

1	5	2	3	3
2	5	2	1	3
3	1	3	3	1
4	3	2	2	3
5	3	4	4	4

The first step is to represent the data in ascending order.

**Table 15.4
Results of the survey by CD plc into the playing of its 'Top Ten' records (ascending order)**

1	2	3	3	4
1	2	3	3	4
1	2	(3)	3	5
1	2	3	4	5
2	3	3	4	5

The mode (the most frequently occurring value)

To achieve the mode reorganise the data into a frequency distribution table, as illustrated in the Table 15.5 on page 183.

The most frequently occurring value is 3, (nine times out of the sample of 25) so the modal value, or mode is '3 times per week'.

The median (the middle value)

For 25 results, the median is the thirteenth result when the values are put into numerical order. In this case the median value is also 'three playings per week'. Look back at Table 15.4.

If there are an even number of observations, then the median is the average of the two central observations.

The arithmetic mean

The arithmetic mean is defined as $\sum x / n$, where x = individual result and n = number of results. So add together the 25 individual results (72) and divide by (25).

Arithmetic mean $= \frac{72}{25} = 2.88$ or 2.9
(1 decimal place only)

This has been an easy calculation since there were few results, and the results were simple whole numbers. Calculations can be accelerated by using pooled data, however. Examine how it is done using the present data.

x	1	2	3	4	5
n	4	5	9	4	3
xn	4	10	27	16	15

$\sum xn \quad 72$

$\sum \frac{xn}{n} = \frac{72}{25} = 2.9$ (1 decimal place)

Two other measures are sometimes determined and quoted, the range and the geometric mean.

The range is the difference between the lowest and the highest value.

For CD and its record, the range is 'from 1 to 5 times per week'.

Table 15.5
Frequency distribution of record playing data

Playings per week	1	2	3	4	5
Frequency of observations	4	5	9	4	3

The geometric mean

This measure is rarely used. It is calculated by multiplying together the values and then taking the appropriate root. For CD this would involve multiplying together the 25 results, then taking the 25th root. This is complicated, so examine a much smaller set of data. Consider the following series: 2 4 3 5.

The geometric mean is calculated by first multiplying the numbers together (2 x 4 x 3 x 5 = 120) then taking the 4th root (3.3). (The 4th root is easily calculated by pressing the square root button on a calculator twice!) So the geometric mean for the data is 3.3, while the arithmetic mean is 3.5.

This method is used to process sets of numbers where the range is large. The geometric mean reduces the effect of the large numbers. It is used in the calculation of share price indices, where there may be a wide variation is actual share prices and it would be inaccurate to give excess weight to the more expensive shares. The geometric mean gives a more balanced picture of overall share price movements.

Now, a typical situation through which the problems of dealing with the spread of data will be investigated.

Spread of data

Consider the Case Study 15.3. The arithmetic mean, of the average incomes of the two groups of customer clearly are different. Confirm that the actual results are as shown. There would seem to be an indication that the more expensive product is bought by the better off buyers. But is the difference in gross income significant or not? This is assessed by examining the spread of the data, by working out the standard deviations for the sets of data. What is a *standard deviation*? First, some statistical theory must be looked at.

The two sets of data above are relatively symmetrical about the average, i.e. there are more or less the same number of customers with incomes greater and lower than the mean. This type of distribution is common and is known as a normal distribution. Normal distributions can have very different shapes. Examine Figure 15.3, which shows two distributions with the same averages.

CASE STUDY 15.3

Consumer incomes and the sales of CD's products

CD plc sells high quality, expensive CD systems and low cost, mass market tape decks. It seems reasonable to assume that the more expensive product is bought by the consumers with the greatest incomes, but CD has no data to support this view. The market research department of CD has done a survey and has interviewed the last 50 customers each who had bought either CD players or tape decks. Part of the interview involved the sensitive question of customer income. The actual question, and the tabulated, grouped results are reproduced below.

Table 15.6

Results of customer income survey for CD plc

Question: Tick one box to indicate your gross income.

(Gross Income = Income before tax or any other deductions)

Income range			Tape decks	CD players
			(Number of customers)	
Under £5,000			0	0
£5,001	to	£8,000	3	0
£8,001	to	£11,000	7	2
£11,001	to	£14,000	10	5
£14,001	to	£17,000	12	8
£17,001	to	£20,000	8	15
£20,001	to	£23,000	4	10
£23,001	to	£26,000	2	4
£26,001	to	£29,000	2	3
£29,001	to	£32,000	1	2
£32,001	to	£35,000	1	1
Over £35,001			0	0
Average income			£16,000	£19,500
Modal income			£15,500	£20,500

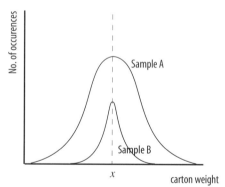

Figure 15.3 *Diagram showing two different normal distributions*

Both distributions have the same mean, but one is much wider than the other. This wideness, or spread, can be measured by working out the statistical values known as the variance and the standard deviation for the data. This is done using the following formulae:

Variance: $\dfrac{\Sigma (x - \bar{x})^2}{n}$

Standard deviation: $\dfrac{\sqrt{(Variance)}}{n}$

Where x = value of an observation
$\bar{x}$ *= average of all observations, and*
n = number of observations.

A measure of the distortion, or skewness of a distribution may be obtained by determining the coefficient of skewness. This is given by the formula:

Coefficient of skewness = $\dfrac{Mean - Mode}{Standard\ deviation}$

The lower the coefficient the nearer to normal the distribution is. Now, an example to work through. Consider the following Case Study 15.4. The average value is 11.5, while the mode is 12. Variance and standard deviation are calculated in Table 15.8.

Variance is 2.09 and SE is 1.44.

The coefficient of skewness is calculated by inserting values into the formula, and gives 11.5 - 12 / 1.44, or − 0.35. The distribution is slightly skewed towards the low side of the average.

Now apply the same operation to the two sets of data obtained about the incomes of CD's customers. It is worked for the CD player, the reader should confirm the results for the tape deck (see Table 15.9).

Class size at school

The policy of the school is to operate with a set size of 12. Very few are actually at this level, but do they conform overall with their own policy. A Business Studies student was set to find out. The resuts of the exercise are shown below.

Table 15.7

Size of block of sets at a school

8	10	12	12	13
9	11	12	12	13
9	11	12	12	13
10	11	12	12	13
10	11	12	13	14

The average value is 11.5, while the mode is 12. Variance and standard deviation are calculated below.

Table 15.8

Calculation of variance and standard deviation

x	f	$(x-\bar{x})$	$(x-\bar{x})^2$	$f(x-\bar{x})^2$
8	1	3.5	12.25	12.25
9	2	2.5	6.25	12.50
10	3	1.5	2.25	6.75
11	4	0.5	0.25	1.00
12	9	0.5	0.25	2.25
13	5	1.5	2.25	11.25
14	1	2.5	6.25	6.25
	$\Sigma\,25$			$\Sigma\,52.25$

Table 15.9

Calculation of variance and standard error for CD customers

x	f	$(x-\bar{x})$	$(x-\bar{x})^2 m$	$f(x-x)(m)$
6,500	0			
9,500	2	10,000	100	200
12,500	5	7,000	49	245
15,500	8	4,000	16	128
18,500	15	1,000	1	15
21,500	10	2,000	4	40
24,500	4	5,000	25	100
27,500	3	8,000	64	192
30,500	2	11,000	121	242
33,500	1	14,000	196	196
	$\Sigma\,50$			$\Sigma\,1,358$

Variance = £271,600 Standard deviation = £521
Coefficient of skewness = − 1000 / 521 = − 1.9.

The distribution is quite skewed towards the low side of the average ie towards the smaller incomes.

The equivalent values for the tape deck buyers and their incomes is:

Variance = £357,700
Standard deviation = £598
Coefficient of skewness = + 0.84.

This distribution is tighter than for CD players and is also skewed the other way.

Summarise the statistics calculated so far (see Tabe 15.10). There is a difference, but is it real. Using the statistical language, is the difference *significant*?

Table 15.10

Summary of statistics for CD and tape deck buyers

	CD buyers	Tape deck buyers
Average	£19,500	£16,000
Mode	£20,500	£15,500
Variance	£271,600	£357,700
Standard error	£521	£598
Skewness	- 1.9	+ 0.84

Significance testing

Significance testing is an important statistical operation. Researchers are often faced with the questions such as 'are the results representative?' or 'are the differences real and significant?'.

First, a little more theory. CD has interviewed a number of people who have bought CD players and tape decks. It has taken a *sample* of buyers from the *population*, or all the buyers. Both groups have means, standard deviations and other statistical methods. Statisticians use different notations for these measures.

Measure	Population	Sample
Mean	μ	$\bar{x}$
Standard deviation	σ	s
Sample size	–	n

The sample should be representative of the population. Examine Figure 15.4.

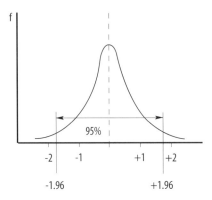

95%

-2   -1   +1   +2

-1.96   +1.96

Figure 15.4 *The normal distribution and distribution about the mean*

Statisticians can demonstrate that, for a normal distribution:

1. for a population of mean (μ) and standard deviation (σ), the sample means are also Normally Distributed, with a mean value (μ) and a standard deviation of $\frac{(\sigma)}{\sqrt{n}}$, where n is the number of observations in the sample.
2. provided the sample size is 30 or more, the sample means are approximately Normally distributed with mean (μ) and standard deviation $\frac{(\sigma)}{\sqrt{n}}$.

The standard deviation of the sample means about the population mean is called the standard error (SE) of the mean. If the sample size is 30 or more, SE can be estimated using the formula $\frac{s}{\sqrt{n}}$.

Significance testing uses these statistical measures. The reader should now understand why sample sizes of '30 plus' are very common. 50 is a good number, provided that such a sample size can be afforded.

Samples of less than 30 can be handled, but this will involve more complicated statistics. Such techniques are beyond the scope of A-Level.

How can this theory be used to measure the significance of any findings? One simple method is to set up a 'null hypothesis', i.e. assume that the difference shown, or the trend is not real, is not significant. Consider the two questions posed.

Is the result representative?

Modern weights and measures, and trades description legislation makes weight control vital to many firms. If a carton is claimed to contain 500 g of product it must do so, subject to clearly defined limits. Examine and work through the following Case Study 15.5.

A filling machine fills by volume. Variations in the bulk density of the product and the actual volume filled results in packages of different weight. The development department will be able to set the machine up so that the packs conform to the law.

First, set the machine to fill about 500 g on average. When the machine has settled down, take 50 cartons and weigh the contents. Results are shown below.

Pack weight (g)	495	496	497	498	499	500
Frequency	1	2	3	6	15	10

Pack weight (g)	501	502	503	504	505	506
Frequency	7	3	1	1	0	1

Now confirm the following statistical measures for this data.

Sample mean ($\bar{x}$) = 499.54 g
Sample standard deviation (s) = 1.96 g
Standard error (SE) = $\frac{1.96}{\sqrt{50}}$ = 0.28 g

CASE STUDY 15.5

Detergent filling and carton weights

A firm sells detergent in 500 g packets. It must ensure that 99% of all cartons contain 500 g of the product. How should the machine be set up?

Was the machine set to a mean of 500 g? Carry out a 'Z' test ie work out the following equation:

$$Z = \bar{x} - \frac{\mu}{SE} = 499.54 - \frac{500}{0.28} = 1.6$$

The Z test assesses if the null hypothesis is valid or not. The greater the Z value the more likely is it that the situation is real, i.e. that the sample is a valid part of the population. In this case it will indicate whether the machine was correctly set or not.

The Z value here is rather low. Statisticians have established that the following rules detailed in Table 15.11 apply. There is a more than 5% chance that the machine was not set to fill 500 g, but was actually set slightly below that. Using the results will mean that the firm errs on the safe side.

Table 15.11
Rejection values for various confidence levels

	Confidence level (%)	Reject if Z value exceeds (SEs)
Significant	95	1.96
Highly significant	99	2.58
Very highly significant	99.9	3.29

The machine must be set so that a carton weight of 500 g is obtained at the 95% confidence limit. 95% confidence corresponds to two standard errors.

Let us return to the results. At the 95% level the machine filled cartons in the range 499.54 - 2(1.96), or 495.62 to 503.46 g. The set weight needs to be increased to 504.38 g to be safe. The lower 5% confidence limit will then be 500 g.

Is the difference significant?

Return to the original problem with CD over its buyers of CDs and tape decks. A reminder of the position is illustrated in Table 15.12.

Are the two sets of buyers different? The null hypothesis is that they are not. If they are from the same population the results may be combined.

SE can be estimated as follows:

$$SE = \sqrt{\frac{S_1^2}{n_2} + \frac{S_2^2}{n_2}} = \sqrt{\frac{521^2}{50} + \frac{598^2}{50}}$$
$$= \sqrt{12,580.9} = 112.16$$
$$Z\ value = 19,500 - 16,000 / 112.16 = 31.2.$$

Table 15.12
Summary of statistics for CD and tape deck buyers

	CD buyers	Tape deck buyers
Average	£19,500	£16,000
Mode	£20,500	£15,500
Variance	£271,600	£357,700
Standard error	£521	£598
Skewness	− 1.9	+ 0.84

This indicates a real difference, with a very high degree of confidence.

Remember, statistics is concerned with probability, with confidence limits. It can tell the user if situations are likely, but it can never be 100% accurate. The 'unlikely' will occur occasionally, without warning. Always remember the limitations of statistics.

Forecasting techniques

Much of marketing research is concerned with obtaining data and information about the situation today. The other major function is to look into and predict the future. This scientific process uses a number of established forecasting techniques. It is then the responsibility of marketing and the other decision makers in the firm to take decisions on company actions in the light of these predictions. Forecasting may be qualitative or quantitative.

Qualitative methods

Many firms and government bodies employ experts to advise about the future. The treasury employs a series of economists as advisers. This type of group can be used in a number of ways.

The Delphi technique

In the Delphi technique, groups of experts are examined through a series of questionnaires. Each series of questions is derived from the answers to the previous ones. Results and opinions are pooled and a consensus view is eventually obtained. Experts do not see the answers from the other experts, nor do they meet as a panel. This eliminates all group dynamics, and no expert can be influenced by the others.

Panel discussions

In panel discussions the experts meet with the express objective of their coming to a consensus view.

These techniques are often applied to economic and political considerations.

Quantitative methods

The main quantitative method, known as time series analysis involves examining data, identifying trends hidden within it, then predicting these trends into the future. Sales information is particularly suitable to such analysis.

The sales of products are influenced by many factors. Some products are subject to seasonal influences. The result is that sales, on a monthly or quarterly basis are often variable and it is difficult to deduce trends. The technique known as time series analysis can be used in an attempt to identify real trends. This involves breaking down data to identify three components, or influences for change.

The trend

The underlying movement behind the statistics is called the trend. Are sales really falling, rising or are they static?

Seasonal variations

Are there any parts of the year where sales are particularly strong or weak, i.e. are there any seasonal variations? Christmas often has a significant effect, but so may the summer holiday season, the harvest or the start of the school or university terms and year.

Random variations

These are 'one off', or random events that can occur and will mask the other influences or trends. Such incidents as the Great Storm, an election, crashes of the stock market or the pound leaving the ERM (European exchange rate mechanism) may significantly affect the sales of a firm.

These components can be exposed by using the technique of 'moving averages'. How does this work? Examine and work Case Study 15.6.

Underlying trends can be extracted from the data by taking averages, or arithmetic means to be precise. Average sales for the five years of trading have been encouraging. Examine Table 15.14.

CASE STUDY 15.6

CD plc and its sales of video tapes

CD plc has been selling video tapes for five years. Sales, on a quarterly basis, have been variable, but there are indications of regular growth, overlaid by a real seasonal effect. The directors want the position classified. Quarterly sales data is presented below in tabular form.

Table 15.13
Quarterly sales data for video tapes
(units - £000s)

Year	Q1	Q2	Q3	Q4
1988	10	8	16	28
1989	24	22	23	33
1990	34	32	30	36
1991	42	42	40	38
1992	36	37	40	40

Table 15.14
CD plc and Annual Video Tape Sales (Units - £000s)

Year	1988	1989	1990	1991	1992
Sales	15.5	25.5	35.0	40.5	38.3

Sales have been rising for the last four years, but now seem to be falling. A more accurate picture can be obtained by taking moving averages, i.e. averages of successive four quarter periods. This information can be further refined by averaging successive pairs of such moving averages. This has been done for CD's sales data and is reproduced as Table 15.15. These results are presented graphically as Figure 15.5.

Table 15.15
Sales of video tapes in moving average form

Period	Sales	4 period moving total	8 period moving total	Moving average trend
Q1/1	10			
Q2/1	8			
Q3/1	16			17.25
Q4/1	28	62		20.75
Q1/2	24	76	138	23.37
Q2/2	22	90	166	24.87
Q3/2	23	97	187	26.75
Q4/2	33	102	199	29.25
Q1/3	34	112	214	31.37
Q2/3	32	122	234	32.62
Q3/3	30	129	251	34.00
Q4/3	36	132	261	36.25
Q1/4	42	140	272	38.75
Q2/4	42	150	290	40.25
Q3/4	40	160	310	39.75
Q4/4	38	162	322	38.37
Q1/5	36	156	318	37.75
Q2/5	37	151	307	38.00
Q3/5	40	151	302	
Q4/5	40	153	304	

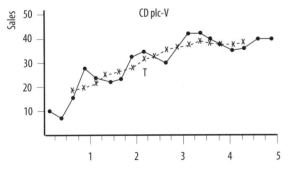

Figure 15.5 *Plot of sales of video tapes against time showing various trend lines*

The trend line can now be seen clearly. The best estimate of the future is obtained by extending or extrapolating the trend line forward. Remember about presentation, though, that the *actual* trend line must be clearly distinguished from the *forecast future* sales pattern.

An estimate of the seasonal effects can be obtained by subtracting the trend figure for a particular quarter from the actual quarterly sales figures. The resulting differences represent the seasonal effects. This has been done for CD's sales figures. The results are shown in Table 15.16.

Table 15.16 Estimate of seasonal effects on video tape sales

	Q1	Q2	Q3	Q4
	0.63	(2.87)	(1.25)	7.25
	2.63	(0.62)	(3.75)	3.75
	3.25	1.75	(4.00)	(0.25)
	(1.75)	(1.00)	0.25	(0.37)
Av.	1.73	(0.68)	(2.19)	2.60
	1.7	(0.7)	(2.2)	2.6

CD seems to gain sales in the first and last quarters of the year, but lose them in the middle quarters. Thus the winter seems to 'encourage' sales. The seasonal effects do not seem to be static, though, so CD should observe this trend closely. Seasonal effects may well change with the state of the product, particularly its stage in the life cycle. This seems to be happening here, and the seasonal effects seem to be reducing as the product becomes much better known. The sales pattern is consistent with a product in the maturity stage of its life cycle.

A final word on the extrapolation of data. Forecasts can be 'optimistic', the 'most likely' or 'pessimistic'. In this case, sales seem to be at a critical point. It is safer to assume a pessimistic case, and then plan to take strong marketing action in an attempt to rectify it. There is another possible situation, though. The product may already be in the early stage of decline. In this case the product should not be supported any more, but the marketing effort applied to new or growing products.

This analytical technique has provided information for management. It has provided another base for decision making, but it does not in itself take decisions. Professional judgement is still required.

The last stage of the market research operation is the presentation of its findings.

Presentation of data

Much research data is presented in tabular, graphical or chart form.

Tables

All readers will be familiar with tables, and they have been widely used in this book already. Remember, tables should have titles and, if they contain other people's or firm's information, the source should be acknowledged. The units should always be clearly marked.

The aim of using tables is to present data in such a way as to make it easier to read and use. Tables have no set format, so the drafter should always remember what the table is trying to achieve.

Graphical presentation

Graphs have an obvious visual impact and are excellent for showing trends. Graph drafting again should follow some conventional rules.

- Give each graph a title, and a source if appropriate.
- Plot the independent variable on the horizontal or X axis. It follows that the dependent variable will be on the vertical, or Y axis.
- Each axis must be fully labelled, and the scale fully stated.

Scales may be arithmetic, logarithmic or a combination of both.

Care must be taken when reading graphs as they can be misleading. Examine 15.6 which illustrate some common traps.

Be careful over actual and forecast data. Are the

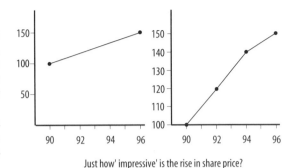

Just how' impressive' is the rise in share price?

Figure 15.6 *Actual vs forecast information*

scales what they seem? Is the comparison valid? Are the scales actually the same. Warning: the apparently simple and informative graph can be a trap.

Diagrammatic presentations

Some data can be presented, or summarised on pie charts, bar charts or histograms. Remember each must be correctly titled, and the source of the data acknowledged.

Pie charts

A pie chart is a circular diagram where the size of the slice represents the size of the variable being represented. If data from two time periods is to be compared, then the difference between the totals can

CASE STUDY 15.7

Presentation of annual profit data for the divisions of CD plc

The directors of CD plc are considering the layout and presentation of their profit data for the next annual report and account. The actual raw data is shown in the table below.

Table 15.17

Profit data for CD plc by product division (Units – £000s)

Year	1992	1993
CDs	120	230
Audio tapes	200	180
Video tapes	250	320
Equipment	85	125
Computer tapes	75	95
Total	730	950

It was decided to use pie charts. Since a circle is made up of 360° the pie 'slice' sizes can be worked out as follows:

Table 15.18

Calculation of chart angles for 1992

CDs	360 x 120/730 = 59°
Audio tapes	360 x 200/730 = 99°
Video tapes	360 x 250/730 = 123°
Equipment	360 x 85/730 = 42°
Computer tapes	360 x 75/730 = 37°
Total	360°

be represented by the areas of the circle. Examine and work through the Case Study 15.7.

It was decided to use pie charts. Since a circle is made up of 360° the pie 'slice' sizes can be worked out as shown in Table 15.18. Confirm that the corresponding angles for 1993 are 87, 68, 121, 45 and 39° respectively.

It was decided that the diameter of the chart for 1992 should be 4 cm. The diameter of the chart for 1993 should then be increased in proportion to the square root of the ratio of the total profits, e.g. profit has increased from £730,000 to £950,000. The ratio of the profits is 1: 1.30. Diameter of the chart should be increased in the ratio of 1: √1.3. So the new diameter should be 4 x 1.14 or 4.56 cm. The resulting presentation is shown on Figure 15.7. Do not forget that pie charts should be titled and credited, just like any other diagram.

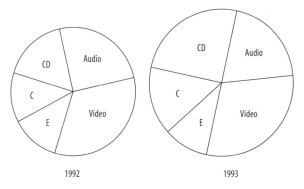

Figure 15.7 *Illustration of a pie chart*

Bar charts

In a bar chart the height of the bar represents the variable being presented. The width of the bar has no significance, but it is conventionally always equal. Bar charts can be presented in a number of different ways. Examine Figure 15.8 where CD plc's profit data is shown in a series of bar charts. Do not forget the title and credits. Also look out for any misleading scales.

The bars on a bar chart 'sit' on an axis. The bars do not touch as the support axis is just that, a support, not a scale.

Histograms

A histogram is a form of bar chart where the area of the 'bar' represents the variable. If all the bars are the same width then the height again represents the magnitude of the variable. The 'bars' touch as the bar sits on a scale.

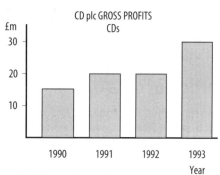

Figure 15.8 *Illustration of a bar chart*

Histograms are widely used when presenting statistical data. Consider the set of data in Table 15.19, which represents the examination results for a class of 25 students. This data is presented in the form of a histogram in Figure 15.9.

Table 15.19
Results of business studies trail examination (ordered data)

52	56	56	57	58
61	62	62	63	64
64	66	67	68	68
69	69	69	71	72
74	75	77	81	93

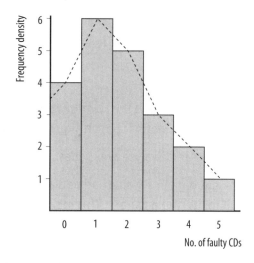

Figure 15.9 *Illustration of a histogram*

The line joining the tops of the columns is known as a frequency polygon.

As always, do not forget the title and credits. Draw neatly: it takes no more time, and remember that good presentation helps clarity. It is part of the marketing operation, the marketing of the research findings themselves.

Distortion of data

Data presented should be truthful. This is not always done, and some forms of presentation will give a misleading impression. For example, pie diameters which do not represent the data. The diameter usually represents the total factor being presented. Examine Figure 15.10, and the data upon which it is based.. Overall sales have actually fallen, not risen.

Profits(£m)

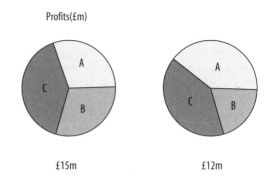

£15m   £12m

Figure 15.10 *Misleading use of pie charts*

SUMMARY

Having studied this long but important chapter, you will be able to:

▼ Define marketing research, and differentiate clearly between *desk and field research*.

▼ Describe the information gathering process. In particular you will be able to design surveys, and ensure that you get the correct consumer profile.

▼ Comment on the analysis of results.

▼ Define and use a range of averages, namely:

– *Mode*

– *Median*

– *Arithmetic mean*

▼ Describe in outline the *normal distribution*, and be able to use the *standard deviation* and other simple statistical techniques to analyse data.

▼ Draw up and analyse *time series*.

▼ Present data using alternative diagrammatic forms, and be able to comment on their suitability and accuracy. This includes:

– *Pie charts*

– *Graphs*

– *Bar charts*

– *Histograms*

Questions and activities

Technical terms and glossary

In the section below you are given a series of technical terms and their meanings. They have been scrambled, though. You must match up the terms and the definitions. When you have them correctly paired, transfer them to your vocabulary or glossary book.

You are also advised to transfer any definitions obtained during the exercises in the case studies into this glossary book.

Technical terms

1. Desk research
2. Field research
3. Market research
4. Consumer panels
5. Representative sample
6. Socioeconomic grouping
7. Random sample
8. Quota sample
9. Mode
10. Median
11. Arithmetic mean
12. Significance testing
13. Pie chart
14. Bar chart
15. Histogram
16. Normal distribution
17. Standard deviation
18. Time series
19. Index numbers
20. Marketing research

Definitions

A. The most frequently occurring observation in a frequency distribution.
B. Group of consumers used by market researchers to evaluate a product. They will produce reports and answer questionnaires about the product.
C. A continuous probability distribution having a symmetrical bell shape.
D. Market research performed using existing, or secondary, data. It is quite cheap, but may be inaccurate.
E. A form of diagrammatic representation in which the frequency of occurrence of an event or reading is represented by the length of a vertical or horizontal bar.
F. Collection and analysis of data about all aspects of marketing.
G. The mid-point, or the middle number in a set of observations when they have been arranged in order.

H. A way of dividing consumers according to their general levels of income, or class. In other words, their economic characteristics.
I. Market research carried out through the collection and analysis of new, specific data. This process, using primary data, is expensive but potentially very accurate.
J. The commonly used name is the average. The sum of all the results divided by the number of observations.
K. Specific numbers of respondents are required to be interviewed from each division of the sample. Specific people are not required.
L. Sets of data which vary with time. Useful for determining trends.
M. A means of showing changes in quantity with time in ratio form. Numbers are unitless, so can be compared easily.
N. A group which has the characteristics of the population from which it is drawn.
O. Collection and analysis of data relating to the properties of the market concerned.
P. A way of presenting data. Presentation is as a circle, and where the magnitude of a variable is shown by the angular size of the 'slice'.
Q. A diagrammatic representation of frequency distributions. Similar to a bar chart, but now the area of the bar represents the magnitude of the variable being displayed.
R. A method of sampling where every person has an equal chance of being selected.
S. A measure of the spread of a set of data around the mean value.
T. Determining whether a result could have come from sampling error, or as a result of bias, or whether it is a real affect.

Short answer questions and essays

1. Explain carefully the difference between field and desk research.
2. Explain the difference between consumer panels and discussion groups.
3. What is the difference between a quota sample and a random sample? When are they suitable for use in market research?
4. Differentiate clearly between the mode, the median and the arithmetic mean.
5. (*Essay*) What is meant by the phrase 'significance testing'?
6. Explain the differences between pie charts, bar charts and histograms.
7. What is a time series, and how can it be used to identify trends?

8. A business producing a range of products has total sales of £100 million in 1986. For their annual report they wish to present this information in diagrammatic form. State one method they might use. (Associated Examining Board, 1987 Paper 1).

9. (*Essay*) How might NOP go about preparing a public opinion poll about voting intentions?

10. (*Essay*) 'Businesses often present data for the use of customers, shareholders and other interested parties in the form of diagrams and charts. Sometimes this material is designed to hide as much as it reveals.'

(a) Supporting your answer with examples and sketches, explain how a diagram or chart can be misleading.

(b) Why might a business want to 'hide as much as it reveals' to interested parties? (Associated Examining Board, 1993, Paper 2).

16
Product planning and development

Preview

▼ In this chapter you will be introduced to the major strategic decisions taken by marketing, and the tools used to make this decision-making process simpler. The vital importance of cash generation will be stressed again. You will then be introduced to:

▼ New *product development* and product portfolio management. The statistical nature of this will be explained. The need for patent cover will be noted.

▼ A procedure for analysing situations known as *SWOT* analysis.

▼ A procedure for categorising the cash generating potential of products based on the 'Boston matrix'. You will be introduced to the notion of products as *'cash cows'*, *'stars'*, *'dogs'*, and *'question marks'*. The likely position of such products in their life cycles will be outlined.

▼ The operation of product differentiation and market segmentation as means of cash generation maximisation. Again, the significance of these decisions on the operation of the *'four Ps'* will be examined.

▼ The use and operation of *decision trees*.

▼ The chapter will end by giving you the opportunity to try out some of these new techniques.

Every firm should have a *corporate plan*, or set of long-term objectives. This may be called a '*mission statement*' today, but it means the same thing. Marketing, as part of the firm, has to prepare its plans to meet these basic objectives.

Businesses have two main objectives. They want to survive and then to make a profit. Firms have to plan not only for today but for the future. They have to plan for the birth, life and death of their products. They will have to spend money in advance of sales for some products, so will have to plan for the positive generation of cash by others. Marketing, therefore, is involved in cash flow management, since its products and actions both generate and consume cash.

Many firms have only a single product, but others have a whole range of different ones. As has been shown earlier, all products have a limited life cycle. This cycle, or the position of a product within it, has a pronounced effect on the ability of the product to generate cash for the firm, e.g. products in the introductory stage will consume cash, but ones in maturity should generate it. Firms, therefore, cannot just count on the future but have to plan the management of existing products and the development of new ones. They have to plan to exploit their product portfolio to maximise the cash flow for the firm. A new definition:

A product portfolio is the number of products and brands sold by the firm.

The firm, on the advice of the marketing management, will have to commission commercial research and development into products and markets. It will then have to set up technical research and development to work on the production process and the economic production of the products. Precise timings are impossible. It will be expensive and will consume cash at a great rate. New products will come forward unpredictably, and there is no guarantee of success. Let us look at product development in more detail.

New product development

Product development is an expensive and slow process. It is worked in stages, i.e.:

- *Idea development* – brain storming, and other creative processes.
- *Screening* – sorting the potentially good from the unsuitable.
- *Business analysis* – just how might the product fit into the portfolio.
- *Development* – turning a good idea into a producable, saleable product.
- *Testing and selection* – making sure the firm has got it right.
- *Production and launch* – selling it to the public.

It is a process of diminishing returns. Many more ideas have to be produced to get one product through to the launch stage. Examine Figure 16.1.

There is only one 'winner' from so many ideas. The probability of a successful new product is increased by working on more and more product ideas. Notice it is the probability that is increased, there can be no guarantee. The products which 'fail' might be good products but just will not fit the objectives of the company, or may be too expensive.

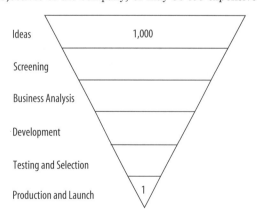

Figure 16.1 *Illustration of the product development model*

These can be protected if the firm takes out a patent, and can be used later, franchised or even sold to another company. Market research will have a large role in this field of work, particularly in the area of product testing. Another new definition:

A patent is a grant of ownership rights by a government to a person or a company in respect of the invention of an entirely new product or process, or a significant improvement to an existing one.

The new product cycle can be long. Some products require a test market. This is where a product is made in production quantities on a small-scale industrial plant, then sold under 'realistic' market conditions against competition in a selected and controlled part of the market. This work is expensive, and the competition will try to disrupt the market as much as possible. It will only be done where the last stage, production and launch, will involve significant capital and revenue expenditure. A test market can give valuable information to the firm about the acceptability of the product and its marketing and marketing mix. It is also useful to production enabling them to refine the process and the packaging. It can also reveal serious errors in the overall marketing forecast and plan. The test market for Cadbury's Wispa Bar illustrates this well. They had seriously underestimated the demand for the product, and sold out in hours. The test was halted, and the whole plan revised. The product was a success, but even this short launch was long enough to alert the competition who worked on their own competing brands.

Development involves risk, and cannot be avoided. Predictions can be made, with some measure of statistical accuracy, but there is no guarantee. Life is such that new products never come quickly when they are most needed! The chances of success, and the likely cost, can be examined using *probability analysis*. Consider the example of Case Study 16.1 and follow the workings very carefully.

How many ideas needed per launch? Multiply the odds together, i.e. 8 x 4 x 4 x 4 x 2 x 1 = 1,024 different ideas needed. Why? It needs two tested products to get one successful launch. Eight products (4 x 2) that have passed development will be needed to stand a chance of getting two to the testing stage, and so on back to the 'Think Tank'.

What will it cost? It is 'testing and selection', followed by the 'final production and launch' which are expensive. Idea development, because of the large number of ideas needed, will consume a large sum of money, though.

FMCGs and the development of new products

CD plc has been considering diversifying into the processed foods market, a significant segment of the FMCG market. It has commissioned a market research company to examine the patterns and costs of product development leading up to successful launches. The report contains the following tables:

Table 16.1

Product development history – foods market

Development stage	Success ratio	Cost per product tested (£)
Idea development	8:1	500
Screening	4:1	500
Business analysis	4:1	500
Development	4:1	100,000
Testing and selection	2:1	200,000
Production and launch	1:1	1,000,000

Table 16.2

Product development cost calculations

Development stage	Success ratio	Number needed	Cost (£)	Total cost
Idea development	8:1	1,024	500	512,000
Screening	4:1	128	500	64,000
Business analysis	4:1	32	500	16,000
Development	4:1	8	100,000	800,000
Testing and selection	2:1	2	200,000	400,000
Production and launch	1:1	1	1,000,000	1,000,000
TOTAL				2,792,000

Costing involves working out the number of operations and then totalling them. Examine Table 16.2 carefully.

Product development is clearly expensive. Remember that there is no guarantee that even after the expenditure of nearly £3 million a firm will have a successful product.

Now confirm that if the success ratios are changed to 10, 8, 4, 4, 2 and 1:1 and the costs per stage to £500, £600, £700, £100,000, £250,000 and £1,200,000 respectively, an expenditure of about £4 million will be required on average, and the 'think tank' will have to come up with, on average, 2,560 ideas per successful launch.

Cost control must be exercised very strictly in this area of market research and development.

How are decisions made? How may the present situation be analysed?

SWOT analysis

This is a system for examining the situation at the moment. The individual or firm will consider its:

- Strengths
- Weaknesses } internal – of the firm
- Opportunities
- Threats } external to the firm

at a moment in time.

'Strengths' would list the assets of the firm in terms of skills, systems and the like. CD plc could list its production ability in the field of electronics, along with its strong domestic selling ability in the retail consumer goods trade.

'Weaknesses' would be just the opposite, areas of potential trouble. CD plc might list a lack of cash for expansion, or an inability to call in its debts.

'Opportunities' are areas where the firm sees potential markets. Again, for CD plc, they might list expansion into Europe.

'Threats' might come from European producers, and imports from the Pacific Rim.

This is a simple concept, but a useful one. It may be used by individuals as well as firms. It concentrates and orders the mind.

Product portfolio development

Let us first review the life product cycle and see how the position here effects costs, revenue and cash flow. This is done in chart form in Figure 16.2. Note how only products with good sales in maturity are capable of generating significant cash for a business.

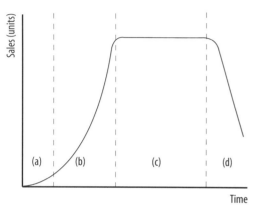

(a) Product life cycle

Phase Title	(a) Introduction	(b) Development	(c) Maturity	(d) Decline
Sales (units) Price Marketing Expenses	Low Low V.high	Growing Rising High	Steady-high High-'List' Low Spasmodic	Falling Steady Nil
Cash Flow	Negative	?	Positive	Positive, Fall

(b) Cash Generating Potential

Note: If sales in maturity are less than forecast, cash flow will fall, and may be zero. Product will have to be examined and possibly cut.

Figure 16.2 *The product life cycle and its relationship to the cash flow characteristics of a product*

New products are expensive to launch and consume resources, but mature products generate them. A firm needs a steady flow of cash, so aims to have a range of products in its portfolio at different stages in their life cycle, plus some in reserve. It will be researching extension strategies, examining cash flow, reviewing product contribution and making plans for portfolio changes.

Products can be categorised in relation to their cash earning potential. There is a good model known as the Boston matrix (developed and published by the Boston Consulting Group, hence the name). This examines products in relation to market share

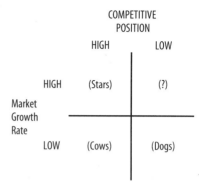

(Source: Boston Consulting Group)

Figure 16.3 *The classification of products according to their cash earning potential or the Boston matrix*

and market growth rate. It effectively places products in the life cycle and is concerned with resource generation. It is illustrated as Figure 16.3.

Products are categorised into one of the following four groups:

Stars

Stars are products that are probably selling well, and growing, but are still in their development phase. They are absorbing resources rather than generating them, but are considered to have considerable potential for growth, cash generation and profitability. They should develop into 'cash cows', provided their sales continue to develop.

Cash cows

Every firm must have these. They are probably developed 'stars'. They will be in the mature phase of their life cycle, so volume will not be growing. They will be generating cash and contribution for the firm and supporting the other products and activities in the firm. They may or may not have gone through extension strategies. If they have not, then they are potentially 'long life cash cows', provided effective strategies can be identified.

Not all stars really develop as predicted. They may become only 'question marks' or 'dogs'.

Question marks

'Question mark' products are still in the development stage. They are showing high rates of growth, and are consuming resources rather than generating them. The market looks small, though, so they may never become good or significant cash generators. They need to be watched lest they become 'dogs'.

Dogs

'Dogs' are low growth, low market share products. They may be products in decline, or those in the maturity phase but they have not really been a success. They generate some cash for the firm, but offer no potential for growth.

A firm can operate successfully with one 'cash cow' only for a period. Eventually it will decline, so marketing must plan for its replacement. It will need to test these, so a 'Star' will appear, but probably accompanied by one or more 'question marks'. The 'cash cow' will eventually decline, and will become a 'dog'.

Marketing management will have to make decisions about the launch of products, the birth of 'stars' or 'question marks', the support and nourishment of 'cash cows', and the putting down of 'dogs'. None of these decisions are easy.

The effect of good product planning on cash generation within a firm is illustrated in Figures 16.4. Good planning will minimise the fluctuations in cash flow, while bad management and product selection can make it worse. An excess of 'stars' could easily result in overtrading and the bankruptcy of the whole business. Here is a reminder of what overtrading is:

Overtrading is the operation of a business at such a rate of expansion that it exhausts its available working capital. It goes into liquidation when it fails to meet its debts.

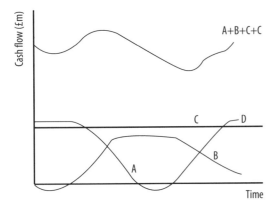

Figure 16.4 *Product planning and cash flow*

There are other strategic marketing decisions which profoundly influence the operation of a business, and the activities of the marketing department.

Market segmentation and product differentiation

Marketing segmentation and product differentiation are techniques used by some firms and marketing departments to maximise the earnings potential of its products. Remember the need to maximise cash generation for the business.

Product differentiation

Product differentiation is the means by which suppliers attempt to distinguish their products from those offered by the competition.

Many firms sell similar products. The firms aim to differentiate their versions from the rest by means such as brand building. They will exploit and promote a colour, shape, perfume or even name. Note that many of these attributes can be registered or protected by a trade mark or registered design. Coca Cola have registered the name, the bottle shape and the wavy lines on the cans. Soap and detergent manufacturers register names and shapes of soap bars. Advertising is designed to persuade the customer that their product is the best. An excellent example is summed up in the phrase 'Don't say brown, say Hovis', i.e. do not buy any brown bread, specifically demand Hovis. Most recently the manufacturer has tried to build on this reputation to sell Hovis white bread, and exploit the Hovis name for quality and reliability. Successful product differentiation enables a firm to charge a higher price for the product than if it was sold as a commodity. Overall, in spite of the fact that its expenditure on a differentiated brand might be high, it generates more net cash than the unbranded commodity. Remember the economics of demand. The manufacturer is trying to make demand more inelastic, or less sensitive to price, so that it can increase sales revenue. It is trying to turn its product into a 'cash cow', a protected, guarded 'cow' at that.

This operation is largely the responsibility of marketing through advertising and other communication techniques. It is a speciality of the FMCG industry, and the consumer goods industry. The motor trade is a good example. A car is a car, but the manufacturers sell more than just a means of transport. Let us see how even CD plc use this technique Examine Case Study 16.2.

This technique leads on to the next one.

CASE STUDY 16.2

CD plc and its marketing of audio tapes

CD plc manufacture audio tapes in a whole range of quantities and lengths. They are not strongly branded, but are sold in parallel with the other range of CD's goods. They had sold well as they were one of the first companies to sell audio tapes.

CD plc had become very concerned that, although its sales were still good, it was experiencing more and more competition, and that its margins were being severely eroded. Marketing were considering ways of increasing the profitability of these products. CD plc already has a name for the provision of high quality, but 'value for money' audio systems, which it sells across a wide range of the market to all age groups.

Task:

Suggest ways that CD plc may achieve their objective. Present your proposals in the form of a short essay.

Market segmentation is the division of a market into identifiable segments each having their own customer profile and buying characteristics. The firm then produces brands specifically for this segment, which it specialises in meeting.

Consider the car market, and the approach of most of the mass market suppliers. Each model of the car is produced in a range of variations and body forms, which sell for different prices. One can get different body forms, different engine types and sizes, and different levels of finish as well as the usual colour choices. There is obviously a demand for these cars, but is there a real need? The different variants sell because:

- The consumers are different.
- The different consumers have different demand levels.
- The market segments can be isolated within the overall market.

The car maker sells more cars and gets more revenue than if only one model was sold. The operation will be profitable if the extra costs involved are less than the increased revenues. Modern production and stock control systems within the motor industry make this much more likely than before. The supplier is able to make each customer think that he or she is unique, and is getting a unique product.

Consider the domestic market for consumer electronic products sold by CD plc. Figure 16.5 shows how this market may be analysed, or segmented.

Some suppliers will attempt to serve all these segments, which will be expensive in terms of

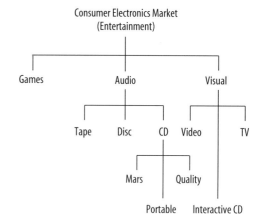

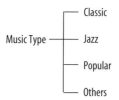

Figure 16.5 *Possible ways of segmenting the consumer electronics market within which CD plc operates*

marketing at least. They will tend to be large and will need to generate a steady flow of money to survive. They may well be national chains, operated by store managers. Others will go for only a small part of the market. They will market in a different way, probably specialising on service rather than advertising. They may also be more flexible in price negotiations. Stores may well be operated directly by their owners. Notice how the decision on segmentation automatically decides how some of the 'four Ps' of marketing have to be utilised, restricting the operation of the marketing department. In other words, the strategic decisions, taken infrequently, limit the tactical decisions that marketing have to take more frequently. Another example of interaction within business.

Analyse your high street. You may well find Comet, Dixons, Powerforce and the like, as well as specialist local suppliers. Compare and contrast the way they utilise the 'four Ps'.

This process can go too far. Segments get smaller and smaller, which can lead to production and cost difficulties. Car manufacturers, again, have countered this by selling 'special', a version in a unique finish which will be sold competitively for a limited period only. In another example, Tie Rack and Sock Shop sell a wide range of a narrow band of goods to a large numbers of customers. The segment of consumers here is the commuter, or captive passing trade.

Some segmentation enables a thoughtful shopper to decide what some firms really do. Black and Decker essentially sell electric motors and the soap makers must keep the utilisation of their general purpose plant up. The more versatile a firm's production plant the more likely is strong market segmentation.

The choice of strategy is wide. Let us examine some decision-making situations and techniques, and see how they can be used. Decision trees will be examined in detail.

Decision making and decision trees

Managements are often faced with multiple choices. They are faced with a series of options, but can only handle one. How can it decide which one to adopt? A useful technique here is the decision tree.

A decision tree is basically a diagrammatic representation of options open to a firm or business. Consider the simple example of tossing a coin, and predicting the outcome. There is obviously a 50/50, or 0.5 chance of obtaining heads or tails. Toss the coin again and there is another 0.5 chance of obtaining heads or tails. What is the likelihood of getting two heads in succession? 0.25, or (0.5 × 0.5) it seems. Look at Figure 16.6.

This confirms the result hinted at above. Now, put this method of analysis in a business situation. This extends the process by using the fact that if one has an activity that should yield a profit of £50,000,

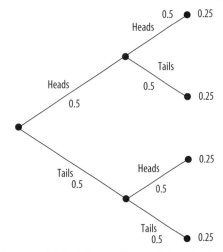

Figure 16.6 Probability tree diagram for coin tossing

but there is only a 0.75 probability of it being achieved at all, the 'most likely' result, overall, is an income of £37,500, i.e. multiply the saving by the probability (see Case Study 16.3).

The most probable decision from the firm will be to replace the worst existing line with new product B. Now work out the likely result if the success factors for the new products were 0.5, 0.25, 0.16 and 0.5 respectively.

Another example set in a rural situation is illustrated in Case Study 16.4.

CASE STUDY 16.3

CD plc and the selection of new CD titles

CD plc is holding its monthly 'label' meeting. It has reviewed the sales and contributions made by its present CDs, and now has to consider the best four new labels proposed by marketing. It has the following data available to it.

Table 16.3 Contribution forecasts (Units – £ per month)	
Worst present product	10,000
New Product A	20,000
New Product B	40,000
New Product C	60,000
New Product D	20,000

Table 16.4 Success forecasts (Units – Probability ratios)	
New Product A	0.5
New Product B	0.7
New Product C	0.3
New Product D	0.2

Market research is also able to assess the likelihood that the new products will be successes. The forecasts for existing products are known through experience to be 90% accurate. This information is reported below.

Table 16.5
Calculation of probable returns to options

	Contribution	Probability	Adjusted contribution
Old product	10,000	0.9	9,000
New product A	20,000	0.5	10,000
New product B	40,000	0.7	28,000
New product C	60,000	0.3	18,000
New product D	20,000	0.2	4,000

CASE STUDY 16.4

The Apple Farm

An orchard owner in Kent has just purchased a new orchard in West Sussex. He has analysed the farm records and has extracted the following data:

Yield: Good Year   2.0 tonnes per acre
        Average Year 1.2 tonnes per acre
        Poor Year   0.5 tonnes per acres

Analysis of Seasons
        Good   0.4
        Average   0.4
        Poor   0.2

What yield can be expected, overall?

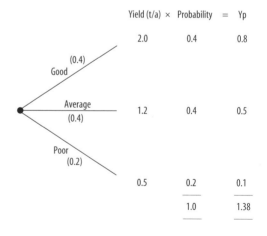

$$\text{Average yield} = \frac{\Sigma Y\rho}{\Sigma\rho} = \frac{1.38}{1} = 1.38 \text{ tonnes / acre.}$$

Figure 16.7 Decision tree for orchard yield

Question and activities
1. Draw a decision tree.
2. Add statistical data.
3. Resolve the problem.

The farmer can expect to obtain 1.38 tonnes per acre in the long run. Actual output, in any one year may be 2, 1.2 or 0.5 tonnes per acre, though.

SUMMARY

Having studied this chapter, you will be able to describe some of the strategic decisions and actions taken by Marketing. In particular, you should be able to:

▽ Describe the concept of a *product portfolio*.

▽ Outline the *product development process*, and explain its costs and probability problems.

▽ Explain the relationship between the position of a product in its life cycle, its marketing plans and the consequential generation of cash.

▽ Describe the *Boston matrix*, and be able to differentiate between '*cash cows*', '*stars*', '*dogs*' and '*question marks*'.

▽ Show how a firm must have an optimum distribution of these types of products in its portfolio.

▽ Distinguish clearly between *product differentiation* and *market segmentation*.

▽ Outline the principles and uses of *decision trees*.

Questions and activities

Technical terms and glossary

In the section below you are given a series of technical terms and their meanings. They have been scrambled, though. You must match up the terms and the definitions. When you have them correctly paired, transfer them to your vocabulary or glossary book.

You are also advised to transfer any definitions obtained during the exercises in the case studies into this glossary book.

Technical terms

1. Product portfolio
2. Patent
3. Trade mark
4. Registered design
5. Boston matrix
6. Cash cows
7. Stars
8. Overtrading
9. Product differentiation
10. Market segmentation
11. Decision tree
12. Brand
13. Research and development
14. Competitive advantage

Definitions

A. The division of a market into smaller identifiable segments.

B. A pattern or shape that is the legal property of a firm or individual, and is protected from use by others.

C. The study of original ideas, and their conversion into practical products.

D. The range of products that a business offers for sale at the moment.

E. Well-developed products with large markets and market shares which yield much sales revenue for the firm.

F. A diagram that utilises the costs/benefits and probabilities of various options and acts as an aid to decision making.

G. A form of legal protection granted, on payment of a fee and the submission of the correct paperwork, to a new invention or a significant improvement of an existing one.

H. The means by which producers try to distinguish their own products from those offered by the competition.

I.   Up and coming products that show early signs of becoming significant cash generators.

J.   A grid showing the cash generating position of firms against market share and sales growth rate.

K.   Operating a business at such a rate that all its working capital is used up and the firm becomes insolvent.

L.   A name given to a product which identifies its supplier to the customer.

M.   A registered design, shape or logo which is the legal property of a firm or individual.

N.   The possession of a brand or a firm which give it a marketing edge over its rivals.

Short answer questions and essays

1. (*Essay*) (a) Why might a firm possess a range of products at different stages in their life-cycle?   (6 marks)

   (b) Why is it that some firms find it difficult to achieve such a portfolio?   (19 marks)

(Associated Examining Board, Business Studies (A), Paper 2, November 1992)

2. State *three* reasons why a firm might decide to diversify its product range.

(Associated Examining Board, Business Studies (A), Paper 1 June 1993))

3. State *two* ways in which a few firms may come to dominate a market.

(Associated Examining Board, Business Studies (A), Paper 1, June 1993))

4. (*Essay*) Outline the process of new product development.

5. (*Essay*) Distinguish clearly what a company would protect with a patent, a trademark and a registered design. Give three examples of each to be found in your home.

6. (*Essay*) Describe the 'Boston matrix'.

7. (*Essay*) How can the process of building a product portfolio give rise to overtrading in a firm?

8. Describe clearly the difference between a commodity and a brand.

9. (*Essay*) Why and how do market orientated firms attempt to discriminate their products.

10. What is a market segment?

Data response questions and case studies

Read the article and answer the questions which follow.

Success through marketing

'The three factors that determine the strength of our business', said Sir Alistair Grant, 'are scale, efficiency and competitive advantage.'

Sir Alistair joined Unilever's Batchelor Foods straight from the army in 1958 where he learned the importance of marketing. He became a brand manager with full responsibility for the marketing of one of Unilever's many brands of consumer goods. (Unilever's brands include famous names like Birds Eye Frozen Foods and Persil detergents.)

The key thing that Sir Alistair drew from Unilever was the importance of the brand. It was the job of the brand manager to preserve the brand's reputation. He explained that as brand manager:

• you have control of the brand for only three to five years, during which time your main job is not to maximise the short-term profit of the product, but to retain its competitive advantage;

• you have to decide how the brand can best be positioned in the market, and to extract whatever profit is available during the time you are in charge of it;

• most importantly, you have to ensure that when you hand over the brand to your successor, the consumers' attitudes to it, and its competitive advantage, are in better shape than when you took it over.

Sir Alistair went on to say that it was only possible to achieve this if you got full backing from the company, and were not forced into fierce personal competition for resources with the other brand managers. He said that fighting other brand managers for capital, marketing budget and the attention of the sales team is a waste effort. There are bound to be winners and losers and that is no good for the product, the manager or the company. It is the job of senior management to allocate resources to each brand in a fair and orderly way, and leave you free to put all your effort into marketing your own brand as effectively as you can.

(Source: *Marketing Business*, November 1992)

(a) Explain the terms
    (i) 'scale' (2 marks) (ii) 'brand' (2 marks)

(b) List *three* benefits to the consumer of the use of branding.   (3 marks)

(c) Discuss how the brand manager might use the marketing mix to successfully retain a products 'competitive advantage'.
        (10 marks)

(d) Discuss two possible disadvantages to the brand in the long-term, that might result from maximising the 'short-term profit of the product'.   (4 marks)

(e) Briefly explain two possible effects that 'fierce personal competition' could have on the morale of brand managers.   (4 marks)

(Associated Examining Board, Business Studies (A), Paper 1, June 1994))

17
Pricing policy

Preview

▼ This chapter examines the pricing decision in the context of marketing.

▼ It will examine the concept of a 'right' price for a product.

▼ It will examine the factors that affect this 'price', and will go on to investigate various pricing methods, and their affects on company performance.

Pricing, demand and the concept of price elasticity of demand has been looked at earlier in this book. It will now be examined in more detail, and firmly in the context of the marketing operation.

Marketing has to make many decisions, but the pricing decision is one of the most critical. If the price is set too high the product will not sell because it is too expensive. If the price is set too low sales may be lost because the potential buyer considers that it is too cheap.

Price is the most consumer sensitive item in the marketing mix ('Product, Place, Price and Promotion', remember!). It is only part of the mix, however, and must be considered within context all the time. It is a *dependent variable*.

What is meant by the price of a product? Most products have a 'list price', or 'recommended price'. This is not always the price that is actually paid. Some firms give discounts against the list price, others will offer to buy the consumer's old product, and the trade-in value has a strong influence on the actual price paid (see Chapter 9). Other products, such as houses and cars, are influenced by the prevailing interest rates. Here it is often the monthly repayment which is critical rather than the price itself.

The price must be 'right', but what is the 'right' price? What influences it?

- the product itself
- the state of the economy
- the state of the market

- the competition
- the position of the product in its life cycle
- the policy of the firm selling it.

Most products are sold to make a profit, so the price should exceed the costs of producing it. As was seen earlier, however, it is not easy for a firm to know the costs of production, especially for a multi-product firm. Again, as was seen earlier, costs of production depend on the level of production achieved, but the level of sales will depend on the price selected, the price of competing goods and the state of the economy. Such a complex problem that most firms decide a price in an unscientific way.

The product itself

Some products are more price sensitive than others. Essential goods, like food, have to be bought, but luxuries are much more price sensitive. Other goods go in pairs, as substitutes or complements. Jam sales tend to increase with bread sales. When beef is cheap and sells well, lamb sales fall – a complex picture.

The state of the economy

Businesses do not have control over the state of the economy. At an individual level this is true, but the actions of industry, commerce and trade, along with the policies of the government, do. Confidence is an important factor, as was illustrated by the situation in UK in the late 1980s and the early 1990s.

When an economy is booming, when there is economic growth and incomes are rising, prices are of little importance. When demand is strong prices will be high, and will even tend to rise. Examine the prices of houses in the south east of England in the late 1980s. They went up and up, and it was less important to control costs. Interest rates were low so mortgage repayments were also low. Ownership was the important thing as it was thought that property could always be sold at a profit. All parts of the economy boomed as the demand in one area generated demand elsewhere. Confidence was high, and demand was multiplied throughout the economy. Marketing was easy in this situation, particularly for a quality product. However, it was all based on inflation, or rising prices, and the bubble eventually burst.

The whole model reverses when an economy starts to decline. Sales drop, profits drop, firms close and people fall out of work. The amount of money in the economy falls, so demand declines. Lack of confidence stops people buying and the process accelerates. Price becomes paramount now. The buyer demands keener and keener prices, better bargains, before money will be spent. This lesson, once learnt, is hard to forget. The UK consumer is now price conscious, and will even bargain over price. The consumer has become aware of his power and in exercising it!

Unfortunately, in spite of efforts of politicians and economists for generations, economies tend to cycle from boom to slump, and back again. This is known as the **business cycle**. Firms have to take this into account when deciding their pricing policy within their overall marketing strategy.

The state, or characteristics of the market

All products are sold in some form of market. Some sellers have a market all to themselves. This is a monopoly market, and many exist. Rail travel, postal services, electricity, gas and coal are examples of effective monopoly situations in the UK, at least until imports are taken into consideration.

A *monopoly* supplier can decide the price of its product without having to consider the competition. The buyer, however, will decide how much the monopolist actually sells. Even in the case of 'necessities' such as water, the usage will be

controlled more carefully as the price rises. Remember, a monopolist is constrained by the demand curve for the product.

Monopolists can increase their income, and hence profits, by adopting a policy known as *price discrimination*. Here the same product is sold to different markets at the same time but at different prices. Consider the economy cabin in a transatlantic airliner. Passengers will have paid one of a whole range of prices – full economy, ABC fares, and even standby fares. The differences can amount to over £500, but, in flight, all passengers are treated the same. British Rail does something similar with its off-peak tickets, and theatres sell cheap tickets at the last minute. The aim in all cases is to increase the number of customers. In the case of a theatre the marginal cost is nil, since all its costs are effectively fixed. Any income from a seat at the last minute is better than its being empty. Even for a transatlantic flight the marginal cost is very low and is the cost of the *additional* fuel used to carry the *extra* weight of the passenger.

The monopolist does not have its own way all the time. The government is aware of the risks and has set up the Monopolies and Mergers Commission to control them. Any firm with more than 25% of a market is considered to have monopoly powers, and the commission can take action to control its prices and hence profits. Also, if a merger might generate a group with monopoly power, the merger itself will be referred to the Commission. Examples are the possible takeover of VSEL by GEC, and the merger of Halifax and Leeds Building Societies.

As the government has privatised many of the services in the UK it has also established regulators to ensure that the public is not exploited. No such bodies were in existence when the firms like British Gas, British Telecom and the water boards were state owned.

In summary, a firm in a monopoly situation can set its price as it wishes, subject only to the demand curve for its product.

At the other end of the market spectrum are the commodity markets or the stock markets. In this situation the product sold is exactly the same wherever it is bought, and the buyers and sellers know this, e.g. copper is copper, and an ICI share is an ICI share, regardless of where it is bought. Price is not a variable in the marketing mix, and sellers have to compete on service, and the market fixes the price. Price will rise if the product is in demand, but will fall if there is excess supply. Economists consider these to be nearly 'perfect markets'.

Demand has been examined earlier. Let us take a quick look at supply.

Supply can also be expressed by an equation:

$$Supply = \int \begin{array}{l} \textit{Price, price of factors of} \\ \textit{production, technology, weather,} \\ \textit{season, price of other products.} \end{array}$$

Price of agricultural products will depend more on supply than demand, unless the marketing boards get to work. Many, like fruits and fish, are at the mercy of the weather. Consider the price of strawberries at Wimbledon time if there is a huge storm over the south east England in a huge glut.

Thus, in a perfect market the seller has no real control over the price of the commodity, but in a monopoly it has complete control. These extreme cases of competition are rare. In between there are the more common situations of limited numbers of suppliers, where the competition matters.

The competition

Most firms sell in competition with others. A firm entering an established market will probably consider setting a price near that of the competition. Some markets, where only a few firms supply the product or service, may actively avoid using price as a marketing weapon. These are known as *oligopolistic markets*.

In oligopoly a price tends to be established. There is nothing to be gained by changing price. The products or services offered are so similar that one firm would lose its customers if it raised its price. A cut by one would result in a price war with no benefits to anyone in the long run, so the process tends to be 'sticky'. This tends to be the situation in the petrol distribution industry. Prices move with the price of crude oil, and there is little price competition at the filling stations. They do practice non-price competition, however. Look at the use of coupons, stamps, etc., and even the sale of coal!

In most situations in the retail market a number of firms produce almost identical products. They try to differentiate their product from the competition by building its image, or brand. In these circumstances price is part of the brand image, and will not be changed often. Again price is not a strong variable in the marketing mix.

Firms may seem to collude, or set their prices together. Look how petrol prices always go up or down together. It cannot be proved, however, in spite of frequent attempts by the Monopolies and Mergers Commission.

The stage in the life cycle

Price is not static through the life cycle. The firm will have planned the price it wishes to sell the product for when the product is mature. The pricing policy adopted in the other stages can vary, however.

Introductory phase

The launch price in the introductory phase is the most critical. The options open depend on the product. A firm has the most options when its product is unique, new to the market. The firm can now decide if it wishes to follow a skimming or a penetrating policy. Figure 17.1 illustrates the possible results of these launch pricing methods.

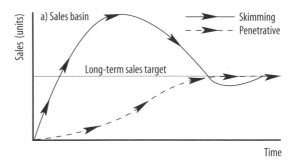

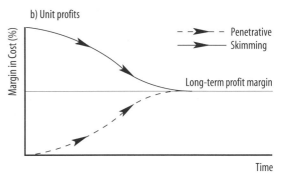

Figure 17.1 Effect of penetrative and skimming pricing on the sale and revenue of a new product

Many FMCGs are launched with penetrative pricing, particularly sweets and chocolate products. Many new magazines are also launched at a penetrative price, but it is no guarantee of success.

Low prices can be difficult to set as the consumer usually resents price increases. A common method of setting the penetrative price is the put a 'special price' sticker on the product. This states that the recommended price is say 55p, but there is a special 'introductory offer' price of 24p. When the offer is removed, the amount actually paid by the consumer will rise, but the official list price is unchanged.

High value electronic goods are often launched with skimming pricing.

Development stage

Price will tend to rise or fall during the development stage, depending upon the launch policy. A firm may have to react to the actions of the competition at any time, but it is probably most likely to occur in this stage of its product's life cycle.

Maturity stage

Price should be established by the maturity stage. It may be changed occasionally in this stage as a means of promoting the product and bringing it back into the mind of the consumers, however.

Decline

Decline is the 'no action' stage. The price will simply follow changes in costs. All cost increases will be passed on to the consumer as far as possible.

The policy of the firm

Some firms have established strong reputations for price and quality. In the FMCG field some retailers have a policy of selling high quality products at a 'reasonable' price. Others have built a reputation of 'value for money'. Some sell branded goods 'cheap', with no frills, others sell a limited range of such goods at even lower prices. Some firms offer 'free' credit, or 'buy now, pay later' deals.

Notice that the pricing decision for a consumer product is being made by the retailer, not by the producer. The producer has no say in the price here, and it is illegal for the price to be fixed in this way. 'Resale Price Maintenance' is illegal for most products in the UK.

Price is a key decision. It is not as independently variable as it might seem, though. The first price is

critical. Once a price/quality image is established it is difficult for a firm to shift it. The Mini car has suffered during its life from being launched at too low a price. It never really earned the profit it should have, in spite of its sales. Consumers resented efforts to increase the basic price, switching to 'better value' products.

Price is an absolutely critical decision at the launch.

Industrial pricing

All the discussions so far have assumed competitive markets for consumer goods. Industrial capital goods can cause different pricing problems, and generate a different range of solutions. In many cases each product is made on a one-off basis, so is unique. There is often competition for the contract, so price is important. It is only part of the requirement, though, and price has to be looked at along with reliability and delivery. Pricing methods which are based on cost estimates include:

- cost plus pricing
- absorption pricing
- benefit pricing

The final contract price in this industrial situation will be the result on negotiation.

Retail pricing

Retailers tend to adopt mark-up pricing.

Mark-up pricing

Retailers buy products from wholesalers and manufacturers and sell them to the customer. They have to cover their buying-in costs in their price, plus the costs of the premises and of the selling effort. The firm handles this by adding a 'mark-up' to their buying-in price to fix the selling price. If they achieve the level of sales forecast when fixing the mark-up they will make a profit.

CASE STUDY 17.1

Retail outlets for CD plc's products

a) Eurovision have been appointed as agents for CD plc's products. The wholesale price of the new CD player is £500 excluding VAT which is charged at 20%. Eurovision have a policy of adding 33.3% to their price to determine their selling price. What price will they charge, with and without VAT?

Cost Price – £500.

Selling Price – £500 x 133.3% = £666.66 before VAT.

VAT due = £666.66 x 0.2 = £133.33

Consumer Price = £666.67 + £133.33 = £800.

Thus the consumer will pay £800 for the CD player. £133.33 (16.7%) of it will go as VAT to the government, £166.33 (20.8%) will be retained by Eurovision, and £500 (62.5%) will go to CD plc.

b) CD increases its price to £550, or by 10%. What will happen to the retail price?

Cost price – £550

Selling Price – £550 x 133.33% = £733.3 before VAT

VAT Due = £733.3 x 0.2 = £146.7

Consumer Price = £880.0

Price has increased by £80, or 10%. The customer will pay £800 for the CD Player now. £146.70 (16.7%) will now go as VAT and CD will receive £550 (62.5%) of the total. Eurovision will now retain £183.30 (20.8%) as its gross profit. This is an increase of £13.40, or 10%.

Prices are easy to fix. If the trade prices rise, so will the retail price. Examine Case Study 17.1.

Note that if the price increase was particular to CD only, say the result of an increase in import costs, and that the costs for Eurovision have not changed, they will increase their profit at no additional effort.

The mark-up method is simple and easy to use, but can lead to a retailer thinking too much in percentages and not enough in terms of money. A reduction in the second retail price above might increase sales significantly. It will depend on the price elasticity of demand of the product (see Chapter 9).

A confusion often arises here – the difference between *margin* and *mark-up*. The *margin* is simply the mathematical difference between the price and the cost of a good – *however the price and the cost has been determined*. The *mark-up* is part of a method of fixing a price. If the mark-up method is used, and a mark-up of 50% on costs has been agreed, then the price will be set at 'cost + 50%'. The mark-up and the margin is 50%. If the price had been fixed using the value method, then there would be no mark-up, but there would be a margin. Examine Case Study 17.2.

CASE STUDY 17.2

Eurovision and the establishment of its mark-up

Eurovision are planning to sell CD players, tape recorders, TVs and computers manufactured by CD plc. They have made the following sales forecasts, and have predicted their costs as follows. They wish to make a net profit of £2,000 per month.

a What mark-up should they add to their prices?

A) Sales forecasts (units per month)

Item	Sales	Purchase Price	Total Payments
TVs	350	20	7,000
CDs	300	12	3,600
Tape decks	200	25	5,000
Computers	400	25	10,000
TOTAL			25,600

B) Cost estimates for business (units: £ per month)

Rental on property	2,000
Labour costs	2,500
Services	750
Publicity	250
Rates and insurance	1,000
TOTAL	6,500
Profit	2,000
TOTAL	8,500

Purchase price x mark up = £8,500

£25,600 x mark up = £8,500

So, required mark - up = 8,500/25,600 = 33.2%, say 33%.

Actual sales only reach 75% of the forecast. Will Eurovision make 75% of the forecast profit?

Assume that the costs stay the same.

Gross profit = £25,600 x 0.75 x 0.33 = £6,336. So, the firm will make a net loss of £164 instead of a net profit of £2,000. It is the profit which is lost first.

The answer is 'No', they will go into a loss situation. Increasing the mark-up and so raising prices may make the situation worse. Again it is a matter of elasticity.

Mark-up will be low in the case of high turnover items, but large for low turnover, expensive goods. A mark up of 33.3% is quite common, giving the gross profit as 25% of the price paid by the customer.

Mark-ups can reach 100% or more for some luxury items.

The mark-up on a particular product will vary from outlet to outlet, region to region subject to the level of competition being experienced.

An impression of the gross mark-up applied by some stores can be obtained from an examination of their annual reports and accounts. The Profit and Loss Account contains the raw data. Examine Table 17.1.

Table 17.1
Extracts from Profit and Loss Accounts for stores (units – £ millions)

	Tesco 1992	M & S 1992	Sainsbury
Sales (excluding VAT)	7,097.4	5,793.4	8,695.5
Gross profit	661.5	1,959.5	868.8
Gross mark-up (%)	9.3	33.8	10.0

Clear differences which reflect the difference in the product mix being sold. Does it tell the reader anything about the pricing policies, though?

SUMMARY

Having studied this chapter, you will be able to:

▼ Discuss the meaning of 'price' in a marketing context.

▼ Explain how the 'right' price depends on a series of factors, namely:

– *the product itself*
– *state of the economy*
– *state of the market*
– *the competition*
– *the position in the life cycle*
– *the firms pricing policy*

▼ Outline alternative pricing policies, for industrial and retail goods, namely:

– *cost plus*
– *absorption*
– *benefit*
– *mark-up*

▼ Describe in outline how supply interacts with demand to establish the price in commodity markets.

Questions and activities

Technical terms and glossary
In the section below you are given a series of technical terms and their meanings. They have been scrambled, though. You must match up the terms and the definitions. When you have them correctly paired, transfer them to your vocabulary or glossary book.

You are also advised to transfer any definition obtained during the exercises in the case studies into this glossary book.

Technical terms
1. Monopoly
2. Price discrimination
3. Oligopolistic market
4. Penetrative pricing
5. Skimming
6. Cost plus pricing
7. Mark-up
8. Absorption pricing
9. Benefit pricing
10. Pricing policy

Definitions
A. A pricing method for a new product where a low price is set initially. The aim is to go for sales volume/market share at first.
B. The amount, usually a percentage, added to the buying price to set the retail, or resale price.
C. In the pure sense, a market that is controlled by a single supplier. Power develops, though, for a firm which controls 25% or more of a market.
D. Pricing method where price is set according to what it is thought a buyer will be prepared to pay for the benefit obtained.
E. Price is set in relation to a simple, measurable unit. This is often 'time worked'.
F. Selling the same product at the same time to different customers at different prices.
G. Setting the initial selling price high so as to generate the maximum profits initially.
H. The pricing method where a set sum is added to all costs to fix a selling price.
I. A market where a few suppliers provide basically identical products to the customers.
J. The decisions taken by a firm regarding its objectives in relation to price within the marketing mix.

Short answer questions
1. What does 'the right price' for a product depend on?
2. What conditions must be met if a supplier is to practise price discrimination?
3. Why might a manufacturer of a potentially fashionable new item of consumer electronics adopt a policy of skimming?
4. Who might use penetrative pricing to launch a new product?
5. Discuss the meaning of the term 'price' in relation to the purchase of a house or a car.
6. How does the state of the economy alter the 'right price' for a product?
7. Can a monopoly supplier sell as much of his product as he likes at the price that he decides?
8. How does the price of a product vary through its life cycle?
9. Why is absorption pricing so often used by car maintenance firms?
10. Give three examples of suppliers that practise price discrimination effectively.

Data response questions and case study
Read the following case study carefully, then perform the tasks set.

CD plc and the launch of a recordable CD system
CD plc is considering launching a new recordable CD system onto the market. No such system exists on the market at the moment and is unlikely to do so for at least five years since CD holds a strong patent on the system.

Production costs show strong economies of scale for the variable element. Fixed costs, however, are not so flexible and there are expensive pre-launch costs, particularly R&D costs. CD insist that these are all recovered within five years of launch.

Cost data is as follows:

Fixed Costs: £100,000 per year
Pre-Launch Costs : £5 million
Variable Costs: Production Range
First 1,000 per year £400 each

1 to 3,000 per year	£350 each
3 to 5,000 per year	£250 each
Over 5,000 per year	£200 each

Demand can be expressed by the relationship: (Units – Demand per year in units)

$$\text{Demand} = 18{,}000 - 0.6(\text{Price})$$

CD plc have a maximum capacity of 10,000 units per year for the next five years. The limiting factor is the supply of the control chips. Supply can only be increased by a factor of five, so a new major demand would have to be developed.

Questions and activities

1. (a) Consider the effects of various pricing policies on the potential profitability position for CD and its launch of Recording CD Systems.

   (b) Consider the possible advantages and disadvantages of CD licensing its systems, particularly the Recording CD Chip, to competitors in the future.

2. Read the following extract on the marketing of the Cadbury Wispa bar and answer the questions which follow.

Marketing the Cadbury Wispa bar

The gigantic brands in the 'pure' chocolate market had, without exception, origins dating back to before the Second World War. Cadbury's Dairy Milk was launched in 1905 and has sold prodigiously ever since. Some twenty years later Cadbury launched Flake, which was discovered as a by-product of manufacturing milk chocolate.

These two products set the pace in the market for 80 years. There have been many attempts to launch a product to stand alongside CDM and Flake. None succeeded until the late 1970s when Cadbury started a secret R&D project.

It was found that the latest technology applied to chocolate manufacturing could confer a different texture and new eating characteristics on their classic milk chocolate product.

All the pre-launch research suggested that the product was a winner. However, as years of bitter experience have taught many manufacturers in this market, having a product that the public likes is not always enough. The complete marketing package is just as critical

Nothing new under the sun

This was the attitude of most consumers to chocolate products. They simply did not believe you could produce anything new. Reversing this belief was the problem facing the Young and Rubicam advertising agency when Cadbury brought them the product named Wispa in 1980.

In October 1983 the product was launched. Cadbury spent heavily on television advertising and on a massive poster campaign. Wispa is now the third largest brand in the total confectionary market and 11 weeks after launch spontaneous awareness among consumers reached 73%. Whichever way you look at it the product is a superb technical accomplishment, unique in a fiercely competitive market.

(Adapted from a Cadbury advertisement, *The Economist* March 1986)

(a) Give three examples of what would be included in 'the complete marketing package'. (3 marks)

(b) The initial launch may well have been accompanied by special pricing deals. What factors might the company have taken into consideration when setting the long-term price? (5 marks)

(c) Cadbury now have three major confectionary products instead of two. What advantages does this give the company? (3 marks)

(d) Outline the factors that the company might take into consideration before embarking upon a European launch of the product? (9 marks)

(Associated Examining Board, Paper 1, November 1987)

18
Distribution policy

Preview

▼ This chapter will investigate first the two meanings of distribution within Business Studies, i.e. the range of outlets through which a manufacturer wishes to sell its product, and the process of storage and transport of goods from a factory to the retailer and eventual consumer.

▼ It will then examine the various distribution channels which are used. It will clearly define and establish the roles of the *wholesaler*, *agent* and *retailer* within the distribution channel.

▼ The chapter will then examine some quantitative techniques which can be used to assist with decision making in the area of distribution. In particular it will study the two *operational research* procedures known as *transportation techniques* and *simulations*.

Distribution within business studies has two meanings:

1. The range of outlets that a manufacturing firm expects its products to be sold through.
2. The process of storing and moving products from manufacture through to the final customer.

Distribution can involve high costs and so has a significant effect on profits. The storage and movement of goods has become an industry itself, known as *logistics*.

The range of outlets

Within the marketing mix, a firm will plan how its product is to be sold. It will decide how many outlets it will use, and where they will be. A manufacturer of an exclusive product like a high performance, expensive car will select a limited number of outlets and liaise with them. On the other hand, the producer of a product like chocolate which is bought on impulse will want as high an exposure as possible. It will aim for sales through as many outlets as possible.

How might Camelot wish to place its National Lottery machines? As wide as possible, to catch as many impulse buyers as possible would seem logical.

A firm may report that it has achieved 70% distribution. This means that it has managed to get its product into 70% of the outlets that it plans to use.

The distribution process

Every firm which makes a product has to decide how it is to be sold. In particular it has to decide the distribution channel to be used, and who should do it. The objective is to maximise the supply of the product to the customer, while minimising the cost of storage and distribution. Specialist firms exist today who will handle products for businesses. Examples are Cristian Selvesen who specialise in frozen foods, and Exxel who distribute many of the country's newspapers.

The full distribution process is concerned with stocking, warehousing, materials handling, transport and order processing as well as the distribution channel itself.

The distribution channel

All products have to have a manufacturer or producer, and eventually have to have a customer or consumer. Between these two ends of the distribution channel may be found *wholesalers*, *retailers* and *agents*. Sometimes, however, the goods go direct and there are no 'middle men'. The actual route used by a firm will depend on the nature of the product itself, the characteristics of the market, the relative costs and effectiveness of the different channels, and the traditions or policies of the firm itself, and the industry or trade that it is part of. Distribution involves wholesalers, retailers or agents. What do each of these organisations do?

Consider the market for groceries and household goods in this country. A vast range of products are produced by many manufacturers, and they are available from a full range of outlets of very different sizes. Now consider a single producer of say laundry products. It could supply each and every retailer, in every corner of the country, regardless of the size of the order. It will be a large-scale operation but with no economies of scale. The large bulk orders to the supermarkets will be profitable, but the small orders to remote village shops will be supplied at a loss. This is illustrated in Figure 18.1, which shows that the last orders, the small ones in reality, result in the firm operating at a loss for a period.

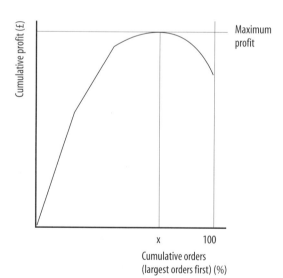

Figure 18.1 *The effect of order size on the profitability of distribution*

The firm maximises its profit after sales have reached point x. The sales obtained and processed beyond this result in a loss. The manufacturer wants

sales to reach 100%, but wants its profits to be greater than before. This is one of the reasons for a wholesaler to service the smaller customers or retailers.

A wholesaler is an organisation that buys goods in bulk from the manufacturers and resells them to retail outlets. It takes ownership of the goods concerned. It tends to service the smaller customers in an area. It acts as bulk breakers and risk takers.

The manufacturer will set a minimum order quantity, and if a shopkeeper wants less than this

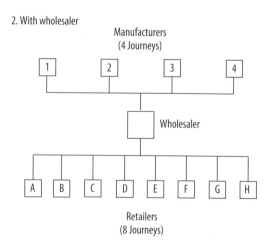

Figure 18.2 *Diagram showing the role of the wholesaler as a bulk breaker*

then it must do its purchasing through the wholesaler. Thus the wholesaler acts as a *bulk breaker*: it splits large orders into smaller lots. It also reduces the handling and transport done by the manufacturer. It now only has to make one large order to a region, rather to a lot of small deliveries. It is easier to organise and cheaper (see Figure 18.2).

The wholesaler is also a *risk taker*. The wholesaler buys the goods from the manufacturer so carries some of the financial risk. If a new product is introduced, then this investment is an encouragement to the wholesaler to promote and sell it on.

The retailer deals with the customer. Information and education is provided. Few manufacturers own shops or retail outlets. There is an obvious conflict if they do. Few firms manufacture a range of goods that can fill a shop. The products of other manufacturers need to be stocked, some of which will be direct competitors. Problems of pricing and supply will result. Also the skills needed to retail and manufacture are very different. Economies of scale cannot apply, so firms tend to specialise in one aspect of business only. The major retailers in the country such as Marks and Spencer plc, Sainsbury plc and Tesco plc specialise in distribution and selling, but produce nothing themselves. (The nearest they get is to break up items like meat and cheese!) Thus, a summary and definition of a retailer:

A retailer is a business which holds a particular product or range of products for sale directly to the consumer.

As the size of retailing has grown, and as large supermarkets and chain stores have developed, so power has swung from the manufacturer to the retailer. They often now make more profit than the supplier – another example of the effect of size.

Both wholesalers and retailers add a profit margin to their costs as a reward for their services. (See Chapter 18.)

The more important distribution channels are:

* Manufacturer – wholesaler – retailer – customers
* Manufacturer – wholesaler/retailer – customers
* Manufacturer/wholesaler – retailer – customers
* Manufacturer – retailer – customer
* Manufacturer – wholesaler – customer
* Manufacturer – customer
* Agent – retailer, or agent/retailer combined (Agents are intermediaries. They do not own the good or service at any time.)
* Agent – wholesaler – retailer.

Choice of distribution channel

As has already been mentioned, the choice of channel depends on many factors. One of the factors is control.

Control of the market, or trading conditions

In all but a few very special businesses, particularly publishing, it is illegal for the manufacturer to fix the price charged later in the distribution chain. This has not always been the case, and before the laws on retail price maintenance, little price competition took place. If a producer now wants to maximise its control over its selling prices then it must keep its distribution chain short and under its control. It can do this through agencies.

Greater control can be achieved by the granting of franchises. The franchiser grants the right to sell to the franchisee, but under strict conditions, which may include price. Well-known franchises are McDonald's, Body Shop and Tie Rack. It is not often realised that most motor cars are sold through franchises.

The nature of the market

A large national market will require a different distribution system to a small local one. It can be seen, therefore, that the importance of distribution will increase as a business grows and expands. This is another consequence of size, and failure to manage it can lead to a growing firm going out of business.

Specialist products, such as high quality hi fis for instance, need different distribution channels to mass production products. Compare and contrast the selling of Bang and Olufsen equipment with that of Fidelity, for instance. B and O sell through *single* exclusive dealers in major towns, with little or no price competition. Fidelity, however, will be found in many outlets and chains, and at different prices. (There may be some limits, however, especially as so many chains are combined. The market is moving towards a monopoly, through the oligopoly stage.)

Cars tend to be sold through exclusive outlets. Pricing policy is essentially set by the manufacturer or agent, rather than the dealer itself. Price tends to be a condition of holding the dealership.

When considering the distribution of a new product, a firm must examine the channels used already for similar goods. Consumer patterns are difficult to change, so the firm will have to have a good reason for going other ways.

The type of product

As has been mentioned already perishable goods have to be distributed fast, so their channels tend to be short and direct. Convenience goods, or those likely to be the subject of impulse buying, will be distributed through as many different channels as possible.

New products can be difficult to distribute, and wholesalers and retailers may need inducements. Large firms, and those with a high reputation will have a distinct advantage. This is clearly another effect of size.

The nature, size and policy of the company

Large firms have the opportunity of choice, while the smaller firms will find self-distribution excessively expensive. Large firms went through a stage where they performed their own distribution, but know more and more use specialist firms. Consider the manufacture and selling of frozen foods. These tend to be seasonal, and all require expensive refrigerated storage (the average cold store operates at - 40°C!) and distribution. The equipment is expensive to set up and operate. Efficiency comes with high utilisation, so specialists have a competitive edge. Through split loads and multi-purpose and multi-product stores high economies of scale and operation can be achieved, and the low costs passed on profitably to both parties.

The economics of distribution

A business has to decide how and where its product is to be distributed, i.e. national or limited regional distribution, sold through wholesaler and retailer or direct to the consumer. It will have to store and dispatch this product. So it then has to decide if it will do this itself or if it will employ professionals for some or all of the process. How can a firm help itself come to such decisions?

Rent or buy decisions

Firms are often faced with the choice of hire or buy for transport and storage facilities. If it decides to do all operations itself it will be faced with a high initial capital investment for warehouses and vehicles, and then the ongoing operating costs for labour, fuel, licences, etc. If it decides to hire, however, it will save the capital costs, but will incur a relatively high rental fee. The initial investment has to be justified by the reduced operating costs. So, the problem resolves into another example of investment appraisal.

Payback, average rate of return, as well as discounted cash flow techniques can be applied to produce a measure of the 'return'. Break-even analysis can also be applied. Look back at Chapter 6 if you do not remember these methods.

This type of analysis will only give a part of the picture. Do not overlook the following points:

1. The policy of the firm. Does the firm usually stick to its core activities? Is it the policy of the firm to aim for full vertical integration? Consider the major retail groups in the UK. They tend to hire transport and specialised depots. Their skill is in buying and selling products, maximising cash generation, and maximising earnings from short-term investments.
2. The renting firm does not have to provide a logistics management system to control its operations. It will not have to develop or purchase the necessary skills. It will not have to employ extra staff so will not increase its payroll. Labour is expensive to recruit, select, hire, maintain and possibly make redundant later.
3. Firms will base their analysis and calculations on forecasts of sales, sales patterns, own and third party costs, and economic trends. They will probably need to consult experts and specialists about the trends in the transport and building field. Projections are likely to be inaccurate.
4. Hiring is a variable cost, so will not change with output or capacity. Vehicles and buildings are a fixed cost, so any contraction in the market will raise unit costs.

These are never easy decisions to take. The numerical/financial information is a guide only.

If CD do decide to go ahead they will have to decide the siting of warehouses, the holding of stocks and the routing of transport. These again are not easy decisions, but the new science of logistics can be a great help. Much of the logistics is beyond A-Level, but some simple techniques are included. The techniques covered include transportation techniques and simulations.

The transportation technique

Route planning and transportation is a key operation within many businesses. Transport and space have to be used effectively and profitably. Consider Case Study 18.1 which illustrates a common problem.

This type of problem can be solved using transportation techniques, one of the more common techniques of operational research (OR). How is this done? Follow this worked example very carefully.

CD plc and the managing of its products

You are the planning manager for Freight, a storage and transport contractor. You manage four warehouses, Anywhere, Backwater, Convenient and Delay. You also are contracted to take the output from three of CD plc's operations, Xerces, Younger and Zeta. The firm has a fixed price contract with CD plc. The warehouses obviously have limited capacity, but CD plc have a predetermined quantity of products to be processed each day. What is the best use of warehouses, routing of transport vehicles to give the minimum cost solution?

Example: OR personnel are trained to be systematic and thorough. Their methods tend to follow the same pattern. Do not take short cuts, but follow the step-wise process carefully.

STEP 1. *Collection of all the basic data*

The OR engineers must establish, in this case:

- The quantities to be handled from each of the three factories.
- The capacities of each warehouse available for CD plc's products.
- The costs of transportation from factory to sites, and between sites.

The data for this case can be expressed as shown in Table 18.1.

The first check is to ensure that capacity, or the supply of space at 825 tonnes, is equal to or exceeds the load, or demand for space, which is fixed by contract at 825 tonnes. There is capacity, just.

STEP 2. *Allocate product to stores, using the cheapest routes first*

Table 18. 1

Cost of transporting the full truck load of goods between warehouses and factories (£ per trip)

		Warehouses			
		A	B	C	D
Capacity (t/day)		150	180	210	285
Factories	Load (t/day)				
X	210	51	60	39	36
Y	270	45	63	78	75
Z	345	45	42	45	51

Go on doing this until all the customers goods have been allocated. This is done for the case in the calculations below.

Cheapest journey

> *XD @ £36 – Allocate all X's product.*
>
> *(X all covered)*

Next cheapest

> *ZB @ £42 – Allocate 180 from Z*
>
> *YA @ £45 – Allocate 150 from Y*
>
> *ZA @ £45 – Full*
>
> *ZC @ £45 – Allocate 165 from Z*
>
> *(All Z covered)*
>
> *YD @ £75 – Only space for 75 from Y*
>
> *Balance to C @ £78 – All Y covered.*

This has been basically a trial and error process.

This is clearly a process that can be computerised. For more complex and realistic problems a computer has to be used as the manual method becomes too cumbersome and time consuming.

Now for another analytical method which can assist decision making.

Simulation methods (or Monte Carlo method)

Most analyses are based on forecasts. Decisions are taken based on predictions of what might happen in the future. One way of attempting to help these decisions is to construct a model, then run it, preferably through a computer, to assess the importance and significance of a range of possible variations. This method is particularly useful in queueing at a sports stadium. It can investigate the effect of the number of gates on the time taken to reach the stadium. It can equally be applied to the design and provision of dispatch gates at airports, loading and unloading bays at factories and warehouses, or even the pressures on oil terminals. How does it work? Examine Case Study 18.2.

CASE STUDY 18.2

CD plc and its delivery arrangements at stores

CD plc is planning to make its own deliveries to city centre store. These usually have only one loading bay. The potential contract specifies a delivery time for the firm and allows 30 minutes only for unloading. In most cases the stores have no parking space. Can the job be done in the time? What is the likely consequence of being early and having to pay parking fines?

The method requires first a thorough analysis of present situations. In this case the OR staff of CD plc analysed arrival and unloading times at the stores concerned, but with other firms with very similar loads. The results of some 700 observations are summarised in Tables 18.2 and 18.3.

This data will form the statistical base for the subsequent modelling and simulation. The next step is to set up the simulation. This is done using random numbers. Random numbers are what they purport to be. Numbers in random order. They are computer generated, and published in books. (Premium Bond prize numbers are generated by

Table 18.2

Analysis of delivery times at sample stores

(– = Early arrival, + = Late arrival) (units – Minutes)

Arrival time	Frequency	% frequency
− 10	6	2
− 8	20	7
− 6	52	17
− 4	62	20
− 2	65	22
0	41	14
+ 2	30	10
+ 4	12	4
+ 6	7	2
+ 8	3	1
+ 10	2	1
TOTALS	300	100

Table 18.3

Analysis of unloading times at sample stores
(units – minutes)

Unloading time	Frequency	% frequency
20	10	2
22	20	5
24	35	9
26	60	15
28	75	19
30	80	20
32	55	14
34	35	9
36	20	5
38	10	2
TOTALS	400	100

computer, by ERNI or electronic random number indicator.)

Number ranges are now applied to the earlier sets of readings. The actual numbers are best distributed according to the cumulative frequency distribution data.

The OR engineer is now in a position to commence the simulation. A table is set up and the following process observed:

- *Delivery 1.* Select a random number from the table (60). Enter Table 18.5 and read off the corresponding arrival time (− 2 minutes). Select another random number (98). Enter Table 18.6 and read

Table 18.4
Section of a table of random numbers

60	10	51	20
98	09	47	07
80	88	86	23
89	30	49	51
08	19	20	73
19	37	82	73
06	67	18	33
51	92	10	37
37	94	42	66
47	58	96	05

off the corresponding unloading time (36 minutes). Thus, the simulation 'predicts' that the first arrival would be early, but would overrun its delivery time allowance.

Table 18.5
Analysis of delivery times at sample stores
(– = Early arrival, + = Late Arrival) (units, minutes)
random number range added

Arrival time	Frequency	% Frequency	Allocated Nos
– 10	6	2	01 – 02
– 8	20	9	03 – 09
– 6	52	26	10 – 26
– 4	62	46	27 – 46
– 2	65	68	47 – 68
0	41	82	69 – 82
+ 2	30	92	83 – 92
+ 4	12	96	93 – 96
+ 6	7	98	97 – 98
+ 8	3	99	99 –
+ 10	2	100	00 –
TABLES	300	100	

- *Delivery 2.* Select the next two random numbers in the series, 80 and 89. repeat the above process and identify the times of (zero) and (34 minutes) respectively.

The process can now be repeated for as many simulations as are required. A full simulation is shown on Table 18.7. This is clearly another operation just made for the computer!

What does this simulation predict? Trucks will probably arrive early, but will marginally underuse the 30 minutes unloading time. Total elapsed time

Table 18.6
Analysis of unloading times at sample stores
(units – minutes)
random number range added

Unloading time	Frequency	% Frequency	Allocated Nos
20	10	2	01 – 02
22	20	7	03 – 07
24	35	16	08 – 16
26	60	31	17 – 31
28	75	50	32 – 50
30	80	70	51 – 70
32	55	84	71 – 84
34	35	93	85 – 93
36	20	98	94 – 98
38	10	100	99 – 00
TOTALS	400	100	

varies from 24 to 40 minutes, with an average time of 32 minutes. A reasonable solution may be for CD to negotiate a 40-minute slot with the stores, then instruct its planners to arrange for an arrival time 10 minutes after the start of this period.

It is possible to subject this information to still further analysis. The arithmetic average and the standard deviation can be calculated. Thus confidence limits can be established. Confirm the following results of such statistical operations:

Arithmetic mean: *31.4 minutes*

(Mode: 34 minutes. Median value : 33 minutes)

Standard deviation of sample: *4.3 minutes*

Standard deviation of population: 4.4 minutes

5% Confidence limits   *± 8.8 minutes*

1% Confidence limits   *± 13.2 minutes*

Remember it is a simulation, not a prediction of what will happen. It is based on observed data, though, but this must be collected systematically and scientifically for the method to be able to produce realistic results. The simulation can be run again and again to build up the significance of any predictions. It is a very useful technique, though.

Finally, a very special example of a distribution problem area - that of export trading. Here the goods and materials have to be sold and then delivered outside the country of manufacture. This presents a full range of special problems.

Table 18.7
Simulated operation of CD plc's delivery operation

Delivery number	Arrival interval Random No.	Arrival interval Simulated time	Unloading Random No.	Unloading Simulated time	Total Time
1	60	−2	98	36	38
2	80	0	89	34	34
3	08	−8	19	26	34
4	06	−8	51	30	38
5	37	−4	47	28	32
6	10	−6	09	24	30
7	88	2	30	26	28
8	19	−6	37	28	34
9	67	−2	92	34	36
10	94	4	58	30	34
11	51	−2	47	28	30
12	86	2	49	28	26
13	20	−6	82	32	38
14	18	−6	10	24	30
15	42	−4	96	36	40
16	20	−6	07	22	28
17	23	−4	51	30	34
18	73	0	73	32	32
19	33	−4	37	28	32
20	66	−2	05	22	24

Problems of export business

Selling to export markets can cause considerable problems, as well as giving the obvious advantages of increased sales from an enlarged market. The problems can be summarised as:

* Exchange rate difficulties
* Currency exchange difficulties
* Culture clashes
* Language difficulties
* Regulation compliance
* Representation.

First, though, two more definitions are given. The trade in goods in known as *visible trade*, while the trade in services is known as *invisible trade*.

Visible trade is the importation and exportation of tangible goods. Examples would be machinery, vehicles, minerals and diamonds.

Invisible trade is the buying and selling across national boundaries of services. Examples would be travel and tourism, insurance, shipping and banking.

This is accounted for on a national basis through the calculation and publication of the Balance of Payments Account. (More of this in Chapter 43.)

Exchange-rate difficulties

The product will be sold in a foreign country that uses a different currency. How is the price to be set, and is it to be fixed or variable? The producer/exporter sells in pounds Sterling, say, but a buyer in the USA will want to pay in US dollars. Exchange rates usually vary, so how will these fluctuations be accommodated? Look at Case Study 18.3. (The situation in Europe in this case is fictional, at least at the time or writing. It could happen, though!)

Situation (a) A Sterling contract. *The price is £520 so the price in USA is now $520 x 1.8, or $936. The rise of 156, or of 20%, will probably cause sales to fall.*

Situation (b) A US dollar contract. *The price in now set at $780. CD will now only get £780/1.8, or £433 for the system now. The loss of £87 could eliminate all CD's profits. It may not be very keen to keep selling to the US.*

Exchange rates respond to changes in the supply and demand of a currency on the FOREX market. These demands and supplies are the result of trade in goods and services, and the action of international speculators who trade in money itself. Some countries attempt to 'fix' the value of their currency, which is of value to traders in general. This will only work for a short period, so then governments have to change the value of their money. They will have to devalue or revalue their currency.

Devaluation of a currency

The devaluation of a currency occurs when the government of a country operating a fixed exchange rate system reduces the value of its money against other currencies.

If the UK was to devalue (it will not now, since it lets the value of Sterling 'float' and find its own level) then one would get more Sterling for each unit of another currency. UK exports would become cheaper.

CASE STUDY 18.3

CD plc and its exports of recordable CD Systems to the USA

CD plc has launched its system very successfully into the UK. It is now considering expansion into Europe and the USA. Europe is no real problem as prices are now set, following the latest EU laws, in ECU's for trans-border internal transactions. The value of the ECU varies only slowly, and then as a result of transactions of the Euro-currency Market of the new European Bank. USA is different. Exchange rates very frequently and significantly.

CD's price to its dealers for its system in UK is £500. Exporting will add £20 to this for transport, improved packing, insurance and administrative charges. Current exchange rate is £1 = $1.50. The price to the US dollar was set at $780 therefore.

The US dollar weakened on the world market, and the exchange rate rose to £1 = $1.80. What will happen to CD and its revenues if the selling contract was written in Sterling or US dollar terms?

Revaluation of a currency

When a currency is revalued, the government increases its value against other currencies.

As was seen earlier, the UK 'floats' its currency. Movements of the exchange rate under this system are called depreciations and appreciations. A currency depreciates when its value falls. It appreciates when its value rises.

Companies can be flexible and use adjustable contracts. Alternatively, they can work on the 'futures' section of the FOREX markets to procure currency in advance at a known price. They can also take out options on the future purchase of currency. The buyer has the right, with a future, to buy currency at a later date at an agreed price. These options are saleable and also do not have to be exercised. They represent a relatively cheap way for a company to insure against fluctuating exchange rates.

Exchange difficulties

Some countries limit, or even ban, the amount of foreign exchange that can be transmitted from the country to pay for goods or services. Ignorance of these laws could mean that a firm's goods cannot effectively be paid for. Banks can give advice, as can the governments of the countries concerned. Exporting companies have to be very careful about when they send goods overseas, and how they will accept payment. 'Cash before delivery' is a good rule. An 'Irrevocable Letter of Credit' may be an alternative.

An Irrevocable Letter of Credit is a document issued by a bank that guarantees payment for goods in a specified currency on receipt of proof of delivery by the customer.

An exporter of goods to, say, India would ask the importer to obtain a Letter of Credit from a bank in India. The bank would guarantee the sum in Sterling, so would ensure that the buyer has the cash, and that the foreign exchange would be made available, and pay it to the exporter on receipt of the correct documentation.

Culture differences

Cultural backgrounds are, of course, different between countries. Some differences are small, others large. These must be allowed for by an exporting company, after it has found out what the differences are. It is the company's responsibility to do this, and will be responsible for any mistakes made in this area. Some matters are obvious, like the ban on pork products in certain countries. Books and magazines can easily cause offence, as can much of the modern Western dress. Companies wanting to enter new export markets need to research this aspect. This can be done using the Trade Representatives of our Embassies or High Commissions abroad. Export Agents can be consulted and employed if required, but these must have a good track record. (The UK has High Commissions in the Commonwealth countries, and Embassies in all others where it has diplomatic relations.)

Language difficulties

A firm will have to get all its publicity translated into the language concerned. This must be done correctly and expertly. Technical language can be a problem. Product names have to be watched very carefully – some do not translate very well, and may be offensive or even indecent in other language. This really ties in with cultural differences.

Regulation compliance

Some countries have very different safety regulations to the UK, and these have to be complied with. Others lay down strict manufacturing and design standards which can be difficult to meet. These may be genuine, or may be designed to make imports difficult. Meeting these regulations can be very expensive.

Free trade is said to exist between countries when they may trade freely, without any limits or restrictions being applied. Countries/companies could then specialise in the production of their most efficient goods or services, for the benefit of the world as a whole. This situation rarely exists, however, although the organisation formerly known as GATT – the General Agreement on Tariffs and Trade, now the World Trade Organisation (WTO) – is pledged to maximise it. The EU, on the other hand, has set a protective 'wall' arround itself and so denies free trade. This is another example of conflict in the business world.

Imports may be regulated into some countries. The importing government may impose taxes, called tariffs, or quotas on imports. Two new definitions:

An import tariff is a tax applied on imported goods. It may be **ad valorem** *– a percentage based on the value of the item, or 'specific' – a set sum per item.*

Import tariffs usually have to be paid in local currency, and will push the price of the imported item up in comparison with the locally made version. The EU applies a tariff on most imports into the EU. The money collected, whether in UK or in France, goes to the administration in Brussels.

A quota is a numerical limit on imports.

The UK operates a voluntary quota with Japan on the import of Japanese cars into the UK. UK-made Japanese cars are exempt, obviously.

An exporter will need a licence to be able to export to a country with a quota on the goods concerned. The shipping company will need to see this before it will accept a load.

Some countries will restrict the port of entry for a product or group of products to a particular port or airport. This example of bureaucracy must be complied with.

Representation

Goods do not sell themselves, so a sales force will be needed. This can be very expensive to set up, especially if the language has to be learnt. The trade system has to be known if the selling is to be successful. One answer is to use specialist overseas agents, but these must be known to be reliable. Agents based overseas may be best, particularly if they are themselves part of a British or multinational company. Firms such as UAC (United Africa Company, a part of Unilever), PZ and Leventis, all who operate throughout West Africa, spring to mind. Firms entering exporting for the first time must check the credentials of overseas agents very carefully before appointing them, and parting with any money.

There are thus many problems and traps which is why relatively few UK firms do look abroad. Those that do consider the world as the market, and gain economies of scale. This is of advantage to the firm itself as its profitability will rise. Customers in the home country will also gain through lower domestic prices.

Certain countries have become powerful exporters. UK was in the days of the Empire and the early Commonwealth. The USA is, but its sphere of influence is falling. The growth area is the 'Pacific rim'. We all know about Japan, but sales from China, Korea and Taiwan are all growing very fast. Companies in these countries are export orientated, and get positive encouragement from their governments.

SUMMARY

Having studied this chapter, you will be able to:

▼ Explain the two meanings of *distribution* within marketing.

▼ Explain the principle of the *distribution channel*, and outline the roles of *wholesalers* and *retailers*.

▼ Show how the distribution channel selected varies with the type and nature of the product being handled.

▼ Examine the economics of distribution, and be able to handle 'rent-or-buy' decisions.

▼ Model distribution using transportation techniques and simulations.

▼ Examine the problems associated with export trade i.e. the distribution and sale of goods overseas.

Questions and activities

Technical terms and glossary

In the section below you are given a series of technical terms and their meanings. They have been scrambled, though. You must match up the terms and the definitions. When you have them correctly paired, transfer them to your vocabulary or glossary book.

You are also advised to transfer any definitions obtained during the exercises in the case studies into this glossary book.

Technical terms

1. Distribution channel
2. Wholesaler
3. Cash and carry warehouse
4. Retailer
5. Agent
6. Direct selling
7. Logistics
8. Operational research
9. Simulations
10. Middle men
11. Quota
12. Tariff
13. Irrevocable Letter of Credit
14. High Commission
15. Floating exchange rate
16. Fixed exchange rate
17. Depreciation of currency
18. Revaluation of currency

Definitions

A. A person or company employed by another to act as an intermediary in the buying process.

B. A slang term for all those people or companies who come between the manufacturer and the eventual consumer.

C. A document that guarantees payment to a supplier of a good or service from an overseas customer in the seller's currency on presentation of delivery papers. It is usually issued by a bank.

D. The route or road down which goods flow from manufacturer to customer. 'Shortest' route is direct, the 'longest' may involve three or more 'stations'.

E. The application of mathematical and statistical techniques to industrial processes as a means of establishing optimal operating systems and procedures.

F. An outlet, often confined to wholesale trade, where no credit is given and no delivery can be arranged. Prices are usually very competitive.

G. The Office of the Representatives of the UK government in Commonwealth countries, and vice versa.

H. A physical limit on the number or quantity of a good or item that may be imported into a country during a period of time.

I. A firm which buys in bulk from the producer, breaks this bulk down, and resells in smaller quantities to retailers.

J. The trading method where the manufacturer of a product deals directly with the final user.

K. A tax applied by governments on goods and services that are imported into that country.

L. The science of the transport and storage of goods.

M. That outlet in the distribution chain where the goods finally come into contact with the final buyer or consumer.

N. Mathematical models used to develop the most effective solution to the problem being modelled.

O. The fall in value of a currency that occurs in a system of free floating exchange rate.

P. An exchange rate system where a currency is allowed to find its own level of the FOREX market.

Q. The action of a government when it raises the value of its currency, and so establishes a new 'fixed rate' for its currency.

R. The system where a government sets a value for its currency, then takes action to keep it there. It does not always work!

Short answer questions and essays

1. What are the usual roles of a wholesaler?

2. (*Essay*) What is meant by 'free trade' between countries? (Associated Exmaining Board, Business Studies (A) Paper 1, June 1994)

3. The exchange rate quoted in a newspaper showed £1 equal to 2,090 Italian Lire and 323 Greek Drachmae. Calculate how many Greek Drachmae are equal to 1 million Lire. (Associated Examining Board, Business Studies (A) Paper 1, November 1993)

4. What types of product will be distributed through a market?

5. Distinguish between an old style wholesaler and a modern 'cash and carry' outlet.

6. Why do furniture manufacturers cut out the wholesaler?

7. (*Essay*) What factors will be taken into consideration when a firm first establishes its distribution channel?

8. How do wholesalers take on some of the risk of a new product launch?

9. (*Essay*) In 1989 Jaguar cars blamed their poor profit performance on the fluctuating value of the US dollar. Explain why fluctuations may have had such an impact and analyse what could

be done to improve the position in the future. (Associated Examining Board, Business Studies (A) Paper 2, June 1991)

10. (*Essay*) (a) Supporting your answer with numerical examples, explain the impact of a currency devaluation on the prices of goods.
(b) What might be the impact upon UK firms of a common European currency? (Associated Examining Board, Business Studies (A) Paper 2, November 1993)

Data response questions and case study

Read the article and answer the questions that follow.

Lorry builders win £70 million export order

Two lorry builders have won a £70.5 million order for 2,440 vehicles to modernise the road haulage fleet in Zimbabwe.

The order, one of the largest lorry export contracts for a decade, provides valuable work when domestic orders have slumped by 30%.

Finance for the deal has been largely provided by an aid package from the British government's Overseas Development Administration.

AWD-Bedford will supply 500 complete 13-tonne vehicles from its Dunstable works early next year. Another 1,500 similar trucks will be despatched in knock-down form over the next 12 months. AWD's contract is worth £46 million. The order is equal to six month's production at 1990's reduced levels.

Engines for the vehicles will be manufactured by Perkins at Peterborough, Cambridgeshire.

ERF, the quoted truck builder at Sandbach, Cheshire, will supply 440 of its six-wheeled heavy tractor units under a £24.5 million contract during the financial year ending March 1992.

(Source: Adapted from *The Times*, 22 December 1990)

(a) List three additional costs that AWD-Bedford and ERF may incur with this export order as compared with a domestic order. (3 marks)

(b) Explain two advantages to the lorry builders of this order by the Overseas Development Administration. (4 marks)

(c) How might other firms in the production chain benefit from this order? (9 marks)

(d) Examine factors, other than price, which influence the sales of British manufacturers' goods. (9 marks)

(Associated Examining Board, Business Studies (A) Paper 1, November 1992)

19
Marketing communications – advertising

Preview

▼ At last, the topic that many people think is 'marketing'. You know now that advertising is not marketing, but just one component of the marketing mix. It is important, though.

▼ In this chapter you will study the purpose and aims of advertising, and see how it is organised. This will be as only one component of the marketing mix, however. You will then examine the advantages and disadvantages of the different forms of advertising available, and also look at the costs. The principle of 'effective advertising' will be developed.

▼ The problems of setting a budget for advertising will be examined. The chapter ends with a section on the economics and ethics of advertising.

Most firms, particularly those manufacturing goods for the domestic customer, do not have any direct contact with the consumers of their products. Goods are sold to wholesalers and retailers. The final customer buys the product from the retailer. Communication between producer and customer is difficult, but necessary. The main communication process for the manufacturer is advertising.

The main purpose of advertising is to increase awareness of something. Detailed objectives will vary from company to company, and from one type of organisation to another. Specific objectives might be:

- to increase demand
- to develop brand recognition
- to increase market share
- to increase the frequency of use of a product
- to inform about a new use for a product
- to develop the overall image of the company
- to support a change in price
- to keep competition out of a market.

This list is not exclusive. Can the reader identify any more? Examine some advertisements in a magazine or on TV and try to put them into the categories described above.

Advertising is part of the 'promotion' component of the marketing mix. It is extensively used for FMCGs and consumer durables. Its design and application varies as the product progresses through its life cycle.

Advertising is an information transmission process. It is designed to educate, inform or remind the consumer about a product, or to encourage and tempt the potential one.

Advertising is the high profile part of marketing. Many people confuse advertising and marketing, and even believe that advertising is marketing. Some firms do little or no advertising as such, but their marketing effort is vast. Consider both Rolls Royce plc and Marks and Spencer plc. These firms until recently did very little advertising. Their marketing effort, including market research, has been prominent.

Advertising can be done in many different ways. It can be a very expensive operation, and there is no guarantee of success. Advertising is part of a marketing campaign. All the components of the campaign will interact, and there will be a synergistic effect, i.e. the results of the campaign mix will be greater than the sum of the results of the component parts.

There are usually three groups involved in advertising. The first group is the advertiser, the firm that produces the product, and is the group that pays. The next group is the advertising agency, who designs the advertisements themselves, and lastly there is the media company, the company that owns the papers, TV or poster sites where the advertisement will appear.

This advertisement for a telephone banking service appeared in The Guardian *newspaper.*

The purpose of advertising

Most advertising is designed to assist in the selling of something, but this is not always the case. The government advertises sometimes simply to *inform*. It informs the population of the perils of using TVs without licences, travelling on trains without tickets, smoking or 'drinking and driving'.

All advertising has an element of *education* within it. It also may *remind, congratulate* or *tempt*.

Advertising will have a quantifiable purpose. This enables the campaign to be evaluated. The costs of the campaign have to be paid for by increased profits arising from sales growth. An increase in sales alone may not be enough. Consider the following:

Effective advertising comprises an advertising programme where the increase in contribution from the product or service is greater than its costs.

This is a simple statement, but very difficult to evaluate.

Public service advertising has to be looked at slightly differently as there may not be a direct financial benefit. Success may be recognised through increased immunisation rates, a reduction in the sales of cigarettes or an increase in the sales of specific licences.

The workings of advertisements

The advertiser always wants to attract a potential consumer, and get him or her to do something. The process can be summarised by remembering the mnemonic 'AIDA'. This covers the stages through which a successful advertisement takes the customer. Each advertisement is targeted at a particular segment of the population. Others will see or hear it, and will pass through some of these stages. The target will act on all of them, *if* the advertisement is a success.

A successful advertisement will first:

1. Attract the *attention* of the reader or viewer. Having got this,
2. Capture the *interest* of the potential target.
3. Develop some *desire* for the product or service,
4. So that he or she takes the *action* that the advertiser wants.

The first letters of the words in italics spell out 'AIDA'. Just consider a few of the advertisements you remember. How do they attract *attention*? Music is one way, with the repeated tune or extract – what does 'Take your breath away' bring to mind, or the Tetley tea bag music? Pictures are also a powerful magnet. Depending on the target audience pop groups, sports persons, and models in various stages of dress or undress can be relied on! This grabs the attention of the potential customer, and without this the rest of the process cannot start. Observe that the attention grabber need not be related to the product or service at all. It is 'bait' really.

Having attracted the attention of the reader, viewer or listener it is then necessary to build on this and develop *interest*. This will be done through the 'copy' and the design of the advertisement. The 'story line' is important, just remember the 'Gold Blend' series. Was the interest in the coffee or the story?

Now the *desire* must be developed. Psychology comes in here, as does careful design again. The car will be the 'top of the range' model, but what about the price. 'Prices start at £x' is common, but not for the model shown. The potential customer will be drawn to the coupon at the bottom, or encouraged to go and visit the store.

What is the potential customer supposed to do? What *action* are they after? The obvious action is to go out and buy the product, and this is the desired action for many fast moving consumer goods (FMCGs). The buyer is supposed to recognise the product from a mass display and pick it out and buy it. The direct 'buy' action is not always the only desired action, however.

Car advertisements are designed to get the customer to send for information or to go down to the local garage. They are not designed to sell cars as such, the sales personnel do this much more efficiently on a one-to-one basis later. The double glazing or conservatory advertisements are not designed to get you to buy directly, but to 'invite' a representative to call and give 'advice'. The action required is for the potential consumers to identify themselves to the firms concerned. This enables the firm to target the remainder of its selling effort more efficiently and frequently on a one-to-one basis.

Advertising and the product life cycle

Marketing campaigns, including the advertising within them, vary with the position of the product in its life cycle. Consider the marketing of a completely new product. Consider the situation when the very first microwave oven was marketed, or the first electronic typewriter. When the first one was actually launched nobody knew what it was for. The product was clearly at the very beginning of its life cycle, in the *introduction* phase. If sales are not achieved the product will die, so the prime action at first was to inform and educate. The advertisement had to tell the potential buyer what the product did and what the advantages of owning one were. They had to get attention and interest, but they specifically had to educate and inform.

This form of advertising can be very expensive. It can be better if two products are launched together so that the education costs can be shared. Competition helps here. A good example was the electric typewriter where IBM 'Golf Ball' had to carry all of the education costs. It was IBM's invention, but they prepared the market for subsequent competitors products. It can be expensive and lonely to be first. Some firms even have a specific policy of not being the first on the market with a product.

Advertising here tends to be used in blocks and for a period of time. It may amount to saturation in some cases. The objective is to reach as many potential consumers as possible. TV advertisements may be broadcast more than one per day, with repeats every day for say a week.

When a product reaches the *maturity* stage the problem is different. The product is known, so education is not necessary. The aim now is to remind the consumer about the product. The advertisement can even congratulate the consumer on having bought one before – now go out and buy another or a 'new improved' version.

Advertising will now come in short infrequent bursts, as the product is known. The consumer needs to be reminded, however. Square Deal Surf, a detergent powder, is an interesting example. It was sold as a low price, high quality product. Costs were kept down as LB&A planned not to spend money on advertising it. All went well at first, but the consumer needed to be reminded, through advertising, that the brand was not advertised.

The *development* stage presents a particular problem. There will now be a mixture of potential customers who are either new to the product, or already know about it. Advertisements now have to be dual purpose, or the firm has to run two different advertisement at the same time.

When a firm has a product in the *extension strategy* zone it has the task of reeducation. To some it will be a new product, but to most it will be an extension of the well-known original.

There is no problem with advertising in the *decline* stage of the life cycle. Recognise that the product is there, and do not advertise it. When did you last see advertisements for grate polish? Yet this product is still available in hardware stores.

Advertising and the product type

Advertising is a much more important part of the marketing mix to some product groups than others. The biggest spenders are in the FMCG industry, whilst the least is spent by the manufacturers of industrial durable goods. Advertisements for engine oil are far more frequent and well known than those for oil refineries! Examine Figure 19.1 which illustrates the different levels of spending on advertising and the other selling methods for the grouping of goods that was developed in Chapter 2.

A) Advertising

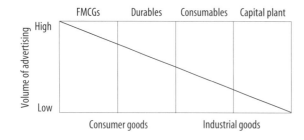

B) Technical Advice, etc.

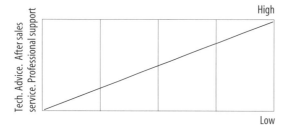

Figure 19.1 Comparison of advertising expenditure by industry and goods

The advertising company

Advertising is part of the marketing activity of a firm. It is handled from within the marketing department. The power and position of marketing within a company will depend on its type, or overall philosophy. A market orientated company will give the marketing department prominence as it puts satisfying the customer today and tomorrow as its first priority. On the other hand, marketing will have little say if the firm is product orientated. Two more definitions to learn:

Market orientation: A philosophy of management which places consumer needs before production needs.

Most successful manufactures of FMCGs fall into this category, as do most long-established multiple retailers.

Product orientation: A philosophy of management which puts the production of the product before the needs of the potential consumer.

Firms working this way find it very difficult, if not impossible to change with the times.

Products will usually be the responsibility of a brand manager, particularly within the FMCG industry. The brand manager will be responsible for the overall marketing policy of the product, will plan the advertising campaigns and will develop the advertising. Much of the detailed work will be handled by advertising agencies.

An organisation chart for a typical department within a large, market orientated firm is shown as Figure 19.2.

Figure 19.2 Organisation chart for marketing department of CD plc

Marketing tends to be very task and achievement orientated. Successful brand managers are in demand, and unsuccessful ones do not survive long. Rewards are high, but so is the risk element.

The advertising agency

A business can perform all its advertising functions itself, or it can employ the services of advertising agencies. Some advertising agencies are household names, particularly after their work for certain political parties. (Remember, a party political broadcast is an advertising operation with a strong 'buy' message!) Just think of Saatchi & Saatchi, J. Walter Thompson or McCann Erickson.

An advertising agency will create advertisements, test their efficiency, organise the production of the copy, film or other advertising medium, book the space and then monitor its performance. A typical organisation chart for an agency is shown in Figure 19.3.

The interface between the companies is the brand manager for the company and the account executive for the agency. Strong personal relationships often develop, and the advertising account will often move with the people.

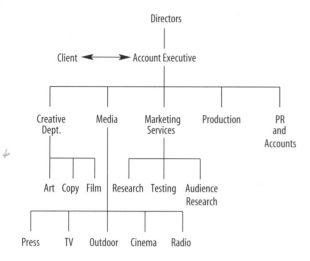

Figure 19.3 Organisation chart for advertising agency

Agencies get reputations for handling certain types of products. Agencies are paid for their services. They also receive commissions from media owners for the space they book on behalf of their clients. Fifteen per cent is a common rate of commission and, as will be seen later, will lead to a good income for the active agency.

Advertising media

The media are the places where advertisements can be displayed. There are many to choose from, but are likely to reach different audiences.

Everyone knows of TV advertising, but much advertising is handled by the press, magazines, posters, radio and cinema. In fact most money is spent on press advertising in this country, and mainly in the local press. Most money is spent on the classified advertisement section by individuals and small businesses.

Advertising is expensive. Costs are published for all UK media in the publication BRAD, British Rate and Data. This subscription-only publication contains the costs for all media, and is updated monthly.

The choice of media depends on the product to be advertised, the market at which it is aimed, and the amount of finance available for the campaign. The aim is always to reach the maximum number of potential customers for the smallest possible outlay. The advertisements will be targeted towards the consumer profile that the market research people have identified. It follows, therefore, that 'consumer

profiles' for the various media are important. BRAD helps here, supported by information from ABC, the Audit Bureau of Circulations, another subscription-only publication, and JICNARS.

Viewers, circulation, and consumer profiles are constantly changing. An advertising agency will keep fully up to date with this dynamic situation and will be able to give authoritative advice on media planning. This type of work is either not cost effective for the small company, or beyond its capacity.

The choice of media is important. Each different media has advantages and disadvantages, and the costs differ vastly. Careful selection is essential. Advertising media can be analysed by considering four distinct characteristics:

- character
- atmosphere
- coverage
- cost.

Cinema advertising

For many years cinema advertising was the only media that gave the advertiser the opportunity to use colour, sound and movement but its importance has declined as cinema audiences have shrunk. TV advertising has largely taken its place, and developed it. The wide use of videos for viewing films has not yet spawned a video advertising industry, however!

TV advertising

TV advertising was confined to the showing of advertisements in limited slots between programmes in the UK. There are no advertising magazines, as there are in other countries. Very limited sponsorship of programmes is now possible, but this is restricted to a name mention only.

This media enable all techniques to be used – colour, sound, movement, words. The coverage is good, but the costs are high. Advertisements have a very short life, and long campaigns often have to be used. Specialist markets are difficult to target economically.

The country is split up into TV regions where different companies operate the system. A national campaign is very expensive.

Some regions are very useful for test marketing. The smaller areas, which can be isolated and measured are popular and Tyne Tees is a good example. London and the South East sees little of this market as this region covers about 25% of the UK market.

Table 19.1 gives examples of costs of TV advertising. Remember these are for the TV time only. The firm still has to pay for the design and production of the film. The cost of media time does put this in perspective, though.

Table 19.1
Cost of TV advertising

Year	Nov. 87		May 91		Aug. 92	
Station	ITV	Ch. 4	ITV	Ch. 4	ITV	Ch. 4
Anglia	6,400	2,200	11,200	11,200	11,210	11,210
Central	15,520	6,220	17,850	17,850	20,750	20,750
Granada	14,410	6,240	17,000	7,650	17,000	7,650
London W. End	16,000	24,000	21,250	8,500	21,250	8,500
Thames	28,000	8,000	41,600	20,810	46,750	22,100
TVS	11,960	–	16,930	–	18,700	–

(Basis: 20 second slot. Peak rate. Basic)

(*Source*: BRAD)

Commercial radio

Commercial radio was not legal within the UK for many years, and the most well-known stations were transmitted from offshore. This changed in 1973, when Capital Radio started the first legal service in the UK.

Radio in the UK is very regional, so coverage, other than in the region is limited. Programmes tend to be restricted, and the audience limited. The character of the station sometimes limits the range of listeners, and hence potential customers that is reached, and costs reflect this.

The press

The press has two main components, national and regional, and can also be broken down into daily and Sunday publications.

Table 19.2
Cost of newspaper advertising

	Nov. 87		May 91		Aug. 92	
	Cost/page	Circ.	Cost/page	Circ.	Cost/page	Circ.
Telegraph	24,640 – 1,146,917		32,000 – 1,095,240		33,510 – 1,041,796	
Times	11,500 – 442,375		15,000 – 424,991		17,000 – 388,196	
FT	18,368 – 209,278		24,640 – 289,336		26,880 – 294,597	
Sun	23,562 – 3,993,031		28,000 – 3,725,729		28,000 – 3,526,879	
Mirror	24,500 – 3,122,773		28,300 – 2,989,237		25,900 – 2,868,246	
Sundays						
The Ind.	12,000 – 222,361		12,000 – 402,004		14,000 – 386,559	
Mirror	22,770 – 3,013,285		27,200 – 2,783,384		28,500 – 2,753,596	
Telegraph	17,920 – 720,902		23,000 – 588,102		24,000 – 565,882	
Times	31,000 – 1,220,021		47,000 – 1,220,693		47,000 – 1,190,860	
News of W.	25,000 – 4,941,966		3,1500 – 4,888,111		31,500 – 4,712,112	

(*Source*: BRAD)

National press

By definition the coverage received in the national press is total. National advertising is very useful for introducing new products. Papers have a short life, so the advertisement must have a high impact. The lead time to get copy in is short, though, so there is potential for snap or opportunist advertising. There tends to be a strong pattern to the readership, and character and atmosphere is strong here. Simply compare and contrast the *Financial Times* with the *Daily Sport*! Colour is now available. Obviously all press advertising is silent and still.

Sunday publishing has a strong advertising content, especially the colour magazines. The colour magazine, which was a marketing/advertising led development, is mid-way between press advertising and magazines. Readership profiles are important as the advertiser must place the advertisement in the appropriate paper. These national papers are read in the home and have a relatively long life.

The press is used widely for advertising appointments, with the specialist papers being used for specialist jobs. Examples are job advertisements for teachers in *The Times Educational Supplement*, accountants in the *Financial Times*, and secretaries in *The Times* and the *Evening Standard*. *The Daily Telegraph* is known for its management appointments section on Thursday, with *The Sunday Times* being the paper with the name for weekend coverage of the same market. This market has become well developed with known specialisations. Relevant coverage is now good.

Regional press

The regional press is the domain of the classified advertisement and promotions for mainly local firms and services. Though the publications are regional they tend to have a longer life than the national press. They are more likely to be read in the home, and may have a wider readership age range.

Magazines

Magazines have a life as they are read at leisure, often more than once and by more than one reader. The quality of paper used and the printing is often very high. Lead time can be long, and space has to be booked well in advance for the popular quality magazines. They can contain sample sachets of certain products, such as a new face cream, and patch cards that contain a small quantity of a new perfume, but advertisements are nevertheless 'still and quiet'.

There is a vast and growing range of magazines in the UK. Almost every taste is catered for, and it is possible to target an audience strongly. Magazines are themselves classified as general interest, specialist, and the trade press. Most have a clear character and atmosphere. The cost tends to increase in direct proportion to their coverage on an overall basis. Note that a magazine that gives near 100% coverage for a small, specialised market will be cheap.

The retail and trade magazines are very useful for promoting products. They are often given free to the appropriate user, and so are paid for by the advertisers. This is a clear indication of their effectiveness.

Examine Table 19.3 for some examples of readership, circulation and costs of advertising space.

Table 19.3
Cost of Magazine advertising

	Nov 1987		May 1991		Aug 1992	
	£/page	Circ.	£/page	Circ.	£/page	Circ.
Yachting World	885	45,317	1,164	30,452	1,164	27,182
Country Life	1,456	48,342	1,765	50,335	1,870	46,236
Newsweek					1,170	–
Time			2,000	–	2,950	821,057
Pract.H'holder	1,650	47,358	2,028	40,634	2,129	34,664
Am. Gardener	1,175	90,368	1,520	81,971	1,670	96,575
Good H'keeping	4,090	345,321	5,360	366,235	6,580	391,449
Home & Garden	2,780	198,188	3,525	206,328	4,120	138,449
She	2,464	212,115	3,320	236,297	3,890	283,731
Autocar	1,030	56,307	2,090	91,546	2,090	83,265
Pract. Photogr.	879	10,116	1,355	120,750	1,355	110,041
Angling Times	2,630	106,557	3,465	125,099	3,643	116,106
Golf World	1,112	85,321	1,695	97,654	1,865	–
Cosmo	3,900	375,894	6,600	42,665	6,950	472,480
Vogue	4,330	180,836	6,560	173,076	7,250	181,912
Hello	–		4,005	346,540	5,355	444,257
M-Claire	–		3,100	182,340	3,400	222,671
Woman	11,900	1,061,967	12,500	805,511	112,500	716,758
Economist	2,350	85,666			3,450	97,903
N. Scientist	1,570	84,543			2,700	78,000

(*Source*: BRAD)

Remember that these costs are for the space only. They do not include the costs of designing and developing the copy, nor the costs of producing the necessary art work and photographs.

Poster advertising

Poster advertising is still a popular media, and good sites command a high price. Posters may be placed on hording, in bus shelters, on buses, trains, taxis, underground trains and stations and even parking meters and litter bins. It is hard to avoid seeing advertisements somewhere.

Posters can be in colour if required. Their main advantage is their long life. They can be seen frequently by the same potential customers and so have a cumulative impact.

Advertising trailers are a new development. These can drive around the region, or can be parked at the more infrequent event, e.g. sports events, pop concerts.

Costs are summarised in Table 19.4.

Table 19.4
Cost of outdoor and poster media

	Aug. 92	Nov. 87	May 91
Adtracters Ltd.	£300/day	–	£300/day
Taxicabs (London) – Outside	3,500/taxi-yr	20/taxi-mth	–
– Inside	25/panel mth	4/panel mth	£21/mth
Posters			
Adshell – Bus Shelters (5,000)	£434,000/2 wk	£97,500	£180,000
Bus (LT) DD Bus-sides	£56/bus. mth	£50/bus mth	£56/b.mth

(*Source*: BRAD)

Other media

Advertisements can be distributed through advertising catalogues in the press, through Prestel and Seefax, and through direct mail or door-to-door delivery. The 'In Flight' and 'House' magazine market is also developing. Certain credit card companies now issue magazines whose main aim is advertising to its customer base.

There are some even more unusual spaces today. Banners behind aircraft, the sides of balloons and airships, and all around sports stadiums if the performance is to be filmed or shown on TV.

The advantages and disadvantages of the major media are summarised in Table 19.5.

The advertising budget

The decision on how much to spend on advertising is one of the most difficult ones for management to take. Advertising should not cost more than it generates, i.e. the increased profits should be more than the costs. Advertising effectiveness is also extremely difficult to measure, so a cost/profit balance is very difficult to determine. Sometimes the objective is not related to sales volume, so this sort of evaluation is impossible.

In some cases the high advertising expenditure is designed to stop or deter competition entering the market. This is a '*barrier to entry*' to the market, and is common in *oligopoly* and *monopoly* markets.

Decisions have to be taken, though, and the more common methods used are as follows:

Table 19.5
Summary of advantages and disadvantages of main types of advertising media

Media	Advantages	Disadvantages
Newspapers	• low cost/high coverage	• still and silent
	• lasting	• poor picture quality
	• assumes image of paper	
	• limited colour	
Magazines	• colour of quality	• slow production process
	• readers can be targeted	• still and silent
	• lasting	
	• can be linked to features	
TV	• high coverage	• expensive
	• colour and movement	• no life
		• hard to change
		• advertisements
Posters	• wide coverage	• static
	• colour possible	• have 'old fashion' image
	• captive audience (trains, tubes, etc.)	• must be easy to read and simple

But are advertisements studied or ignored?

Percentage of sales

Percentage of sales is a common method, but is somewhat illogical. If sales fall for some reason, so will the advertising expenditure. An increased budget would seem more logical in this situation.

It can be used in markets dominated by a few manufacturers, an oligopolistic market. Here the normally high percentage used by all the manufacturers act as a deterrent to potential customers. If this is allied with a process with significant economies of scale, the defence can be almost perfect.

Match the competition

Matching the competition is a very negative approach. If followed too rigorously then the small firm can be pushed into serious cash flow problems.

It is also a process which makes a marketing breakthrough difficult.

What the firm can afford

Spending what the firm can afford may seem very logical, but much depends on the policy or philosophy of the firm. Advertising could come well down the priority order in a product orientated firm. Here an increase in production cost would result in a drop in the advertising budget.

There must always be an objective behind the advertising. If the budget does not allow this to be met, then the objective must be reset. Spending too much or too little is a waste of expenditure.

The 'task' method

One of the more scientific measures is the 'task' method. The firm sets definite objectives, then draws up full marketing plans to achieve it. It then sets its advertising budget within the overall product and marketing budget. If the firm cannot afford the full expenditure, it will then have to trim its objectives.

Measurement of effectiveness

This is not easy. A firm is trying to measure the effects of its actions, but such attempts are hampered, quite deliberately, by the firm's competition. The task of identifying the effect of one variable in a situation where many factors are changing is almost impossible. Quantitative data is therefore scarce and potentially unreliable. Refer back to the demand model developed earlier. Demand has several determinants and advertising is only one of them. The effectiveness of advertising will also depend on the state of the economy – another factor which is never static.

This is a difficult problem, but one which is so important that it has to be faced. A number of methods are used. Market research personnel attempt to measure:

Awareness and recall

Which advertisement has been seen and remembered? This will be tested prompted and unprompted, i.e. list ten TV advertisements you watched last week, or did you see the advertisements for product X? There can be big differences between these two measures.

Attitude

Attitude is an attempt to see if the advertisement has supported or established a favourable attitude towards the firm and its products.

Counting

Some forms of advertisement ask the potential customer to take action. The number of coupons returned can be counted, and it is for this reason that many return addresses are given a reference, i.e. reply to Department ST 7. This would tell the firm that the letters are a response to its seventh advertisement in *The Sunday Times*. Equally the number of visitors to a showroom can be recorded and analysed.

Economics and ethics of advertising

Advertising is such a strong part of life in our economy, and that of the western world, that it is hard to be able to evaluate this topic objectively. All market and mixed economies exhibit choice in their markets, and where there is choice there is marketing. It is only in the old communist economies, where there was no choice and no advertising as such, that the other case can be examined. Here advertising was replaced by propaganda to ensure that their populations believed themselves to be better off than the west. The situation in Russia today, however, does little to advance the argument either way.

There is a lot of controversy about the need for ethics in advertising. There is also a lot of politics. Be careful when considering this problem, and keep clear of dogma. Pure economics answers are also not really relevant to the real world of Business Studies. It is an important topic, all the same, and must be considered.

Advertising clearly is a cost, and costs eventually have to be paid by the consumer.

This is true, but it is not true that without advertising, and the other marketing activities, prices would be lower. Advertising increases demand for a product. In industries where there are strong economies of scale this will lead to reduced costs. Competitive pressures will ensure that these savings are passed on to the consumer. Competition will also lead to improved and better quality products, and price stability. The sole supplier, especially a state supported one, has no encouragement to change, be efficient, or even consider price reductions.

Research and development is expensive. Only the profitable firm can afford this. Advertising can assist in building the brand loyalty necessary to success, and then inform the consumer of the new products.

Advertising is an industry and creates employment, but consumes scarce resources.

Again, this is true. It might be a case of wasted resources, but equally they may be productively generating more demand, and hence more work for others. The incomes paid to all the staff in advertising will recycle back into the economy, as they are also consumers.

Without advertising there would be no commercial television or radio, a very reduced press and magazine sector where prices would be much higher, and fewer sports events. In spite of the BBC, a duller world would result. Some may consider this to be a good thing, but it is a matter of opinion. It is very doubtful whether party political broadcasting would also be banned!

Advertising has to be controlled.

Again, this is a true statement. It does not mean that all advertising is bad. Advertising informs and persuades, so the information must be true. This is true of all advertising, even government advertising.

Advertising is controlled directly and indirectly through a series of laws and control bodies. All advertisements are subject to the Trades Description Act, and some come under the jurisdiction of the Weights and Measures Regulations. Control bodies, such as the Advertising Standards Authority, and the law demand that advertisements are 'legal, decent, honest and truthful'. Certain techniques, such as subliminal advertising, the transmission of frequent but very short advertisements which the viewer does not even notice, are illegal.

Advertising and its claims have led to consumerism. Consumer groups have been set up to 'look after the interests of the consumer' and publish reports on quality and value for money. They are also popular TV programmes today.

Just because the industry is regulated it does not mean that it is against the public interest.

Advertising is an unreliable guide to quality.

This is true, but so are price, distribution and reputation unreliable guides. The buyer has to judge himself. '*Caveat emptor*' – 'buyer beware' – is the motto!

Advertising may encourage materialism and consumerism.

This may be so, but it is very doubtful if it causes it. The individual is entitled to use his or her money in any way. Advertising of products can hardly be accused of setting the moral, ethical and political standards of a country. Advertising and marketing are followers here, not leaders.

The case is clearly unproven.

SUMMARY

Having studied this chapter, you will be able to:

▼ Discuss the purpose of advertising.

▼ Explain how advertising works, using the mnemonic AIDA.

▼ Develop how advertising changes as a product flows through its life cycle.

▼ Discuss the develoment of advertising campaigns, and the role of advertising agencies.

▼ Describe the major types of media used, and their specific purpose, namely:

– *TV advertising*

– *Cinema advertising*

– *Commercial radio*

– *Press: papers and magazines*

– *Posters*

▼ Consider how an advertising budget may be set, and how its effectiveness may be determined.

▼ Consider the ethical aspects of advertising.

Questions and activities

Technical terms and glossary

In the section below you are given a series of technical terms and their meanings. They have been scrambled, though. You must match up the terms and the definitions. When you have them correctly paired, transfer them to your vocabulary or glossary book.

You are also advised to transfer any definitions obtained during the exercises in the case studies into this glossary book.

Technical terms

1. Effective advertising
2. AIDA
3. Market orientation
4. Product orientation
5. Advertising agency
6. Advertising media
7. Advertising budget
8. Recall
9. Brand recognition
10. ABC
11. Brand manager
12. BRAD

Definitions

A. The places and systems that are used to support advertisements.

B. Advertising which generates more additional profit than it costs.

C. The strength by which a specific product is recognised by the consumer through its name, design or other unique characteristic.

D. A UK publication which lists all advertising media in UK, with its costs and exposure, if relevant. Means 'British Rate and Data'.

E. Acronym explaining how an advertisement works. 'Attention, Interest, Desire and Action'.

F. The amount of money a company puts by to cover all its advertising.

G. A philosophy of management which puts the production of the product ahead of the needs of the potential customer.

H. A member of the management team of a company who is responsible reputation and sale of one or more of a company's products.

I. A philosophy of management which places consumer needs before production needs.

J. The ability of a viewer to remember, prompted or not, a particular advertisement.

K. Name of company which specialised in providing details of the circulation of magazines, etc. It stands for Audit Bureau of Circulations.

L. A company which specialises in the provision of a full range of advertising services for others.

Short answer questions and essays

1. (*Essay*) Differentiate, using examples, between product and market orientated businesses.
2. Discuss three different objectives of advertising.
3. Describe how an advertisement is designed to affect the observer.
4. How might you describe 'effective advertising'?
5. (*Essay*) How does the nature and type of advertising change as a product passes through its life cycle?
6. Describe the advantages and disadvantages of four different advertising media.
7. (*Essay*) On what basis may a firm set its advertising budget?
8. (*Essay*) How might the effectiveness of a particular advertisement be measured?
9. Who controls the quality of TV advertising?
10. Who or what is JICNARS?

Data response questions and case study

1. Read the articles below and answer the questions which follow.

Unilever well spread for upturn

A USEFUL publicity coup was scored last week by Unilever, the Anglo-Dutch consumer products giant behind the new vegetable-fat spread, I Can't Believe It's Not Butter.

Soap-opera-style television ads, which were to have marked the spread's UK launch, were banned by the Independent Television Commission because of their reference to butter. Unilever responded with full-page newspaper ads which look to have created rather more and cheaper publicity for the product which, despite its extraordinary name, has been highly successful in America.

(From The Sunday Times, 3 November 1991)

BT rebuked over price cut advert

AN ADVERTISEMENT headlined 'BT is bringing prices down' was criticised yesterday after complaints that the telephone company was actually raising some charges.

The rebuke from the Advertising Standards Authority included a request that BT avoid 'exaggerating', and that it should present its price structure in a way that could be easily understood.

The advertisement, which ran to about 600 words, appeared in the national Press last summer after BT announced its latest price structure.

'We take any criticism by the authority seriously and we will take full account of their comments in preparing future advertising materials', a BT spokesman said.

(From *The Independent*, 22 January 1992)

Benetton attracts controversy over new campaign

SUPPORT was growing in the advertising industry yesterday for a voluntary boycott of a campaign by Benetton, the clothing company, after the leak of its latest advertisement depicting a dying Aids victim.

Several magazines have already refused to run the campaign, poster companies were warned yesterday that it was 'unacceptable' and the Advertising Standards Authority said it was likely to cause offence and distress.

One senior industry source told The Independent that agencies and publishers were speaking privately about a voluntary media-wide ban. 'It is cynical and it is deliberate and it has gone too far', he said of the Benetton campaign. Another source, close to the company's founder, Luciano Benetton, had told executives he intended to court controversy.

(Adapted from *The Independent*, 25 January 1992)

(a) Distinguish between advertising and publicity.
(4 marks)
(b) What do the articles tell you about the Advertising Standards Authority in terms of:
(i) its role (3 marks)
(ii) its effectiveness? (6 marks)
(c) Give three reasons why a near-monopoly, such as British Telecom (BT), consider it necessary to advertise. (6 marks)
(d) Discuss two arguments against the use of advertising. (6 marks)
(Associated Examining Board, Business Studies A, Paper 1, 1993)

2. Read the extract and answer the questions which follow.

MINERAL WATERS IN THE UK

During the 1970s, Perrier (UK) built the market almost single handed, aided by the 'Eau so successful' advertising campaign. By the early 1980s, there were five major competitors each contributing to spending on advertising and stimulating market growth. In 1983, there was a major marketing windfall – a national water strike – which caused the market to leap by almost 50% in one year. At the same time, the market began to segment on a price basis, as the premium brands gained national distribution through grocery outlets and own labels were introduced.

UK mineral water market

(millions litres)

1980	25
1982	34
1984	65
1986	105
1987	150
1990 (Estimate)	210

Today, the ownership of the mineral water brands can be divided between those companies which have a diversified product range, e.g. Nestlé, Cadbury Schweppes, and those who are purely mineral water producers (e.g. Perrier, Highland Spring).

While product life-cycle theory suggests that volume growth will inevitably slow down, the Chief Executive of Perrier (UK) estimates that the average Briton will be drinking ten litres of bottled water a year within two decades (Financial Times, 1986). A British Market Research Bureau (1986) survey showed that 34% of UK adults claimed to drink bottled mineral water. 25% of those claimed to drink it once a month or more

The UK Consumer and Derived Brand Benefits

Forty-one per cent of UK mineral water is consumed by Londoners, perhaps due to the fact that the original 'eau' campaign was targeted upon 'image-conscious trendies' who saw mineral water as a status symbol.

As the distribution base broadens (56% of national sales are now distributed through major multiples - Mintel Market Intelligence, 1988) and the market structure changes, it seems likely that with increasing consumer demand, a mass market will develop from the niche position previously occupied.

There is considerable evidence to suggest that other environmental and social factors are also encouraging these structural changes.

(Source: *The Quarterly Review of Marketing*, Summer 1989)

(a) What factors might affect a grocery outlet's decision to introduce 'own label' products?

(5 marks)

(b) Assume that total advertising expenditure in the UK Mineral Water Industry was £2 million in 1986 and £2.5 million in 1987. If other factors stay the same, calculate the advertising elasticity of demand for the UK Mineral Water Market between 1986 and 1987, and comment on the significance of the result. (5 marks)

(c) How might those 'who saw the mineral water as a status symbol' have been targeted by the marketing department? (4 marks)

(d) How might marketing strategies change as the distribution broadens and the market structure changes to a mass market from a 'niche position' in the market. (3 marks)

(e) What factors other than marketing might have led to the increase in sale of mineral water?

(3 marks)

(Associated Examining Board, Paper 1, June 1992)

3. Advertising prices change frequently. They will vary with the circulation and coverage of the media, as well as the costs of producing the advertisment itself. The following are some selected costs for March 1995

Daily National Papers	–	*Whole page*
The Daily Telegraph	–	£36,500 (main paper)
The Times	–	£19,000
Financial Times	–	£35,700
The Sun	–	£35,000
Sunday National Papers	–	*Whole page*
Sunday Telegraph	–	£27,000
The Sunday Times	–	£47,000
New of the World	–	£35,700
Magazines	–	*Whole page*
Good Housekeeping	–	£7,600
She	–	£5,100
Cosmopolitan	–	£7,500
The Economist	–	£5,100

(*Source*: Direct Telephone Survey)

Questions and activities

(a) Compare this data with that in the chapter. Examine any relationship between cost and circulation. Predict the circulations for the papers, etc. in March 1995.

(b) Up-date the rest of the data, using any resources you can. (Consult BRAD in the library, if there is one, telephone the newspapers, TV companies, etc.) Analyse any trends you reveal.

20
Marketing communications– selling, sales promotion and merchandising

Preview

▽ This chapter introduces another important communication process for marketing – *selling, sales promotion* and *merchandising*.

▽ The chapter examines the role and function of a *sales force*. It then describes and defines *sales promotion* and merchandising, and studies the many forms that are available of these to marketing.

Advertising is directed by the producer of a good or service at the potential consumer by indirect or impersonal means. Selling, sales promotion and merchandising act directly at the point-of-sale. They are another aspect of the promotion component of the marketing mix. Advertising is designed to 'pull' the potential consumer into the retail outlet. It is the job of the sales force, the sales promotions and all the merchandising activities to then 'push' the customer into buying the good being promoted.

Sales policy and selling

Firms have to manage the actual selling of their products. They employ a sales force under the control of a sales manager or even sales director. This group of staff is responsible for achieving a predetermined level of sales. The sales director is a member of the senior management team within the marketing department. The sales director will be responsible to the marketing director.

Many firms used to employ large forces of salesmen who visited customers regularly. The sales force provided the direct personal contact that some products required. They presented and sold new products to the retailers and they also acted as order takers for existing products. They were in direct competition with the sales staff of the competition for

space in the stores concerned. They would reassure the storekeeper that the new products would be fully supported through advertising, and would offer inducements so that the products would be stocked by the store. They were also part of the market research establishment as they gathered intelligence about the market and the competition.

Sales forces are expensive to organise and operate. With the increase in the importance of multiple retailers and supermarkets the role of the sales force has changed. It is now more economic to use specialist sales staff to introduce new products, and to collect reorders by telephone. Personal contact is still maintained and the whole process is more economic. The supermarkets are a special case, and they are usually handled at director level and at their head offices. Modern stores now reorder by computers which are directly linked to the tills.

Sales forces were organised around territories. Each salesperson had an area of responsibility, and a sales quota which had to be achieved. The size of the area and the number of calls that were planned to be made depended upon a number of factors. These included the density of the market, the size of the outlets, and the complexity of the product.

The importance of the sales effort varies with the type of product being handled. It is the main marketing activity for industrial consumer goods and other very technical products. The salesperson, who may well be called a consultant or a sales engineer, requires considerable technical support and often visits to the factory are involved. At the other end of the scale, in the FMCG industry, the salesperson has been largely replaced by the telephone.

Payment of sales forces

The payment of salespersons has presented problems. They may be paid a salary only, commission only, or a combination of both. Commission, or a sum of money related to sales, encourages the salesperson to sell, but it can encourage a short-term view of selling. Salary only may not give sufficient inducement to sell. The combination package is thus the most common. The commission rates will often vary with the level of sales; the more that is sold the higher the commission rate. The salesperson has a target level of sales set and agreed, and the commission will vary about this level. Advertisements will be seen for sales staff quoting a payment such as £25,000 'OTE'. This means 'On Target Earnings', i.e. if the target is reached the total of salary and commission will be £25,000 per annum. Note that it does not state what the target is, how commission is related to this, what the size of the basic salary is, or how difficult the target is. There is a lot to find out about what seems to be an attractive package.

The salary, with or without commission, is only a small part of the cost of a sales force. To this must be added the statutory payments for pension and National Insurance, the cost of a car and its operating costs, travelling and hotel expenses and considerable telephone or fax bills. Add to this the sales office costs and it can be seen how expensive selling can be. Because sales forces are expensive, they have to be used sparingly.

Use of sales forces

Sales forces have decreased over the last decade. They have been replaced in many areas by telephone selling. Their use now is product related. Sales forces are far more likely to be found handling industrial goods than consumer goods. They are rare now for FMCGs, though they may be used, on a contract basis, to launch new products to the trade.

Sales promotion

Advertising is designed to inform and persuade the customer to take some action. It is designed to pull the potential customer into the shop or store. The work of the sales force has ensured that the product is in the store for the potential customer to buy. The potential customer has thus been given a small push

Discounting and special offers are used by many retailers to attract customers into their shops.

towards the required sale. Sales promotion and merchandising are designed to strengthen this push and to ensure a sale is actually made.

First, a definition of sales promotion:

Sales promotions are selling techniques which persuade and motivate customers to buy at the point-of-sale.

Sales promotions are aimed and designed to increase sales. They may be directed at the final customer/consumer, or at the wholesalers and retailers. They work through:

- encouraging consumers to sample the product, or to purchase it another time
- persuading more outlets to accept and sell the product
- encouraging the customer and the sellers to hold more stock.

This technique is widely used by the FMCG industry.

Promotional methods

Sales promotions tend to have a very quick impact on sales, but the improvement can be short lived. They can even generate a drop in sales later as consumers have bought more of the good earlier to take advantage of the offer. Remember the Hoover offer which offered free air tickets to USA with any purchase above about £120. The offer seemed more attractive than the product. Sales surged initially, and stocks sold out, but later sales went very flat. The effect on sales for promotions in general, and for the Hoover offer in particular, are shown in Figure 20.1.

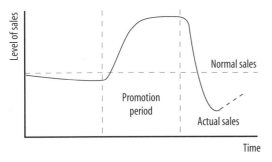

Figure 20.1 *Representation of the effect of a promotion on sales*

Note the dips in sales below the trend line as the promotion is cut. Advertising campaigns, on the other hand, tend to produce a slow but lasting

growth pattern, as illustrated in Figure 20.2. Compare and contrast this with Figure 20.1.

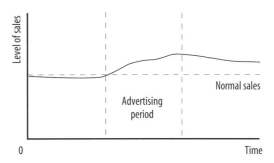

Figure 20.2 *Representation of the effect of a advertising on sales*

Sales promotions are often aggressive and attempt to influence and change buyer preferences at the point of purchase. Sometimes, however, they are defensive and are designed to keep buyer loyalty. There are a full range of promotional methods for a firm to choose from. The most common promotions, with explanations, are discussed below.

Branding

Brand names are difficult to build up. Brands are a guarantee of quality to the confirmed user. Brand building and image are important to the seller and the buyer.

Branding is a positive attempt at product differentiation, i.e. trying to establish that your product is really different to all the competition.

Free samples

Free samples are self-explanatory. A small sample may be put through the letter boxes of all the houses in an area, given away by a demonstrator in the store, placed in hotels or given as sachets in magazines. It is very effective, but is very expensive to carry out especially if special packs are needed.

Users must know where additional supplies may be purchased.

Labelled price reductions

The labelled price reduction is the situation where the product carries a 'special price' tag on the label. These are popular with the trade as there are no problems of coupon redemption. They are also popular with producers as they provide a means of giving a special introductory price without actually reducing the list price.

It is only likely to be successful if demand for the

product is price sensitive. It also tends to be very short lived in its effect, even for sales promotions.

'Money off the next purchase', or with two special labels are popular with the producer. They encourage the repeat purchase, but a significant number of coupons are never used. Most readers will be aware of that drawer in the kitchen filled with out-of-date offer coupons!

Branded offers

Branded offers form a popular, well-known product is used to support or 'carry' a free sample of another non-competing product. The two products, which may be produced by the same firm, are often banded together. An example might be a cream alternative with a jar of instant coffee, or a pack of dental floss with a tube of toothpaste. It is hoped that the buyer will try and like the free sample.

Another variation is the 'two-for-one' offer, or 'buy one, get one free' offer. Sales volume will clearly rise, but not sales revenue. It may prevent the buyer from purchasing a competitor's product, though.

Premium offers

There are three main variations on the premium offer: free gifts, 'send away' offers and self-liquidating offers.

Free gifts may be placed in the product itself, as is popular with breakfast cereal producers, or given out at the check-out. Coupons may have to be collected sometimes and then exchanged for goods. This promotion is popular with petrol companies as it encourages customers to collect and thus become regular, almost tied, purchasers.

'Send away' offers involve no transactions at tills, so are popular with the store. Again, many coupons get forgotten, even though the item was bought to get the offer later.

Self-liquidating offers are those where something is bought. Money has to be sent with the proof of purchase. The buyer obtains merchandise, say towels or a clock, at no cost to the primary good supplier, say a detergent producer.

Competitions

Competitions are very appealing to some consumers. Prices may be very attractive, but there will be few of them. Competitions may require answers to very simple questions, with a tie break activity – often a slogan – or be essentially a draw. Newspaper Bingo is popular, as is Portfolio in *The Times*. The lure of something for nothing is strong!

A variation is to put coupons in products which

entitle the lucky winner to a major free gift. It has been used successfully in the detergent industry and with similar products. Great care has to be taken with the distribution of the limited number of winning tickets, as bunching could be an embarrassment. (On the other hand it could cause a huge increase in demand in a little village store!) Good examples have been 'Make-Money' by Shell and a whole range of 'soft drink in cans' offers.

Personality promotions

A prize is won if you have the required product when the personality calls. This is expensive, so is restricted to big brands from major suppliers.

This is only a limited selection of the major promotions. Marketing attempts to develop or invent new promotions as their very newness will be an attraction. Some promotions come and go. Trading stamps and cigarette coupons used to be very popular. The buyer was given stamps proportional to the money spent in the shops or garages, and the stamps could then be exchanged for goods from a catalogue. They are no longer popular at all, and the major stamp businesses have disappeared.

Promotions have different effects, and some are more suitable for some purposes than others. These facts are summarised in Figure 20.3.

a) To get consumer trial of new or exisitng product	Free with-, in- or on-pack premium
	Money-off voucher
	Money-off offer
	Sampling
	Propriety promotion
b) To obtain repeat purchasing	Any premium offer of a collectable item
	Competition
	Free mail-in
	Free continuous mail-in (coupons)
	Money-off voucher
	Self-liquidating promotion
c) To obtain long-term consumer loyalty	Continuous self-liquidating promotion
	Trading stamps
d) To increase frequency or quantity of consumer purchase in the short run	Competition
	Free-on, with-pack premium
	Free mail-in
	Personality promotion
	In-store self liquidator
	Money off offer
	Shop-floor promotion
	Tailor-made promotion

e) To move high stocks out of stores	Competition
	Free with-pack
	Free mail-in
	Shop-floor promotion
	Tailor-made promotion
f) To get consumers to visit premises	Free gifts
	Money-off voucher
	Shop-floor promotion
	Tailor-made promotion
	Trading stamps
	Proprietary promotions
g) To get increased distribution	Trade promotion. Possibly also consumer push.
h) To obtain increased stock levels/ stocking in depths	Trade promotion, plus right consumer push
Trade promotions	Gifts, money off, holidays, etc., inducements/incentives

Figure 20.3 *Which promotion to use and why*

Merchandising

Merchandising involves the display, packaging and store layout for the goods. It is done at various levels, at the level of a particular good, a group of goods, or for a whole store. These are very important communication methods to the FMCG industry, just look at your local supermarket.

Store merchandising

The major retailing trend over the last 20 years has been away from small shops where the customer is served by the owner or sales assistant towards large, self-service establishments. The centre of gravity of shops has moved from the town centre to large, out-of-town complexes.

Opening hours have increased: 12 hours per day, seven days per week is not uncommon. The consumer will not easily tolerate shops that close for lunch any more. As more and more people work the the more useless the conventional 9 a.m. to 1 p.m., 2 p.m. to 5 p.m. set of hours has become.

The design and layout of the modern supermarket is no accident. The total design is aimed to attract the customer, to expose the customer to as many different products as possible, and provide opportunity for the customer to maximise his or her purchases. How is this done?

- Put essential purchases away from the door.
- Put the special offers, the loss leaders, at the back of the store.
- Put the high volume sellers at eye level.
- Put selected items in special displays at the end of rows of shelves.

Many of the large multiples decide on the complete layout of their stores and issue precise details to be followed.

Shelf and product merchandising

As has been mentioned earlier, the position in a store matters, as does the position on the shelf. Merchandising is all about maximising the impact of a product upon the potential consumer.

Pack design

Packaging is that part of the marketing mix concerned with the visual impact of the product. Packaging is presentation, and making the most of the presentation. A pack has to be instantly recognisable, often to potential consumers who may not yet be able to read. Remember, with products like sweets, biscuits and breakfast cereals, the consumer, the child, is not always the purchaser.

The packaging designer has less freedom today over the shape of the carton than before. Many pack and tin sizes are now subject to European Commission Regulations. Such packs carry the 'E Mark'. The manufacturer then has to get the required quantity of the product into that carton. This removes one option for the designer, but also makes possible deception harder.

Some products, like chocolate bars, are packed into small outer cartons for protection and sale to the retailer. These outers are often designed to double as a display carton for use in the store. The products are impulse buys, so the greater the impact the greater the sales are likely to be. The smaller outlet will often sell the product directly from these outers which may be set directly on the counter.

Shelf and store support

Manufacturers often supply advertising materials for use in the shop. Posters and stickers are common, and some industries supply special display cases. These are common for cigarettes, ice cream, and soft drinks. Often the user is tied to the products of the supplier only.

In certain industries the supplier will supply the name board for the shop which will obviously carry the name of the supplier.

Manufacturers offer assistance to stores on layout and display. This is all aimed at getting the maximum impact out of its products.

SUMMARY

Having studied this chapter, you will be able to:

▼ Differentiate clearly between the marketing communication processes known as

- *Selling*

- *Sales promotion*

- *Merchandising*

▼ Describe the changes in selling policy which have occured over the recent years.

▼ Discuss the advantages and disadvantages of sales forces, and their methods of payment.

▼ Examine various sales promotion techniques, examples of which are:

- *Branding*

- *Free samples*

- *Special offers*

- *Competitions*

- *Personality promotions*

▼ Evaluate the various types of merchandising available to a firm, and to be able to distinguish between:

- *Store merchandising*

- *Shelf and product merchandising*

Questions and activities

Technical terms and glossary

In the section below you are given a series of technical terms and their meanings. They have been scrambled, though. You must match up the terms and the definitions. When you have them correctly paired, transfer them to your vocabulary or glossary book.

You are also advised to transfer any definitions obtained during the exercises in the case studies into this glossary book.

Technical terms

1. Sales force
2. Commission
3. Sales promotion
4. Branding
5. Premium offers
6. Personality promotions
7. Store merchandising
8. Product merchandising
9. Tele-sales
10. OTE

Definitions

A. The modern technique where sales persons contact potential customers over the telephone.
B. Design of a product or its packaging so as to maximise its impact on the potential customer.
C. 'On Target Earnings': the income a salesman should get if the sales target is met.
D. That group of people in a company who go out and try to sell the product or service. They may or may not deal with the eventual consumer.
E. A means of helping consumers to identify a particular supplier's variety of good or service.

F. Using a well-known personality to attract potential customers to a product or store.
G. A way of paying sales forces. A set sum of money will be payed for each unit of a product or service sold.
H. A series of methods that a company may use at the point of sale to encourage the potential consumer to buy.
I. A method of sales promotion utilising free gifts, coupons or other self liquidating offers.
J. The science of the design of a shop, store or warehouse to maximise sales.

Short answer questions and essays

1. (*Essay*) Discuss the problems associated with the payment of sales staff.
2. (*Essay*) How has the use of sales forces changed over the last 20 years or so?
3. What is sales promotion?
4. (*Essay*) Describe and explain, using examples wherever possible, four different means of promoting sales.
5. Who makes money when a company offers a telephone competition?
6. (*Essay*) Describe, in detail, how a supermarket utilises merchandising to boost sales in its stores?
7. (*Essay*) How might a manufacturer of a food product merchandise its product in a supermarket not owned by itself?
8. (*Essay*) Examine and discuss the layout of a modern supermarket shelf system.
9. (*Essay*) What is sales promotion designed to do?
10. Why may petrol companies have found coupons and voucher saving schemes successful as a means of boosting sales?

21
Marketing communications – after-sales service and guarantees

Preview

▽ This chapter will look at the marketing opportunities at the end of the marketing process, beyond even the point of sale.

▽ It will examine the possibilities and dangers for producer and buyer alike of using after-sales service and the guarantee as a marketing weapon. This will all be set in the legal context, but the reader is encouraged to follow this through by studying Chapter 22.

The field of *after-sales service* and guarantee is an area for marketing to use, especially for large expensive items; in the consumer durables field for example. The manufacturer has to satisfy basic legal requirements, but is free to 'give' more if this is thought by marketing to be sensible.

The responsibilities and opportunities for a firm do not end when it has sold its product or service. In all cases the business has a legal responsibility towards the consumer. In most cases the seller and the maker of the goods are different and both have a responsibility. Goods must be of *merchantable quality*, be safe and, if appropriate, work. If a watch does not function properly shopkeepers cannot avoid their responsibilities by claiming they did not make it.

Sometimes manufacturers and sellers can use this area as an opportunity to impress the buyer, and give the consumer another reason for buying their product rather than one from the competition. After-sales service can be offensive or defensive in marketing terms. No firm can avoid its legal responsibilities.

Legal responsibilities

All firms have to comply with the Trades Description Acts, the Weights and Measures Regulations, the Fair Trading Act, the Unfair Contract Terms Act, and the Sale of Goods Act. Every sale forms a contract. Look at Chapter 22 very carefully.

Goods must be safe and functional. They must conform to the appropriate safety regulations, and may carry the appropriate marks and *British Standard* numbers. They must also do what they claim they are sold to do. They must be of 'merchantable quality'.

Consumers have the opportunity of taking cases to the *Office of Fair Trading*, the *Citizens Advice Bureau* and the *Trading Standards Department* in the region. Hire purchase and other credit sales are covered by their own law.

Products sold with a *Guarantee* or a *Warranty* are covered by Law, and no guarantee can take a consumer's *Statutory Rights* away. Guarantees are enforceable in law and if it is not complied with the customer may legally cancel the contract and demand that the purchase price be returned. This is not the case with a warranty, and here the manufacturer only has to replace or repair the goods.

Statutory rights are the basic rights that a consumer has to product quality, etc., as enshrined in the area of Consumer law.

Many firms and industries go beyond providing just the legal minimum requirements. Various trade associations have set up *codes of practice* covering the operation of their trade or business. Major ones are to be found in the areas of cars and car repair, mail order trading and package holidays. Some, like ABTA, the Association of British Travel Agents, which covers the operation of the travel agency business in UK, carry bonds to protect the consumer in case of problems.

Marketing opportunities

The marketing department has the opportunity to use first the guarantee, then after-sales service as marketing weapons. They are part of the marketing mix, so their use must be integrated with the other factors, or weapons, being exploited. How might this be done?

Consumer durables, and industrial capital goods are expected to last. Many need servicing and the occasional repair to keep them operating. Thus many of these goods are sold with a guarantee, and with the opportunity to pre-purchase service. This can be used by firms as another marketing weapon. Firms may also offer a range of accessories, an operating handbook with full operating instructions, and even an installation service. This is the 'total product' concept of marketing.

The guarantee

The buyer always has statutory rights. However, additional guarantees may be offered.

Here the manufacturer guarantees the function or operation of the unit for a period. One year 'parts and labour' guarantees are common in the consumer durables area. They will be found 'as standard' with many items of stereo equipment, TVs, computers and most domestic electrical goods. The buyer is automatically covered against faults, which will be rectified free of charge, occurring during the first year of *normal operation*. This can be difficult to define!

Extended guarantees are becoming a real marketing tool today. These can be given away 'free', or may be sold as an optional extra. Look at the following examples.

Free extended guarantee

These are now quite common in the motor trade. Bodywork and anti-rust guarantees are popular, some for up to six years. Most have a sting in the tail, though – the buyer must register the car for an annual inspection, and have any damage repaired. The cost of this is met by the purchaser, not by the guarantee, so the warranty is not quite as good as it seems.

Mechanical guarantees can seem to be free also, but watch if they are for parts and/or labour. The major cost of a repair is usually labour, particularly if a call-out charge – the charge made for having a fitter/mechanic call at the buyer's house – is involved. The charge can be based on a minimum of £50 for just coming out, then additional £35 for every 15 minutes on site. Work out the labour cost for a job which takes 45 minutes. If the part that had to be changed cost £5, a parts only guarantee is not very satisfactory.

These guarantees look and sound good, but read the 'small print'. They can be used very effectively, though, and significantly increase the chance of a sale.

Paid extended guarantees

Here the purchaser is invited to buy an extended warranty. The normal one-year can be extended to say five years for a price. This type of extension may be sold quite aggressively, but buyers must be careful. Such guarantees can be expensive, and really give cover, or insurance against a very low risk. When associated with a low initial price for the good it is a case for extreme caution. Extended guarantees to suppliers are usually a form of insurance. They do not carry the risk themselves, nor do they run a service department. They sell a policy for a firm which does, and they take a commission for selling the policy. (Notice the similarity between this and holiday selling with insurance.) A competitor's product may seem to be cheaper than yours, but in reality it may not be the case when the guarantee is included. Examine Case Study 21.1. At what price should CD plc sell their unit?

CASE STUDY 21.1

CD plc and the sale of CD players

CD plc were launching their new solid state CD players for the Christmas market. These were very reliable units, significantly better than any competition at the time. The main competitors were seen to be units made by Badmans and Mony, who both use extended guarantees aggressively as part of their marketing mix. The present market situation is as follows:

Table 21.1

CD market and prices

Supplier	Basic price	Extended warranty	Commission	Total price
	(£)	(£)	(£)	(£)
Badmans	450	150	50	600
Mony	380	175	75	555

The real answer should start 'it all depends', and it does depend on many factors. Based on competitive pricing, though, they could adopt a price of £560, and give and promote a 'free three year guarantee'. This places them between the competition who charge an effective £600 and £555. The suppliers, however, only get £500 and £455.

The same situation applies to holidays. Many of the major companies offer big discounts on list price, but insist that insurance is purchased from them. This is expensive, and buyers who shop around can often get a better price for the same holiday, with insurance. Look at Table 21.2, which illustrates such a situation. There is a basic legal principle which applies to many transactions known as *caveat emptor* or 'buyer beware'. This is just one of those areas.

Table 21.2

Comparison of holiday package prices

Company	Basic price(£)	Insurance(£)	Total to buyer(£)
A	550 – 10%	80	580
B	540	20	560

A competitive and really free package can be valuable to the buyer, though. Consider Jaguar cars, which had a reputation before Ford's takeover, for unreliability. They offered the following, free:

- three-year mechanical/electrical warranty, including special RAC membership
- full overseas emergency assistance
- three years paint and surface warranty
- six years corrosion (perforation) warranty

Nobody expects to have to pay out much. Is this a way of marketing an improvement in quality, without actually saying it was ever poor?

After-sales service

After-sales service can be expensive for the customer to obtain as repair firms are in short supply now. Offers are good if service is needed regularly, like for cars, but of doubtful value if problems are occasional. Consider a few industries.

Motor trade

Less and less regular servicing is needed now, since it has been designed out. Manufacturers set prices and schedules which approved garages have to follow. This cuts out the problem of potential overcharging.

Some firms now offer free servicing deals, for one or two years. These can be valuable, especially when the servicing is expensive. Watch the terms and conditions, though. Is it parts and labour, or just one of them.

Good servicing builds a good reputation for the dealer and supplier. It encourages, but does not guarantee a repeat purchase.

Electrical goods

This can be a problem in this 'throw away' world of today. Electrical contractors are rare. The supply boards used to offer a service, and some still do. The Gas Board, or British Gas has offered service for years, but there is an obvious safety factor here.

The utilities do offer reasonably priced service contracts, to the advantage of both parties. The consumer gets work done, and the utility gets continuity of work for its workers.

SUMMARY

Having studied this chapter, you will be able to:

▼ Discuss the legal and marketing aspects of the provision of guarantees, both from the point of view of the supplier and the customer.

▼ Explain the options open to marketing for free and priced extended guarantees.

▼ Explain the role of after sales service contracts within the marketing mix.

Questions and activities

Technical terms and glossary

In the section below you are given a series of technical terms and their meanings. They have been scrambled, though. You must match up the terms and the definitions. When you have them correctly paired, transfer them to your vocabulary or glossary book.

You are also advised to transfer any definitions obtained during the exercises in the case studies into this glossary book.

Technical terms

1. British Standards
2. Statutory rights
3. ABTA
4. Extended guarantee
5. After-sales service
6. Guarantee
7. Merchantable quality
8. Normal operation
9. *Caveat emptor*
10. Warranty

A. A legally binding promise by the seller of a product that in the event of the product failing to work it will be replaced or repaired free of charge. The promise is usually 'time limited'.
B. The organisation that good travel agents belong to. Membership, which has to be earned, gives a guarantee of quality.
C. Basically another name for a guarantee.
D. Latin phrase meaning 'buyer beware'. When applied to purchasing it means that it is the buyer's responsibility to check before purchase.

E. An extension of the legal quality cover given by a producer. This may be a free or a paid extension.
F. A private body in UK which sets up standards for a whole range of products, services and operations. Specific documents are numbered, e.g. BS1500.
G. A legal limit on the cover of a guarantee. The good must work efficiently when it is used as it was designed and sold to do. A very contentious area!
H. The provision of maintenance, spare parts and even training which is provided and used after the item is sold.
I. The rights that a purchaser has which are set out in the various legal statutes.
J. One of the bases of product law. A purchaser has the right to a good that is safe and is capable of doing what it is described as being capable of doing.

Short answer questions

1. What minimum legal rights does a customer have when purchasing an item in a store?
2. Who prepares British Standards?
3. Who use codes of practice to regulate their activities?
4. What is a guarantee?
5. How can marketing use extended warranties as a marketing weapon?
6. When an item is returned to the retail outlet where it was bought, but has been found to be defective, who has a legal liability to put it right?
7. How can after-sales service be used to boost the marketing of a product?
8. What types of product are best suited to marketing using extended guarantees?

22
The legal aspects of marketing

Preview

▼ This chapter looks at the laws that impinge upon marketing.

▼ It looks briefly at the international aspects, then closes by reviewing the self-regulatory systems.

This chapter is designed to give the reader a broad outline of the laws surrounding marketing. It does not attempt to analyse the law in detail.

The law has a lot to say in the area of marketing. This covers the whole marketing operation, as well as the sale itself. It also has international aspects now, as the UK is a member of the European Union (EU). Marketing is also subject to a number of 'internal' codes of practice.

The most general law applicable is the Law of Contract. This is a very broad area of common law, and specifies what constitutes a contract, e.g. a contract of sale. It can be the subject of a book on its own! More specific laws are:

Selling laws

Sale of Goods Act 1979, Supply of Goods and Service Act 1982, Sales and Supply of Goods Act 1994

The most basic requirements of a contract for the sale of goods are that the goods are:

1. of 'satisfactory quality'. This means that they must be reasonably fit for their normal purpose.
2. 'fit for any particular purpose' made known to the buyer. Walking shoes should be waterproof, for example.
3. are 'as described'. If you order a red car, you must be supplied with a red one.

The Consumer Protection Act 1987

Legislation requires that prices be displayed in a particular way. It controls what may be described as a 'special offer' and as a 'sale price'. Monitoring and enforcement is through the Local Trading Standards Officers.

Resale Prices Act 1976

The Resale Prices Act restricts the right of producers to control the eventual selling price to the consumer to a very few special trades such as newspapers and books. Before this new law price competition between retailers was almost impossible. Producers could stop supply to retailers who cut prices.

Consumer Credit Act 1974

This controls credit transactions including hire purchase up to £15,000 credit. The buyer is given set rights, including a 'cooling-off period' in some cases.

Trade Descriptions Act 1968 and 1972

These Acts make it a criminal offence to:

1. apply a false description to a good, or supply goods with such a description
2. give a false indication of the price of a good
3. make a false statement as to the provision of goods, services, etc.

Fair Trading Act 1973

The Fair Trading Act provides for the appointment of a Director of Fair Trading. This is the Act that controls competition, or the amount of a market held by one company. It looks at potential monopoly situations which are those that control over 25% of the market or more. Reference may be made to the Monopolies and Mergers Commission.

The Act also examines anti-competitive practices, i.e. those which restrict, distort or prevent competition. Possible anti-competitive practices are:

*   *Predatory pricing.* Temporarily selling at prices below cost, with the intention of driving competition from the market.
*   *Tie-in sales.* A stipulation that a customer must purchase part or all of a second product from the supplier of the first.

Exclusive supply, or selective distribution in certain situations.

International aspects

The UK is now subject to EU law. It has been affected by the Single European Act, and more laws are inevitable. Just what is the definition of a 'sausage,' a 'banana' or a bar of chocolate? All these questions have taxed the minds of EU bureaucrats as they attempt to harmonise the laws of member states since goods lawfully on sale in one country cannot be excluded from markets of other EU member states, even if they contain additives or colouring which was previously banned in the target market.

Self-regulation

Advertising itself is subject to more self-regulation than specific legal laws.

Commercial broadcasting is subject to the rules of the Independent Broadcasting Authority (IBA). These state that advertisements have to be 'legal, decent, honest and truthful'. Advertisements themselves are subject to the rules of the Advertising Standards Authority, which operates the British Code of Advertising Standards.

It is generally accepted in this country that advertisements should concentrate on the merits of their own product, and not be involved in criticising or 'knocking' competitors' products. Doing so would be risky, as damages would be liable under the laws of tort unless the statements could be proven.

SUMMARY

After reading this chapter, you should:

▽ Be able to list and describe the major laws affecting marketing, namely:

– *Sales of Goods Act*

– *Prices Act*

– *Consumer Credit Act*

– *Consumer Protection Act*

– *Trades Description Act*

– *Fair Trading Act*

▽ Be aware of the international dimension.

▽ Be able to discuss some of the self-regulation methods used in marketing.

23
Methods of production

Preview

▼ This chapter will introduce the reader to the basic methods of production available to a business, namely: *job production, batch production, flow production*.

▼ It will discuss their characteristics, and their advantages and disadvantages, both for the firm and for its workers.

▼ It will show how a firm may decide to change from one method to another. Such an action is a major change for a business, so a decision will not be taken lightly. (It is an opportunity to use break-even analysis again!) The interrelationships between firms in production will also be discussed briefly.

All products have to be made. They have to be produced as efficiently and as effectively as possible. Once *Marketing* and the Board have decided on the specification of the product, it is the responsibility of *Production* to decide how it will be made, in what quantity, and when. Production then has to manage the process, and to continually strive to identify better and more effective ways of producing its present and future products.

This chapter will examine the various basic methods of production. Subsequent chapters will study various analytical and control techniques used in production.

There are three basic ways of organising production:

1. *Job production.* Here a product is made one at a time. Each product is often unique.
2. *Batch production.* Products are manufactured in identical groups.
3. *Flow production.* Products are made in stages, often as they pass along an assembly line. Chemical processes may be continuous.

Job production tends to be expensive and slow. It produces a low output, and is not suitable for repetitive work. It is ideally suited to the production of 'one offs', or items tailor-made to a specific person or location. It is often cheap to set up, as it depends more on human capital, the skills of specialist tradesmen, than on financial investment. It is frequently a labour intensive operation.

This is not always the case, however. Consider the production of the Trident submarine in the UK. Only three may be built, one at a time, using vast amounts of fixed capital as well as skilled labour. No export market here!

Flow production, on the other hand, produces a large quantity of an identical product cheaply, but often after a high level of capital investment. It is a capital intensive method of production. The major human investment has been put in at the design and development stage, many processes being operated by computer control these days.

Batch production lies between these extremes, and combines many of the facets of both. Now, the methods of production are examined in more detail.

Job production

Most products will have started their life cycle being produced by job production methods. The first prototype for a car which will eventually be mass produced will be hand-made by job production. Some luxury cars, like Aston Martin, are still made by job production even when in production. The output is low, and the amount of individuality in the models sold is high.

Job production involves making one product at a time, usually on a 'one off' basis. Repeat orders for the same item are not usually expected, if they are even possible. Products are usually 'made to order', with little stocks of finished goods being available.

The scale of operation can vary widely. Quality furniture, luxury yachts and even warships are often made by job production methods.

Job production has some key demands on production staff and their equipment.

- Production personnel have to be flexible in their work, and skilled in more than one operation.
- A wide range of equipment and machine tools will be needed.
- However, utilisation of such plant and equipment will probably be very low.
- Much time will be spent setting and altering machines, rather than using them productively.

It is an area where a high proportion of jobs will be done by hand, or with simple hand tools. High levels of mechanisation will not be justified. It is an area of production where real craftsmen will be found.

Job production will tend to be expensive, i.e. unit costs are high. However, the low potential sales volume means that there may be no viable alternative method of manufacture.

Batch production

As the demand for a product increases so job production becomes impractical. At some stage batch production will be started. Units will now be made in groups – five aircraft at a time, six luxury cars, seven 50-ft yachts or even eight sideboards. Now each work unit performs its task more than once. A machine tool will produce a set of parts before it is reset, a series of items will be spray painted before colour is changed, or a batch of refrigerators will be tested together prior to packing and dispatch.

Units do not have to be identical as the process can cope with some individuality. Unit costs are lower than for job production, but some flexibility in production and planning is lost.

Batch production is widely used in the chemical, food and pharmaceutical industries. Products are made in tanks, mixers, vats, etc. in quantities from a few kilogrammes up to hundreds of tonnes. Batches, however, can be identified, tested, analysed and accepted as such, and identified later through their batch numbers. Examine the pharmaceuticals you may have at home and identify their batch number. Look at a tin of beans: it will have a batch identity code on it somewhere, though this is not always obvious. The code may be a set of marks on the label. Look at Figure 23.1, which shows such a code on a marmalade label. (Do not confuse this code with the bar code. This is normally just an identity label, and does not usually even carry the price in code.)

Figure 23.1 Batch identity on marmalade jar

Under batch production workers and craftsmen still have to be flexible in their skills and approach to work, and be prepared to carry out a range of tasks during a day. More specialised equipment can now be used, however, with less reliance on manual methods. (Some craftsmen see this as the start of de-skilling, an area of clear potential conflict.) The factory, and it will be a factory now rather than a workshop, will have lost some of its flexibility.

Flow production

As demand for a product rises flow production methods will eventually be considered. Operations are now made in sequence, and products made, stage by stage, along some form of manufacturing or

The ship-building, motor and chemical industries use a wide range of production methods.

assembly line. Flow production may be fully continuous, or batch sequential.

Flow production methods produce identical products at very low unit cost. They are usually very expensive to set up, and may be hard or time consuming to change for another product. They trade cost effectiveness for flexibility. They are also considered by some workers as completely de-skilling.

Continuous production

This is the most specialised of all production methods. Consider an oil refinery. It operates round the clock for the whole year, produces products it is designed for at very low unit cost. It cannot switch products at all easily, and can even find a change of crude oil raw material hard to cope with.

Modern high-volume petrochemical plants, breweries and soap and detergent works are likely to operate continuous processes. It is more common to find a combined batch/continuous plant being operated. Often processes such as mixing will be operated in batches, while spray drying or distillation will be done continuously. Packing is frequently done this way, and batches of approved products are packed or bottled at high speed on modern machines. Speeds of 500 units per minute are not uncommon in the detergents, soft drinks and pet food industries. Notice even at this stage the firm will be faced with a choice. Does it use a single high speed unit, with low unit costs, but a complete reliance on a single machine, or more but slower machines, with a higher unit cost, but with potentially more reliable production? In either case the result is a high volume but very uniform product with a very low unit price.

Sequential, or flow line production

This is the method widely used to produce large quantities of mechanical items or assemblies. The item is made step by step, the growing product passing from work stage to work stage. Tasks can often be mechanised, machines be set almost permanently, and the work rate paced by the speed of the assembly line. Flow line methods impose many limitations on the product and its management.

This method of manufacture, which is also known as mass production, is widely found in the automobile industry, the manufacture of consumer durables, and office equipment.

Flow line methods can be seen as completely de-skilling. Jobs are broken down into simple, routine tasks. This led to boredom and frustration among workers, with the inevitable strikes and other labour disputes. Flow line methods are now often manned by groups of workers, who do a range of jobs on rotation. The price for the very low unit cost of the product is motivational problems with the work force. (More of this in the chapters on the management of people.)

The modern flow line assembly plant is a highly organised and flexible place. A modern car plant is capable of making, or rather assembling, a whole range of models and colours, and the output accurately reflects the demand pattern of the market.

Care must be taken in designing a flow line plant.

Linked stages will have compound efficiencies. For example, if a plant consists of three linked machines, each of which is expected to operate for 80% of the year, then the combined efficiency of the compound unit will be $(0.8 \times 0.8 \times 0.8)$, or just over 50%. The compound unit will not function for about 50% of the time. Look at the Case Study 23.1. The output will be found by calculating the compound efficiency, and then multiplying it by the slowest unit rate.

CASE STUDY 23.1

CD plc and the assembly of video tapes

CD plc assemble video tape cassettes using a process which involves six operations. The process is described in the table below, which also gives unit efficiencies and maximum outputs. At present the plant is fully integrated, with no buffer stock points between any units.

Unit	Efficiency (%)	Output (units per hour)
1. Moulder	90	50
2. Tape inserter	80	60
3. Sealer	85	50
4. Labeller	95	80
5. Boxer	75	80
6. Shrink wrapper	85	80

What is the reliable output of the plant at present?

(0.9 × 0.8 × 0.85 × 0.95 × 0.75 × 0.85) × 50 =
18.5 units per hour.

Now for your turn. What will the potential output be if the line is split into two, with unlimited buffer space between the sections, after units 2 or 4?

Original flow lines were very demotivating for the workers. They were very de-skilling as jobs were reduced to a single operation. Breaks would not be taken unless the whole line was shut down. The modern line overcame this. The key aspects of a good line today are:

- The line is divided into sections, each section staffed by a *team* of workers.
- Each member is capable of doing *all* the jobs in the section.

- Each team member *rotates* through all jobs.
- The team members man the section as they wish, and can organise individual breaks as required.
- The team appoints its own Section Supervisor.

Here is production practice and motivation theory working closely together – another example of interaction and interdependence. Even with this, though, modern flow line production units need:

- flexible attitudes towards employment and jobs from trades unions
- efficient and effective management and communications
- 'JIT' ('Just In Time' method of stock control) and 'TQM' (Total Quality Management approach to production and operations.) (See Chapter 24.)

An intermediate step between batch and flow production is batch-flow. Small batches of a product are now made together, and moved as batches from work area to work area. There are fewer work stations than in a true flow line unit, and the work done may be more skilled and specialised. Unit costs are higher than full flow line would be, but lower than one off production. It is an especially useful method for the production of a product where demand is a little low, and where quality is a selling point. Morgan Cars use this method, and they sell on quality, design, and the 'hand made' nature of their product.

The development of production

Firms have become more and more specialised in what they do. Consider the major international car makers of today. Ford, General Motors, Toyota or Renault, for example. These businesses have specialised in designing, assembling and selling cars. They do not manufacture all the parts, though. They are seen as the manufacturer, but they sub-contract the manufacture of components to firms who specialise there. They might obtain tyres from Dunlop, electrical equipment and lights from Lucas and spark plugs from Champion. Two new definitions:

A prime contractor is a person or firm who contracts, or enters into a legal obligation, to supply a major good or service. The prime contractor assumes total responsibility.

A sub-contractor is a firm or person whom the prime contractor will contract to do some of the work covered by the main contract. The sub-contractor is responsible to the prime contractor.

Look at the board outside a major building project in your area. You will see the heading 'Prime Contractor', say Laing or Trafalgar House, who will manage the project and do some of the work. Many trades, however, will be sub-contracted out. They are employed by Laing to perform a task, not by the company who has ordered the project from Laing.

Here is final set of examples, which has been seen before. Marks and Spencer sub-contract the manufacture of their clothing to specialist tailoring firms. They specialise in design and selling. They also sub-contract the manufacture and supply of chilled foods to a company named Northern Foods. (It is interesting to note that Northern Foods also supply Sainsbury, Tesco and other supermarket chains.)

The supplier/contractor relationship can be cyclic. Many firms go through phases of integration, when they purchase their sub-contractors to produce an integrated business. They then might well go through a phase where the order of the day is the 'core business'. The previous sub-contractors may well be sold off again. Look at Boots, which is reported to be selling its pharmaceuticals manufacturing and research business to Zeneca, presumably so that Boots can concentrate on its retailing business. Zeneca, the former pharmaceuticals division of ICI, will specialise even more in R&D and production of pharmaceuticals. It has no retail arm, though.

SUMMARY

Having studied this chapter, you will be able to:

▽ Describe, with examples, the differences between *job, batch* and *flow* production.

▽ Explain the advantages and disadvantages of the methods.

▽ Outline the cyclical nature of many production decisions.

Questions and activities

Technical terms and glossary

In the section below you are given a series of technical terms and their meanings. They have been scrambled, though. You must match up the terms and the definitions. When you have them correctly paired, transfer them to your vocabulary or glossary book.

You are also advised to transfer any definitions obtained during the exercises in the case studies into this glossary book.

Technical terms

1. Job production
2. Batch production
3. Flow production
4. Continuous production
5. Job rotation
6. Prime contractor
7. Sub contractor
8. Core business
9. Cyclical changes
10. Compound efficiency

Definitions

A. A method of production where products are made in large quantities. Work is done in stages, and the item moves, or flows, form work station to work station until it is complete. This method of production is capital intensive.
B. Changes that effect business that occur on a regular basis. Changes can be external (political and business cycle) or internal (centralisation followed by decentralisation).
C. The firm that takes full responsibility for a job or project, but cannot do all the work itself. The firm specialises in project management essentially.
D. A method of production where individual items are made one at a time, on an individual basis.
E. A firm which does work for another firm, but not the firm which will eventually pay for it. The job has been passed on to them.
F. A manufacturing process where the product is made in a never-ending stream. A very specialised method, and usually very expensive and capital intensive. An example would be an oil refinery.
G. This is the resulting output potential when more than one machine are joined together, and they all have to be functional for production to be possible.
H. A production method where small groups of product are made together. An example is a baker's oven.
I. A means of improving the motivation of workers working on batch or flow processes. Rather than have to do a single part of a task all the time, the worker is trained so that he/she can move from one task to another and relieve monotony.
J. That product or part of a multi-product business that the management consider as the key element of it.

Short answer questions and essays

1. Differentiate between *job*, *batch* and *flow* production. Give three examples each of products made by these three methods.
2. (*Essay*) Why are so few products made using continuous processes?
3. Describe the changes that have had to be made to make flow production operations more efficient.
4. (*Essay*) Why do firms periodically concentrate on their 'core activities'?
5. (*Essay*) Why did Trafalgar House not do all the work on the Dartford Bridge?

Data response questions

CD plc make and assemble CDs at their factory in Reading. The pre-recorded discs and the plastic covers and printed materials are brought in from their factories, and the final product is only assembled at Reading. It is a mechanised process and the stages, their output potentials and expected efficiencies are shown below.

Stage	Output potential (per minute)	Overall efficiency (%)
1. Disc inserter	10	85
2. Label setter	15	80
3. Overwrapper	12	75
4. Cartoner 10s	2	80
5. Bulk packer – 12 x 10s	1	70
6. Transit wrapper	1	75

(a) Prepare a flow diagram to illustrate the above process.
(b) What output can CD plc expect to get from the above close coupled plant?
(c) What could CD plc do to increase output without having to purchase any more of the above plant?

24
Stock control and valuation

Preview

▼ This chapter will first introduce and describe the large range of materials that a business may hold in stock. The importance of stocks to a company will be described, particularly the large drain on cash that they have. It will then go on to develop a means of controlling stocks. Brief outlines will be given of methods used in a number of industries today.

▼ The modern 'no stock' method of production or '*just-in-time*' (JIT) operations will be outlined. Quality management will be introduced, in particular BS5750 and the later international ISO9000, and their interrelation with stock levels and control.

▼ The final section of the chapter will concentrate on the problems of the valuation of stock, and will describe the methods based on *LIFO* (last-in-first-out), *FIFO* (first-in-first-out), and AVCO (*average costing*).

Every firm holds stocks of something. Manufacturing firms hold stocks of raw and packing materials, as well as stocks of finished goods. There will also be stocks of spare parts for all the plant and equipment, as well as stocks of fuels and lubricants. The office will have its stock of stationery. It is not uncommon for up to 60% of a factory's space to be taken up by storage areas and warehouses. Stocks, therefore, are expensive both in themselves and in terms of the buildings and staff required to keep them safely and securely.

To summarise: businesses hold stocks in some or all of the following categories (note that some are directly product related and others are processor operations related):

- raw materials
- packing materials, and packaging materials
- part finished goods, or work-in-progress (WIP)
- finished goods
- tools, spare parts, etc.
- consumables, such as lubricants, gases, fuels, etc.
- stationery.

Stocks of materials tie up a large proportion of the cash resources of a firm, especially if there is a long period between their purchase and the receipt of cash after their eventual resale, even though by now there will be added value included in the price. Note that some companies will demand 90 days credit on sales, in other words they will not pay for goods until 90 days, or nearly three months after receipt.

Firms hold stocks of materials for a number of different but important reasons. It is vital, however, that these reasons are not over-valued and excessive stocks bought and held lest cash flow problems result. The major reasons for holding stocks are:

To enable materials to be bought cheaply
This is the application of one of the purchasing economies of scale. By buying a larger quantity, but more infrequently, a keener price is obtained. The supplier gains by getting more revenue more quickly, so is prepared to share this gain, in part, with the purchaser. The volume of stock, perhaps equivalent to three months' use, then has to be stored so that it does not deteriorate, and also cannot be stolen. A careful balance has to be made between the cost of

storing the materials and the quantity discount obtained. The opportunity cost of the money tied up must also not be ignored. It is essential that the firm's buyer, or purchasing officer, has this information and balance in mind when planning and negotiating purchases.

To ensure that materials are always available for production

A firm will run out of materials if it produces faster than planned, or if a delivery of raw materials is late, or is rejected as being of inferior quality. A 'base' stock is held, therefore, to cover for this and reflects the time taken to *change* order quantity in response to changes in demand for the product, the *variability* in delivery times, and the *probability* of materials being substandard. It is a statistical exercise, and an important one. Observe the link with quality. Today stock and quality control are moving closer and closer together. (More of this when 'just in time' ordering is considered later in the chapter.)

Similarly raw materials may not be available evenly throughout the year so may be stockpiled at times of availability.

To enable production to run efficiently

Production processes often have to work within a limited range of outputs, and for long periods of time. A steel blast furnace, once fired up, cannot be halted without a major rebuild and relining being necessary. A modern oil refinery or petrochemical plant works 24 hours per day, seven days per week, 52 weeks per year. Since it is most unlikely that the finished product will be required to this pattern, stocks of finished goods have to be held.

To enable sales to respond quickly to changes in demand

Sales departments will sell from stock, rather than from production, enabling surges to be coped with quickly. Equally, for seasonal products, production must go into store for sale and use later. Two examples of seasonal products:

1. *Fireworks.* Sales occur over a two-month period in the UK. Stocks have to be built up and held for up to 10 months. The alternative of producing the product all in the two-month sales period will require too much investment in both money and human capital.
2. *Wheat.* All the year's requirements will be produced in one short period of time. A huge quantity of grain has to be held in silos for up to a year. (With the EU farm policy this can now be for well over one year.) Observe here that the decision on production target quantity is made up

to nine months before 'production' – the time before ordering of seed and eventual harvesting.

Consider the problems that may be met. The fireworks company must make enough product to meet any sales requirement. The grain merchant must have enough silo capacity to hold all the season's production.

The calculation of stock levels, and the complete control of stocks, is a complex process. This process is only outlined in the sections that follow. It is done against the background of a real company, CD plc, setting up its control system for the plastic monomer it uses to make its tape boxes.

Step 1: Establish a minimum stock level

This is the minimum amount of stock that a firm expects to have, on average. The quantity is largely a matter of company policy, but will reflect the variability of delivery period, quantity and quality of the item. It will also respond to the likely variations in the sales forecasts. The more inaccurate a forecast is seen to be, the more stock it would be prudent to hold, especially for a material on a long delivery.

This is an important measure as it establishes the basic stock level, and hence cost for a company. The firm will have to finance this amount of stock, on average, all the time. Decisions have to be based on the fact that the more that is held the smaller the risk of going out of stock and losing sales. On the other hand, the working capital requirements are increased. If this grows too much the business will fail, as it will if it cannot meet its orders. A compromise is necessary. An examination of the stock levels of a business can tell a lot about the operating philosophy of a company.

Assume that CD plc decided that it should hold a minimum stock of 200 tonnes.

Step 2: Establish an economic order quantity

Should a firm place one order per year for materials in bulk, or order small quantities each day? This question is answered on the basis of company policy, and an economic balance. The balance can be resolved by analysis. Consider the costs and benefits of holding stock.

Stock holding cost

As order sizes increase the value of the stock on site increases. This calls for more working capital, with increases in financing costs. More space will be needed to store the materials in, with the inevitable increase in building and land costs. Since the time that an item will be kept will increase, better quality storage space may be necessary, with higher quality security provisions.

Stock ordering costs

These fall as the quantity ordered increases. The two major reasons for this are the reduction in price that goes with larger orders (the effect of bulk buying), and the reduction in administration costs as the number of orders and the resulting paper work is reduced. This will effect many parts of a firm other than buying. Security, quality control, goods inwards and accounting will all see their work reduced as order size increases.

These two effects can be evaluated and plotted (examine Figure 24.1). They can then be combined, giving a graph of total cost against order quantity. It is then simple to read off the *economic order quantity*.

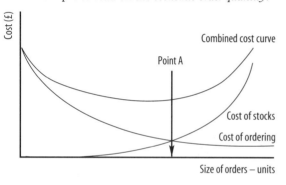

Point A = Economic order quantity, i.e. the quantity where costs are minimised.

Figure 24.1 *Diagram showing the relationship between costs and benefits of order size*

Thus the firm has established its *minimum stock level* and its economic order quantity. These combine by simple addition to establish the firm's *maximum stock level*. It is this figure which establishes the total space requirements for storage for a company, as it has to be able to store the maximum it can expect to hold.

The basic components for a stock control chart are now established. Examine the basic chart shown as Figure 24.2. It has been demonstrated that the firm's economic order quantity should be 800 tonnes. Combine this with its minimum stock level of 200 units, and its maximum stock level becomes 1,000 tonnes.

The firm would order 1,000 units of the material initially, and start production when it has arrived and has been passed as fit for use. Material will be used

each week, and stock levels will fall. Assume that CD plc uses 400 tonnes of monomer each week. This can be recorded on the stock control chart developed earlier. Look at Figure 24.3. This shows that CD plc will meet its minimum stock level after two weeks.

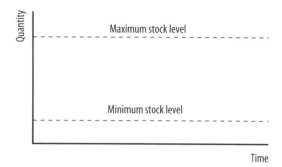

Figure 24.2 *Basic stock control chart (1)*

The next key step is to decide when the next order should be placed.

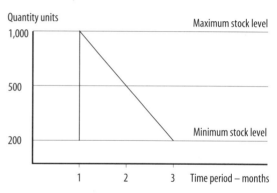

Figure 24.3 *Basic stock control chart (2)*

Step 3: Establishment of the reorder point

New materials have to be ordered so as they arrive in the factory in time for use, but not too early. They should arrive, ideally, just as the stocks are reduced to the minimum stock level established earlier.

The firm needs facts to enable it to plan this. It needs to establish how long it takes between ordering an item and receiving it. This will always be longer than the delivery time quoted by a supplier on any quotation or tender. The firm needs to know:

- the time for internal company procedures to prepare and issue an approved company order

- the time taken for the supplier to prepare the order
- the time taken to transfer the materials from the supplier to the buyer
- the historical accuracy of the data.

Assume that this works out as one week for the example firm. Thus the next order for materials has to be ordered one week before the minimum stock level is reached. Look again at the Chart, now updated as Figure 24.4. One week before Point A is reached, the stock level will have been reduced to 500. This can be used to trigger the reorder process. When stocks reach 500, which can be read from the control chart, the stock controller will automatically issue a new order for the material.

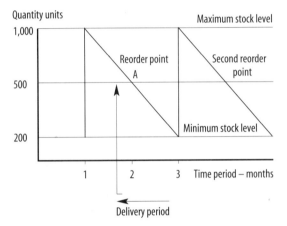

Figure 24.4 *Basic stock control chart (3)*

Thus, the purchasing department of CD plc will monitor the chart very carefully, and issue a new order for 800 tonnes of monomer every time that stocks fall to 500 tonnes. Deliveries will arrive regularly, and the factory will be able to remain in continuous operation.

In the real business world the use and sale of materials is not regular or according to plan. Also deliveries are early or late, and sometimes of insufficient quantity. An 'actual' stock control chart may well look like the one reproduced as Figure 24.5.

Stock-outs may occur. They should be infrequent and only of short duration. It can be argued that unless a few stock-outs do occur the firm is holding too much stock.

Modern trends are for stock levels to be kept as low as possible, thus minimising the amount of working capital that is required. This development

eventually led to the operation of JIT, or the 'just-in-time' method of stock operation.

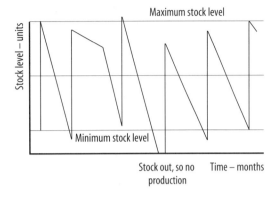

Figure 24.5 *Representation of a typical real stock control chart*

Just-in-time (JIT) operations

JIT is more than simply a method of stock control, it is a form of management philosophy. It was started by a few large companies, and has developed into a system where companies and suppliers cooperate and work together, to the benefit of all parties. It demands that the buying company has a detailed picture of its sales and production patterns, and of its likely variations. It also demands that the supplier produces a high quality product all the time.

Companies that operate JIT arrange the deliveries of materials 'just-in-time' for them to be used on the production line. Thus there is no time for quality control before the item or materials are used, so this has to be done at the supplier's factory. This means in practise, that the two firms cooperate over quality. The supplier, in return for a long-term contract, will often install new, high quality equipment to improve its methods and quality. Notice the development of a partnership between a customer and a preferred supplier. JIT has resulted in a move away from strictly competitive tendering, with the order going to the cheapest supplier, towards the use of 'preferred suppliers'. The supplier now has some security upon which it can invest in its production methods and quality. Firms end up working in groups for the advantage of all the members of the group. Note that competitive tendering is still the norm within the public sector!

Suppliers have to be able to respond quickly to changes in demand. They will have to hold stocks now instead of the customer. It will all be reflected in the price.

JIT puts a great requirement on total quality operations. This has led to the development of BS5750, and the later international ISO9000, which lays down a set of operational, procedural and quality standards. Firms that comply with these and pass the necessary inspection will be granted BS5750 status. This is becoming a requirement to supply many businesses, especially those in the public sector.

JIT has been used successfully by some major motor car companies, and those involved in electronics and computers. The potential saving for the firm is huge, both in money terms and in space requirements. The extra costs are easily justified. It is a total change in management philosophy, so there is much resistance to its introduction in the more traditional businesses.

Stock control methods

Stock can be controlled, or monitored, using a stock card. This may be literally a card which is updated by hand, or a file within a computer system. The heart of all systems is the paper work, and the effectiveness of the system depends on keeping the records up to date.

Manual stock control

The stock card has columns for receipts (deliveries) and issues. Examine Figure 24.6, which represents a stock card at CD plc for plastic CD cases. A new order was issued on 6th March, and was received on 21st March. Note the relationship:

Opening stock + Receipts − Issues = Closing stock

and observe how it can be used as a checking procedure.

Stocks will be checked by physical checking and counting at least once per year. This process, which is called *stock taking*, is required to establish the actual quantity, and hence the value, of the stocks that will be included in the firm's Balance Sheet. In many large companies the process of stock taking is a continuous one. Checks are made all the time, but in different parts and departments of the firm. When the accountants and auditors are satisfied, fair accounts for the business can be prepared.

Stock taking, particularly when it is done by external and independent persons, serves also as a check on possible theft and fraud.

Manual cards have been used by many firms for a

Checking whisky stocks in a warehouse.

ITEM _____   CODE NUMBER

_____   _____

Date	Opening stock	Delivery/receipt	Issues	Closing stock	Signature
1.3.93	Zero				
1.3.93		10,000 (Batch 1)	0	10,000	PK
2.3.93			1,000	9,000	JPF
6.3.93			3,000	6,000	GM
9.3.93			1,000	5,000	JPF
12.3.93			2,000	3,000	JPF
17.3.93			1,000	2,000	GM
20.3.93			1,000	1,000	GM
21.3.93		10,000 (Batch 2)	0	11,000	PK
25.3.93			2,000	9,000	PK
30.3.93			2,000	7,000	GM
31.3.93			1,000	6,000	GM
			Month End	6,000	PK
1.4.93	6000				
1.4.93			2,000	4,000	PK
10.4.93			1,000	3,000	GM
14.4.93		10,000 (Batch 3)		13,000	PK
16.4.93			6,000	7,000	JPF

Reorder quantity: 6,000 units

Approved by   GJB

Date   2.4.93

Opening stock + Receipts − Issues = Closing stock

    0   20000   14000   6000

Prices paid	
Batch 1	£10 each
Batch 2	£15 each
Batch 3	£20 each

Figure 24.6 *CD plc Stock control department: stock card for plastic cases for CDs*

long time now. The time involved, and the risk of errors, increases as the number of items that need to be controlled increases. This has led to automated or computerised systems.

Computerised systems

Stock control was an ideal activity to computerise. Networks and methods were clearly understood, but the real snag was time and order processing. The computer's big advantage of speed could be effectively utilised. Consider the modern large spare parts department at a major motor car dealership. Consider, too, the modern supermarket with its vast range of items on sale, and its minute stores, other than the display shelves themselves.

The modern computer till in the local supermarket is a key part in the company's computerised stock control system. All tills are connected to the master computer. All deliveries are fed into the system, then, as sales are recorded, stock levels are adjusted. The use of a *bar code* means that the stock level can be adjusted before the customer has actually paid for the item and taken it from the store. The computer then generates new orders, and also analyses and monitors the sales patterns for all lines, and indicates sales and cash flows. The supermarket's computer can also be used to order tins or other packing materials which the supplier of a product will soon need. This is an excellent example of cooperation and interdependence.

Observe that a computer can also be used to monitor the performance of staff. It can record the rate at which a till operator handles items, both in items per minute, and value. Selected, or 'identified' staff can then be offered training: another example of interdependence.

So stock can be controlled and orders issued. The stock still has to be given a value, though.

The objective of most stock control systems today is to keep the business concerned operating efficiently and effectively with the minimum possible level of stocks. This will keep the stock element of the working capital requirements down, and release cash for more important purposes – cash control again, note! This leads naturally to the problem of putting a value on stocks. Why is it a problem?

Valuation of stocks

Stocks clearly cost money to buy, and have a price at that time. They will have to be valued later so that they can be recorded in the accounts. Stock value is important as it is shown directly in the Balance Sheet, where it is one component within the group of 'Current Assets'. It is also used in the preparation of the Profit and Loss Account, and has a direct impact on the amount of profit a firm 'makes', or is able to declare, and hence the amount of tax it eventually pays to the Inland Revenue. Stock valuation is the subject of strict controls, therefore, both by the Accountancy profession and the Inland Revenue Department of the Government.

Accountants follow the practice of *prudence* and value stock at '*Cost or net realisable value, whichever is the lower.*' For example, a firm buys a material, a plastic polymer, at a price of £6,000 per tonne. It is still in stock after two years, by which time it has been replaced by a better material. The original polymer now can only be sold for £3,000 per tonne.

It thus has to be valued at £3,000 per tonne in the accounts, and the 'loss' of £3,000 per tonne has to be accounted for.

To understand the position of the Inland Revenue the various methods of valuing stock must be studied and their implications for tax examined.

Stock valuations can be based on a *FIFO, LIFO* or *average cost* basis. The need for these different methods of valuations arises from the fact that the prices of stock will vary with time, and that different batches or deliveries of materials are rarely stored separately and used strictly sequentially. Thus the typical warehouse will contain items of different ages, and different prices will have been paid for them.

In today's world, prices are normally expected to rise with time, the effect of inflation, although they can fall sometimes.

FIFO – first in, first out

Under this procedure it is *assumed* that the oldest material, the *first in*, is used first so is the *first out*. The material in the store will be the newest, and usually the most expensive.

Consider the example in Figure 24.6, but now price the first batch of materials at £10 each, and the second at £15 each.

During the month 20,000 units were delivered, but only 14,000 used. Since the first batch was 10,000 units, FIFO assumes that all these have been used, so that the closing stock are all the 'new' ones for which £15 each was paid. The closing stock will be valued under this method at £15 x 6,000 or £90,000.

Further, assume that each item was sold for £25. The gross profit can be worked out using the following formula:

Gross profit = Sales revenue – Cost of sales
Cost of sales = Value of opening stock + Cost of purchases – Value of closing stock

So, considering the data in Figure 24.6:

Cost of sales = £(0 + 250,000 – 90,000) =
£160,000
Gross profit = £25(14,000) – £160,000
= £(350,000 – 160,000)
= £190,000

If it is further assumed that the government levies tax at 25% on profits, the company will eventually pay £47,500 in tax to the Inland Revenue.

To summarise, FIFO will value the stock at £90,000, produce a profit of £190,000, and give a tax liability of £47,500.

LIFO – last in, first out

This method assumes that the newest or freshest materials are always used first. Thus the material left in the warehouse will be the oldest and usually the cheapest. Refer again to the example illustrated in Figure 24.6.

When the second batch of 10,000 were delivered, there was still some 1,000 of the first batch left. The last 5,000 used were from the latest delivery. Since there was still old stock left, the whole of the 6,000 closing stock would be valued at £10 each. Thus the closing stock now has a value of £60,000.

The same formulae still apply, but observe the changes that result from the adoption of LIFO.

Cost of sales = £190,000
Gross profit = £160,000
Tax liability = £40,000

So LIFO results in a lower tax liability than FIFO, but shows a lower profit. Does this matter? Examine the cash flow position. Observe that this is the same regardless of the stock valuation method used.

Cash inflow – £350,000
Cash out – £250,000
Cash surplus – £100,000
Plus a stock of 6,000 units

Since LIFO results in a lower tax liability than FIFO, most firms would prefer to use LIFO. They may do so, provided they say so in the annual accounts. The Inland Revenue, however, will recalculate such accounts to FIFO before assessing the tax liability of any business.

Average value method (AVCO)

In this method the average value of the stock is worked out each time a new delivery is received. Refer back to the example again. On 21st March, when the second order was received, CD had 10,000 units for which it had paid £15 each and 1,000 units for which it had paid only £10. Thus the average value of the stock is determined as follows:

(£15 x 10,000) + (£10 x 1,000) / 11,000
= £150,000 + £10,000 / 11,000
= £160,000 / 11,000
£14.55

On 21st March CD would change the value, or transfer price of the units from £10 to £14.55. Now consider the changes that would be made on 14th April.

When Batch 3 arrived CD had 3,000 of the old stock with a value of £14.55 and the new batch of 10,000 with a price, or value of £20 each. The new average price for stock valuation purposes would be:

(3,000 x £14.55 + 10,000 x £20) / 13,000
£43,650 + £200,000) / 13,000
£243,650 / 13,000
£18.74 each

The value of the items in stock will have been increased from £14.55 to £18.74 with the arrival of the third order.

Thus this method gives a value between the other two. Small stocks and large orders result in a value similar to that derived from FIFO. Large stocks with small deliveries produce a result similar to that derived by LIFO.

This method is no more accurate than the others. It seems more accurate because of the apparent precision of the values. This is the result of arithmetic, however, not accuracy.

Remember the definitions of the three stock valuation methods described above:

FIFO: A stock valuation method which assumes that goods are used from stock in the order that they are received so that the cost of goods sold is based on the cost of the oldest goods in stock, but the value of the closing stock is based on the prices of the most recent purchases.

LIFO: The reverse of FIFO. Now goods are assumed to be used on the basis of 'newest first'. Cost of goods sold is based on the costs of the most recent purchases but the value of closing stock is based on the price of the oldest item available from store.

Average value – AVCO: This method requires that the value of stock in a store is calculated, on an average basis, each time a delivery is made to the store. It is not recalculated after each withdrawal from the store.

Firms may choose a method of stock valuation, state it in their reports, then stick to it. This is an example of the *consistency concept* in accounting.

Now, a task for you to close this chapter. Examine Case Study 24.1 and do the exercises.

CASE STUDY 24.1

CD plc and its stocks of plastic cases

You are the management accountant for CD plc at its Repton factory where compact discs are made. You are preparing a report on the high cost of stocks, and have highlighted the stocks of plastic cases.

Records from the warehouse for three months were examined, and are summarised below.

1 January 1994	Opening stock	15,000 cases	1 March	Receipt	20,000
3 January	Issue	10,000	10 March	Issue	5,000
6 January	Issue	5,000	20 March	Issue	5,000
12 January	Receipt	20,000	30 March	Receipt	10,000
20 January	Issue	10,000	Prices paid. 1st Order		£25 per case
30 January	Issue	5,000	2nd Order		£28 per case
3 February	Receipt	20,000	3rd Order		£32 per case
20 February	Issue	5,000	4th Order		£38 per case

Questions and activities

1. Draw up a stock record card for this item.
2. Value the stocks on the basis of FIFO, LIFO and average cost.

SUMMARY

Having studied this chapter, you should be able to:

▼ Explain why stock control must be performed.

▼ Establish a process for stock control based on the control chart.

▼ Describe the modern just-in-time method for stock control.

▼ Illustrate the use of a stock card, either manually or computerised.

▼ Explain the problems of the valuation of stocks, in particular the method known as:

– FIFO – 'first in, first out'

– LIFO – 'last in, first out'

– Average value method

Questions and activities

Technical terms and glossary

In the section below you are given a series of technical terms and their meanings. They have been scrambled, though. You must match up the terms and the definitions. When you have them correctly paired, transfer them to your vocabulary or glossary book.

You are also advised to transfer any definitions obtained during the exercises in the case studies into this glossary book.

Technical terms

1. Reorder point
2. Minimum stock level
3. JIT
4. Stock taking
5. FIFO
6. LIFO
7. Average cost basis
8. Net realisable value
9. Stock card
10. Economic order quantity

Definitions

A. A method of stock valuation where it is assumed that the newest goods are used first. Cost of goods sold is based on the cost of the most recent purchases, while stocks are valued using the price of the oldest item theoretically available.

B. The predetermined stock level that will trigger the reordering of the material concerned.

C. A modern method of management where stocks are minimised, and materials are organised to be delivered 'just in time' for use.

D. That quantity of material for an order that results in the best combination of savings and costs for the firm.

E. The process of physically counting all items and materials held in the stores of a firm. It needed to confirm the paper records.

F. A method of stock valuation where the loaded, or weighted average cost of items is used.

G. The lowest level of stock that a firm has determined it must have to minimise the risk of stock outs closing the factory.

H. The amount of money that would be received, after deducting all costs incurred, if the stocks of a firm were sold in bulk.

I. The method of stock valuation which assumes that materials are used from stock in the order that they are received. Stock value will be based on the newest items, but cost of sales on the basis of the oldest.

J. The heart of a manual stock control system. Used to record all deliveries and issues of a material from a warehouse, and to trigger reordering.

Short answer questions and essays

1. What do firms hold stocks for?
2. What types of things do businesses hold in stock?
3. (*Essay*) Explain the significance of 'JIT'.
4. (*Essay*) Describe how a method of manual stock control using cards might work.
5. Why is the valuation of stocks such a difficult task?
6. What is the difference between FIFO and LIFO?
7. (*Essay*) When might it be wise for a firm to carry high stocks of a raw material?
8. (*Essay*) How would a firm determine its economic order quantity for a raw material?
9. (*Essay*) JIT reduces the money tied up in stocks for a firm. What other changes does its adoption have on a business?
10. (*Essay*) A company's annual costs of goods sold is £5.5 million. Average stock value is £695,999. Calculate the stock turnover ratio. (Associated Examining Board, 1992/1)

Data response questions

Airways Ltd are retailers who sell mobile telephones. During January to March 1992 they decided to concentrate their selling activities on the 'Meteor' model, which experienced several cost price fluctua-tions during the period. The company found that because of this it had to adjust its own selling price.

During the period the following transactions took place:

1 1st January: An opening stock of 50 telephones was obtained at a total cost of £8,250.
2 10th January: Initial sales were good so extra telephones had to be obtained from abroad; 200 telephones were purchased at a cost of £135 each but in addition there was a freight charge of £3 each, as well as a customs import duty of £5 each.
3 31st January: During the month 180 telephones were sold at a price of £175 each.
4 1st February: A new batch of 120 telephones was purchased at a cost of £170 each.
5 28th February: The sales for February were 120 at a selling price of £215 each.
6 2nd March: A further 220 telephones were purchased at a cost of £240 each and these were subject to a trade discount of 12.5% each.
7 31st March: 250 telephones were sold during March at a price of £230 each.

All purchases were received on the dates stated.

The accountant of Airways Ltd decided he would apply the first in, first out (FIFO) and weighted average (AVCO) methods of stock valuation in order that the results could be compared.

Questions

(a) Calculate the stock value at 31st March 1993 using each of the methods indicated (if necessary, calculate to one decimal place).

(16 marks)

(b) Prepare the trading accounts using each of the above methods for the period January/March 1993. (8 marks)

(c) What considerations should an accountant bear in mind in deciding on a stock valuation? Reference should be made to relevant accounting concepts. (20 marks)

(Associated Examining Board, Accounting June 1992)

25
Quality control

Preview

▼ This chapter will develop the operation of quality control (QC) within manufacturing and service companies. Comparisons will be made between the older, product related and statistically based QC methods, and the newer 'total quality' approach.

▼ A series of well-established sampling and testing procedures will be described. The chapter will go on to discuss the role and position, organisationally, of QC within the firm.

▼ BS5750 (ISO9000) will be introduced, and its implications for businesses discussed.

Basic quality standards are established by law. Products are covered by laws relating to both function and safety.

The quality of a firm's product or service is critically important, particularly in the more competitive and open markets of Europe today. Quality control, or QC as it is often called, and quality management is growing in importance day by day. QC has been changing very rapidly over the last 20 years, so much so that two clear approaches are now identifiable – classic and modern.

Quality matters because it involves costs. It is a revenue cost in its own right, and the more QC is done, the greater will be the total cost. However, the production of defectives increases the average costs of the satisfactory products, but provided they are detected and removed from stock, they do not affect sales and reputation directly. If they get on to the market the firm can easily lose its reputation. Then, even if strong steps are taken to improve quality, the poor reputation sticks. So, poor quality costs money, but so does the process of controlling quality. An optimum must exist, therefore. Examine Figure 25.1 which shows the minimum.

The cost of defects must include an element for the reputation of the firm. It is hard to evaluate in advance, but seen easily with hindsight! Required quality is a marketing responsibility. Marketing staff must specify the requirements in the light of their

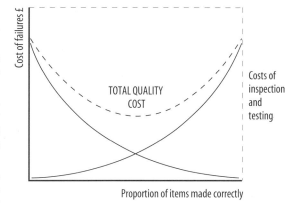

Figure 25.1 The total cost of quality

placing of the product, and the marketing mix being used. Once set, production must follow it until it is revised by marketing. It is not production's responsibility to set the standards, just meet them. QC has the job of checking. How is this done?

The classic QC operation

Traditional QC procedures are based on the sampling of materials, both raw materials and finished goods, for analysis and testing. 'Acceptable' products are allowed to pass through to the next stage of the process, or to be sold. QC was carried out by specialist staff independent of production. Production staff were responsible for process control to ensure that the product was being made correctly. The final judge was the QC department, which was usually responsible directly to the Site General Manager, or the Chief Executive of the firm if he or she was based there.

Classic QC was a statistical exercise involving the drawing of representative samples for testing, and coming to conclusions based on the results obtained. What is a representative sample, and how is it taken? Can it be taken in one operation, or is it more economic to test in parts – screening followed, if necessary, by detailed examination? Two basic methods are possible, and both of them involve a knowledge of statistics.

1. 'Yes-no' test method

Statistics can be used to determine a suitable sample size. This sample will give an indication of the accuracy of the sample, and hence all the products, subject to a known accuracy, i.e. take a sample of 50 tapes and test for defectives. If one defective is found, reject the batch. If no defectives are found, pass the batch for packing. This method will not be accurate. Some good batches will be rejected, and other bad ones passed. This is illustrated in Figure 25.2.

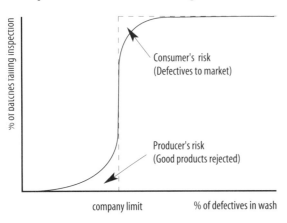

Figure 25.2 Deviation of packed weight from range of powder fillers

This method can be revised, and made potentially more accurate. (Note, it can never be 100% unless 100% testing is done, and even then all tests are performed with 100% accuracy!) This is based on two-step, or sequential testing.

2. Two-step testing

The first stage is the same as the above. If a failure is found in a batch, then this batch will be tested 100%. This method reduces the waste of 'good' products, but has only a small effect on the number of defectives which passed through the net.

Now, how can QC deal with a weight problem?

Weight control

Many products are sold by weight, and a weight is printed on the packet or carton. The purchaser believes that is the weight being bought. The Law stipulates what tolerances are allowed in relation to this Declared Weight. Any packing machine will

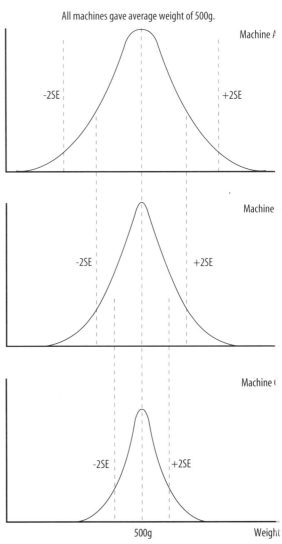

Figure 25.3 Deviation of packed weight from range of powder fillers

produce a range of weights. The machine will produce packets with a range of actual weights. How does QC cope with this? Again, a two-step approach, and the reader will see the beginning of the modern methods here.

- Test alternative machines, and select the one with the tightest distribution of weights. This is back to standard deviation work. Look at Figure 25.3.
- Check the selected machine in detail, and determine its packing performance at a series of different set weights, in other words, produce a table of set weights and the corresponding values of 1, 2 and 3 standard errors.
- Draw a QC chart for the machine. Legal requirements demand that the machine be set so that the set weight is + 2 standard errors over the declared weight.

This seems simple enough. Work your way through the Case Study 25.1.

These methods of QC will minimise the risk of poor quality goods, or sub-standard goods leaving a factory. They will do nothing, however, to reduce the number of defectives being made. This is where modern QC methods come to the fore.

Modern quality control methods

The old QC procedures were based on the belief that a process was inherently faulty, and that poor quality, or substandard product would be made at some time. Procedures were designed to identify the level of these errors, and to then enable appropriate action to be taken.

Modern QC is more concerned with avoiding the production of defectives than with detecting them after they are made. This role still remains, though, as '100% error free' is not really practical. How has this change come about?

It would be fair to say that the lead has come from Japan, but with the assistance of the industrial engineering profession and some very old-established

CD plc and the packing of desiccant bags

CD plc packs silica gel into small bags. These are used to keep the air in transport packages dry. CD plc sells these to many other firms. It sells three sizes of bags – 100, 250 and 1,000 g sacks. How should the filling machine be set so that the packs will be legal? The QC department have produced a packing profile for the new high speed filler to be used. This is shown in Figure 25.2.

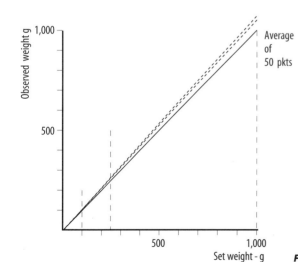

Declared weight	100	250	1,000
Set weight	120	280	1,000

Figure 25.4 Height control chart for desiccant filler

firms. The first step in the evolution of modern methods was quality circles.

Quality circles

Firms set up multidisciplinary teams – quality circles – in the workplace to analyse and critically review the design of a component or item used in the factory. These informal groups of managers and workers, shopfloor workers and office staff, engineers and accountants, looked for ways of making things 'better'. In other words, they looked for ways of making things quicker, easier, cheaper or more reliably. This was done in a blame-free atmosphere, positively. They collectively improved things where they could. The results were improvements in quality, reliability and costs.

This started as a section operation, but gradually spread to departments and even businesses as a whole. It also started in production, and concentrated on products, or parts and components. The more enlightened managements soon saw that it could be applied to systems and methods in all areas of the firm, not just production.

At the same time as this was going on, stock control has been moving from the use of large buffer stocks to 'just-in-time' methods of operation. This made it harder and harder to check materials as they arrived, and pushed the QC frontier back into the supplier's territory. At the other end of the factory, production had less and less time to check their outputs before they were sold. The accountants wanted the working capital kept ever lower, and finished goods stocks were squeezed as well. A real need for total quality management had come to light. Quality had to be guaranteed both in the factory, but also from the suppliers. The scope of work and role of QC had changed.

Total quality management (TQM)

Some firms now started to develop and use the systems that were to become the key elements of modern quality management. They tackled the problem both internally and externally.

Internal operations

QC was widened and made responsible for examining all methods and procedures in the company to ensure maximum reliability and quality. Both of these measures had to be raised. Standard procedures were developed and codified, and work methods and practices were altered so that these were followed. Designs were critically examined, and weaknesses eliminated. The result was a product that was as reliable as possible, and of the quality required, uniformly. Thus the firm had: *standards*, *methods* and *procedures* which were adhered to. Training was given, where needed. The only problem left was the quality of the raw materials and components bought in.

External operations

The purchasing company went out to its suppliers and offered assistance. It encouraged them to follow the same practices and procedures that they used. They even put in their own QC and production staff to help. This was done on a positive basis, and the benefits were shared.

Firms in the service sector were in the lead here. Stores such as Marks and Spencer offered 'assistance' to their suppliers. The initial reaction was not always good, but, in the end quality and reliability improved. Efficient, quality manufacturing firms resulted. Modern computer firms who use subcontractors act the same way. QC was becoming integrated between supplier and buyer. This then led to another significant operational change.

Meeting these new standards often involved the supplier in considerable costs. Firms would not readily accept this, so buying practices also tended to change. The buyer would not put everything out to competitive tender, but would operate with a group of preferred suppliers, provided they met the buyers quality standards. Two definitions:

A competitive tender is where suppliers are invited to quote for the supply of a good or service, and the one offering the lowest price is granted the order.

This system squeezes the margins of suppliers, but it also gives them no security. Suppliers would not be

Inspection lab at a modern electronics firm.

encouraged to invest in new efficient machinery, even if they could afford it.

A preferred supplier where the purchaser builds up a relationship with the supplier over quality and price. The supplier is granted 'preferred' status, and are guaranteed orders, provided they can guarantee the quality of their product.

Firms are now able to invest as they have a guaranteed income. Any testing done will be done using the old statistical methods. Often even this is not done, but the supplier has the responsibility to replace components eventually found to be defective. Chilled foods being delivered to a supermarket for sale that day will not be quality tested as such. The temperatures in the chilled transport container will, though, and if they are too high the load will be returned – and not paid for. This shows the power of the supermarket buyers; it is an economy of scale to them, remember.

This system has been formalised through BS5750. This British Standard, which is now reinforced and essentially replaced by the international ISO9000, lays down a procedure for total quality to be followed. Firms may adopt this, pass a test to confirm that they satisfy the requirements of the standard, and are granted a licence to confirm that they conform to the standard. Many buyers, particularly those in the public sector, including local government, insist on the holding of a BS5750/ISO9000 licence before a firm can be granted an order. (Can the seller insist that the buyer holds BS5750?)

Legal testing

Certain products have to be tested formally, and in a set way, and detailed records kept. This particularly applies to the pharmaceuticals industry.

Drugs have to conform to a whole series or laws and regulations. Basically they have to be made in identifiable batches and fully tested. Double testing is usual, and results have to be kept. They also have to be signed by the QC manager to confirm their accuracy, with legal consequences if they are wrong. The final product sold to hospitals or chemists have to carry a batch number and date.

Many pieces of equipment also have to be tested regularly and certified. This covers steam boilers, pressure vessels and even fire extinguishers. This testing is usually carried out by insurance company inspectors.

SUMMARY

Having studied this chapter, you will be able to:

▽ Compare classical and modern methods of *quality control.*

▽ Show how QC will be a cost compromise.

▽ Outline how tests and machines may be set up to give acceptable results using QC procedures.

▽ Describe how modern QC developed through *quality circles* and *TQM* (*total quality management*).

▽ Briefly explain how BS5750/ISO900 came about, and its implications for business today.

Questions and activities

Technical terms and glossary

In the section below you are given a series of technical terms and their meanings. They have been scrambled, though. You must match up the terms and the definitions. When you have them correctly paired, transfer them to your vocabulary or glossary book.

You are also advised to transfer any definitions obtained during the exercises in the case studies into this glossary book.

Technical terms
1. Weight control
2. Total quality management
3. Quality circles
4. Competitive tender
5. Preferred supplier

Definitions
A. An arrangement where a firm grants a supplier a special status. This enables the supplier to commit capital to the production of the item as sales are ensured, provided quality is adhered to.

B. A firm invites others to sell it a good or a service. The contract will be granted to the firm with the lowest price.

C. The modern system where quality procedures are applied to all aspects of a business – design, systems and purchasing as well as the product itself.

D. The operation of a QC system to ensure that the correct quantity of material is filled into a pack.

E. A group of people in a business who are assembled to examine a good, service or system and advise on ways of making it better.

Essays
1. Is 100% quality control possible?
2. What does a quality circle do?
3. What affect has BS5750 had on businesses today?
4. Why is it difficult to know in advance that a shot-gun cartridge will work? How did this problem lead to the development of non-destructive testing?
5. Why does the government insist on batch records of pharmaceuticals?

26
Work study and industrial engineering

Preview

▽ In this chapter, you will see how work study evolved in the manufacturing environment of the early 1900s. The various techniques, such as method study and work measurement, will be developed.

▽ The link with motivation will be explained.

▽ The chapter will close with a discussion of the development of the modern industrial engineering profession.

The production department has the responsibility of producing the good or service required as cheaply and as economically as possible. It must strive at all times to identify improvements in its processes and procedures. It has the considerable help of the industrial engineering department in doing this.

Industrial engineering is the profession concerned with getting the most out of the factors of production being used in any process. It looks for better and more efficient ways of doing things. It looks at how people and machines are used, how jobs are done, and how they interrelate.

Industrial engineering is a 'new' profession. It was developed by F. W. Taylor in the early 1900s. He pioneered a 'scientific approach' to problem solving, particularly in the manufacturing field. His methods were based on observation, analysis, selection and design. This is summarised in Figure 26.1.

Taylor looked at jobs and the people who did them. He also examined the effects of payment methods and other methods of motivation on the efficiency of the production process. The profession has developed steadily from these beginnings, and is now a powerful force in firms who are aware of its value to all concerned.

What does it do?

The traditional industrial engineer is often seen as the man with the stopwatch and clipboard. Harder work and fewer jobs follow in his wake. This view is common, but wrong. Information gathering is still an

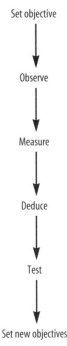

Set objective

Observe

Measure

Deduce

Test

Set new objectives

Figure 26.1 *Model of the methods of F. W. Taylor*

important aspect of the work, but it is the analysis that matters. Statistics are a powerful tool of the industrial engineer, as are advanced simulation and probability models. Let us look at some of his work. First, the classic or basic procedures.

The Channel Tunnel under construction.

Classic industrial engineering

Classic industrial engineering has often been considered as simply time and motion study. This is really best examined as *work measurement* and *method study*.

Work measurement or work study

This is where the stopwatch comes in. Work is measured against time so that performance standards may be set. This can cause considerable problems with the workers. Unless it is introduced to them properly they see it simply a means of getting more from them, or even of reducing their numbers. Here is *conflict* again and as has been seen so much before, set in the context of *change*.

This type of study can reveal problem areas. One problem may be where too much time is wasted, or a disproportionate amount of time is spent on one phase of a job. The study has revealed a need for an operational change. A high cost operation is not always caused by slow labour. This gives rise to the next action – method study.

Method study

This is the process of examining the job itself in an attempt to find a better alternative. A logical, stepwise approach is essential. Such a process may be as follows.

1. Observe and record the present method of working in detail. This might involve time measurements again, so very careful preparation must be done. The reason for the exercise must be explained to the workers and their representatives.

2. Examine the method carefully. Quality circles can be used here. The wise industrial engineer involves the present workers in this exercise, and listens to their comments and worries.
3. Develop new methods of handling the job. Again, get the quality circle going. Set up a team from the relevant department to help, and be responsible for suggestions.
4. Set up the new methods and procedures, and test them. This will reveal any teething problems so that they can be ironed out in advance of mass use. The process may have to cycle round again sometimes.

The procedures looked at so far have concentrated on either the man or the job as separate entities, as unrelated components of the production process. This is not the case, usually, so a combined approach is often necessary. This leads to ergonomics and motivational studies.

Ergonomics

Ergonomics is the study of the relation between man and machines, or the workstation. Why has the cockpit of an airliner changed very little in terms of space as the craft has become bigger? Because it has been ergonomically efficient for some time. Everything the pilot has to reach is in the right place, without his really having to stretch.

The seat itself, however, has changed as a result of ergonomics. It is more comfortable, effective and safer than originally. The instrument panel has also altered in response to the advances in technology. Finally, working conditions in the cockpit itself have been examined. Modern airconditioning is the response to modern safe conditions.

On the shop floor, ergonomics looks at how workers relate with machines. Workstations have been redesigned, seats made more comfortable and suitable. A problem remains in the modern office, though, the design of a really safe and comfortable computer workstation still needs to be achieved.

Motivation

Modern work study and industrial engineering are concerned with the effect of motivation on the worker, and hence output and efficiency. This is covered fully in the part of the book involved with personnel. Here it will simply be mentioned that team working may be introduced instead of single workers doing boring, unstimulating repetitive jobs. Job rotation may be suggested. It is also valuable as far as motivation is concerned to involve workers in the Industrial Engineering itself.

Industrial engineering and payment

Work study practitioners can get involved in work on payment schemes.'Equal pay for equal work' is a common call. What is 'equal work', though? This is where job evaluation comes in. The jobs in a company will be examined in detail, and characterised and measured against predetermined standards. Jobs with similar point scores can be given the same pay and conditions.

Job evaluation will look at factors such as skills required, initiative needed to be applied, exposure to the customer, the need to make decisions, to name but a few. The danger is that the results look very scientific, but this is not really the case as the relation between the attributes, and the ranking of professional skill, must be subjective.

Work study can be used to aid the setting up of some complicated payment systems. Work measurement can be used to set up a simple piecework system, or a more complicated basic rate plus output related bonus system.

Modern work study

Traditional work study has been developed in modern firms. The use of industrial engineers is obvious. Work has become driven by long term objectives, and is carried out on a fully integrated basis.

Industrial engineers will be involved in the development of new facilities as part of the project team. They will be specially involved in areas such as warehousing and distribution. The aim is to get the job or project right before it comes on line rather than tamper with it later. They may even organise quality circles. They have become a member of the firms management team.

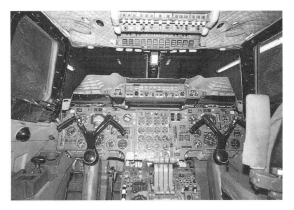

The flight deck of Concorde, the result of ergonomic design.

SUMMARY

Having studied this short chapter, you will be able to:

▽ Outline the development of work study from Taylor's research in the early 1900s.

▽ Explain the differences between work measurement and method study.

▽ Desccribe the development of the work of ergonomics.

▽ Show how work study can link in with payment schemes and motivation.

▽ Outline the development of work study into industrial engineering.

The reader will be very aware of the need to involve the workers in all aspects of work study and industrial engineering.

Questions and activities

Technical terms and glossary

In the section below you are given a series of technical terms and their meanings. They have been scrambled, though. You must match up the terms and the definitions. When you have them correctly paired, transfer them to your vocabulary or glossary book.

You are also advised to transfer any definitions obtained during the exercises in the case studies into this glossary book.

Technical terms

1. F. W. Taylor
2. Work measurement
3. Method study
4. Ergonomics
5. Industrial engineering
6. Job evaluation

Definitions

A. The study of the interface between people and machines or technology.

B. The founder of work study. An English engineer.

C. The modern science of work study, etc. Now includes logistics, systems development and factory design as well as the classic work/method study activities.

D. An aspect of work study which involves the application of measurement techniques to establish the time it takes for a trained worker to carry out a particular job.

E. A set of procedures to assess the relative worth of groups of jobs in an organisation so as to place them in rank order.

F. The systematic recording and analysis of the way in which a job is performed.

Essays

1. Who founded work study, and when?
2. Differentiate between work and method study.
3. What is ergonomics?
4. How have quality circles helped to develop the science of industrial engineering?
5. 'Industrial engineering has the capacity to kill motivation.' Discuss.

Data response questions

Read the extract and answer the questions that follow.

Manufacturer Opens Door to Modern Practices
A Midlands manufacturing firm has agreed the most wide-ranging productivity deal of recent years in the engineering industry.

The agreement will allow it to update working practices among 9,000 manual workers at three Midlands plants.

Managing Director Bill Hayden described the Coventry Browns Lane assembly plant, the firm's biggest, as among the worst he had seen outside the Soviet Union.

Workers will receive a 12.5% pay rise this year and 7% or the rate of inflation next November. 4% of this year's deal covers the end of antiquated practices such as the production quota system. This allowed line workers to go home after producing a specified number of units. Now they will work full shifts, doing other jobs if necessary.

The working week will also be reduced by an hour to 38 hours next November and to 37 in November 1992, adding pressure to other Midlands engineering firms to follow suit.

A pilot scheme brings in group leaders for teamworking. The group leader will receive an allowance and will back up salaried supervisors.

Line workers will take over responsibility for simple maintenance and to improve quality control.

The agreement contains a commitment to accept ongoing changes including the improvement of processes, quality and skills levels. Quality improvement groups are part of this.

The firm is also giving its workers a direct incentive to reduce unofficial stoppages, with a bonus of £26 a week for good behaviour.

Although the rises will fuel fears of inflation, plus demands in other companies, the firm can argue that productivity improvements pay for its 4%.

The changes are part of a business plan to boost production. It wants to triple output to 150,000 units a year over the next 10 years.

(*Source*: Adapted from *Personnel Today*.)

(a) What is meant by 'productivity'? (2 marks)
(b) Explain how 'productivity improvements pay for its 4%'. (4 marks)
(c) Identify in the agreement:
  (i) *two* features that may reduce worker dissatisfaction; (2 marks)
  (ii) *two* features that may lead to worker motivation. (2 marks)
(d) Explain how the features you have identified in (c) above relate to Herzberg's Theory of Motivation. (6 marks)
(e) Discuss *one* reason why improved job satisfaction may *not* result in improved productivity. (4 marks)
(Associated Examining Board, Paper 1, June 1992)

27
Network planning or critical path analysis

Preview

▼ Chapter 9 examined ways of estimating and predicting the costs of projects. However, it ignored the time effect. Clearly time is money, so the duration of any task or project has to be controlled carefully. This chapter will look at ways of planning the time taken for projects. In particular it will examine the process known as *critical path analysis*.

▼ The chapter will conclude with a section which shows how the procedure can be expanded to control the use of resources, such as manpower, and to monitor the costs.

'How long will it take to build the Channel Tunnel?' 'The new petrochemical plant is running 10 months late.' 'The new road scheme for the by-pass was completed 5 months ahead of schedule.'

All such statements presuppose that a system for estimating the duration of projects existed, and that it could be used for control purposes. An estimate was made, then the actual compared to this. The above projects were probably controlled using critical path analysis or CPA. What is CPA?

plane, it had to build a factory to make it in and a runway so that the product can be flown and delivered. All activities were planned and phased so that the factory was built to cope with the expanding production, and the runway and control system was completed just in time for the first flights. Just how does it work?

Network planning is a control technique. It has two major components, the preparation of the master plan, and the use of this plan to control the operation.

Critical path analysis

Critical path analysis (CPA) was probably invented in USA during the Polaris Project. This was the scheme to develop a complete weapon system – rockets for launch underwater, submarines, control and communications systems, dockyards and maintenance facilities. This complex exercise required complex solutions and PERT (Programme Evaluation and Review Technique) was devised. This is a systematic planning system based on a logical stepwise approach. It is similar to budgeting in that the project, now, is split up into short, identifable and manageable parts.

Consider another example. When Boeing developed the 747 it not only had to design the

The master plan

The preparation of the master plan, or network diagram, can be divided into four stages, namely:

- activity listing
- activity timing
- logic diagram preparation
- timing of network

The basis of the system is the breaking down of the project into a set of activities. Each activity has a start and an end. The duration of the activity is known, as is the way these activities interlock. A drafting code is used, and this is illustrated in Figure 27.1.

The process will now be illustrated, using changing of a wheel on a car as an example. First, the activity list.

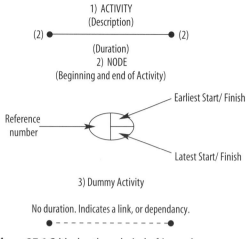

1) ACTIVITY
(Description)

(Duration)

2) NODE
(Beginning and end of Activity)

Earliest Start/ Finish

Reference number

Latest Start/ Finish

3) Dummy Activity

No duration. Indicates a link, or dependancy.

Figure 27.1 *Critical path analysis drafting code*

Activity listing

The task is to change a wheel. List all the stages, or activities, that this involves. This is best done on a form which can then be used as a computer input document. Examine Figure 27.2 below for the wheel change. Note any dependencies, or jobs which have to be done before another can start.

Observe how the task has been broken down into 16 different activities, and that five dependent activities have been found. The next stage of the system is to ask the person responsible for each activity how long it will take. In this simple example one person does a job. In the realistic case project managers or supervisors who are responsible for teams or parts of the work are asked. The timing has to be given by someone with responsibility for

No	Activity	Code Time	Notes
		(minutes)	
1.	Remove Jack	1	
2.	Place Jack under car	3	
3.	Raise Car	2	Slacken Wheel Nuts First
4.	Lower Car	2	After wheel on and nuts finger tight.
5.	Remove Jack	1	
6.	Replace Jack in Boot	1	
7.	Remove Spare from Boot	4	
8.	Remove Old Wheel	3	Nuts must be off
9.	Place New Wheel on Studs	2	
10.	Place Old Wheel in Boot	3	
11.	Remove Wheel Brace	1	
12.	Loosen Wheel Nuts	4	Before wheel is raised
13.	Remove Wheel Nuts	2	
14.	Replace Wheel Nuts	4	
15.	Tighten Wheel Nuts	3	Car back on ground
16.	Replace Wheel Brace	1	

Figure 27.2 *Activity listing 'changing a wheel on a car'*

achieving it. Note that timings have been added to Figure 27.2.

The next stage is to draft the network diagram.

The logic diagram

The planner uses his or her professionalism to draft a diagram that represents the logic of the task, or the dependencies between activities. The result for the tyre change is illustrated in Figure 27.3.

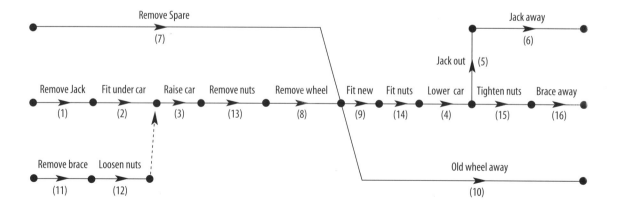

Figure 27.3 *First draft logic diagram for changing wheel*

Conventions have to be followed when drafting a logic diagram. These conventions are:

- Projects must have a single starting point and a single end.
- Activities and dummies must run forwards.
- Activities must be identified by a unique pair of numbers. This sometimes means that dummy activities have to be used.
- The number of the start of an activity should be lower than the number of the end of the activities.
- All activities, other than dummy ones, must have durations.

- Description of the activity is written on the activity line.
- Time/duration of an activity is written below the activity line.
- There must be no 'danglers', in other words activities that do not tie in to another.

How are dummy activities used? Why are they used? They are necessary to keep the logic of the system, and also to keep activities fully and uniquely identifiable. Examine Figure 27.4. When these rules and principles are applied to the first draft, a final draft logic diagram results. This is shown as Figure 27.5 The timings have been added, ready for the timing of the network. The activity codes can now be added to the activity listing table. Look at Figure 27.6.

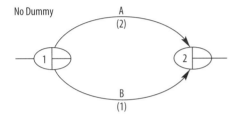

No Dummy

Both activities, A and B would be coded 1-2
and beyond analysis
USE A DUMMY

With Dummy

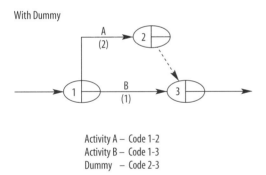

Activity A – Code 1-2
Activity B – Code 1-3
Dummy – Code 2-3

Figure 27.4 *Use of dummy activities*

No	Activity	Code	Time	Notes
			(minutes)	
1.	Remove jack	0-1	1	
2.	Place jack under car	1-3	3	
3.	Raise car	3-4	2	Slacken wheel nuts first
4.	Lower car	8-9	2	After wheel on and nuts finger tight
5.	Remove jack	9-10	1	
6.	Replace jack in boot	10-12	1	
7.	Remove spare from boot	0-6	4	
8.	Remove old wheel	5-6	3	Nuts must be off
9.	Place new wheel on studs	6-7	2	
10.	Place old wheel in boot	6-12	3	
11.	Remove wheel brace	0-2	1	
12.	Loosen wheel nuts	2-3	4	Before wheel is raised
13.	Remove wheel nuts	4-5	2	
14.	Replace wheel nuts	7-8	4	
15.	Tighten wheel nuts	9-11	3	Car back on ground
16.	Replace wheel brace	11-12	1	

Figure 27.6 *Activity listing table 'changing a wheel on a car'*

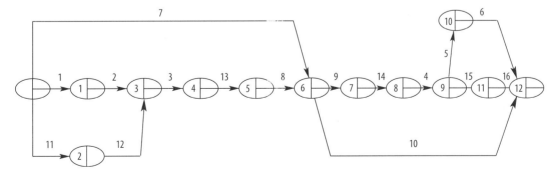

Figure 27.5 *Final draft logic diagram for changing a wheel*

Timing of a network

This is done in two stages, the forward and the backward pass. The 'forward pass' works on the earliest time that an activity can start. It uses the upper 'wings' of the 'beetles'. Examine Figure 27.7.

Activity D, or (3 – 4) as it can be identified by its reference numbers, cannot start until both C and B are ended. Its start is dictated by the latest of the two completion times, in this case week 5. Thus D can start at week 5, but no earlier.

The 'backward pass' works on the latest times that activities can start without affecting the completion time for the project as a whole. It uses the lower 'wings' on the 'beetles', and starts at the end of the last activity. Examine Figure 27.8. To finish at week 8, activity D must start by week 5 (8 – 3). Activity B can now start at any time up to week 3 (5 – 2), but Activity C must start on week 1, (5 – 4). The project must start at week 0.

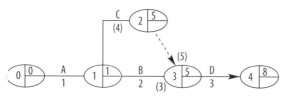

Activity D cannot start until Activities B and C are complete.

Figure 27.7 *Example of forward pass network timings*

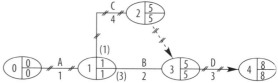

Figure 27.8 *Example of backward pass network timings*

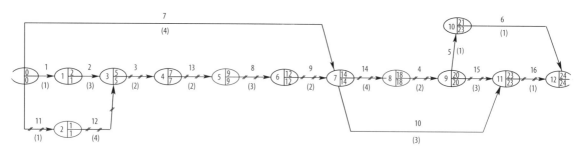

Figure 27.9 *Timed network for wheel change*

Note that for the path A – C – D the timings in the 'beetles' are the same. In other words the earliest and the latest start times are the same. Each activity is critical, and A – C – D is the *critical path*. Note how it is marked. If there are any problems over materials, or any critical activity is late, resources could be diverted from B, but only to the point where it becomes critical.

The same exercise has been applied to the wheel change example, and the results are shown in Figure 27.9.

The critical path goes through the following activities:

11 – remove the wheel brace
12 – loosen wheel nuts
 3 – raise car
13 – remove wheel nuts
 8 – remove old wheel
 9 – place new wheel on studs

14 – replace wheel nuts
 4 – lower car
15 – tighten wheel nuts
16 – replace wheel brace

The whole operation takes 24 minutes. The operation is now planned, and the 'management' have a basis for making changes if they wish. If the project has to be completed more quickly, then some activities on the critical path will have to be accelerated. It may be possible to release resources; look at the non-critical activities. They have extra time available to them, or they have float as it is called. This can be free float, that which the activity has to itself, and is not linked or chained with others.

All activities not on the critical path have some float. This may be 'free', or part of the 'total' float of a line of non-critical activities. Two more definitions for the personal glossary:

Free float is time by which an activity may be delayed or extended without delaying any subsequent activity.

Total float is time by which an activity may be delayed or extended without delaying the completion of the project.

Look at the example that has just been worked through. Activity 6-12 is predicted to take three minutes, but has 12 minutes to do it in. It has nine minutes of free float, therefore. It can waste nine minutes without affecting anything else.

Activity 0-1, on the other hand, has only total float. It has one minute in hand, but if it uses it, then Activity 1-3 has no float at all.

Float management is important, and float should be preserved. It is best to set the target for all the activity managers to pass on as much float as possible to the next activity manager. (Apply this philosophy to your own work planning and pattern of study. Start as soon as you can, finish as fast as you can – accurately – then use any spare time (float) as you wish!)

Work your way through Case Study 27.1.

CASE STUDY 27.1

CD plc and its expansion project

Part 1.

You are the project manager for CD and are responsible for planning the expansion of their factory at Reading. You have considered the project in detail and have prepared the following activity list.

		Code	Duration (Weeks)
1.	Design Expansion	1-2	4
2.	Clear Site	2-4	2
3.	Design Civil Works	2-3	1
4.	Procure New Building	2-5	13
5.	Do Civil Works	3-5	5
6.	Procure Plant and Equipment	2-6	20
7.	Procure New QC Equipment	2-7	15
8.	Erect Building	5-6	4
9.	Instal Plant and Equipment	6-8	10
10.	Train QC Staff	7-8	2
11.	Test Plant and Equipment	8-9	3
12.	Start Production	9	

Figure 27.10 Activity list for CD plc and its expansion at Reading

You also have prepared the following dependency information.

Dependency: a) 1 must be complete before any other activity can start
b) 5 requires that 2 and 3 be complete first
c) 8 requires that 4 and 5 be complete first
d) 9 requires that 6 and 8 be complete first
e) 11 requires that 9 and 10 be complete first

Figure 27.11 Dependency data for CD plc and its factory expansion at Reading

Tasks:

1. Prepare a network diagram, and time it fully.

2. Identify the critical path for the project.

Control

Just getting to a Network Diagram has some value for a business. Using it for control multiplies the gain significantly. The simplest control method is to get reports at regular intervals from the managers responsible for the activities, then to compare actual with forecast. Naturally the first examination will be of activities on the critical path. If the project is going late, then plans will be made that will concentrate effort where it is most effective. Look at Case Study 27.2.

CD plc and its expansion at reading progress report and control

PART 2. Twenty weeks have gone by, and you have just received the monthly progress report. This is reproduced below.

Date - Project Week - 20				
Activity Code	Started	Weeks to Complete	Finished	New Duration
1-2	Yes	–	Yes	
2-4	Yes	–	Yes	
2-3	Yes	–	Yes	
2-5	Yes	1	No	
3-5	Yes	–	Yes	
2-6	Yes	5	No	
2-7	Yes	–	Yes	
5-6	No	4	No	
6-8	No	–	No	12
7-8	No	–	No	1
8-9	No	–	No	2

Figure 27.12 Progress report for expansion project at Reading CD plc

Tasks:
3. Prepare a report for your director showing the status of the project.
4. Comment of the likelihood of the project finishing on time.

Network planning clearly controls time. It can also be used for resource allocation and even budget cost control.

Resource allocation

If the activity list is expanded to include the resources needed to complete it, such as skilled and unskilled manpower, tools, plant, materials to name a few, then the computer will produce a report of requirement against time. This may reveal problem areas in, say, skilled pipe fitters. The network will allow simulations to be run with different allocations of fitters, and the optimum solution determined.

Cost control

Add a capital cost element to the activity list and the budget will be allocated over the network. Costs can

then be compared, and variance analysis carried out. The computer will prepare another report, now of cash outflow against time. This could be very useful in identifying any potential cash flow problems.

Critical path analysis is a very useful tool for management. Project engineering has become more and more complex, and has generated a new profession, that of planner. Good project managers are planners, and can handle PERT and the like. They can be responsible for vast amounts of money, as a factory development can easily cost £100 million today. Imagine you are the project manager for the development of the Boeing 777, or more fancifully, for a NASA space station. You will have to be confident with figures and computers, but also adept at dealing with people at all levels of the company. A responsible and interesting job.

CPA was developed for advanced technical projects, but it is not confined to work of this type. It can, and should be used for all types of project beyond a certain size. It can be used for relocation projects, distribution exercises and even for the development of systems themselves.

What is the size limit? PERT really comes into its own when the project cannot be handled by manual methods. One is looking at 100 activities, as a general rule.

What alternatives are there to PERT? What was used before it was invented?

Bar charts

A bar chart is simply an activity list transferred to a time-scale. The problem with it is the difficulty of showing, or seeing the dependent activities. Bar charts work well for simple projects, but not for complex ones.

Gantt chart

A Gantt chart is another form of bar chart, but is used mainly for production planning. It schedules orders or activities against time, and also shows the availability of machines or plant. Again, dependent activities are hard to detect.

Both of these methods are difficult to use for real control as they are difficult to change or computerise. There is no indication of the critical path from either method. It is this aspect that makes PERT so valuable.

SUMMARY

Having studied this chapter, you should be able to:

▼ Outline the history of critical path analysis (or PERT), or network analysis, as it is sometimes called.

▼ Prepare an activity list, logic diagram and fully timed network from tabulated data and a statement of dependencies.

▼ Identify the critical path on such a network.

▼ Prepare a status report for a project based on an activity progress report.

▼ Outline alternative methods to PERT, and describe their limitations.

Questions and activities

Technical terms and glossary

In the section below you are given a series of technical terms and their meanings. They have been scrambled, though. You must match up the terms and the definitions. When you have them correctly paired, transfer them to your vocabulary or glossary book.

You are also advised to transfer any definitions obtained during the exercises in the case studies into this glossary book.

Technical terms

1. Activity
2. Critical path analysis
3. Node
4. Free float
5. Total float
6. Gantt chart

Definitions

A. A means of project planning where a timed logic diagram is used to find the duration of the path determining the minimum time that the project can take to complete, on the basis of the time estimates built into it. It is then used for the monitoring and control of the project concerned.

B. A term used in critical path analysis to indicate the total amount of free time belonging to a chain of dependent tasks.

C. A term used in PERT to define a single, controllable job or task.

D. A term used to define the amount by which a single job may go late without affecting the times of subsequent jobs, or the completion of the project as a whole.

E. An alternative to a network. It is planning using a special linked form of bar chart.

F. The beginning and end of an activity. It is a point in time, and a reference mark.

Essays

1. What is critical path analysis?
2. 'It should be the objective of all activity managers to pass on as much float as they can to the next manager in the chain.' Discuss.
3. How can network analysis be used to assist in resource analysis?
4. What is the difference between free and total float?
5. Discuss the alternatives to PERT for a project planner.

Data response questions

1. Draw a network that conforms to the following activity dependencies:

A is the start of the project
B, C and D follow the completion of A
E and G follow B
F follows C and D
H follows E and F
I follows G and H
J follows I

2. The activity durations that accompany the activity list in above is as follows:

Activity	A	B	C	D	E	F	G	H	I	J
Duration (weeks)	2	3	6	4	10	6	3	7	3	3

(a) Draw a fully timed network diagram.
(b) Determine the critical path.
(c) Prepare a full float analysis for the project.
(d) Which activity is nearest to being critical?

28
The legal aspects of production

Preview

▼ This chapter shows how the law impinges on the firm in the area of production. It discusses the two aspects involved, *employee law* and *product law*.

▼ It also discusses some of the voluntary codes of practice which are applied in the area of production.

The firm has a liability in law to its workers. It also has a liability for the product to the buyer and consumer.

Employee law

Employment law itself is not considered in this chapter. Working conditions are subject to a very complex law.

Health and Safety at Work Act 1974 (HASAW)

This law created the Health and Safety Commission, and the Health and Safety Executive. In 1994, the latter were busy with the accident with the boarding ramp at Ramsgate, and the railway signalmen's strike and the use of staff to operate the signals.

The Act is concerned with:

1. Securing the health and safety of persons at work, whether employers, employees or self-employed persons.
2. Protecting the general public against risks to health and safety arising out of, or in connection with, the activities of people at work.
3. Controlling the keeping and use of dangerous substances.
4. Controlling the emission into the atmosphere of noxious or offensive substances from prescribed premises.

Factories Act 1961

This is gradually being replaced by HASAW. This Act is the basis for a vast range of Orders.

Offices, Shops and Railways Premises Act 1963

Environmental Protection Act 1990 and Water Resources Act 1991)

These acts control the disposal of waste by factories or other business premises.

Product law

This involves Trades Descriptions and Weights and Measures regulations, as well as consumer safety laws e.g. the Consumer Protection Act 1987.

The Weights and Measures Acts (1963 and 1979)

These Acts define 'short weight' and empowers District Councils to inspect equipment and products by the trading standards inspectors.

The Consumer Protection Act

This Act specifies how things should be made, and from what. It sets down testing and enforcement procedures. The Act is operated through regulations. Examples of some are:

- Pedal Bicycle (Safety) Regulations 1984
- Upholstered Furniture (Safety) Regulations 1980
- Children's Clothing (Hood Cords) Regulations 1976
- The Electrical Blankets (Safety) Regulations 1971

The Environmental Protection Act 1990

Firms are now under a legal obligation to maintain air quality both within and without the factory or work place. The liability continues down to company car and vehicles.

Codes of practice

The production and working of certain industries is regulated by a number of voluntary bodies. There are many of these, but a few examples are:

- Code of practice between ABTA Tour Operators and the buying public.
- Code of practice for the motor industry, published by Society of Motor Manufacturers and Traders.

Pressure can be applied by bodies, or pressure groups, such as the Consumers Association and Greenpeace.

SUMMARY

Having read this chapter, you should:

▼ Be able to describe the major laws which regulate working conditions, namely:

   – *Health and Safety at Work Act*

   – *Factories Act, and offices, shops and Railway Premises Act*

▼ Be able to describe the major laws affecting factory operation, namely:

   – *Weights and Measures Act*

   – *The Consumer Protection Act*

   – *The Environmental Protection Act and Water Resources Act*

▼ Be aware of some of the Codes of Practice followed voluntarily by some firms and industries, namely:

   – *ABTA Code of Practice, Motor Industry
     Code of Practice*

and also be aware of independent pressure groups, such as the Consumers Association.

29

An introduction to the work of the personnel department

Preview

▼ In this chapter the principal roles of the personnel department will be analysed.

▼ The part played by the personnel manager will be examined, as will the responsibilities of employers towards their employees and vice versa.

▼ Finally, the difficult issue of change and the skills needed to adapt to this will be looked at.

The scope of personnel management

The evolution and increasing specialisation of the manpower and personnel functions have followed similar patterns to those developed elsewhere in this book.

Personnel management concerns itself with the *human resources* for, as industry develops, work becomes more specialised, thus requiring more detailed knowledge on the part of those selecting recruits. Skilled labour is a scarce commodity. You therefore need specialists to *recruit*, *select* and *train* employees to the practical specifications of jobs within the firm.

Employees may belong to organised groups, such as trade unions or professional bodies, and this also contributes to the specialisation of the personnel function. Other procedures, such as nationally agreed wages levels and conditions for health, safety, redundancy and productivity are increasingly dealt with by specially trained and experienced members of the management team.

As the personnel function has developed in its importance, so has the use of specialist theories and other social science disciplines. Psychology, sociology and organisational theory are now applied to the methods of selection, training, motivating individuals and controlling the performance of working groups. Personnel specialists are therefore responsible in modern industry for both the welfare of employees and for advising senior management on the standards of reasonable working conditions required by both the law and trade unions. They also help try to ensure that work is satisfying to the individual by making full use of his or her skills, aptitudes and abilities.

This requires specialist knowledge of motivational theory, psychology, organisational and communication theory and job design. The full discipline of personnel management, therefore, can be divided into two broad areas:

1. The psychological and sociological theory concerning itself with the motivation and interaction of people at work.
2. The practical procedures, administrative details, laws, etc., which are applied in organising and retraining people at work.

The role of the personnel manager

The management of people forms a part of every manager's job, but the personnel manager provides the specialist knowledge, advice and service for the other members of the management team. By providing such an input the personnel manager is allowing his colleagues to make decisions against the best possible background, and as such will make the most effective use of human resources available.

The personnel manager should have a clear understanding of the economic factors affecting the success of the organisation, particularly the cost effectiveness of manpower and associated expenditure.

The personnel manager is both concerned with the long-run economic success of the firm and the welfare of its employees. This may be a difficult balance to keep. As someone responsible for welfare they have access to confidential information; as senior managers they will see the financial predictions of the organisation.

Responsibility to the employer

Like all employees the personnel manager owes primary loyalty to the employer. His responsibilities normally centre on the following:

- Advising on good practice concerning terms and conditions of employment, staffing, the labour market, the organisation of work, training and development, employee benefits, welfare facilities and the working environment.
- Promoting good working relationships with trade unions and employee representatives.
- Encouraging the development of effective consultation and communication at all levels in the organisation.
- Respecting the employer's requirements for the confidentiality of information given to him.
- Promoting non-discretionary employment practices, and common standards of justice in the treatment of individuals by the corporate employer.
- Constantly updating the professional skills and knowledge in respect of new learning and legislation in the field of personnel and the impact of technological, economic and social change on people at work.

Responsibilities to the employees

The conduct and practice of a personnel manager should promote a desire among other managers to use their expertise in problems they encounter elsewhere in the organisation. This should allow the personnel manager to:

- Offer counselling of individual employees on such issues as development, discipline and career opportunities.
- Try to provide the best possible opportunities for all employees.
- Ensure privacy and confidentiality of personal information, and subject to any legal requirements keep this in the best interests of individual employees.
- Ensure that current and potential employees are given full and accurate information concerning employment within the organisation.
- Have concern for all employees and their dependants.

The personnel manager will also need to liaise with other professional bodies, government departments, institutions, employer and trade associations, trade unions and other associations. As such the personnel manager should be trying to enhance the reputation of the organisation.

Managing people – an introduction

People are the most fundamental asset of the organisation. They tend, alas, to be the most expensive and are those most likely to be blamed when things go wrong. It is time to address an obvious issue, namely, 'are organisations only as good as the people they employ'? What is an organisation?

An organisation is: 'A collection of interacting and independent individuals who work towards common goals and whose relationships are determined according to a certain structure.'
J.G. Duncan, *Organisational Behaviour*, 1981.

Each of us has personal 'goals' and these must be tailored to help achieve organisational *aims* and *targets*, but it is important to appreciate that organisations are human creations. They consist of people rather than pure material assets. Strategies based on a market share or financial performance are not 'divinely given', they are human-driven. It is individuals working within organisations who produce, develop strategies, make decisions, etc. As the manufacturing sector has declined in importance, so arguably the need for organisations to be more people-based has increased. Consumers now demand quality or 'add-on' value, so companies are more dependent on the skills and talents of those employees who enhance the value of the product.

It is never easy to quantify people, whereas a Balance Sheet can quite easily be analysed and errors highlighted. All too often, managers fail to appreciate the role of people in a successful organisation. But some early management theorists did take note of this. For example, Fayl (1930) considered the traditional manager performed the following functions (see Chapter 41):

1. *Planning:* producing a framework for future decisions.
2. *Organising:* bringing together the correct resources and developing an organisational structure to allocate the tasks.

3. *Directing:* achieving tasks either individually or through delegation to others.
4. *Controlling:* maintaining performance levels by monitoring and evaluation.

Despite this quite broad-based attitude, it does appear that early theorists, e.g. Taylor (1911) saw organisations not as a collection of people, but as groups of machines, worked by an easily controlled unit, namely a person. A guaranteed route to commercial success was to despoil all functions, provide an environment of bland surroundings and minimise movements. Human failures were the direct result of unnecessary movements, fatigue and poor physical environment. The fuel of man was money and financial reward was the only motivating agent. In the period before the Second World War, the school of thought based on financial reward was paramount in most organisations. Those responsible for developing management styles seemed slow to appreciate the changing role that work played in people's lives. Increased output may have been recorded, but the view of people at work was distinctly unflattering and inadequate. Unlike machines, people have feelings and emotions which influence both their behaviour and responses to a situation. People can decide on effort rates, are naturally creative and can be innovative. Successive generations learn from one another and certain social skills must be acquired.

People are different from machines: human beings can 'fail' for far more reasons. Charles Handy (1985) listed over 60 different factors which influence the behaviour of people at work. He stressed that these factors have a direct bearing on an individual's effectiveness and therefore the performance of the organisation.

The main areas for study are shown in Figure 29.1. Before embarking on a detailed study, a brief introduction to each will be beneficial.

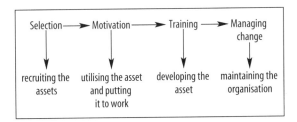

Figure 29.1 *Managing people: the main areas*

Selection

An organisation is only as good as the people it employs. An obvious statement, but it needs to be made. Selecting the right person for the job involves more than just placing an advertisement in a local paper. Management must be aware of the individual's skills, education and professional qualifications. These must be matched to what the organisation requires. The organisation must have a clear idea of the talents needed for an individual to perform what is required of them. This is known as a person/skills match approach to selection. Employees have to accept direction. They must 'fit' into the environment, be capable of working with others, relate to the organisational style, culture and climate. Different organisations have different cultures, and employees will expect differences between both occupations and firms.

Making a mistake is costly and the disharmony of a poor person-environment fit is likely to result in low job satisfaction, lack of organisational commitment and employee stress, all of which affect organisational outcomes, e.g. productivity, high labour turnover, absenteeism, and individual problems such as physical, psychological and mental well-being.

Despite the importance of selection and the sophistication of the range of skills required, many organisations still form their opinions based on a single interview. Research suggests that 'first-opinions' are important to selectors, so a decision could be made in the initial four or five minutes. The balance of the process merely reinforces the 'accept' or 'reject' decision. In times of high unemployment, there may be less pressure on selection to get it right, but with falling birth rates and more people seeking early retirement, the task of selecting the right person may become more crucial. Organisations have to remain competitive and must be responsive and accommodating to the changing needs of their workforce if they are to maintain, retain and develop their human resources. Such advances as flexible working hours, home-based work, job share, child care facilities and training programmes will play a major role in attracting and retaining staff in the future.

Motivating

Selection is merely the first step. Individuals must now be encouraged to perform to the best of their abilities. Money may be the primary reason for working, but it is not the only one. Apart from money, people go to work for:

- *Activity:* so providing an opportunity for people to use their skills and knowledge.
- *Variety:* it relieves the boredom of being confined to the home.
- *Temporal structure:* it gives a meaning and a structure to the day.
- *Social contact:* it provides an opportunity to interact with others.
- *Status and identity within society:* it provides a sense of recognition with the society.

The take-up rate of 'home-based' work is still low, and it appears that people enjoy going to work, even though home working offers greater employee flexibility and reduced travelling time. These in turn offer cost savings to organisations in reducing overheads in such items as rents and maintenance. However, people seem to like social contact, variety and a feeling of purpose. Managers need to be aware that 'people work to meet their expectations that work should be meaningful and intrinsically rewarding and motivating'. Ideas that arose in the Far East, e.g. trust, consensual divisions and greater worker autonomy are now being more readily adopted by Western organisations. The key themes of human resource management (HRM) are: *autonomy*, *involvement* and *commitment*. The best functioning organisations are those which act to improve the quality of work life for their employees by enriching and enlarging jobs to make them intrinsically satisfying and rewarding, rather than simplifying them.

Training

Correct decisions can be made regarding who to select and how to motivate, yet employees may still lack some of the skills needed to perform their jobs. Training is therefore an essential part of managing people. Training refers to the process of teaching, via a system, employees to acquire and improve job-related skills and knowledge. This may concentrate on manual skills, interpersonal skills and other less specific issues.

A lack of correct training will probably result in unnecessary and costly 'on-the-job' learning, production shortfalls, errors and wastage. It may also

result in unsafe practices or dissatisfaction in the work itself. An important result of inadequate training is the likelihood that a good employee will leave. Training for your future needs a sensible long-term investment that pays obvious returns.

Managing change

The speed of change is great. Just consider the impact of technology on language. In a little over a decade, 30,000 new words have been added to the *Oxford English Dictionary*. This is greater than in any previous decade, including the 'revolutionary' 1960s. The impact of new technology, globalisation of markets and political change have meant that the correct action for today may be incorrect for tomorrow. The need to change was perhaps the largest single need of most organisations during the 1980s, and those who survive through to 2000 and beyond will be those who successfully adapt to change during the 1990s.

The *management of change* has become an essential part of a manager's brief. Recognising and responding to change is likely to result in a multitude of organisational outcomes. It may include:

- Reformulating corporate philosophies and market strategies.
- Developing new products.
- Introducing new technologies, systems and procedures.
- Restructuring or downsizing.
- Pooling resources and expertise to expand on market position by collaborating, acquiring or merging with other organisations.

All of these will affect the working lives of employees and the internal culture of the organisation. If such changes are to be successful, then they must be effectively implemented and must gain the acceptance and commitment of the majority of the workforce. Failure to respond to change will probably have unfavourable consequences for both the employees and the organisation. Obviously change is stressful, yet reaction to changing circumstances is imperative. A brief analysis has been made here of the major issues facing managers as handlers of people.

SUMMARY

Having studied this chapter, you will be able to:

▼ Describe all the basic functions of a personnel department.

▼ Explain the responsibilities of an employer to his employees and vice versa.

▼ Outline the main reasons why modern management face a perpetual climate of change.

Questions and activities

Technical terms and glossary

In the section below you are given a series of technical terms and their meanings. They have been scrambled. You must match up the terms and the definitions. When you have correctly paired them, transfer them to your alphabetical vocabulary or glossary book.

You are also advised to transfer any defini-tions obtained during the exercises in the case studies into this glossary book.

Technical terms

1. The personnel manager
2. Feelings and emotions
3. Autonomy, involvement and committment
4. The management of change
5. Add-on value

Definitions

A. Those qualities which make humans different from machines.
B. The critical awareness of consumers that allows them to demand high quality products.
C. The individual responsible for recruiting, selecting and developing employees.
D. The key themes of human resource management.
E. Recognising and responding to the changes with an organisation.

Short answer questions

1. What did Fayl consider to be the main functions of a manager?
2. Explain the term 'PE-fit'.
3. Why, in your opinion do people go to work?
4. Outline the major issues a manager may face as a result of change within the organisation for which he works.
5. Briefly describe (a) the responsibilities an employer has towards its employees and (b) the responsibilities an employee has towards his or her employer.

30

Establishing the criteria for personnel management

Preview

▽ In this chapter the processes and documents needed to embark on a recruitment and selection process will be covered.

▽ Special attention will be given to the role of job analyses, job descriptions and job specifications.

This chapter concentrates on how an organisation *recruits* staff. Before being able to begin the process of selection, however, you need a base from which to work. In this area of an organisation you work from a *job analysis*.

Job analysis

Job analysis can be defined as the systematic and rational collection of information about a job in such a way that it can be set out and used to select, train and reward personnel.

To ensure the correct compilation of a job analysis, the course set out below is normaly followed:

1. Study the job, describe it and break it down into a logical sequence of steps.
2. The components needed to complete the task are then listed under headings, e.g. skill, knowledge required, physical and mental effort required, safety hazards and any special aspect, such as danger.
3. The range of responsibilities is determined in terms of materials, finance and subordinates. Each particular aspect of the job is given a rating on a point-scale ranging from 1 to 10. This analysis is then used as the basis for the job specification, which is a full description of the factors required in a person to do the job.

To ensure successful job analysis it must be undertaken with the full cooperation of trade unions and workers.

The most commonly used method of determining job analysis is direct observation. Perhaps the most successful method of analysing a job is to observe the process directly, either by personal observation or video record. Obviously, the full cooperation of all involved is essential. It is normal for a period of 'rehearsal' to take place, so that those being observed grow accustomed to the monitor and work 'normally' and not at the pace or in the style they feel will impress observers.

It is normal to follow up observation with a personal interview, so allowing the observed to fully explain the actions that have been observed. The immediate supervisor may also be interviewed, thus enabling him to explain their responsibility for what has been observed. Problems do arise with direct observation, especially when supervisors have little, if any, experience of the jobs being observed. Difficulties can also appear as workers fear bias and distortion, as they expect a significant change to their work pattern.

Almost all job analyses of technical or engineering jobs require a thorough examination of the types of materials used in the job process, the machinery, tools and layout, the speed at which the work is carried out and its influence on subsequent productivity, improvements can often be made by close observation of such issues as layout and tool usage.

An examination of the flow of paperwork

supporting the job will usually be required. An examination of the clerical system reveals:

- blockages and bottlenecks in the flow of raw materials and semi-finished parts
- over-use of some machines, while others lie idle
- repetition of processes or illogical flow sequences of actions
- imprecise or unclear working instructions
- insufficient explanation of how the task should be performed
- inadequate safety standards, or patterns of accidents with particular machines and/or processes.

Not all jobs allow direct observation. In order to study the majority of managerial, professional or supervisory jobs other methods have to be used, for example:

1. a questionnaire
2. a personal or panel interview
3. a self-recording work diary

Clearly, 1 and 2 are open to considerable distortion and inaccuracy. A questionnaire has the additional disadvantage of being prone to poor response rates.

The 'diary' approach is quite popular, but checks have to be made, otherwise some people will list a working day that struggles to fit into the 24 hours available.

Job descriptions and specifications

Job description

Once a job has been analysed, a job description can be written. This normally consists of:

- job title
- broad scope and main tasks of job
- number and status of subordinates
- to whom the job holder reports.

The description therefore seems to place the specific job in the formal chain of command.

Job specification

This begins with the job description, and concentrates on the major responsibilities involved in the particular employment (see Figure 30.1).

Job title _____   Size of job _____
Location _____   1. number of subordinates _____
                          2. budget responsibility _____
                          3. production responsibility ____

Position in organisation   Limits of authority
Responsible to _____   Without the permission of a
Responsible for _____   senior the job holder cannot:
                              _____
                              _____
                              _____

Specific responsibilities
75 per cent of time
   1. _____
   2. _____
   3. _____
   4. _____
10 per cent of time
   5. _____
   6. _____
   7. _____
15 per cent of time
   8. _____
   9. _____
  10. _____

Working conditions
1. Physical: sitting, standing, working, driving, etc.
2. Environmental: noise, heat, cold, dirt, wet, etc.
3. Hours: shift, holiday work, emergencies, etc.
4. Health risks

Figure 30.1 *An example of job description proforma for a managerial/supervisory post*

Other issues normally included are frequency of duties, working environment, safety hazards and an indication of any special tools or machinery required. Finally, the performance standards of a particular worker are set out in the job specification.

Personal specification

For the purpose of recruitment and selection, details of the job specification are often re-drawn in terms of type of personality best suited to a particular job.

The specification contains all the attributes that a suitable candidate would be expected to have to fill a particular vacancy.

Using job analysis

A job analysis can be used in various ways within the organisation.

Organisation and manpower planning

A job analysis allows management to compare job with job, and so eliminate overlapping areas of responsibility and authority. Duplication of task centres can be prevented and more precise manpower requirements developed. The degree to which current manpower is being economically used can also be gauged so that:

- excess labour can be eliminated
- overtime can be reduced
- interchangeability and rotation can be more carefully planned
- personnel can be moved about more freely, so enhancing job enlargement and enrichment policies.

Recruitment and selection

Job analysis provides the detailed information upon which recruitment and selection of candidates for vacancies can be undertaken. Such attributes as intelligence, skill and experience can be measured against the actual requirements that have been revealed by the job analysis.

Personnel development and training

A job analysis also provides information necessary to allocate personnel to special departments, or assign them to special tasks in order to provide them with the required experience for special tasks or promotion. Job analysis is the basis of job rotation and enlargement schemes and is most useful for the selection of potential candidates for promotion. From the information provided, specific training schedules can be developed. This, in turn, reduces training time, so saving the company money.

Job evaluation

This concentrates on the ranking of merit or complexity of a number of jobs within an enterprise. Without job analysis it would be difficult to establish rank order. Once the ordering has taken place, appropriate salary and wage levels can be allocated.

Safety and health

Job analysis is used to identify hazards, dangerous or inadequate working conditions and operations.

SUMMARY

Having studied this chapter, you will be able to:

▽ Explain the construction and use of a job analysis.

▽ Describe the content of a job description.

▽ Analyse the use of job specifications.

▽ Explain the importance of a job evaluation exercise.

Questions and activities

Technical terms and glossary

In the section below you are given a series of technical terms and their meanings. They have been scrambled. You must match up the terms and the definitions. When you have correctly paired them, transfer them to your alphabetical vocabulary or glossary book.

You are also advised to transfer any definitions obtained during the exercises in the case studies into this glossary book.

Technical terms

1. Job analysis
2. Job description
3. Job specification
4. Job evaluation
5. Direct observation

Definitions

A. The most commonly used method of job analysis construction.
B. A systematic and rational collection of information about a job in such a way that it can be set out and used to select, train and reward personnel.
C. A statement that describes all the responsibilities involved in a particular job.
D. The ranking in order of merit or complexity of a number of jobs within an organisation.
E. A description that places the specific job in the formal chain of command.

Short answer questions

1. What is meant by the term 'job analysis'?
2. Outline the main components of a job description.
3. For what purposes might an employer use a job specification?
4. Why might a job analysis be of use when deciding on pay rates?
5. Why might a direct observation method of job analysis be unsuitable for certain types of jobs?
6. Could security videos be used for working day observations?

31

The recruitment of personnel

Preview

▼ In this chapter careful consideration will be given to the ways in which employers can recruit employees.

▼ The various sources of potential employees will be analysed, and suggestions made as to how best to attract high-calibre candidates.

▼ Attention will also be paid to the important topics of application procedures and interview techniques.

▼ Finally, the construction of a formal contract of employment will be analysed.

Once a job analysis has been conducted and the need for the post established, the recruitment can commence. This is the process by which the supply of potential candidates is secured by the firm order to fill the vacancy. Most companies operate a chain of events.

The recruitment chain

For the selection/recruitment chain (see Figure 31.1.) to work effectively three interrelated factors need to be considered:

1. The company's organisational or corporate policy relating to recruitment at the various categories and levels of manpower required.
2. A constantly up-dated analysis of vacancies and job specifications.
3. Critical analysis of the sources of manpower supply and recruitment and the standard of recruits who present themselves for interviews.

```
Job analysis  →  Recruitment  →  Interview
Selection     →  Placement    →  Induction
```

Figure 31.1 *Recruitment chain*

Most companies have a clearly established policy on recruitment. Such a policy is normally discussed with trade unions and staff associations before being put into operation. As already noted, there are two main ways of developing a recruitment strategy, these are *internal recruitment* and *external recruitment*.

So, why do some firms opt for an internal strategy, while others concentrate on external sources? To answer this question an analysis must be made of the advantages and disadvantages of both processes.

Internal recruitment

This tends to be more easily introduced in strongly unionised firms, or where job mobility is low. It has certain advantages.

- *Good for employee morale.* By promoting from 'within', the company is clearly demonstrating a policy of rewarding current employees. This should encourage hard work, as individuals feel more highly valued.
- *Use of manpower.* The efficient use of a company's manpower through a policy of job enlargement and job rotation means that skills, knowledge and aptitude can be fully utilised.
- *Costs.* By promoting from an already recruited work force the company avoids the costs of advertising and selection.
- *Accuracy.* It may be possible to recruit from a

better level of knowledge regarding individual's abilities.

- *Labour turnover.* This may be reduced if personnel perceive they have opportunities for promotion within the organisation.

There are also disadvantages of internal employment. Those most commonly raised are:

- *No 'new blood'.* There is an absence of new people and new ideas. This may stifle initiative, reduce flexibility and increase resistance to innovation and change.
- *Cost.* Whatever the previous experience of the internal appointee they may require costly training.
- *Bad feeling.* There is a danger of creating jealousies, rivalries and cliques among staff competing for too few promotional opportunities.

External recruitment

Why might an organisation adopt an external recruitment policy? In the fast changing world of modern business it is quite common for a 'new post' to be created. The current employees do not possess the necessary skills to recruit for the post.

A specialist agency provides higher grade and more specific personnel. They often prepare job descriptions, interview, test and decide on rank order, before sending applicants. Such a comprehensive service has to be weighed against the type of position to be filled.

Sources of external recruitment

Two sources of personnel exist, namely external and internal. If the firm does not recruit from internal sources, then it must seek sources for recruiting adequate personnel. These sources include:

Informal contacts

Informal contacts such as personal friends of employees fall under this category. A more expensive form of 'contact' comes under the title of '*headhunting*', i.e. when people in employment elsewhere are approached and asked if they would like to work for the company. This tends to occur for senior positions and may involve the offering of a *golden hello*, i.e. a sum of money or a set of conditions designed to attract the person. Obviously, such recruits, regardless of status, have to be vetted carefully. Friends may be an expensive form of recruitment.

Educational establishments

Educational establishments include schools, colleges and universities. They can be a valuable source of both basic manpower and the potential reservoir of talent which can be trained and developed by the company.

Most companies try to build and maintain links with these establishments. This may be through visits, sponsorship and lectures. Many big organisations visit universities in what is known as the 'milk round', where they try to recruit those approaching graduation. It is obviously advantageous to have your company known by those nearing employment, but employers have noted some disadvantages. These include:

1. High training costs and formal introduction (induction) costs, may well be a long process.
2. All who come only possess potential; they have little, if any, proven ability, and as such may fail when confronted by the real world of work.
3. Those recently qualified may be anxious to succeed and will seek early promotion. If opportunities do not arise, costly recruits may leave and go elsewhere.

Experienced manpower has to be recruited from other sources. They may include the following.

Trade unions and professional bodies

By dealing directly with known organisations the quality of a potential recruit can usually be predicted. Employers often prefer to advertise in the appropriate journals so that their advertisements are aimed at a particular market segment, rather than covering the market in general. Obviously, you are limited to the range of journals available.

Government agencies

Government agencies include Youth Training Schemes and the Professional and Executive Register. Once again you can normally be assured of a certain quality of recruit and at a reasonably low cost. As with all 'trawling' exercises you are limited to who is out there and actively seeking work.

Advertising for prospective employees

The following section has some factual analysis. Buy a newspaper, or borrow one, or go to a library. Look at the structure of a job advertisement.

Analyse what appeals to you and why. Here is a list of some points to look for:

- title, description and postal details
- experience, skills, formal qualifications required
- conditions of work, salary and other benefits
- how to apply

Content

A successful advertisement will run through an obvious sequence and identify quickly and without misinterpretation the major characteristics of the job and the person you are looking for. A standard format is impossible to compose, but College Dynamics have decided on the one shown in Figure 31.2.

Table 31.1
Advantages/disadvantages of certain placements

	Advantages	Disadvantages
National newspaper	Fast, wide, direct circulation. High quality presentation	Costly, too wide circulation The page is full of other job advertisements
Local press	Quick, builds up local connections Direct, read by interested parties	Quality, tends to be read by non-management candidate
Local radio	Direct, repetitive Hits people when they least expect it	Control of presentation Too fast for full appreciation
Professional/ trade journals	Correct readership The right people read regularly	Long gaps between publication dates Slower circulation

Whatever medium you choose make certain you get on the page most likely to be read by your target group. In 'the tabloids' many advertisements for manual and semi-manual jobs are placed in the part of the paper dealing with football pools and horse-racing.

Selection

The process of selecting from among those who have applied can be a complicated one. This will involve decisions on a set of information-gathering techniques that will enable selectors to measure candidates against the predetermined requirements of the job. Normally, the method of application will be central to this process. Recruitment drives cover a wide range of skills, but some central attributes will be common to all. These will include: intelligence,

STRUCTURE	ADVERTISEMENT	REASON
Logo/Motto	'Serving the people'	Building recognition Provides an instant 'flavour' of the organisation
Bold type	JOB/S ON OFFER	Attract people quickly!
Smaller type: Clear concise easy to understand	KEY COMPONENTS ESSENTIAL REQUIREMENTS	Lead interested people through all important information quickly!
	TERMS, BENEFITS CONDITIONS, LOCATION, OTHER DETAILS	
Highlight direct contact and address telephone number	APPLICATION PROCEDURE 'Serving the people'	

aptitude, attitude, mental and verbal reasoning, leadership skills and where necessary, reaction to stress. For certain categories of appointment the face-to-face interview will be very important.

Most positions will require a *reference*. These can be slightly problematical as people already in work may not wish to tell current employers that they are seeking employment elsewhere. A firm must be aware of candidate-chosen references, which normally reflect the person as 'not to be missed'. In some organisations, references are not called for until a position is offered and then the telephone is used.

The selection procedure will be inadequate unless it is used as an opportunity to explain clearly to all candidates the precise nature of the job and any special conditions appertaining to it (e.g. unsociable hours). When considering a selection procedure it must be used as a *two-way exercise* and candidate participation must be encouraged.

Within the programme will be an in-built *follow-up* procedure, noting that the company is selecting the best people available and that they are performing at their best during employment with the company.

It must be established precisely what is needed. The conventional way of proceeding is:

- Design an application form/letter of application.
- Ask for references.
- Request a medical check (though this may be done once a position is offered).
- Carry out interviews.
- Make a selection.

The next step is to decide which tools to use and in what order to use them. To assist in this the company must establish the *main criteria*. These will include:

1. *Candidate experience.* It is a two-way procedure. The type of selection procedure needs to fit their expectations. For example, the lower-skilled applicants will not expect an IQ test, while those who left school some time ago may be suspicious of formal written tests!

2. *Specific attributes.* Make certain these are verified, preferably by senior management. A person's word or an old certificate does not necessarily prove current competence.

3. *Time.* The aim must be to produce a procedure that minimises time but meets with candidate's expectations and a thorough examination of a candidate's suitability. However, it must never allow appointments to be made in a hurry. It is best to re-advertise if the correct candidate does not apply.

4. *Cost.* The length of the procedure obviously influences its cost. The company is concerned with *cost effectiveness*, so if the validation requires time then the procedure should be allocated the funds to do the job properly.

5. *Order.* It is best to see this like an athletics event that requires people to negotiate a series of hurdles. The company needs to sort out unwanted applicants and yet attract as wide a field as possible. This careful balance is usually best achieved by the following steps:

- Put key criteria early in the procedure – a medical check is essential for an HGV driver.
- Cut numbers at the start of the procedure – use the address form and CV procedure to sift out.
- Make the candidate do the work – collate as much as possible on the forms, tests, etc. so saving lengthy interviews.
- Be aware of people's feelings – do not just 'reject', but provide them with an opportunity to illustrate their abilities. Always acknowledge receipt of an application form.

Application form procedures

Most posts have a certain amount of basic information that is required about them. Usually a form provides this. In other cases, especially in low paid jobs, a simple question and answer session will suffice.

Letters of application allow the candidate to express himself in an unstructured way.

Handwriting, coherent expression and a sound style can at least be seen. It is a 'pen picture' of someone's character – look at the paper, layout and preparation – all are good indicators. However, most candidates will tailor their content to suit what they think you want to see.

To try to overcome some of these problems, organisations often use *application forms*. These enable standardisation of information and allows comparisons to be made. The form will be a core element of any subsequent interview and any gaps can be quickly filled in with accurate questioning. The successful candidate has provided the basis of their personal records and even those who are unsuccessful can be kept 'on file' and re-examined against future vacancies. The data contained on the forms can be extracted and used to monitor labour flows and changes in the types of person seeking application. This will improve their targeting at a later date.

An application form normally contains:

- Title of the job.
- Applicant's name, address, place and date of birth, telephone number, place of work.
- Marital status, number of children, nationality.
- Education, professional training, qualifications, membership of professional bodies.
- Employment and experience, salary, level and jobs together with reasons for leaving.
- Medical history and name and address of referee(s).
- A space for candidates to explain why they are applying for the post, and their interests, hobbies, etc.

The form must be an efficient and easily understood document. Particular care must be paid to:

- *Contents.* Everything on which the firm wants information must be covered.
- *Layout.* Research scientists normally require large boxes for educational background, canteen assistants seldom do.

References

These are normally called for in the majority of positions being offered, even if they are only telephoned for a brief description of an applicant's character. They can come in various forms:

- *Unselected.* Beware, as these usually paint someone in the most glowing of terms.
- *Letters.* These are usually in response to a specific

response. Most referees are refreshingly honest though the pressure is on them to be 'nice'. Once again it is an unstructured document and may not cover the material you actually want.

To try to overcome the unstructured problem of letters some companies produce a reference proforma which is forwarded to the named referee. This allows specific targeting of information, but you must also be careful to stay within the law – defamation is not a part of law that most reference writers understand. Care must be taken not to offer a dissatisfied employer the chance to 'offload' someone onto the company and you will never fully appreciate whether it is a personal reference or one merely churned out by a clerk in the personnel department. To be sure, the telephone reference is always available. Direct contact, with a named individual, and careful listening are always the best way to test the suitability of a candidate.

Their final test may be to screen on medical grounds. Send candidates to a trustworthy physician and only proceed when an 'A1' form is received. The most common form of selection procedure is an *interview*. These are usually planned in detail and are the end result of previous preparation. The company is just as much on show as the candidate and care must be taken (see Figure 31.3). Now for the interview itself. The unsuccessful candidates have been 'screened out' and, hopefully, there will be a number of candidates from whom to select.

The interview

The interview must perform a measurement function. The procedure, questioning and discussion are designed to both obtain information and test achievement. The interview is also the time most people assess personality. Such a range of requirements needs careful preparation and skilful application.

A style will be set. It may be 'stress-orientated' or more relaxed, but in both the resources used must complement the process. Numbers involved will vary according to the nature of the job and the type of testing being used. Certain pitfalls must be avoided at all costs, some of which have been encountered before. They are:

1. *Be aware of first impressions.* Once these are formed, they condition us and influence our judgement.

Identification
Name
Address
Telephone number
Date of birth
Name of post applied for
Recruitment source

Education
Schools attended: name and dates
Examinations passed
Higher education: name and dates of institutions attended
Examinations passed
Other qualifications and courses attended: name and dates

Occupation
Name and addresses of all previous employers
Dates of employment (month and year)
Job title
Synopsis of main responsibilities
Final salary
Reason for leaving
Recreation
Hobbies, sports and other pastimes

Miscellaneous
Health record: history of illness plus attendance record in last job
Driving licence/possession of own car
Positions of responsibility held (at school/college/socially)
Notes in support of application

Figure 31.3 Checklist of application form data.

2. *The interviewer has opinions as well.* Some will be convinced that all good storemen are over five feet ten tall! It would be interesting to look in a laboratory to see how many scientists actually wear glasses!

3. *Stress*, which is obviously apparent in an interview, makes people behave in unusual ways. Most begin by being nervous and tense, then the 'best impression' behaviour will emerge and answers will be tailored to what the interviewer wants to hear. The interviewee will therefore exaggerate some points and minimise others.

4. *Interviews may last a long time.* An 'interview performance' can only be maintained for a short time.

All interviewers have their pet likes and dislikes, but several systems have been devised to help standardise attributes and their measurement. The most commonly used are the National Institute of Industrial Psychology's seven-point plan and John Munro Fraser's fivefold grading system. Both use the technique of identifying a series of factors against which candidates will be assessed during the interview:

NIIP seven-point plan	John Munro Fraser's five-fold grading classification
1. Physical appearance	1. First impression and physical
2. Attainments	2. Qualifications
3. General intelligence	3. Brains and abilities
4. Special aptitudes	4. Motivation
5. Interests	5. Adjustment
6. Disposition	
7. Circumstances	

The three Cs

The 'three Cs' form a good guide to the basis of interview technique:

1. *Contact.* Establish rapport, then people will talk. Silence does not help!
2. *Content.* Listen to what is said. Does it really relate to what you want? You must digest and match.
3. *Control.* Rapport without a sense of purpose is worthless. It is not a friendly chat. Care must be taken to steer the content in the correct direction. The company wants to discover strengths, weaknesses, levels of commitment, and gain the maximum amount of assessable information (see Figure 31.4).

The questions and the methods of asking them will also be important. Some tips are:

- Questions can be open-ended – you must listen carefully to the answers.
- Questions can be linked, so developing a progressive pattern.
- They can be probing, putting some 'stress' into the situation.
- They can be logical, again developing a sequence.
- Occasionally ask *no questions* – silence can bring out some unexpected reactions in people!
- Keep the flow going – respond, indicate agreement, etc.
- Do not interrupt.
- Try not to ask ambiguous or multiple questions – they do not often receive clear answers
- Ask as few yes/no questions as possible.
- Do not openly criticise.
- Wherever possible sit still; do not suddenly begin cleaning your ears!

At the end of this complicated process an *evaluation* must be made.

Throughout the entire exercise the firm will have been evaluating but usually the end of the interview signals the formal drawing together of information and feelings. Interviewers must be careful not to be influenced by 'looks' – a handsome person is not necessarily clever; the old prejudices in us all must be carefully noted: there is usually little evidence to support such beliefs! 'Nice people' may make good friends, but they may not fit into the organisation in the way you want. Likewise, not all 'red heads' have a fierce temper. Everyone is influenced by 'negative attitudes' and they continue to infiltrate our opinions. It may be hair length, shoe cleanliness or nails; whatever the demarcation point is, you must be aware of its subtle influence. That is why many interviewers seek a second opinion before making a choice. The process of seeking is now moving towards a conclusion, but some positions may require *testing*. There are various kinds open to us:

Type of test	Observations
Performance	Can this be measured against agreed 'terms' and, if so, how?
Aptitude	How have these been monitored before, can you test/simulate, or do you have to rely on experience, plus the reference?
Knowledge	Do qualifications actually prove this? Have you asked questions that allow for useful responses?
Intelligence	How does one measure this and of what use is a 'raw score'?

What do you want to achieve?

The firm must be clear as to what precise roles need to be performed by a certain type of person.

Making the final decision

- *The discussion.* Involve all who have had an input in the procedure. This may be best achieved by a document, followed by a meeting.
- *Notification.* How will the successful candidate be told? Will there be any conditions prior to final acceptance?
- *The follow-up.* Inform the unsuccessful in a way that does not totally lose their interest.
- *The law.* Has the company met all the requirements of the various Employment Acts?

Types of selection interview

There are several types of interview. They are

One-to-one

One-to-one interviews are where an individual interviews each applicant separately.

Job title: Safety and security manager   Department: Personnel   No. employed in this position ....
Division: Personnel services   Date of completion ....

	Essential	Desirable
Physique, health and appearance		
Height	Minimum 5 ft 8 in.	Minimum 6 ft
Build	–	Proportionate to height
Hearing	Normal	
Eyesight	Normal colour vision	Perfect eyesight
General health	No serious complaints	
Grooming	Well turned out	
Dress	No eccentricities of dress	
Voice	Clear speech	
Sex	Male	
Attainments General education	Sufficient for reading and writing reports and preparing budgets, and for mixing easily in management level. Sufficient understanding of employment and health and safety legislation	BEC National or Higher National Award in Business Studies with employment law options, or equivalent
Job training	Interpretation and enforcement of criminal and civil law Protection and security of property, etc.	First aid certificates. Report-writing. Budget preparation. Insurance practice, as relevant to the company and its employees
Job experience	Police Inspector or above or commissioned rank in armed services, police or provost branches, or senior security officer	3 years' experience
General intelligence Tests		
Top 10%		
Upper 20%		Upper 20%
Middle 20%	Upper middle 40%	
Next 20%		
Bottom 10%		
General reasoning ability	Ability to relate the security function to other organisational operations	Ability to reason in the abstract
Special aptitudes		
Manual dexterity	–	Understanding of mechanical devices
Skill with words	Sufficient for written and verbal reports	Fluency in interpersonal relationships backed up by sufficient business
Skill with figures	Sufficient for budget preparation	knowledge to be able to form meaningful relationships with other managers
Artistic ability	–	
Musical ability	–	
Interests		
Intellectual	Sufficient interest in the topic to keep up to date with legislation and practices	
Practical constructional	Sufficient knowledge of processes and machinery to be able to identify unsafe practice	
Physically active	Must be mobile	Participation in physically active pursuits
Social	Must be capable of maintaining positive attitudes to health, safety and security	Evidence of wider contacts than work alone
Aesthetic	–	
Disposition		
Acceptability	Must be acceptable to employees at all levels	
Leadership	Must be able to influence and persuade others	
Stability	High degree	
Self-reliance	High degree	
Circumstances		
Age	40–50	45–50
Marital status	–	Married
Dependants	–	
Mobility	–	
Domicile	Must live near enough to work irregular hours and to be called out in emergencies	
Other points	A car or some other vehicle is essential if he is not within walking distance of work	

***Figure 31.4** Personnel specification, based on the NIIP seven-point plan*

Panel, multiple and board interviews

Panel, multiple and board interviews involve the candidate being interviewed by more than one person. A panel interview tends to be composed of several people and is usually conducted in a more formal manner than the interview by one or two managers.

This type of interview has several advantages: namely, specialists can ask in-depth questions on their own areas of interest, more than one personality is confronted by the person being interviewed and indeed some panels deliberately perform different roles, and more than one person is involved in the final decision.

Panel interviews may be stressful for the candidate and it is not easy to create a relaxed environment. Board interviews are particularly stressful because of their formal nature and the number of people involved.

Successive interviews

Successive interviews are where the candidate is interviewed by one person, first, then passes on to the next interviewer, then the next, and so on.

This method can be tiring for the candidate and questions may be repeated along the chain. Candidates can also learn what is expected and answers may be prepared. As already noted before the final decision is reached it may be necessary for a test, or series of tests to be undergone. These may include tests for aptitude, skill, personality or intelligence. Other forms of selection include examination, role playing or monitoring the person performing the actual tasks. Once all the required information has been collected, it has to be summarised and rated. The latter issue is often done on a scale out of 10. It is important to keep a record of why a particular candidate was chosen and why the others were rejected. This formalised closure to the process allows the employer to:

- keep reserves, in case the first-choice does not accept the offer
- keep accurate records, in case any external body should require them, e.g. the Equal Opportunities Commission
- take a flexible approach – candidates may have been interviewed and, though unsuitable for a particular job, might be suitable for other jobs in the future

Medical examination

A medical examination (including a chest X-ray) is legally required for those entering full-time employment who are under the age of 18, and for certain categories of especially dangerous work. Most large firms, local authorities and state industries require a medical examination. Such an examination serves three functions.

1. It ensures the candidate is physically fit to meet the demands of the job.
2. It identifies people carrying contagious diseases.
3. It provides the company with a record of the employee's medical history and condition at the time of commencing employment. This might prove extremely important on subsequent occasions if claims are made against the company for injury or ill health.

Employment of the disabled

Most application forms ask for details of physical disabilities. Any subsequent medical examination is not designed to bar the employment of personnel who suffer from any physical handicap. The Disabled Persons (Employment) Act 1944 lays down the following obligations:

1. A register must be kept of all persons who are handicapped by their disability and retaining employment.
2. All establishments which employ more than 20 persons are required by law to accept a quota of disabled people equal to at least 3% of their labour force.
3. The employer can dismiss a disabled employee only if he can show very convincing reasons (other than the fact of the employee's disability)
4. Certain types of employment have been reserved for the disabled alone to fill.
5. A rehabilitation scheme has been provided for the disabled.

Perhaps the major problem emanating from this Act is that not all disabled people wish to be registered as such. Also, a number of jobs specially designed for the disabled require regular and long hours and so are physically tiring.

Making the offer of employment

An offer of employment made at the final interview must be confirmed in writing as soon as possible. The written offer of employment forms the basis of the individual's *contract of employment*.

A contract of employment

A contract of employment is a formal agreement entered into by an employer and an employee. The employee undertakes to perform certain duties in return for an agreed remuneration. The employer, by entering into a contract, undertakes very specific duties as regards the health and safety of his workforce, and is responsible in law for wrongs committed by his employees acting in the course of their employment. Until the 1963 Contracts of Employment Act, an employer could, in theory, dismiss a worker with only one hour's notice. Under the Employment Protection (Consolidation) Act 1978 an employee is entitled to access to the following conditions of employment (once they have remained in employment for 13 weeks).

1. the name of both employer and employee
2. the date on which employment officially commenced
3. rate of pay and method of calculating pay
4. how and at what intervals payment is made
5. the normal working hours
6. sickness benefits
7. holiday pay
8. payment due on termination of the contract
9. details of any pension scheme applicable to the employee
10. the exact title of the job.

The Act also lays down the period of notice which the firm is obliged to give in terminating employment.

1. One week if employed for between six months and two years.
2. Two weeks for two to five years employment.
3. Four weeks if employed for five years or more.

In turn, the employee must give the employer at least one week's notice of his intention to terminate employment if he has worked for the firm for more than six months.

The employee may seek redress in a certain way if he has any grievance during the course of his employment.

The employee has the right to join an accredited trade union; and finally, the contract must include a note specifying any disciplinary rules applicable to the employee, or where these may be found.

Within any organisation conditions of work and pay are subject to change. As such, contracts need to refer to up-to-date documents, which have to be made available (usually from the personnel department) on request.

Induction

Upon arrival at a company most new employees are given a period of time to be shown all the essential tasks, rules and regulations concerning their new job. This induction process normally takes the form of a series of talks, lectures, films, handouts, brochures and other forms of help. The induction normally lasts for the first few days of the employment and may be followed up by a brief interview a few days after the process has finished.

CASE STUDY 31.1

Personnel management

At College Dynamics we have used part-time, female workers as the major part of our workforce. The main method of payment has been a small basic rate, supplemented with an output bonus and a quality bonus. (The basic rate is per hour.)

We recently underwent a certain amount of internal re-organisation. A section-leader (female) retired, and another woman, in her late forties was promoted to fill the vacant position. It was felt that the promotion was a just reward for the individual concerned and a sensible policy for the company. At the same time a younger man was appointed to the position of production superviser. He was thus a new tier of management to whom the newly promoted female worker was responsible. He was told to expand output while improving quality.

For the first six months things went smoothly and the employees settled well into their new positions. During this period the section leader appointed a deputy, a man, who had been with the company for five years. The person concerned was a well-liked individual. By the early part of the New Year things were starting to go wrong. The production supervisor and the section leader were barely on speaking terms and cooperation was strained. The problems seemed to be personal rivalry and that the section leader felt that the production supervisor was using her ideas and taking the credit for himself.

Further difficulties began to emerge. The section leader's reputation for breaking subordinate confidences was spoiling the harmony among her colleagues. She then decided, without consultation, to re-draft the job specifications of her own position, and she did the same to that of her deputy. Her deputy was put in charge of day-to-day operations on the production line. Alas, the accounts department reported that the line was considerably overspent against budget. The final straw was reached when the section leader decided to 'warn' two employees who were considering joining a union that they would face the sack. A heated debate followed and the personnel manager was called for.

Questions and Activities

1. Obviously College Dynamics has problems and they need to be faced immediatley. What do you think are the real causes of the difficulties?
2. Imagine that you were asked by the Chief Executive Officer (CEO) to put forward proposals for solving the problems. Send your proposals in the form of a memorandum.

SUMMARY

Having studied this chapter, you should now appreciate:

▼ The types of selection procedure available.

▼ The compilation of application procedures.

▼ Interviewing for new staff.

▼ Making a formal offer of employment.

Questions and activities

Technical terms and glossary

In the section below you are given a series of technical terms and their meanings. They have been scrambled, though. You must match up the terms and the definitions. When you have them correctly paired, transfer them to your alphabetical vocabulary or glossary book.

You are also advised to transfer any definitions obtained during the exercises in the case studies into this glossary book.

Technical terms

1. The scientific approach developed by F.W. Taylor.
2. Temporal structure
3. Add-on value
4. Job rotation
5. The personnel manager or director
6. The recruitment chain
7. Internal sources of recruitment
8. External sources of recruitment
9. A reference
10. The 3 Cs
11. Panel, mutiple and board interviews
12. A Contract of Employment

Definitions

A. The individual within the organisation respons-
    ible for recruiting, selecting, training and
    developing the employees.
B. The critical awareness of the consumer that
    allows them to demand high quality products.
C. A theory that workers are only motivated by
    money.
D. The giving of a meaning and structure to an
    individual's day.
E. A process whereby employees move jobs at
    regular intervals, but always to jobs at the same
    level of complexity.
F. A type of selection interview that involves more
    than one interviewer.
G. Contact, content, control.
H. Sources of employees from within the
    organisation.
I. The process by which an employer seeks to
    obtain a new employee.
J. A formal document that supports an applicants
    request for consideration.
K. Sources of employees from outside the
    organisation.
L. A legally binding document that formalises a
    specific offer of employment.

Data response questions

1. Outline the advantages you associate with the
    internal recruitment of staff.
2. Compose a job application form for someone to
    work in a company's stores. They must be
    capable of simple clerical tasks, and have some
    experience of computerised stock records. The
    position will probably be most suitable for
    someone aged 20–25 years of age.
3. Describe the rights afforded to workers under
    the current employment legislation.
4. The Board of College Dynamics has decided to
    appoint a Credit Control Manager. The starting
    salary will be £20,000. The company is looking
    for a young graduate, or the equivalent, with
    approximately three years experience in credit
    control work. Training in the company systems
    will be offered to the successful candidate. The
    new employee must have a clean driving licence
    and be prepared to travel around the country.
    (a) Design a suitable advertisement for
        inclusion in a local newspaper.
    (b) Compose a short check list of the main
        issues needed to be covered in the interview.

Short answer questions

1. Briefly describe the content of a good job
    analysis.
2. What should a job description contain?
3. Give a brief description of the main purpose of a
    job evaluation programme.
4. Define the terms:
    (a) headhunting
    (b) golden hello
    (c) milk round
5. Describe what a good job advertisement should
    contain.
6. Outline what information you would expect to
    find in a reference.

32 Training and development

Preview

▼ The chapter also examines the aims of training, how it is organised, the various methods used, some research findings on the subject and the measures taken by government to provide people with training.

▼ This chapter will cover the definition and purpose of training, the organisation of training schemes, supervisory training and modern research, state employment and training measures.

Definition and purpose of training

Until relatively recently the traditional image of training had been firmly based on the rather narrow topic of 'vocational training'. It was thought necessary to provide people with practical skills, and leave 'learning skills' to the time spent in school or college. The more modern approach still includes 'skills' but great emphasis is given to the need to develop the individual. In doing so attention is paid to knowledge, aptitude and personality as well as pure skill.

Training is initiated to prepare the individual and the work force for:

- job rotation, extension and enlargement of current tasks
- transfer from one working group to another, from one branch/department to another and from one speciality of the firm to another
- promotion.

Training also seeks to familiarise staff with new processes, forms of organisation, administrative procedures, and to enable the company to be productive and market new products in increasingly competitive markets. It may also be undertaken to help resolve specific problems. These may include low productivity, high levels of waste, inadequate health and safety standards, too many accidents and general inefficiency.

Training covers all levels of the work force, from the non-skilled through to senior management. It can be carried on:

- within the plant/office/site
- external to all of these
- in specialist institutions.

Training can be:

- continuous
- part-time
- block release
- full-time for a specific period.

Its main purpose is to increase the general efficiency of those who have undergone the training process, and should promote:

- greater job satisfaction
- reduced labour turnover
- less absenteeism and sickness
- better adherence to practical and financial objectives.

Why train?

Training can, and often does, cost considerable sums of money. So, why do firms bother? The reasons are:

1. To prepare employees for their jobs and the

place where they fit into the organisation (induction training).

2. To prepare more established members of the company for new tasks and techniques.

3. To help resolve 'gaps' that analysis has suggested exist in the 'skills bank' possessed by either individuals or the total employee force.

4. To enable manpower to adapt more easily to innovation and change.

5. To promote, transfer or upgrade individuals or groups of workers.

The organisation of training

As with any activity of a business, its training programme costs money and has to be viewed against agreed targets. It must be undertaken at the minimum cost consistent with the objectives laid down by the senior management. It is essential therefore that the personnel department is clear on the following points (see Figure 32.1):

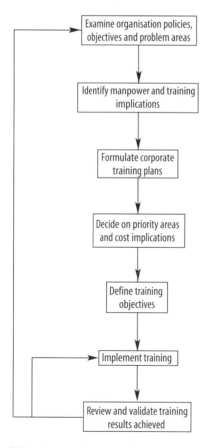

Figure 32.1a A systematic approach to the assessment of organisational training needs

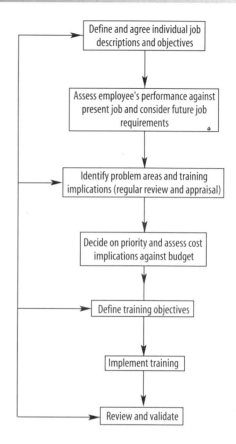

Figure 32.1b A systematic approach to the assessment of individual training needs

- the objectives of its training programme
- the budget to which it is expected to work
- the relationship between the proposed training and the individual's/group's working environment.

The training must be relevant and specific and those providing the training must be aware of the social and technical background from which the trainees come and to which they will return.

Implementing the training programme

In recent years a reasonably clear pattern has evolved as to how to implement a training programme. This normally appears as follows:

1. Jobs have to be defined and analysed as part of a formal programme.

2. From this review standards of performance are established, so training can be matched against these.

3. Trainees are selected on current performance

and predicted potential. Personal prospects of the individual have to be matched against the job and training specification.

4. Any apparent difference between current ability and future expectations has to be identified and the training gap isolated.

5. Training programmes are then designed to meet specific needs of individuals or groups. Records must be kept which monitor both progress and allow for weaknesses to be identified and corrected.

6. Performance is measured at intervals throughout the training, and at the end.

The assessment of training gaps is a relatively easy process when dealing with pure knowledge or specific skills, but as will be seen later, it becomes more difficult when moving onto higher order managerial skills and what are known as interpersonal skills.

It must also be remembered that manpower planning influences training. The 'long-term' has to be addressed, so consideration must be given to the proposed expansion/contraction of the labour force over the coming years, and where possible to the implications of technical change. This is essential in situations where expensive training must take place over two or three years on a more or less continuous basis.

Developing a training programme

Before embarking on a training programme any company has to address several questions. These are:

1. Will the training be carried out within the company?
2. Is the training to be carried out by an external agency, e.g. college or professional organisation?
3. Is the training to be on a joint basis, shared between the firm and an outside agency, and if so, where is the training to be held?

The decision will probably depend on:

- The facilities and staff expertise already available within the company.
- The practical resources available within the company, e.g. workshops, manuals, etc.
- The level of commitment to training with the company and the probable long-term status of training within the enterprise.
- The facilities that exist for training within the immediate vicinity of the firm. An availability of specialist facilities in the locality could be an enormous advantage.

- The objectives of the training programme designed for the various individuals.

Internal/external training

Internal training seems to be best suited to situations where a majority of the following are present:

- Adequate technical facilities are available within the firm and are at least as good as any available in local training establishments.
- The training to be undertaken is work or production based.
- Training can be organised for short and specific time periods.
- Training is very highly specialised and not required very frequently.

External training is undertaken when:

- The expected duration of training is long, requires intellectual inputs and has definite qualification objectives.
- A high level of academic attainment is a necessary part of a training programme.

It will be obvious that most firms operate a training programme that draws on both internal and external sources. Large firms tend to have educational training facilities, while smaller concerns tend to be more reliant on local training institutions. The significance of specially tailored short courses is now apparent, and often these are designed to tackle specific issues, such as the 'Market in Europe'.

Methods of training

Not all companies can afford specially designed training programmes. Some still train within the working environment, using skilled operators or supervisors as the trainers.

On-the-job training

On-the-job training is often called 'sitting next to Nellie'. The essential features of this form of training are:

1. There is very little clear distinction made between work and training. The trainee is expected to both work and train simultaneously.
2. Everything used by the trainee is 'real', i.e. they learn in a real work situation.
3. The trainer is an experienced worker, who trains by showing how something is done. This is usually done in a practical and immediate way.

Individual job description/ objectives	Name of job holder	Problem areas/ training implications	Training objectives	Priority	Training plans/methods	Estimated cost	Action required (target date)	Action taken and results achieved

Figure 32.2a Individual training plan

Organisation policies objectives and problem areas	Manpower and training implications	Training objectives	Priority	People affected (groups/individual)	Training plans/mentods	Estimated cost (target date)	Action required achieved	Action taken and results

Figure 32.2b Corporate training plan

This type of training has a number of advantages, which include:

- By being at the place of work it is realistic and not divorced from the working environment.
- It is direct.
- Hopefully, a 'one-to-one' relationship builds up between trainer and trainee, so helping both learning and motivation.
- It is less costly than other forms of more formal training as it takes place alongside work.

The disadvantages are considered to be:

- The trainer may be a poor teacher, who shows little real interest in transferring knowledge. Indeed, he may even teach poor or wasteful forms of work.

- Poor quality work or inadequate machinery may mean that the trainee learns bad habits.
- There is a danger that those who have worked for the company for some time will pass on their attitudes and opinions to the trainee. Not all of these will be desirable.

Skill training

Sitting next to Nellie is most commonly used when operatives have to learn a correct series of responses to complete a task. To transfer more complicated skills normally requires a more detailed analysis of the separate movements of hand and eye to determine just exactly how the task is completed. This process is known as 'skill analysis' and forms the basis of much operative or craft training.

The use of a detailed skill analysis can reduce training time, cut training costs and eliminate the problem of low motivation and retention during long periods of training by preparing carefully graded sequences of training exercises.

Discovery method

The discovery method of training relies on trainees finding out what is required of them. It most certainly encourages initiative, but it is dependent on the ability of people to be self-disciplined and well-motivated. One further risk is that trainees may, unwittingly, train themselves incorrectly. The process may be time consuming and create waste.

Traditional forms of training

More traditional forms of training include demonstrations, lessons, lectures and coaching. Such methods allow a great deal of information to be given out in a short period, and they resemble those used in school.

Like all styles of training they can be criticised and these traditional methods are normally thought to have the following defects:

1. They are basically passive forms of learning and the feedback process is not obvious.
2. Such traditional methods rely greatly on hearing and seeing and are therefore not very dynamic. As such they do not stimulate or motivate for very long periods of time.

To overcome some of these criticisms most firms now encourage the use of videos, role play and trainee participation.

Other methods of training

Simulation

The cost of exposing someone to a complete experience of the training issue may be prohibitive, e.g. airline pilots. In such situations the trainee is placed in a simulated situation. This allows for a full range of situations to be posed and trainers can monitor, and if need be correct, as the trainee responds.

In-tray exercises

This method is most frequently used for clerical and administrative trainees. The trainee is given an 'in-tray' of documents, etc., and told to deal with what arises from the materials.

Assignments

These are specific tasks given to the trainee. They in turn must use their initiative to react in the way they consider to be correct. A report is normally compiled at the end of the assignment and this is used to assess the validity of the reactions.

All of these methods concentrate more on involvement, which should promote interest and motivation. They rely considerably on self-motivation, self-regulation and controlled learning. It is felt that such qualities help the retention of information and knowledge.

Programmed learning

These are 'self-study' schemes, which are based more on 'distance-learning' than classroom participation. Materials are normally read and then tested against assignments. The advantages of such programmes are:

1. The trainee learns at their own pace, free from the pressures of 'peer group' expectations.
2. The materials can be sent direct to the student, so allowing for a speed of receipt that suits the individual's progress.
3. Research suggests that retention and long-term recall are both high in this form of learning.

The system works best where there is a relatively large amount of 'static' materials. Subjects liable to constant change are not so well covered by manuals, test units, etc.

Attitude testing

We shall return to the attitudes of people and management awareness later in this chapter, but at this stage it is worth noting that people's feelings need careful monitoring just as much as their skills. Managers have to prepare employees for change and must be aware of individual needs when communicating issues. Attitude training attempts to change often deeply-held beliefs. Sensitivity training concentrates on deliberately putting the trainee in 'tense' situations. This should promote the need to try to analyse why other people react in certain ways. Some of the methods used include:

1. *Role-play.* Here trainers are required to act out pre-determined parts or roles. These often reflect simulations of work situations. Once again an important underlying theme of this form of training is to encourage trainees to appreciate why individuals behave as they do in response to orders, instructions and such issues as an 'industrial relations' problem.
2. *Case study work.* This centres on pre-prepared stimulus material, which is reacted to by trainees. Their reactions are then analysed and suggestions/comments made.

3. *Training groups.* This is sometimes known as 'T-group' training, and involves a small group of trainees meeting to consider each other's behaviour. Participants are free to say whatever they wish. Proponents of such training put forward the following advantages:

- They help change attitudes by showing what others think of each other.
- They demonstrate the importance of group influence on behaviour and attitude.
- They help individuals to communicate and use their 'social skills'.
- They may show the observers qualities, such as leadership potential, in the participants.

However, it must be remembered that a basic 'open session' in honest opinion can lead to fairly heated debate.

Some recent findings on how to make training effective

By 'effective' it is meant that the trainee genuinely improves their performance and is satisfied with the end result. To try to achieve this, recent research has found that acceptance and subsequent best results are strongly influenced by the following:

1. The trainee's immediate superior should be fully involved in the training schedule. The superior should take as active a part in the training as possible.
2. The trainee must be able to see the job related relevance of the training. Ideally the training should be centred round particular problems of the actual workplace in which both the superior and the trainee find themselves.
3. Training succeeds best where it is practical in nature and not a mere set of academic tests.
4. Trainers themselves have to be involved with the problems actually faced by the superior and the trainee. They must, in turn, relate their experiences to the problems, so promoting motivation and knowledge retention.

Not all training schemes can and do reflect the above list, but most do try to reflect as many as possible. Some courses have to be dry and academic and 'off-site', but the content must be seen as relevant and correct.

The role of the state in training

The ever-changing nature of what is called the 'economy' does not promote the best climate for firms to spend money on training. A reluctance to commit money is understandable, and in a cost-cutting regime training is an easy budget to reduce.

To try to overcome this reluctance most governments promote training. This is set against a background of the following:

1. A continued fall in the number of 16–19 year olds being available for employment. This is forcing change onto firms as they must now 'attract' young people and train their current employees to be flexible.
2. The large numbers of unemployed people need to be found ways of re-entering the workforce. Human resources are a key component in international competitiveness.
3. A reduction in the workforce, coupled with an ageing population means a change in pension funding is inevitable. This has been referred to as 'the demographic time-bomb' and must be addressed, for most advanced economies are not generating sufficient wealth to meet the real value of future welfare expectations.
4. Certain trends are beginning to appear in the labour market. These include an increase in employment in the service industries and a decrease in jobs available in what has been known as the 'manufacturing sector'. More new jobs are part-time and often taken by female labour, workers are having to become more flexible in their work patterns, and more people will work 'from home'. We will return to these trends later in the book.

Training for employment

Young people and those no longer quite so young but unemployed enter the Youth Training Programme through a variety of routes. This is normally started by attending a Job Centre. They will then be sent to an approved training agent, e.g. a school or college. The training agent will be responsible for counselling, assessing and providing a personal action plan for the individual and then placing him/her with a training manager, who will be responsible for the actual delivery of training. Trainees within the programme are paid a training allowance.

Job clubs

Job clubs are designed to help people seek work who are not sure how to tackle the issues involved in trying to find it. At a job club a group of unemployed people meet and try to help each other find work.

Figure 32.3 *The state's role in training*

They have access to telephones, free stationery and postage. Skilled support staff are available at the club and they can advise on the best techniques of searching for a job and succeeding at interviews.

Enterprise Allowance Scheme

Under the Enterprise Allowance Scheme, unemployed people who want to set up their own business are paid an allowance for the first year. They also receive free advice from business people and other members of the local Training and Enterprise Council (TEC).

Education has also been changing to meet the new demands of the labour market. Concentration is now on making young people more flexible on the skills industry requires. To try to meet this demand new qualifications such as GNVQ (which are school/college based), NVQs (which are work based) have been introduced. They are designed to be more practical or vocational in their content than the normal GCSE and GCE 'A' levels. Their standards are designed to be similar to the more formal qualifications and can be used as transfer qualifications to sixth forms and at their 'higher' levels to university. As stated earlier this area of training is constantly changing, and it is advisable to keep as up to date as possible.

CASE STUDY 32.1

Training and staff development

From: Chief Executive

To: Assistant Personnel Manager

Ref: Supervision/Management Training

I would be grateful if you would forward to me in fourteen days time a staff development programme with the following headings

a   Introduction of supervisory staff

b   Senior managerial training

c   Intensive executive training in the areas of: computing, communications and stock control

d   Day release provision for Junior clerical staff

I.D. Leadwell, Chief Executive Officer

SUMMARY

Having studied this chapter, you should be able to:

▼ Explain the purpose of training and developing employees.

(continued)

▽ Describe the organising and implementing of training programmes.

▽ Explain the methods of training available.

▽ Understand the role of the state in training.

Question and Activities

Technical terms glossary

In the section below you are given a series of technical terms and their meanings. They have been scrambled, though. You must match up the terms and the definitions. When you have them correctly paired, transfer them to your alphabetical vocabulary or glossary book.

You are also advised to transfer any definitions obtained during the exercises in the case studies into this glossary book.

Technical terms

1. Simulation exercise
2. Distance learning
3. Off-site or off-job training placements
4. Skills gaps
5. Sitting next to Nellie
6. Role-play exercises
7. NVQ
8. T-group meetings
9. Training and Enterprise Council
10. Internal and external training

Definition

A. The two main types of training programmes.
B. Closely observing everything done by an individual.
C. An exercise that tries to copy what will probably take place.
D. Studying in the home or place of work and not at a specialist educational institution.
E. Acting out certain situations, so allowing mistakes and correct actions to be monitored.
F. A small group of trainees that meet to discuss each other's reactions, progress, etc.
G. A locally based organisation that is designed to promote training and job opportunities.
H. A national examination, with a 'vocational bias', that is designed to prepare young people for the world of work.
I. Training programmes that take place away from the place of work.

J. Clearly identified areas of skills where the organisation has no one, or too few employees capable of performing the necessary tasks.

Short answers questions

1. Give a brief description of what a training programme should be preparing an individual for.
2. Why would a job analysis exercise be of use to the training department?
3. Outline the advantages of an internally based training programme.
4. Outline the advantages of an externally based training programme.
5. What is meant by 'on-job' training?
6. What is meant by 'off-job' training?
7. Why might an employee be interested in pursuing a programmed learning package?
8. Do you consider it important that a trainee's immediate superior should be aware of the trainee's development programme? Give reasons to support your opinion.
9. What is the role of the Job Centre in youth training?
10. Could job clubs liaise more closely with schools/colleges, and if they did what might be the advantages?
11. Suggest five reasons why training is an easy target for cost-cutting.

Short essays

1. What do you understanding by the terms: 'in-tray exercises', 'role-play'.
2. Analyse the benefits and dis-benefits of the on-job and off-job systems of training.
3. What contributions can training make to the overall efficiency of the company?
4. The TEC scheme has received considerable praise from some quarters, yet corporate and government expenditure on training continues to fall – why?

33
Appraising employees

Preview

▼ In this chapter the exercise of appraising employees will be analysed. All organisations have to develop systems that enable employees to be assessed and their performance rated.

▼ Usually, such exercises are part of a regular procedure and are carried out by the employees immediate superior.

There are three basic approaches to appraising:

1 *The traits approach.* This approach attaches most weight to the personal qualities expected of someone carrying out the specific job. These *personal* qualities include: appearance, punctuality, leadership and cooperation.
2 *The results-orientated approach.* This calls for some agreed form of 'result' to be available, e.g. sales figures, and against this performance is assessed.
3 *The job-behaviour approach.* This concentrates on such indicators as effective performance and attitudes to work and behaviour. The superior tries to measure the individual's performance against agreed 'norms'.

A further distinction may be made. In an *open system*, the appraisee has the opportunity to discuss his performance with the superior, so he can contribute. In a *closed system*, the superior assesses without discussion so there is no appraisee contribution.

Why do we appraise?

A regular review of employees' performance is a useful management tool. Such an exercise should provide accurate information about the quality and skills of the workforce, and therefore help in human resource planning. Most organisations have both written and unwritten 'values', and part of any review should concentrate on both *results* and *style*. Recognition of the style being achieved tends to reinforce the behaviour.

An appraisal programme may also help to identify what is required from the training programme, as areas in individual performance where effectiveness could be improved can be targeted. Key skills can be identified, and employees can be trained towards these. Such is the pace of technological change that most employees require re-training at regular intervals. By identifying 'gaps' in an individual's performance we can establish the best way(s) of enabling them to achieve a higher level of contribution. Such issues as 'relations', or even 'domestic issues' can be discovered, and hopefully, resolved. By interviewing the individual the manager should be able to discover potential and so build *succession trees*. The 'results' of an employee's performance give the manager an objective base from which to consider the individual's potential.

The exercise of talking should improve communications, so reducing the barriers that may arise. Constructive dialogue should promote an increase in the way both parties see each other. This in turn should improve individual motivation. A few well-chosen words of encouragement and recognition can have a positive effect on morale and job satisfaction. An employee given the opportunity to 'improve' against known criteria is more likely to work towards the necessary improvement.

In addition, the 'meeting' of employer and employee representatives allows for disciplinary necessities. It would be a mistake to simply use an appraisal for a 'telling-off' but constructive discussion of difficulties can help reduce tensions and stop the need for further action. Whatever theorists say there is a link between appraisal and pay! If pay is in anyway 'merit related', then some formal structure must exist for deciding merit. Some managers try to divorce pay from performance analysis. Indeed, they may let several weeks elapse between the two meetings, but many employees see a clear link between their agreed performance and future pay awards. Like any system an appraisal needs careful pre-meeting preparation. Advocates must be aware of certain pitfalls. These include the following:

Administrative problems

People need to be trained in appraisal technique and it must be accepted that time will be required to conduct a worthwhile appraisal programme.

Assessment problems

Interviewers must be aware of certain pitfalls, such as:

* *Bias.* People do have likes and dislikes, and these can influence their opinions.
* *Halo effects.* We like certain types of people and they receive our 'blessing' regardless.
* *Stereotyping.* We judge everyone against an image we consider applies to all.
* *Negative information.* One poor answer is allowed to colour everything else.
* *Leniency.* Being over-generous, even when the answer is obviously poor.
* *'Playing God'.* Making moral judgements on the behaviour or appearance of someone else.

The above are more likely to arise in traits systems, but they can appear in results-based programmes. We need to give careful consideration of how we decide *who* is the real personality behind a success, or a failure; and what other characteristics may have influenced performance, e.g. poor materials, a declining market, or even the attitude of the appraiser!

Implementation problems

Some employees will see appraisal as the 'promotion interview', but this is seldom the case. Disappointment may therefore creep in and the resultant frustration can be dangerous. Another problem may be that of training. A well-organised employee can dictate the course they need, but it may not actually be the best course for their 'training'.

The pitfalls of linking pay to appraisal have already been discussed. Whenever one is appraising, all parties must be aware of the precise system, its objectives and its methods of evaluation, otherwise it will all be a waste of time.

Shall we introduce appraisal?

Most institutions already have appraisal systems, but if it is one to be developed there must be a strategy. To be successful, the firm must have a clear idea of what it wants to achieve from the appraisal, so in an odd kind of way, it is necessary to start at the end.

For any system to work it must be 'accepted' by the majority. This can only be achieved if three conditions are met.

1. All those using the system must be trained in its use. They must know how to operate it, and in the case of an 'open' system, have skills in assessing and interviewing.
2. The system must be seen to be used for purposes intended. It must be seen to be working.
3. Each appraiser must, in turn, be appraised.

Once the organisation has accepted the above, it must decide *what to appraise.* Here are some things to think about.

Traits-orientated appraisals

Traits-orientated appraisals tend to be *subjective* as it is one person's perception. How can an individual actually improve their character or personality? After all its been with them for quite a long time! It is therefore normally more successful to show them ways of improving their work rate, which may in turn affect their own self belief and therefore their personality.

Results-orientated appraisals

Results-orientated appraisals are concerned with measurement. But what do we measure? How do we measure? Do we accept certain constraints, difficulties, etc?

Job behaviour-orientated appraisals

Again, what is a 'good performer'? What measurements do we use?

As you can see, each system has its problems, and 'how' and 'what' to assess has not been decided. Normally, one of the following is used:

Job description

This is usually based on identifying *key tasks*, i.e., those which have a major bearing on the achievement of a particular job. Once key issues have been identified, standards of performance can be assessed. Success, or lack of it, can be seen and acted upon. Using job descriptions allows for a blueprint of what is to be achieved, but does it identify how any improvements should be implemented?

Panels

Groups of managers, who are familiar with the organisation and its requirements, can gather together and decide on a list of traits (attributes) or results (outcomes) against which an employee can be appraised. They can also follow the jobs approach and decide how an individual is appraised. Problems exist with this method, as 'panels' normally have to deal in 'compromises' and may miss essential issues through a lack of knowledge.

In-depth interviews

These are quite common and often concentrate on specific issues, e.g., crucial aspects of the job. By developing a list, the superior can identify the important issues, but it is time-consuming and calls for a degree of skill in interviewing and cross-questioning.

Critical incident technique

This technique centres on selecting at random certain employees and asking them to describe the most difficult problems they have confronted in, say, the last 90 days. Common issues should emerge, and these can receive management attention.

Document analysis

An analysis of current documents circulating within the company will show which problems are arising. This is sometimes called the *content analysis technique*, and provides a starting point from which to measure performance.

The methods described above can, of course, be used in tandem, and are seldom imposed in isolation.

Keeping records

All systems seem to impose the need for keeping records. The following are the main ways of keeping accurate information.

Description

The appraiser completes an unstructured report describing the appraisee's performance. There is a risk that important material may be left out and 'delicate' issues may also be excluded.

Check lists

Check lists offer a structure in that they provide a list of what must be covered. They should be constructed to reduce the use of such words as 'good' or 'fair', for these seldom mean the same thing to two different people. One way around this problem is to stress that the appraiser must include both *strengths* and *weaknesses*, giving a more balanced analysis. It may also be advisable to instruct appraisers to state what they considered to be 'deciding' factors when they reached their decisions.

Ratings

Ratings centre on a score being given to each section of a check list. Again care must be taken when deciding on words used. Numbers can be 'massaged' to achieve a score which means very little. However, a clearly defined set of numbers may be linked to pay levels and this is quite a popular combination in business.

Comparisons

From a list of scores a rank order can be extracted. This allows for comparison. We must be aware of the obvious, namely that someone will always be top, and someone else bottom. The latter may be a first-class employee, but try as they might they cannot move up the league table.

There is probably no one system we should adopt. What we should do, however is avoid:

- imprecise definitions
- a lack of deciding factors
- an opportunity to despatch someone to the permanent position of bottom of the league.

Holding appraisal interviews

The major points to remember regarding holding appraisal interviews are:

Preparation

Regarding preparation, we must be sure of:

- What is required
- The key results we expect to see emerge
- The standards we will use to assess employees
- The current standards of employee performance and from where these are to be drawn
- Problems beyond the control of the employee
- Strengths to build on
- Weaknesses to be corrected
- The mechanics of the reporting system, and arrangements for subsequent reporting and action.
- The policy of the firm regarding pay, training, transfers, promotion, etc.
- Select the best place to hold the interviews.

Implementation

One new situation we have to confront is that both parties may 'know each other', so we must be aware of not taking anything for granted. Care must be taken to ask the type of question that encourages in-depth analysis and an awareness of perceived weaknesses. Questions will be open and probing, so encouraging openers on:

- achievements
- disappointments
- problems
- possible actions

Silence and encouraging nods can be used to good effect to keep the appraisee talking.

Report writing

Without effective follow-up even a well-conducted appraisal exercise is a wasted opportunity. It is normally advisable to complete the report immediately after the interview. Aim to be: *accurate*, *precise*, yet *comprehensive*. Keep all promises made in the interview and always try to respond in the time set.

Analysis

The information contained on the appraisal documents will be of interest to several parties within the organisation. After all, it should show an accurate picture of the current state of the business affairs. Managers responsible for training, planning, etc., will obviously need to be informed and analysis can direct management time towards those problems that require attention.

We must not see appraisal in 'isolation', for a good manager is constantly assessing the situation. This in turn means he is probing performance, evaluating and acting upon findings. Regular feedback and guidance should be a part of any manager's workload.

As well as not seeing appraisal in isolation it must not be viewed as a 'one-off' operation. Review, reassessment and re-analysis are most important. Indeed, we should be asking such questions as 'Is the appraisal system doing what was intended for it?'

SUMMARY

Having studied this chapter, you should be able to:

▽ Describe the various types of appraisal used.

▽ Explain why organisations use appraisal.

▽ Explain what use an appraisal exercise is.

▽ Understand how to administer an appraisal procedure.

▽ Describe the 'follow-up' to the initial interview.

Questions and activities

Technical terms and glossary

In the section below you are given a series of technical terms and their meanings. They have been scrambled, though. You must match up the terms and the definitions. When you have them correctly paired, transfer them to your alphabetical vocabulary or glossary book.

You are also advised to transfer any definitions obtained during the exercises in the case studies into this glossary book.

Technical terms

1. Key task identification
2. Some of the problems associated with appraisal
3. A succession plan or tree
4. A closed system
5. A traits-orientated approach

Definitions

A. An assessment of personal qualitites such as appearance, punctuality, leadership and cooperation.
B. A system in which the superior assesses without discussion with the appraisee.
C. The process of developing a plan as to how the appraisee will perform what functions in the future.
D. Bias, halo effects, stereotyping, negative information, etc.
E. The task of identifying important parts of a job, and deciding what standard must be reached for each of these.

Short answer questions

1. Why might you choose a traits-orientated approach as opposed to a results-orientated approach?
2. Outline the main reasons why an employer conducts an appraisal exercise.
3. What do you understand by the term 'succession plan or tree'?
4. Briefly describe the major 'pitfalls' an appraiser must be aware of before starting an appraisal interview.
5. How can an organisation best gain acceptance for an appraisal programme?
6. Why might job descriptions be an important part of the appraisal procedure?
7. Briefly list the 'pros and cons' of the following appraisal methods:
   (a) in-depth interviews
   (b) critical incident technique
   (c) document analysis
   (d) panels
8. 'Preparation is paramount in appraisal.' Do you agree with this statement and why?
9. Why is it important to:
   (a) report back to the employee quickly;
   (b) regularly update your actions after the interview;
   (c) develop communication, so not allowing the interview to be a 'one-off' exercise?
10. Why do employees link appraisal to pay?

34
Remuneration, discipline and employee welfare

Preview

▼ An organisation must devise ways of paying employees. These need to be acceptable to both the employer and the employees.

▼ In this chapter the various methods of payment and other benefits will be analysed.

▼ As well as pay or remuneration other benefits are normally offered to employees and these must be examined and their effectiveness measured.

Remuneration: a pay structure

Remuneration involves the company in devising a system of internal differentials between various levels of pay, for various jobs, based on some form of scale. A clearly defined pay structure and cost calculations helps employees know where they are within the organisation. It normally encourages individuals to believe that a degree of fairness exists, and that financial reward is not merely at the discretion of a particular superior. The arrival of legislation to promote equal pay between the sexes makes a structure even more important.

How then does a company devise a formal pay structure? We can go for an *ad hoc* formula. This is often based on 'what we can afford' and may be based more on personality than on an individual's skills. Such a structure normally reflects 'seniority' but in theory a junior employee could acquire a higher salary than someone more senior. An *ad hoc* structure may also give rise to jealousy and distrust among employees . The company may therefore wish to consider some form of externally imposed pay levels. These clearly state 'the rate for the job' and are agreed at a national level of negotiation. Such a structure still allows the company to reward above the externally imposed pay levels but not below it.

A more 'locally' negotiated structure may allow the company a greater sense of reality and flexibility. Unions in certain localities may have to be monitored and they may have adverse effects on *differentials*.

All of the structures so far analysed are based on a starting amount and differentials emerge from this. The problem of who earns what is left to the company to determine, even though the award may have little to do with the actual job being done. The impact of the problem has promoted the '*job-evaluated*' system, which starts from trying to establish the relative worth of jobs, using the job content as the main deciding factor. This means that such factors as *responsibility, working conditions, skills and training* are taken into consideration. But how are these valued? We could look at the *whole job* and *rank* it against others, or compare it against predetermined grade descriptions to find where a certain job fits.

A grade description for job evaluation

Grade	Description
1	Simple, manual tasks closely supervised
2	Simple, light manual, some personal responsibility
3	Some manual effort, some discretion
4	Some manual work, some responsibility for the work of others

The above is simple to apply, but it is *subjective*. It is not always easy to separate tasks and disagreements may arise. At best it provides a 'pecking order', but it is seldom satisfactory.

If the company appoints a panel to decide, then they might reduce the problems. The panel must represent all interests, and they normally compare jobs in pairs, so establishing which of the two has the greater value. This approach is known as the *Inbucon Consensus Method*.

The company may opt for a process that attempts to analyse a job in its various bits and then score each component. To achieve such a structure they need to decide on what is significant, divide these into individual factors, assign weights/scores, divide the factors into degrees or levels, select jobs to be reviewed and view these against agreed job (benchmarks), e.g.:

Factors	1st degree	2nd degree	3rd degree	4th degree	5th degree
1 Skills required					
general reasoning ability	5	10	15	20	25
dexterity and motor skills	5	10	15	20	25
training and previous experience	15	30	45	60	75
education required	15	30	45	60	75
2 Responsibilites and mental requirements					
alterness to details	5	10	15	20	25
attention needed	12	24	36	48	60
effect on other operations	10	20	30	40	50
responsibility for materials	5	10	15	20	25
responsibility for safety of others	15	30	45	60	75
responsibility for work of others	15	30	45	60	75
3 Effort required					
physical demands	5	10	15	20	25
abnormal position	5	10	15	20	25
4 Job conditions					
disagreeableness	5	10	15	–	–
unavoidable hazards	5	10	15	–	–

Source: M. Armstrong and H. Merlis *A Handbook of Salary Administration*

The most commonly used categories are those of the HAY MSL guide chart profile. It uses know-how, problem-solving and accountability as its principal group headings.

Against each of these points are awarded, with each 'degree' being added to by a factor of 15 points. As with previous systems it is still open to accusations of subjectivity, e.g., who decides what is a 'benchmark' job? However, the company does now have a framework on which to base negotiations.

Another 'banding' system is that devised by Paterson. He centred his analysis on decision-making, hence a job will be classified against the following bands.

- Band E – policy making.
- Band D – programming, planning how to carry our policy.
- Band C – interpreting, deciding how to implement plans.
- Band B – routine, deciding which tasks need to be done.
- Band A – automatic, allocating techniques and tasks to others
- Band O – Defined, following a defined procedure to carry out a task, making decisions on how to follow the procedure.

This system once again gives the company a clear base, but does it allow for such features as skills, experience, responsibility and an ability to communicate with others? It probably would not be the correct system for non-managerial positions.

Criticisms of this system include the following:

- A job will be placed on a high grade even if only a part of it involves coordinating other people.
- Employees may try to formalise informal relations, so that they appear to have more responsibility than they actually do.

One further method needs to be analysed, namely the *time-span of discretion*, i.e., how long it takes for a marginally substandard decision to have an obvious effect. This system was developed by Elliott Jacques, who considered that 'the longer the time the more an employee should be paid'.

He then developed a wage index, based on what he considered a 'fair rate' linked to responsibility. Critics have charged this system with similar failings to those of Paterson's, in that some jobs do not have obvious decision-making contents. Also, when delegation is well-established a subordinate may earn more. However, time is more objective than some of the other methods that have been analysed. Here is a re-cap on the major problems of trying to measure pay and to set levels:

1. Systems tend to be *subjective*.
2. Systems must be constantly *updated*.
3. Systems that have universal *application* are difficult to develop.
4. Jobs of equal size may not be of equal attractiveness to employees. This will make recruitment more difficult. A way through this dilemma is to allocate *weights* to tasks, so reflecting the current importance the firm places on a job.
5. A fixed system can make it difficult to reward extra performance because it has little *flexibility*.
6. To get unions to agree it is normally best to

encourage maximum *worker participation*.

7. It is legally very difficult to pay someone less than they once received, even if a new grading system now says they should. This leads to what is called *red circling* (i.e. paying present employees on the old rate, but recruiting new members on a lower rate).

8. Job evaluation establishes an *order*; it does not necessarily tell a firm how much someone should be paid.

So, why should a firm bother to establish a pay structure? The major reasons put forward in favour of a structure are:

1. It provides a *framework* on which to discuss pay.
2. It gives *consistency* and *acceptability* in negotiations.
3. A 'good' system should enable us to reward the factors considered to be of importance.
4. The spin-offs from such an exercise should be beneficial, so improving *employee understanding*.

The best procedure to follow for introducing a formal pay structure is:

1. Examine the results of a job evaluation exercise.
2. Group similar jobs together.
3. Decide on grades needed.
4. Review current grade structure.
5. Decide on the range of payments to be included.
6. Consider current market rates.
7. Cost the new structures.
8. Implement the new structure.

Whatever system the company imposes it will need to have an agreed form of payment. The methods available to it are:

- *Wages*. Payment on an hourly, daily or weekly rate. Bonuses will be considered a little later.
- *Payment by results (PBR)*. These are designed to reward employees for the amount they produce, or for the time they take to do a given job. Most systems work on deciding a *base output*, and extra output is rewarded at an agreed rate. Some systems merely reward by a proportional increase as output uses, while others reward by an increasing amount that goes up in steps as output rises beyond the base.

In practice, the company is merely applying Taylor's principle that money motivates'. Supporters claim that high wages produce high output. It is an accurate system, and promotes self-sufficiency. However, critics point to the establishment of 'group norms', it may also lead to a drop in quality, but an increase in quantity. So quality and design up-dates must be both monitored and introduced.

- *Measured daywork*. This system is designed to even out differences in weekly earnings. It works by setting an agreed level of performance, so when an employee reaches a certain level, he is paid at the rate for that level of performance. Several rates are set and employees progress through these as their skills develop. Critics say that much depends on supervision and the various personal pressures imposed on the individual to meet targets e.g. imminent holidays!

Should the pay structure be based on a *day rate* or *flat rate*? These provide an agreed rate in return for a given period of work, e.g. £3.50 per hour, or £120 per week. Rates change via collective bargaining. Pay varies according to hours worked, and *not* output.

This system is normally most applicable to machine controlled work, or where output control is beyond the employees direct influence, e.g. raw material supplies. It does not necessarily reward effort, and needs careful introduction. It is normally best to agree standards before commencing and to have known grievance procedures set up in advance.

Salaries are normally paid on a monthly basis. They are paid at a flat rate, and differentials normally reflect promotion.

Whatever system is chosen the really important issue is *how well it is introduced*. The 'message' the scheme conveys is paramount to its acceptance.

Some systems use a *fixed-incremental* scale, i.e. that individual moves through a series of known salary increases. These are often related to age and/or experience. Such schemes are not known for their incentive qualities as employees move through the grades as of right. Others are based on *variable incremental systems*, which allow an element of discretion. Staff are rewarded for various behavioural characteristics. Critics point to an *ad hoc* system that does not have clear boundaries. One other option is that of the *fixed merit system*, which is based on a fixed and agreed formula. Performance appraisal is used to determine the progression. Once again it is important to set clear, understandable and largely acceptable standards. The last system open to us is *variable-merit system*, which is merit-related and does not have a fixed formula or rate. Within the overall budget a manager is free to reward individual performance.

Is there a rate for the job?

Most firms try to establish a rate for the job by referral to published surveys, though they may also conduct private surveys to support their findings. Whichever surveys they use they must be aware of:

- bias in the survey(s) chosen
- comparison of their own company situation with the findings of a 'general' response
- the existence of 'fringe benefits' which distort the figures shown
- averages being moved upwards by a few highly paid individuals
- outdated figures, concepts, etc.
- different laws, customs, etc., affecting the data.

Even with all these shortcomings, most firms use surveys as indications of where to set pay levels. However, when doing this they must consider:

1. *Their company's pay policy.* Are they to be 'market leaders', followers or nicely balanced in the middle? They may choose to put a greater emphasis on other conditions than just money.
2. *Costs.* Do they have the money to be a market leader?
3. *Collective bargaining.* How do they consult their workers? Are their exmployees well unionised? If so, this may shape the pay structure.
4. *Differentials.* Do they have wide boundaries of pay differences, and how do they decide who earns what?

All are difficult decisions. But the following must also be considered:

- equal pay legislation
- various Wages Acts, e.g. 1986
- entitlements, e.g. maternity pay
- holiday pay
- statutory sick pay.

Employee benefits

The basic rate of pay is only part of the remuneration package. Employers must now look at other benefits an employee may receive when awarding any of the benefits that follow. They must take into consideration:

- *Tax.* It will cost companies considerably more to increase an employee's pay than the actual amount offered. This is because they have to meet increased National Insurance and pension contributions.

- *Expectations.* Most employees now expect sick pay and pension contributions as a part of their standard conditions. Employers must therefore design benefits that are both attractive and not too costly.
- *Retention.* They must beware of what Americans call 'golden handcuffs', that is paying benefits that keep an employee with them after they have served their use, e.g. a subsidised mortgage scheme. Companies should induce loyalty, not pay rewards for previous success.
- *Motivation.* Employers do not want employees to leave. The individual who enjoys status will see certain 'perks' as signs that they have 'arrived'. These can form part of a benefits package.

A benefits package

Before finalising the pay arrangements, employers need to consider:

1. *Objectives.* Are they aiming solely at current employees, or should they have one eye on future staff? They need to decide on:
- employee retention
- tax implications
- costs
- motivational value
- prestige factors.

2. *Policy.* Are they going to pay low basic rates that are boosted by benefits, or the reverse, or a 'balanced' approach? They have to decide on the precise policy option.
3. *Costs.* The benefits must be affordable and some, e.g. pensions, will require a lengthy commitment from the company.
4. *Employees' needs.* What does the employee expect and can the company meet these expectations? Will share option schemes be acceptable to current shareholders? Bonus payments need discussion. Employers need to listen carefully to their employees, who may have good ideas that could be very cost-effective.
5. *Impact of decisions.* A benefit to one group may not be good news to another group. Morale and productivity may suffer. Demands for equal treatment may not be possible.

What can a benefit package include?

1. *Bonuses.* These may be a pure addition to basic pay at, say, Christmas, or a sum paid for continued good service. They may be based on some agreed 'merit' payment or a sum paid to a specific group for a successful job. They could take the form of a profit-sharing bonus,

323

reflecting the recent 'success' of the company, or may be payable to all working in a particular plant or department. At executive levels a bonus may be a sum related to profit.

2. *Share schemes.* Rather than a pure monetary bonus employers may offer shares in lieu. This tends to introduce employees to the fact of profit and the risks inherent in making one.

3. *Pension schemes.* These are another popular form of benefit. Past employees can receive a certain percentage of their highest earnings multiplied by the length of service they gave. An employer can provide the 'flat' or 'standard' rate, or he may enhance the scheme, so giving the employee extra income on retirement.

4. *Loans.* An employee can be loaned money on preferential rates of interest, or even interest free. The sum could be used for such costly outgoings as a season ticket on the railways. Careful account must be taken of the Inland Revenue rates on such loans, but once again such a policy should boost retention, alleviate financial concerns and so increase performance.

5. *Discounts.* These tend to be most common in retailing, where employees can purchase items at a reduced rate. This tends to promote a greater sense of identification with company products, and offers free publicity if people see employees using corporate products. Employers may offer allowances, such as travelling or in special circumstances, may provide a one-off sum, e.g. housing re-location payment.

6. *Payments in kind.* Perhaps the most obvious example here is the *company car*. Such a benefit may either be solely for business use, e.g. a salesman's car or as part of remuneration, e.g. the Chairman's Rolls-Royce.

The benefit may take the form of a *health-care scheme* where companies pay for a range of medical facilities. Some senior personnel have received *household items*, such as furniture, as part of a package. Another familiar benefit is an '*expenses account*'. In reality it is a re-imbursement for costs incurred in carrying out duties, but there are ways in which this form of allowance can become a benefit, e.g., all credit card payments met without individual items being queried. Business trips, especially if accompanied by one's spouse, may also be seen as a perk, while a more traditional extra is a '*luncheon voucher*'.

The part that any or all of these payments play in the total remuneration package depends on company policy, as will the last category – *time off*. Most employees have automatic holiday allowances, which on average cost about 2% of total employment per week granted. Leave to attend higher education, or some other facility not normally related to work is often referred to as sabbatical leave. Flexible working hours or *flexitime* is becoming quite widely used. It enables the employee to decide, within reason, how he works his contracted week. Most organisations operate a 'core time' period, e.g. 10.00 am to 4.00 pm, and state that these hours must be worked each day. Others allow more latitude, in that they state a minimum working week and let the employee decide how to spread the work. The advantages of such a scheme, which fits more to clerical surrounds, appears to be:

- It puts the responsibility on the employee to regulate their own attendance.
- It allows the employee flexibility to attend appointments, for example at the dentists.
- It allows travel outside rush hours.
- It allows employees to control the pattern of their work, e.g., the need to collect young children from school.

Employers have also added a drop in one-day absenteeisms, a fall in labour turnover, retention improvements, easier recruitment and a general improvement in industrial relations to the list of advantages. They also indicate that assembly lines, shops and other companies where the customer controls the demand are not easily converted to flexitime.

Most employers honour sick leave, if it is supported by official medical documentation. The largest causes of 'lost days' are matrimonial disputes, the common cold and alcohol.

Women expecting a baby are entitled to *maternity leave*, providing they have worked for the employer for two continuous years. In most European countries a similar arrangement exists for fathers, namely *paternity leave*. Elsewhere in a working life the individual may be granted compassionate leave, for illness or deaths in the family, or special leave, e.g., to get married.

Attention will be given to the implications to business of the increase in leisure through a shorter working week in the section covering the social changes effecting business.

Discipline

Managing a work force involves many different and testing actions. Among the most difficult are those that concentrate on having to discipline, or even dismiss, an employee.

A dismissal arises when one of the following occurs:

- When an employer terminates the contract of employment of an employee, with or without notice. Termination without notice may be called *summary* or *instant* dismissal.
- *When an employee can be instantly dismissed.* This can occur if an employee is found
  - fighting
  - attacking a superior
  - drunk at work
  - stealing
  - in gross violation of their expected behaviour.
  Any of these can result in the employee being 'fired on the spot'.

  Grievance procedure: Notification of this is normally included in the Contract of Employment. Each employee must be aware of their rights to seek further opinions if they consider they have been unfairly treated. Normally, an employee may choose someone to accompany them to a Grievance or Arbitration Meeting. This may be a solicitor, union official, or simply a friend. If the employee still disagrees with the decision of the arbitrator they may seek permission to take the issue to an Industrial Tribunal. This is not a court, but does have powers to recommend re-instatement, or more normally a payment in lieu of loss of earnings.
- When an employer terminates a contract, in such a way as to force the employee to leave. This may be subsequently found to be *forced* or *constructive* dismissal.
- When an employee comes to the end of a fixed period of employment, and the contract is *not re-newed*.

One of the important aims of any manpower plan should be to minimise the risk of employing too many people. Such a surplus is known as having people who are *redundant*. Legally, this arises if the work for which they are employed has come to an end or diminished. Management normally tries to minimise the effects of redundancy because of the dramatic impact this inevitably has on people's lives.

Causes of redundancies

The redundancies can be caused by:

- Market fluctuations.
- Changes in the availability of raw materials.

- Technological advances.
- Government action.
- Changes in the cost of labour relative to that of other resources.
- Mergers, which normally result in duplications of certain posts which then have to be tackled.
- Cost reduction or 'down sizing' exercises which concentrate on reducing cost bases, of which in most organisations labour is the largest single cost.
- Rationalisation – as plants/outlets are amalgamated.
- Relocation of output.
- Financial collapse.

All of these may cause employers to consider making people redundant.

The costs of redundancy

To the individual the feeling of shock or rejection can be very strong. Feelings of insecurity and inadequacy are well documented and society has to find taxed income to pay benefits. The 'economy' suffers lost output and the cost of paying those who become unemployed.

The company may also suffer shock. It may become 'defensive' and such stresses as a 'loss of morale', negative employee reaction, loss of public confidence and the cost of handling such a delicate issue may seriously undermine corporate confidence.

The unions may 'fight' redundancies both from the individual's point of view and the obvious reduction in their own influence. The confidence of the company may be dented by a sustained period of high levels of redundancies.

How can redundancies be prevented?

1. Allocate redundancies to 'natural wastage', and only seek 'wastage' via those 'prepared to go'. Key positions will require filling regardless.
2. Concentrate on part-time or temporary employees.
3. Retire those nearing or past the 'official' age.
4. Offer work-sharing programmes.
5. Transfer people.
6. Offer retraining.
7. Seek voluntary redundancy.

Handling redundancies

A company must have an agreed procedure. This should concentrate on:

- Consultation.
- Full disclosure of information.

- Clear identification of who is to be selected, e.g., 'last in, last out'.
- Specification of how those affected are to be notified, paid and what their legal entitlements are.
- Specification of any bonuses being offered to 'go'.
- An outline of how those affected may seek time off to find new employment.
- A statement regarding 'alternative' employment which may be available elsewhere within the organisation.

The company:

- must give legal notification
- must notify about training/re-training offers
- must offer counselling
- must notify any financial inducements available
- must try to rebuild morale
- must try to avoid adverse publicity
- must re-organise quickly
- must minimise costs to the company and country
- must keep to the letter of the law.

Legal requirements

Since the 1965 Redundancy Payments Act the employer has a legal obligation to pay some redundancy payments to employees (see Chapter 44). Under the 1965 Act a scheme was created that was financed by employer contribution. At least one half of all redundancy payments are funded by this scheme, the balance being contributed by individual employers. The Act provides the *minimum* requirements and these are now included in the Employment Protection Consolidation Act 1978. They are as follows:

- Up to two years' services does not entitle any employee to a minimum payment (both full-time and part-time employees).
- For each year's service, (where the employee has worked for over two years) for ages 18 to 22, half a weeks pay (i.e. half of average weekly pay).
- For each year of service between 22 and 41, one week's pay.
- For each year of service between ages 41 and 65 (60 for women) one and a half week's pay.

Many firms pay additional sums to these. In general this is a sound policy as it helps reduce labour and trade union hostility to the introduction of labour saving techniques and the firm gets a reputation for being a fair and generous employer. The payment of a once and for all sum may be less expensive than a period of industrial unrest.

Note that an individual wishing to resign from his/her job may do so without giving a reason – although the Personnel Department may ask to be told why 'in confidence'.

CASE STUDY 34.1

College Dynamics – shopfloor problems

A disagreement has developed over how much and by what method of payment College Dynamics should pay casual workers in the period prior to Christmas. We normally attract students for this type of work and they do not pay tax. They may use our subsidised canteen, providing they are working five-hour shifts and attending work for all normal working days (Monday to Friday).

The assistant personnel manager wants to pay a straight £3.25 per hour, with no guaranteed hours or other benefits. The production manager prefers £3.75 per hour for a guaranteed 35-hour week, providing (a) staff report for training by 5th December and (b) meet quality requirements at the end of the training programme. He then hopes to attract some back next year.

Question

Briefly outline, in the form of a memorandum, your reasons for supporting one of the two proposals. Your memorandum should be addressed to the chief wages clerk.

College Dynamics – 'Top people' package

'Our executive package requires an overhaul. So let us see how we improve the terms and conditions of those at head of division level and above.'

This is an extract from a recent Board meeting minutes.

As personnel director you are both responsible for proposing certain advantages and will be a recipient of most of them! To date at the level mentioned we provide

1. a company car
2. subsidised lunches
3. one week's holiday above company average

and at Board level we add

1. a 'top-up' to the pension scheme
2. one spouse accompanied flight per six undertaken by the executive.

Question

You have to balance cost against incentive. Prepare your initial notes on what other benefits may be fitting to the two levels of management.

SUMMARY

Having studied this chapter, you should be able to explain:

▼ The various forms of payment systems available.

▼ How pay is determined.

▼ How an individual may be paid.

▼ Other forms of inducements that do not necessarily involve money.

Questions and activities

Technical terms and glossary

In the section below you are given a series of technical terms and their meanings. They have been scrambled, though. You must match up the terms and the definitions. When you have them correctly paired, transfer them to your alphabetical vocabulary or glossary book.

You are also advised to transfer any defintions obtained during the exercises in the case studies into this glossary book.

Technical terms

1. A system of reward that establishes a structure and bench marks
2. A pay structure
3. Collective bargaining
4. Golden handcuffs
5. Paterson's banding criterion

Definitions

A. A way of devising a system of internal

differentials between various levels of pay, for various jobs, based on some form of scale.

B. Analysing jobs by component parts and then allocating a score to each component.

C. The process of banding that is based on decision-making.

D. The system of negotiation that allows a few to represent the interests of a larger group.

E. The payment of a benefit that keeps an employee within an organisation regardless of their ability.

Short answer questions

1. Define the terms.
   (a) differentials
   (b) job-evaluation
   (c) *ad hoc*
   (d) rank
2. Describe what is meant by the Inbucon Concensus Method.
3. What are 'benchmarks'?
4. Briefly outline the major characteristics used in the Hay MSL method of pay determination.
5. Why might you support the adoption of the Paterson Band Approach of wage determination?
6. Explain what is involved in the time-span discretion method.
7. Define:
   (a) worker participation
   (b) red circling
   (c) payment by results
8. How might payment by results be combined with management by objectives?
9. Distinguish between:
   (a) day rate and piece rate
   (b) measured daywork and a fixed incremental scale
10. Outline the principal ways in which an employer can determine his rates of pay.
11. When may an employee be instantly dismissed?
12. Outline the causes of redundancy.
13. Why is redundancy considered a 'costly' exercise?
14. Define:
    (a) natural wastage
    (b) re-training
    (c) grievance procedure
15. What advice for a redunancy procedure would you offer an employer faced with 'laying-off' personnel?
16. Briefly describe the minimum legal entitlements made law under the 1965 Redundancy Payment Act.

35
Manpower planning

Preview

▽ In this chapter the important subject of manpower planning will be analysed. This will centre on the application of planning principles such as requirements, changes and developments.

▽ Firms are also concerned with reacting to changes in manpower requirements and disposing of any surplus and with the various aspects of training and developing existing and, where known, future manpower resources.

The background

The firm is about to be engaged in an area of business that involves morals and events that influence real people's lives. Even without these controversial issues, manpower planning is a complex exercise. Perhaps now is a convenient time to ask why.

- People have minds - they are all individuals.
- They are capable of expressing both individual and collective expressions.

- They are dynamic.
- Their availability varies with economic, social and political conditions.

It is not surprising that such a list tends to make the task of tracing the individual in an organisation who is responsible for manpower planning a rather difficult one. Indeed, in many organisations a 'piece-meal' system has evolved. For example at College Dynamics, manpower needs are currently dealt with as follows:

- *Production manager:* exercises day-to-day control over motivation and discipline and plans holiday cover.
- *Personnel manager:* plans recruitment and training.
- *Operations manager:* dictates team sizes, rota systems and inter-section transfers.

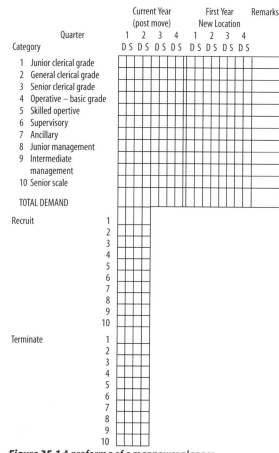

Figure 35.1 *A proforma of a manpower planner*

Alas, the dissolving of control tends to mean that unlike other forms of planning manpower requirements are often less comprehensive, involve some needs being ignored and others merely sketched over. Perhaps the complexity of people partly causes this poor coverage, but some of the blame must lie with the all-too-normal separation of responsibilities. What is certain is that a firm cannot present a series of guidelines in the hope that a single individual or department will put them into practice. They face a difficult task in developing a corporate manpower plan, but its implementation will be even more difficult.

Perhaps a good place to begin this exercise in establishing a new manpower policy is to ask what the purpose and objectives of the newly forged system will be. It will be aiming to ensure that the right numbers and types of manpower are available to meet the current overall company sales and production plan, and will be available to meet future plans. The system will also be responsible for making certain that the company can react favourably to future threats and opportunities and offer job satisfaction to, and assist proper motivation of, all employees. In short a more formal definition may read as follows.

A manpower policy is a set of planning techniques that are concerned with acquiring, developing, utilising and disposing of manpower in the most efficient ways known, ensuring that the right numbers and types of personnel are available and will become available to meet needs and group satisfaction and motivation to employees.

The main objective is to make any change as smooth a process as possible. Personnel must forecast needs regarding quantity and quality of employees required to reach the performance objectives of the other functional areas of the organisation. The planning process attempts to forecast the need, on both a short and long-term basis, in order to achieve the following:

- recruitment needs
- training needs and objectives; staff development
- a planned approach to redundancies and redeployment
- management development and succession planning
- labour cost-planning, including payment systems and levels of productivity
- space requirements; buildings and equipment

Manpower planning is an essential part of the organisational corporate planning process. It is continuous, constantly adjusting and readjusting in just the same way as marketing or finance. It must also react to such changes as population changes, skills changes, competition and technical changes. Most organisations use such a plan to forecast:

- recruitment
- selection
- training

Their policy will concern itself with such issues as:

- Internal promotion and current staff development.
- External appointment.
- Short and long-term job description alterations.
- Training, both its functions and its cost-effectiveness.
- Negotiation of topics such as manning levels, payments, productivity, redundancy and the careful implementation of all agreements.

Internal and external needs

The internal and external labour markets

The first task will be to analyse all those currently 'in post' and build up job descriptions; these can be matched at a later date against the new requirements. A register of each employee's central purpose must be created. This can then be expanded to a detailed *job description*. At this stage in the exercise the firm must think about why each job exists. By asking the question they are forcing themselves to look more closely at both duties and time spent.

Next they must look at the groupings of responsibilities. Realignment may be possible, especially among higher grade personnel. Certain key ratios may be used:

Labour turnover

Wastage rate

This is the number of employees per annum leaving the firm, as a percentage of the average number per department, section, etc., employed during a period, e.g., month or year:

$$\text{Wastage rate} = \frac{\text{Number of employees leaving the firm per annum}}{\text{Average number of employees per department section}} \times 100$$

Stability index

This is a measure of the number of employees who have remained within the firm for more than one year and is calculated as follows:

$$\text{Stability index} = \frac{\text{Number of employees with one years service}}{\text{Number of employees with the firm one year ago}} \times 100$$

By identifying high wastage and turnover the firm can trace signs of problems and seek reasons for these. These could include:

- general working conditions
- poor supervision, bad management/worker relations, or inadequate management
- poor induction, lack of direction of work force
- poor job expectations and prospects.

External features may also influence labour turnover. This may involve:

- better employment prospects elsewhere
- better conditions offered elsewhere
- a poor worker perception of the company

A high turnover of labour is a costly problem and may well lead to more serious problems. Costs incurred include:

- lost recruitment and selection costs
- training, administrative and induction costs
- lost productivity during training, induction and replacement
- costs of sub-contracting work, overtime or diversions of skilled labour
- scrapped or spoiled work

Nevertheless, total stability of the labour force produces stagnation and a loss of the essential dynamic element within the work force.

Sickness and accident rates

By calculating sickness and accident rates the firm can cost the days lost through them and may compare them on an interdepartmental or inter-company basis.

By calculating the average number of accidents that can be expected per employee's working life comparisons can be made. These can be against individuals, firms and industries. Above average readings may indicate:

- unsatisfactory working conditions or safety standards
- lack of supervision or poor management
- inadequate safety training
- the employment of unsatisfactory workers.

Costs are always central to employee effectiveness, so the firm must analyse how much employment actually costs them and whether they are investing the shareholders' money wisely. They

may also look at the proportion of their labour which is *direct* and *indirect*. It is also a perfect opportunity to analyse age, sex, length of service, training potential and other features of the labour force.

In most circumstances *corporate planning* will be conducted against a more flexible and less predictable backdrop than that at College Dynamics. Manpower planning must be moulded into corporate planning and shaped to reflect:

- *Financial issues. Turnover, gross and net profit, return on investment.*
- *Product development, both of new and established lines.*
- *Market share. Desired, probable and productivity targets.*
- *Location change.*
- *Employee change. Birth rate, education programmes, internal and external training.*

The more accurate the information, the more successful the planning. The firm will need to constantly test and re-appraise; the 'survey' should not be the only manpower exercise. The corporate policy will shape the manpower needs but, in turn, the manpower plans will influence corporate policy; if the skills required are not found, then further decisions are faced.

By listing job specifications and noting those currently filling them, the firm can establish two important facts:

1. Are they efficient at their assigned tasks?
2. What new tasks will appear in the future?

This will enable the firm to *identify its manpower needs*. Such an exercise is not a once-for-all; a whole range of other factors will enter the calculations. These must include:

- Market fluctuations – demand changes.
- Raw materials availability – production changes.
- Technical advancements – some jobs will go, others will arrive.
- Government policy – Acts quite often create jobs (e.g., the Health and Safety Act).
- Mergers and takeovers – some people will find themselves 'surplus to requirements'.
- Internal changes – strikes, dismissals, resignations.
- Changes in cost of labour relative to other resources – all are vulnerable to the computer!

Obviously some of these changes are foreseeable and can be planned against. Others are more difficult, but the statistical exercises covered elsewhere in the book can be applied. Manpower planning can be subjected to time series analysis (see Chapter 27), probability testing, linear programming and where possible a form of network analysis. Certainly *succession analysis* is the recipient of mathematical testing and the results are used to control the flows of personnel both through the enterprise and to certain specific areas. The length of time an employee spends in one department will be influenced by where they are supposed to be within the corporate structure at a certain date.

Manpower supply

Internal

The firm is trying to identify its existing manpower position and to predict what proportion (and where possible, who) of their existing workforce will remain with them. What information will they need to know?

- *Age* – concentrations, imbalances.
- *Skills* – both broad (clerical) and specific (computer literacy)
- *Training* – how can you concentrate and improve existing employees, monitor advancement and improve new arrivals?
- *Turnover* – relate leaving to age, reason for leaving and length of stay. This is a major indicator for waste control.
- *Succession* – who will succeed who and when.

College Dynamics is not large enough to support a single manpower planning department, but personnel will have to liaise with the corporate planning department when setting its objectives.

Once again, CD is building up a picture of what it has and then it can compare this with what it will be aiming to achieve. This in turn will dictate its training and development programmes.

CD must also monitor what is available outside the company, and how it intends to recruit its future requirements.

External

The information required here is considerable. Among the data that will be collected are:

- Population profiles within a certain radius of the firm. Such variables as density, age and sex ratios, occupational categories, socioeconomic grouping, residential developments and the expected growth prospects will be collated.
- The education system and its output.

- Local employment levels.
- Skills profiles within the area.
- Competition for recruits, current rates of pay.
- Local transport facilities and attitudes to travel.

Obviously, a lot of information will be required in order that CD can make the decisions as to the ability of current staff to meet future requirements and where new recruitment will be needed.

When the company has arrived at a manpower plan it must put it to good use. One of the major uses to which it can put its findings is *long-term planning*. Its records must now contain details on:

- natural wastage
- redundancies
- recruitment
- internal transfers
- training
- promotions

Timing will be essential, so that CD's short-term requirements can be planned in detail and the long-term in outline. Once again, the corporate plan must be taken into account. Why should CD bother with such records?

- Sudden actions usually cost more money.
- Employers have a moral responsibility to announce changes as early as is possible.

Effective manpower planning will also concentrate on *shift* planning. Systems must be devised to give maximum coverage and to allow for different team sizes at different times during the week. The rotas have to be balanced so that over a period each rota covers an identical pattern and so that from the individual's position the maximum number of working shifts and the changeover from one shift to another are reasonable. They must seek opinions on such issues as the most acceptable period between people's rest days.

Concluding the exercise

The task of establishing the manpower needs of College Dynamics is drawing to a conclusion, but before it announces its findings it must check certain features of the exercise.

The first area to scrutinise is that of the *information* flow that has been used. Beware of people fitting their objectives to suit what they think you want to hear, and of others seeing the exercise as a thin disguise for redundancies. Both sides should be involved in the process as early as possible, so promoting their involvement and hopefully their understanding.

A further problem with College Dynamics is that it has no previous experience of planning at the corporate level. Hopefully, this exercise has established the need for planning elsewhere in the organisation.

CD has assumed that the information it has used is accurate; if it is not CD will know who to blame!

College Dynamics has probably been pushed into the real world of collating data that refer to the labour market – remember accurate information produces efficient management. It has carried out the exercise in a short space of time and without the use of experts. Both might be considered somewhat risky.

Despite all its planning, uncertainty still exists; all it can do is monitor trends and be prepared to react. By conducting a sound manpower analysis it has constructed a firm base from which to make future predictions.

CASE STUDY 35.1

Manpower planning – creating the supply

College Dynamics has evolved quickly and at no time did the senior management ever sit down and formally decide on a recruitment policy. Its continued expansion means that it must now address the need for a clearly defined policy on seeking recruits to the company.

Imagine that you have been given the responsibility of preparing a short report on the policy options open to College Dynamics and the advantages and disadvantages of the routes open to the company.

Your report should be presented in the form of a memorandum and forwarded to the Personnel Manager.

SUMMARY

Having studied this chapter, you should be able to:

▼ Understand the construction of a manpower plan.

▼ Explain internal/external sources of personnel.

▼ Describe how a manpower plan is used.

Questions and activities

Technical terms and glossary

In the section below you are given a series of technical terms and their meanings. They have been scrambled. You must match up the terms and definitions. When you have correctly paired them, transfer them to your alphabetical vocabulary or glossary book.

You are also advised to transfer the definitions obtained during the exercises in the case studies into this glossary book.

Technical terms

1. Labour turnover
2. Stability index
3. Manpower needs
4. Direct and indirect labour
5. Succession analysis

Definitions

A. Sources of recruitment.
B. A measure that determines how long employees are staying with the firm.
C. A plan that determines who will fulfil certain jobs when they fall vacant.

D. The number of employees leaving the firm per annum.

E. A plan to forecast the demand for and supply of employees.

Short answer questions

1. Why must we consider people as being different from machines?

2. Outline what you understand by the term 'manpower policy'.

3. What are the major targets of a manpower planning process?

4. Define the labour wastage rate. Why might a Personnel Manager be interested in such a ratio?

5. Briefly describe the 'external' features which may influence labour turnover.

6. Why might a 'high' labour turnover prove a costly exercise for a company?

7. What is meant by (a) direct labour? (b) indirect labour?

8. How must manpower planning be moulded into Corporate Planning and what other issues must it reflect?

9. Outline the information needed to construct an 'internal' manpower supply analysis.

10. Define
    (a) succession analysis
    (b) stability index
    (c) skills profiles

Data response questions

A company has recently moved from its traditional site in the centre of a town to a newly opened industrial estate on the outskirts of the town. Following the move there has been a sudden increase in the level of labour turnover.

1. As personnel manager, write a report to the managing director, using a suitable format to cover the following areas. (6 marks)
   (i) How labour turnover may be calculated. (2 marks)
   (ii) Why the company should be concerned about the recent increase in labour turnover. (7 marks)
   (iii) Possible reasons for the increase. (6 marks)

2. What steps would you, as personnel manager, need to take to establish clearly the nature of the problem? (6 marks)

(Associated Examining Board, Business Studies (A) Paper 1, June 1987)

36

Industrial relations, trade unions and employers' organisations

Preview

▼ Industrial relations cover the economic, social and political relationships which exist between management, employees and government. It includes the relationships of such organisations as the Trades Union Congress, the Confederation of British Industry and various government departments and ministries.

▼ The functions of trade unions are important to the smooth working of all industrial relations.

▼ Our objectives in this chapter are:

– to develop an outline of the range of industrial relations

– to describe the various functions of trade unions

– to briefly outline the role of trade unions in modern economies

– to compare and contrast the functions and services of unions with those of employers organisations.

Introduction

Let us begin by outlining what is meant by the term 'industrial relations'.

Industrial relations

The relationships that exist between the various parties that are involved in the 'commercial world' are becoming ever more complex. Companies have now expanded to cover national and international markets and it is no longer easy to analyse one company as a sole entity.

The term 'industrial relations' can be used in two ways:

1. To include all the various social and human relations that evolve between individuals, managers and employees, trade unions officials, members of work groups, etc., within the industrial environment.

2. To include the more formal structures and procedures which develop through collective bargaining, rules, procedures, discipline requirements and other regulations.

In essence, industrial relations are mainly concerned with *conflicts of interest* between managers, employees and government. If the central feature seems to rest on conflict, then it is true to say that much of the detail concerns itself with communications, resolving disputes, and seeking compromise. Industrial relations are in a constant state of flux, and it is important to keep up to date with developments through newspapers and relevant journals.

The structure of trade unions

The evolution of trade unions has tended to run in parallel with industrial development. In the nineteenth century unions were often craft based, small and aimed at trying to achieve reasonable working conditions for members. The craft unions concentrated on restrictive practices (preventing other workers, who were not members of the union, from performing the work done by union members). This in turn tended to keep wages relatively high. Traditional crafts are now in decline and this is reflected in the trend within union structures to represent more general skills as required by scientific-based technology.

Another feature of the Industrial Revolution in Britain was the development of 'general unions'. As workers moved into the new industrial towns of the North, so the need for 'representation' emerged. Working conditions were poor and exploitation undoubtedly took place.

The twentieth century has seen the emergence of industrial unions, which attempt to recruit members of whatever skill, trade, etc., that work within one industry. Such unions normally show characteristics of:

- Highly specialist workers that cannot be easily transferred to another industry.
- Promotion takes place within the same industry.
- The 'tight-knit' structure produces well-organised unions that often have considerable political strength.

Another fairly recent development has been the emergence of 'white-collar unions'. These unions normally embrace grades of workers who would probably classify themselves as 'staff'. Such industries as banking, insurance and teaching now have large percentages of their participants in various trade unions. The growth in this type of trade union is apparent in most industrialised countries, and several social and economic reasons appear to have promoted their development. These include:

- The success of 'blue-collar unions' (craft, general and industrial unions) in improving working conditions for their members has been a natural spur to other sectors to organise.
- The fear of pay differential erosion between clerical workers and manual or semi-skilled workers has led to many seeking the strength of union membership.
- Technology has changed many traditional occupations. Automation has reduced the status of some workers; once again they have sought security from trade union membership.

- Public sector industries have encouraged union membership.

There has therefore been a general tendency for unionism to increase and for the size of the unions to grow in response to the growth and size of manufacturing and commercial concerns, economic conditions and changes in the relationships of one class of worker with another. The trends now seem centred on 'open' access to unions, where they will accept all classes and grades of workers and pure 'pay negotiation' may no longer be the preoccupation of union officials.

Positions within a trade union

Shop steward

Trade union organisation is centred on the place of work and the post responsible for representing workers at this level is the shop steward. This position is elected, and normally voluntary and unpaid, though some senior shop stewards are paid a salary. Election of a shop steward has to be ratified by the union. Under the Employment Protection Act 1975 a shop steward must be allowed time off to carry out his duties. These duties include:

- collection of union dues from members
- encouraging union membership
- furthering the objectives, policies and instructions of the union
- dealing with grievances that arise at the workplace
- negotiating with management
- representing the union and work force to management
- acting as an intermediary between work force and management
- acting as an intermediary between employees and official union representation
- representing the union at various committees that monitor workplace safety, etc.

Their essential role is to represent the members of the union and like all officials they have a variety of 'sanctions' at their disposal. How they use these tends to rest on the nature of the relationship between the steward and 'the management'. A well-informed and able shop steward can

- settle local disputes quickly and without resort to lengthy negotiations or Head Office intervention
- keep issues to the workplace and not allow a 'mushrooming effect' to take over
- be a 'sound-board' for management regarding possible future policy
- be the link between management and workers for

an ever-increasing level of skill, technical ability and awareness among working people.

The shop steward does have restrictions on the use of power and influence:

- Remember, the post is voluntary and they are subject to annual re-election. So, they have to stay 'popular'.
- Company policy, e.g. pay restraint, has to be followed, and as the recognised voice of the union, reaction to such a policy may not make the steward very popular with the rest of the employees. Energetic shop stewards can encounter difficulties from foremen, supervisors and even junior management, as their presence may be seen as a 'threat'.

District and Executive Committees

The local branch of the union elects members to the district committee, which is usually headed by a full-paid district secretary, who in turn passes resolutions to the annual conference. The Executive Committee is responsible for the day-to-day affairs of the union. It is based at Head Office, where a permanent staff are under the control of a General Secretary. Members are elected for periods of one to five years and the range normally reflects geographical, trade and male/female membership ratios. The Executive Committee carries out the following functions:

1. to generally administer the union
2. to control union funds
3. to take responsibility for wages, and negotiations and conditions of employment at national level, and consider the effects of national economic policy on their numbers.

Conference

The senior policy-making forum of a union is its annual conference. Here the Executive Committee and elected representatives of local branches debate and pass resolutions that will shape future policy.

Trades Union Conference (TUC)

Unity is the essential feature of union influence, and in 1868 a central, organising body was founded. It was known as the Trades Union Congress. Its main functions are:

1. To debate and formulate national policy on issues involving wages, conditions and all things economic and political which affect union members.
2. To influence government economic and financial policies.

3. To promote, as does any other pressure group, a favourable image of trade unions.
4. To provide research, publicity and representative facilities for all affiliated unions.

The TUC is not affiliated to the Labour Party and it does not generate a political fund, neither does it discriminate against members who may prefer the philosophy of other political parties. The total membership of the TUC is approximately 8.5 million.

The day-to-day affairs of the TUC are controlled by a General Council, which consists of 35 members representing the trades into which the affiliated unions are classified. They are elected to office by the annual congress, and their functions include:

- The approval of all industrial, economic and legislative matters involving the movement.
- The co-ordinating activities for the trade union movement in general.
- Dealing with inter-union relations and disputes.
- Monitoring a liaison with government and the Confederation of British Industry.

Trade unions and society

The trade union movement exists to further the interests of its members and to improve the general conditions of employment in industry.

As such it represents only a proportion of what may be called society, but then so do employers and managers. Modern enterprise is very complex and the interrelated nature of all industrial and social enterprises compel both unions and employers to consider their wider responsibilities to the welfare of society at large.

How trade unions have helped shape society:

1. They have produced a steady improvement in basic wages and conditions, regardless of whether the workers are unionised or not.
2. They have contributed considerably to the advancements made in universal education, health care and the standards of health, safety and hygiene now apparent in all types of workplace.
3. They have helped raise living standards and have therefore increased levels of demand for goods and services. This has contributed to the long-term profitability of firms in which members earn their living.

Against these advantages, which call for careful consideration, can be set several disadvantages:

1. A loss of individual freedom as the worker signs into a body that requires solid unity.

2. The possibility of 'militancy' and various practices (demarcation disputes and inter-union rivalry) that may actually harm wage standards and job security.
3. The democratic structure can only be truly open if all participate, and unions, like other organisations, do suffer from apathy among members. This, in turn, may lead to a small minority dictating the policy that will affect the majority.

Employers' organisations

Individual employers normally join together for two purposes:

1. To attempt to influence employee/employer relations involving conditions of work, remuneration, and other trade union matters.
2. To attempt to influence matters of trade between firms, such as pricing, supply and relations with government.

Most employer organisations have 'federated' status, i.e. by becoming a member the firm agrees to accept certain rules and policy statements. Some small firms belong to 'non-federated' organisations, whil some very large organisations remain unattached to any one concern.

Of the nearly 2,000 employer organisations in the UK the following is an approximation of membership terms:

- A member has to work in the particular industry.
- The firm must be prepared to cooperate with the association, and abide by its rules and policy decisions.
- The business must provide proof it is reputable

Firms that fail to meet such requirements may be subject to:

- a public statement being made by the federation that voices disapproval
- expulsion
- withdrawal of the special facilities offered by the federation
- denial of access to the association's strike fund

Membership of a trade association or federation normally affords the firm the services of:

- information exchange between members
- common action in reaction to specific circumstances
- special research facilities
- formal representation of views and interests in discussions with trade unions

- assistance in negotiating, especially when a dispute arises
- assistance in dealing with industrial relations problems
- negotiations of a common pay structure throughout the industry
- representations of employers' interests to government and official bodies.

Like trade unions, employers' associations have a small number of permanent and semi-permanent officials, arranged in a hierarchical system of local, regional and national committees.

Confederation of British Industry (CBI)

This was formed by an amalgamation of various federations in 1965. The Royal charter of the CBI lays down its principal objectives as:

1. The production of general financial, economic, fiscal, industrial, commercial, labour and social welfare policy.
2. To act as a point of reference for all those institutions seeking the views of employers within industry.
3. To develop the contribution of industry to the national economy.
4. To develop the efficiency of British industry and to provide the services necessary for this.
5. To maintain a close relationship with government and trade union bodies.

The membership of the CBI is diverse, covering over 12,000 individual manufacturing firms, over 300 trade associations and employer's associations, banks, wholesalers, retailers and distributors, as well as the major nationalised industries. It is governed by a Central Council, which like the TUC is representative of the membership. Its daily work is also done by a number of specialist committees, covering all aspects of economic, industrial, commercial and political life. It also has representatives overseas, e.g. Brussels.

Remuneration and conditions

In this section we will:

- cover what is meant by remuneration
- describe and analyse the major methods of payments used
- briefly cover the law relating to equal pay
- outline the conditions of work normally evident in companies.

Remuneration

A payment made by an employer to an employee for time spent at the workplace actually involved in tasks for which the employee is formally paid, or for actual work done, is known as a *wage*. There are two basic forms of remuneration, namely:

1. A wage based on time, which is normally expressed as a rate per hour.
2. A piece rate system in which work is paid according to the number of tasks completed, or pieces of work finished.

Whichever system is chosen, it determines the *basic rate* of pay.

Most wage systems now operating are a mixture of the two. To increase the basic rate employers can:

1. Establish a basic minimum rate of pay. This can be negotiated at national, industry or plant level.
2. Pay a 'waiting-time', this is often used in piece-rate scales, as workers lose money if delays occur which are not their fault.
3. Pay overtime or multiple payments (e.g. double time) for work done outside of normal working hours. It is paid at a higher rate than the normal working rate.
4. Pay a shift-payment for employees working night, evening or unsociable hours.
5. Allow 'special payments' for such things as dirty conditions, hazards or a special condition to the job.
6. Award 'seniority payments' for long service, age or retention in the company.
7. Pay 'cost of living allowances' to compensate for increases in basic prices.
8. Offer 'bonus payments' for extra productivity.
9. Offer various other payments for travelling, special clothing, or luncheon vouchers.

The workers always need to be aware of their 'extras' growing faster than their normal basic rate, for this can make them vulnerable to income falls if demand for the firm's products drop. The increase in extras above basic rate is known as *wage drift*, and is a common feature during periods of cost-push inflation (see Chapter 43).

Payment by result

An efficient wage system tries to relate awards earned to the actual production achieved by the individual worker. Normally, this means that the more you produce the more you earn. The majority of what are known as payment by result (PBR) schemes involve the employee receiving a basic rate for the job, and in addition a payment which varies with output.

Most PBR schemes are based on thorough job analysis and evaluation, which in turn allows for standard times to be decided upon. Additional payments are then made if the standard, or normal time is reached with set targets met.

The advantages of PBR are:

- With no increase in the work force the productivity increases.
- The work study needed to evaluate the scheme usually produces a better method of production which will increase efficiency.
- The extra incentives tend to require less supervision and disciplinary procedures virtually disappear.
- In industries where the work can be accurately measured the output increases.

This last point illustrates some of the problems encountered by PBR. Generally, there has been a decline in the use of PBR schemes for the following reasons:

- It is difficult to determine how much productivity is influenced by better working conditions, machine type, work study, etc. As such the standard output is difficult to set.
- Keeping the momentum going after initial successes tends to be difficult.
- The needed flexibility of workers can lead to transferred workers finding themselves actually losing money. As production schedules alter, or as products change, so individuals find their rewards alter.
- Setting uniform standard rates can be difficult and may be open to charges of 'favouritism'.
- Successful earners in non-supervisory grades may earn more than junior managers, and that can also cause tension.
- Maintenance staff are not often paid by PBR, and can earn less than operative employees. Good maintenance obviously influences productive capacity, so allowing operative workers to earn good bonuses. To try to overcome this problem some managements pay a 'lieu bonus' to maintenance workers, i.e. they receive a bonus influenced by the operative output.
- Once a PBR system has been set up, workers quickly establish their own work norms irrespective of the standard set for the job by analysis. Groups produce their own rates and sanctions against those who fail to meet them, e.g. damage to personal possessions. By making a low 'norm' the workers guarantee their employment so maintaining group unity and reducing work pressure.

- Safety standards and the quality of work may suffer.
- Friction may arise if individual earnings fluctuate owing to bottle necks caused by other workers or systems.

Group bonus schemes

Instead of setting output targets, some companies set a bonus for the group as a whole. There are several advantages to this type of scheme. These are:

- Group morale and cohesion is maintained
- Where the work group consists of people who possess different levels of skill this PBR system can be used. It also allows for job rotation for those willing to move from one type of job to another within the team.

These schemes normally work best where the group number is small and skill differences are minimal. An extension of a group bonus scheme is to use the basic idea to cover the whole factory, so that the bonus is given and divided if total factory production exceeds a given figure.

Measured day work

Another criticism of PBR schemes is that the main thrust for higher productivity rests entirely on workers. Measured day work offers higher wages in return for higher productivity and, as the enterprise has committed itself in advance to increased wage costs, management is forced to provide a steady flow of work and remove all obstacles to efficient production. One of the merits of this type of scheme is that supervisors are given a vital role to play, in that they, and junior management, are made responsible for checking reasons for individual failure to reach the required production target.

Salaries

A salary is a payment made to a member of the firm's staff. It is normally a fixed payment, paid at the end of a calendar month usually directly into the recipient's bank account. A salary rarely includes the additional payments included in a wage. A salary usually increases in steps as the recipient grows older, increases in experience, or receives promotion. A certain amount of outmoded class attitude surrounds the differences between wages and salaries. The former are the domain of the labourer, whilst white-collar workers receive a salary. In reality the distinction is blurred for the following reasons:

- In some industries wages are higher than salaries

- Wages are now often paid by cheque

Redundancy and employment legislation have now increased the security of wage earners. White-collar workers now suffer redundancies, indeed they often score more highly than wage earners. This trend may have been a major reason behind the unionisation of white-collar workers.

Some salary earners receive payments for the length and complexity of their training. The qualifications they need to fulfil their jobs are used by some salary earners to justify part of what they earn, e.g. doctors and accountants. It is therefore difficult for salary structures and yearly increases to be related to productivity. This tends to be compounded by part of the work not being directly equitable with productivity, e.g. supervisors fulfil many complex roles, and not all are easily related to output increases. One of the reasons for the traditional confidentiality of salary rates is that rates are not always related to identifiable and rational aspects of the production process.

In recent years, job evaluation and work study have been applied to salaried jobs and the most widespread scheme being used is known as *merit rating*. This attempts to reward staff for their intrinsic worth to the company, or for the complexity and responsibility of the job done. Tasks are normally analysed into skills, qualifications, experience, knowledge, span or responsibility, creativity, etc. A scale is established, e.g. 1 to 10, and each aspect of a job is allocated points and individual employees are then ranked according to their performance in the posts. Each range of points refers to a salary scale and the work's basic salary scale fixed accordingly. Such schemes need maximum backing from staff associations and trade unions, as there will always remain an element of subjectivity in any system.

Payment of wages and salaries

How an employer pays an employee is basically covered by the Truck Acts (1831–1940) which stresses that workers should be paid by 'coins of the realm'. However, deductions can be made for: lodgings, medical facilities, food cooked and provided by the employer, fines for spoilt work or lateness, subscriptions to relevant bodies or journals and statutory deductions (e.g. income tax). An amendment in 1960 allowed for payment to be made by cheque, giro, bank credit, money or postal order, if the employee gives their written consent.

Equal Pay Act 1970

This Act requires equal pay to be given to men and

women where they are employed in identical work, or in work of exactly the same value as established by job evaluation. Failure to implement equal pay schemes can result in the employers being made to pay arrears of up to two years' pay or damages, as determined by an industrial tribunal.

In the future the United Kingdom will become more integrated into Europe via the European Single Market. The European Union tends to have substantial amounts of social and economic legislation. This should lead to a gradual erosion in the differences between male and female rates of pay. Such a move for equality may result in increased wage costs as more women enter the work force. A further possible consequence may be yet more pressure on female pay rates to rise as women are sought to fill the gaps not being filled by a decline in young workers. The range of facilities now being offered by employers to potential female employees continues to grow.

Conditions of work

Historically, conditions or terms of employment have concentrated on two main elements, namely, hours of work and holiday entitlements. However, we will include analysis of fringe benefits, holiday entitlements, and pension schemes. We have already covered redundancy payments and health and safety will follow later in this chapter.

Hours of work

Under law there is no legal restriction on how long an adult may work. The *Factory Acts* cover women and young persons, and place some restrictions on overtime and holiday entitlements. Some categories of male, adult workers have restrictions imposed on them by statute, e.g. airline pilots, lorry drivers and shop assistants.

In most occupations the trend in working hours has been to see a reduction. The average working week has fallen from 44 to between 38 to 40 hours per week, and it may fall to near 35 hours before the end of the century. The continued reduction in working hours is supported by those who believe it:

• reduces boredom and fatigue and actually boosts the quality of production
• increases the quality of workers' leisure activities
• forces management to install technology so boosting output
• forces unions to accept productivity related pay deals
• will ration what work is available as work becomes less in total, with machines taking over, and a

shortening in the working week.

For some workers anomalies still exist, these include:

1. Longer average working weeks still exist for manual workers.
2. As working weeks have declined so overtime payments have risen.

The first point is a direct reflection of the attitude shown to manual workers. The second seems to be the result of the need to meet fluctuations in demand, the need to maintain productivity despite a shortage of labour, to allow for maintenance to be carried out and to supplement basic pay rates for shop-floor workers. (Perhaps the real reason centres more on inefficiency, high labour costs and low basic rates, but that is not part of this chapter!)

Shift work

There has been a move to expand this in some industries, as it is considered more economic to run a plant on a continuous 24-hour basis. This, in turn, requires workers to operate the machinery on a shift basis. To meet demand and pay back capital costs employers are increasingly under pressure to produce in long runs. They therefore resort to:

1. a continuous three or four shift system, so allowing for a 168-hour week
2. a permanent night shift
3. an evening shift that uses mainly part-time workers
4. variations of the above.

Shift work does have the advantages of continuous work at full capacity, so providing the opportunity for higher earnings, increased productivity and reduced overtime, but there are problems, e.g.

1. Maintenance costs may rise as machines are under constant use.
2. Mechanical failures in one shift may be blamed on other shifts, so causing internal conflict.
3. Welfare facilities, e.g. a canteen, have to be provided for all shifts.
4. Public transport may not be easily obtained when the night shift operatives require it.
5. Constant exposure to night work may cause fatigue and even upset the body's metabolism. An individual's social and home life may also suffer.

Flexitime

In recent years a growing number of firms have introduced a system where the employees have some control over when they start and finish work. Generally, the following conditions apply:

- A core time is agreed upon, and all workers must be present during that time. Outside the core time they are free to arrive and leave as they wish.
- Lunch breaks can be varied.
- The normal starting time is not before 8.00 am and the normal leaving time is not after 7.00 pm.
- A standard number of working hours must be recorded during an accounting period (e.g. one month).
- Hours worked over and above the standard period may be converted into holidays.

Flexitime has been most easily adopted in commercial and service industries. It has received less favourable application in the manufacturing sector. Its main advantage is, of course, flexibility, and this helps improve morale, reduce absenteeism, sickness rates and staff turnover. It has proven very popular where a large proportion of the workforce are women and have family commitments.

Fringe benefits

Fringe benefits which, unlike a wage, can be paid in kind, include company cars, subsidised meals, cost price company products, low interest mortgages and many other advantages.

The company hopes to attract high calibre staff, retain their services and keep morale and motivation high. There is a risk of envy and jealousy and once they have been awarded they are almost impossible to remove. They do allow workers to receive an 'increase', even when the law bans money increases in wages and salaries.

Negotiating and collective bargaining

In this section we will concentrate on:

- Explaining and analysing the nature of collective bargaining at the workplace.
- Describing the main forms of industrial action used by unions within the free bargaining process.
- Explaining the role of the state in industrial bargaining.

Collective bargaining

The term applies to any situation in which a group negotiates with another group to decide wages, salaries and conditions of work. Terms agreed by

such negotiations have been freely entered into by the parties and are normally considered morally binding on all parties (see Figure 36.1).

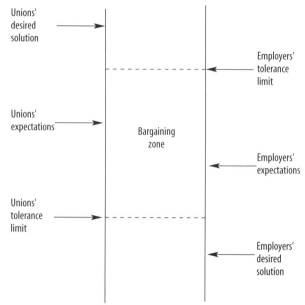

Figure 36.1 *Desires, expectations and tolerance limits that determine the bargaining zone*

In most factories, plants and offices, collective bargaining concentrates on wage levels, working conditions, disciplinary procedures and negotiations as to the amount of work to be done by particular groups over a given work period. The negotiations normally involve representatives from both management and unions, and the latter may be represented by the shop steward. Recent trends have moved towards greater use of local bargaining as they allow for accurate representation. Conditions can be based on the local conditions, so allowing for accuracy, specific knowledge, speed of decision-making and on enhancement in status for those who conclude the discussions.

At an 'industry' level the process involves union representatives and employer's federation representatives and are common in industries that rely on time-rate rather than piece rates. This type of bargaining tends to concentrate more on establishing minimum and maximum sums leaving final details for local or plant level resolution. By deciding on the limits the process should help reduce wage drift and the opportunity for excessive local demands.

Some companies are not covered by either formal wage council bargaining or by industrial councils. They rely on direct talks with their own workers.

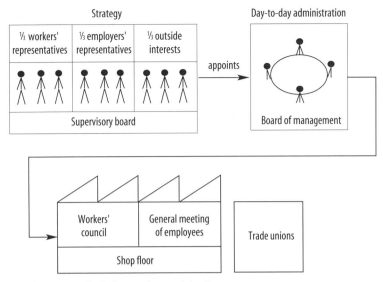

Figure 36.2 Possible two-tier company including worker participation

In the United Kingdom an example of this is Ford (UK) Co.

Another trend that has become established in bargaining procedures is the concentration on productivity agreements. These schemes link pay awards to the achieving of genuine productivity increases. They may also be based on: removing excessive overtime, abolishing demarcation lines, reducing the number of workers performing each task and generally trying to increase efficiency, job mobility and the standard of output per worker. In turn, workers expect to gain higher and more stable rates of pay, increased holidays, higher fringe benefits and some insurance against redundancy once overtime claims have been reduced.

Productivity agreements have also become necessary as:

- There has been an increased need to lower costs to remain competitive.
- Successive governments have tried to control inflation by keeping price rises to a minimum. If profit margins are to remain satisfactory, then costs must be controlled.
- There is a continued need to try to get more people employed, to reduce the waste of unemployment.

Industrial conflict

Both individuals and groups have different expectations and objectives. In a free society people are free to air their views. This is probably bound to cause conflict, so it is not surprising that much of the image portrayed by industrial relations seldom seems to rest on harmony.

Representing one group's interest may lead individuals into difficult negotiations, and if these talks are not satisfactorily resolved certain courses of action may occur.

Non-strike action

To strike, or withdraw labour, is normally the last resort. Other courses of action exist. They include:

1. *Go slow.* This is where workers consciously slow down the rate at which they work.
2. *Work to rule.* When workers perform no extra duties other than those which they are legally required to do. Every rule and regulation is interpreted as it is written, so reducing any cooperation and slowing down the average rate of work.
3. *Blacking.* This involves refusing to handle goods, materials, parts, etc., that have come from, or are destined for, a sector of the industry in dispute with management.
4. *Secondary picketing.* This relatively recent development, which is now largely illegal, involved members of one union picket trying to stop workers not directly involved in the dispute from entering their place of work. Such action was designed to dislocate the output yet further.

Other tactics which may arise when relations are strained include: increased sickness rates, absenteeism, accidents at work, increased labour turnover, a decline in quality and excessive waste.

Strike action

The withdrawal of labour has traditionally been the last resort open to workers in disputes with management. Until comparatively recently it was seldom used by grades of worker above the manual/unskilled labourer, but now it is a tactic of other grades as well. This change seems to have been influenced by:

- The success among manual operatives in obtaining higher wage levels.
- The need for non-manual workers to maintain differentials as the manual category caught up with them.
- The greater involvement of women in the campaign to achieve better conditions at work.
- The awareness that group action usually succeeds where individual action no longer does.

There are quite a number of different types of strike action. They are:

1. *The official strike.* This is when all legal requirements have been met for calling a strike (see later) and a satisfactory conclusion has not been reached. The strike receives full union backing, and strikers may receive union strike pay.
2. *General strike.* Here, the whole trade union movement withdraws its labour on a national scale. This is a drastic situation, and has only happened once, in 1926.
3. *Lightning strike.* This means an immediate stoppage, without due notice. The work force usually 'downs tools' and leaves the premises. They are rare, and normally flare up quickly. Most are settled quickly.
4. *National strike.* This is when all members of one union strike on a national basis.
5. *Sit down strike.* Here, the workers stop work but refuse to leave the premises. Strictly speaking, such disputes are illegal.
6. *Sympathetic strikes.* This is when the workers have no immediate disagreement with their own employers, but withdraw labour in support for workers in other industries or plants.
7. *Token strike.* These tend to be short and specific, say one hour on a particular issue. They indicate the attitude of people, and perhaps serve as a warning that something needs to be done – quickly!

8. *Unofficial strike.* This is when union members take strike action without official union backing or support. They are often locally based and are called as a result of a particular incident.

Why do strikes happen?

Almost all strikes are the result of a series of complex and sometimes confusing events. It is difficult to identify a single issue in many strikes, although the majority occurring in 1994/5 were due to the imposition of new contracts containing controversial items like wage reductions. Often the strike is the final event in a long-running dispute. We can group probable causes into:

1. *Immediate and recognisable issues.* These tend to be obvious, e.g. a grievance regarding working conditions.
2. *Socio-economic issues.* These may result from reactions to the effects of inflation, employment levels, prices, living standards or some techno-logical change.
3. *Inter-union disputes.* These may arise from competing shop stewards trying for leadership, which in turn causes rivalry at shop floor level. Sometimes, union leaders have conflicts, and this may lead to industrial action.
4. *Management action.* Such difficult issues as redundancy or discipline may cause a reaction, as might the need to introduce more democratic and consultative methods of regulating working arrangements.
5. *Political ideology.* Few examples exist of this. Workers may well disagree with government policy, but they normally use democratic means to register this.

Research suggests that in most industries strikes are caused by a mixture of:

- unfair, irrational and chaotic wage structures
- slow or inadequate grievance procedures
- union rivalry within plants

Most industries suffer few, if any strikes, and maintain production on a constant basis.

How do we stop strikes?

Some countries have resorted to strict legal controls over strikes, but wide-ranging research suggests that this approach tends only to increase bitterness.

A Royal Commission on Industrial Relations in 1968 suggested that strikes in British Society could be reduced by:

1. introducing a ballot before strikes could be called
2. a cooling-off period being introduced before a strike could be called
3. negotiations being concentrated at local level
4. management concentrating on 'participative' styles
5. unions being re-designed to reflect industries and not skills.

Perhaps some form of 'non-strike agreement' should be introduced? A number of white-collar unions have negotiated 'no strike' agreements. From a union point of view these have a number of advantages:

- The sheer cost and dislocation of strikes does not benefit anyone.
- Regular wage increases can be incorporated as part of the agreement.
- Fringe benefits can be included in the package.

Management also gain from such agreements, as they have guarantees on output and can plan ahead assured of little chance of serious disruption. Alas, 'blue-collar' and 'manual workers' seem less keen to enter such agreements. The old suspicions continue, and both 'sides' do not seem to trust one another.

Industrial relations and the state

Few governments, regardless of their beliefs, have been keen on involving themselves in industrial relations.

State intervention has tended to concentrate on:

- stopping blatant abuse or exploitation
- protecting the weakest members of society
- introducing regulations and organisations designed to reduce tensions.

Membership of the European Union (EU) has also resulted in our participation in some Europe-wide initiatives, such as the establishment of European Worker Committees (EWCs).

Various Acts have entered the Statute Book. These include:

The Industrial Relations Act 1971

The Act was intended to cover:

- The rights of employees to a formal contract of employment and terms of service.
- Regulations of trade unions and employer associations.
- A reform of collective bargaining.
- Legal procedures for the conduct of and use of strikes.

- The setting up of an Industrial Relations Court and Industrial Tribunals to regulate the conduct of industrial relations.

The Act also established an industrial relations code of practice. This defined the rights of employees. Its main areas of concern were:

1. *The agency shop.* This was a situation where all workers had to belong to a certain union. If they refused, they had to pay a subscription equal to the union due.
2. *The closed shop.* This was a situation where to actually obtain a job at a particular place of work, a worker had to belong to a certain trade union. Such agreements obviously maximised union membership and some managements liked them as they made negotiations simpler. Unions argued that all workers share the benefits of negotiations and should therefore pay for the upkeep of those who represent them. Others felt it was morally wrong to force someone to participate against their will.
3. *Unfair dismissal.* The Act laid down conditions which employers had to satisfy in order to begin dismissal procedures. A course of action had to be agreed, in advance, with both unions and management and every employee had to know the procedure. Employees had also to be informed of what could lead to dismissal and the opportunities for appeal.

The Act was met with considerable hostility from unions, who felt their ability to defend members' rights had been reduced. They also cited loss of shop steward status, and loss of advantages of closed shops.

The Act made collective bargaining legally binding on both employees and unions alike, and although parts of it were later repealed, the 1971 Act still forms the fundamentals of the code of practice on which most United Kingdom industrial relations are based.

Subsequent legislation

1. *Trade Union and Labour Relations Act 1974.* This repealed the 1971 Act and abolished the Industrial Relations Court. Legal immunities were restored to Trade Unions and closed shops legitimised.
2. *Employment Protection Act 1975.* This increased workers' rights to lay-off pay, maternity pay and job reinstatement and time off to carry out union duties and take part in union activities. It established the Employment Appeal Tribunal to hear appeals from the industrial tribunal's findings. It also gave statutory status to the

Advisory, Conciliation and Arbitration Service (ACAS) which was set up in 1975, and widened its powers in helping to avoid and settle industrial disputes. The Act also required employers to consult trades unions about proposed redundancies.

3. *Employment Protection (Consolidation) Act 1978.* This did not alter the existing rights of employees, but consolidated the law on individual employment rights contained in the Acts already mentioned. This Act remains the key Act in current law.

The Employment Act 1980

The objects of this Act, passed by the Conservative government, were to redress the balance of power between the trade union movement and management, and to increase the independence of action and freedom of the individual worker. Although this Act has since been repealed it established many principles and procedures which were to be embodied in later Acts. These include:

Secret ballot

Secret ballots were to be used by unions for any of the five purposes listed below:

1. Decisions to call a strike, or to end a strike, or to initiate other industrial action.
2. Elections to executive committees of the union.
3. Elections of full-time union officials.
4. Amendments to union rules.
5. Decisions on the amalgamation or merger of one trade union with another.

The objective of these provisions was to increase the influence of moderate trade union opinion and, hence, to decrease the power of radical members. (Secret ballots had been a feature of most large unions' methods of conducting business for the previous two years. The National Union of Mineworkers, for example, had used a secret ballot for a number of years.)

Codes of practice

The Employment Secretary was empowered to issue codes of practice, without necessarily having the concurrence of the trade unions. Codes of practice were to be issued on picketing, the closed shop and recognition issues.

Such powers had minimal effects on industrial relations, because:

1. Both the TUC and CBI already issued their own codes.

2. The trade unions had always resisted any attempt to have their affairs regulated by the law.
3. The codes themselves were weak because no actual criminal or civil proceedings could flow from them directly. They could only be referred to in a civil or criminal case that might arise in the normal course of union or management activities.

Exclusion or expulsion from trade unions

Where a trade union membership agreement existed (i.e. a closed shop), an actual or potential employee would be able to complain to an industrial tribunal that application for membership of the union had been refused unreasonably, or that he had been expelled unreasonably from the union. What was 'unreasonable' had to be decided on the merits of the particular case, but mere compliance with union rules would not, in itself, be a test of reasonableness.

Appeals against the tribunal's decision would be made to the Employment Appeal Tribunal on a point of law as well as fact.

Compensation

Where a tribunal finds that an employee has been unreasonably expelled or debarred from joining a union, he can be awarded compensation according to the following provisions:

1. The employee must have attempted to find alternative work, i.e. he must have attempted to mitigate his losses.
2. Deductions can be made for any aggravating circumstances of the case brought about by the action of the employee himself.

Unfair dismissal

Employees who claim that they have been unfairly dismissed must show that they were dismissed, as well as that they qualified for protection. Employers must show that they had a valid reason to dismiss. The burden of proof has shifted slightly; now the employer must show that the dismissal was in accordance with equity and that the substantial merit of the particular case warranted dismissal. The qualifying period before an employee can bring a case is now two years.

This small change in the emphasis of the law is unlikely to have any startling impact on it, or on the justice or injustice done to individual workers. What the section does is to make it marginally easier for an employer to shed new and unsatisfactory employees.

Dismissal and trade union membership

The Act made it unfair to dismiss an employee for refusing to join a trade union on grounds of conscience or other deeply held personal beliefs. The rule applied to existing, as well as to all future closed shops.

Basic awards

An employee who is dismissed unfairly but suffers no loss no longer receives compensation for the unfair dismissal. The basic award is restricted to lost redundancy entitlement, which itself may be cut if:

1. The employee has refused reasonable employment.
2. It appears just to reduce his award because of the complainant's own conduct.

Maternity

The sections of the Act which refer to maternity rights required an entirely new form of documentation to be set up, which is both expensive and time wasting. It was made much harder for a woman to return to work after the birth of her baby.

Picketing

The law has been changed drastically in this respect. To be lawful, a picket must now be:

* in contemplation or furtherance of a trade dispute
* outside or near the picket's own place of work
* carried on by accredited trade union officials
* conducted in an orderly and peaceful fashion.

Secondary picketing

The Act removed the immunity at law of trade union members and officials for induced breach of contract (other than an employment contract) in all cases of secondary action outside the place of work of an employer not directly affected by an industrial dispute with his own work force. This section of the Act was contested bitterly by trade unions.

The Employment Act 1982

This Act has been repealed but again needs our attention because it established many points which were embodied in later Acts.

The main terms of this new Act came into force on 1st December 1982. Its aims are to:

1. Increase the legal protection of people dismissed

from work for not being trade union members in a closed-shop situation.
2. Promote the regular review of closed-shop agreements by the use of a secret ballot of the work force.
3. Prevent clauses from being written into commercial contracts concerning trade union membership and recognition at the place of work.
4. Make trade unions liable for damages if they organise unlawful industrial action (for example secondary picketing).
5. Restrict lawful trade disputes to those between workers and their actual employers about pay and conditions of work only.
6. Encourage consultative machinery to be set up which will allow employers to consult directly with their employees.

The Act repeals Section 13(2) of the Trade Union and Labour Relations Act 1974 which had recently been interpreted in the courts as providing *no redress* against workers who occupy or sit in at their place of work.

The trade union movement as a whole is opposed to the terms of the Act, although it is seen by the government as introducing a mild dose of democracy into industrial relations. Nevertheless, there is no doubt that it represents a fairly severe attack on traditional union power.

Other legislation affecting industrial relations

A number of other Acts have contributed to the overall Employment Law picture. Some of the more important are:

Social Security (No.2) Act 1980

Among other provisions, this Act provided that the families of persons on strike should have their social security benefits reduced by £12 per week and that this figure would be raised in line with average price increases. The underlying assumption was that a union should support its striking members and should make up the sum deducted. The objective was to make strikes financially more costly for unions and perhaps to force them to charge more realistic dues to their members who might then begin to take a greater interest in the democratic processes whereby union leaders are appointed and union policies formed.

There is an understandable feeling that the public should not be asked for unlimited financial support for strikes, from which they are often the chief sufferers. The unions argued that similar arguments could be applied to payments to the families of convicted criminals and that strikers should not be treated more harshly than criminals.

Social Security Act 1986

Whilst the Wages Act attempts to free firms from legislative restrictions and reduce the administrative costs of wage payments, the Statutory Maternity Pay Scheme which became law in April 1987 places the duty of payment for maternity leave, etc. on the shoulders of the employer in a more cumbersome way than before.

This legislation introduced a two-tier system of payment – an earnings-related element and a flat-rate payment – and eligibility for entitlement will depend on length of service with the current employer. Full entitlement is earned only after 24 months' full employment. Employers recoup money paid under this system by deductions from the company's National Insurance returns to the Inland Revenue.

The scheme also allows some considerable flexibility as to when maternity leave is taken, so that, for example, women can take much of their leave entitlement before the actual birth if they so choose.

The Trade Union Act 1984

This act required secret ballots to be held for certain leadership positions within a trade union. Ballots also were required to confirm industrial action, to maintain the union's immunity for tort liability. Unions were also required to hold ballots to maintain a political fund.

The Employment Act 1988

This act continued the policy of union reform, giving new rights to Trade Union members with regard to the union leadership, e.g. the right not to be induced to take part in industrial action where no ballot was held. Individual members were also given the right to inspect the union's accounts. The act also set up a commission for the protection of the rights of Trade Union members.

The Trade Union and Labour Relations (Consolidations) Act 1992

The purpose of this act was to codify all the existing Trade Union acts and to put all this legislation together in one new statute. Major changes were made immediately after this statute was penned.

The Trade Union Reform and Employment Rights Act 1993

This act tightened up on procedures on union balloting and use of union funds. The Act's major

aim, however, was to implement a 1992 EU directive on pregnant workers to bring UK law into line with EU law on this issue. A new right was introduced in this Act, giving 14 weeks maternity leave to all employees, regardless of length of service or size of business, for example. The Act strengthens the position of pregnant employees or those who have recently given birth, against discrimination on the grounds of pregnancy or childbirth. Such dismissal will be automatically regarded as 'unfair'.

The impact of the new employment Acts

Initial reluctance to use the new laws

The evolution of the industrial law is altering the balance of power between the trade unions and the state, but the powers provided by the 1980 and 1982 Employment Acts appear to have been little used during the year-long miners' strike, which ended in 1985. Old law proved the most decisive weapon (for example Trade Union Act 1871, Conspiracy and Protection of Property Act 1875, Trustee Act 1925); employers hesitated to use the new laws, and many of the most important cases were brought by working miners to enforce their rights as union members and to enjoy freedom of work unhampered by picketing.

Sequestration

Cases brought under the Trade Union and Labour Relations Act 1974 clearly demonstrated the power of sequestration, once a receiver had been appointed. The willingness of foreign courts to cooperate with the sequestrators was a significant factor here. The main cases highlighted the difficulties of placing union funds outside the control of English law once a receiver had been appointed to look after the rights and welfare of union members as a whole, and established that no limit exists to the fine a court can impose on a union for contempt of court.

Union rules

Even though a strike is classified by the courts as a trade dispute, it can still be in breach of union rules. If a strike is called in breach of union rules, strikers may not call it official and could fail to qualify for strike pay. A national strike requires a national ballot with 55% of the membership voting for strike action.

Breach of the Peace

Police have the legal right to turn back potential pickets, even at a considerable distance from the scene of an industrial dispute, if they have reasonable grounds for suspecting a breach of the peace.

Dismissing strikers

The conditions under which an employee may be dismissed as a result of being on strike are laid down in the 1982 Employment Act. They are as follows:

1. There must be an industrial dispute.
2. The employee must have taken industrial action or been locked out.
3. All employees taking part in the industrial action must be dismissed at the same time.
4. If there is selective re-employment within three months, those not offered re-employment can claim unfair dismissal and the employer will have to justify his refusal to re-employ.

Following the decision in Brown vs Southall and Knight (1980) dismissal has also to be clearly communicated, not necessarily in writing but by some clear 'overt communicated act'. An offer of reinstatement has also to be made to all the employees, but not necessarily at the same time; workers may be re-engaged by stages.

To summarise, an employer may avoid unfair dismissal if:

- all striking employees were dismissed at the same time
- re-engagements take place within three months of dismissal and an offer is made to every dismissed employee (though not necessarily simultaneously)
- re-engagements take place after this three-month period, in which case no unfair dismissal claim can be brought.

The decline of union power

Since 1979, the power and authority of the trade union movement in the UK have seriously declined. There are several reasons for this shift in power.

1. Through the effects of mass unemployment in decaying industrial areas and also in the engineering and metal industries of the North West and West Midlands, and with unemployment endemic throughout industry, actual trade union membership numbers decline; when young workers perceive that the unions cannot protect their livelihood they refuse to join the movement.
2. With declining membership, union revenues also decline, so that the organisation lacks the necessary financial muscle to sustain long industrial disputes in order to safeguard members' rights and improve their conditions of employment.
3. General unemployment and the fear that it will spread, breed apathy and doubt among the rank and file.
4. Government legislation has severely curtailed the power of the large unions to engage in secondary picketing or call a strike without a secret ballot and, by outlawing the closed shop (except in special circumstances), has weakened the grasp of the unions on the work force at plant level.
5. Public opinion and the hard facts of political reality have both turned against trade unions. Union action which severely inconvenienced the general public has made unionism unpopular, as has union identification with the extreme left of the Labour Party. This unpopularity has placed a strong anti-union Conservative government in power; hence the wide popularity of their 'anti-union' legislation.
6. Finally, there are the effects of modern technology. Industrialists have been rapidly changing one factor of production (high-cost labour) for low-cost capital investment in the form of automation and computerisation. This has undoubtedly increased unemployment in those industries (for example the car industry) where union militancy was at its most powerful. One further effect of automation is that its adoption encourages the formation of small or paternalistic firms in areas not associated with union strength.

Health and safety

The number of working days lost through illness and accidents exceeds those lost through strike action by over 20:1. In 1991 over 23 million days were lost through accidents and illness, whereas only 761,000 days were lost through strikes. Consequently, any measures which reduce accidents will increase productivity, save money and add to the welfare of the working community. Over 500 people are killed at work each year.

Types and causes of industrial accidents

The annual report of HM Factories Inspectorate, the body responsible for the implementation of the various provisions of the Factory Acts, the Offices, Shops and Railways Premises Act 1963 and the

Health and Safety at Work Act 1974, has divided the types of accident suffered at work into the following main categories:

- Cuts and abrasions, which account for well over 40% of all industrial accidents.
- Strained, pulled muscles and sprained ligaments (25%).
- Injuries sustained through falling objects.

The report also indicates that most accidents are caused by incorrect lifting of materials rather than incorrect use of machinery or dangerous or unguarded machinery.

Generally, management is responsible for accidents caused by poor or unsatisfactory working conditions (unguarded machinery, inadequate safety guards, lack of protective clothing, etc.) while workers themselves, provided they have been adequately supervised and trained, are responsible for injuries sustained through unsafe acts (failure to wear protective clothing after clear and unambiguous instructions to do so, unauthorised removal of machinery guards, etc.).

Safety organisations at work

These are usually concerned with three related aspects of the works environment:

- Adequate training and instruction of the individual worker for a specific set of tasks.
- Control and maintenance of the working environment to ensure that accidents and injuries at work are kept to a minimum.
- Setting up an organisational procedure and minimal standards to be jointly operated by management and representatives of the work force, to ensure adequate health and safety standards.

Safety programmes

Safety programmes will usually include:

- Appointment of a safety officer, whose main functions are to direct schemes to prevent accidents, to report on accidents in a specialised and thorough manner as quickly as possible, to alert both management and workers to health and safety hazards and to take preventative measures.
- Analysis of accidents and continual review of safety measures required, according to the changing conditions of the factory or workplace.
- Provision of adequate facilities and regulations, training and continual safety training.
- Provision and continual amendment of safety

manuals, posters, information and literature disseminated to all concerned.

Health, hygiene and industrial disease at work

Health and hygiene programmes have not been very highly developed in British industry, though thorough programmes exist in the United States, Germany and Sweden and are run in close co-operation with the trade union movement.

Objectives

The objectives of such policies, where they exist in particular industries (for example mining), are:

- Prevention of occupational contagious disease, and the control of health hazards which are the direct cause of such disease.
- Health and medical education.
- Provision of rehabilitation and medical services and the funding of research programmes into both physical and mental health at the workplace.
- General provisions – those companies in Britain which pay particular attention to the health of their work force (they tend to be the larger private concerns and utilities, for example, mining, steel, chemicals and the asbestos industry) usually make the following general provisions:

(a) medical examination before employment begins
(b) medical check-ups during employment, especially for those in special occupations (for example foundry workers)
(c) the provision (often on a regional basis) of special medical and paramedical specialists (dermatologists, physiotherapists)
(d) research programmes, literature and dissemination of information.

Legal requirements

The legal provisions governing health and safety at work, which lay down the minimum requirements, are contained in the following statutes:

- The Employers' Liability Act 1969
- The Factories Act 1961
- The Offices, Shops and Railway Premises Act 1963
- The Health and Safety at Work Act 1974
- The Health and Safety Act 1992

These Acts lay down three duties which employers have to their employees:

1. To provide a place of work which is safe from danger and health hazards.
2. To ensure that all plant, machinery and tools are safe to use.

3. To ensure a safe system of work by inaugurating adequate safety measures and safety regulations in written form, and to involve workers, managers and trade unions in the safety procedures of the factory.

The Acts also lay down penalties for breaches of these fundamental common law duties.

General terms of the Acts

- Cleaning, painting and refurnishing of premises at prescribed intervals.
- Minimum floor space which must be provided per person employed.
- The minimum standard temperature, humidity and ventilation at work.
- The provision of separate toilet facilities for men and women, together with the provision of drinking water.

- Provisions as to excessive lifting and handling, together with six-monthly inspection of lifts and hoists.
- The notification of accidents to the Factories Inspectorate if they have resulted in death, or if the employee has more than three days' absence from work.
- The guarding of machines and provision of protective clothing or devices (e.g., ear plugs to guard against excessive noise).
- Clear passageways on all stairways and gangways.
- Regular checking of fire exists and fire appliances.
- The presence of first aid boxes for every 150 people and the employment of a qualified person to handle first aid.
- Powers given to the Factories Inspectorate to carry out inspections before the premises are used as a factory during the day or night and the right of the Inspectorate to inspect documents, records, machines and general conditions of work.

CASE STUDY 36.1

What kind of work force do we want?

CD is seriously considering opening a new factory in South Wales. The area is well known for its hard-working work force and its single union agreements with Japanese employers.

We are not sure whether to commence talks on a 'single union' deal, indeed we are not certain whether we should recognise unions at all.

Draw up a SWOT analysis on the proposals of moving to a new location and signing a single union deal.

SUMMARY

Having studied this chapter, you should be able to:

▽ Explain what is meant by industrial relations.

▽ Explain the role of trade unions and other organisations.

▽ Describe remuneration and conditions of work.

▽ Explain what collective bargaining is.

▽ Describe the nature of industrial conflict.

▽ Explain how industrial relations, the state and the legal requirements are linked.

▽ Describe health and safety regulations at work.

Questions and activities

Technical terms and glossary

In the section below you are given a series of technical terms and their meanings. They have been scrambled. You must match up the terms and the definitions. When you have correctly paired them, transfer them in your alphabetical vocabulary or glossary book.

You are also advised to transfer the definitions obtained during the exercises in the case studies into this glossary book.

Technical terms

1. Conflicts of interest
2. Shop steward
3. TUC and CBI
4. PBR
5. Collective bargaining
6. Flexitime
7. Secret ballot
8. Secondary picketing

Definitions

A. Asking the members' opinions in a way that allows them to vote as they wish.
B. The union representative at shop floor, or plant level.
C. A process where the interests of a number are represented by a few.
D. Being allowed to work the majority of your contracted hours when you wish to work them.
E. A system of payment that is closely linked to the quality of output.
F. The two major organisations representing the interests of employees and employers.
G. The arrival at a situation where opinions may represent opposing interpretations of a situation.
H. Attempting to interfere with workers not directly involved in the dipute.

Questions

1. Distinguish between blue- and white-collar workers.
2. Explain what is meant by the term 'payment by results'.
3. What is meant by the terms:
   (a) flexitime
   (b) collective bargaining
   (c) secondary picketing
   (d) work to rule?
4. When is a woman entitled to maternity pay?
5. Outline the main reasons why the influence of trade unions changed during the 1980s.
6. Under the Health and Safety regulations what responsibilities does an employer have to its employees?
7. Explain the terms:
   (1) sequestration
   (2) closed shop
8. What do these abbreviations stand for?
   (1) TGWU
   (2) TUC
   (3) CBI

Short answer questions

1. Explain what you understand by the terms:
   (a) craft unions
   (b) industrial unions
2. Describe the role of the shop steward in industrial relations.
3. How do the services offered by employers associations differ from those offered by unions to their members?
4. The role of shop steward is a difficult one. Their membership bring their troubles to them and they have to sort out chaos. Management expect them to 'keep the peace'. Quite often they are the restraining influence on both sides of a conflict.
   (a) Why do shop stewards have trouble thrust upon them?
   (b) Why do management rely on shop stewards and how might this affect the position of a supervisor?
5. Explain what you understand by the terms:
   (a) Joint industrial councils
   (b) Wage councils.
6. Why and how have the roles of trade unions changed in the last 10 years?
7. Would a wider application of productivity bonuses be a means of improving the efficiency of industry?
8. List the arguments for and against full-scale worker participation in industrial decision making.
9. Briefly describe the various ways in which an employer can recruit to fill a vacancy in the organisation.
10. Outline the recent changes which have taken place in the provision of maternity leave.

Data response question

Read the article and answer the questions which follow.

Unionised firms consult more widely

Employees in unionised companies are consulted on a wider range of issues than in those without unions, according to an ACAS report. 5

The survey of 600 private sector firms shows that employee consultation in unionised workplaces adds to collective bargaining rather 10 than supplanting it. Unionised workplaces have also been more likely to witness an increase in the scope of consultations over the last three years. 15

However, managers at many companies, both union and non-union, told researchers that they consulted workers on a growing range of issues to do 20 with running the business.

'It appears that the general process of consultation may have become more important in their thinking and approach 25 to employee relations in recent years,' says the report.

Topping the list of companies with the most extensive range of issues for consultation were 30 the British bases of foreign firms, mostly European. This bears out the view that an employer from a country with a well-established statutory frame- 35 work for consultation will be more likely to have absorbed the culture of consultation.

The survey explores the myth of the non-unionised in- 40 ward investor riding roughshod over the British workforce.

The report makes it clear that, although British management is doing a great deal more 45 in the way of communicating with employees, it is clearly being outstripped in most respects by foreign firms operating in this country with a 50 more open and participative management approach.

The report says that a minority of establishments, not all of them small employers, 55 had developed little or no formal or regular means of actively seeking the views of their employees.

(Adapted from *Personnel Management Plus*, March 1991)

(a) Distinguish between 'employee consultation' and 'collective bargaining' (lines 8 and 10)
(4 marks)

(b) What might make consultation between managers and employees in unionised workplaces more likely than in *non-unionised* workplaces?
(6 marks)

(c) Explain *four* benefits managers might hope to gain by adopting a 'more open and participative management approach' (lines 51-2).
(8 marks)

(d) '... although British management is doing a great deal more in the way of communicating with employees, it is clearly being outstripped in most respects by foreign firms ...' (lines 44-49).

Discuss the business implications of this statement for British firms. (6 marks)

(Associated Examining Board, Paper 1, June 1993)

37
Motivating people at work

Preview

▼ The importance of well-motivated employees can never be overstated. In this chapter the complex issues of how employers motivate and communicate with employees will be analysed in detail.

Motivation

Motivation is a complex process by which human behaviour of both individuals and groups is directed towards a previously agreed target or objective. It is assumed that people work towards satisfying a need, and that their behaviour reinforces this course of action (see Chapter 26). Likewise, a group of individuals will work towards achieving a specific target only to the extent that to do so satisfies their own personal needs.

It was thought until comparatively recently, that financial incentives (wages) were the sole motivating factor. However, other factors now seem to influence motivation. The formation of unions, which gave workers a greater influence over their financial interests, also gave other issues more influence. For their part, employers realised that a better-off workforce was a vast potential market for the very goods they produced.

Much of the early work into non-financial motivators was done by A. H. Maslow, a US psychologist. He divided human needs into the following:

- *Physiological needs.* These are our basic needs that enable us to maintain life, e.g. food and drink. At work, such needs are satisfied by wages and salaries, which must be sufficient to buy the fundamental needs of life (food, shelter and clothing). The values placed on these can vary according to culture, but as economic wealth is created a set of 'standard' demands do start to emerge.
- *Safety needs.* At work these include the security of a job, pension schemes, and the actual safe environment.

- *Social needs.* These include the desire to be liked, appreciated and to have friends. We also like to associate with others of similar interests.
- *Ego needs.* These include the desire to work independently. To be accepted as someone who has a 'value' and a status, and the opportunity to exercise control and power. At work, such needs show themselves in the desire to fulfil desires.
- *Self-fulfilling needs.* These are our 'creative' desires and equate with the need for us to fully utilise our talents, skills, knowledge and training in order to contribute something distinctive and unique to the work one is employed to do. (see Figure 37.1.)

Classification	Description
Level one Physiological or basic needs	Needs essential to the continuance of life. The grouping includes food, water, heat, sleep, etc.
Level two Safety and security needs	Needs essential to self-protection. The grouping includes shelter, insurance, rules, etc.
Level three Social needs	The needs for friendship and acceptance. This grouping includes companionship, affection, friendship and support.
Level four Ego or esteem needs	The need to be held in esteem by others. The needs grouped here include recognition, respect and status.
Level five Creative/self-fulfillment needs	The need to make full use of individual skill and abilities. The needs grouped here include achievement

Figure 37.1 Classification of needs based on Maslow

Maslow's needs fall into a hierarchy, as shown above. He argued that, once one set of needs have been achieved, so the individual would move to satisfying the next set, and so on. He also accepted that individual needs change, and do not remain static.

How can Maslow's hierarchy theory be applied to the workplace?

The implications of Maslow's findings, are that once an individual has satisfied his financial needs he will look for other *intrinsic* rewards. His effort will clearly be influenced by the ability of the organisation to satisfy the needs of security, social life and creativity. It is difficult to believe that repetitive assembly line or office really satisfies more than pure financial needs. No matter how high the financial motivation the individual morale will probably be low. This may show itself in aggression, poor work, absenteeism, sickness and even a strike action. Dissatisfaction pervades through all levels of worker and is a dangerous enemy.

If it is assumed that the base needs are met through one's part in a productive process, then how do the other needs receive attention? Social needs can be satisfied by the individuals' freedom to join working groups, associate with others, be part of a working environment that actively supports others and the status or prestige that is attached to a particular role, or even an organisation. Some organisations have tried to make work more meaningful with such innovations as job analysis, appraisal, promotion schemes and techniques of accountability that include *management by objectives*, which involves subordinates setting their own targets and objectives after consultation with their superiors.

Herzberg's theory of motivation

Herzberg was a social psychologist, who developed a theory of motivation based on interviews he undertook with accountants and engineers. Each group was asked what had led to satisfaction and dissatisfaction in their places of work. The responses were broken down into: *positive* job events, which lead to *satisfaction*, and *negative* job events, which resulted in *dissatisfaction*.

The results can be summarised as:

1. The *positive* experiences had *intrinsic* sources, such as achievement, recognition, the nature of the work itself, promotion, personal growth and these were mentioned far more often than extrinsic sources.
2. The *negative* experiences had *extrinsic* sources,

such as company administration, supervision, relations with peers, supervisors, status, security and they were mentioned nearly twice as much as intrinsic sources.

Herzberg argued that the factors which provided the source of satisfaction at work were different from the factors which can result in dissatisfaction. He called the extrinsic sources, which cause dissatisfaction the *hygiene factors*, while he labelled intrinsic factors causing satisfaction as motivators. The implications of his investigations are:

- If intrinsic factors are correctly manipulated and balanced by appropriate job design, then this will result in feelings of satisfaction and high motivation.
- The manipulation of extrinsic factors will not produce satisfaction, but the absence of dissatisfaction.

So, high pay will not lead to a feeling of high job satisfaction, but a challenge, a sense of personal achievement, will.

Critics of Herzberg's findings concluded that:

- The theory concentrates on personal satisfaction and not on productivity outcomes.
- Those interviewed were qualified professionals and there is little evidence that such findings naturally apply to manual workers.
- The research may have been undermined by the simple fact that most people ascribe unfavourable events to factors outside themselves and favourable events to something from within. (See also Figure 37.2.)

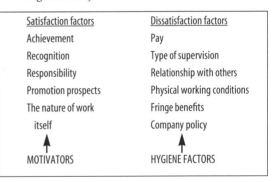

Satisfaction factors	Dissatisfaction factors
Achievement	Pay
Recognition	Type of supervision
Responsibility	Relationship with others
Promotion prospects	Physical working conditions
The nature of work	Fringe benefits
itself	Company policy
↑	↑
MOTIVATORS	HYGIENE FACTORS

Figure 37.2 Analysis of factors for worker satisfaction

Expectancy theory

This school of thought suggested that people are more influenced by how they perceive an issue. The core of the theory relates to how person views three relationships:

- efforts at work

- performance
- reward

The strength of the belief of how an action will influence the individual is known as the 'valence'. The strength of any particular outcome of effort and performance is termed 'reality'. Both reality and valence are dependent on how the individual perceives a situation. If we see promotion as linked to security and not ability, we will not necessarily direct our maximum efforts to achieving this goal. Effort or motivated behaviour will occur when the individual perceives that such attributes lead to effective performance and attractive rewards. However, efforts may not lead to effective performance, because there are other factors which affect personal performance. These include managerial style, organisational efficiency, capital investment, technology and training. Once again these rewards can be either *intrinsic* (satisfying the individual's personal needs) or *extrinsic* (pay, conditions of work, etc.). As already outlined it is the intrinsic rewards which are likely to satisfy the individual worker. The main findings of Vroom and others were:

- An individual will only act when he perceives that the action will lead to a desired and attractive outcome.
- How an individual perceives reality is the key to the motivating process.
- Satisfaction at work follows effective job performance, and not the other way round.

The results of Vroom and others' work have been work schedules that emphasise such intrinsic factors as variety, autonomy, task identity and positive feedback.

We will now examine some possible non-financial ways of motivating workers.

Job enlargement and enrichment

The first of these, job enlargement and enrichment, concentrates on extending the tasks asked of an employee at the same level of complexity and responsibility as in the past (see Chapter 30). Job enrichment entails greater responsibility, and the greater use of skill, knowledge or qualifications than before. Both are practised to ease feelings of frustration, dissatisfaction and the monotony of various work patterns. They are designed to provide for the greater satisfaction of human needs as defined by Maslow. Job enrichment consciously attempts to increase the intrinsic satisfaction received from work. To extend and enrich a professional job is comparatively easy to achieve, but enlargement or enrichment of manual workers is both less practicable and cost effective. Their work tends to be tied to specific production methods. A further problem arises if organised labour fears such development as an erosion of traditional job demarcations. Even when union backing is achieved it may be difficult to enrich a job unless such action is supported by obvious productivity increases. One way around such a difficulty is to introduce a scheme of *job rotation* (i.e. to train operators in several skills so that jobs can be exchanged round a group of workers at regular intervals). Such a method has several advantages:

- It allows for greater satisfaction to be achieved through individuals seeing all parts of a particular process.
- Workers become more versatile and are therefore of more use to management.
- Production methods can stay the same; its the workers that change.

Of course, they may find that productive workers are not highly satisfied workers, and highly satisfied workers may produce less. Some probable reasons for this are:

- If managers and workers do not share the same interests, then productivity will be low.
- Certain 'outside' factors may influence the work effort. Such issues as unemployment, high wages, labour mobility, skill mobility, fear of losing jobs.
- The influence of 'group norms' tend to produce agreed work levels that individuals accept.

Nevertheless, organisations should concentrate on the provision of reasonable job satisfaction for their employees. If they do not, then they may experience low morale, dissatisfaction, sickness, accidents and generally low productivity rates. The firm itself will be at risk of being labelled one of little vision towards its employees. Such an image may influence customer perception and could reduce the desire of potential applicants to seek employment. It seems probable that prospective employees will be greatly influenced by working conditions and job satisfaction.

The working group

The analysis so far has concentrated on the individual. Now the analysis must make reference to the social environment of the workplace.

A more meaningful way of developing ways of managing people is to see them as part of a social group. Individuals respond to the actions and interactions of other members of the work force. Each of us is in regular, close and continuous contact with groups of people. To be classified as a group a collection of people must illustrate the following conditions:

- There must be face-to-face communication and individuals must be in close proximity to one another over a long period of time.
- Individuals' work must form a deliberate part of a sequence that has an obvious relationship to others.
- There must not be great divisions of status, education, skill, culture or class background.
- The group must not exceed 10 to 15 people.
- Signs of an 'external threat' will cause the group to 'close ranks' and be self-supportive.

Types of group

People normally are members of the following groups:

1. *Primary groups.* These are small groups who have freely chosen to be together, or carry out common activities. They form face-to-face relationships and can develop informal relationships
2. *Secondary groups.* These are larger groups and usually have quite a formal structure, with a leadership hierarchy. They often have precise economic, social or political aims and are formed to achieve a precise task. They are formal in their relationship structure.
3. *Interest groups.* These are groups which come together because of some common interest, relationships or goal. Normally, they consider themselves to have some clearly recognisable feature, e.g. skill or professional qualification. As a group they develop common reactions and develop policy, rules, regulations, etc. to maintain their individuality.
4. *Peer groups.* These are groups of people of the same age, who share the same cultural values, interests and moral beliefs and who are usually intensely loyal to one another.

Managers must be able to appreciate the characteristics of groups, for they are an essential element in industrial psychology. Research repeatedly shows that values, norms and expectations of groups are an important referral point for the individuals that belong to them. In other words, the group influences the individual even when it is acting quite independently (see Figure 37.3).

Figure 37.3 *The relationship between human needs and activity*

Elton Mayo

The first specific research carried out with group influence was supervised by Elton Mayo, at the Hawthorne Plant of the Western Electrical Company in Chicago, between 1927 and 1932 (see Chapter 40). The work developed from a study on the influence of light levels on productivity. Early results of changes in light levels were found to be unsatisfactory, as other 'subjective' factors had influenced the outcome. To try to isolate these factors a number of women were put into a room and the light levels and work speeds monitored. The results of the research, which lasted five years, were:

- Early analysis showed an increase in output and then this declined.
- The physical changes had little effect on productivity.
- Productivity responded to changes in the social climate. This was brought about by isolating a group of girls, who in turn did not feel 'over-supervised' and developed interpersonal relationships.

As a consequence of this research a further 20,000 employees were interviewed to find out their attitude to work. The data revealed:

- Workers' attitudes to their work were a key factor in determining productivity.
- Workers' attitudes were greatly influenced, if not created by, membership of a particular working group or groups of which they had membership. The establishment of group norms were the dictating factor, regardless of payment and bonus schemes.
- Once a group's productivity norm had been established, efforts above it were derided by group members, while those who fell beneath the norm were described as 'shirkers'.
- An 'appointed' supervisor was considered to be just that, a mere management representative and seldom the real leader of the group. This drafted-

357

in leader usually struggled to balance the conflict of satisfying his superiors, while maintaining the goodwill of the work force.

- Contrary to management's instructions, workers often helped out one another on a voluntary basis and rotated jobs.
- Unofficial leaders who emerged from within the group were far more influential than the management-appointed supervisors.

This very important piece of research has been applied to many working situations. The majority have endorsed the importance of social relationships between individuals within a working group. Organisational specialists now recognise that most employment is carried out in a socio-technological system that is characterised by three related factors, namely:

1. *The technical environment* – the process, physical environment, etc.
2. *The social environment* – personal relations at work
3. *The economic environment* – payments, bonuses, etc.

An awareness of working groups are of value to both employee and employer.

Employee

- They allow the satisfaction we need through friendship, esteem, etc.
- They provide a social structure and pattern to relationships.
- They enable us to establish boundaries, codes, modes of conduct (group norms) to which we can refer when making a decision.
- They offer 'support', i.e. protect individuals against the intrusion of outsiders.
- Group membership can provide individuals with opportunities for leadership, self-expression and personal esteem.

Interest groups tend to be exclusive and can be aggressive towards outsiders who do not share their values. Groups also tend to resist change in their normal patterns of conduct. Unofficial leaders emerge from within the group and they may be antagonistic towards the official, management appointed leadership.

Managers

For managers the implications are:

1. To maintain peaceful industrial relations it is best to try to ensure that the formal structure of authority fits with the informal structure of

prestige and authority conferred by the informal group.
2. The maintenance of good working conditions and fair relationships with workers normally allow the work force to feel more sympathetic towards corporate objectives. They will probably incorporate the company's objectives within their own.
3. Any change under consideration should be introduced gradually and after full discussion with the workers. Such a course should allow for full cooperation by workers.
4. High levels of production are more likely to come from group-based organisational structures than from those based on individuals.
5. Careful planning is required when setting group targets, for you do not want to set one group against another.

Motivation

The early theories of motivation can be categorised under three headings:

1. *Satisfaction theories.* Satisfied workers are productive workers.
2. *Incentive theories.* Workers work hard given specific rewards.
3. *Intrinsic theories.* Workers work best when given a worthwhile job and allowed to get on with it.

Satisfaction theories

Satisfied workers tend to stay in the same organisation and this is probably the result of their being mentally satisfied. An employer who pays attention to conditions of work and worker morale will normally gain its benefits of less labour turnover and absent employees. Hopefully, this will result in increased productivity, but it is not guaranteed. Under this heading can be grouped theories that are based on an acceptance that people work best when they like their leaders, or are satisfied with the group with whom they work.

Incentive theories

These are based on the belief that the individual will increase his efforts in order to obtain a desired reward. The majority of these theories concentrate on money as the principal motivator. For these to work the individual needs to be able to relate to the rewards and sees them as being worth the extra effort. Workers must feel assured that increased efforts can be related to the individual and that the rewards are to their liking. The final feature that underpins the theories is that the increase will not become the new accepted minimum.

Such schemes tend to work best when the owner is directly concerned with the 'shop-floor' output or the worker is involved in small-batch production. A failure to make the reward seem worth the extra effort will really only push workers into a 'satisfaction theory' situation, and if the extra effort merely becomes a new minimum the tensions could well rise.

Intrinsic theories

These theories are based on the observations of Maslow, and his 'hierarchy of needs'. Maslow proposed that needs are only motivators when they are unsatisfied. Needs are achieved in an order, but research suggests that needs become less powerful as they are satisfied. Aldefer, who put forward only three categories of needs (existence, relationships and personal growth) pointed out that each of us may have different levels of each.

McGregor and Likert proposed that the high order needs are more prevalent in modern man. They felt that a primary motivator was the need to consider the job "your job!". Freedom in determining what the job involves and how it is carried out are major motivators. People like to feel involved and able to participate. Rewards tend to lie in the task or in how the individual relates to the group. Managers should strive to create conditions where effective performance is a goal in its own right rather than merely a means to a further goal. The manager should be seen as a colleague, consultant and resource and not merely the boss.

Research into the effectiveness of these theories suggest they struggle when:

- Technology prevents direct individual control over the job.
- Individuals have little say.
- Individuals desire authoritarian leaders.

It is therefore not surprising to discover that such theories appear most acceptable when people of high educational backgrounds are working on challenging problems, e.g. research and development assignments.

Are these theories accurate?

Most of these theories rely on relatively unproven assumptions about human behaviour. Schein categorised their development as being closely related to industrial history. He traced a pattern of 'evolution'.

His opening category is *rational-economic man*,

Job satisfaction is one of the primary motivators of individuals at work.

who is capable of being made to do almost anything. This form of human is passive and must be manipulated. Organisations must organise such an irrational individual. A small group, who do not require such constant control, will form the leaders.

Next in line is the *social man*, who gains his satisfaction from his relationships with others. Work in itself is not sufficient, it is social relationships within the job that count. Such individuals concern themselves with leadership styles and group behaviour.

This category is followed in the procession by *self-actualising man*, who is mainly self-motivated and tends to dislike external controls and pressures. Left to their own devices these employees will integrate personal goals with those of the organisation.

The penultimate category is known as *complex man*. This is Schien's favourite and centres on man being variable. He has many motives which have at any one time a hierarchy, and this can change as time and situations alter. Fulfillment of all needs in any one situation may not be necessary. Personal response to management will depend on how the policy is considered appropriate.

Levinson, Jacques and Zaleznik took Schien's work a stage further with their *psychological man*. The complex individual passes through development stages that include both physiological and psychological features. Personal ego promotes a desire and this is based on hunger, sexuality and aggression. Man strives to meet his ideal. The gap between what the individual wants and what organisations provide decides how well we feel we have achieved. This dictates the feelings of pride, guilt, etc., for work is part of personal identity and we must be afforded chances to achieve in order to be 'motivated'.

Conclusion

Those favouring the satisfaction and incentive theories will seek to negotiate. They will look towards such facilities as conditions of work and fringe benefits. Those favouring intrinsic theories will look towards creating individual opportunities within the correct working environment. The table below gives some more details of early research into why people work. Its findings may appear a little obvious but they are interesting.

Nancy Morse and Robert Weiss interviewed a random sample of 401 employed men in the USA in the early 1950s to explore the function and meaning of work.

Question: If by some chance you inherited enough money to live comfortably without working, do you think you would work anyway or not?

	Total	Age 21–34	35–44	45–54	55–64	64 +
would keep working (%)	80	90	83	72	61	82
would not keep working (%)	20	10	17	28	39	18

Question: Why do you feel that you would work?

	Interest or accomplishment	To keep occupied	Other
professional/managerial (%)	44	37	19
working class (%)	10	71	19
farmers (%)	18	64	18

Question: Suppose you didn't work, what would you miss most?

the people I know through work, friends, contacts (%)	31
feeling of doing something, would be restless (%)	25
the kind of work I do (%)	12
feeling of doing something important, worthwhile (%)	9
regular routine (%)	6
feeling of interest, being interested (%)	5
other (5)	6
nothing (%)	6

Question: How satisfied are you with your job?

	Very satisfied	Satisfied	Dissatisfied
professional/managerial (%)	42	37	21
working class (%)	27	57	10
farmers (%)	29	56	15

From Morse and Weiss, 'The function and meaning of work and the job', *American Sociological Review*, 1955.

An alternative approach

The range of theories before us can make understanding a little difficult. Let us therefore try to develop a model that gives us a base from which to work. The analysis begins from a position where an individual deals with individual decisions, to do or not to do something, to go or not to go, to apportion or not to apportion his time, energy, etc. Man is, to some extent, an independent unit capable of some control over his own destiny and how he responds to pressures. In turn he can select the paths he chooses to reach them. Some versions of this approach have been given the name *path-goal* theories.

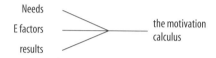

This model merely states that each individual has a set of needs and of desired results. He decides how much 'E' (effort, energy, excitement, expenditure, etc.) to invest by doing a calculation. The process of calculation is not often as deliberate as the model suggests, but is a start for further analysis.

Almost all theories of motivation make some assumptions about individual needs, or drives. They have been categorised, listed, and titled in a variety of ways. Some of the most useful lists are:

1. *Maslow's* hierarchy of needs; simplified by Aldefer.

2. *Roethlisberger and Dickson* amplify Maslow. They add on to physiological and safety needs the following:

   - friendship and belonging needs;
   - needs for justice and fair treatment;
   - dependence – independence;
   - needs for achievement.

3. *Herzberg's* two-factor theory. Herzberg maintains, on the basis of his research studies, that in any work situation you can distinguish between the factors that dissatisfy and those that satisfy. The interesting thing is that they are not the opposites of each other. Dealing with the dissatisfying factors does not turn them into satisfying or motivating factors. In general, the dissatisfying factors are things to do with conditions of work – company policy and administration, supervision, salary, interpersonal relations and physical working conditions. He called these the *hygiene* or *maintenance* factors. They are the necessary conditions of successful

motivation. The satisfiers are achievement, recognition, work itself, responsibility and advancement. These he called the *motivators*. Good hygiene deals with the question 'Why work here?', only the motivators deal with 'Why work harder?'

4. *McClelland* and his co-workers have looked at the way people think, in many cultures and many sections of society. They have grouped the responses into three categories, each representing an identifiable human motive or need. These are:

- need for achievement
- need for power
- need for affiliation.

Most people have some of each in their thoughts, but seldom in the same strength.

- *The need for power.* Most managers have a high need for power (as defined by McClelland's tests). High need for power by itself will often lead to unconstructive authoritarianism. Combined with, in particular, need for achievement it can lead to productive and satisfying results. Some degree of need for power seems to be a necessary condition for managerial success. Having it, however, does not guarantee success!
- *The need for affiliation.* The individual with a high need for affiliation *alone* will tend to be more concerned with developing and maintaining relationships than with decision making. These people are often seen as ineffective helpers, probably because they are not task-orientated enough. However, some need for affiliation is probably present in most. It is present but is seldom dominant in successful individuals.
- *The need for achievement.* The individual with high scores on this need will like personal responsibility, moderate and calculated risks and feedback on how he is doing. Unless moderated by other needs the high need-achiever may tend to become too individualist to be very successful in any organisation where other people's contentions need to be harnessed.

5. *Robert Ardrey*, working from his observations of animal populations, arrived at three basic needs (*identity, security* and *stimulation*) in his book *The Territorial Imperative.*

These categories of needs should not be thought of as exclusive. Anyone can add to these lists. One psychologist, Murray, listed thirty needs, which perhaps is too wide a spread to be useful in analysis. The valuable aspect of most of these particular lists is that ways have been developed for measuring them. The really important points to remember about needs are:

- That each individual has his own set, sets that may differ widely;
- That the relative importance of each need in the set may change over time. For instance, in times of redundancy, the security needs suddenly come to the fore so there is little point on relying on self-actualisation as a motivator.

It is interesting to speculate on the origins of particular need hierarchies, or individual differences. This would lead us deeper into personality and behaviour theory than would be appropriate in this section. But at least we can list the influencing factors that must be thought of in any consideration of an individual's set of needs.

- *Heredity/early environment.* Recognised by all theorists as crucially important, it is notoriously hard to disentangle the effect of one from the other. Physical talents are more easily attributed to heredity, aspiration levels and ego ideals to environment.
- *Education.* By changing an individual's set of models through his educational surroundings the priority rating of his needs can be changed. McClelland has also applied an educational approach to the raising levels of need for achievement.
- *The individual's self-concept.* The individual's assessment of his personal capacities, of his place in society, of his degree of aspiration, will affect the strength of each need. The self-concept itself is largely the result of early environment, education, and the people he has chosen to model himself on – parents, teachers, friends.
- *Experience.* The individual's experience in life, his age, the degree to which he has in the past satisfied some needs, will affect all his current need set. Needs not satisfied by experience at the appropriate stage in life often remain dormant unnaturally long. The 40 year-old adolescent may never have had the opportunity to rebel when he was young.

The motivational calculus

This calculus is central to the problem. It determines how much 'E' is given to any individual activity or set of activities. Most motivational theories have been concerned with expenditure of effort. Whichever 'E' word one addresses, motivation theory has to explain how the allocation decided upon has been arrived at. Naturally, the calculus is different for each individual, but certain essential elements can be identified:

- the strength of each of the needs
- what the 'E' will lead to (expectancy)
- the ability of the 'E' factors to reduce the need(s) in the first element (instrumentality).

To these we must add that all reactions contain an element of subjectivity and that the relationship between the need, expectancy and instrumentality is *multiplicative*, i.e. if one receives no real attention the whole sum is zero.

We also have boundaries of behaviour. We may act instinctively (unconscious reactions) and in a calculating way (conscious reactions). The former normally leads to the individual reacting to the most immediate need (e.g. the next drink). The time-span can vary from the immediate to an indefinite. The longer the period the more the needs that have to be considered. e.g. a drink becomes more thought-provoking when weighed against one's health.

Age and experience may have influences on the conscious calculus. Younger people often aim for the 'immediate return', while older people see a longer perception. Failure to secure long-term needs may cause negative mental reactions such as a breakdown.

To be fair, few of us could take the pressure of constantly re-appraising our calculus. The majority of people base reactions on precedent. They react in the same way to similar situations. What interests the manager are those decisions which alter a previously established pattern or cause the individual to react in ways not previously recorded.

Predicting human beings is never easy, but the good manager needs to be able to identify those issues that will develop a management by objectives. By involving people the manager is forcing/enabling them to make part of the results relevant to the individual's personal calculations. Recent research has suggested that the setting of targets or objectives is not as successful as once thought. Even 'high-achievers' are not thought to set high individual targets, but actually lower their targets if they can achieve similar rewards. This observation is

deepened by other research that suggests the best objectives to be those that have emerged through feedback or a definite knowledge of results. Managers must set objectives and keep the participants fully informed. Our model can now be extended:

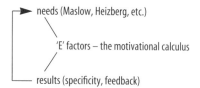

needs (Maslow, Heizberg, etc.)

'E' factors – the motivational calculus

results (specificity, feedback)

Again, it must be remembered that nobody passes through this calculus every time a decision is made, but it is thought to be the underlying principle against which we make decisions. One further observation needs to be made, namely the part played by groups in the decision-making process of the individual. This is known as the *psychological contract*. There is an unstated psychological contract between the individual and the organisation. This contract is essentially a set of expectations. Individuals expect things back from organisations and then in turn the organisation expects certain things from the individuals. The latter has three important factors:

1. Most individuals belong to more than one kind of organisation. In turn the individual has more than one psychological contract. As such, the individual need not satisfy all needs from one contract.
2. Organsiations often consider a contract to be all-embracing while individuals do not. This can lead to feelings of exploitation from an individual point of view while the institution may consider the individual lacks involvement.
3. The individuals' calculus only becomes predictable if and when the psychological contract is viewed in terms similar to both parties.

Evidence for the calculus

Kolb, Winter and Berlew found that when business school students were committed to a new goal (instead of having it imposed) and also got more feedback from each other, the percentage of successful students rose from 5 per cent to 61 per cent.

Kay, French and Myer found that when specific goals for self-improvement were included in appraisal interviews 62.5 per cent were achieved compared with 27.3 per cent when they were not included.

Row and Russell demonstrated in an experimental game situation that constant *failure* to achieve targets resulted in individuals ultimately setting lower targets for themselves than when they were reasonably successful in meeting their targets, i.e. we lower our goals if we find we cannot reach them.

Hoppe found that *success* in a problem-solving exercise led to a rise in the level of aspiration for 69 per cent, while *failture* led 50 per cent to lower their aspirations.

Lewin pointed out in 1936 that goals are not accepted by the individual unless they are thought to be attainable. He also underlined the fact that one's colleagues, or peer groups, have a big influence on the level of our goals. A high-achieving group will raise the aspirations of all its members.

Gebhard demonstrated that continued success increased the desirability of the goal. In other words, if you think that your effort or energy will be rewarded (high expectancy and high instrumentality) it is only natural to feel that it is all worthwhile.

It is possible to categorise organisations according to the type of psychological contract which predominates. These are:

- *Coercive.* These arise in such institutions as prisons, where individuals are held against their will. The contract is not voluntarily entered into. The regime is based on control, punishment and power. Failure to comply can result in withdrawal of personal liberties. 'E' factors tend to be enforced by fear of punishment.
- *Calculative.* The contract is now a voluntary one. An exchange of goods or money takes place for services rendered. Management can reward by use of 'desired' things, e.g. promotion. Most people work under such a contract. Its ability to increase 'E' is difficult as threats tend to move the contract back to the coercive category.
- *Co-operative.* Under this form, management delegates part of the day-to-day running of the organisation. The individual has greater control over the pursuit of goal attainment. The increased trend in such contracts has met two obstacles, namely:
  - goals though meaningful to management may not seem so important to those lower down the organisation
  - responsibility has its worries and not all individuals want such features to be a part of their contract.

In short, you cannot impose on someone a contract without it becoming coercive.

What is the role of money?

Is money the all-embracing issue the early theorists thought? It obviously differs with individuals and research based on self-reporting suggests money does not come top of the list.

It is difficult to compare or assess without some recourse to monetary boundaries. People certainly seem to hold opinions on what is fair (or as Herzberg considered 'equitable').

Certainly money received at regular intervals reinforces efforts. The truth is difficult to identify but most of us have an idea of our 'worth' and we react favourably to rewards directed at increasing that strongly held self-belief or target.

Do we have an idea of what we are?

Levinson believed this and suggested that our ego-ideal (or idea of what we could be) was a major motivating factor. In the UK it remains to be seen how the 'customer' perception of doctors will alter as the National Health Service becomes more money-driven. A further issue needing consideration is personal reaction to a failure to achieve an innermost desire. What follows is another attempt to distinguish reasons why people work, but this time it concentrates on the personality of the individual.

Holland has described how people with different orientations tend to choose different work environments to suit their skills and needs.

1. *Realistic.* The realistic person seeks objective, concrete goals and tasks and likes to manipulate things – tools, machines, animals and people. They are best suited by agriculture, engineering, outdoor conservation work and similar practical jobs.
2. *Intellectual.* Ideas, words and symbols are important to these people who are best suited to tasks requiring abstract and creative abilities, suggesting science, teaching or writing.
3. *Social.* These people are best known for their interpersonal skills and interest in other people. Social work and counselling are possible careers and so is the organisation of others.
4. *Conventional.* The conventional person copes with life by following the rules and selecting goals approved of by society and customer. Accounting, office work and administration often suit them well.
5. *Enterprising.* High energy, enthusiasm, dominance and impulsiveness are the hallmarks of these people, leading to occupations such as sales, politics, entrepreneurial business or foreign service.
6. *Artistic.* The artistic person uses feelings, intuitions and imagination to create forms and products,

leading most obviously to the performing arts, or writing, painting and music.

(*Source*: Holland, *Making Vocational Choices*, 1973, p.171)

Unemployment's threat to psychological success

Peter Warr of the University of Sheffield has listed the nine likely psychological effects of unemployment, as established by research.

1. *Financial anxiety.* Two-thirds of working-class people have their income reduced by a half or more.
2. *Loss of variety.* There are fewer places to go to, fewer things to do. Most unemployed people sleep more and do more housework and television-watching.
3. *Loss of traction.* There is less structure in life to draw one along, and fewer goals and tasks that have to be done.
4. *Reduced scope for decisions.* There is more freedom but less to be free about, fewer options.
5. *Less skill development.* There is usually less outlet for one's skills.
6. *More psychological threats.* More rejections from job interviews, credit applications, and social meetings.
7. *More insecurity.* Particularly about the future.
8. *Less interpersonal contact.* Social contacts are cut because of lack of money and there is no work to go to.
9. *Loss of status.* And the self-concept that goes with a work role.

These factors, Warr points out, do not apply to all people equally. Those who were less committed to the job, who were older or younger, those who were middle-class, female and healthy: these all seemed to suffer less than the others. To be working-class, middle-aged and totally committed to your job was bad news when unemployment hit.

(*Source*: P. Warr, 'Work, jobs and unemployment', *Bulletin of the British Psychological Society*, 1983)

So the fear of being made redundant may also motivate us.

CASE STUDY 37.1

College Discs

Memorandum
To: Assistant Personnel Manager
From: Personal Assistant to CEO
Ref: Poor output returns

The CEO has noted the low output returns for the second of our two day-time shifts.
He wants to know:
(a) why such low returns have been recorded
(b) what has been done to rectify this matter

He draws your attention to:
(a) The recent wage increases awarded to line workers, regardless of shift.
(b) The new equipment installed on the line.

Please reply to these points by 3 pm on Friday.

J. Parkinson

Questions and activities

You have received this somewhat blunt memo on Tuesday afternoon. Plan your reaction to such a correspondence.

Your answers should concentrate on:

1. what, in your opinion, motivates line workers
2. the differences between the two shifts
3. the increased labour turnover noted among those workers allocated to the second shift that clocks on at 8.00 pm
4. the apparent hostility to the new equipment
5. the rumours of distrust among the workers to the new line foreman
6. problems regarding adequate public transport at 6.00 pm.

SUMMARY

Having read this chapter, you should now be able to:

▼ Explain all the factors relating to how people are motivated at work.

▼ Describe the ways in which employers can try to motivate employees.

Questions and activities

Technical terms and glossary

In the sections below you are given a series of technical terms and their meanings. They have been scrambled. You must match up the business term and its definition. When you have got them correctly paired, transfer them to an alphabetical vocabulary book or glossary book.

You are also advised to transfer the definitions obtained during the exercises in the case studies into this glossary book.

Technical terms

1. Hierarchy of needs
2. Intrinsic rewards
3. Extrinsic rewards
4. Group norms
5. Motivational calculus

Definitions

A. A modern process that tries to explain all the factors that motivate.

B. The order of basic human requirements.
C. The accepted practice or standards of a collection of individuals.
D. Individual needs that are 'personal' in nature.
E. Individual needs that are not directly related to the individual.

Short answer questions

1. Outline and illustrate the theory of motivation put forward by A.H Maslow.
2. How did Herzberg's ideas differ from those of Maslow?
3. Why might an employer use job enlargement and enrichment to motivate employees?
4. Describe why Mayo considered groups to be influential in the motivation of employees.
5. Explain:
   (a) E factors
   (b) Rational man
   (c) an individual's 'self-concept'
6. Why do some psychologists consider unemployment a threat to an individual's success.

38
Leadership

Preview

The analysis of the 'human side' of business continues with a description of those styles of leadership apparent in organisations.

The nature of leadership

Leadership is the process by which an individual influences, motivates and controls the behaviour of others towards a specific set of objectives. The style most frequently used in the past was autocratic, in that it was based on issuing commands or orders, which were reinforced with sanctions or punishments for those not obeying. The traditional view of leadership emphasised power divorced from authority, combined with a rigid hierarchical group structure, in which loyalty was expected of all subordinates. Most leaders in industry are officially appointed. Their essential task is to ensure that the organisation meets the targets set by its policy makers.

As has already been discovered, 'unofficial' leaders emerge in a group structure, and their objectives may not necessarily be compatible with the objectives of the organisation. The most successful official leader should therefore strive to direct the group in such a way as to *minimise conflict* and *achieve organisational objectives*, by directing the activities of subordinates so that they obtain a degree of satisfaction from their work situation. An official leader depends on a number of institutional and psychological factors associated with his position. He has rank, status, title and prestige, and through the authority that accompanies these he can both punish and reward. It also assists his role if he has more obvious technical skill or knowledge than the subordinates, so that they consider he has the ability to hand. The possession of most or all of these does not necessarily qualify a person to be a successful leader. Other factors influence the ability to lead. These include:

1. The *situation* in which the leader finds him or herself. An effective leader in one situation may not be the right leader in another. Leaders are not necessarily born, they are products of a particular set of conditions.
2. The *style* of leadership exercised will influence the degree of authority and power afforded to the leader.
3. The presence of *unofficial* leaders and *group norms* may be incompatible with achieving organisational objectives.

The majority of research into leadership suggests that leaders cannot be understood apart from the characteristics of the group they lead. The *personality traits* of the leader are only one of a number of individual variables which determine the leadership at any one point in time. Leadership is therefore dependent on the total socio-technological environment in which both the leader and the led find themselves.

To fully appreciate this complex analysis students need to explore how *unofficial leaders* emerge.

- They are usually appointed by the group, because it is felt that they best illustrate the values and requirements of the situation facing the group.
- The group feel the leader is the most competent person to achieve their goals, regardless of whether they are the organisation's objectives.
- The unofficial leader clearly identifies with the values, beliefs and life-style of the group. An official leader may come from entirely different surrounds to those he leads.
- The unofficial leader communicates directly and frequently with the group.

- More than one unofficial leader may emerge, as the role may determine the individual.
- Unofficial leaders are dependent on the group for their authority and power. They have no formal structure on which to base their control. Failure to maintain support can cause a dramatic loss of authority.

Leadership and management styles

At one end of the leadership style spectrum come *autocratic* managers. They:

- act in a dictatorial way
- issue orders
- rely on legalistic procedures and sanctions
- maintain a rigid status distinction between them and their subordinates.

Others may be described as *paternalistic*, in that they act autocratically but make conscious efforts to:

- Organise in a way that is 'best for everyone'.
- Provide a lot of welfare facilities.

Nevertheless they seldom encourage free exchange of ideas, and consider decision-making to be the sole domain of management.

Another form of leadership is known as *laissez-faire*. Here managers:

- provide little direction and control
- leave decision-making to the group.

Critics of such a style point to the problems of poor working relations, a lack of cohesion and subsequent poor work performance.

With *democratic* leaders comes a concentration on:

- open discussion
- objective setting within a formal but relaxed structure of authority.

This usually promotes cohesion within the group and good working relations.

There is also the bureaucratic, *scientific management* style, where:

- the authority of a manager stems from their position in the organisation
- the effectiveness of the group depends on the structure, training and experience rather than the leadership style.

A *charismatic* leader is one who derives power from a magnetic personality. The removal of such a

leader normally means the end for the group. There can thus be violent fluctuations in group performance.

McGregor's Theory X and Theory Y

Douglas McGregor was an American management consultant who divided management style into two distinct types, namely X and Y (see Figure 38.1).

- *Theory X.* This was associated with the autocrat, who assumed that workers disliked work, avoided effort and responsibility, and had to be forced to work by the threat of control and punishment. Such managers placed great emphasis on status, prestige and a hierarchical structure of command. Subordinates were expected to show loyalty and gratitude and individual aims were supposed to mirror those of the company. Under such a system, only fundamental material needs could be satisfied.
- *Theory Y.* This was associated with a less formal style of management: one closer to being democratic. Work is both necessary and rewarding to the individual. Working groups need little external control, provided management is capable of giving positive and flexible motivation. Self-regulation can therefore be practised by groups, and such a regime will lead to cooperation and the attainment of corporate objectives. Maximum opportunity is provided for the satisfaction of Maslow's ego and self-actualisation fulfilment needs.

McGregor's finding closely corresponds to those of Burns and Stalker, who classified Theory X as *mechanistic* and Theory Y as *organistic* styles of management. The latter concentrated on directing responsibility and authority to tasks in a fluid, informal and flexible way. Theory Y was dependent on the requirements of the circumstances, so making little use of rigid, formal hierarchical structures.

Mechanistic management works best where:

- stable economic conditions exist
- the work flow is steady
- operatives are organised on an assembly line basis.

while organic management is best where:

- new technology is complex
- new products are being introduced
- rapid change is apparent.

been further developed by a number of modern management theories. They include:

N.R.F. Maier

N.R.F. Maier put forward the idea that decisions based on human groups could be analysed according to the quality and the acceptance of the decisions affected by them. He considered quality to refer to:

- logical, rational, practical, technical aspects of the decision. These concentrated on financial and technical issues.

The acceptance related to:

- the depth of the decisions, once made, and how this is acknowledged as correct and legitimate by the subordinates who have to carry out the tasks and fulfil the targets set by such decisions.

Peter Drucker

Drucker, who did the majority of his work in the 1950s, built on the theories of Fayol and Taylor. Drucker subdivided his findings into various categories.

- *Setting objectives for the organisation.* Objectives had to be measurable, agreed to by subordinates, communicated to all employees and performance evaluated. Such objectives had to be linked to a mission statement that involved all of the business.
- *Organising the work.* The business must be divided into manageable parts, activities and jobs, which fit neatly into a structure capable of quick response to all changes in the business environment.
- *Motivating people.* This was seen as essential if management wants to get the best from the company employees. Good managers could balance all objectives and still motivate individuals to achieve the targets. Drucker regarded all business as having one overriding function, namely economic performance, i.e. long-term survival based on profit and customer satisfaction. Again, a 'good' manager was aware of time dimensions and the need to prioritise. Once again Drucker stressed the need to be aware of individual objectives, recognition and the need to motivate individuals, while at the same time being aware of the need to meet the corporate objectives (see Figure 38.2).

Theory X and Theory Y

Douglas McGregor in the 1950s enunciated two sets of propositions and assumptions about man in the organisation.

THEORY X

1. The average man is by nature indolent – he works as little as possible.
2. He lacks ambition, dislikes responsibility, prefers to be led.
3. He is inherently self-centred, indifferent to organisational needs.
4. He is by nature resistant to change.
5. He is gullible, not very bright, the ready dupe of the charlatan and the demagogue.

The implications for management are:

1. Management is responsible for organising the elements of productive enterprise – money, materials, equipment, people – in the interest of economic ends.
2. With respect to people, this is a process of directing their efforts, motivating them, controlling their actions, modifying their behaviour to fit the needs of the organisation.
3. People must be persuaded, rewarded, punished, controlled; their activities must be directed.

THEORY Y

1. People are not by nature passive or resistant to organisational needs. They have become so as a result of experience in organisations.
2. The motivation, the potential for development, the capacity to assume responsibility, the readiness to direct behaviour towards organisational goals, are all present in people. It is a responsibility of management to make it possible for people to reorganise and develop the human characteristics for themselves.
3. Management is responsible for organising the elements of productive enterprise in the interest of economic ends, but their essential task is to arrange the conditions and methods of operation so that people can achieve their own goals best by directing their own efforts towards organisational objectives.

(*Source:* From D. McGregor, *The Human Side of Enterprise*)

Figure 38.1 *Douglas McGregor's Theory X and Theory Y.*

The way in which managers react to work situations naturally affects both the quality of decisions being made and the quality of output that follows. This has

Charles Handy

Handy argued that the functions of any manager are so varied that a definition is meaningless. The manager, in his mind, had three essential tactics, which are:

1. *General practitioner.* In the same way as a doctor diagnoses, so a manager must identify symptoms, decide what to do, begin treatment and monitor results. Such treatment might be centred on financial issues, personnel changes, patterns of work organisation structure or changes of procedure.
2. *Dilemmas.* Handy considered that managers faced four of these:
   - the organisational culture, i.e. deciding which style is best suited to particular tasks and the people involved
   - time-horizons – balancing the needs of the short-term with those of the long-term
   - trust-control – how far does a manager keep in sole control, and how much does he delegate
   - commando leaders' – junior managers show a liking for working in teams, which have clear objectives and bureaucratic control, while more senior appointees prefer order and structured forms to control and monitoring.

FORCES IN THE MANAGER

e.g.

- Attitude toward shared decision-making
- Confidence in subordinates
- Personal leadership inclinations
- Feeling of security/confidence in uncertain situations

CHOICE OF LEADERSHIP STYLE

Forces in the situation
- Types of organisation
  - how managers are expected to behave
  - size and spread of work unit
  - need for confidentiality
- Group effectiveness when working together
- Difficulties encountered
- Time pressures

Forces of subordinates
- Need for independence
- Readiness to accept responsibility
- Interest shown
- Understanding of and identification with organisational goals
- Degree of acceptance of shared decision-making

Figure 38.2 *Formal leadership: choice of leadership styles*

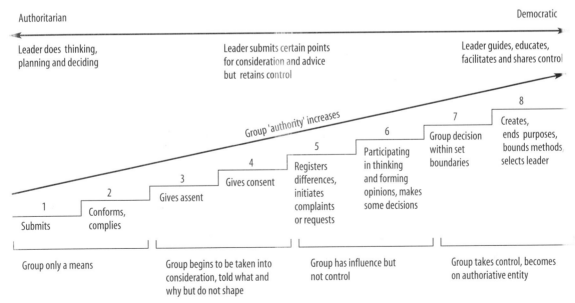

Figure 38.3 *Types of response to leadership*

3. *A person.* The 'manager' is now a professional, often highly trained. Those beginning their careers require rewards for using their skills. In other words managers have their own objectives which the organisation must recognise if they are to retain high quality employees. Against this is the growing awareness that 'no one has a job for life' and the pattern is emerging of a small group of highly effective permanent staff being employed who are supported by part-time, outside workers, who enjoy few of the benefits of full-time contractual workers (see Figures 38.3, 38.4 and 38.5).

	Autocratic			Democractic
Harbison/Myers	autocractic	paternalistic	consultative	participative
Likert	system 1	system 2	system 3	system 4
Tannenbaum/ Schmidt	leader control	shared control	shared control	group control
Vroom	leader decides	consults	shares	delegates
Hersey/Blanchard	telling	selling	participating	delegating

Figure 38.4 *Some other observations on leadership styles*

Figure 38.5 *Adair's ideas on leadership*

The three circles

John Adair has perfected a very successful model of leadership training in Britain based on the three overlapping circles that are involved in any leadership situation:

He emphasises the importance of distinguishing the *individual* from the *group*. There will seldom, if ever, be a perfect match between the needs of the individual, the group and the task. The leader's job is to be aware of the tension and to manage it. To do this he needs a *functional* approach which has eight elements:

- Defining the task
- Planning
- Briefing
- Controlling

- Evaluating
- Motivating
- Organising
- Setting an example

The training is organised around precept and practice in each of these eight areas. Style, as Adair points out, is more than and different from the business of taking decisions, which is relatively straightforward.

(*Source:* J. Adair, *Effective Leadership*, 1983)

CASE STUDY 38.1

'We never encountered this open disagreement when everything was centred in the hands of CJ,' remarked Colin Mansfield, the Chief Packer.

He was tired of explaining everything to everyone and never quite knowing who should know what. When the General Manager had been a loyal company man of many years service, everything had run like 'clockwork'. Everybody knew exactly where they stood, liked it, and never asked for more than the odd notice on the canteen board.

Then came the new boy, university educated and full of ideas. All memos now had to be circulated and active participation was the key phrase. Channels of communication had to be maintained and consultation shown to have taken place before decisions could be made. Changing a light bulb now seemed to take ages as all involved had to have their say. Thank goodness they had no Greens among them, or they would have endless debates on long-life bulbs. Despite this open approach the ordinary worker felt little real improvement, just more paperwork and greater chance of failing to do what had now become expected of them.

'Bring back the autocrat', cried Colin, 'it was predictable and I, for one, liked it that way.'

'Colin', said the new General Manager, 'you obviously feel strongly about my changes. Here is one of my college essays on leadership and involving your team. You may like to read it and write me something on it. Say 500 words on how these new-fangled ideas can be properly applied to College Dynamics.'

A red-faced Colin had not realised that the 'new boy' had been listening to his little attack on Mr Modern.

Question

Yes, you have guessed, you are Colin and you have got 500 words to explain how such management styles are supposed to improve manager-worker relations and output.

SUMMARY

Having read this chapter, you should be able to:

▽ Describe the various types of leadership used in organisations.

▽ Explain the advantages and disadvantages of these styles.

▽ Discuss some of the theories put forward to explain why the various styles are relevant in certain circumstances.

Questions and activities

Technical terms and glossary

In the section below you are given a series of technical terms and their meanings. They have been scrambled. You must match up the terms and the definitions. When you have them correctly paired, transfer them to your alphabetical vocabulary or glossary book.

You should also transfer any defintions obtained during the exercises in the case studies into this glossary book.

Technical Terms

1. Personality traits
2. Autocratic
3. Democratic
4. Theory X and Y
5. Mission statement

Definitions

A. A theory of management that divides workers into two distinctly different groups.
B. A style of leadership that is based on one person and little delegation.
C. Qualities considered necessary for a leader.
D. A clear statement of an organisation's objectives.
E. A style of management that is open, democratic and encourages communication.

Short answer questions

1. Outline the major characteristics associated with some considered to be:
   (a) an autocratic leader
   (b) a *laissez-faire* leader
   (c) a democratic leader
2. How might McGregor's X and Y definitions influence a leaders style.
3. What new ideas to leaderhsip theory did Drucker and Hardy introduce?
4. What do you understand by the terms 'mechanistic management' and 'organic' management?

39
Communication

Preview

▽ The art of good communications is central to the running of any organisation.

▽ Various styles of communication have evolved, and do not only involve language or writing.

▽ The various types and style of communication each have their own virtues and pitfalls.

▽ Alas, even with a well-organised system of communications mistakes do occur, and managers have to deliver bad news as well as good.

One of essential qualities of management is the transmission and exchange of all types of information necessary to the efficient running of a business organisation. The task central to all forms of communication is to transmit information that is clear, unambiguous and understandable to the receiver for whom it is intended, and who is required to act upon it.

An effective management must seek means of effective communication. This depends upon engaging the attention of the intended receiver, the degree to which the receiver understands and appreciates the importance of the message and the degree of motivation to act upon information received.

Managers not only communicate, they also have the responsibility of appointing work to subordinates. To achieve this, all appointed work must be carried out efficiently and part of the manager's authority must be transferred to the individual or group responsible for completing the work and meeting the objectives.

Many managers favour the maximum use of what is known as *delegation*, though it must complement organisational efficiency. The main advantages of this approach are as follows:

1. Greater flexibility in decision-making, so enabling a company to meet the needs of the fast-changing business and technological change.

2. A greater sense of participation and motivation among subordinates.

3. Greater commitment from participants once decisions are made.

4. The skills of management are developed through the exercise of authority.

In any act of delegation it is the responsibility of the manager to clearly define the limits of the authority delegated, so ensuring that subordinates know precisely where their limits are and that up to these they will be supported. Whatever may happen, the manager remains responsible for the decisions made by the subordinate but he must not interfere, or he will destroy the advantages of delegation.

Participation

Many management theorists support the use of participation in the decision-making process. Indeed, they promote bringing more and more people into the decision-making structure. The exponents of this belief cite the following as the reasons for their support:

1. Consultation and participation are essential for involving people in the decisions that affect

Effective communication is essential in business as well as in government.

them. By doing this from the top (unions) to the bottom (individuals) it is seen as an essential part of 'modern' management.

2. The increasing complexity of modern, industrialised societies means that one set of workers are more dependent on other groups. Working people now demand a say in what affects their lives and their families lives.

3. It is now recognised that purely financial decisions do have a 'human dimension' and do cause hardships to individuals.

4. Resistance to change is likely to be lessened if people understand why something is happening.

5. Employees now appreciate how much they contribute to the profitability of the company and know that they are a valuable asset. They therefore expect a say in what is to be done.

6. Modern education levels, industrial practices, and possibly the access to information all tend to encourage individual independence. They also make us more aware of our democratic rights.

Those who oppose this more 'open' approach to management put forward that:

- It is too involved for all but a few workers to fully understand and appreciate.
- Management is the steward of the shareholders' assets and has the responsibility for profit-maximisation. The work force does not have such a responsibility and therefore does not need an input to high level decision-making.
- Workers tend to take a short-term view of what needs to be done. The long-term is the territory of management, and as such it is their responsibility to encourage innovation and risk.
- Many workers, and some union leaders do not

consider it is their responsibility to make decisions. They argue that as there are always likely to be areas of difference between management and workers, negotiation rather than top-level participation is the legitimate role for workers.

Dealing with innovation and change

People and groups to which they belong, tend to be rather conservative by nature, and once values and norms have been established it is difficult to change them. Change, even of a minor issue, can be both frightening and threatening. Its effects are unknown, unpredictable and uncertain. Yet, in the fast pace of industrial change people do have to alter their ways. New skills have to be acquired, old ideas of status and position must be re-appraised. Indeed, innovation is often so rapid that individuals find themselves unable to adjust to new ideas and events. It is here that management meets new challenges. Authoritative, formal, highly structured chains of command and very long lines of communication do nothing to reduce the effects of change. Indeed, they may actually reinforce resistance. To meet change successfully management must:

- Create flexible and democratic chains of command that communicate with all those affected.
- Encourage participation and consultation in advance of change and agree schedules for the introduction of change.
- Identify all the probable effects of change and plan well in advance for the introduction of whatever is intended.
- Offer practical assistance, re-training and financial help for such things as re-allocation and new forms of work.

Only a well-established programme of participation and trusted procedures for comm-unication can create a climate within which change can be adequately handled. Management must aim for maximum acceptance and minimum dislocation.

In the event that some employees simply cannot cope with the anticipated change, a sensible redundancy package should be produced.

Throughout all of these aspects of management one essential quality is required, namely an ability to communicate. In the last part of this chapter we look at the various methods of communications available to managers and workers alike.

We must now turn our attention to the fundamentals of communication. First, the various methods of communication must be examined.

Methods of communication

Methods are equal ways of doing things, while systems are a group which form some sort of connected structure. Combine these and we can see that any organisation is a combination of systems, through which managers have to communicate. These systems tend to be complex, and are not often obvious – the effective communication has to be aware of their individual characteristics. The main methods or systems of communication which are found in industry are now discussed.

Line management

This management system is a form of communication that follows the hierarchy of the organisation. A pyramid or tree structure is developed and tight allegiance to it is promoted throughout the company. An example of a communication system based on the hierarchy of the organisation is shown in Figure 39.1.

Figure 39.1 *An example of a communication system based on the hierarchy of the organisation*

This system is often known as a 'chain of command' method of communication, as essential information flows downwards or upwards. The use of such a system tends to reduce the risk of confusion or misinterpretation, but both superiors and subordinates must be clear to whom they report and from whom they receive instructions. Oral instructions often form the impetus of line management, but most instructions are supported by 'paperwork', in either minutes from a relevant meeting, or a direct memorandum.

One source of confusion in communication is a misunderstanding between the terms 'line' and 'staff'. Line authorities exercised by any manager, over his immediate subordinates carries the ability to enforce an instruction. Staff authority is exercised by a staff manager only over other managers who report to a line manager in common with him, and only carries a right to advise (see Figure 39.2).

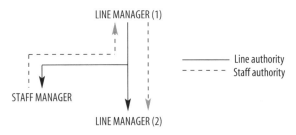

Figure 39.2 *Authority and status*

Group briefings

Group briefings augment the normal one-to-one forms of communication. In these one communicator tells a number of people a set of instructions. The communicator is normally of a senior status to the group and more often works from a written brief agenda or instructions.

Such groupings are normally best held when:

- something important has to be communicated
- only on special occasions
- there is 'good' as well as bad information (e.g. redundancies)
- they are brief – say 30 minutes at maximum
- they allow for questions, usually at end.

As with all communications, briefings are most effective when the message is presented as shown in Figure 39.3.

Figure 39.3 *Making communication effective*

Participative decision-making

Any decision in any organisation will come either directly from its leader, or from a member of the company. The precise form used will depend upon:

- the situation
- knowledge of subordinates
- the nature of the decision
- the philosophy of the organisation.

Recent developments in management thinking have promoted the idea that the more people share in decisions which affect their working lives, the more they are motivated to carry them out. Participation seems to heighten people's:

- enthusiasm
- involvement
- commitment
- sense of responsibility.

Although the ultimate decision may rest with a superior, the consulatation has forged an essential link in motivating individuals. Most organisations therefore actively encourage meetings which pass information *upwards*. The advantages of these meetings are that:

- employees' contributions are actively encouraged
- employees' experiences and ideas can be funnelled into the decision-making process
- employees and managers gain an opportunity to meet and discuss their options.

Decisions can be immediate, or communicated to the relevant members of the group, or the committee. The latter not only pass information upwards and downwards, but sideways (laterally) and illustrate the need for all communications to be coordinated. We must always remember that as well as being subordinates we are also coordinators with one another.

Published communications

The identification of employees with a common company image or *corporate identity* is now a feature of business. Such a process can include the *logo* (a change which recently cost BP £72 million), through to letterheads, colours and in more tangible forms, 'house' magazines, reports and journals. The early forms of house journals tended to concentrate on downwards and sideways communication, but that is now changing. Increasingly, magazines are being used to feature items on people, their personalities, opinions and attitudes. The individuals chosen are not only senior management, and employees are actively encouraged to make suggestions. Such communication is not reserved for the written form; the video, public presentation and other forms of welding a recognisable image are all part of publicly communicating the virtues of your organisation. The use of in-house magazines can be to test employee opinion on a range of items. These include:

- issues requiring management attention
- morale

- statistical information
- employee expectations from training
- acceptance/disagreement of previous management actions
- management performance.

Often this form of probing is achieved through a questionnaire. By actively encouraging feedback, the management are promoting participation, and gaining first-class information directly from those most affected.

Grape vines

All organisations house these! Alas, the passing of a message from one individual to another often involves *distortion*. The more people involved the greater the risk of distortion and informal communication is particularly suspect to exaggeration and little personal additions or subtractions. The existence of these perfectly normal modes of communication can also be considered beneficial. They should serve the purpose of passing information upwards, so passing a form of judgement on how well the official channels are actually working. Informal channels can also be used to 'test' or 'sound out' opinion. In modern politics the terms 'a source close to the Minister' usually means his Press Secretary. This offical will put an item into the minds of journalists, who in turn produce stories about what might happen. The 'feedback' in public reaction and media coverage is then matched against policy and the idea dropped or proceeded with.

These informal contacts are particularly important for lateral communication. The meetings that develop within any organisation are an essential part of the pooling of experiences and opinions of those who actually work for the enterprise. So, communication can be both *formal* and *informal* and can be developed through a series of systems that concentrate on face-to-face individual contact, groups and the general public perception of the organisation.

Towards effective communication

The art of communication is a complex issue and space does not permit a very full coverage. We therefore try in this section to outline certain styles, which if adopted will aid more effective communication.

Speaking

The normal advice given to someone about to address a group is illustrated in Figure 39.4.

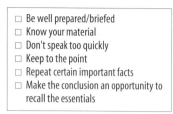

☐ Be well prepared/briefed
☐ Know your material
☐ Don't speak too quickly
☐ Keep to the point
☐ Repeat certain important facts
☐ Make the conclusion an opportunity to recall the essentials

Figure 39.4 How to speak effectively

Preparation

It is advisable to have an *aim*, or *objective*, i.e. what you really mean to communicate. This usually necessitates some form of *plan*. No real rules exist for the design of a plan, but it seems sensible to have a clear beginning, middle and end. It may be necessary to do some background reading about the people you are to communicate with and reconnoitre the place in which you are to meet. It is always reassuring to know the seating, lighting, acoustics, probable distractions and the working of any equipment you may make use of. In brief, devise a workable plan, do your homework and know what you want to say.

Clarity

Clear thinking actually results in clear instructions. It is therefore essential to concentrate on analysing, selecting and evaluating your opinions a long time before you actually utter them. To communicate well one needs a decisive approach, which combines an ability to be lucid with that of being honest.

Simplicity

Always try to be uncomplicated. An essential skill for this is the ability to be able to see to the heart of the matter and then be capable of relating this to others.

Colourful

A central feature of this is to be energetic and apparently keen on the topic. Wherever possible show enthusiasm, illustrate a creative mind and use language that complements your delivery.

Naturalness

This skill greatly influences the delivery of our communication. It is a complex mixture of stance, language, breathing (intonation) and gestures. To this is the need to add emotion – try to stimulate interest, curiosity, anger or passion.

Listening

Most of us are poor listeners. In what ways is this apparent?

* summary dismissal
* too critical of deliverer's approach
* selective listening
* interrupting
* mind wandering
* being distracted
* deliberately avoiding a difficult issue
* bowing to emotions
* simply 'nodding off'

Let us look at each in turn:

Dismissal

Most people have clear-cut likes and dislikes. A certain type of person will always condemn 'long hair' as a characteristic of a male they do not want to listen to. It is probable that we never meet anyone who is incapable of teaching us nothing, yet we do dismiss people with alarming speed and ease.

Delivery

A stance, an accent or a particular characteristic should not deter us from listening, but it does.

Selective listening

This is rather like our ability to consider summers of some years ago to have been warm or sunny. They seldom were, yet we choose to filter out unpleasant parts. Our brain behaves in a similar way with what we want to hear.

Interruptions

To disturb the flow of communication probably destroys the understanding. Most exchanges of information have natural pauses, and then interruptions can be pursued.

Mind wandering

Very few people can actually think of two things at the same time.

Distraction

Poor seating, noise, heat or cold, sunlight or gloom: all can play their part in destroying attention. The better the listening the less obvious the distractions and probably the better the understanding.

Difficult issues

Lazy listeners seldom take in the full story. Alas, some issues have to be persevered with.

Bowing to emotions

Certain word patterns conjure up particular pictures in peoples' minds. Once their imagination has wandered it is doubtful if their retention will be high.

Nodding off

Tiredness does affect our listening and the old commodity of will-power will have to be raised to the surface.

To improve listening it seems admissible to concentrate on:

- an interesting topic
- good content
- controlled delivery
- identifying ideas
- flexibility
- making the receivers listen – try to outweigh distractions, exercise their minds and encourage them to think along with you.

Writing

This obviously important part of business communication is often spoilt by a combination of the following:

- *Curtness.* Beware of being over-brief and apparently unconcerned for your reader.
- *Sarcasm.* Not a popular form of humour to receive.
- *Silliness.* Try not to use phrases like 'I'm surprised by your childish reaction to…'.
- *Rage.* Annoyance in one direction usually provokes a similar reply.
- *Suspicion.* This usually surfaces in the form of doubting someone's motives. It seldom builds mutual respect.
- *Insult.* Few people set out to be deliberately rude, but accidental rudeness has just the same effect.
- *Patronising attitude.* Wherever possible never 'talk down'.
- *Familiarity.* The use of a person's first name is never an easy issue.
- *Presumptions.* It is advisable to check someone's desire to do something before you ask them to do it.

The most common form of written business communication is the report. When compiling such a document it is probably best to remember the contents of a letter sent by Winston Churchill to all departments. He advised that colleagues should:

- make reports as short as possible
- use short, crisp paragraphs
- only put statistics in appendices
- use headings to show the main point in each paragraph
- end with the shortest of concluding remarks.

Reading

The manager is constantly receiving reports and other written documents. An ability to read and digest quickly and fully is now a major skill of effective decision-making. To formulate an ability to take in large numbers of words quickly we have to learn the art of *perusing*. This consists of fast, accurate and permanent reactions to the words in front of you. Such a skill can only be enhanced with practice, but two complementary features are the ability to read quickly and an exposure to what is considered 'good' reading. Many schemes exist for improving reading speed and perusal can be improved by ignoring old habits such as reading every word. Look at summaries or headings and try, if possible, to gauge an author's style, for then you should start to see where he/she is saying something important. The following may help improve the speed of reading.

- Look at the title, summary, illustrations and the preface.
- Look at structure of work, e.g. chapter length.
- Sample-read a chapter – note the tone, word use and how it actually appeals to you.
- Begin reading and slotting together the key elements.
- Sweep across the text in systematic waves.

Leading a meeting

Managing the exchange of information and ideas is an implicit part of any manager's life. In addition, he/she must lead and seek to forge a working union of minds, wills and actions. However a leader emerges (democratically or appointed) he/she will be responsible for the conduct of a meeting. The leader will need to address certain questions, namely:

- Why is the meeting being held?
- Who is coming?
- What is to be discussed?
- What must be decided?
- What is the 'power' of the meeting?

The leader's needs for 'chairing' a meeting will centre on:

- an ability to clarify
- an ability to summarise
- an ability to seek concessions.

and their ability to succeed in these will depend on their skill in:

1. *Initiating.* Good listeners put forward ideas and look for feedback, and this is essential if he/she is to proceed through the agenda with confidence.

2. *Planning.* To plan means to allocate resources to contracts to achieve objectives. A structure appears from within a plan. Plans involve setting priorities. Plans must also coordinate delegation and set agreed codes for behaviour. A plan begins before the meeting (place, etc.) and ends after it (follow-up procedures).

3. *Control.* Like all captains a good leader must keep his ship on course. This requires a subtle mixture of the carrot and the whip. One essential part of this process is to summarise and identify what still needs to be achieved. The leader must act as the funeller of feelings, emotions and their characteristics and seek to steer the meeting to a satisfactory end.

4. *Support.* It is never easy to air an opinion in front of others, and a good chairperson must encourage participation by all those who wish to make a contribution. The standards set by the leader will normally influence those used by others.

5. *Informing.* This is a two-part process, in that it concerns informing those present and passing on the conclusions of the meeting. These functions give the leader the important role of both a channel for the opinion of others and a filter.

6. *Evaluating.* Leaders have to set standards and decide upon the feasibility of what has been proposed. This necessitates the ability to follow through the consequences, quite often with considerable speed. One further part of this function is to note agreement, or consensus. In many organisations, consensus is arrived at via a note.

As noted earlier the style of leadership adopted by the individual will have considerable influence on how they react to the responsibilities contained within the above.

Developing effective communication skills

What is communication?

A very simple but accurate way of defining communication is that it is 'the transfer of a message from one party to another so that it can be understood and correctly acted upon'.

Communication in management has become a central concern to people in all walks of life, not least the place of work.

Why is communication so important?

It is likely that you will come up with reasons why poor communication is not effective. Try to think of the positive aspects of communication. These can be divided into two areas:

1. *Management* considers communication important as good communication will increase *efficiency*.

2. *Staff* consider communication important as good communication will increase *involvement* and thus, motivation.

Examples of poor communication

Stories of poor communication are commonplace and never more apparent than in the game 'Chinese Whispers'. This demonstrates how a message which is passed on unclearly is distorted into one which makes sense to the receiver, and hence the famous story of a message sent in the last days of a military advance on enemy lines. The message was: 'Send reinforcements, we're going to advance.' This was delivered at HQ as: 'Send three and four pence, we're going to a dance!'

Communication: some definitions

'Communication is the transfer of a message from one party to another so that the message is received, understood and acted upon.' (Drucker)

'Communication is defined as the process of transmitting understood information among two or more people. As such, it always involves at least two parties – a sender and a receiver. Technically speaking, communication is successful only when mutual understanding results, that is, when one not only transmits information, but also makes oneself understood by others.' (Bedeian)

'Simplify communication. When speaking of a certain lawyer, Abraham Lincoln remarked, "He can compress the most words into the smallest ideas better than any man I ever met." As more of us assume information-producing jobs, there is going to be more information. And information overload is one sure way to immobilise people. We all need to work hard to keep our communication as simple and brief as possible. Keep all written communication to an absolute minimum. Question every line of every form, report and

memorandum and ask, "Does this cause anyone to take any useful action?' If not, get rid of it. Communicate to others in language they understand." (le Boeuf)

The key word must, therefore, be *understanding*. Communication is not effective unless it means the information concerned is *understood* (see also Figure 39.5).

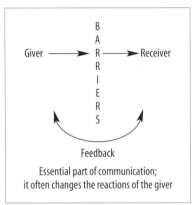

Figure 39.5 *Communication – A model*

Characteristics of the communication process

Regardless of the types of communication that you must undertake, each type follows a predetermined process. That is, the communication flows from one individual to one or more individuals and is thus a two-way process. This physical process takes place both when a message is sent and when one is received. More specifically, however, the communication process involves more than just sending and receiving. It contains certain characteristics that are common to any oral or written communication situation. These characteristics are illustrated in Figure 39.6.

The information source is a speaker or writer who develops an idea or observes some fact, object or experience and wishes to convey this idea or experience to another individual. This idea or experience is encoded or translated into a message and transmitted or sent through a channel or medium, such as a spoken or written word. The message is received by the listener or reader and decoded or interpreted. Based on the interpretation, meaning is

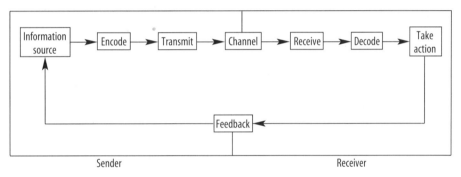

Figure 39.6 *Characteristics of a communication*

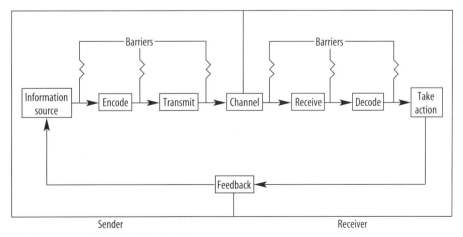

Figure 39.7 *How barriers might affect communication*

given to the message and provides feedback to the speaker or writer. A model of this communication process is shown in Figure 39.7.

Barriers in the communication process

An assumption that may be drawn from the model shown in Figure 39.7 is that there has been a free flow of information from the sender to the receiver. This assumption is not always realistic, however, since problems occur that inhibit or impede the free flow of information from the sender to the receiver. When such problems occur, message understanding and interpretation is often affected. These problems are often described as barriers to effective communication.

An important point to remember is that communication barriers may develop within the sender, within the receiver, between the sender and receiver, or in situations external to both. In other words, these barriers can be classified as intrapersonal, interpersonal or organisational.

Intrapersonal barriers arise within the sender or receiver. For example, the user or receiver of a report may lack adequate knowledge of the systems design to understand the report.

Interpersonal barriers, however, occur because of the interaction between sender and receiver. An example of the interpersonal barrier would be the hostile attitude of a client's employee toward an external consultant, arising from the possibility that the employee's job could be changed as a result of the consultant's recommendations.

On the other hand, organisational barriers develop as a result of the communication environment. The barrier may occur when a relatively junior member of staff meets with a director. The status or position differences between the two may have an impact on the communication exchange.

A. Types of communication processes

Overcoming barriers to communication

Adjust to the world of the receiver

Try to predict the impact of what is going to be written or said on the receiver's feelings and attitudes. Tailor the message to fit the receiver's vocabulary, interest and values. Be aware of how the information might be misinterpreted because of the prejudices, the influences of others and the tendency for people to reject what they do not want to hear.

Use feedback

Ensure that a message is received back from the receiver which tells how much has been understood.

Use face-to-face communication

Whenever possible talk to people rather than write to them. That is how to get feedback. Adjust or change your message according to reactions. Verbal criticism can often be given in a more constructive manner than written reproof which always seems to be harsher.

Use reinforcement

It may be necessary to present a message in a number of different ways to get it across. Re-emphasise the important point and follow up.

Use direct simple language

This seems obvious. However, many people clutter up what they can say with jargon, long words and elaborate sentences.

Suit the action to the words

Communication has to be credible to be effective. When someone says they are going to do something, they must do it. Next time, they are likely to be believed.

Barriers to communication

Hearing what we want to hear

What people hear or understand when someone speaks to them is largely based on their own experience and background. Instead of hearing what people have told them, they hear what their minds tell them they have said. They have preconceptions about what people are going to say and if what they say does not fit into their framework or references they adjust it until it does.

Ignoring conflicting information

Individuals tend to ignore or reject communications that conflict with their own beliefs. If they are not rejected, some way is found of twisting and shaping their meaning to fit preconceptions. When a message is inconsistent with existing beliefs, the receiver rejects its validity, avoids further exposure to it, easily forgets it and, in his memory, distorts what he or she has heard.

Influence of the group

The group with which individuals identify influences their attitudes and feelings. What a group hears depends on its interests. Staff members are often more likely to listen to their colleagues, who share their experiences, than to outsiders.

Words mean different things to different people

Essentially, language is a method of using symbols to represent facts and feelings. It is difficult to convey meaning; all they can do is to convey words. Do not assume that because something has a certain meaning to one person, it will have the same meaning to someone else.

Non-verbal communication

When people try to understand the meaning of what others say, they listen to the words but they use other clues which convey meaning. Individuals attend not only to what people say but to how they say it. They form impressions from what is called 'body language': eyes, shape of mouth, the muscles of the face, even posture. They may feel that these tell us more about what someone is really saying than the words they use. But there is enormous scope for misinterpretation.

B. Types of non-verbal communication

Being a better listener

It is not easy to become a good listener, and the benefits are considerable. They include:

- a better grasp of what the speaker is saying, and thus more information for the listener
- better working relationships, because they understand more accurately and because people appreciate their attention and interest
- more effective solution of problems or disagreements
- more likelihood that people will see through their own problems or difficulties clearly by having the opportunity to talk and think them through.

The guidelines in this section should help the reader to become a better listener. All the guidelines apply when they are the sole listener, such as in a one-to-one discussion or interview; most apply equally well when they are a member of an audience or at a meeting.

Preparation
- Eliminate distractions (noise, views, people, etc.) and concentrate on the speaker.

- Allow enough time to listen – be ready to respond, but not too hastily.

Attitude
- Find an area of interest in what is being said. If the listener is to make a worthwhile attempt at receiving ideas, they need a conscious objective. A good listener knows what is sought from a communication, but is also flexible enough to change the original purpose if necessary.
- Try to judge the content of a message rather than the person sending it.
- Keep an open mind about the speaker and the subject. Put prejudices on one side. Only evaluate when the listener has thoroughly understood.
- Concentrate on the meaning of what is said, not just the words themselves.
- Listen analytically. Look for central ideas, themes, links, necessary details. Use the extra speed of thought compared with speech to give the listener time to mentally summarise what they have heard and weigh it up. But be careful not to switch into 'think mode' for too long and so miss the speakers' next words.
- Listen for the feelings behind what the speaker is saying. Be sensitive to what the speaker is communicating non-verbally.

Demonstrate listening

Let the speaker know the audience is listening and provide encouragement. This is even more important when there is only one listener or a small group:

- Keep a posture that looks alert and attentive but not threatening.
- Keep looking at the speaker nearly all the time but do not look as though you are judging or ciriticising.
- Encourage by the occasional smile, nod, 'yes, I see', etc. at appropriate points, but do not overdo this one.
- Seek clarification of the meaning. This can be done by asking questions, reflecting or summarising.
- Mirror the body posture and speech of the speaker. This helps build the rapport between the listener and the deliverer (see Figure 39.9).

L-I-S-T-E-N: a summary

L – Look interested and show encouragement by:
- facing the speaker
- keeping eye contact
- staying relaxed
- leaning forward slightly
- maintaining an open posture.

	Type I	Type II	Type III	Type IV	Type V
Leader	Any	Probably C	Probably E	Usually C	Any
Speed of learning a procedure	Relatively slow			Quick	Slow
Speed of solution	Relatively Slow	Slow		Quick	Slow
Mistakes not corrected: flexibility to change	Quite good	Weak		Often inflexible	
Originality of ideas. e.g. for brainstorming				Low	High
Number of messages sent	Fairly large			Small	Large
Satisfaction/morale	Usually good	Not high		C often high; remainder low	All equal

Figure 39.8 How we learn our communication skills

I – Inquire with questions
- clarify the speaker's meaning
- ensure all get the full story
- remember the various types of questions open to the listener.

S – Stay on target
- stick to the point by remembering the purpose. Listen for the central theme of what is being said: wait for the complete message – don't prejudge, don't 'yes, but …' be patient!

T – Test understanding
- ensure everyone really does understand what the speaker is saying. Restate to make sure: 'So what you're saying is …'

E – Evaluate the message
- identify the speaker's purpose and analyse what is said
- reasoning
- flaws
- generalisation
- emotional appeals
- facts and assertions
- complete or partial
- information source
- up-to-date
- reliable
- language

- use of familiar words/jargon
- body language
- consistent with verbal message
- voice-related indicators
- tone
- pitch
- speed of delivery

N – Neutralise feelings
- stay calm: retain self-control
- don't get heated or emotional
- keep an open mind

Questioning techniques

Open questions
Open questions allow a wider range of answers which often require several sentences or a longer explanation. Many questions which ask for an opinion, and explanation of events or procedures, or the reasoning behind a particular decision fall into the category of open questions.

Purposes/uses
- to gather information
- to get the customer to open up
- to get information without creating defensiveness
- to allow the customer to express a personal point of view.

Examples

- 'I read in the press your intention to acquire X Ltd. In the event of this being successful, how would you see the integration of this company into the group?'
- 'What impact will the recent regulation changes have on your company?'

Problems

1. conversation can wander into side issues
2. it can become overloaded with information
3. a person may find it difficult to respond: especially if she/he is not used to open questions.

Closed questions

Closed questions are designed to require a specific answer. They narrow the range of possible answers and focus on a particular point in discussion. Questions which can be answered with yes or no, a single word, or a simple phrase, fall into the direct question category.

Purposes/uses

- to gather specific information
- to give the other person a clear idea of what you want to know from him/her
- to eliminate misunderstanding of what answer is required
- to guide the discussion towards a specific problem

Examples

- 'Do you have any major capital expenditure in the foreseeable future which requires funding?'
- 'Do you require credit facilities next year?'
- 'Are XXX Bank providing you with a good service?'
- 'Are your current banking requirements being met by your existing banking relationships?'

Problems

1. they can be seen as threatening
2. they can arouse defensiveness and when people are defensive, communication becomes difficult. Thus the effect of increasing defensiveness is usually a less productive discussion.
3. they can actually result in getting less information. Using too many direct questions may make you sound like a prosecuting attorney or a police sergeant.

Clarifying questions

A clarifying question asks for more information or a more complete explanation of what has just been said. It is often used when the listener finds a statement unclear or the previous answer incomplete. Questions which ask for examples or a second explanation of the same point fall into the category of clarifying questions.

Purposes/uses

- to promote full information
- to help prevent misunderstandings
- to clarify points which have been made
- to ensure that the meaning of the words expressed is understood
- to show interest in the other person's comments.

Examples

- 'I'm not sure I understand your thinking on this; could we review it once more?'
- 'You say it always happens; do you mean every time or ...?'
- 'I think I understand your point; could you give me a couple more examples?'

Problems

1. can be time-consuming
2. if over-used, person may feel you are not listening.

Non-verbal communication (body language)

Communication – the value of non-verbal powers

The most effective way people can communicate with each other is by face-to-face, two-way conversation. Apart from being able to get immediate feedback and having the ability to question and clarify, they are able to observe the whole wealth of non-verbal communication signs which can add to, or detract from, the verbal message.

They unconsciously look for signs to confirm what they are hearing and, equally, give signs for a listener to pick up. The actions and postures they adopt are to a large extent automotive responses, but they can choose, once they are aware, to use non-verbal techniques consciously as a very powerful tool in communicating.

A note of caution must be sounded before looking at particular aspects of non-verbal language. It is very easy, perhaps easier than with other forms of communication, to misinterpret the signs that are seen. Folded arms and crossed legs may be a defensive barrier indicating unease, but equally, they may indicate merely a comfortable posture. An indication of mood or underlying feelings can be gained, however, from groups or clusters of non-verbal signs. It would be wrong to concentrate on one aspect of non-verbal communication, such as bodily postures and ignore other areas, such as eye contact. Remember also that non-verbal communication covers a lot more than just body language. In this section we will look at the use of non-verbal language as an aid to more effective communication and as a tool available to us in the working environment.

How does he actually feel?

When communicating it is important to gauge the mood of the other party. In some circumstances, such as an interview, it is very important that we are able to assess how the other person is feeling. Many moods are expressed by automotive, non-verbal responses.

Some of the limitations of non-verbal signs become obvious. Do the averted eyes, for example, mean suspicion or defensiveness? Do the hand to face gestures you see mean evaluation or cooperation? Do the money jingling, flesh pinching signs that are seen mean nervousness or expectancy?

We must at all times look at body signs over a number of areas to assess the true feelings of the other person. Just as important, we must be aware of our own non-verbal language. Are we supporting our verbal communication or providing a contradiction? Can we control our physical actions or do moods become transparently obvious?

Certain facets of a person's appearance can be controlled. The expression on someones face, for example, can be set to suit their mood – but they are less capable of changing what their eyes perceive. They are aware of their upper body but their lower body, legs, ankles and feet also have significant messages which they are less likely to control. Think of the interview situation where the interviewee is sitting at some distance with his whole body from head to foot clearly visible. How vulnerable does he feel and how much more easy is it for someone to assess him?

It is much more than body language

It is wrong to assume that non-verbal messages are limited to our bodies. There are two areas of immense importance that we should understand and use. One is personal space, the other is timing.

Everyone is surrounded by their own cocoon of personal space, inside which other people step only with consent. If somebody stands, or sits too close to us, we feel uncomfortable.

In a room there are fairly strict areas for individuals: the manager behind his desk and the member of staff in front; perhaps a neutral corner round the coffee table. Individuals transfer from one area to another by agreement. If they move to somebody else's zone without agreement they could create mistrust and suspicion.

The timing of questions and responses is another critical area. People feel comfortable with a four- to five - second gap between question and answer. If they are pushed to answer in a shorter period, they feel rushed; if they take longer, a gap develops and they begin to feel uneasy.

As the gap increases, so does the tension. The pressure on both the questioner and the questioned is heightened and the need for response becomes more and more important. If they combine timing with eye contact they are able, as an interviewer, to increase the pressure on the interviewee.

After a period, direct eye contact becomes an embarrassment. When one person meets another they look at each other's eyes for initial reaction. An automatic response signal is a minute dilation of the pupil signifying acceptance. They search for this. When you meet somebody wearing dark glasses do you feel at ease or uncomfortable? When speaking to people we constantly check contact for signs of reassurance. When we are uneasy we avert our eyes. When we wish to increase contact we look more intently. People with close emotional bonds look into each other's eyes and can express sentiment without the use of words.

A combination of these two aspects – direct eye contact and silence following a question – can produce intense pressure. Incorrect use of these techniques can destroy an atmosphere between two people.

To touch or not to touch?

People meet, shake hands and form an opinion, based purely on the firmness, limpness and style of contact. The double handshake, the forearm grip, the shoulder grab – these are all forms of touching which are practised and are accepted, and convey an initial impression.

Yet touching can cause unease and revulsion. Does a secretary want her employer to put his arm around her? However, touch in appropriate circumstances may be welcomed and give assurance. In this area, more than any other, its use must depend on personal relationships.

The important message must be awareness and sensitivity. Touching can increase rapport; it can improve relationships; it can be comforting. However, it is important that we realise its limitations and dangers and use it with care.

Body language and differing cultures

As our society becomes increasingly cosmopolitan and we mix with many more nationalities we must be aware of the different interpretations of non-verbal signs from country to country. Eye-to-eye contact in the UK is the norm but in Nigeria it can be considered a mark of disrespect.

Gestures made with the body are capable of many varied interpretations. The success sign of thumbs up is an obscene sign in Saudi Arabia. The circle formed by fore finger and thumb, to us indicating excellence, is offensive in France.

Just as any other method of communication is capable of misinterpretation, the same is true of non-verbal signs. They are an aid to face-to-face communication and no more. The signs can be misconstrued, but to ignore them would be to ignore the wealth of information they contain. By being more aware and using our non-verbal powers consciously we can improve the effectiveness of face-to-face communication.

Remember, perhaps 70% of your message can be communicated non-verbally. Body language is the art of seeing what the other person is thinking!

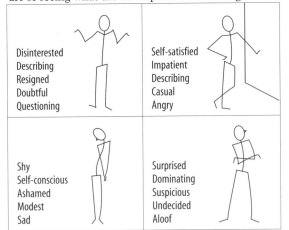

Disinterested
Describing
Resigned
Doubtful
Questioning

Self-satisfied
Impatient
Describing
Casual
Angry

Shy
Self-conscious
Ashamed
Modest
Sad

Surprised
Dominating
Suspicious
Undecided
Aloof

Figure 39.9 Some of the most used forms of 'body language'

Non-verbal communication

- *Body contact.* Less common in UK but accepted in many other countries. A touch on the arm signifies support or a warning. Use with care in the UK!!
- *Physical proximity.* The more intimate a group becomes the closer they stand or sit together.
- *Orientation.* With regard to seating: across a table – formality/conflict; diagonally – less formal/friendly; side-by-side – cooperative/very friendly.
- *Body posture.* May signify interest, boredom, aggression.
- *Gestures.* Hands, feet or arms. The greater the

emotion the greater the gestures.
- *Head nodding.* Effective non-verbal for expressing agreement, understanding or acceptance that a message has been understood.
- *Facial expressions.* Eyes, mouth, blush – show relief, surprise, anger, boredom, happiness, neutrality.
- *Eye movement.* Again a variety of messages going from shiftiness to happiness. No eye contact is seen as a sign of nervousness. Too much eye contact is seen as aggression.

Managing conflict and developing trust

An important part of the 'communications game' is dealing with people under difficult circumstances. The business jargon for this is *conflict management*. College Dynamics have developed a training programme that tries to improve personal ability to handle conflict. It has identified five major types of reaction to a situation:

1. *Compete* – go out to win at all costs; concerned for objectives only.
2. *Compromise* – settle for 'half a loaf'.
3. *Accommodate* – yield or subordinate own concerns to those of the other party.
4. *Collaborate* – work towards mutual problem-solving, recognising both parties' goals.
5. *Avoid* – deny, suppress or put aside differences.

These possible reactions tell us something of your character or personality.

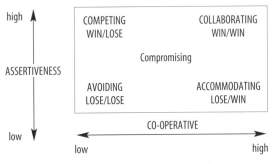

Figure 39.10 How will a manager manage conflict?

Inter-group reactions

Now on to *inter-group* reactions and conflicts. Most people find it easier to operate in a small rather than a large group. Contact is close, communication more personal. Status, importance and acceptance are personal. Status, importance and acceptance are easily seen in a small group. However, people need to conform with the rules of the group because to be aggressive with a group may cause rejection. People do not like to lose, yet they have to prepare group members for the possibility that their opinion may be rejected. Once a possible defeat is seen they tend to adopt certain reactions. These may include:

- seeing the best in ourselves and the worst in others
- concentrating with other groups against a common enemy
- assuming the worst about other groups
- ignoring the views of others
- looking for scapegoats
- reducing levels of communication.

To avoid inter-group conflict at work people need to be conscious of these possible feelings and try to avoid them. How should CD aim to achieve this?

1. ensure that goals are clear
2. ensure that situations are created where groups can reach their goals through working together.

To lose is not an easy situation to accept. Trying to ensure that employees do not lose can give rise to conflict of interest. If one party gets their own way and the other does not, then we have a win/lose outcome. Alas, the loser probably becomes determined to win next time. Another possibility is a lose/lose outcome; both parties are stubborn, so neither gets the way they want. The most desirable result is a win/win outcome, with both parties getting the essentials of what they want. Perhaps neither gets totally what they want and have to concede something. To achieve this best solution requires *trust* between the parties and we must now consider how trust can be built between two parties.

A possible list of positive behaviours includes:

- Be prepared to accept that others have different values, perceptions and expectations. You should not feel rejected personally if other people disagree with your opinion.
- Get to know and hopefully understand those with whom you have to work.
- Do not automatically assume you are right and they are wrong.
- Make sure you know your goals clearly and try to arrange situations where both parties who are potentially in conflict can achieve their goals. Try to seek common goals.
- Keep good communication between groups and individuals so people know what is going on.
- Learn to be a good listener.

Sometimes, whatever someone tries conflict does arise, so what can CD do when a disagreement develops?

Basically, CD needs to:

- identify the conflict and its causes
- recognise key issues
- acknowledge the benefits to both parties of resolving the conflict
- search out the best method of resolving the conflict.

Management theorists have suggested five ways of resolving a conflict:

1. *Ignore it* – allow it to 'cool off' and it might go away.
2. *Smooth over it* – play it down and maintain harmony. However, resentment may bubble away beneath the surface.
3. *Use power of dominance* – usually a quick solution. However, this may result in a win/lose situation, leaving one party feeling hard done by.
4. *Compromise or negotiate* – each party gives up something in order to reach the agreed solution. Both parties must reach a necessary goal, or else a win/lose situation will result.
5. *Collaborate on a joint solution* – where this is possible it usually results in a win/win situation. However, there must be the time and ability to make it work. In effect collaboration is a more positive form of compromise.

The best method is going to depend on a particular situation and the people involved. The aim should nearly always be to try to reach a win/win conclusion if possible.

Trust

This is essential in the building of a successful team or group. Look at the list and think of a relative or colleague and put a tick against the three issues easiest to trust him/her about.

The trust we find easiest to have for one another is

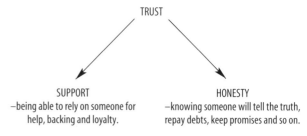

Figure 39.11 Building trust

usually of two kinds as shown in Figure 39.11.

If trust is to be stable and lasting then it has to be a two-way feeling. Actions tend to speak louder than words. Telling someone they are trusted means nothing if they are constantly checked on! Some organisations define every function in precise detail, but these are seldom happy places in which to work. In practice, every leader has to trust his or her subordinates to some extent and, because of the reciprocal nature of trust, this necessitates that they must be given good reason for trusting the leader. The most effective are normally the most trusting and trusted. It is probably more difficult to build trust than to destroy it. Individuals do not build up a credit balance of trust; one act can wipe out the whole balance and make it almost impossible to start again. There are a number of factors which can help trusting relationships;

- truth, honesty, openness
- common interest, mutual benefit to be gained
- knowledge of how people behave
- knowledge of the other person's past behaviour
- necessity: it can force people to trust one another
- being prepared to take a risk
- being prepared to make the first move.

Let us go over the basic principles of communication from a manager to a subordinate. The purpose of such communication is:

1. *To increase knowledge or understanding.* Every time someone tells an employee about a new process, record or even product, they are trying to increase their knowledge. In turn this should develop the employee's understanding of the firm and their role within it. The manager may or may not want them to change their behaviour as a result of the communication.
2. *To influence or change attitudes.* Changing people's attitudes is never easy. They may try a direct 'command' but increasingly the practice is to put forward the consequences of non-acceptance. By stressing the possible outcome the manager is trying to gain a positive reaction from the employee and therefore an acceptance of what has to be done.
3. *To investigate or influence action or behaviour.* It could be argued that all communication is aimed at achieving this end. By changing under-standing and/or attitudes people are trying to produce the necessary change in behaviour. Certain communications, such as a referee's whistle, require immediate response, while others take more time to produce the called-for response.

Is the nature of work changing?

Not many people really know what kind of job they want. Schools and colleges try to make students decide, but many simply cannot make up their minds. The decision of how to earn a living is made against a number of criteria. Think for a moment about the following:

- What sort of organisation would you like to work for?
- What size of organisation would you like to work for?
- What type of working conditions would you expect?
- What kind of benefits will you want to receive?

Readers have already noted that the pace of change is increasing, so not only does one have difficulty deciding what to do, but the ground rules may be changing. Ask yourself if (a) a job for life will be feasible for much longer (b) a basic salary will be the major form of reward or will 'merit' pay be the major determinant of your pay (c) your work will remain the same, or will flexible conditions become the main form of organisation?

In most of the principal European economies certain trends are becoming clear. The two most obvious are more temporary and contract workers and more flexible working patterns. Why are such changes arising? It seems that productivity, flexibility and cost control are the three driving forces. These have surfaced in various forms, including:
- an increased emphasis on the flexible firm
- the growth of 'contracting out'
- an increasing emphasis on skills and training
- the 'collapse of some skills'
- the increased spread of 'teleworking'
- the increased use of 'performance-related pay'.

There is a need to look in more detail at each issue.

The flexible firm

This increasingly popular form of organisational structure needs us to distinguish between three types of workers, namely core, peripheral and external:

- *Core.* These are normally multi-skilled workers, who work full-time and who receive good pay, conditions and benefits.
- *Peripheral.* These are short-term, temporary and part-time workers, who receive less favourable pay, conditions and benefits.
- *External.* These are not employees of the firm, e.g. temporary workers who are often contracted out and self-employed.

The flexible firm will cut its labour costs to a minimum by limiting the number of core workers compared to peripheral and external workers.

Contracting out

The new, flexible firm 'contracts out' non-core facilities. Gone is the need to control every function of the organisation. The flexible firm delegates some non-essential functions to outside agencies. Contracting out can help reduce the size of an organisation, reduce central costs, and increase operational efficiency.

Women in the workplace

Only as recently as 1985 men outnumbered women in full-time employment by 45%. By the early 1990s the figures had drawn close to being equal. This trend has within it certain interesting features: (a) Women tend to be less likely to be core workers. (b) Almost half the female workforce are in part-time jobs. (c) A high proportion of women are in relatively low-paid jobs.

Fewer women currently occupy senior or management positions. This may be because management is seen to possess male characteristics such as drive and aggression.

The pressure is now on personnel departments to change their practices by introducing provision for child care and extended periods of paternity as well as maternity leave. Social stereotypes are beginning to change, albeit slowly.

Increased emphasis on skills

The education providers are constantly under pressure to increase 'vocational training' in schools. It has been suggested that a failing of the labour market is that young people leave school with inadequate skills to fit into a job. Job-related training varies according to employment status and age. Part-time and older employees are less likely to be offered training.

The collapse of skills

The process of continuous change shows itself in various ways. One of the most important is downsizing (reducing the size of an organisation) and employing fewer highly skilled people while making those employed do more. This does not only apply to blue-collar workers. More senior managers are being forced to confront the basics of their responsibilities. No longer can they focus on the 'high powered' parts of their job description, they now must turn their attention to basics and concentrate on seeing the product through to consumer satisfaction.

Teleworking

The communications revolution has changed the way people work. No longer do they require constant checking. The end result is the main goal of competitivity. Teleworking, with its potential for productivity gains, fits well into performance-related pay, devolution of responsibility and setting clear quality standards and targets.

The increased use of performance-related pay

These forms of payment are based on performance appraisal techniques. Management jobs are the most affected by performance-related pay. Performance is normally assessed against working objectives. Individual objectives are normally called 'account-abilities'. In turn short-term goals may be attached to each objective. A system of scoring is often worked out to measure performance against objectives and these enable attainment levels to be distinguished. Bonus payments are often aligned to target achievement, as are increments.

So, what does this mean for the labour market and the future of College Dynamics? It now seems easier to acquire labour in times of expanding demand and lose it when a downturn takes place. The labour market is more flexible than it once was. Perhaps it is now so free that 'social dumping' will arise, i.e. firms with more investment to countries with lower employment standards, and presumably, costs.

College Dynamics must be aware of change and react to the growing flexibility of the labour market. Does it need to slim down its core workers and look to peripheral workers? As ever, the issues of ethics and morality are not far away from an 'essential business decision.

CASE STUDY 39.1

'All the new machines are here, but keep quiet about them till I say so.' This was the immediate response of Ted Smith, Office Manager, College Dynamics, on receipt of the new disc cover printer. 'I know it's German, but just look at the technology. This will cut costs and give us a lead in the market. The Big Boys will want our discs now.'

This must be a common event in most industries but does it deliver all the advantages the manager hopes for?

Two weeks after this initial conversation a carefully worded memo appeared on the general notice board. Within hours of its appearance Ted was embroiled in some heated discussions.

He felt that all workers should be pleased, indeed they should be proud to have such modern equipment in their works, but all he had received was a deputation asking about job security, redundancy and who was capable of working such space age gear?

At six o'clock on a dark November evening Ted sat and looked at a blank sheet of paper. How was he going to (a) resolve the situation and (b) tell the CEO that the normal good industrial relations no longer existed.

Questions and activities

(a) Explain why you think Ted Smith found himself in such a predicament.

(b) How would you have approached the introduction of new machinery?

(c) What courses of action are now open to Ted to rectify the tensions that now exist?

CASE STUDY 39.2

Moving out east

'The Pacific Basin is where we want to be', was the opinion of Peter Scarsbrook, our Sales Director. 'Income is rising to over US$4,000,000 a year, and at that level even the car manufacturers become interested, so we should already be there, and I don't just mean Japan, but think of South Korea, Malaysia, Singapore, Taiwan, and one day Thailand, Vietnam, Cambodia and ultimately China.'

'You may have a point Peter, but how do we get our message across when English is not the mother tongue?' ask the CEO.

'But it is. The most popular music is in English, and then there's Star TV, BBC World Service Radio and TV, Voice of America and don't forget sattelite – all of them broadcast in English.'

'Yes, but aren't they more conservative than us?'

'True, but the pace of change is fast, and we provide the basic product. Its what others put on them that reflects the culture, tastes, understandings, and so on. Please let me prepare a market report.'

'O.K. Peter, but you must pay particular attention to how we effectively communicate our brands in a part of the world where CDs seem to be made just about everywhere.'

'Thanks. I'll have it ready for the next meeting.'

So, Peter has quite a challenge. Think about what he has to achieve.

Questions and activities

(a) He discovers some very encouraging market figures, but notes intense competition. Design a 'flier' for the first mailshot to record producers, shops and other main users. You should stress the strong points of College Dynamics products.

(b) Outline the main barriers you feel College Dynamics will confront when trying to build an effective communications network with such a diverse group of countries many miles from the UK.

(c) Develop ways of reacting to these problems, so aiming to establish CD discs as one of the 'major players' in the fastest growing market in the world.

CASE STUDY 39.3

Tomorrow's World

CONFIDENTIAL

The day of the job for life is fast disappearing. Core-workers will be in a minority and contract employees will work from home and communicate via technology. Flexible working hours will suit the former and the latter will have to adapt.

If we are to remain competitive we must adapt to the changes in the labour market. Such changes will need careful handling, but everyone's future depends on us accepting 'downsizing' and adapting to the new work patterns.

The above is an extract from a memo sent by the CEO of College Dynamics to all directors. It is to form the basis of a major item for discussion at the next Board meeting.

Questions and activities

1. Define:
   (a) core worker
   (b) contract worker
   (c) flexitime
   (d) downsizing
2. Why are College Dynamics ideally suited to adapt to the new work patterns?
3. What problems might College Dynamics encounter in the introduction of such radical change?

SUMMARY

Having studied this chapter, you should be able to:

▽ Explain the importance of communication in business.

▽ Describe the methods of communication available.

▽ Explain what being an effective communicator means.

▽ Explain what being an effective listener is.

▽ Describe how to lead a meeting.

▽ Explain the barriers to effective communication.

▽ Explain the managing of conflict and the developing of trust among employees.

Questions and activities

Technical terms and glossary

In the sections below you are given a series of technical terms and their meanings. They have been scrambled, though. You must match up the terms and the definitions. When you have them correctly paired, transfer them to your alphabetical vocabulary or glossary book.

You are also advised to transfer any definitions obtained during the exercises in the case studies into this glossary book.

Technical terms

1. Line and staff managers
2. The main causes of poor written communication
3. Closed questions
4. Delegation
5. Corporate identity (including logos)
6. Body language

Definitions

A. A process of communication that passes down the formal chain of command the responsibilities for performing certain tasks.
B. A formal relationship that allows authority to be used over immediate subordinates, as opposed to a right to advise and only have authority over those who report to the same line manager as the individual.
C. An identification system that is used through all an organisation's operations.
D. Curtness, sarcasm, silliness, rage, suspicion, insult, patronising attitude, familiarity and presumptions.
E. Questions designed to require a specific answer.
F. The art of seeing what the other person is thinking or feeling.

Short answer questions

1. Explain what is meant by the term 'delegation'.
2. Briefly describe why some theorists promote the idea of 'participative management'.
3. Distinguish between someone in (a) a line position and (b) a staff position.
4. Explain and give examples of 'corporate logos'.
5. What makes a 'poor listener'?
6. What advice would you give someone who is to chair or lead a meeting?
7. Briefly describe the main barriers to effective communication.
8. Why is non-verbal communication such an important part of any dialogue between two or more parties?
9. What is meant by the term 'open questions' and why must these be used with care?
10. Explain what is meant by the term 'closed questions'. What are the main purposes of such questions?
11. When faced with a probable defeat what range of reactions covers the behaviour of most people?
12. Why is the development of trust so important in a manager's objectives?
13. Define:
    (a) contracting out
    (b) core workers
    (c) teleworking
14. What do you understand by the term 'social dumping'?

40
Organisations – individual and corporate goals

Preview

▼ In this chapter the formation of goals and objectives for both the individual and the organisation forms the major theme. How and why do people seek to achieve targets or objectives and why are these so important to the organisation for which they work?

▼ Such targets can be both of a formal and informal variety and the importance of these to the institution must be analysed.

What are organisations?

Try to think of anything to which you belong that does not have a formal structure to it. It is not an easy task. So, what is meant by organisations? One definition is:

Organisations are groups of people who coordinate their activities and efforts in the pursuance of some purpose.

To understand this definition more fully care must be taken to analyse it in detail. First, organisations consist of people, and as such are *social structures*. True, all companies make use of assets such as buildings, but these have been created by man to meet human desires. When we say 'organisation' we are really referring to groups of people who make up and influence the behaviour of this thing we call an organisation. In reality, we are including shareholders, directors, managers, clerks, skilled and unskilled workers. Secondly, groups of people 'coordinate' their activities and efforts. The ability to coordinate distinct but interrelated activities is an essential feature of all organisations. If people act as separate entities then they are not 'organised' in the accepted sense of the word. So, for a business to operate 'effectively' someone must devise a system that coordinates all the activities that the business is engaged in. This process is made somewhat easier if firms have *goals* that are clear and identifiable and have good planning, good organisation of functions and jobs, good communication of information and effective control of all activities.

Companies can organise people and coordinate their efforts, but it must be for a purpose. Usually, they specify the purpose, however complex, and direct operations towards achieving this. Let us try this in action.

Objective/goal/target: to achieve a profit

This looks simple, and College Dynamics has decided that all projects must make a percentage return on capital. But how does it achieve this ambition? It needs to decide on such issues as price, quantity, reputation, image, competitor reaction, employee satisfaction and financial limitations. These are all valid considerations and each has to be seen on both its own merits and how it affects others. Indeed, if the analysis moves away from a pure production organisation and looks at a hospital, we find the difficult issue of 'best health care within the financial resources available'. Literally, a life-or-death situation is confronted.

So organisations have goals, or objectives. But are these necessarily the same for everyone and does each employee accept these as applying to them? Work organisations are the most complex and a great deal of study is needed in order to begin to understand them. To better understand the complexity of organisations it is best to think about how they develop. College Dynamics has expanded by amalgamating the skills, knowledge and resources of others. The founders of CD could not have expanded the business without the help of others. They have relied on formal assistance from others in just the same way as a hospital doctor needs porters, nurses, etc. in order to function efficiently.

As CD has grown bigger it has tried to foster good relations with its employees, but are the aims of each individual at work microcosms of the aims of the organisations for which they work? They do not all hold the same values; seldom do they have similar powers of influence, or possess identical intellectual capabilities. It is not surprising, therefore, that there exist great differences between the aims of individuals at work and the overall goal of the organisation.

How do people view work?

Here is a theoretical view of work:

- Work consists of groups of individuals coming together at distinct times to perform specific tasks.
- People are recruited by organisations to perform specific tasks which match with certain skills and abilities that the individuals possess.
- The sum of all the individual tasks equals the corporate task of the organisation.
- Controlling and coordinating all the individuals (often called the management function) resides in getting the individuals to achieve what the organisation requires.
- The system of control confers rights, status and obligations on individuals within the organisation.

This may appear to be a somewhat complicated way of describing an organisation, but look around, and see if you disagree with this list as the way in which a school or college operates.

To move on from this list and try to understand how an organisation functions, we begin to focus attention on how employers get each individual to respond in accordance with those objectives. It is difficult to conceive ongoing consensus between employees and employers about the function and interaction of their various roles. Such a consensus may not actually exist, but that does not stop us from trying to achieve it.

Goals

Each person has a list of goals, but how they select these is a complicated issue. They begin at their births, for this is when they start to formulate what is called a *value system*. One's innermost feelings will in turn be influenced by the family, school and culture. To these they need to add such influences as personal wealth, health and the type and level of education received, for each will have an influence on their value system. Abraham Maslow looked at how individuals behaved at work and what factors influenced behaviour. He concluded that individuals have needs which they are striving to satisfy. He listed some *primary needs*, e.g. physiological, food and drink, companionship, continuing the species, warmth and so on. His *secondary needs* concentrated on psychological matters and included the need to be recognised and valued, to achieve, to be creative and to make a contribution to society. Individuals will often use their place of work as a means of satisfying some of these needs, but the actual nature of the needs will vary. Each individual travels with their value system and this determines what they want from their jobs. Some will be mainly motivated by money, as this will allow them to satisfy many of their physiological needs and some psychological needs as well. People may want status, or a chance to be seen to have 'achieved' things. At CD, the chief executive and the senior shop steward may have genuinely different goals and yet work for the same organisation. Both will subscribe to certain formal goals of the organisation, e.g. production targets, but on another issue such as wage levels, they view the potential outcome very differently.

The beliefs people hold and the objectives they seek are personal, yet some feel empowered to influence others. Individuals, however, seldom have a great deal of power to influence others, but acting in groups they can influence the course of events. This is increasingly obvious in countries new to the 'democratic' process. An individual's true ability to influence is determined by a number of factors, e.g. wealth, independence, education, personality, articulation, and perhaps most importantly how their value systems conforms with those they seek to influence. The power of one individual will vary according to the situation and the role being played. Individual's goals are therefore a product of their own value system plus their assessment of their ability to influence others in relation to specific situations or issues. It seems most likely that individuals seek to satisfy their own goals first and then those of the formal organisation (see Figure 40.1).

Group goals

What exactly is a manager? Here is E. Brech's definition:

Management is the responsibility for the effective planning and regulation (or guidance) of the operations of an organisation, such responsibility involving:

1. *The installation and maintenance of proper procedures to ensure adherence to plans for the accomplishment of defined objectives.*

2. *The guidance, integration and supervision of personnel comprising the organisation and carrying out its operations.*

Fine words, but what exactly do they mean? The central theme of this, and other situations, is that *defined objectives* shape *business policy*. It is doubtful if anyone would disagree with this, as long as they remain aware of the existence of other goals at the organisational level. Good determination is clearly intertwined with the need to plan the direction in which the institution is moving. This *planning process* is concerned with forecasting needs, defining objectives, anticipating problems and developing feasible solutions. The ability to forecast is very important to any business and it clearly illustrates the process of defining objectives. Once the plan is functioning the management compares its forecast with reality and appraises the performance. Control is achieved by examining the nature of the differences and the action to be taken, if necessary.

Formulating goals in business

Firms vary in size, purpose, structure and accountability. However, a list can be made of probable common factors that influence goal determination. The list can be subdivided into inputs and outputs.

Goal formation attempts to set an organisation in its environment by identifying the needs and problems that it faces in relation to its surroundings. All managers must be aware of the changes forced upon them by such issues as technical change, environmental concerns and social changes.

It is difficult to quantify the impact of each criteria, but that senior management will consider all of them when formulating policy. Not only must policy-makers be aware of internal input factors, they must identify the external issues that have an impact on their organisation. Thus, other organisations, such as trade unions, have a part to play in policy making.

Formal goals

Not all organisations have clearly defined formal goals. Some manage to succeed without them, while others have diluted their targets down to a *mission statement*, or outline of where, how, when, etc. the business is going. Goals present us with a measurement tool. Managers can assess performance and, hopefully, avoid wasting time on unnecessary activities. An organisation without formal objectives might:

- waste time pursuing ends that contribute little, if anything, to the organisation's enhancement

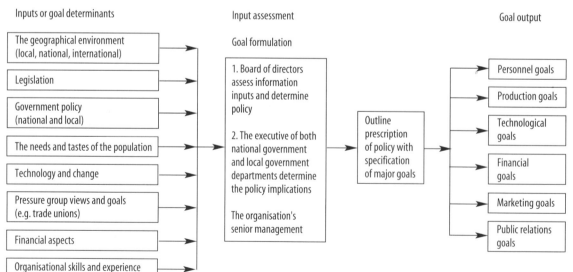

Figure 40.1 Outline of the process of goal formulation in formal work organisations

- be unable to define precisely, so leading to conflict and difficulty in reconciliation
- be able to persuade others that 'success' has been achieved when it has not
- be incapable of forecasting the future, and so not be aware of setbacks and opportunities.

A conclusion

The traditional view of organisation structures is that of the need to ensure that the sum total of the efforts of individuals within the organisation is in accordance with the corporate task, and that management are responsible for achieving this. This assumes that management possesses the ability to mould all employees into a unified team. This team supposedly has ambitions to achieve just a single goal, namely the stated aims of the organisation.

However, it has been noted that individuals have needs (goals) that may run contrary to the corporate targets. This is perhaps best illustrated by some management opinion that 'all trade unionists are trouble-makers'. As such, each member should be 'weeded-out', and once this is done the team will be united.

Others take a view that any organisation is made up of groups of workers with varied interests. This school of thought reduces the belief of 'only one correct way' and develops a style of management that focuses on ways in which many interests and objectives can be kept in a satisfactory state of equilibrium, in the sense that leadership can reconcile its objectives with the direction in which the organisation is moving. Such a belief admits to the legitimate existence of many sources of leadership and many focuses for loyalty. As a consequence, an organisation is seen as containing a whole hierarchy of goals, often of a conflicting nature.

These two obviously different perceptions of how people react within an organisation are important in the way in which judgements are formed. If organisations view people in a *unitary* way, then the hierarchy of the organisation will be centred on clearly defined goals, e.g. at departmental level, and these objectives will go largely unchallenged. A clear structure will run through the organisation and each function will have a clearly stated specification.

If, on the other hand, a *pluralistic* view is held, then the organisation will be less rigid and will be more open to flexibility in order to meet changing situations. The business is 'organic' in nature. So, it has been noted that things called *goals* exist within organisations. These are not easy to describe. On the one hand, goals exist at a number of levels, from

those of individuals to the stated goals of the whole organisation. It has also been noted that some goals are clearly visible, while others are hidden.

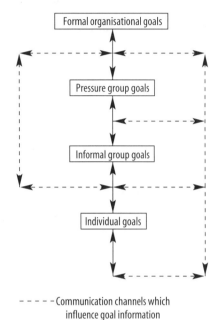

Figure 40.2 *The hierarchy of goals*

So, College Dynamics has noted certain trends in the organisation's development (see Figure 40.2):
- People have goals or objectives.
- Companies have objectives and they are not always compatible with those of their employees.
- Each individual brings clearly personal goals which normally have a wide range of objectives.
- Individuals form two kinds of grouping within the structure of the formal work organisation, namely formal and informal groups.
- These groups have goals, some of which are clearly stated, while others remain suppressed or deliberately hidden.
- Informal groups of workers can make their grievances known through official channels.
- CD senior executives determine the goals that form the organisation. They decide on the corporate goals and then develop policy to achieve these. They are also responsible, wherever possible, for gaining the acceptance of the individuals who are asked to perform the tasks.
- Management is also responsible for noting how each job contributes to the achievement of the corporate objectives, and they must do everything possible to see that these are attained.

SUMMARY

Having read this chapter, you should be able to:

▽ Identify how individual goals emerge and how they fit into the running of an organisation.

▽ Distinguish between formal and informal goals.

▽ Explain the relevance of group goals to achieving the targets held within the corporate mission statement.

Questions and activities

Technical terms and glossary

In the sections below you are given a series of technical terms and their meanings. They have been scrambled. You must match up the business term and its definition. When you have got them correctly paired, transfer them to an alphabetical vocabulary book or glossary book.

You are also advised to transfer the definitions obtained during the exercises in the case studies into this glossary book.

Technical terms
1. Goals
2. Value systems
3. Group goals
4. Unitary
5. Pluralistic

Definitions
A. Considering an organisation to have a hierarchy that is based on clearly defined goals, e.g. at departmental level.
B. A set of targets or objectives that both individuals and organisation aim to achieve.
C. A less rigid form of organisation, that is flexible in order to meet changing circumstances.
D. The innermost feelings each of us possess that influence the way we see things.
E. Setting an organisation in its environment by assuring the needs and problems it faces are addressed by a manager.

Short answer questions
1. What is an 'organisation'?
2. Define and illustrate what is meant by the term 'goal'.
3. Why should an organisation develop what are known as 'formal objectives'?
4. Which other groups influence the ways in which an organisation develops its formal goals/objectives?
5. Distinguish between a 'unitary' based organisation and a 'pluralistic' based organisation.
6. Why might the style of leadership used influence the goals of the organisation?
7. How does the 'mission statement' influence the organisation's goals?
8. Why might individuals' goals and corporate goals not be the same?

41
Organisations – theories and models

Preview

▽ This chapter will cover the principal theories/approaches to organisations.

▽ It will also analyse the interrelationships between organisational goals, structures and purposes.

▽ It will analyse possible weaknesses in organisational structure.

▽ We have already noted how goals are an integral part of any organisation, and here we will note the relationship between these goals and the structure of organisations.

What is a formal organisation?

Like other areas of Business Studies, definitions tend to be cumbersome, but they are needed. Schein defined a formal organisation as the rational coordination of the activities of a number of people for the achievement of some common purpose or goal, through the division of labour and function, and through a hierarchy of authority and responsibility.

The classical model of management

The earlier analysis of the evolution of College Dynamics noted the interlocking nature of individuals and formal and informal groups within work organisations. Although this analysis may not be perfect, it is the best anyone has got, and it probably formed the base from which F.W. Taylor formulated his famous scientific model of management (see Chapter 26). Taylor aimed for an organisation which would achieve greater efficiency and effectiveness than those operating in his day. He made two fundamental assumptions:

1. People are primarily motivated by financial reward.
2. Organisations must incorporate the following:

- a clearly defined division of labour
- highly specialised personnel
- a distinct hierarchy of authority.

Taylor approached his study in a systematic way. He developed methods of analysing work. Together with F.B. Gilbreth he developed techniques for studying and measuring work. His study was based on watching men handling pig-iron at the Bethlehem Steel Company in America. His conclusions led him to put forward a four-principle analysis of how organisations functioned. He believed organisational design should be based on the following:

- All functions of work should be measured in the smallest feasible element and the organisation of work should be structured around the efficient operation of each of these elements.
- People must be carefully selected to perform the work required at its best.
- Close supervision of workers will be required to ensure that they perform their work as determined by the first point above.
- Management is accountable for all actions of subordinates. (See Figure 41.1.)

Taylor was successful in increasing the output of pig-iron from 12.5 to 47.5 tonnes per man. This conclusion founded both a motivational theory and the foundations for an organisational theory that became known as the *classical model*.

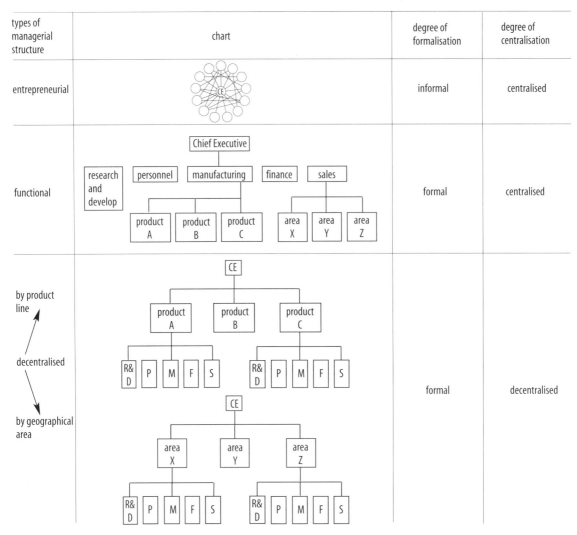

types of managerial structure	chart	degree of formalisation	degree of centralisation
entrepreneurial		informal	centralised
functional		formal	centralised
by product line decentralised by geographical area		formal	decentralised

Figure 41.1 *Examples of the basic managerial structures.* (Source: Weinshall, A., 'Application of two conceptual schemes of organisation behaviour in case study and general organisational research', Ashridge Management College, New York 1971.)

Taylor concluded his motivation theory on two main aspects; the physical capabilities of employees, and economic incentives linked to work performance. He concluded that rewards closely related to work efforts bring forth the maximum performance from individual workers. Taylor viewed people and machines as complementary to one another. The operatives were as much a part of the machine as the control handles, buttons, cogs, tools, etc. People were appendages to the machines they operated. In turn this made efficiency and motivation a relationship of the physical limits of human performance controlled by such limitations as loads, pace and fatigue. Pay was linked to performance and an average target was set. The

school of management that grew from this early principle focused its attention on the following main characteristics:
1. division of labour.
2. unity of command.
3. a distinct set of rules that influence the relationship between labour and authority.

Such a belief, or set of beliefs, were first written about by Adam Smith in 1776. The major premise is that the more a particular job can be broken down into its smallest component parts, the more specialised and the more skilled a worker becomes at carrying out his part of the job. The classical administration theory based on this observation centred on a 'specialised' work being more efficient so making the organisation more productive. These early theorists concluded that such a system would work best if controlled by a single command structure. People were felt to work best if situated in a known role within a hierarchy. A clearly defined *span of control* was essential and a formal hierarchy was delivered via a pyramid of authority (see Figure 41.2).

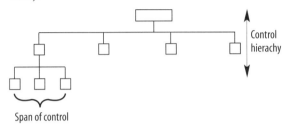

Figure 41.2 A pyramid of control

A pyramid of control

Workers under the pyramid system are grouped together according to task. All those performing the same task are treated alike and this shows itself in a structure based on departments that perform the same *function*, e.g. personnel, marketing, etc.

The second principle of this school of thought concerned the value of the product being made. An expensive version, even if produced alongside a less expensive form, would be controlled by a separate and autonomous hierarchy. In simple terms the product class distinguished who controlled it.

The third principle centred on geographical separation. All jobs in a specific geographic area were grouped together. An example of this was a military base in an overseas territory, where one single command structure controlled all servicemen, regardless of whether they served in the army, air force or navy.

Problems of the classical model

Taylor formed his opinions with two main factors of influence: (a) organisational assumptions, and (b) analytical tools to measure work efficiently.

The selection of the two principles of classical management though raises the question 'Are other issues equally important when determining an individual's output at work?' What of personal skills, the work culture of the country, politics, economics, technology – the list seems endless. Should we view people as appendages to machines? Does boredom affect performance? Such questions begin to make others ask about the influence of:

- health
- financial problems
- family problems
- political sympathies
- the working environment
- ... and other issues.

These questions gave rise to the human relations model.

The human relations model

The human relations model had its birth in the studies of Elton Mayo at the Western Electric Company, Chicago, between 1927 and 1932 (see Chapter 37). He was interested in perfecting the Scientific Model. To do this he centred on working conditions. He experimented with the levels of lighting at the workplace, hours of work and the number of rests. His initial findings were somewhat confusing, as lighting differences did not always match the output changes, but Mayo concluded that 'at least equal attention should be given to the behaviour of the people doing the work as to the detailed analysis of the work done'. No simple and direct relationship was found to exist between the physical working conditions and the rate of production. No evidence was gathered to support the idea that increased output follows from a relief of fatigue. What Mayo did discover was the importance of small groups. When people related well to one another a cohesive group emerged and work standards improved.

Mayo concluded:

1. A worker's output is not determined by his physical capacity but by his social capacity.
2. Non-economic rewards play a central role in determining the motivation and happiness of the individual workers.
3. The highest degree of specialisation is by no means the most efficient form of division of labour.
4. Workers do not react to management and its honours and rewards as individuals, but as members of a group.

Today, such findings may not seem radical, but Mayo's cohesion led to significant changes of such organisational issues as the following.

Division of labour and specialisation

A breakdown of jobs into parts considered the satisfaction the workers received from performing. People work best when they have self-respect.

The physical layout of work organisation should not ignore the informal group relationship. Mayo's work on the relay assembly rooms study suggests the need to structure work situations so that workers can form satisfying relationships with each other and with the management of the organisation.

Leadership

The organisation cannot ignore the informal leadership impact on the setting and enforcing of group norms. The Scientific Model placed leadership solely in the hands of 'management', but the research conducted in the bank wiring room study indicated that informal leadership influences can be stronger than the influence of management. So, no matter how much we study the ways in which a work programme is to be conducted, the human factor could negate most things unless recognised as a part of the necessary planning.

Planning

In both of Mayo's studies he placed emphasis on fully explaining all matters to workers. In turn the workers stressed that part of the good relations that emerged was the result of the care taken to communicate with them. The workers considered that the interest shown in them was a motivational force and increased their effort and commitment.

The bank wiring room study supports these findings, though from a 'breakdown' situation workers had established an output they felt was 'acceptable' to management. In fact these targets were beneath that required by management, but they had failed to communicate this to the workers.

From Mayo's studies, it can be concluded that organisations must be viewed as social environments which stimulate individuals to work towards organisational goals. This conclusion is based on these main beliefs:

1. Cooperation with a social grouping will tend to minimise conflict. The organisation should try to influence the social groupings, or else they may adopt plans that are contrary to the interests of the organisation. Nobody believed that an awareness of the informal group would remove conflict, but there was evidence to show it would be significantly reduced.
2. The 'engineered' social groupings will mainly allow the satisfying of both organisation and individual goals.
3. An organisation that can marry individual and organisational goals will experience positive human behaviour, e.g. high productivity and low absenteeism.

Central to this belief was the assumption that the most satisfying place to work would also prove to be the most efficient. The human relations school put a new dimension into people management, namely the belief that people act as individuals, as members of groups and as individuals performing job roles which attempt to meet required standards. The allocation of work needs to take account of people's expectations; it needs to actively seek their approval. Any amount of scientific design does not generate human acceptance. Managers must be aware of boredom and frustration. People find some tasks intolerable. Subsequent frustration can lead to aggression.

By combining the classical and human relations theories managers can obtain a clear picture of how an organisation works; it appears that the two systems, namely a formal organisation and an informal organisational structure, operate within one.

The classical school concentrates on the formal organisation, for it is a design produced by managers. Such an organisation will concentrate on division of labour, a hierarchy of supervision and control, systems of rules and regulations and patterns of administration.

The informal organisational structure is that recognised by the human relationists. It is concerned with the pattern of relationships which exist between people who work in a formal organisation in addition to those determined by the rules. The informal organisation is concerned with understanding relationships and behaviour which result from the interaction of people and work with the formal organisation. It centres on what determined human behaviour. Why are some people more effective than others as leaders? What leads to boredom, frustration and aggression and just how important are informal groups to the formal organisation?

Now try discussing the following:

1. If the human relations school are right, then the most important structure is a *working group that works together*. This means that the group should have a work pattern that is both demanding and interesting so as to minimise boredom and frustration. Second, the group will show a desired level of delegated authority to control the majority of the work activities for which it is responsible. To achieve this the pyramid structure would probably require flattening (a reduction of levels) so reducing the isolation and the necessary increase in authority at each level. Such a structure would simplify the communications

networks and therefore would increase the chance of attaining both the industrial goals and those of the company.

Mayo's studies showed the importance of both formal and informal leadership; it was crucial that the dominant leader be acceptable to the group, and not a mere management appointee. So, would an involvement of the working group in selection actually increase the chance of the individual appointed being accepted by the group? The changes with the group might also affect the cohesion. How would a newcomer fit in? Would the structure remain positive? These are some of the questions that the human relations approach asks of organisational structures.

2. It is doubtful if any organisation is in reality a 'happy family'. Can a more acceptable leadership style or group membership actually reduce the impact of say, technological change which will inevitably result in job losses? Likewise, will a patient approach to management produce an understanding response from the workers concerned, particularly from those threatened with redundancy?

3. Is the human relations approach equally applicable at all levels in an organisation? We need to consider whether groups of shop floor workers react in similar ways to groups of senior management. In what ways is the behaviour likely to be different and why?

Structural functionalism

A group emerged that felt that human relations was an unacceptable interpretation of human behaviour. And they could not believe that a formal work organisation, consisting of many groupings of different individualism, could all work harmoniously towards common goals. They felt that there were too many different goals existing to allow for a harmonious conclusion. At best it seemed realistic to hope for a minimising of the impact of individual goals that run contrary to organisational goals.

This became known as the 'structuralist' viewpoint. Structuralists argued that the human relations approach presented an incorrect picture of the world of work. Structuralists argue that organisations are large and complex social units consisting of many interacting subgroups or units. The goals of subunits varied widely. Sometimes they produce harmony, but frequently they are opposed to each other. The human relations school represents an 'ideal' model that made work pleasant, so reducing conflict. Structuralists consider that people working for a third party can never really be wholly satisfied at work.

The structuralist view revolves around a belief that work alienates people. The process results from the following:

- Workers do not have a direct share of ownership of the land, assets, etc., that is the organisation. This minimises involvement.
- The trend towards increasing specialisation at work reduces the ability of people to appreciate the complex picture of the organisation. The high fragmentation of individual jobs makes work seem meaningless to the individual.
- Regardless of delegation, workers are inevitably controlled and do not control themselves. They do not determine how their efforts will be rewarded, or the environment in which they work.

Structuralists stress the need to minimise the alienation of workers. This functionalist approach is concerned with the concept of order in formal work organisations and how to maintain this order regardless of changes in personnel. The structural-functionalists concern themselves with the relationships between the parts and the whole of an organisation, and in particular how stability is achieved and maintained. They reanalysed Mayo's studies and put forward two propositions to be considered:

1. He failed to analyse the conflicts of interest evident between the various groups of workers.
2. He failed to analyse the unintended actions and results that occurred

The fruit of these considerations centres on what makes people have such a diversity of interests and beliefs. Without this we are in a position of order-simplifying both the nature of people and the organisations within which they work. The structuralists argued that the importance of informal norms and goals is that they result from the beliefs and perceptions of individuals making up groups, and that there will be conflicts of interest and differing values.

The unintended consequences have been studied by Merton, who concluded that:

1. Behaviour is not always what it seems.
2. The consequences of actions may be different from those intended.
3. What is thought bad shows up on analysis to be vital.

4. Conflict can spur people to adapt to change; indeed it may act as a safety valve, in that it contributes to stability.

What, then, does this approach to organisational behaviour ask us? It certainly should make us concerned about how peoples' aspirations fit into the daily running of an efficient organisation. Can managers actually forecast the response of people, or must they accept an element of chance? Is an 'ideal' work system possible?

The systems approach

It is what goes into a system that interests the structuralists. They normally centre their enquiries on the ability of the organisation to adapt to change, the contribution of each subsection to corporate goal attainment, and the ability of different functions to merge into a corporate whole. The essential feature to appreciate is that the approach is open, namely it is attempting to show the dependence of one system on another. It stresses the interrelatedness of various events and reminds us that just to relate to one narrow variable to another without taking into account the social context in which they function is illogical (see Figure 41.3).

Let us look at some attempts to classify this far-reaching theory. Talcott Parsons centred his ideas on the essential issue of order, what he saw as the result of a merger between personality, culture and social

Figure 41.3 *Concepts of a system*

system. Their interlocking produced an overriding central value system in society. This acts as the core of any society and gives it stability and continuity. Thus general behaviour is more or less permissible and society continues regardless of changes in membership. People hold to these values or beliefs and like the stability they bring. Most of us have firm beliefs on such issues as family, murder and war. Parsons considered that organisations worked in the same way as any other social system. He searched for a connection between central values and corporate organisational goals. He felt that this was achieved by

defining clear roles. He concluded that the value of an individual's job within an organisation is determined by the expectations which the individual role occupants bring to their jobs.

Parsons' functional requirements of organisation

Parsons also tried to explain the link between organisations and society. He stressed a 'common core' of values to both organisations and society. But stability is also achieved through adaption, cooperation, and coordination of the component parts of work organisations (see Figure 41.4 and 41.5).

A practical application

Another exponent of this school, S.O. Shainghassey put it in a more practical way. He saw it as focusing on two interrelated functions:

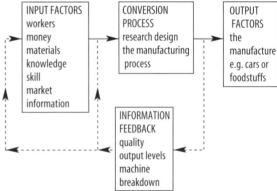

Figure 41.4 *Interrelations of factors within an organisation*

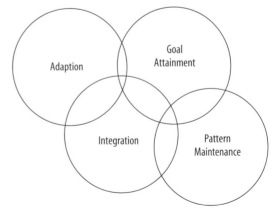

Figure 41.5 *Parson's functional requirements of organisations*

The decision making activity **+** *communication activity*

The essential features of an attempt to apply a system concept in practice he summarised as:

1. specify objectives
2. identify the subsystems
3. analyse the decision areas and establish information needs
4. design communication channels for the information flow
5. group decision areas to minimise the communications burden

How can we summarise the functional approach to organisations theory? Probably with some difficulty! The best way is to see it as a jigsaw approach. It attempts to break things down to their essential elements and then assemble these into patterns of interrelationships. To this must be added a communications process that enables all who need to know, to know exactly what is required of them.

Max Weber and the ideal bureaucracy model

Weber was probably the most influential of the structuralists. He concentrated on the maintenance of order within the structure of formal work organisations and in particular the distribution and acceptance of power among the various positions. He pondered on the question 'Why do individuals accept authority?' Acceptance is a noticeable part of history, and even though it may now be less than it once was, people still obey. Is it a personality that induces acceptance? Weber felt that in modern societies people gained acceptance through authority. He concluded that individuals will grant to others the legitimacy to use power over them if the reasons are logical and conform to the framework of values they hold. We accept rules if they are seen as necessary to a specific situation. Situations vary and so does acceptance.

Weber's theory says that people will obey if the consequences of not obeying are sufficiently unacceptable, but this is not willing acceptance and the commitment to the task may lack real effort. *In essence, this theory means:*

Power + *legitimacy* = *authority.*

SUMMARY

Having studied this chapter, you should be able to:

▽ Explain the significance of the scientific, systematic school to the development of organisation theory.

▽ Describe how the human relations school (Mayo) emerged from the Taylor era.

▽ Trace the development of the structuralist and systems approach through to the observations of Weber.

Questions and activities

Technical terms and glossary

In the sections below you are given a series of technical terms and their meanings. They have been scrambled. You must match up the business term and its definition. When you have got them correctly paired, transfer them to an alphabetical vocabulary book or glossary book.

You are also advised to transfer the definitions obtained during the exercises in the case studies into this glossary book.

Technical terms

1. The systematic school or classical model
2. Span of control
3. Human relations school
4. Structural functionalisation
5. Weber's observation

Definitions

A. The number of people for whom you are directly responsible.
B. Power + legitimacy = authority
C. A school of thought that was based on the importance of working conditions.
D. A school of thought that centred on money as the principal motivator and system as the best way of organising an enterprise.
E. An area of organisational theory that believed it more realistic to aim for minimising the impact of individual goals that run contrary to organisational goals.

Short answer questions

1. Define what is meant by the term 'organisation'.
2. Outline what you understand when a management theorist refers to:
   (a) value systems
   (b) primary systems
   (c) secondary systems
   (d) group norms
3. Explain the term 'Mission Statement'.
4. What were the main principles on which F.W. Taylor believed an organisation was based?
5. How did the human relations school differ in their approach to organisational theory from that put forward by the scientific school?
6. What changes in management beliefs did the structural functionalists introduce?
7. Outline the major ideas of those known as 'Systems Approach' supporters.
8. How did Max Weber believe an individual gained authority over others?

CHAPTER 42

Developing human resources

Preview

▼ One other part of management that must be covered is that of *team building*.

▼ Managers must concentrate on achieving the maximum from each one of their employees, that is, their human resources.

Building teams

A team is composed of members interacting towards a common goal and is characterised by communication patterns, a shared sense of collective identity and a group structure made up of the roles of members and standards of behaviour.

The test of a team's effectiveness is the capacity to achieve useful results. Effective teams require careful and methodical construction but they can perform at a level far beyond that which a collection of individuals can achieve. As a result of specialisation, group dynamics and high performance norms, the team fulfils its potential and satisfies individual needs for care and support (see Figures 42.1, 42.2 and 42.3).

Figure 42.2 *Pressures on the modern manager*

Stage 1: Forming

The group is not yet a group but members seek each other out. The group orientates itself to the task with discussion of how to go about accomplishing it and suggestions on the information and resources that are needed. This is a period of testing and discovery to find out what kind of behaviour is appropriate and members tend to defer to the leader or dominant member for guidance.

Stage 2: Storming

This is the conflict stage in which members try to

Figure 42.1 How managers create working opportunities

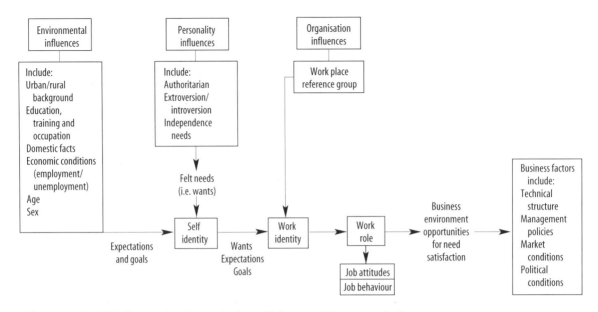

Figure 42.3 *Possible influences that shape attitudes and behaviour within an organisation*

express their individuality and resist group pressures and influence. There are often emotional responses to the demands being made, especially if the group is under pressure to achieve results.

Stage 3: Norming

At this stage, members develop ways of working and a sense of group identity begins to emerge. There is a willingness to listen to and accept the view of others. Group standards and member's roles emerge.

Stage 4: Performing

The group gets on with its task and solutions are found to problems. The team develops a functional but flexible structure and roles are interrelated. Interpersonal conflicts have been sorted out and the team is highly task-orientated.

Leadership is a critical part of a successful group's development into an effective team unit. Particularly at the early stages of development, members need feedback, encouragement and reassurance from the leader. The leader will also have to clarify objectives, suggest procedures and set standards. Further development requires a positive climate to help the team come through the storming stage and opportunities need to be created for the team to meet and share information and allow members to take part in the decision-making process.

The Johari Window shown in Figure 42.4 is a useful device to increase a person's understanding of how others see them. To use it, particular types of

behaviour should be located in one of four boxes on the basis of whether the behaviour is known to yourself and known to others. It requires the user to accept help and advice from others on behaviour of which they are unaware.

An effective team is not composed of very similar people. Members of a team will have their own specialist skills which characterise their functional role. They will also have their team role which relates to their personality. A successful team needs a balance of functional skills and a balance of personalities (see Figures 42.5, 42.6 and 42.7).

	Behaviour known to self	Behaviour unknown to self
Behaviour known to others	PUBLIC	BLIND
Behaviour unknown to others	HIDDEN	UNCONSCIOUS

Figure 42.4 *The Johari Window*

Team building or team development has matured as a viable management tool, useful for improving performance and profitability. The methodologies and the approaches have changed and will continue to change as new developments and refinements are made in the management process relative to individual and group behaviour, strategic and tactical planning and the dynamics of the business environment.

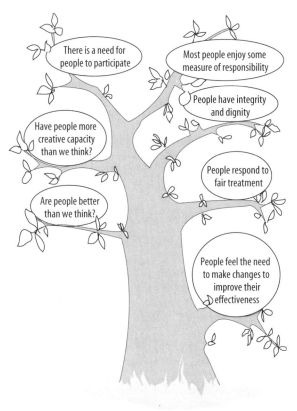

Figure 42.5 Making a decision – some food for thought

- Avoidance
- Dominance
- Smoothing over
- Appeal to higher authority
- Establish policies and rules
- Appeal to neutrals
- Changing the flow of work
- Inter-group confrontation
- Selection and training
- Bargaining
- Consumer problem solving

Figure 42.6 Managing conflict – a blue print

Kinds of change

- Methods of work
- Policies and procedures
- Standards of work
- Economic changes (salaries, etc.)
- Equipment changes
- Organisational changes
- Transfer of personnel
- Status and social changes
- Location
- Environmental

Resistance by management

- Negative view
- Unconscious dissension
- Apathy, indifference
- Free translation
- Pet project attitude
- Authoritarian approach

Conditions contributing to resistance to change

- Shortage of personnel/equipment during implementation
- Failure to justify reason for change
- Top management pressure for fast installation of change
- Lack of participation
- Poor planning for redeployment of people
- Insufficient guidance of people affected
- Lack of enthusiasm by management
- Lack of advance information

Why people resist change

- Economic reasons:
  Fear of unemployment
  Fear of reduced hours
  Fear of demotion and reduced pay
- Personal reasons:
  Resentment of implied criticism that present methods are inadequate
  Fear that skill, knowledge and pride will be reduced
  Fear that job will be less interesting or challenging
  Fear that harder work will be involved
  Resistance because of lack of understanding
- Social reasons:
  Dislike of making new social adjustments
  Dislike of breaking present social ties
  Fear that new social situation will bring reduced satisfaction
  Dislike of outside interference
  Resentment of lack of involvement
  Change seen as benefiting only the organisation

Conditions for reducing resistance to change

- Management support and belief in change
- Evidence of how workers have been well treated in the past when changes have been made
- Commitment through understanding, involvement, and communication
- Information given on:
  What is to be done
  Why it is to be done (advantages and disadvantages)
  How it is to be done
  When is it to be done
  Who is to be involved

Figure 42.7 Resistance to change: checklist of factors

Groups and teams

When does a group become a team? Most can answer that instinctively and will probably be right. Teams have just the right number of people. The relationship between them is characterised by trust. Their abilities dovetail and they are conscious of this interlink and know each other's skills and abilities. Where there is temporary absence, members cover for each other. Less communication is necessary because members know things without being told. The team's needs tend to be satisfied, and each member has a strong sense of responsibility for their own and the team's collective work.

Is there any way of affecting the development from group to team? To start with, the members will certainly need a good measure of luck; an employer who will not move key members out and make other changes which frustrate team efforts is very rare in business today.

Finally, one can look at certain special functions which groups need to have one (or more) of their members fulfil to keep the group process going. Team working is a process: it takes place over time and needs both regular maintenance and special roles to tend to the various parts of the process.

Practical and theoretical concepts of successful teams

The reasons why successful teams flourish are varied and complex. Successful teams bring together a mature range of competencies, experience, attitudes and values which create a tightly coordinated pattern for different purposes.

'Top Teams' need to be seen as whole entities in the round, for each members' attributes both contribute to and feed off the others. The Ashridge Team-Work Research Unit in the UK very recently pieced together all the evidence they could find from other people's work and their own in order to put together a comprehensive picture of what qualities make a successful team. Although this is an idealistic and visionary picture in terms of best practice, it does identify a wide range of recognised qualities associated with 'top team' success.

Characteristics of successful teams

Successful teams all have several things in common, whether they be sport teams, business teams, military teams or whatever.

Here are eight characteristics which have been identified and which will help you to analyse the 'health' of your own team:

- a mission or charter
- common objectives
- interdependence of members
- an effective relationship to the environment
- an identifiable decision-making system
- well-motivated members
- an effective leader
- well-organised, effective meetings.

High performing or 'top teams' tend to have the following goals or aims:

1. They are persistent and obsessive in the pursuit of their goals, but creatively flexible in their strategies for getting there. They are continually returning to the question, 'What are we trying to achieve?'
2. They confront people or situations which lie in their path. They are tenacious and inventive in their efforts to remove all obstacles.
3. They are committed to quality in performance and all aspects of team working. They have very high expectations of themselves and of others.
4. They display significant understanding of the strategy and philosophy of their apparent organisation or that part of it which is important to success.
5. They are inspired by a vision of what they are trying to achieve. This provides a strong sense of purpose and direction. They also have a realistic strategy for turning the vision into reality.
6. They actively build formal and informal networks which include people who matter to them and who can help them.
7. They are driven by success. They exude the energy, excitement and commitment that being successful releases. They also thrive on the recognition that success brings.
8. They are action-orientated. They respond quickly and positively to problems and opportunities and are optimistic even when the going gets tough. But above all they do not wait for things to happen to them. They go out and make things happen.
9. They are committed to the success of their parent organisation. They thrive in an open culture where responsibility and authority is delegated to them to produce agreed results.
10. They have a significant influence on the parent organisation. The power to influence is not based on formal authority but on the team's credibility. Team and organisation feed off and learn from each other.
11. They work best with principles and guidelines as procedures rather than rules. In this way they preserve one of their key qualities – flexibility.

12. They distinguish the important from the urgent, and while valuing change, flexibility will make routine those activities which can be dealt with most effectively in that way.
13. They value leaders who maintain the team's direction, energy and commitment. They expect the leader, with their help, to fight for support and resources from key figures within the parent organisation.
14. They are able to sustain communication and momentum as well when they are working apart as when they are working together.
15. They pride themselves on being creative and innovative and on being prepared to take legitimate risks in order to achieve significant gains.
16. They understand why they are successful but are never satisfied with that. They are constantly looking for ways to 'do things better'.
17. They value people for their knowledge, competence and contributions rather than for status and position.
18. They will always try to work with others rather than working for or against others.
19. They sometimes seem arrogant – and this can be the cause of their downfall!

Definition of success teams

'A team is a group in which the job and skills of each member fit in with those of others, as in a jigsaw puzzle pieces fit together without distortion and together produce some overall pattern.' (B. Babington-Smith)

'Teams are groups of people who cooperate to carry out a joint task. They may be assigned to different work roles, or be allowed to sort them out between themselves and change jobs when they feel like it.' (M. Argyle)

Qualities of successful teams
* appropriate leadership
* suitable membership
* commitment to the team
* constructive climate
* concern to achieve
* clear corporate role
* effective work methods
* well-organised team procedures
* critique without rancour
* well-developed individuals
* creative strength
* positive inter-group relations.

Forces that enhance group cohesiveness
* friendly group atmosphere
* similarity among members
* interdependence among members
* high status
* attractive group goals
* small group size.

Forces that diminish group cohesiveness
* threatening environment
* low public image
* disagreement over group activities
* membership in other groups
* unpleasant group experiences
* competition with alternative activities
* disagreeable group demands.

Figure 42.8 attempts to illustrate the forces that diminish group cohesiveness.

In the early 1970s, R. Meredith Belbin started to investigate what made a management team successful, as opposed to what made an individual manager successful. Over the next nine years he carried out detailed research with teams in training situations and related the results to real management teams in a variety of organisations in both the public and private sectors.

His research is continuing but in 1981 he published the initial results. The key points from his work are as follows.

What is a team role?
Belbin defined a team role as the way in which members with characteristic personalities and abilities contribute to a team.

He established that there were a limited number of useful team roles, and that a team's success depended on how well the individual roles were discharged and how they interlocked with each other.

Personality traits
Much of Belbin's research was supported by personality measures used to give an insight into the individuals in the teams. Among the measures he used were:

* mental ability/intelligence
* introversion/extroversion
* anxiety/stability

Later, these basic measures were extended to consider other factors such as creativity, dominance, and trust in others.

Category	Positive norm	Negative norm
1. Enterprise and personal pride	Group members stand up for the company when it is unfairly criticised.	Group members do not care about company problems.
2. Performance/ excellence	Group members try to improve, even when doing well.	Group members are satisfied with the minimum acceptable performance.
3. Teamwork/ communication	Group members listen and seek the opinions of others.	Group members talk about others behind their backs rather than confronting issues.
4. Leadership	Group members ask for help when they need it.	Group members hide their problems and avoid superiors.
5. Profitability and cost effectiveness	Group members are concerned with increasing profitability and cost effectiveness.	Group members do not care about profits; that is someone else's problem.
6. Colleague relations	Group members refuse to take advantage of one another.	Group members do not care about one another's well being.
7. Consumer relations	Group members feel the customer is No 1.	Group members are indifferent to customer satisfaction.
8. Honesty and security	Group members refuse to tolerate pilferage or lax security.	Group members are unconcerned with pilferage or security.
9. Training and development	Group members care about training and development.	Group members talk about training and development, but do not take it seriously.
10. Innovative change	Group members are always looking for better ways to do things.	Group members do not have new ideas.

Figure 42.8 Ten categories of work group norms with positive and negative examples

The Apollo syndrome

Initially Belbin concentrated on the concept of mental ability and put together teams of people who all had above average intelligence and who scored high on critical thinking faculties. He called these 'Apollo' teams after the American lunar success.

However, Belbin's Apollo teams did not share the success of those they were named after. Belbin's Apollo teams were usually a dismal failure, ending up in the bottom half of the 'league'!

There were three key reasons for the failure of these teams:

1. They were difficult to manage, disliking any form of imposed organisation.

2. They were prone to destructive debate, spending too much time trying to persuade each other to their point of view and finding flaws in other people's arguments.

3. They had difficulty reaching decisions – probably because of the destructive debate.

On the few occasions when an Apollo team did well, it was noticed that:

- The Chairman was slightly cleverer than other members of the group; a tough, discriminating individual who could hold ground without dominating.
- Team members usually had complementary skills, and cooperated in their use. For example, financial information would be jointly handled by one person with high skills in numeracy and another with high analytical skills.
- There were few, if any, dominant members of the team.

'Pure' teams

Belbin also experimented with other teams composed of people with major characteristics in common. He tried four types, none of which were particularly successful.

1. *Stable extrovert teams.* These worked well together and enjoyed their work together. They had a versatile approach and used resources well, but were inclined to euphoria and laziness. Their results were good on the whole, but individually they were rather dependent on one another and on others.
2. *Anxious extrovert teams.* These were dynamic, entrepreneurial, good at seizing opportunities, and prone to healthy argument. However, they were also easily distracted and liable to rush off at tangents. Their results were good in rapidly changing situations but unreliable at other times.
3. *Stable introvert teams.* These planned well and showed strengths in organisation. Their weaknesses were that they were too slow-moving and liable to overlook new factors in a situation. Their results were generally indifferent.
4. *Anxious introvert teams.* These were capable of producing good ideas but tended to be preoccupied and lack cohesion as a team. Their results were usually poor.

The concept of team roles

As the research continued, Belbin looked at more and more factors and gradually evolved the concept of team roles: the idea that a successful team needs a variety of people within it and that, based on their characteristics and ability, each should have a specific role. Eventually, he established eight team roles.

The eight team roles

1. Coordinator (formally called chairman)

This role is one of presiding over the team and coordinating its efforts to meet external goals and targets. Focused on achieving the task goals but doing so by knowing each team member's strengths and weaknesses, and trying to use each member as effectively as possible in achieving the team's objectives. They encourage everyone to contribute and impart a sense of purpose to the team.

Coordinators are usually of above average intelligence but not outstanding creative thinkers. They talk easily, and are easy to talk to. They are good listeners. They will set the agenda and control group discussions, but without being domineering

STABLE EXTROVERT	ANXIOUS EXTROVERT
Work well together	Dynamic and entreprenurial
Enjoy working together	Good at seizing opportunity
Versatile approach	Enjoy healthy argument
Inclined to laziness	Easily distracted
Results rather good but dependent on one another and others	Tend to rush off and go in all directions
STABLE INTROVERT	**ANXIOUS INTROVERT**
Well planned	Produce good ideas
Organisational strength	Pre-occupied, lack of cohesion as a team
Too slow moving	
Overlook new factors	

Figure 42.9 Pure teams

(see Figure 42.9).

They will listen, sum up group feelings, spell out group verdicts and, if a decision has to be taken, will take it firmly after everyone in the team has had a say. Their personality traits are: stable, dominant, extrovert.

2. Shaper

This role is the one of concentrating the task through to completion. This role is an alternative to the coordinator type of leader, and a team needs one or the other – not both. Shapers are better than Coordinators when a team needs a leader to push

people into action, to galvanise them. Otherwise the Coordinator type will usually lead a team to produce better results.

Shapers are full of nervous energy: emotional, compulsive, impatient and easily frustrated. They enjoy and welcome challenges, are often argumentative, and can be quick to sense a slight, or feel there is a conspiracy against them.

They will usually put forward more ideas and will try to unite ideas, objectives and practical considerations into a plan for decision and action. They want action, and want it now.

They are often seen as arrogant and abrasive and have a tendency to steam-roller other members of the team. But they do make things happen. Their personality traits are: anxious, dominant, extrovert.

3. Plant

This role is the major creative one in the team: the source of ideas, suggestions, proposals – often distinguished by their originality.

Effective plants are likely to be the most intelligent and imaginative members of teams. They concentrate on major issues, seeking new lines of approach, but often miss out on detail and make careless mistakes.

They can be uninhibited at times, prickly, and may cause offence to other team members by the way in which they criticise ideas. Conversely, they are bad at accepting criticism themselves. They may also shoot off at a tangent on ideas that catch their fancy, but that do not contribute to team objectives. Their personality traits are: high IQ (especially on critical thinking), reserved.

4. Monitor-evaluator

This role is the one of the team's critic, carrying out a measured and dispassionate analysis of the team's ideas and proposals. Although unlikely to come up with a creative proposal, the monitor-evaluator is the one likely to prevent the team committing itself to misguided action. Effective monitor-evaluators are perceived to be of high intelligence with skills in assimilating, interpreting and evaluating large volumes of complex material. Sometimes their evaluations are delivered tactlessly and despairingly which can dampen team members' morale while making monitor-evaluators unpopular.

They are generally not ambitious, although they can be competitive, and typically lack warmth, imagination and spontaneity. However, they are solid, dependable, and rarely wrong in their judgements. Their personality traits are: high IQ, stable, introvert.

5. Implementer (formerly called company worker)
This is the role of turning decisions into defined and manageable tasks for people to do. The emphasis is on what is feasible: the logical extension of the objective into an achievable plan. This is an essential role for team effectiveness.

Implementers are noted for their sincerity, integrity and tenacity, and have a disciplined approach to their tasks. What upsets them is the sudden change of plan: because they like stable structures, they tend to flounder in quickly changing conditions. Sometimes a little inflexible, but usually prepared to adapt their proposals to meet agreed plans and procedures.

If anyone in the team does not know what has been agreed, or what is to be done, it is the implementer that will be able to tell them. Their personality traits are: stable and controlled.

6. Resource investigator
This is the role that liaises with those outside the team: collecting information and ideas; exploring new possibilities in the outside world. This person stimulates ideas and innovation, but not with the same originality as the 'plant'.

Resource investigators are probably the most likeable team members: relaxed, sociable, with a positive, enthusiastic outlook. Drawbacks are their tendency to lose interest and to spend too much time on irrelevancies. They can also become bored, demoralised and ineffective if not part of a team. Their personality traits are: stable, extrovert.

7. Team worker
Probably the most supportive role in the team. A good listener who helps and encourages others; building on their ideas rather than demolishing them or producing rival ideas.

Team workers are the cement of the team. They are sensitive to other people's needs and worries, perceive emotional undercurrents, and strive to produce unity and harmony within the team. An excellent counterbalance to the friction sometimes caused by the 'shaper' or the 'monitor-evaluator'.

Not usually competitive and may even be seen as soft and indecisive. But they have a noticeable effect in times of stress and pressure. Their personality traits are: stable, extrovert, low in dominance.

8. Completer/finisher
The one who is not content until every 'i' has been dotted and every 't' crossed. This person is not at ease until a personal check on every detail has made sure that everything has been done, nothing overlooked – a 'perfectionist'.

'Completer/finishers' are not assertive but maintain a sense of urgency which galvanises others into activity. They are self-controlled but apt to be impatient with more casual members of the team who are not so compulsive about meeting deadlines and doing things properly. They are important assets to a team provided they do not get bogged down in detail and lower the morale of other members of the team.

Their personality traits: anxious, introvert.

Our preferred team roles
The fact that there are eight team roles does not mean that there must be at least eight people in a successful team! We can each fulfil more than one role; and we can often switch to an alternative key role if someone else in the team is filling our first preference role. The important thing is that all the key roles are being carried out adequately.

Winning teams
Those teams that produce the best results have some characteristics in common:

- a good coordinator in the chair, or a shaper
- a very creative and clever plant - but only one!
- a fair spread of mental ability: coordinator, plant and perhaps one other such as monitor-evaluator, above average; the remainder below average
- a spread in personal attributes that gives good coverage of the various team-roles, with at least:
  – one completer/finisher
  – one implementer
  – one resource investigator
  – one team worker if the leader is a shaper and preferably one extrovert and one introvert
- a good match between an individual's attributes and team responsibilities
- a willingness to adjust roles according to the strengths and weaknesses of other team members. (See also Figure 42.10.)

Using the research results
We may find we do not have a winning team, but what can we do about it? It is rarely possible for us to completely reconstruct the team so that its members all have complementary role strengths. Some of the things we can do to overcome roles that are not adequately filled in a team are:

- Get team members to fill roles that may not be their preferred ones but that are, nevertheless, ones in which they have reasonable strength.
- Fill a missing role by an alternative method; for example: use 'brainstorming' if the team lacks a

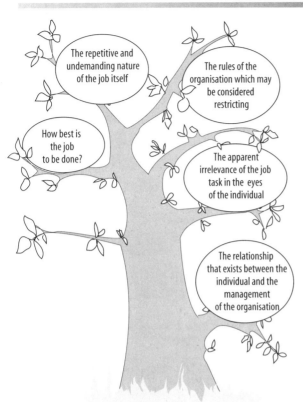

The repetitive and undemanding nature of the job itself

The rules of the organisation which may be considered restricting

How best is the job to be done?

The apparent irrelevance of the job task in the eyes of the individual

The relationship that exists between the individual and the management of the organisation

Figure 42.10 *Causes of frustration*

'plant'.

If we find, however, that there are problems caused by people being in the wrong team roles or in conflicting team roles, we may have to try to change some team members or have people negotiate their team roles.

Some examples of such circumstances:

- an ineffective coordinator
- conflict between coordinator and a shaper both trying to lead the team
- overlapping roles, such as two plants

Belbin's model only helps managers identify any problems. They must still decide how to resolve them. Belbin's eight team members and their qualitites are shown in Figure 42.11.

SUMMARY

Type	Symbol	Typical features	Positive qualities	Allowable weaknesses
Coordinator (chairman)	CH	Calm, self-confident, controlled.	A capacity for treating and welcoming all potential contributors on their merits and without prejudice. A strong sense of objectives.	No more than ordinary in terms of intellect or creative ability.
Shaper	SH	Highly strung, out-going, dynamic.	Drive and a readiness to challenge inertia, ineffectiveness, complacency or self-deception.	Proneness to provocation, irritation and impatience.
Plant	PL	Individualistic, serious minded, unorthodox.	Genius, imagination, intellect, knowledge.	Up in the clouds, inclined to disregard practical details.
Monitor-evaluator	ME	Sober, unemotional, prudent.	Judgement, discretion, hard hardheadness.	Lacks inspiration or the ability to motivate others.
Implementer (company worker)	CW	Conservative, dutiful, predictable.	Organising ability, practical common sense, hard-working, self-discipline.	Lack of flexibility, unresponsiveness to unproven ideas.
Resource investigator	RI	Extroverted, enthusiastic, curious, communicative.	A capacity for contacting people and exploring anything new. An ability to respond to challenge.	Liable to lose interest once the initial fascination has passed.
Team worker	TW	Socially orientated, rather mild, sensitive.	An ability to respond to people and to situations, and to promote team spirit.	Indecisiveness at moments of crisis.
Completer/ finisher	CF	Painstaking, orderly, conscientious, anxious.	A capacity for follow-through. Perfectionism.	A tendency to worry about small things. A reluctance to 'let go'.

Figure 42.11 *Summary of team roles.* (**Source:** *R.M. Belbin,* **Success in Management,** *1981*)

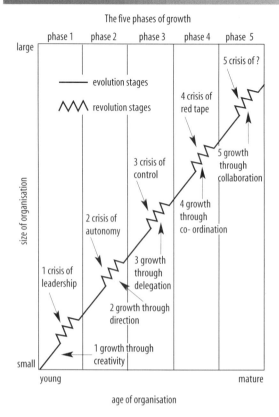

The five phases of growth

phase 1 | phase 2 | phase 3 | phase 4 | phase 5

large

5 crisis of ?

—— evolution stages

4 crisis of
red tape

ᴧᴧᴧ revolution stages

3 crisis of
control

5 growth
through
collaboration

size of organisation

2 crisis of
autonomy

4 growth
through
co- ordination

1 crisis of
leadership

3 growth
through
delegation

2 growth through
direction

1 growth through
creativity

small

young   mature

age of organisation

Figure 42.12 *The pains of success*

New recruit in CD's pay office

Kate Schofield, a new employee, has impressed our Personnel Manager. She is always ready five minutes before her shift, and is prepared to work overtime. At 5.00 pm she is still working, while others are not!

Alas, the other workers do not like Kate. She is beginning to be ignored and the odd worker has been guilty of giving her bogus, time-consuming jobs to do. Kate has been saddened by this behaviour and is considering giving in her notice.

Questions
(a) Analyse the attitude of Kate's work colleagues in terms of group norms
(b) What can we do, if anything, to help Kate to be more acceptable to her colleagues?

Having studied this chapter, you should be able to:

▽ Describe the fundamentals of what makes a good team.

▽ Explain how to keep a team working efficiently.

▽ Discuss the relevance of teams in modern business.

Questions and activities

Technical terms and glossary

In the section below you are given a series of technical terms and their meanings. They have been scrambled, though. You must match up the terms and the defintitions. When you have them correctly paired, transfer them to your alphabetical vocabulary or glossary book.

You are also advised to transfer any definitions obtained during the exercises in the case studies into this glossary book.

Technical terms

1. Span of control
2. Non-economic factors
3. Maslow's hierachy of needs
4. The structuralist approach
5. Mission statement.

Definitions

A. A system of understanding human behaviour that is based on a hierachy of obtainable needs.

B. A precise message or statement that enshrines exactly what the organisation stands for and wants to achieve.

C. A clearly defined range of authority within a formal organisational structure.

D. A group of rewards that are part of Mayo's theories that do not involve direct monetary payment.

E. A group of theories based on the belief that workers are alienated at work and need 'control';.

Short answer questions

1. Why is the Johari Window considered of use in predicting human behaviour?
2. Briefly analyse and apply the main skills needed for a successful team.
3. Explain and evaluate why groups cease to perform as a cohesive unit.
4. What did Belbin mean by his 'Apollo Syndrome'?
5. Describe the qualitites needed to be a good coordinator.
6. What should be the end results if we find the correct blend of personalities for our team?
7. Apply Maslow's theory of motivation to work in any industrial location of your choice.
8. Briefly explain what you understand by the terms:
   (a) Job enrichment
   (b) Job enlargement
   (c) Job rotation
9. What are the implications to management of the findings of Macgregor?
10. What specific features would you advise to be included in a new system of communications to be introduced at College Dynamics.

43

The economic
environment of business

Preview

▼ Attention must now be turned to an analysis of the environment within which business has to operate.

▼ Careful consideration must be given to such issues as nationalised industries, foreign trade and certain external influences on the economy.

▼ Similarly, the internal features, e.g. government finance, must also be analysed and understood.

The changing pattern of demand in the United Kingdom

Oil, petro-chemical and chemical industries have all increased output by considerable amounts since the beginning of the 1970s, followed closely by electrical engineering, the computer industries and precision engineering. Production in mechanical and heavy engineering remained fairly steady, not sharing the same rate of growth exhibited by the industries based upon advanced technology, a high capital utilisation, or investment in scientific research.

Industries based on primary products, including coal and steel, have declined in output and importance, as has shipbuilding. For as the demand of society becomes more sophisticated and technology changes, advanced forms of industrial production enable the provision of services to expand, while basic primary product industries tend to decline. This has led to a loss of employment in some areas, which in turn reduces disposal, income and demand.

Trends

- Since 1970, there has been a rapid and accelerating decline of non-traditional secondary industries based on heavy engineering, so that by 1982 the UK was a net importer of manufactured and semi-manufactured goods.

- A rise in the importance of North Sea oil both as an internal source of industrial fuel and power (reducing UK oil imports) and, since 1982, as an export commodity. But this is a finite product and North Sea oil production is set to decline. Past revenue from this asset has largely been absorbed in the payment of benefits to those unemployed. The new fields to the west of Scotland will extend the lifetime of this asset.

- A move from comparative advantages in manufacturing to a comparative advantage in the provision of services (particularly financial services).

Such trends appear to have been common to all industrialised countries who underwent similar changes during the 1970s and 1980s.

Patterns of employment

Employment changes reflect the patterns of production within the economy. Employment in industries such as coal, iron and steel continues to decline, but the number of people employed in finance, science and professional services has increased faster than in any other sector of employment. Economic changes force the working population to seek jobs in white-collar occupations and service industries rather than in basic production; this is a feature of all advanced industrial societies.

New technology and unemployment

The micro-electronic revolution

Since the mid-1970s, commercial opportunities in the computer and electronic fields have been transformed by the application of the silicon integrated circuits to electronics, and the development of micro-electronics. Hence, the existence of College Dynamics!

The advantages claimed for this relatively new industrial technology are:

- The introduction of new products.
- Improvements in the manufacture of old-style products.
- Clean, safe and automated production methods, can be applied over a wide area of industrial production.
- Widespread use of advanced telecommunications systems, a direct form of notification.
- Improved information storage and retrieval.

New technology is advantageous, but we must be aware that some will receive the disadvantages. On balance, however, it appears that wealth increases as technology is applied to productive processes.

- Although some jobs will be lost, others will be created.
- Failure to adopt the new technology will in any case create unemployment in the face of foreign competition. The newly industrialised countries – NICs – some of our major competitors.
- Countries which had the most impressive record for industrial innovation also lead the field in industrial productivity and employment prospects.
- Reduced prices and higher wages in the sectors of industry adapting to the new technology will work to increase domestic demand. Exports should increase as the price of goods become competitive.

But, there are disadvantages as well:

- The adoption of automation in certain industries (chemicals and engineering) is likely to be very rapid indeed because of high wage costs. Personnel are therefore likely to become redundant faster than new jobs can be created.
- Somebody trained for one type of job may not find alternative employment in another unrelated industry unless the state provides very substantial help in the form of retraining, financial aid for moving from one locality to another, and information about the employment opportunities available.

- Can there be a smooth transition from a field of declining employment to one of expanding opportunity? This implies that the educational institutions and training agencies are fitted to train and provide the right type of person to fit the new job opportunities.
- Our whole attitude to work is likely to undergo radical change as a result of having to adopt new technologies. For example, it may be that our amount of leisure time might have to increase whether we like it or not, in order that the amount of work available can be shared.

Income and expenditure

Personal disposable income and consumer expenditure has almost doubled over the last 30 years. This has led to an increase in the average standard of living. One of the features of a rising standard of living is that, as the disposable income rises, the amount of money spent per household on foodstuffs as a whole does not increase, extra income being used either to buy more luxury goods or more sophisticated convenience foods.

The quality of food eaten in Britain also reflected changes in the pattern of demand as income rose; far less money was spent on bread and cereals, expenditure being switched to oils, fats, dairy produce, fruit, meat and bacon. The figures tend to reflect the general rise in the standard of living and changes in technology. A further example is provided by the steady decline in the number of black-and-white television sets purchased and the increase in colour sets bought.

General trends

What, then, are the long-term trends summarised as follows.

- British industrial society is in the process of fundamental transition from one phase of an industrial revolution – largely dominated by primary products – to a period of growth based on advanced technological industries. These changes are accompanied by a decline in older industries.
- Industrial development is likely to be accompanied by a high rate of unemployment because of the accelerated rate at which automated and semi-automated production methods (which are capital rather than labour-intensive) are being introduced into modern industry.
- In all industrial countries, including the UK,

industry is undergoing profound change as a result of increased competition, the drive to find new markets, the formation of free trade areas such as the EU, and the practicality of instant global communication via satellites. The main developments can be summarised as follows:

- the formation of large multinational companies operating in areas far from their home base.
- a move towards takeovers and mergers and larger sized trading units
- the development of global branding
- a drive to push costs down and deliver customer benefits and value for money
- a reduction in the workforce and a levelling of managerial hierarchies.

Trends in United Kingdom manufacturing employment

Why have these changes occurred in employment patterns?

A number of reasons for the relative 'de-industrialisation' of the UK have been put forward. One school of economists argue that the prime cause of de-industrialisation in the mature economies is the rapid industrialisation of nations such as Mexico, Brazil, Korea, Taiwan and the Philippines, which are known as newly industrialised countries or NICs, mentioned earlier.

It is argued that low labour costs, coupled with advanced production technology, enable such countries to outbid more mature industrial nations in world markets. Many of these countries have easier access to growing markets in South America, Africa, South-East Asia and China than do the nations of Europe. The 'Pacific Basin' is not an easy access area for a firm based in Western Europe.

However, de-industrialisation in the UK began long before the newly industrialised nations started to capture a significant share of world markets.

What of the development of new technology? Micro-electronics and automated systems are certainly beginning to flush out high-cost labour. Again, this development began ten years after the first sign of the rapid decline in manufacturing employment.

Other factors attributed as causes of the decline in manufacturing employment are:

- The rapid growth of the public and service sector in all modern economies (hence the pressure for cut-backs in public sector spending).
- The growth of foreign competition in the wake of low productivity, poor marketing and over-priced goods; hence the call for import controls to defend home markets and employment.
- The rapid development of North Sea oil, which has caused a shift of investment away from the manufacturing sector.
- Shortage of investment funds, owing to excessively high interest rates and a reluctance for people to invest savings in industry. UK savings tend to flow into 'property', i.e. building services.

The public sector

In recent years, manufacturing has become less important in the total economic activity of the nation. Public sector and service employment have grown correspondingly. Manufacturing is predominantly an employer of men. The public sector and service industries, on the other hand, employ mainly women. Jobs in manufacturing are mainly full-time, often heavy, relatively unskilled work, while those in the public sector are often part-time, semi-skilled, 'white-collar' work.

The reasons for public service growth appear to be:

- A rise in demand for welfare services of all types as unemployment remains at 2.5 million.
- Increase in criminal behaviour – particularly juvenile crime linked to deprivation and unemployment.
- Demographic changes, i.e. the growth of an ageing population.
- Higher expectation of public service provision linked to the general rise in affluence of the majority of the population.
- Rising rates of divorce and numbers of single parent families.
- The rising costs of technology – particularly in the NHS.

One of the major problems of any society for the future is to generate sufficient wealth to sustain projected levels of public spending.

Competitiveness

Up to the early 1970s, Britain's manufactured products were no more expensive than foreign products. This was because, over the long term, devaluation of the pound and appreciation of competitors' currencies tended to balance rising manufacturing costs in Britain.

The UK car industry illustrates this particular problem. Its difficulties appear to have been:

- chronic labour troubles within the industry

- restrictive practices
- over-manning
- the poor status of middle management and supervisory grades
- poor pay structure (skilled workers and production engineers).

By the mid-1980s, the exchange rate had ceased to compensate British manufacturers for lack of competitiveness in world markets. High interest rates, combined with the North Sea oil bonanza, attracted foreign money and caused appreciation of sterling. There are two ways of halting this appreciation.

- by encouraging an outflow of capital by restricting North Sea oil development and investing the profits of North Sea oil abroad
- by expanding the economy, i.e. stimulating home demand to offset losses in exports.

Both courses of action are dangerous. Investment overseas is risky, and there is no guarantee that substantial profits will flow back to the UK. Expanding the economy faces the danger of massive stagflation, i.e. high levels of unemployment coupled with rising inflation. So, the UK has had to address change and adapt.

The UK economy has undergone considerable change. An analysis must be made of the various sections of the economy. The public sector is where the analysis begins.

Nationalised industries

Most countries in the world have nationalised industries. These are firms owned and run by the state through a board of directors. There are no public shareholders, all capital being held by the state in trust for the public. They are directed, ultimately, by a government Minister.

Nationalised industries should not be confused with the State or public corporations. These are not involved with trading with the public, nor do they report directly to a minister. Examples of such corporations are the Bank of England, the Post Office and the BBC.

Nationalised industries do not produce public goods like defence, or the major merit goods such as education and health. Nationalised industries produce public goods for the government; they exist primarily to trade with the public.

Thus, nationalised industries are those public corporations:

- whose assets are in public ownership, and vested

in a public corporation
- whose board members are not civil servants
- whose boards are appointed by a secretary of state
- which are primarily engaged in industry or other trading activities.

In most economies production is split between the private and public sectors of the economy.

In the UK the recent Conservative governments have carried out a policy of privatisation, or denationalisation. Businesses which have been privatised include:

- British Steel Corporation
- Electricity Generating and Marketing Boards
- British Gas
- British Telecom
- British Airways
- National Freight Corporation.

Why should there be nationalised industries? Why should they be privatised again?

Justifications for nationalisation

1. *Prevent the abuse of monopoly power.* A state monopoly can adopt marginal cost pricing, to the benefit of the consumer. In the same area comes the ability of such a firm to sell to the public at special, low prices. It can give special prices to 'needy' customers. The firm will probably make losses but these will be financed by the government – social benefits and costs, again. However, this amounts to a subsidy for the product or service.

   Such monopoly firms will be able to supply or serve minor markets, where a profit would not be possible, for example, rural rail and postal services. A private firm would either not supply, or would charge an excessive price for the service. (Unless they received a subsidy from the government.)

2. *Strategic reasons.* Some industries have to be kept operating, for reasons of defence or the supply of basic power services. A good example is the nationalisation of Rolls Royce by the government when the aero-engine company went bankrupt. Most UK military aircraft use Rolls Royce engines.

3. *Economies of scale.* Natural monopoly industries are 'best' organised as nationalised industries to avoid wasteful competition, for example, the electricity or gas industries.

4. *Capital aspects.* If a firm requires finance from the state, for research and development, or unprofitable investment in, say, the railways,

it might as well be publicly owned.

5. *Employment reasons.* A private firm will put its product and its costs as objectives before employment. It cannot be expected, without assistance, to continue to employ labour when new capital would be more effective and efficient. Nationalised industries, through the adjustment of objectives and targets including financial ones, can put employment first. The cost of this form of subsidy may be less, both financially and socially, than the costs of unemployment.

Arguments against nationalisation

1. *Inefficiency.* There is no motive to be efficient, no incentives. Since most are monopolies, they have little real competition anyway. Add to this the bureaucracy that will usually develop, and raise costs, and a potentially inefficient industry results. The industry is not exposed to the pressures of the market, and does not have to match or beat any competition. The monopoly may even exploit the consumer simply because it is state owned, and outside any organisation to protect consumer interests. The newly privatised industries were established with this protection, but the old state organisations did not have it. The consumer did not have the advantage of OFTEL until BT was privatised.

2. *Political interference.* This really is politics, but should politicians try to run or manipulate trading industries? It would all seem to hinge, economically, on monopoly power and efficiency, since most nationalised industries seem to be monopolies.

How do nationalised industries price their products?

Marginal cost pricing

This is often quoted as a plus for nationalised industries, but it has its reverse side. Marginal cost pricing, in itself, is no guarantee of social and financial efficiency. The basic theory is shown in Figure 43.1.

Nationalised industries exist almost everywhere. The most common are postal services, followed by the telecommunications industry, railways and airlines. The latter is often a matter of national prestige rather than pure business reasons.

National income accounting

In order to make an analysis of how an economy works, we need to be able to measure it. How do we measure the value of the economy? This involves us in what economists call macroeconomics.

Macroeconomics deals with the economy as a whole, and looks largely at changes in the levels of output, employment, income and prices, and the effect these have on the economy. It is essential, therefore, that there is a means of measuring an economy, a means of determining how well the factors of production are being worked.

The 'size' of an economy is measured in money units, and is known as its national income (Y). Economists, journalists and politicians are always

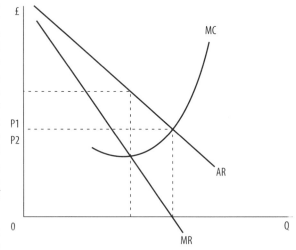

Figure 43.1 *Marginal cost pricing: how a 'nationalised' industry prices its products.*

talking about GDP (gross domestic product) and national income. What is it? Where and how is it measured? Consider the diagram below:

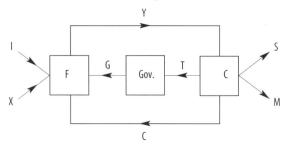

Where:

Y = National income	*I = Investments*
T = Taxation	*X = Exports*
S = Savings	*G = Government*
M = Imports	*expenditure*
C = Consumers' domestic consumption	

When an economy is in equilibrium, i.e. the money leaving the circular flow is exactly matched by the injections entering it, the value of all the goods and services produced in it must be the same as the level of sales in the economy, since they must be the goods bought. This must match the money being earned by the factors of production employed in this production process, as this is the money used in these transactions. This leads to the three ways that national income is calculated:

1. *Income Method.* The sum of all the income received by the four factors of production (land, labour, capital and enterprise) in the domestic economy in a year. This is given the code of NI.
2. *Output Method.* The total value of all goods and services produced in the domestic economy in a year. This is given the code of NP, since it is often called the national product.
3. *Expenditure Method.* The total of all spending on domestically produced goods and services in a year. This is coded as NE.

It follows that since they are all measures of the same thing, they all should be the same for any given year, i.e.:

$$NI = NP = NE$$

Because of the great difficulty in measuring the national income of an economy, the numbers rarely come out the same. (Just imagine trying to add up all of the salaries, wages, rents, profits, etc., paid or earned in a single year in UK. The Inland Revenue would be a good place to start collecting data, provided they were allowed to release such information, and provided all the records were absolutely reliable.) The problem is resolved rather neatly. It is assumed that the expenditure method result is correct, and the other totals are adjusted to bring them into line by adding or subtracting a residual error, RE. So:

$$NI + RE = NP + RE = NE$$

The residual error applied to the two totals may not be the same, since it is most unlikely that the two different methods will come up with exactly the same level of 'inaccuracy'. Remember, this is all based on an assumption. There is no reason why it should be the most accurate of the three results.

It must be remembered that assets such as plant and equipment, buildings, cars, etc., wear out with time. This has to be allowed for, and these items eventually have to be replaced if the level of existing output is to be maintained. This allowance is known as depreciation, or capital consumption. It must be deducted from national income calculations to give a true picture.

1. Transfer payments, income which is not a reward to a factor input for 'work' done, are excluded. Thus state or private pensions are ignored, as are sickness and unemployment benefits, pocket money and allowances paid to children and students.
2. No allowance is made for voluntary work, or for the notional value of the work done by people who look after the home. There is no means of accurately assessing these non-monetary activities, so they are left out.
3. Incomes are counted before income tax is paid, or 'gross' as it is called. Also, the profits made by companies before dividends are paid, and before tax is deducted are included. The result is the gross profit of the firm concerned. Surpluses made by nationalised firms are also included gross, as would be any losses made by these organisations.
4. Some firms and individuals have money overseas, and receive rents, interests, etc., from these investments. Equally, some groups in this country pay similar accounts to overseas organisations. (A Japanese firm operating in UK may pay an annual dividend, or some form of technical fee to its parent company in Tokyo.) This has to be allowed for through an entry known as 'net income from abroad'.
5. Allowance has to be made for any change in value of stocks held by firms. Any increase in value due to inflation has to be deducted from the account.
6. A strange one: the owners of houses in this country are assumed to benefit from a rental income, even if they are owner occupiers. Thus a notional sum is added to represent this.

Output method

- Double counting must be avoided. This can be done by including the value of final products only, i.e. those goods and services that are consumed, not incorporated into other goods, or resold. An alternative method is to count the value added by firms only.
- Taxes and subsidies are not a problem here, provided the value added method is followed. These sums are not part of value added, so results are automatically calculated at factor cost.
- Distortions due to imports and exports have to removed. Exports leave the country direct, but bring money into the economy, so must be recorded and added into the output result.

Equally, imports which will be picked up in the calculation of output or consumption must be deleted, since now the money value of them leaves the country where they are sold.

Expenditure method

- Only final expenditure is included. This has to be adjusted to factor cost, as indirect taxes such as VAT and excise duty, and subsidies distort spending, so have to be removed or added back as appropriate.
- Expenditure on stocks has to be adjusted for. This is output not sold to a customer, so the 'value of the physical increase in stocks and work-in-progress' has to be added to this account. (If stocks are actually consumed, as they would be if demand exceeded production and stocks existed, then their value would have to be deducted as they were not produced in the same period.)
- Government expenditure on transfer payments must be excluded. Only its spending on goods and services should be included.
- Adjustment has to be made for imports and exports again.

National income accounting

What use is there in knowing the national income for an economy? In theory it enables the growth of an economy on a year-by-year basis to be measured, and also to compare one economy with another. First, though, some dangers and qualifications.

Real or money income?

The national income for a country rises by 5% over a year. Has the economy grown? It all depends on the changes in prices which may have taken place over the same period. Let us assume a rise in prices, overall, of 5%. It is now clear that the national income, as measured or in money terms, has risen. The consumer or the economy is no better off, though, as any increase in income has been swallowed up by inflation. So, the 'money' national income has risen, but the 'real' national income was unchanged. If the rate of inflation was 8%, then the real national income would have fallen.

So, a comparison of figures for Y for various years needs a knowledge of inflation rates over the same period before they can be of value, and to enable valid conclusions to be drawn from them. The data for national income, or GDP, has to be adjusted for price changes. The government calculates the GDP deflator, and applies this. The GDP deflator is a variation of the Retail Price Index used by the UK government, and is a measure of the level of inflation in an economy. It is also normal to use figures standardised to a set year. Examine the example below to see how it might be done:

Year	1	2	3	4	5
Money GDP (£ billions)	100	120	140	180	210
Percent change in prices (GDP deflator)	-	10	15	20	10
Index	100	110	127	152	167

Year 2 is to be the base year

	1	2	3	4	5
Adjusted index	100	110	127	152	167
	110	110	110	110	110
=	91	100	115	138	152
Real GDP (£ billions)	100	120	140	180	210
	0.91	1.00	1.15	1.38	1.52
=	110	120	122	130	138

National income and the standard of living

National income is a total of income for the whole economy. Standard of living, however, relates to the level of earnings of individuals. So to use the national income (Y) as a measure of standard of living, the figures for Y have to be divided by the size of the population; i.e. Y has to be expressed as Y per head of population. For year-by-year comparisons real Y has to be used.

So, if national income of an economy stays constant for a period, while, over the same period the population rises, then standards of living have probably fallen. Populations as a whole tend to change slowly, especially in modern, developed countries. It can be a real problem in undeveloped countries where Y itself is small to start with, and population also tends to grow relatively rapidly.

Remember, for year-by-year comparisons real income has to be used.

Distortions of measures of national income

Distribution of income

Assessing standard of living by dividing national income by the population assumes that the distribution of incomes within the economy is uniform. This is virtually never the case, and the problem is at its peak in developing economies. Here a very small proportion of the population have a large proportion of both wealth and income.

Wealth is usually distributed more unevenly than income. It would be normative to say 'more unfairly'.

This problem can be illustrated using the Lorenz curve shown in Figure 43.2.

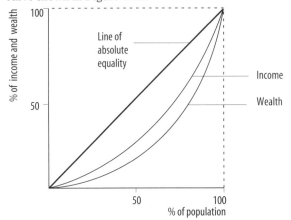

Figure 43.2 *A Lorenz curve showing various forms of equality/inequality in income and wealth distribution*

Non-monetary transactions

Non-monetary transactions can have a distorting effect on national income, or rather any assessments of standard of living based upon it. For example, housepersons do not earn wages but do contribute significantly to the national income through their spending. Some economists estimate that the contribution made by housepersons in the UK could amount to some 20% of our GDP.

Agriculture can cause problems here. In developing countries subsistence farming is the norm. People grow food basically for their own use, with only the small surplus, if any, being sold. This means that there is little contribution to national income from the agricultural sector. In developed countries, where farms sell virtually all their produce, the contribution is large. Less developed countries may even add an amount to their measured national income to allow for this, or to eliminate this distortion.

Tax evasion

Tax evasion causes national income to be understated. The 'cash economy' operates outside the official economy and no values are recorded. This is sometimes known as the 'black economy'. This problem obviously varies from country to country. To give a yardstick, the loss to this cause in UK is estimated by some economists to account for some 10% of our GDP.

Leisure

If a worker got the same pay all year, but the working day was reduced from 39 to 36 hours during the period, the worker would be better off; his standard of living would have increased. The same effect can be applied to national income as a whole. This means that a careful watch must be kept on working hours in general, and other leisure-related items.

Government expenditure

Government expenditure is a large proportion of most Western world economies. In this country it amounts to some 45% of GDP. The level of expenditure by government has no direct effect on standard of living. It is what it spends the money on that matters.

Expenditure on defence will not raise the standard of living for an economy as a whole, only for those employed in the defence industry. If money is spent on hospitals and education there will be a direct increase.

International comparisons

This is an important area of analysis, and one where many snags and problems exist. The first problem is that each country will calculate its GDP in terms of its own currency, and will use its own rules and regulations. This raises two immediate problems.

Exchange rate

GDPs must be in comparable units, so some exchange rate will have to be applied. If the exchange rate ruling is not a fair measure of the relative purchasing power of the two currencies; then the results will be distorted, if not actually misleading. If a country was to devalue its currency by 10%, would its standard of living fall by 10%, either immediately or in the long run?

Rules and regulations

Different countries will have different financial years, and different methods of calculating depreciation. The former can be allowed for, provided a series of years' results are available. It will be an approximation, though. This is dealt with very simply: most comparisons are made at the level of GDP, so ignoring the differing rates of depreciation used in different countries completely.

All the problems associated with national income figures apply in the case of international comparisons. In particular, great care must be taken over income distribution, non-monetary activities and the expenditure of the government.

The economic environment

An examination of certain broader issues in the economy must now be undertaken. These will centre on:

- foreign trade
- balance of payments and exchange rates
- the European Union and other international organisations
- money and monetary policy
- inflation and public finance
- economic growth and the challenges facing the developing world.

Foreign trade

The analysis of foreign trade centres on the following facts:

- production of different sorts of goods requires different kinds of resources
- the economic resources are not distributed evenly throughout the world
- some resources are not very mobile.

The resources land, labour, capital and entrepreneurship are what a business makes into something that it hopes someone else wants.

Land, the resources or raw materials, are becoming more and more mobile, subject to the costs of moving them. Vast quantities of oil are moved worldwide, along with iron ore, coal and grain. Some key minerals, like chromium, have to be moved since they occur so rarely. Land and climate are effectively fixed, though.

Labour is becoming more mobile as more countries open their borders. Others close theirs, however, and put up qualification barriers. Many workers are not prepared to relocate from one part of their country to another, let alone internationally.

Capital is much freer now as exchange control regulations are relaxed and removed.

Enterprise has always been the most mobile of factors. The entrepreneur will go to the location that gives the best opportunity for the greatest reward, or profit.

So, why trade? To get goods that countries cannot produce themselves, for example bananas to UK, apples to West Africa. To get goods at a cheaper price, because some countries are able to specialise – e.g. cocoa beans from Africa to UK, chocolate bars to Nigeria.

It can be stated, though, that in theory international trade takes place because factors of production are not fully mobile. This enables specialisation to take place, and the effective division of labour. The early theories came from David Ricardo, who developed the theory of comparative advantage. he used two countries, UK and Portugal, and two products, wine and cloth, on which to base his theory.

Let us examine trade between two countries A and B, of two goods X and Y. This is a trade situation, as the examination assumes that goods will be exchanged for each other. It ignores the effect of price, as such, and of exchange rates between the two countries concerned. The model is therefore in terms of barter trade.

Both countries can produce both goods, X and Y. The table below shows the production of the two countries on the assumption that each in its own country uses the same amount of resources to produce the two goods, i.e. using the same amount of resource in its country, Country A can produce 100 units of X and 30 units of Y. Country B, sharing resources in its country, can produce 15 units of X and 85 units of Y. This effectively means that the two countries are both dividing their resources equally between the two products.

Good	X	Y	Opportunity cost
Country A	100	30	3.33:1
Country B	15	85	0.18:1
Total	115	115	
Ratio A:B	6.6:1	0.35:1	

Country A is clearly better at producing X and Country B at producing Y. Country A then has an absolute advantage in X, and Country B an absolute advantage in Y. Assume that the countries specialise in that way. The model then becomes:

Good	X	Y
Country A	200	0
Country B	0	160
Total	200	160

Clearly, more of both goods are now available. Countries A and B need to trade to gain the advantage, since the goods are clearly not in the right price. They can trade profitably at any price within the opportunity cost ratio shown above. Assume trade takes place at a price of 1Y for 2X, and that 80 units of X are traded for 40 of Y therefore. Country A exports 80 units of X and exchanges them for 40 units of Y, which it imports.

The final position will be as follows:

Good	X	Y
Country A	120	40
Country B	80	120
Total	200	160

Both countries have clearly gained from trade, as both had an absolute advantage to use, or exploit. This model has ignored transport costs, or rather has assumed that they are zero. This is not the case in the real world.

This can be illustrated on a diagram. In the diagram (see Figure 43.3), line AB is the production possibility frontier for country A, line CD the frontier for country B. Specialisation and trade enables country 1 to achieve point b, a move from point A. Line AE is the 'effective' production possibility frontier for country A now.

Country A has clearly gained from the exercise as

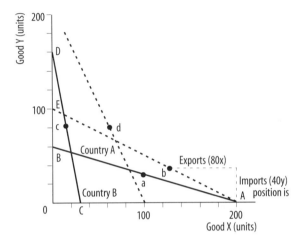

Figure 43.3 *The production possibilities for countries A and B*

has country B where its correspondingly effective production is shown by Point d. Now, another situation which is not so clear-cut:

Good	X	Y	Op
Country A	60	30	2.0:1
Country B	40	10	
Ratio A:B	1.5:1	3.0:1	

Country A is clearly best at both goods. It is 'best best' at Y, though. It is said to have comparative advantage here. Country B, however, is 'least bad' at the production of X. It is said to have a least comparative disadvantage here. Assume specialisation takes place this way:

Good	X	Y
Country A	0	60
Country B	80	0
Total	80	60

Not too encouraging, but let trade take place at a price of 3 to 1, and that 30X is traded for 10Y. The model again:

Good	X	Y
Country A	30	50
Country B	50	10
Total	80	60

Country B is clearly better off, but is A? It was as 60X and 30Y but now has 30X and 50Y. It has half as much of X, but two-thirds as much again of Y. It has traded thirty units of X, therefore, for twenty units of Y. This is an opportunity cost ratio of 30:20, or 1.5:1. It operates itself at 2:1, so if it had tried to get 50 units of Y by switching production internally, it would have been worse off, i.e. it would have ended up with 20 units of X and 50 units of Y. It has gained from trade, therefore, provided it actually wants this combination of goods. This is illustrated again in the diagram below (see Figure 43.4).

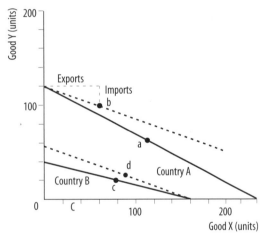

Figure 43.4 *Trade switching – does it pay?*

Countries trade when they have a comparative advantage, and then trade between themselves at a price within the range of their individual opportunity costs. If the opportunity costs of the two countries is the same, there will be no gains from trade. This is a simple two-country, two-product economy and trade is only between themselves. In reality, countries produce a multiplicity of products, and trade between a whole range of countries

The multi-product, multi-country situation aids trade as it is more likely that a country will then be found that wants the extra goods being produced. Multilateral trade is much stronger than unilateral trade, but the chains can sometimes cause problems if they break (see Figure 43.5).

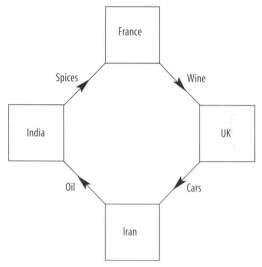

Figure 43.5 *A model of a free trade flow.*

It is also possible to combine the concepts of indifference analysis, opportunity cost and comparative advantage to answer the price question. Examine Figure 43.6.

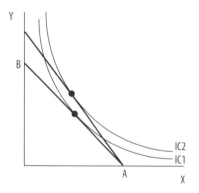

Figure 43.6 *Does a country gain from international trade?*

AB represents the country's pre-trade production possibility frontier, and AC its post-trade frontier. IC1 and IC2 represent two indifference curves for the country for goods X and Y. The country will select mix 'a' before trade, and 'b' after trade as these will give the country the maximum benefit from the mixes of goods.

The gains from international trade

It is claimed that international trade will increase competition, and hence reduce costs and increase consumer surplus. Factor prices may move closer together on an international basis. (For skilled, professional labour, this will become an international resource and will be priced on a worldwide basis.)

The more efficient units will be able to exploit economies of scale and produce more cheaply still, to the benefit of all. There are such things as diseconomies, remember, and lower costs do not automatically get passed on to the consumer. The consumer should get a wider choice of goods and services, and domestic monopolies should be removed.

Foreign trade

Free trade seems to have a lot to offer the economic world. There is an organisation dedicated to encouraging it called The World Trade Organisation (WTO), previously known as GATT, but trade is still not free by any means. At the same time other international organisations are setting up both free trade and protectionist organisations. This is happening in Europe with the growth of the EU and EFTA (the European Free Trade Area). The EU is a customs union. There is completely free trade internally, but all member countries are protected by a common external tax barrier, or tariff. EFTA has no internal controls, either, but here each individual country will apply its own tariffs. other trade groupings are aiming to act the same way – free trade for members, but protection against the 'outside world'. Trade is boosted internally, between the member countries, but is diverted away from the external, non-member countries.

What hampers free trade?

There are many barriers to completely free trade, some natural and some artificial. It is the latter which cause the most problems, but there are arguments in their favour in particular situations.

Tariffs and quotas

These are limitations on imports. A tariff is an import tax, and a quota is a physical limitation put on the number or quantity being imported. For example, the tariff on imports of whisky into a country is 10% of the import price at the country's port; the quota on the importation of cars is 10,000 units per year from all other countries. These both raise the price to the consumer, who loses consumer surplus, and give a larger market to the more expensive local producer. In the case of a tariff the local government gains an income. A tariff may be *ad valorem*, that is a percentage of the money value of the imports, or 'specific', that is, a tax paid per unit of quantity imported. This produces different tax and cost profiles (see Figure 43.7).

The effect of tariffs and quotas on market price is shown in Figure 43.8.

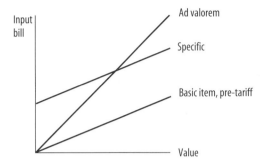

Figure 43.7 *Different types of tax*

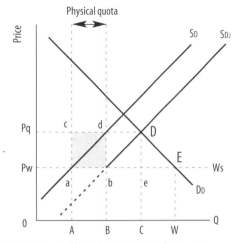

Figure 43.9 *The effect of quotas on market prices*

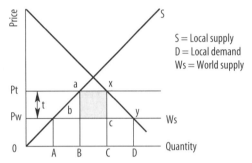

Figure 43.8 *The effect of tariffs on market prices*

The world's supply is so large that any increase in demand from one country will have no effect on its price. Supply is perfectly elastic in terms of price. With no tariff the price in the country would be Pw, the market size would be 0D, but only quantity 0A would be supplied by the local firms.

The government imposes a tariff on imports of value t. Thus the price of the imported commodity is forced up to Pt. The market shrinks to 0C, but the local market now fills 0B of it – i.e. a larger share of a smaller market.

The winners and losers? Examine the area PwPtxy. This is the loss of consumer surplus, so the buyer has clearly lost out. Where has the consumer surplus gone, though? The quantity BC has been imported against a tariff of t. So area abdx is the tariff paid, and is a gain for the government. Note that this is effectively paid by the consumer, not the importer, as it is in the area of lost consumer surplus. PwPtab is transferred to the local producer as economic rent. Consumer surplus, bounded by xyc, goes to nobody, and is lost. It is known as the 'deadweight loss' of the tariff (see Figure 43.9).

The government imposes a quota, by volume, of AB. This quantity enters the country at price Pw, then imports stop. Domestic suppliers can start to sell again, and the domestic supply curve is re-established, SD2, and the market stabilises at price

Pq. The market has shrunk to 0C, though. Again consumer surplus has been lost, and area PqDEPw represents this loss. This analyses as follows: abcd – to the importer who gets Pq for the product, where Pw would have been sufficient. PqcaPw – to the domestic supplier. dDeb – again to the domestic supplier. DeE is again lost to all. It is the deadweight loss of the quota. There is no revenue for the government this time, only the cost of administering the system. It does give a physical fix to the level of imports, though, which a tariff does not. Governments also have the means of paying a type of negative tariff to their own producers. It can, and sometimes does pay subsidies to firms who export goods or services. It can also give them tax exemptions, which have the same effect. It can do this through a 'duty free' port. Here factories who export can operate tax free. If they sell locally they will be liable for tax, but not if they export.

These barriers, when applied on a group basis, will tend to cause trade diversion. Trade will be diverted from the cheaper external country to the cheapest of the member countries, but the price will be above the best prevailing world price. In the EU this is being circumvented by many external suppliers, who are setting up production facilities within Europe. This does tend to give some benefits to both members and outsiders, particularly to the member country in which the 'foreigner' decides to locate.

Political frontiers

The border itself, with its formalities, is a problem and a cost. This is aggravated by language and legal difference.

Currencies

Exchange rates, which are now only very weakly

related to trade, distort the advantages of free trade. In this general area, some countries still impose exchange control regulations. (The UK abolished all exchange control regulations in 1979.) This will limit the amount of imports that can be paid for in foreign exchange.

Nationalism

Governments can discriminate in favour of local firms when they are the buyer themselves. They can use limited tenders to do this, or complicated local requirements. This is again considered as a major distortion within Europe at the present. Certain industries hardly operate on an international basis within the EU. Telecommunications is a good example as it is largely state owned and operates to different national standards.

Justification for protectionism

1. *Cheap labour, and dumping.* It is an abuse of free trade if a country sells goods at below their costs of production, or as a result of the use of artificially cheap labour, i.e. slaves. Cheap labour is not sufficient reason for protectionism. Cheap to whom? What is a low wage in the UK may be a fortune in the Far East. Low labour costs are an advantage that should be exploited, and is one way that a comparative advantage can develop.

2. *Infant industries.* Newly industrialised countries, and new industries themselves, will need protection from the established world giants. They will need protection from competition initially. The danger is that they become dependent on this protection, and become lazy and not as efficient as they could be. A consumer gains initially, but it can become a transfer of consumer surplus to economic rent. (Rent becoming permanent.)

3. *Strategic implications.* Even if a country could produce steel or munitions or aero engines cheaper than everybody else total specialisation would not take place. These and other strategic industries must be kept on a national basis. The pressure is to minimise the number of strategic industries. Today food is a good example, and could be put forward as a reason for the Common Agricultural Policy of the EU.

4. *Unemployment.* Trading off cheap goods for unemployment hardly seems logical. Protectionism, again, tends to reinforce inefficient practices. Unemployment may be valid as a means of giving a transition period, but not really in the long term.

5. *Balance of payments.* Short-term tariffs and other barriers can be applied in an attempt to cure balance of payments problems, when more is being spent on imports than is being received for exports. Exchange rate will move against the country as well.

6. *Source of revenue.* Tariffs are a significant source of revenue to some governments, who are then reluctant to remove or reduce them. They have to be set to allow goods in, though, or there is no revenue at all.

There is clearly a balance to be drawn here. How it is resolved will vary with the countries concerned, and their production efficiency. The more efficient the country, the more it is likely to push for free trade conditions.

The European Union and other international organisations

History and background

European cooperation started at the end of the Second World War. In 1946 the organisation of European Economic Cooperation (OEEC) and the organisation of European Cooperation and Development (OECD) were formed. This led to the founding of the European Coal and Steel Community. This was a 'trial run' for the eventual full Community which was founded in Rome in 1957 when France, West Germany, Italy, the Netherlands, Belgium and Luxemburg signed the Treaty of Rome. At the same time EURATOM, the European Atomic Energy Commission was formed. The objectives of the original EEC – now the EU – were:

- The elimination of customs duties and quotas between members.
- Common external customs tariffs and commercial policy.
- Free movement within the community of people, services and capital.
- Common agricultural and transport policies.

Offices were set up, and a bureaucracy to manage the 'club'. The EU is financed by the member countries through a scheme which included:

- Paying all import duties and agricultural levies on imported produce to the EU.
- Paying a portion of the VAT (value added tax) charged in the country to the EU. (It is a condition of membership that VAT is charged within all member countries.)

As has been said, the EU is a customs union. The members have agreed to remove all tariffs and other barriers to trade within the group, and to apply a uniform rate of external tariff. The alternative group set up in Europe is EFTA, European Free Trade Area. This is a 'Free Trade Area'. Here members have no internal tariffs, etc., as for a customs union, but can apply their own individual external tariffs.

Advantages of the EU

- Greater specialisation and economies of scale will be possible (community rather than nationally based).
- Greater competition within the community.
- Increased exports, for the more efficient EU countries.
- More investment.
- Much improved economic prospects.

Many of these potential savings have been quantified by a committee set up to look at the full effects of the 1992 agreement known as the Cecchini Report. There is no reason why the advantages should be distributed evenly throughout the Community.

Disadvantages of the EU

- Europe may become inward looking and ignore the 'outside world'.
- Diseconomies of scale might become more prominent.

The organisation of the EU

The EU has six key components:

- *The Commission.* This is based in Brussels. It is a non-elected body run by 17 commissioners appointed by the member countries who must 'leave behind all national allegiances' on appointment. It drafts new legislation, and ensures compliance. It employs over 15,000 people and is split into 23 departments. Sir Leon Brittan is the current Commissioner appointed by the UK government.
- *European Parliament.* This has 518 elected members. It is consulted on Commission proposals, but has little executive power.
- *Council of Ministers.* This is a group made up of one Minister from the Parliament of each member country. It is the ultimate decision-making group in the EU. The UK representative on the Council is the Prime Minister. It operates through committees, with different national representatives on each one.

- *Economic and Social Committee.* This is an advisory group of 189 representatives appointed from employers' organisations, trade unions and other 'interested parties'.
- *European Court of Justices.* This is a court that adjudicates on EU matters, and is above national courts. It deals with disputes over implementation and interpretation of EU law. (Do not confuse with the Court of Human Rights which has nothing to do with the EU.)
- *Court of Auditors.* This keeps an eye on the financial side of the organisation.

How EU legislation is decided

Most EU legislation involves the adoption of regulations and directives by the Council of Ministers based on the initial proposals of the Commission.

The Council of Ministers adopts legislation either through the 'slow track' consultation procedure, or the 'fast track' cooperation procedure.

- *Consultation procedure.* Ministers have to agree, after considering the opinions of the European Parliament and the Economic and Social Committee, by a unanimous decision.
- *Cooperation procedure.* This is the new majority voting procedure. Proposals which have been to the European Parliament twice may be adopted by the Council of Ministers by a vote of 54 of the 76 votes available. Each Member has an allocation of votes according to the country represented; i.e. Belgium 5 votes, Denmark 3, Germany 19, Greece 5, Spain 8, France 10, Ireland 3, Italy 10, Luxemburg 2, Holland 5, Portugal 5, UK 10. This procedure may be used for all single market legislations.

Unanimity is required for all matters concerning fiscal harmonisation, most environmental matters, living conditions, enlargement of the EU and the extension of Community powers.

CAP – Common Agricultural Policy

The objective of CAP is to stabilise agricultural prices and therefore incomes and output, to the benefit of producers and consumers alike. In reality it seems to cause over-production, increases costs to the consumer through the costs of CAP within the budget, and keeps inefficient farmers in work. It is a two-part scheme: an intervention scheme for domestic producers to give them a guaranteed income; and an import tariff scheme to raise the price of imports to those of expensive, locally produced goods.

The EU is divided into cost units, and there may be more than one unit in a country. A target price is then set so that the highest cost producer gets a return on the crop. An intervention, or guaranteed price is set at 95% of this. An import tariff is then set that will raise the price of imports to this level, allowing about 5% for tansport costs. This is illustrated in Figure 43.10.

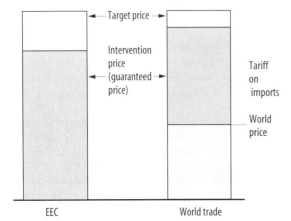

Figure 43.10 *A guaranteed price*

There is no encouragement to increase efficiency. The difficulties come from the small, high-cost farms. The problem area used to be France alone, but many German farms are now causing concern. Costs have run away with the EU budget. New schemes to cut costs involve 'set aside' – the payment for not using farm land. This still favours the small, inefficient unit as the scheme hits large, efficient farms first (see Figure 43.11.)

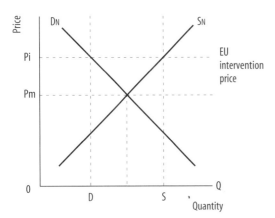

Figure 43.11 *Intervention price*

The free market price, Pm, is ignored and all production is guaranteed a price of Pi. Supply increases to 0S, but demand slumps to 0D. The surplus, DS, has to be bought by the EU and becomes part of a food 'mountain'.

EMS – European Monetary System

This was formally started in 1979, and was an attempt to obtain a greater degree of stability in exchange rates between members of the EU. It is a three-part scheme and includes the unit of account, the ECU (European Currency Unit), the exchange rate mechanism (ERM) and the Credit and Reserves Scheme.

The ECU

The ECU is a currency unit based on a 'basket' of member currencies. It is a weighted basket, where the proportion of a currency in the ECU is proportional to importance in the EU. The $US value of the EU is calculated by converting the basket quantities at equivalent $US exchange rates. For example:

	%		
German Mark	30.1	Luxemburg Franc	0.3
French Franc	19.0	Danish Krona	2.45
Sterling	13.0	Greek Drachma	0.8
Italian Lire	10.15	Irish Punt	1.1
Dutch Guilder	9.4	Spanish Peseta	5.3
Belgian Franc	7.6	Portuguese Escudo	0.8
			100.0

In 1995 the ECU was still an 'artificial' currency. Money in these units does not exist in circulation. It is the unit of account of the EU, though, and is used to calculate subsidies, payments, etc. In particular, agricultural subsidies are fixed in ECUs, and its value in Sterling is fixed by the 'Green Pound' exchange rate against the ECU.

An example: assume a three-currency Common Market with marks (M), francs (F) and pounds sterling (P). Present exchange rates are:

$$P1 = M2 = F2, \text{ so } M1 = F1$$

Assume a trade weighted basket of currency in the ECU of:

$$ECU\ 1 = M\ 0.5 + F\ 0.25 + P\ 0.25.$$

The ECU can be valued in any of the component currencies by inserting the appropriate exchange rates, i.e. value in terms of pounds.

$$ECU\ 1 = 0.25P + 0.125P + 0.25P = 0.625P \text{ or } 1.25\ F \text{ or } 1.25\ M.$$

So, if target price for wheat in the CAP is ECU 150, British farmers will get 150 x 0.625 P, or 93.75 P.

If the currency is revalued, then the value of the ECU in terms of that currency will strengthen against the ECU (less ECUs per unit of currency) and any agricultural or other ECU subsidy will fall in terms of the currency concerned.

The ERM – Exchange rate mechanism

This is the mechanism where member countries 'fix' their exchange rates between themselves into a grid. After the initial values are set, rates may then only vary + or −2.25% of this. Countries have to agree to attempt to run their economies and manage their reserves so as to keep in this band. Other countries are pledged to assist when a currency gets near its limits. Funds are available from the European Monetary Cooperation Fund (EMCF). If this proves impossible realignments may have to be made.

The ERM will only work if the economies of Europe come together, or converge, in economic terms. Rates of inflation, growth, etc., must be in line. There must be almost no pressure on the exchange rate of a currency, even from speculators.

The ERM was founded in 1979. The key to effective operation within the ERM is the rate set at entry. There is reason to believe that the UK entered at too high a rate, with too harsh an effect on the UK economy through the pressure it exerted to keep interest rates high. The period before UK entry was noted for a series of realignments of currencies, but generally the Deutsche Mark rose and others fell. There was a period of fixed alignments after UK entry until 1992. After a huge burst of speculative activity, sterling was withdrawn from the ERM by the British government. Pressure has continued, and another realignment was made in November 1992.

Credit and reserves

Each member has to convert 20% of its reserves into ECUs. This is held by the EMCF, and is used to help countries whose currencies come under speculative pressures.

The single market

The cost factor is an evaluation of the costs being incurred now because of the lack of a single unified market. Apart from tariffs the following barriers must go:

- *Physical.* The intra-EC border stoppages, customs controls and associated paperwork.
- *Technical.* Product standards, technical regulations, business laws, etc.
- *Fiscal.* Differing VAT and excise duties.

Major cost centres are seen as business, financial and telecommunication services, and the production of automobiles, foodstuffs, building materials, textiles and pharmaceuticals.

1. *Border controls.* Some countries are worse than others. Small to medium-sized firms suffer the most. The major cost element is 'business foregone'.
2. *Public procurement.* The opening up of this to competition should reduce costs. Firms will gain from fair, 'lowest cost wins' competiton.
3. *Technical standards.* The worst area is in the telecommunications industry. Note that this is usually a nationalised industry in the EU, and highly protected. The different standards mean that money is wasted on duplicated research and development, and the full benefits from economies of scale cannot be taken and competition is weakened outside the EU.
4. *Taxation rates.* VAT rates, in particular, vary considerably. Consider wine, spirits and tobacco, and the differences between French and British rates. Unification will not be easy.
5. *The savings factor.* Essentially the process will give a 'supply side shock' and will be given to all industry and commerce in Europe. What will be obtained?
   - significant reductions in costs
   - improved efficiency within companies, widespread industrial reorganisation; falling prices
   - new patterns of competition between entire industries, and reallocation of resources
   - increased innovation.

All consumers will be better off, but only some producers. What will be observed?

- more mergers and takeovers
- more joint-ventures.

The Maastricht Treaty

This treaty was signed in December 1991 and sets out the procedure and timetable for further unification in the areas of monetary, political and social policies. A simple summary of the economic aspects are as follows:

1. The treaty sets out a procedure for a single currency as part of a monetary and economic union.
2. Signatories commit their countries to a policy of:

- non-inflationary economic growth
- high level of employment and social policy
- the single economy.

Monetary policy

Monetary policy will eventually be controlled for Europe by the ECB (European Central Bank). Each country will have its own central bank. The ECB will be run by a Council consisting of the Governors of the component central banks. This organisation and arrangement is known as the ESCB – European System of Central Banks. The Central Banks will implement monetary policy (set by the ECB), conduct FOREX operations and hold and manage FOREX reserves. Monetary policy will then be beyond the control of member states, as it now is in Germany.

Social chapter

This follows from the Social Charter of 1989. The objective of the Chapter is to:

- promote employment
- improve living and working conditions
- implement proper social protection
- develop human resources with a view to lasting high employment.

It includes the provision for a minimum wage, equal pay for men and women for equal work and 'paternity' leave.

General agreement on tariffs and trade (GATT)

In 1944 economists and finance experts of the free world met at Bretton Woods in the United States to discuss and plan the reconstruction of the economic world after the traumas of the Great Depression, followed by the Second World War. During the late 1920s and the early 1930s – a period of recession and protectionism – world trade fell from US$3 billion to only about US$0.5 billion. The United States had set very high import tariffs which triggered a trade war and other countries increased their tariffs in retaliation. After the additional trauma of the war, the allies were determined to set up a more secure, free world system. Free trade was a key element of this, and the conference proposed the formation of the International Trade Organisation, the ITO. This was still-born, but GATT resulted instead. GATT was set up in 1947 with an initial membership of 23 industrial and developing countries. On 1st January 1995 GATT changed its name to World Trade Organisation (WTO). It has its headquarters in Switzerland, and its Director General is also Swiss.

Its objectives are:

1. To reduce tariffs and other barriers to trade to eliminate discrimination in trade.

2. To produce a World Free Trade area, which will result if it is successful.

Membership has grown steadily since its formation. There were 96 member countries in 1988, and membership now stands at 108. Obviously it becomes harder to reach agreement as the size of the negotiating group increases – a diseconomy of scale! Membership entitles countries to 'most favoured nation' status, i.e. to trade with other members of the most favourable terms available, to use WTO's disputes procedures to settle trade rows, and to take part in negotiations to liberalise trade. On the other hand, new members have to guarantee that their trade policy will meet WTO's rules, and change their tariffs, quotas and other trade restrictions accordingly.

WTO is paid for by subscriptions from members. The rate is proportional to the share of world trade held by the country concerned. In 1987 this resulted in the United States paying 16% of WTO's costs of US$40 million for the year!

The organisation acts through a series of agreements reached after long negotiations. These negotiations are called 'Rounds', and seven have been completed since its foundation. The eighth, the Uruguay Round, commenced in 1986, and was planned to close out in 1990.

As a result of the agreements made during these rounds, world trade has increased significantly, as have average standards of living in the member countries.

- *Tariff.*
  A tariff is a tax applied to imports. It raises the price in the domestic market from a to b, and increases local production from OA to OB at the expense of imports. The government applying a tariff gains an income of foreign exchange (see

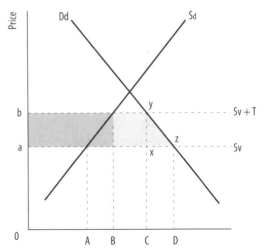

Figure 43.12 The imposition of a tariff

Figure 43.12). There is a loss of consumer surplus that cannot be accounted for, indicated by the triangle xyz.

- *Exchange controls.* Restriction on the purchase of foreign exchange. If you cannot get US dollars you cannot buy US made goods. This was abandoned by the UK in 1979.
- *Bureaucracy.* By setting up complicated procedures importers are discouraged from starting the process. Procedures atports of entry are criticial.
- *Product/service rules.* A new area. Making a product to meet these very tight national rules over safety and other standards can make the cost of exporting prohibitive. This is common in the car market, and has been used successfully by Japan.
- *Quota.* A limit by number or quantity that may be imported. A good method of control, but the government has no income. The Japanese car industry operates a voluntary quota on the importation of cars into the UK.

Market price will be forced up from a to b. The size of the market will shrink, but the domestic producers will get a larger share of it, i.e, local production will rise from OA to OA + BC (see Figure 43.13).

The subsidy will enable the domestic producers to sell on the world market at price b. The domestic market is kept at price a, so the consumer gains nothing from the subsidy. The domestic suppliers now have a market of OB instead of OA.

- *Import deposit schemes.* When applying for an

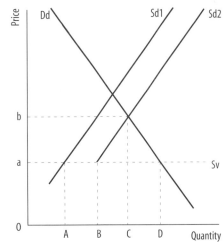

Figure 43.13a *A quota imposed on trade*

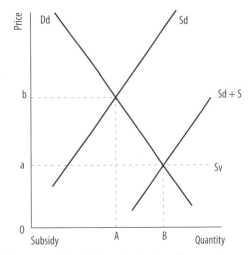

Figure 43.13b *A subsidy paid to local producers*

import licence a large deposit has to be presented. This effectively raises the price of the import, and makes it less competitive.

WTO has concentrated its activities on tariffs up to the Uruguay Round. Average tariffs have tumbled significantly.

Industrial nations' average tariffs (%)

1940	1950	1960	1970	1980	1990
40	26	18	11	8	5

The theoretical basis for the reduction of tariffs, with a resulting increase in trade is shown in Figure 43.14.

With no trade the total market will be OA + OY. With trade it will increase to OB + OZ. The price in

The oil industry is subject to strict quotas and controls.

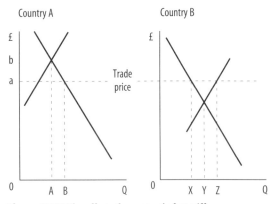

Figure 43.14 *The effect of a removal of a tariff*

Country A will fall to a, the same as in Country B.

WTO promotes 'fair trade' based on the fundamental principle of non-discrimination. Trade advantages negotiated between any two members have to be made available to all members. This would seem to clash with the growing establishment of trade groups. However, free trade areas and customs unions are allowed within the rules of WTO, but a clash, or conflict of interest, seems to be inevitable.

WTO's success has not been uniform. Overall, tariffs have been reduced significantly, but in some areas 'managed trade' has had to be organised. It has been quite effective in the field of textiles, through the formation of the Multifibre Arrangement. This does not eliminate tariffs, but controls the trade in textiles and clothing through a complex series of bilateral quota arrangements between rich importing countries and the poor exporting countries. It has also set up other such arrangements in the area of cars, steel, videos, semiconductors and shoes.

WTO bans dumping, the selling of goods at below cost, and has had some success, e.g. cotton goods from China. It allows infant industries to be protected by 'open' tariffs.

The main problem has been, and still is, agriculture and its subsidies.

Current problems and the Uruguay Round

The membership pattern of WTO has changed, and Third World countries are now more prominent. Some NICs, particularly in the South East Asia region, are very successful in world trade, but have been slow to fully accept their obligations under WTO. However, three areas still constitute a major power block: the USA, the EU, and Japan. The commitments of membership are not always observed as rigorously as they should be!

The series of negotiations known as the Uruguay Round was started in 1986 in Punta del Este, Uruguay. The objectives were:

- To cut the present level of overall tariffs by 30%.
- To reduce the application of export subsidies, especially in the area of agriculture.
- To extend the objectives of WTO to services and intellectual property, i.e. patents, trade marks.

Work in the non-tariff area had first started in the Tokyo Round. This was continued in the Uruguay Round, which covers textiles, clothing, subsidies, intellectual property rights, and new procedures for settling WTO disputes. Agricultural areas had been targeted, but were put off in the end.

The world had a lot to gain from these negotiations. The OEDC (Organisation for Economic Development and Cooperation) estimates that trade restrictions now cost the world US$475 billion each year, but that a successful Uruguay Round would reduce this substantially.

Most countries subsidise agriculture is some way or another. Usually it is done as a means of cushioning a restructuring of the industry, with the now inevitable loss of jobs. The high levels of productivity achieved by the efficient farmers in advantageous areas have resulted in excess production potential for some crops. Small and/or inefficient farmers need subsidies to survive.

This round was finalised in December 1993 and formally signed in Morrocco in early 1994.

International Monetary Fund

The International Monetary Fund (IMF) was set up to provide short-term finance for its rich member countries.

The IMF was another of the Bretton Woods' 'children'. It was a club, with at least 151 member countries for the developed economies of the world. It has its headquarters in Washington, DC, and a staff of some 2,000. The Managing Director is traditionally European. Members subscribe to the fund based on the country's national income. This subscription determines the borrowing capacity of the member, and its voting rights. Power resides as follows: USA 20% of the votes; G7 countries 49% of the votes. (G7 countries are USA, Japan, Germany, France, UK, Italy, Canada; the 'G10' countries add Sweden, Holland, Belgium and Switzerland.)

The IMF's original objective was to provide short-term finance to help member countries through exchange rate crises. At this time the world was using fixed rates, based on the Gold Standard. In the early 1970s it switched to the dollar standard and its 'crawling' peg system. Loans, based on a country's quota, having strings which increase as the size of the loan, expressed as a percentage of the quota, increases. Loans have to be repaid in three to five years.

In 1974 the fund launched its Special Oil Facility, to aid countries in difficulties over the rapid increase in the price of oil. It also launched the Extended Fund Facility for undeveloped countries. This was the first sign of the swing from rich to poorer nations.

In 1982 the debt crisis, brought on by the oil price rises, and the excessive lending of some institutions, hit both the IMF and the World Bank, and they started to work much more closely together.

In 1982, Mexico was in severe economic trouble. It was unable to meet its liabilities to the banks, and could not even pay the interest due on its loans. Mexico was the catalyst, though, as many countries were in the same trouble. Mexico, Brazil and Argentina owed US$220 billion, with combined interest of US$13 billion per year. There was a clash. Debtors could and would not pay, and lenders would not release the debtors from their payments. There was great danger of a financial collapse on a global scale. If Mexico defaulted, then commercial banks would fail. The collapse of Barclays, Midland and National Westminster would have caused economic ruin in the UK, for instance. This could not be allowed to happen, so the IMF stepped in and made the parties compromise. It put in some cash, organised the rescheduling of payments, and then monitored progress. Most of the new debtor economies were not normally covered by IMF finance. The role of the IMF had changed.

A joint body was formed. IMF made a loan, attached 'strings', and then the World Bank added more cash. The World Bank and the IMF both monitor the progress, but the IMF is the leader. The crisis was averted. From 1985 onwards, both bodies have been in a positive situation. Repayments exceed new loans, and world growth is slowing.

The new challenges facing the IMF centre on (a) reducing world debt as a whole, particularly in the poorer or newly industrialised nations, and (b) the new problem of eastern Europe.

International Bank for Reconstruction and Development

The World Bank, or 'The International Bank for Reconstruction and Redevelopment' to give it its correct name, came into being after the Bretton Woods Conference in America. It was set up in Washington, DC, in 1947 to provide long-term finance for the developing countries of the world.

The United States traditionally appoints the president of the bank, and also has a strong say in the appointment of senior staff. European countries, as individuals, have little influence, but the 'voice' of the EU will be greater. It is a commercial bank, and lends money on normal commercial terms for periods from 15 to 20 years to governments or government-supported private sector organisations. It raises its capital through selling bonds and taking deposits from its member countries. The aim of the Bank was first to assist in the reconstruction of Europe, but this was overtaken by the Marshall Plan. Thus its main present objective developed, that is, to promote growth in poor countries.

The Bank splits between lenders and borrowers. The breakdown of this in 1988 was:

Lenders: Japan, USA, Germany (these countries account for some 50% of the lending).

Borrowers: Latin America, South Asia, East Asia (these countries account for about 50% of the borrowing).

In 1987 the Bank lent US$14.1 billion for 127 different projects. It now has more than 6,000 staff recruited from over 100 nationalities.

'Normal commercial terms' were found to be too expensive for the really poor economies, so the Bank started two associates or subsidiaries to give more appropriate aid:

- IDA (founded 1960) – International Development Association. This organisation lends for 50 years at very low interest (under 1%). To qualify, however, the country must have an average GDP of about US$500 or less. There are more countries in this group than you imagine, and in 1987 again they lent another US$3.5 billion for 108 projects. In effect this organisation provides aid rather than loans.
- IFC – International Finance Corporation. This organisation was set up to advance non-guaranteed loans to the private sector. The Bank cannot do this, by the terms of its charter.

The Bank specialises in lending to develop infrastructure, production, agriculture and fishing. It has advanced cash for projects in the areas of family planning. It has developed and changed in character as time has passed. The major agents for change have been the international debt crisis of the 1980's, and the emergence of NICs.

Money and monetary policy

When selling something to someone a debt is incurred. How are such debts settled? Some societies barter, but in more advanced countries we would encounter the double coincidence of wants, i.e. the difficulty in finding a seller of the good we want, who also wants what we have to sell. We may also encounter problems of value. What is a fair price for a good, and who determines a commodities price? Other problems may also arise – namely, storage, value fluctuations and perishable products. So, trying to run an economy on a barter system may not be the most efficient method.

Perhaps we could try collective ownership, so allocating goods and services on some agreed basis of need. This form of allocation was central to the planned economies, and removed private ownership from the economic system. Exchange was replaced by allocation.

The evolution of money rests firmly on something that is generally acceptable in the settlement of a debt. The four characteristics of money are defined as:

1. *A medium of exchange.* The essential characteristic is that it be acceptable in exchange for all goods and services, and at all times.
2. *A unit of account.* This thing (which we will now call money) must enable the values of goods and services to be expressed in terms of common measure. (As we shall soon note, the problems of inflation may undermine this function.)
3. *A store of value.* Money enables people to postpone current consumption by saving. It is therefore desirable that it be capable of storage without cost, risk of physical deterioration or fear of obsolescence; people will only be interested in holding money if they know they can use it in the future. Once again inflation, especially hyperinflation, may cause people to resort to barter or to exchange their wealth into something that has an intrinsic value, e.g. gold.
4. *A standard of deferred payment.* The use of credit is a major advancement in most economies. It enables debts to be postponed. This enables the use of cheques, credit cards and other forms of delayed payments.

Characteristics of money

Money must also suit the convenience of the transaction. Thus, divisibility, portability, uniformity, durability and a high value in relation to bulk are useful, but not essential, characteristics. It is also an advantage if some control is practised over its supply and the opportunity for counterfeiting should be minimised. Few forms of money have a value in themselves (they were once made from precious metals). The only essential characteristic of money is that it be generally acceptable.

The evolution of modern money

Throughout history various commodities have been used as money, e.g. salt. In the UK money evolved from the work of goldsmiths. Those with money (then silver or gold) lodged their holdings with goldsmiths. This 'safe place' offered a further service of enabling debts to be settled by transferring the receipts for gold, rather than the gold itself. These 'pieces of paper' began to have a value of their own, and so the bank note was born. The goldsmiths had more gold in their vaults than customers normally used, so they were able to issue more receipts and so the modern bank deposit, loan and credit systems emerged. As confidence in the system grew, so people were prepared to accept written instructions to a banker to transfer deposits from the account of the debtor to that of the creditor: this formed the origin of the cheque system. This system has reduced any serious risk involved in handling large amounts of bank notes.

The supply and demand of money

A large range of commodities may have some monetary value, but in practice we consider money to be defined in terms of the ease with which it can be converted into cash, i.e. liquidity. By definition cash is perfectly liquid. Your current account at a bank may be drawn on by cheque, so creating a cash sum of money. These deposits are commonly transferred by cheque, but it is the bank deposit, not the cheque which is money. By adding these two we get what is officially described as the narrow definition of the money supply (M0).

Definitions of the money supply
- M0 = notes and coins in circulation plus commercial banks' operating balances at the Bank of England.
- M2 = M0 minus bankers' balances at the Bank of England, plus private sector non-interest-bearing sight deposits with banks and private sector interest-bearing retail bank and building society deposits.
- M4 = M2 plus other private sector sight and time deposits at banks and building societies and private sector holdings of bank and building society certificates of deposit.

These money stock figures measure the level of certain liabilities in the banking sector. Two markets operate within this sector, which with modern facilities and international banking are becoming ever more difficult to decipher, namely the money markets (involved mainly in short-term lending, usually under one year) and the capital markets (the providers of medium and long-term finance for government, firms and individuals).

The banks and credit creation

A bank deposit is a liability, i.e. it represents a claim on the bank for cash. So, if you deposit £100 in cash with a bank, they owe you £100. But they also have an asset of £100 (your cash) and they may use it to generate income. Deposits with a bank may either be passive or active. Our example above is passive, as its value does not change and the amount of money in circulation has remained unchanged. In terms of our money supply measurement the 'notes and coins in circulation' have fallen by £100, while 'private sector sight (current account) deposits' have risen by £100. The same applies to payments by cheques deposited with a bank. Let us say that you deposit a cheque with bank A. It is your salary and is drawn on bank B. Bank A now has an asset, which it can present to bank B for cash. When the cash is paid, the deposit with bank A acts as an asset in just the same way as your original £100 did in the first example. Once again our 'narrow' definition of money is unchanged, sight deposits of one bank have increased, while the other has decreased. The cheque simply serves as the vehicle for transferring deposits. In the Balance Sheet of your bank the transactions would appear as:

Liabilities		Assets	
Deposits	£100	Cash	£100

In practice, cheque transactions account for the majority of transfers of money and in most countries banks belong to clearing houses, who calculate the net indebtedness of each bank to the others each day. The banks then settle their debts via money they hold in accounts at the Bank of England.

Active deposit creation is centred on fractional reserve banking, i.e. an idea that all customers will not withdraw their funds at the same time. The acceptance of this enables the banks to monetise debt, i.e. lend on other people's money, or buy someone else's debt.

Bank advances

A bank can create a deposit by giving someone the right to withdraw money. If your bank lends (or gives in advance of) £100 to another customer, it now has an asset of £100. It is an asset, as the borrower must repay this debt. It has also created a liability of £100, as it has entitled its client to withdraw £100. Thus its Balance Sheet now shows:

Liabilities		Assets	
Deposits	£200	Cash	£100
		Advances	£100
	£200		£200

Buying debt

If you hold someone else's IOU for £100, you could sell it to a bank. The bank would then have an asset worth £100, but it would also have created a liability as you could draw out £100 in cash. This transaction now changes our Balance Sheet:

Liabilities		Assets	
Deposits	£300	Cash	£100
		IOU	£100
		Advances	£100
	£300		£300

In modern banking IOUs can take two forms:

- *Commercial Bills.* Trade is often done on credit. So, the receiver of the goods may not have to pay on delivery. This 'credit' may take the form of a 'commercial bill'. This may be for three months (90 days). The owner of this debt may sell the bill. In doing so, to a bank, he enables the bank to create an asset, and a deposit liability, as you could withdraw the sum owed on the bill. The bank has acquired someone else's debt.
- *Government debt.* The government also sells its debts. Those of less than 90 days are known as Treasury Bills, and those for longer than 90 days are known as gilts. Once again the purchase of these creates both an asset and a liability for the banking sector.

Both of these transactions would be subject to interest. This will be covered in monetary policy.

The principle components of the supply of money are notes and coins in circulation and bank deposits. Many other financial assets are classed as near money.

The demand for money

This comes from households and firms and is thought to comprise of three motives:

1. *Transactions* – to finance current expenditure
2. *Precautionary* – to guard against unforeseen circumstances
3. *Speculative* – when it is believed that the price of other assets is to fall. This motive is influenced by changes in the rate of interest.

The theory which attempts to explain these

motives is known as liquidity preference, or the desire to hold your wealth in the form of liquid money rather than in an interest-bearing asset. This theory determines the rate of interest via the demand and supply of money (see Figure 43.15).

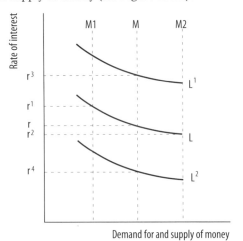

Figure 43.15 *Interest rates and the demand and supply of money*

From Figure 43.15 we can predict that:

- An increase in the money supply *reduces* interest rates ($M \rightarrow M^2 = r \rightarrow r^2$).
- A decrease in the money supply raises interest rates ($M \rightarrow M^1 = r \rightarrow r^1$).
- An increase in the demand for money raises interest rates ($L \rightarrow L^1 = r \rightarrow r^3$).
- A decrease in the demand for money reduces interest rates ($L \rightarrow L^2 = r \rightarrow r^4$).

Economists consider that the speculative demand for money depends on expectations of the future course of bond prices (i.e. an alternative form of holding your money and one which pays interest).

So, if people think that the price of bonds will fall and the rate of interest will therefore rise, the demand for speculative money increases. While, if people think the price of bonds will rise, and interest rates therefore fall, they reduce their holdings of money. In simple terms, the price of bonds and the rate of interest vary inversely. We can transfer this theory into two diagrams (see Figure 43.16 a and b).

We consider that the precautionary (p) and transaction (t) balance are not affected by changes in interest rates.

The major influences on these balances are income, the price level, and the frequency of payments. (The more frequently we are paid the less we require money.) We call these active balances.

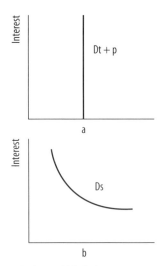

Figure 43.16 *Active and idle balances*

The speculative demand for money depends on expectations, i.e. do we think that bond prices will fall or move upwards?

Normally, when bond prices are considered to be high, we anticipate a fall and a subsequent increase in interest rates. This will increase the demand for money, as we wish to avoid capital losses. We call this balance an idle balance. For the Keynesian application of this theory see Figure 43.17.

Here, increases and decreases in the supply of money at a certain rate of interest do not affect the interest rates, as all wealth-holders believe interest rates to have reached a floor. Any increase in the money supply will flow into idle balances. As interest rates do not alter the level of expenditure in the economy (C + I) monetary policy has been ineffective.

The credit multiplier

By creating credit, banks can alter the level of deposits held by their customers. This in turn alters the money supply. To try to control this ability to create credit the banks are controlled by various regulations. As we have already noted when a bank makes a loan, both its assets and liabilities are increased by the amount of the loan. This in turn increases the money supply. The banks must be careful of repaying deposits and this provides them with a fundamental dilemma, for the more they lend the more profit they make, yet under certain government regulations they must maintain a certain level of liquidity.

The creation and control of credit

The banks are required to hold a cash ratio, i.e. a percentage of their deposits must be backed by cash resources. If this ratio was, say 5%, then for each £100 of cash holdings they could extend credit by £100 x 100/5 = £2000. This would result in a credit multiplier of 20. Hence our formula is:

$$\text{Credit multiplier} = \frac{100\%}{\text{cash ratio}}$$

This ratio is reduced if the public demand more cash. Its function in modern banking explains why banks are always trying to make customers use less cash and more 'plastic'. A more realistic figure for the cash ratio is 10%, but then this gives banks enormous credit creation facilities. The same £100 can create a new loan of £90. This creates a new deposit of £90, increases the money supply by £90 and the process starts all over again. The maximum deposits for an entire banking system = Maximum deposits = Original holdings of cash x Credit Multiplier. Whilst the total loans for an entire banking system = Maximum loans = Original holdings of cash x Credit multiplier – Original holdings of cash. This process is perhaps best illustrated by a simple example:

The cash ratio = 10% and the initial deposit = £100

The individual bank can create a further loan of £90, but the entire banking scheme can create credit of £900, as each new deposit can have 90% of its value lent-on.

Control

In general the more liquid a bank's asset the less profitable it is. Remember liquidity = the ease with which an asset can be converted into cash, while profitability = interest-earning power of an asset. Banks normally hold their assets in the following form:

- cash in tills   *Monetary base*
- balances at Bank of England base
- money at call   *These once*
- treasury Bills   *formed what*
- short-term Commercial   *was known as* Bills the   *the reserve*
- short-term local authority Bills   *asset rate*
- certificates of deposit
- longer-term investments – government stock, etc.; these can be sold at relatively short notice
- advances to customers

- special deposits – taken out of monetary system by the Bank of England.

Banks also have liabilities, i.e. claims on the banks. These usually take two forms:

1. *Current or sight deposit*, which do not normally pay interest.
2. *Deposit or time deposits*, that do pay interest to customers.

These liabilities can be either eligible, which do feature in definitions of the money supply, or non-eligible, which do not feature.

So, banks face a dilemma between liquidity and profitability, and they also come under central government control. The latter is known as monetary policy.

Monetary theory

The decade of the 1980s saw monetary theory gain in prominence in many countries. It was, on occasions, a controversial debate. Keynesians were supposed to believe that 'money did not matter', while monetarists concluded that 'money mattered most of all'. Neither of these two extremes is representative of the real debate, although some Keynesians do give less emphasis to the importance of money in controlling economic activity. The real debate centred on the transmission mechanism, i.e. the means by which changes in the money supply feed through into the economic system.

The quantity theory of money

Classical economists argued that money was 'neutral', i.e. it did not affect the relative prices of goods. They believed that money was simply a medium of exchange and was demanded as such. The formalisation of this came with the Fisher equation, which was written as:

$MV = PT$

M = *the stock of money*

V = *the average times it changes hands in a given period, i.e. its velocity of circulation*

P = *the average money value of each transaction, or its price*

T = *the total number of transactions during the period.*

So, if 100 transactions take place in a given period, with each costing an average of £10, then

P x T = £1,000. If the money stock is fixed at £200, then on average each £1 must be used five times in the period. So, V = 5. T is normally considered to be equal to the level of final output. P is taken as the price level (duly weighted), so PT = the nominal value of national income. V is assumed to be relatively constant in the short term as it is dependent on the institutional arrangements made for payments or income receipts. T is considered to be fixed as it represents the real output of the economy (with a fixed level of technology); it was also assumed that full employment would exist. So, with V and T fixed it can be seen from the equation that changes in M (money supply) directly effect the level of prices (P).

Critics argue that economies seldom adjust automatically to full employment and that wages are not flexible enough to promote this. They also consider the theory of little practical use as it does not take account of the impact of relative price changes of assets ('neutrality') or money illusion (i.e. people not failing to appreciate that a wage increase accompanied by a price increase does not increase income).

Keynesian theory

As we have already noted, Keynesian analysis considered money to be the liquid end of a spectrum of financial assets. People appear to hold money for three reasons (or motives) namely transactionary, precautionary and speculative (see Figure 43.17).

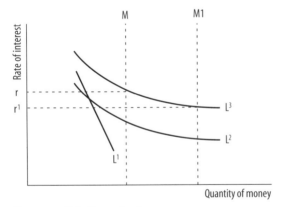

Figure 43.17 The Keynesian theory

- L^1 = very unresponsive to interest rates (precautionary and transactions).
- L^2 = speculative.
- L^3 = total demand for money.

The effect of an increase in the money supply (M1) can be traced and applied to the transmission mechanism. At the prevailing rate of interest people have more money than they wish to hold, so they will buy close substitutes for money, i.e. other financial assets. An increase in the demand for these assets should increase their price, so lowering the price (interest) to r1. The transmission mechanism is seen as a chain reaction along the liquidity spectrum, the demand for the next most liquid asset rising first, with the consequent lower interest rate causing increased demand for the next most liquid asset and so on.

So, the initial increased money balance has a 'ripple effect' along the liquidity spectrum, with diminishing impact on the less liquid end of the range of financial assets. However, decreasing interest rates may affect expenditure on real assets, e.g. falling interest rates may increase the willingness of firms to borrow and invest. If this did arise, then increased investment would raise aggregate demand with an upward multiplier effect on national income. This could in turn cause price rises through an inflationary gap. However, the demand for investment funds is likely to be at the less liquid end of the spectrum, where the impact on interest rates is less marked. Keynesians generally believe that it would need a very large change in the supply of money to effect a significant change in interest rates, and that interest rates do not, in any case, have a very substantial impact on investment expenditure. The money supply has an indirect influence on nominal national income through interest rates and the money supply is therefore an imprecise and very ineffective method of controlling aggregate demand. As we shall see a little later, they put greater emphasis on fiscal policy.

Monetarist theory

Milton Friedman has been the most prominent exponent of what is sometimes called 'the new quantity theory'. In the monetarist view, money (as the medium of exchange) is a unique asset with no obvious close substitute. The distribution of a person's income will depend on each asset's own interest rate (the value of future services derived from holding the good). When the money supply derived from holding the interest rate on money balances falls, this leads to a small but noticeable change in all planned expenditures, be they for goods or financial services. Monetarists believe money to be a substitute for all assets, and not just financial assets (as Keynesians do). Thus, changes in the money supply have a direct effect on all planned expenditures and therefore on the level of nominal national income. Futhermore, the expenditure of all assets is sensitive to changes in their own rates of interest, and it is therefore meaningless to talk of 'the' rate of interest.

Monetarists consider that a close relationship exists between changes in the money supply and the value of national output. They argue that there is a time lag between changes in the money supply and a subsequent new equilibrium. Moreover, such a time lag may be variable, so ruling out fine-tuning. They prefer the 'fixed throttle' approach, which relates changes in money supply to the rate of growth in the real level of output. Adherence to this strategy will enable the economy to operate at a 'natural' level of unemployment without inflationary pressures.

Keynesians challenge both the causality and stability of the velocity of circulation. They admit that a rise in prices may follow an increase in the money supply, but does that imply causality? The main area of disagreement seems to rest on whether the demand for money to hold is responsive to interest rates of other financial assets only (as the Keynesians believe) or of all assets equally (as the monetarists believe). Many empirical studies have been undertaken. Their conclusions tend to point towards the interest elasticity of demand for money being greater than zero, but not as high as Keynesians would promote.

The money supply

We noted earlier that money is currently measured across a spectrum ranging from narrow to broad (M0 to M4). As early as 1976 authorities began setting targets for money growth. The long-run target was to bring money supply increases in line with the level of output. Demand management or fiscal policy was to be used within these monetary limits and had to be conducive with monetary constraint. The initial impact on employment was forecast as negative; but as inflation reduced, so the economy would support better levels of employment. Ultimately, economic activity depends on creating an environment in which effort, enterprise and efficiency are rewarded.

Probably the most telling criticism delivered by the monetarists was the unsettling effects of sudden increases in the money supply and the concurrent interaction between fiscal and monetary policy. A central objection of the monetarists was the size of the public sector borrowing requirement (PSBR). This is the sum borrowed by government to pay for its commit-ments, over and above its tax revenue.

Strictly speaking, any attempt by government to borrow money could raise the money supply, as the debt will need to be financed by the selling of Treasury Bills to banks. These will, in turn, increase their reserve asset holdings leading to increased bank

lending and an increase in the money supply. So, the debt must be sold to the non-bank private sector – hence the increase in National Savings, and other ways of getting private concerns/individuals to hold govern-ment debt.

Increased holdings of non-marketable debt and government securities prevent the government's borrowing feeding into the money supply. However, large-scale selling of government securities must effect long-term interest rates, and it is these which are likely to affect economic activity and therefore investment finance.

Higher interest rates may be necessary to attract new buyers, but this will reduce the market price of existing stock. The problem for the bank is thus how to use the sales of marketable debt to prevent the money supply rising, without making the market so unstable as to deter people from holding stock as they fear a capital loss.

The rest of the domestic borrowing requirement is financed via the banking sector, mainly by sales of Treasury Bills. As a part of the reserve assets, these increase the reserve base and lead to increased bank lending, provided that there are borrowers and the government does not 'take-in' the excess liquidity via either special deposits or other direct controls.

Monetary policy

Monetary policy is designed to influence the cost and availability of credit. The authorities work to exert pressure on the size and composition of bank deposits. The main policies used are:

1. *Changes in the cash ratio.* This is sometimes known as the liquid/reserve asset ratio. If this is increased, then a multiple contraction of deposits follows and this in turn reduces lending. In reverse, a decrease in the ratio will expand deposits and increase lending.

2. *Open market operations.* This involves the purchase and selling of bonds on the open market. If the government sells bonds then a cheque is raised by the purchaser (who is normally a commercial bank), they draw this from their account at the Bank of England. The account is therefore reduced, so reducing their liquidity. A multiple contraction takes place and lending is reduced. Open market operation therefore has an influence on both the demand and supply of parts of the money market,* and therefore on the price of money, or the rate of interest.

3. *Special deposits.* The Bank of England freezes the amount of bank assets. These are placed in

the Bank, where they receive a rate of interest equivalent to that paid for Treasury Bills. This is normallly less than that which could have been earned when the money was used for advances. Once again a multiple contraction of deposits will arise and lending will be reduced accordingly.

4. *Funding.* This results from the government replacing Treasury Bills (as they mature) with gilts, which are long-term stock. The liquid asset (Treasury Bill) has been replaced with an illiquid asset (gilt). Once again the reduction in assets (deposits) will lead to a multiple contraction of credit.

5. *Quantitative and qualitative ceilings.* The bank imposes limits on the total size of the loan and offers guidance as to who may receive a loan.

6. *Bank rate.* At the close of most business days the Bank is approached by discount houses. These act as intermediaries and borrow money from the Bank. They in turn lend the money on to normal commercial banks. This unique feature of the British system works as those in other countries, as the discount houses are charged a rate of the money they borrow, they base their charges on that which has been imposed on them. The Bank reacts to this market cash shortage, but by charging a penal rate to the discount houses they pass on through the market a rate (base) at which they want money charges (interest) to be set. Banks which have borrowed money raise their interest rates and this normally results in a drop in the demand for credit.

7. *The public sector borrowing requirement (PSBR).* A reduction in the PSBR reduces the government demand for loans from the banking system (i.e. fewer Treasury Bills are issued). By reducing its own demand for credit the government reduces the bank's ability to create credit, as the amount of Treasury Bills (liquid assets) are reduced. Once again the method by which the PSBR is financed can also influence the amount of credit creation.

From time to time other policy options are discussed. These include hire purchase controls, windfall taxes on banks' profits and even stricter forms of special deposits. The discussion normally results in things staying as they are.

The banking sector now comprises a wide range of institutions and many are registered overseas. A supervisory role is practised by the Bank of England and they also have the important function of managing the government's borrowing.

Monetary policy involves the use of instruments designed to control the cost and availability of credit and the rate of growth of the money stock. The latter is considered an important element in the control of inflation.

Increased recognition has been given to the impact of fiscal policy on monetary objectives, and this resulted in the adoption of target rates of growth of the money supply, which imposes stricter control on the level and direction of government borrowing.

Inflation and public finance

This topic has attracted more attention than any other. The analysis begins with a definition:

Inflation is a process of a generalised and persistent increase in the level of prices.

Measuring inflation

Inflation is normally measured by changes in the retail price index (RPI):

Item	Weight	Current price (base year = 100)
A	5	110
B	3	120
C	2	130

Multiply weights by current price index: (5 x 110) + (3 x 120) + (2 x 130). Divide the total by the aggregate of the weights:

$$\frac{1170}{5+3+2} = 117 = the\ RPI$$

Are there any beneficiaries of inflation? Although inflation is normally considered a problem, it may have advantages. A buoyant economy may support a low, but stable rate of inflation. This would encourage investment to meet any excess demand, which would imply increased employment, output and growth. If inflation begins to accelerate, or get out of line with major trading rivals then benefits will disappear.

Debtors are normally said to benefit from inflation since the money they repay will have a lower purchasing power than the money they borrowed. In these circumstances debtors make real gains, particularly if they buy assets (houses) whose prices have appreciated.

Profits would, all things being equal, rise. However, other things do not remain equal, and generally real profits fall during periods of sustained price rises. Milton Friedman has argued that governments gain from inflation because of the effects of fiscal drag.

The problems of inflation

Increases in prices can cause a number of problems. These include:

1. *Expectations.* What is expected to happen plays an important role in economics. Firms may react to rising prices by cancelling future investment. They fear cost increases and a reduction in aggregate demand. Rising prices may lead to tighter monetary policy and therefore more expensive money. This in turn may reduce the prospects for exports, employment and investment. The combined effect of these would be a fall in economic growth.

2. *Self-fulfilling prophecy.* People may fear price rises and the adverse effect these would have on their real incomes. Their reaction to this may be to seek wage increases. As wages rise, so costs will increase, and firms may pass these costs on via price increases. Certain groups of workers may fear a slip in money wages to levels beneath those earned by other groups. Increased wage demands may overcome money illusion as workers become more aware of the impact of increased prices on the purchasing power of their money incomes.

3. *International competitivenes.* If domestic prices are rising faster on average than those of foreign competitors, while exchange rates remain relatively constant, then exports become less attractive, while goods being imported into the country have a relative price advantage. Consequently, exports decrease and imports increase causing an adverse move on the balance of payments. To some extent, flexible exchange rates tend to offset the relative price disadvantage, but a lower exchange rate inevitably causes import prices to rise, which may in itself contribute to further inflationary pressures. Government policy is now concerned with exchange rate influence. The sale of Bills is designed largely to influence short-term interest rates which in turn affect the exchange rate.

4. *Distribution of income.* Not all incomes rise in line with the average level of earnings. Those who are most disadvantaged are those in weak bargaining positions, or whose incomes are subject to government control, e.g. pensioners. People who have relatively fixed incomes have a disadvantage and to a certain extent, a redistribution of income in favour of those working in areas of the economy that have a strong bargaining power. There may also be a functional redistribution of income towards those receiving a wage or salary.

5. *Economic efficiency.* High levels of inflation have tended to be accompanied by higher levels of unemployment and lower rates of investment and growth. The economy is therefore effectively trading at less than its optimum output, and living standards are lower than might have been expected.

The theories of inflation

Demand pull

The central feature of these models is that of an inflationary gap, which is caused by 'too much money chasing too few goods'. The demand exceeds an economy's ability to produce. This may result in employers bidding up wages in order to gain factors and this pushes up costs. Cost increases soon become price increases. As these higher prices decrease the real value of incomes, increased wage demands result, thus causing further price rises, and so on. The wage-price spiral may become more vicious as expectations of future price rises are built into wage demands.

In a free-trading economy excess demand could be satisfied by increased imports. However, flexible exchange rates would probably cause import prices to rise, so reinforcing the inflationary trends. We have already mentioned a trade-off between unemployment and inflation. This relationship is shown in the Philips Curve (see Figure 43.18). It was considered that the whole curve had shifted to the right, i.e. to achieve full employment a higher rate of inflation than previously had to be adopted.

Friedman used this observation to develop his expectations-augmented Phillips Curve. This denies

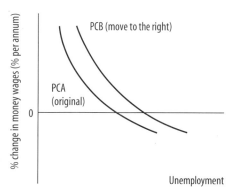

***Figure 43.18** The Phillips Curve*

the existence of any long-run trade-off between inflation and unemployment. Attempts, in the short-run, to reduce unemployment below its natural rate by any form of fiscal reflation (cutting taxes and increasing public sector expenditure) will succeed only at the cost of generating a wage-price spiral. Workers, who will have been tempted to re-enter the labour market, will realise that increases in nominal wages are quickly cancelled out by price increases (see Figure 43.19).

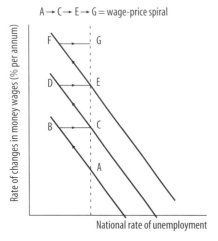

Figure 43.19 *Friedman long-run augmented Phillips Curve*

Recent empirical studies have suggested that in the United States 6% unemployment stabilises inflation, while in Japan this relationship appears to stabilise at 3%. Other studies have suggested that expectations of rising prices are now clearly shown in the prices accepted for the placing of gilts, i.e. the yield curve relationship between short-term interest rates and long-term government bonds.

The generalised level of excess demand that was apparent during the mid-1980s is an unlikely explanation for all the inflationary pressures. An American economist, Schapiro, has suggested that excess demand may be localised in certain expanding sectors. To this may be added those sectors whose raw materials are imported, for during periods of flexible exchange rates they may suffer significant cost increases. Schapiro suggested that large consumers of certain commodities may attempt to acquire commodities up to a point where they cause a supply bottle-neck. The consequent price increases created by this bottle-neck could be absorbed by either shaving margins, or the more likely advantages of increasing returns to scale. So, expansion is accompanied by increased factor costs and not rising prices.

Elsewhere, in industries with similar require-ments, the cost increases may not be absorbed and are passed onto customers. In the cyclical nature of trade, demand will eventually suffer a downturn but these industries may now be open to rising unit costs and are therefore uncompetitive. Without govern-ment intervention the industries may cease, so increasing structural unemployment. Schapiro's analysis clearly recognises the role of imperfections in the labour market and how these perpetuate inflation. It also gives prominence to the effects of structural change within an economy.

Cost-push theories

Cost-push theories are attempts to explain price instability in the context of an economy working at a rate below full employment. Inflation is initiated by an autonomous rise in costs. Price rises are not in themselves signs of cost-push inflation, for they may be the result of excess demand – it is the autonomous nature of cost increases which is important.

The components of inflation are:

- unit labour costs
- other costs per unit of output, e.g. electricity prices
- import prices
- net indirect taxes per unit
- residuals.

The relative importance of these components does change over a period of time. Some possible types of cost-push inflation are:

1. *Profits-push inflation.* This suggests that firms use their monopoly power to increase prices for their own benefit. This was recorded in the late 1980s as being equal to 1/2% on the RPI, but there is little subsequent information to support this.

2. *Wage-push inflation.* This theory implies that labour manages to demand wage claims above the levels of productivity increase. In times of economic growth this can be a substantial influence on wages, especially where 'skills gaps' exist and some workers can bargain for high levels of remuneration. However, in less buoyant times, this ability diminishes, but it does not always reduce as fast as prices have fallen. Hence, even in periods of low inflation it is always worth looking at annual earnings figures.

Other pressures may account for some wage-push inflation. Among the most important is probably relativity bargaining. If this is combined with our earlier analysis of expectations then it is possible to see a wage-price spiral emerge. This would be the result of one group of workers trying to jump ahead in order to maintain their relative wage advantage. This begins to feed into wage expectations and awards rise, fuelling further inflationary pressures. A recession seems to have a distinct dampening effect on this, as does a drop in inflation!

3. *Government-push inflation.* This theory tries to relate previous government policy to current wage levels. A tax increase, e.g. in VAT, may encourage higher wage claims, as workers wish to maintain living standards. A squeeze on real disposable income may also result in a subsequent bout of higher wage claims. The government may have, inadvertently, helped push prices up. The last example of this was the ill-fated 'poll tax', which added at least 1% to the then RPI, so putting pressure on wage negotiations to keep abreast of price rises.

4. *Import-push inflation.* The domestic rate of inflation is directly affected by the price of imported goods. A rise in raw materials, or component prices may feed through into final output prices. This in turn may cause the RPI to increase. The period following a currency devaluation may see increased import prices as the 'J curve' shows elsewhere in economics. This increase in domestic prices may lead to a loss of competitiveness in exports and increased penetration of imported goods. It is also worth remembering that exports may be reliant on imports for a part of their component costs.

Cost-push inflation may initiate an inflationary spiral, but it cannot sustain the process in absence of an expansion of monetary demand. If the money supply is firmly controlled, producers cannot pass on cost increases through higher prices without a reduction in the level of sales which will cause production to be cut back. In the monetarist analysis, as unemployment rises above its natural level, expectations are reduced, and the rate of inflation falls. Thus, monetarists consider cost-push to be a symptom rather than a cause of inflation.

Inflation – an overview

We have noted that inflation is a sustained rise in the general level of prices without any corresponding increase in output. Two major types are distinguished, demand-pull and cost-push. Friedman identifies three types of inflation. These are:

1. *Demand inflation* – inversely related to unemployment, and caused by increases in the money supply.

2. *Core inflation* – inflation that is built into the system, and based on previous recent experience of inflation and/or future expectations if inflation.

3. *Shock inflation* – one-off increase in inflation caused by external factors.

A restrictive monetary policy is designed to reduce demand inflation. This is normally combined with cuts in government expenditure, higher taxation, higher interest rates and credit restrictions. Cost-push inflation normally receives policy options that include incomes policies, reductions in interest rates, reductions in employers' taxes, an appreciation in the exchange rate (if inflation is imported) and a reduction in indirect taxes.

Public expenditure and fiscal policy

The importance of government in economic policy has already been noted. Now we must turn our attention to:

- how governments raise the money they spend
- how governments spend the money they raise.

Public expenditure

This includes both current and capital expenditure of central and local government. We must also include loans and grants made by central government to nationalised industries and public corporations, the contingency reserve (to finance any changes in plans), and part of the interest payable on government borrowing. Despite all the changes of the 1980s, the government still spends over 40% of the gross domestic product.

We expect our government to provide certain essential features of our daily lives, e.g. public goods (defence, roads), merit goods (health, education) and various aids to industry and employment. By spending our money, the government deliberately redistributes income either in kind (health) or directly (social security benefits). Some of our previous analysis has centred on the fact that the levels of and changes in government expenditure do directly influence national income, and therefore have an effect on employment and inflation.

Managing public expenditure

It is now the custom in the UK for the Chancellor (Finance Minister) to announce his expenditure and revenue-raising plans at the same time. For many years the Chancellor has announced his tax-raising proposals in the March following his expenditure announcements in November.

To reach the final requirements for expenditure takes a long time. Each spending ministry must submit proposals to the Treasury. These then come under close scrutiny, and after much debate are passed to the Cabinet for consideration. Once a collective decision has been reached by the Cabinet, a formal White Paper is produced. This is introduced to the House of Commons, debated and finally voted on. Normally, the government requires a majority to implement their proposals.

The sum announced for public expenditure normally contains a contingency reserve, which is an amount set aside to cover any planned changes or unforeseen problems. As the financial year proceeds, expenditure is closely monitored and compared against the expected sums. The Audit Commission actively researches the amounts spent and whether they appeared to achieve 'value for money', and within the House of Commons the Public Accounts Committee can investigate expenditure.

Local authorities also spend large sums of money. They are mainly concerned with education, housing, environmental services, roads and lighting. They are now very closely limited and can be 'capped' if they exceed the spending limit set for them by central government. Local authorities have normally raised some of their own revenue by a tax on property within their area. This 'rates' system of finance has received some alteration, notably the 'Poll Tax', but the current Council Tax is assessed on the value (resale) of the property in which you reside.

Public expenditure is financed by taxation and borrowing. However, borrowing imposes its own constraints in that public expenditure must include payment of interest on debt. Thus, the major determinant of public expenditure is the economy's ability to bear the levels of taxes imposed upon it. Ironically, as the level of economic activity falls, so the statutory obligations on government of certain types of expenditure increase, e.g. unemployment benefits. While improvements in, say, health actually increase life expectancy, they impose an increased welfare burden on the economy and its financial resources.

An essential core of public expenditure is determined by the past level of spending, changes in the structure of population, and the statutory commitments of government. To these we must add the fact that once a project has commenced, it is very difficult to bring it to a halt. Hence, economists consider that a degree of inertia exists within public expenditure and that the uncertain issue of 'political implications' must always be borne in mind. The electorate faces a basic paradox, namely they dislike paying taxes, but they also dislike cuts in services.

Taxation

The principal purpose of taxation is to raise revenue to finance government expenditure. However, the types of taxation chosen can reflect social priorities and the desire to redistribute incomes. We must also remember that the level of taxation is an important instrument in the demand management (see below) of the economy.

The fundamentals of our tax system were first postulated by Adam Smith. He considered that taxes should be applied with equality on those 'similarly placed'. His other principles included that taxes should not be costly or inconvenient to collect, and that a tax liability should be certain. In addition, it is generally agreed that tax should be related to the ability to pay and that its effects should not be detrimental to economic efficiency:

- Tax on income falls broadly into the following types: Taxes on income, e.g. income tax, National Insurance contributions paid by employees, corporation or profits tax and taxes on expenditure, e.g. value added tax, sales tax, excise duty.
- Ad Valorem *or percentage tax*. These are levied as a percentage of the price of a good (e.g. VAT).
- Specific taxes levied on the quantity of the good (e.g. excise duties and a motor vehicle tax).
- *Taxes on capital*. E.g. local rates, capital gains tax, capital transfer tax.
- *Payroll taxes*. E.g. employers' national insurance contributions.
- *Poll taxes*. A lump sum levied equally on each individual.

Taxes are levied in either a direct form (i.e. they are levied on the income receiver and cannot be passed onto someone else) or indirect form (i.e. levied on the seller of a good and can be passed onto someone else). Not all taxes on expenditure are indirect taxes, e.g. stamp duty is paid by the purchaser of the house and not the seller. Taxes are often analysed with reference to their marginal effect.

The marginal rate of taxation is the proportion of the extra £1 of income that is paid in tax. A progressive tax takes a higher proportion of income as income rises, i.e. the marginal rate of tax increases.

A regressive tax is where the marginal rate of tax declines as income increases.
A proportionate tax is one which remains constant as a fraction of income (see Figure 43.20).

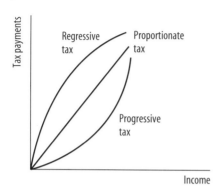

Figure 43.20 *The various types of taxation*

1. *Fiscal drag.* If tax allowances remain the same, people move into highter tax brackets as a result of inflation and successive wage increases. This results in the proportion of income taken in taxes increasing.

2. *Poverty trap.* Households with low incomes receive income-related benefits (e.g. free school meals). So, as earned income rises, they lose some of their benefits. In the worst case a £1 increase in income could result in a £1 loss of benefits or more. This would impost a marginal tax rate of over 100% on the individual. Some people currently unemployed may not find a return to work financially rewarding, as their benefits nearly equate with their proposed wage. This is known as the 'unemployment trap'.

Demand management

Fiscal policy, i.e. planned variations in the level of government expenditure and taxation, may be used to redistribute income and wealth, achieve certain social and political objectives, or control the level of activity in the economy. This final use has been known as demand management.

Successive governments have sought to promote economic growth, maintain full employment, stabilise prices and the exchange rate, and produce a 'healthy' balance-of-payments situation. The priority given to these macro-targets changes with the government and the economic climate. Many economists consider that the achievement of one is probably only acquired at the expense of one, or all, of the others.

The range of policy options known as fiscal policies have normally been used to try to smooth out the fluctuations in economic activity that reduce the prospects for full employment and economic growth. Careful use of the policies was thought to be conducive with high employment and low price infation. Accurate forecasts of expected changes in demand could be accommodated, as policies would be altered according to the future predictions (see Figure 43.21).

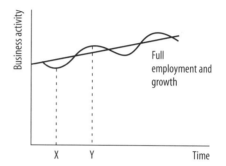

Figure 43.21 *Economic activity*

Counter-cyclical demand management

Figure 43.21 shows the economy in a deflationary period at X. To try to avoid any further reduction in aggregate monetary demand, the government would try to raise it back to full employment equilibrium. It would aim to achieve this without causing excess demand. This latter situation would be most likely at Y, and may be a principle cause of inflationary pressures. This form of demand management became known as 'stop-go' because governments switched from stimulatory to deflationary policies whenever it was thought that the economy was either too slack or too hot. The political cycle (the time between elections) also seems to have some influence on when 'stop' or 'go' policies were enacted. Critics of this form of policy suggested that they might be 'pro-cyclical' so worsening the situation, and not 'counter-cyclical' as its proponents put forward. An example of this would have been a period of 'go', i.e. reductions in taxes and increases in public expenditure, which would have increased employment, but possibly at the cost of rising prices and lost export orders. The alternative action – namely, to cut demand by increasing taxes and reducing public expenditure, may further worsen recession.

What Keynesians call 'fine-tuning' did encounter some problems. Among these were:

• *Data collection* – which takes time.

- *Accuracy* – economic data is notable for its inaccuracies.
- *Forecasts* – even the most complex computer models make wrong predictions.
- *Analysis* – this may be wrong, especially as the analysis usually follows some time after the event.
- *Time* – following on from this is the difficulty of trying to react at precisely the right time. Alas, economies do not wait until you have concluded your research and subsequent analysis.
- *Democracy* – whatever a government wishes to do, it may have to guard a small majority, so it can't always introduce 'painful measures'. Likewise, the length of debate, plus the committee stage may delay implementation.

Fiscal policy

Two broad types of fiscal policy can be distinguished. They are:

1. *Automatic stabilisers.* These run 'counter cyclical' and operate automatically as the level of economic activity alters, e.g. progressive income tax may cause tax revenues to rise faster than income, so having a dampening influence on the level of demand in an inflationary gap. Welfare payments may serve a similar purpose, as payments will rise automatically as demand and employment fall in a deflationary gap. This prevents disposable income from falling as fast as the economic conditions might otherwise have enforced. In theory, automatic stabilisers have little time-lag between the situation arising and the policy being implemented. However, they have to await the event and cannot therefore prevent anything from happening.
2. *Discretionary fiscal policy.* These involve a deliberate manipulation of taxes and government spending to affect aggregate demand. Usually, they are used to remove or lessen inflationary or deflationary gaps possibly removed, by a budget surplus – that is, by decreasing government spending to G1, with the leakage function unchanged, or by increasing taxation to T1, with government expenditure remaining unchanged. Any combination of policies which increases net government income would have some influence on reducing the inflationary gap. Because of the multiplier effect, demand needs only to fall by ab to reduce income from Y1 to Yf. If a deflationary gap had arisen, then a budget deficit (more government spending than receipts) could have been introduced to cure this economic problem (see Figure 43.22).

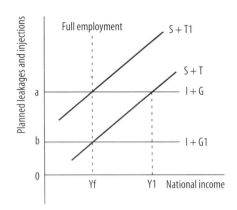

Figure 43.22 *Discretionary fiscal policy*

Tax changes

The deflationary gap we have just described could be attacked by introducing tax changes. Decreases in income tax would increase disposable income, so encouraging a rise in consumption. Once again tax has been used to influence a major component in what is known as aggregate monetary demand. Tax cuts may have an even greater effect if they are directed at the lower paid, as the marginal propensity of such a group to consume will be greater. Alternatively, a decrease in expenditure taxes could stimulate consumption, so leading the economy away from a recession.

Investment

This may be harder to influence but reductions in corporation tax, or increases in allowances, the introduction of 'tax breaks' or other forms of investment incentives may bring forward corporate investment plans. Using taxes to increase the rate of change in consumption expenditure may, through the accelerator effect, induce increased investment.

Trade

Despite the risk of retaliatory measures and being against the ground rules of the EU and GATT, some countries do impose higher sales taxes on imports. Likewise, they reduce taxes on exports, so increasing the trading performance of the domestic economy.

Whatever policy (or combination of policies) is used, it must be remembered that cuts or increases do not feed directly into aggregate demand, since a part of any decrease or increase will be lost through savings or imports.

A second problem is that changes in taxes may affect the marginal propensity to consume, so that the eventual change in national income is less predictable. One further difficulty arises – namely, the consumption function. This means that the full effect of an increase in disposable income may not be evident in the short run. A virtue of tax changes is that they can be reversed, though governments do not normally like to be accused of going against any election pledges they made not to increase or to decrease a certain form of tax.

Expenditure changes

We normally expect an increase in government expenditure to have an immediate effect on demand. As such, it should be expansionary. An example of this is an increase in a welfare payments. These are normally drawn by those with a high marginal propensity to consume. This will enable the income to quickly pass into increased consumption expenditure. Investment expenditure can be increased directly or by offering grants and subsidies.

The major difficulty with expenditure changes is time. It is very hard to find short-term 'cuts', though of course in the long run anything considered too expensive can be postponed or even cancelled. A high proportion of public spending goes on wages and salaries, hence 'cash limits' are imposed on departments, so forcing them to hold down labour costs. A further problem in this sector is that over 50% of public expenditure goes to health, education and social security. Reductions in these sensitive areas can be very damaging to the political standing of a government.

The budget

Changes in discretionary fiscal policy are announced in the budget. During this famous presentation, a review is undertaken of the previous year's economic performance and, in future in the UK, a statement will be made on planned taxation receipts and revenue expenditure. As we have noted, fiscal policy may affect both the level of aggregate demand and the structure of expenditure.

The traditional view of classical economists was that governments should 'balance their books' in the same way as a household. The Keynesian argument was that budget deficits could be used to remove deflationary gaps, and that budget surpluses could be used to reduce inflationary pressures. A deficit would stimulate activity, so increasing employment and tax receipts. In part, the shortfall in government receipts would not have to be covered by borrowing, as increased tax receipts would flow to the Treasury, so financing a part of the deficit. At the same time a reduction would be recorded in welfare payments, so reducing the government's appetite for cash. Despite all the attention given to monetary policy and government borrowing (PSBR), the short-term impact of fiscal policy is still a major part of any Chancellor's 'Budget Speech'.

A neutral budget is one which leaves the level of aggregate demand unchanged, but a balanced budget, i.e. one that increases government expenditure by the same amount as an increase in taxation, is expansionary. This is because an increase in government spending of, say, £1 billion increases the initial level of Aggregate Monetary Demand (AMD) by £1 billion, but the same increase in taxes does not reduce consumption expenditure by £1 billion, since some of the income now taken in tax was previously saved or spent on imports. So, there is an initial net rise in AMD (but of less than £1 billion) which has a multiplier effect.

The national debt

Government revenue goes into the Consolidated Fund, which allocates supply money to various government departments for their approved programmes, and pays a sum to the National Loans Fund towards interest on the national debt. The National Loans Fund is responsible for managing government borrowing, repaying loans, and paying interest. This includes the deficit of the Consolidated Fund. It also manages the government's domestic lending, on which it receives interest, and it finances the monies needed to help support the pound at the required exchange rate.

The net borrowing of the National Loans Fund is the major determinant of changes in the national debt, which may be broadly defined as the cumulative total of outstanding debt of British governments, and comprises all liabilities of the National Loans Fund.

'Liabilities' means the amount of money the various governments have borrowed. This borrowing can take various forms. Individuals buy National Savings Certificates and these form part of the non-marketable debt, as claims to repayment cannot be sold to another person by the original saver. Marketable debt can be 'sold on' before its maturity date. It is usually sold as either Treasury Bills (short-term loans to government) or gilts (long-term loans to government).

The ability to resell government debt, and the fact that the government is very unlikely to break its repayment promise, make these investments popular with lenders. Unlike dividends on shares, the returns are guaranteed and therefore represent a secure form of saving. Hence, such institutions as pension funds and banks invest heavily in the market holdings of government debt.

About one-quarter of the national debt is held by the government itself. This consists of holdings of the National Debt Commissioners, who invest in the National Insurance Fund and ordinary deposits of the National Savings Bank. A further proportion is held by the Bank of England, both as backing for the issue of bank notes, and also as assets of the banking department. This last holding is similar to the holding of government as a form of asset by ordinary commercial banks.

A further part of the national debt is held by individuals, private trusts, other financial institutions, foreign banks and the IMF.

The fund also receives interest from loans it has made to nationalised industries and public corporations. The net figure of financing the national debt is therefore equal to:

Interest on debt + Administration charges – Receipts from loans

This net figure is charged to the Consolidated Fund and is borne by the taxpayer.

In theory the burden of the national debt makes no real claim on national resources for, as one stock matures the government issues another. However, the net cost of servicing the debt is an additional tax burden and so may place a restraint on government spending elsewhere in the economy.

Receipts for overseas holdings are a leakage from the circular flow, and taxes raised to pay the debt may drain financial resources from other sectors, so 'crowding out' investment potential elsewhere.

Increased government borrowing may, under certain circumstances, have the effect of increasing the money supply or raising interest rates. As we saw earlier, many believe that such a combination will be inflationary and have an adverse effect on investment, employment and growth.

Conclusion

Public expenditure includes the final consumption spending, transfer payments and capital formation of central and local government and public corporations. It may be directed towards the provision of public and merit goods, and sums can be spent to aid industry and employment, further redistribute income, and control the levels of economic activity. Attempts in recent years to reduce public expenditure have been reasonably successful, though current sums have been more difficult to control than capital amounts. It may also be the case that policies have been pro-cyclical in their consequences, as they have intensified such problems as unemployment.

Public expenditure is financed by taxation and by borrowing. Recent policy in the UK has shifted the emphasis slightly away from direct and onto indirect taxation. Fiscal policy, the manipulation of planned levels of taxation and government expenditure, can be directed towards structural change within an economy, social priorities, or the management of overall economic activity against such specific objectives as employment, price stability, growth and a favourable balance of payments.

The national debt is, broadly, the cumulative total of past government borrowing. The payment of net interest on debt does increase the tax burden of the economy and may be a cause of a further redistribution of income. Over time, these influences may affect the level of aggregate monetary demand, and payments to overseas residents do, ultimately, serve as a drain on domestic economic resources. Finally, the ways in which government borrowing is financed may cause inflationary pressures as they expand the supply of money and induce interest rate increases.

The policy options open to government have caused controversy. The principle differences between the schools of thought are as follows:

Keynesians

- An economy is basically unstable and the market will not function to self-correct savings in economic activity.
- Inflation is caused by independent cost-push factors and causes increases in the money supply.
- The use by governments of fiscal policy can manipulate economic activity. Budget deficits stimulate the economy while surpluses cause enforced savings.
- Monetary policy can be used only to influence interest rates. Money itself is impossible to define and attempts to control it will probably be irrelevant and possibly cause a loss of output.
- Demand for money is interest-elastic (i.e. is responsive to interest rate changes). Investment is interest inelastic (i.e. is not responsive to interest rate changes).

Monetarists

- Economies are stable and resource allocation is achieved through the price system. A natural rate of unemployment exists.
- Inflation is caused by excessive growth in the money supply.
- Fiscal policy is not successful for it will reflate the economy. You cannot trade off inflation and unemployment. A budget deficit will cause an increase in the money supply and subsequent

inflationary pressures. A large government demand for money may cause interest rates to rise; as the total stock of money (credit) becomes insufficient to meet demand.

- Demand for money is interest-elastic. Investment is interest elastic.

Supply-side economics

Supply-side economics was popular at the start of the 1980s, and its policy options still remain quite widely used. They include reductions in government involvement in the economy, reductions in corporate and personal taxation, private action, reform of trade unions, aid to small businesses; the 'right to buy' council houses; increased emphasis on labour mobility; and the end of any controls on pay, prices and dividends.

Economic growth

What is it?

In its broadest terms, economic growth is normally considered to be an increase in real gross national product (GNP) per head of population. However, most people would consider growth to be an increase in their standard of living. While year by year measurements of GNP do show the effects of recession and recoveries, 'growth' is best thought of as the rate at which output in increasing in the long term. Thus growth can be defined as the rate at which potential output is increasing over time. It is worth noting that few developed countries achieve an annual rate of growth of 3%, indeed many stuggle to pass 1.5%.

How is growth achieved?

Once again economists differ as to the main ingredients of this important issue, but a 'consensus' opinion would concentrate on certain basics. These include:

- a rise in the productivity of existing factors

In the short run this may be achieved by increasing the abilities of firms to organise. For example, a better division of labour could be achieved, or greater economies of scale. In modern economies it may result from more intensive use of capital (e.g. work practices allowing more flexible working hours). Physical working conditions may be improved and thus also boost potential output.

In the longer term the improvements need to be more 'deep-rooted' and may concentrate on better education, improved capital utilisation skills and other investments in human capital that improves the quality of individual output.

- an increase in the stock of factors of production

The size of the labour output can be increased through either an increase in the number of hours worked per worker, or an increase in the working population as a percentage of the total population.

An increase in the hours worked is not the normal trend in developed countries, for as living standards improve people tend to demand more leisure. We may be able to change the record by either altering the ages at which people begin and end work, or by changing attitudes to work among certain groups. This has been most obvious among married women, many of whom now work as well as maintaining a home and family.

Improvements in technology increase a country's ability to utilise its natural resources. In Northern Europe a number of countries have benefited from the discovery of North Sea oil and gas. In other parts of the world marginal land has become workable through the application of modern facilities and pesticides. The impact of natural resources on an economy can be considerable but much will depend on the proportion of value added that stays within the borders of the resource-owning country.

Economists usually distinguish between widening and deepening the availability of capital within an economy. By widening we mean adding sufficient capital to keep a constant ratio between labour and this fundamental factor of production. We are therefore maintaining the existing ratio. When referring to deepening we are describing an increase in the capital–labour ratio. The latter is normally considered to be a major indicator of a developed economy, and an essential ingredient of economic growth.

Some factors that influence economic growth

1. *Technological change.* Societies do not stand still; scientists and other innovators continue to produce more sophisticated ways of producing output. Productivity normally increases as technology improves. Alas, it may also bring an increased risk of unemployment. In reality increases in labour skills, availability of natural resources and improvements in capital tend to develop in parallel, so promoting the need for new techniques.

Economists also consider that certain structures and facilities within economies foster growth potential. The availability of such facilities will also be considered when we examine the problems faced by Third World or developing countries (DCs).

In advanced industrialised countries (AICs) we expect to see certain signs of growth. These, in turn, help to continue the growth process.

2. *Human capital.* The proportion of national wealth being invested in human skills will influence growth. Such institutions as schools, colleges and universities absorb resources, but will hopefully produce better trained workers for future economic progress. The proportion of these people who may emigrate can also influence the growth potential.

3. *Research and development.* Research and development will be an important indicator of growth potential. There is strong evidence to link high research intensity industries with major economic development. The scientific base of an economy is a very important part of its investment in future prosperity.

4. *Financial markets.* A skilled labour force blossoms best when backed by adequate capital investment. AICs have access to stock markets, insurance cover and other specialist facilities.

5. *Infrastructure.* The means by which resources are distributed is also important to growth potential. As such, roads, rail links, air and sea ports all serve to increase the sophistication by which goods and services are made and distributed. The need for such utilities as water, gas and electricity are obvious.

Why is economic growth desirable?

Growth is normally an important objective of economic policy as it enables politicians to predict increased standards of living. It may now be a fact of western European life that people expect rising living standards.

When economies grow, governments receive more revenue and can therefore provide better services for the electorate. They may also concentrate some policy options on the distribution of income. The less well off may receive a greater share of available expenditure than those on high income levels.

It must also be remembered how quickly growth accumulates if compound formulae are applied. For example, a 3% annual growth rate means a doubling of real economic wealth in 24 years. This can lead to a comparatively small national difference developing, over relatively short periods of time, into noticeable

differences between living standards of neighbouring countries. The same economic facts lie behind the inability of poor countries to close the gap with rich counterparts.

The costs and benefits of economic growth

Growth normally results in more being available for consumption. It may also be possible for output to remain static while fewer hours are worked. Hence AICs normally enjoy more leisure than developing countries. Richer countries can afford to keep people in education for longer periods, and allow those at a more advanced stage of life to retire earlier. The range of social services can also be increased.

Nevertheless, a society wishing to maintain high living standards can only do so if they sacrifice some of their current consumption. As such the investment needed to promote future growth has to be valued, and a decision made as to its true worth.

Economic growth also imposes a variety of social costs. The motor car is a perfect example of this. High levels of car ownership can only be supported by high income, yet car production is known to carry certain social costs, e.g. pollution, congestion and the use of fossil fuels. The 'green' or environmental debate is now a major part of modern economies.

Another area of controversy is the pace of economic change. What were only recently agreed practices or skills can become redundant. People now face less secure futures and may have to accept retraining. The social costs of disruption and unwanted breaks may be high for some people.

Growth is seldom evenly distributed. In AICs few accept a reduction in working hours, so others face redundancy. On a more global scale will richer nations ever accept a fall in living standards to enable the poorer countries to close the gap?

Low income countries normally lack advanced banking, money markets and insurance markets. This in turn means that they do not have an active mechanism for encouraging savings and switching these into investment.

The lack of financial infrastructure is compounded by a distinct lack of physical infrastructure: a shortage of good roads, rail, telephones, and other essentials of water, gas and electricity make development even more difficult to achieve.

How can developing countries develop?

The development of developing countries is not easily achieved for they lack many of the essential ingredients for productivity increases. Perhaps they should utilise comparative advantage? Most developing countries have abundant land, so should they specialise in land-intensive primary commodities? Alas, the prices of these tend not to be stable and they are normally determined in centres situated in the developed world. The creation of substitutes also reduces demand for pure commodities, e.g. rubber. Both demand and supply tend to be inelastic, so a small shift in one causes a large change in equilibrium price. Trade cycles, harvests and weather add further complications to this route to growth. The high dependency on certain primary commodities also means a high export concentration. So, perhaps they should diversify: but into what?

Commodity stabilisation programmes offer one possible solution. These are attempts to create buffer stocks, which can be used to promote a more stable flow of commodities, with the consequence of less volatile prices.

Another route to growth may lie via industrialisation. One part of this is the encouragement of import substitution. Barriers to trade are created, e.g. quotas or tariffs, and domestic output is encouraged to expand in order to meet home demand. It may be a dangerous route, as specialisation could be encouraged in areas where a comparative disadvantage exists. Resources may be wasted and it is often very difficult to become internationally competitive. One possible advantage is that an increase in skills is fostered and these can be directed towards export-led growth. Some developing countries have become successful exporters. Such nations as South Korea, Taiwan and Singapore have noticeably increased their share of world export trade.

They now form part of what are known as newly industrialised countries (NICs). They have concentrated on certain product areas and have penetrated many of the more labour intensive markets of the developed world. The result of their success has been a re-emergence of protectionist cries among some AIC producers. If DCs can keep more of the value added for themselves then they can use the money for development. Think about a jar of coffee. Who makes more money, the grower of the beans, or the producer of instant coffee?

Conclusion

This may be the first experience you have had of confronting the difficulties faced by Third World countries. They are considerable, and of course, the economic progress of advanced industrialised countries does not stand still and wait for developing countries to catch up.

They lack applied technology, capital, human resources infrastructure and market opportunities. Perhaps the rich world needs to think about offering greater access to their markets for Third World goods, but that would require fundamental changes in their attitudes. These changes may be forced on them as successive developing countries encounter serious economic difficulties. They cannot meet their debts, so exposing their populations to yet further poverty. Naturally, this can have political consequences. Seeking assistance from the IMF usually means a structural readjustment programme. These normally concentrate on reduced money supply, cuts in public expenditure and the ending of subsidies for both essentials and manufactured products. The short-term effects of such programmes can be very serious for the country, especially, as it tends to hit the poorest hardest.

Consider how you think the following characteristics would adversely affect a developing country:

- low productivity in agriculture
- large proportion of export earnings coming from primary commodities
- poor infrastructure
- rapidly expanding population aged 16 and under
- small manufacturing base.

SUMMARY

Having studied this chapter, you should be able to:

▽ Explain the changing nature of industry.

▽ Describe public sector industry.

▽ Explain national income accounts.

(continued)

▼ Describe foreign trade.

▼ Describe the European Union.

▼ Discuss international institutions.

and you should understand:

– *money and monetary policy*

– *inflation*

– *public expenditure*

– *economic growth and development.*

Questions and activities

Technical terms and glossary.

In the section below you are given a series of technical terms and their meanings. They have been scrambled. You must match up the terms and the definitions. When you have them correctly paired, transfer them to the alphabetical vocabulary or glossary book.

You are also advised to transfer any defintions obtained during the exercises in the case studies into this glossary book.

Technical terms
1. Privatised industries
2. Measures of national income
3. New industrial technology
4. The European Currency Unit (ECU)
5. Newly industrailised countries

Definitions
A. The introduction of new products, new processes and the application of automated, safe and clean methods of production.
B. Countries experiencing rapid industrialisation.
C. Industries that were once owned by the population via the public sector, that are now in private ownership.
D. Income, output and expenditure methods.
E. A measure of currency based on a 'basket' of EU membership currencies.

Short answer questions
1. Explain the main changes that have arisen as a result of the micro-electronic revolution.
2. Outline the major changes that have occurred in UK industrial patterns throughout the 1980s and 1990s.
3. What do you understand by the terms:
   (a) nationalised industry
   (b) privatisation?
4. Why are National Income Statistics calculated?
5. Describe the economic advantages that are put forward to support foreign trade.
6. What barriers exist to reduce the effectiveness of international trade?
7. Why do governments impose restrictions to the free movement of trade?
8. Briefly outline the major economic advantages of being a member of the European Union.
9. Evaluate the effectiveness of (a) the WTO (previously GATT), (b) the IMF and (c) the IBRD to meet the economic targets they are designed to meet.
10. What is the principal purpose of monetary policy and what options may governments use to control the amount of money in circulation?
11. Why should a business be concerned by a persistent increase in the general level of prices?
12. Define:
    (a) demand management
    (b) fiscal policy
    (c) fiscal drag
    (d) poverty trap
    (e) automatic stabilisers
13. How is the national debt financed?
14. What is meant by the team supply-side economics?

15. Outline the basic economic ingredients needed for economic growth.
16. Why do developing countries remain in a cycle of poor living conditions?

Data response questions

Read the article and answer the questions which follow.

(*Note:* Training and Enterprise Councils (TECs) were set up in local areas by the government to coordinate business training and development.)

Norfolk and Waveney TEC Market Research Findings – December 1991

Table A
Norfolk and Waveney – Consumer Spending
(% change) Constant 1985 Prices (£m)

	Total	Durables	Non-durables
1989	3,993	440	3,553
% change	4.0	0.6	4.4
1990	4,055	408	3,647
% change	1.5	−7.4	2.6
1991	4,044	412	3.632
% change	−0.3	0.9	−0.4

Table B
Norfolk and Waveney GDP
(% change) Constant Prices (£m)

	1989	1990	1991
Total GDP	4,803	4,821	4,783
% change	2.9	0.4	−0.8

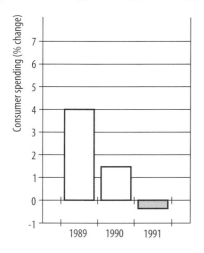

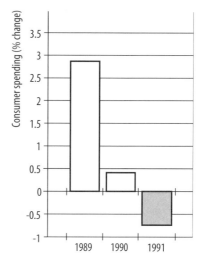

(Source: *Business Strategies Ltd*, London, December 1991. Adapted from *Updata*, Edition 2, Norfolk and Waveney TEC, December 1991.

Trends and projects in local consumer spending in Table A clearly show the effects of the recent recession. Similar trends and projections can be seen when looking at Gross Domestic Product (GDP) for the TEC area in Table B.

It is important to note that there is also a delay expected between the economy showing sustained signs of recovery and businesses feeling confident enough to take on more staff. It is for this reason that rising unemployment could be expected at least in the short term.

Norfolk and Waveney TEC envisages local economic recovery to begin in the first half of 1992 and although short-term labour and skill shortages are not expected, past experience suggests that labour market problems associated with strong economic growth will eventually emerge. The TEC fully appreciates the importance of planning early for the skills needed in a growing economy.

Questions

(a) Using only data from Tables A and B, discuss the effects of the recent recession in the area, already visible in December 1991.   (9 marks)

(b) Explain how these 'effects' might have an impact upon employment in:

   (i) an independent local supermarket (3 marks)

   (ii) a medium-sized engineering firm making components for washing machines and spin dryers   (3 marks)

   (iii) the local tourist industry   (3 marks)

(c) Discuss the 'labour market problems associated with strong economic growth ...' as mentioned in the article.   (8 marks)

(Associated Examining Board, Business Studies (A) Paper 1, 1993)

44

The social environment of business

Preview

▼ The final part of the analysis of business covers such important topics as *regional policy*, *manpower policy* and *policies covering competition*.

▼ The *influence of law* on business will be covered, as will the *social implications* of the ever-changing business world.

The economic system

The availability and quality of the factors of production dictates the ability of business to produce the goods and services required by the population of the country. Insufficiency of one or more of the factors of production, or insufficient demand for the goods and services produced by the system, throws the system out of balance. A lack of national expenditure leads to an under-utilisation of the nation's capital, while an increase enables this utilisation to increase.

To maintain a growing economy, three types of expenditure must be in evidence:

1. Expenditure by consumers on goods and services.
2. Investment by firms and government in new plant, machinery, hospitals, etc.
3. Expenditure by foreign nations on a country's exports.

All three types of expenditure add to the utilisation of the stock of resources at a nation's disposal. The majority of western governments have certain, agreed economic objectives. These normally are:

- to improve living standards
- to reduce unemployment
- to stabilise price rises
- to achieve an equilibrium in the balance of payments

- to achieve stabilisation in the exchange rate
- to promote economic growth.

The macro targets have received considerable attention elsewhere, but before we move on to other economic policies we must first look at standards of living.

Improving the standards of living

There are various problems connected with the concept of a standard of living. First, we must make a distinction between consumption, which is easily measurable in terms of money and the services which are consumed without having to pay the full cost at the actual time of consumption, e.g. education. We must also be aware that certain social factors, e.g. 'being able to walk the streets without fear of attack', also affect our standard of living. Increased levels of pollution, the run down of once prosperous regions, breakdowns in communities, increased crime, etc. all affect our standard of living, but it is difficult to physically measure their impact in pure monetary or economic terms. There are also apparent differences between groups, regions and certain parts of the country. In general, people on fixed incomes, e.g. students, have seen their standards of living fall, while those in full-time employment have seen a rise in their life style. Elsewhere, the end of mining has adversely effected some regions. The standard of living depends upon:

- the quantity of resources available
- the quality of resources available

- the proportion of resources being utilised.

Governments therefore aim to influence the quality and quantity of the nation's economic and social resources currently utilised and likely to be available in the future. Basically, government can stimulate utilisation of resources by policies which encourage expenditure and consumption. We have already studied such important topics as:

- inflation/price stability
- balance of payments
- fiscal policies
- monetary policy
- exchange rates
- the importance of Europe.

Regional policy

When considering the location of industry, we must list those factors which induced particular industries to locate in certain regions: old industries such as coal, steel and shipbuilding decline while new market-orientated industries begin to grow in the Midlands and South East England, where they can obtain resources of capital, skill and labour which cannot easily be shifted from the old declining areas to the areas of growth.

Mobility of labour

One of the central objectives of government policy is to encourage both occupational and geographical mobility of labour. This can be achieved by:

- redundancy payments
- the provision of moving grants, either by central or local government or by private firms
- grants for new housing and generous consideration to house purchasers seeking mortgages when they move from an area of high unemployment to one of expanding work
- national retraining schemes (for example the Youth Training Scheme).

All these policies are aimed at encouraging the individual to move to new work, and reducing the financial and social problems which have traditionally made labour so reluctant to move.

Movement of firms to depressed areas

A second feature of policy is to attempt to get firms to move into depressed areas – again by the provision of government subsidies, investment grants, and loans for factory buildings, and the installation of new, up-to-date machinery. The policy can work in two ways:

1. firms can be pulled into areas of decline
2. by the use of Industrial Development Certificates they can be discouraged from settling in areas already overcrowded or congested, such as the Home Counties and South-East England.

Some people favour a hands-off approach, that is a non-government intervention stance in the economy. The advocates of this type of non-interventionist policy argue that:

- any restriction or inducement to firms to move either deters investment or forces firms into unsuitable locations, so that in the long term they cannot remain competitive with firms unfettered by government regulation
- government benefits are merely short term (see later) so that in the long term new sites become uneconomic, and resources are wasted.

However:

- the free market economists also assume that firms conscientiously seek their lowest-cost location, which in practice they do not
- national collective pay bargaining often prevents a firm from reaping the benefit of location in an area of high unemployment (where wage rates ought to be well below the national average).

In recent years, the ability of firms to reap the cost benefits above has been considerably improved with the decline of mass trade unions and the dismantling of minimum wage legislation.

Difficulties of regional policy

As we have already indicated, a government's regional policy to revive old depressed areas – which may be based upon welfare and social considerations – is not necessarily the same as the commercial objectives of an entrepreneur or businessman left to decide his location for himself. Most firms using advanced technology will require to be near their markets and established where they can use the technical and administrative skills of the industry as a whole.

Further, it is often difficult to balance the costs of regional help against the social benefits involved, and there is also the danger that once a firm has been persuaded to settle in an area in order to provide employment, it may abandon the venture at a future date, leaving the area worse off than ever. Firms refused planning permission to expand in congested areas may simply not expand at all, and a policy which encourages labour mobility out of a depressed area leaves the area more derelict than before.

Finally, the designation of an area as a region in special need of investment will inevitably mean that other areas are deprived of investment, quite possibly those areas on the borders of the special areas themselves.

Some economists would argue that the best way to stimulate industrial growth is not to interfere in the location decisions of the industry or firm but to devote public money to building up sound expanding industries in locations chosen by businessmen themselves according to sound financial and economic criteria, and for the government to provide very comprehensive retraining and re-housing schemes to encourage labour mobility.

Government measures

Over the years governments have created assisted areas which are currently of three types:

1. *Development areas.* Large areas of high unemployment, with declining basic industries, for example Tyneside, the Scottish coal fields, and areas in South Wales.
2. *Special development areas.* Areas of endemic unemployment and social deprivation within the development areas themselves.
3. *Intermediate areas.* Areas where the trend of unemployment is on the increase and there are few signs of future economic growth (for example Manchester and Leeds).

Firms setting up in these areas receive incentives such as grants towards the cost of machinery, building, factories, factory rates on favourable terms, training grants and tax allowances on plant and machinery. All are relatively short term (they are phased out over the life of the asset or over time). Other measures include central government grants to improve the infrastructure, including roads, and the environment of the area – for example the partial transformation of the Liverpool dock area into a national garden centre. Many of these schemes are long term in that they are designed to transform an old industrial area into one which is attractive to service industries, particularly tourism.

Governments can also deter movement into an area of population congestion by using such measures as:

1. The granting of Industrial Development Certificates. Under the scheme, certain types of building can be built without normal planning permission.
2. The building of new towns (30 in the UK since 1946), for example Washington (near Newcastle) and Milton Keynes (serving London).

Finally, you should also remember that almost all aspects of government taxation and expenditure policy have some form of regional significance. A clear example can be found in the case of unemployment benefits; those regions with high unemployment will receive selectively high payments of benefits. Thus, unemployment benefits provide a form of regional policy, with depressed areas receiving relatively more than prosperous areas.

Enterprise zones

An interesting experiment was introduced in 1980: the enterprise zone. A number of local areas were designated as suitable for special help. Details of the assistance to be given to both new and existing firms within enterprise zones are as follows:

- Exemption from development land tax (since abolished).
- 100% capital allowances (for corporation and income tax purposes) for commercial and industrial buildings. The initial cost was about £20 million a year.
- Exemption from general rates on industrial and commercial property, the local authorities concerned being reimbursed for their net loss of rate income by 100% specific grants from the Exchequer (cost about £10–£15 million a year).
- Simplification of planning procedures. It was proposed that there should be a plan for each enterprise zone prepared by the relevant local authority or development corporation and approved, prior to designation, by the Secretary of State. The plan would show which classes of development were permitted in each part of the enterprise zone; it would set out any conditions governing development, for example those needed for health or safety or for the control of pollution; and it would specify any 'reserved matters'.

  Following designation, developers would not need to apply for planning permission for developments that conformed to the zoning and conditions in the plan. They might need approval from the local authority or development corporation for the 'reserved matters', but these would relate to details such as access to a highway. Approval for developments that did not conform to the plan would require individual application in the normal way.
- Speedier handling of requests for 'customs warehousing', etc. Applications from firms within enterprise zones for the customs facilities known as 'customs warehousing' and 'inward processing relief' would be processed as a matter of priority,

and the criteria applied to decisions on 'private' customs warehouses in enterprise zones were relaxed.
- Any remaining requirements for Industrial Development Certificates were abolished.
- The government would reduce to a bare minimum its requests for statistical information.

It was intended that, in general, simplified procedures and speedier administration of control over development would be applied in enterprise zones. However, there would be no lowering of the standards needed to protect health and safety or to control pollution.

Is regional policy a success?
- This is difficult to assess as we cannot tell what would have happened without the policies.
- Not all jobs created are 'new'; many are diverted from other areas where firms might have located in the absence of government inducements to move.
- The cost of creating new jobs is extraordinarily high – at least £36,000 per new job.
- New jobs and industrial investment have slowed down economic and social decline.
- Some foreign investment has been attracted (for example Japanese investment in Wales).
- Britain has used the Regional Development Fund (from the EU) to create jobs in Scotland which are of direct benefit to the environment (for example the £6 million Glendern water treatment and dam project).

Labour and manpower policy

Fiscal and monetary policies attempt to control expenditure and income. The objectives of labour and manpower policy are to raise the productivity of labour in both the short and long term and to fit labour more exactly for job opportunities in the future.

Differences in labour productivity
Differences in labour productivity may be caused by many factors, the most important being:

- the amount of training received by the labour force to perform not only present jobs but also future work necessitated by changes in technology and reorganisation
- the willingness and ability (skill and financial ability) to move from one area of employment to another

- the ability to move from one area of work within a firm to another without trade union restriction
- the amount and pattern of working time lost through strikes, accidents, sickness and absenteeism
- the amount of power and machinery installed, which in turn depends on government fiscal and monetary policy to stimulate investment and expansion
- fiscal policy and differential payments.

The natural rate of unemployment
This is something that economists recognise as an important influence on wage and price trends. It represents a condition where there is neither excess demand for, nor excess supply of, labour as a whole. Such unemployment is due almost entirely to 'frictional' causes and perhaps to some structural changes. It is then assumed that there exists no pressure on wage or price rates.

'Frictional' unemployment means temporary unemployment caused by a local and short-term mismatch between the supply of and demand for labour; it can be unemployment caused by workers leaving work and seeking other work.

Another way of describing this situation is to say that the influences giving rise to pressures for wage and price increases and decreases must balance.

This 'natural' rate is not a fixed level. Because it is associated with pressures to change wage and price levels, it is affected by any alterations in the strength of these influences. For example, if there is a swift and strong upward pull on prices and wages as a result of excess demand, then this will tend to raise the natural rate of unemployment required to balance this effect.

If, therefore, we suspect that the natural rate of unemployment has risen, we must look for causes likely to strengthen the pressures to increase prices and wages.

Effect on wages and prices
Such causes are not hard to identify in Europe. Until the recession began to bite, inflation and the expectation of future inflation were both high. Employers were, therefore, quick to raise wages to retain or recruit workers, in anticipation that they could recoup additional costs through price rises. Unions pressed for wage rises in anticipation of future price rises, and these tendencies have only fairly recently been modified by rising unemployment.

New employment legislation
Political and social measures also tended to weaken

the downward pressure of unemployment fears and strengthen the upward pressures on wages. Legislation increased the legal rights of workers and the powers of unions. It increased the security of people in work and secured rights to financial compensation for unemployment.

At the same time, the penalties for being unemployed were reduced – at least in the short term. Earnings-related benefits, redundancy pay and a wide range of social security benefits softened the financial consequences of unemployment so that there was a greater willingness to risk this possibility, especially as there was a belief that unemployment would be only temporary.

Social attitudes

These have also played a part. In the post-war period, inflation and full employment have been the general rule, and recession and periods of relatively high unemployment have been of short duration. This has further reduced the general fear of long-term unemployment and its power to depress upward pressures on wages.

More general social attitudes may also suggest that wages should rise in the interests of social equity or of income redistribution, almost regardless of the economic function of wages as a price determining the allocation of production factors. If such an attitude is general, it may reduce the perceived importance of indicators of excess supply in some sections of the labour market.

Increased specialisation

The changing structure of industry and employment has tended to produce a more specialised work force.

Unemployment in one occupation is not felt as a threat to other occupations, as the ability of workers to move from one activity to another is restricted by skill and union requirements. One group may thus be able to exploit a worker shortage and be unaffected by excess supply in other occupations. Thus, in many cases the supply of labour for particular jobs has become less elastic.

Until the 1980s the increased importance of union organisation in the public sector also reduced the responsiveness of negotiators to economic indicators. There was a belief that workers in 'socially desirable' services were, or should be, insulated from economic considerations of relative supply and demand in labour markets.

In general, therefore, reduced sensitivity or responsiveness to signs of excess labour supply may force up the natural rate of unemployment, thus allowing prices and wages to rise together and permitting a high rate of unemployment to develop.

This, in turn, has a marked influence in depressing wage and price rises.

Policies relating to competition

Very few pure monopolists invest in the UK. Despite that, many firms wield considerable monopoly power (see Chapter 22). UK legislation, therefore, defines a 'monopoly situation' not simply from a purely economic point of view, but as one where a third or more of the supply of goods and services is controlled by one firm or group of interconnected firms.

UK firms are also subject to EU regulations. Article 86 of The Treaty of Rome prohibits 'any abuse by one or more undertakings of a dominant position... in so far as it may affect trade between member States'. Government policies relating to industrial competition generally have two objectives:

- to limit the growth of specific firms
- to restrict the type of commercial behaviour permitted by business firms – the type of behaviour of particular interest to the government is the collective agreement between firms to fix prices or restrict supply to the detriment of the public, and attempts by individual manufacturers to force retailers to adopt the price dictated by the manufacturer when they, the retailers, sell goods to the final consumer.

Monopolies and Restrictive Practices Act 1948

This was the first piece of anti-monopoly legislation passed in Britain. The Act performed the following functions:

1. It created the Monopolies Commission.
2. It gave the Board of Trade powers to ask the Commission to investigate and report on monopoly in industry, i.e. where one firm supplied one-third or more of any particular class of goods.
3. Parliament was then asked to restrict the power of any firm which was using its monopoly position to raise prices and restrict competition.

Restrictive Trade Practices Act 1956

This Act attempted to regulate agreements made between two or more parties to restrict prices, limit supply, or dictate the terms of sale, process of manufacture, persons or areas to be supplied.

All agreements of this nature have to be registered

with the Director-General of Fair Trading, who has the power to place suspect agreements, i.e. those tending to restrain freedom of trade, before the Restrictive Practices Court. The latter is to decide if the agreement is, or is not, in the interests of the public.

Such agreements are allowed only if the parties to the agreement can prove that:

- the agreement between them protects the public from injury
- the agreement produces substantial benefits for the consumer
- the agreement is necessary to enable fair terms to be negotiated with a supplier or distributor
- removal of the restriction imposed by the agreement would adversely affect employment or reduce export orders.

In fact, the conditions of exception are drawn so tight that very few companies have attempted to evoke them in order to justify restrictive practices in industry.

Restrictive Trade Practices Acts 1968 and 1976

Under the provisions of these two Acts, all agreements made between firms which might tend to limit freedom of competition are to be placed before the Restrictive Practices Court. The Court must be satisfied that the agreement is in the interest of the general public before allowing the firms concerned to continue operating under such an agreement. A new provision of the 1968 Act was that all informal agreements between firms to exchange information about prices, for example, had also to be registered.

Resale Prices Act 1964

Prior to 1964, it was a common practice for large-scale manufacturers to force retailers to charge customers prices for goods decided by the manufacturer, even though the manufacturer contributed goods typically through wholesalers to the retail outlet. This practice was held to be illegal by the Resale Prices Act 1964, on the grounds that obligation existed between retailer and manufacturer through a contractual chain, though a contractual obligation did exist between retailer and wholesaler. The passing of this Act paved the way for a tremendous growth and change in distribution methods which began in the 1960s with the development of cut prices, high volume selling, and self-service supermarket grocery.

The Act stopped manufacturers from enforcing retail prices unless they could prove that were they not to do so:

- the quality and variety of goods offered to the public would deteriorate
- the number of retailers would be reduced
- the conditions under which goods were sold would be dangerous to public health and safety
- after-sales service would be reduced.

Subsequent to the enforcement of this Act, the Monopolies Commission was asked to investigate the practice of manufacturers 'recommending' a price at which retailers should market their goods to the customer. The practice was allowed to continue.

Competition Act 1980

This Act abolished the Price Commission and made minor changes to the law relating to monopolies and restrictive practices. The main effect of the Act was to strengthen conditions of free competition in the sale of goods and services.

Anti-competition practice

This was a relatively new concept in United Kingdom law, and was defined as a course of conduct which is intended to restrict, distort or prevent competition in connection with the production, supply or acquisition of goods and the supply and securing of services in any part of the United Kingdom. The definition is applicable to both the public and private sectors of the economy.

Competition reference

The Fair Trading Act in 1987 provides for a preliminary inquiry by the Director-General of Fair Trading, which results in a report. The matter can then be referred to the Monopolies and Mergers Commission. This is known as a competition reference. The director specifies the scope of the reference. The Commission will then submit its report to the Secretary of State.

During this procedure, the firms under investigation may undertake to cease the anti-competitive practice. Note that an anti-competitive practice can be a course of conduct pursued by one person only. The Secretary of State may not be satisfied with the undertaking made by the firm or person, and will then order the practice to cease. The Act refers to past conduct and also to conduct contemplated in the future. In general, persons are free to bring civil rather than criminal actions (damages or an injunction).

The Secretary of State may refer to the Commission any question relating to the efficiency and cost of the service provided by any statutory corporation where there is possible abuse of a monopoly situation.

Report of the commission

The Commission report:

- gives reasons for their conclusions
- makes recommendations to remedy the situation under investigation
- orders the person or corporation abusing the law to remedy the situation, or prevent some adverse effects specified in the report

All plans are put before Parliament and must be open to the public.

Protection of Trading Interests Act 1980

The Secretary of State may make an order forbidding compliance with any law of an overseas country which seeks to regulate or control international trade, if:

- compliance would damage the interests of the United Kingdom
- the foreign law refers to matters outside that State's territorial boundaries.

Various clauses of the Act protect United Kingdom businessmen from having to pay multiple damages in cases involving the breach of United States anti-trust, anti-monopoly laws.

Industrial policy

Almost everything that a government does in the way of fiscal, economic or social legislation has an effect on a country's industry. However, industrial policy may be thought of as government policy which explicitly seeks the achievement of a particular production objective, or the restructuring of an industry, or the promotion of growth, investment and technical progress in individual firms and industries. Current examples of industrial policy include the closure of uneconomic pits in favour of investment in open-cast mining, the rationalisation of the UK steel industry, and the privatisation of many service and trading companies such as British Gas, British Telecom, the Trustee Savings Bank and BP.

Britain has never had an industrial policy in the sense of setting targets to be achieved by various industrial sectors (like a typical industrial strategy of the centrally planned economies) or even a list of priority industries towards which government would channel investment. Many economists argue that one of the prime reasons for the UK's rapid industrial decline has been the lack of a coherent strategic plan for industry, designed to tackle a specific set of changes, many of which would have wide implications. So, should the 'State' intervene in industrial policy?

The rationale of industrial policy

Free-market economists see little need for a planned, coherent and consistent industrial policy. The production sectors, according to free market theory, are fully coordinated by market forces acting in response to price changes. Behaviour is automatically adjusted to changes in income and the prices which are faced by individual firms; income and price determine what is profitable to produce. Each factor of production - including labour, revolves round an equilibrium price, and the market operates free of any friction. However, in practice the free market is subject to serious imperfections which point to the need for coherent and sustained government intervention.

The imperfections of the market

The growth of monopolies

Here is a classic case of market imperfection: one factor, or a cartel, controls supply, output is restricted, prices to the consumer rise and market resource allocation is distorted. The same general pattern is presented by oligopolies (the predominant type of industrial concern in the UK).

Social vs private costs

Industrial activity generates costs to society at large (for example pollution, alternative uses of land, etc.), benefits (the utilisation of resources, incomes, wealth, etc.) and private costs to the firms (for example the development costs associated with utilising resources). But market resource allocation through the price system via supply and demand relationships takes no account of the indirect effect of such allocation on third parties (for example noise, pollution, traffic congestion). Governments intervene in the working of the market to reduce the social cost to the community (for example health and safety regulations, patent laws, etc.).

But there is also another problem: in a free market, competitors are free to imitate the innovative products of others; the original innovator is thus left with the majority of the research and development costs, but poor or declining marketing opportunities. Hence, if research and development and other innovative efforts are left entirely to the free market, too little of it would be done by the private sector.

There is therefore a need for government support and direction.

Regional imbalances in employment, incomes and social provision

Left to themselves, market forces will quickly produce imbalances between one geographical region and another (contrast South East England with the North East).

Failure of information

The flow of full and accurate information from industry to the consumer in a highly complex society entails a cost to industry which, if left unregulated, it will be reluctant to bear. Again, there is a need for government regulation to ensure the free flow of adequate information from producers to the market (for example consumer law, etc.).

Industries in which either demand or supply is elastic

Many industries would have to bear excessive short-term dislocation if left to face the imperfections of the market. Many firms would go out of business through short-run imbalances between supply and demand. Examples include agriculture, capital-goods industries and machine tools manufacturers.

'Sunset' and 'sunrise' industries

As has been argued earlier, there may be a case for government protection for both declining industries and also infant industries and small businesses.

Almost all attempts at industrial planning since 1945 in the UK, have centred on correcting the type of market imperfections mentioned above. The alternative approach of a coherent overall strategy has not been consistently applied.

Current policy

The Conservative government is sceptical of the value of central planning, and confident of the power of market forces to reveal growth potential. But central direction has not been abandoned altogether.

Government activity, so far as industrial policy is concerned, includes:

- the promotion of service industries by removing the barriers they have had to face, up to the passing of the 1984 Finance Act, in gaining development grants and tax exemptions
- measures to promote small firm growth, mainly though various forms of tax exemptions
- privatisation and competition (remember our earlier discussion)
- regional policy (again see previous discussion).

The European Union and the single market

The European Communities Amendment Act (1986) brought about the move towards a single market (see Chapter 43). The practical impact of the legislation is that from 1992, companies within the EU have been able to trade within a single market larger than any other outside China and the former Soviet Union. This single business environment offers greater opportunities for firms, but has at the same time increased competition and hence uncertainty.

The impact of this competition is felt on a global rather than a continental scale. Even before 1992 companies from the United States, Switzerland, Austria, Sweden and Japan were negotiating company mergers and acquisitions within the EU (for example car plants in the UK) in order to gain access to the new market opportunities created by a single market throughout Europe. Completely new corporate strategies are needed to cope with this scale of change in customers, suppliers, financial providers, transport and frontier controls, health and safety legislation, Community consumer law, trade union legislation and personnel policies.

The central aim of the Single European Act was to provide an economic environment capable of competing on a world stage, and to arrest the decay of European industry into a 'screwdriver' economy, reduced to putting parts together for more technologically advanced United States and Far Eastern competitors.

Basic facts about the European Union

The European Union was created by the Treaty of Rome in January 1958. The combined gross national product (GNP) of all its members made it the second largest economic trading bloc in the world behind North America, and potentially the fastest growing trade bloc. Over 280 of the top 1,000 industrial companies are based in Europe (310 are in Canada, 345 in the USA). Europe has 115 companies earning profits exceeding US$200m per annum.

Despite these impressive statistics, Europe as a whole has a poor technological base, compared to Japan and North America. It is this central weakness which stimulated the formation of a single market. Wealth is also somewhat unevenly spread throughout the Community. It has some of the richest states within its borders, but also some of the poorest.

The industrial weakness of the European Union

Leaving aside the major problems associated with the Common Agricultural Policy (CAP), the main weaknesses of the Community can be summarised as follows.

1. Technological backwardness compared to Japan and North America.
2. The fragmented nature of the Community itself, particularly its political and economic fragmentation.
3. Lack of a really homogeneous market covering all member States.

These, in their turn, have led to related competitive weaknesses.

- Waste of resources in terms of research and development to adapt products to meet the different quality standards imposed by different countries.
- Obstacles to the free flow of goods and labour across the Community.
- The dangers associated with protectionist policies during periods of general recession.
- Lack of trained European managers and a European labour force.

The Single European Act

The broad terms and conditions of the Single European Act are as follows.

- Majority, rather than unanimous, decisions to be made by the EU Council of Ministers.
- To update the Treaty of Rome in respect of:
  - economic and social legislation
  - common policies regarding the environment
  - cooperation between institutions within the EC
  - political and monetary cooperation and uniformity – a common currency.

Sharing the wealth

The Act recognises that some areas of the Community are wealthier than others and better able to benefit from a single common market (for example the South East of Britain, Northern France, the Ruhr and the Benelux countries). Very substantial amounts of aid are available to outlying regions to develop their infrastructure.

Deregulation

The Act deregulates areas of law which restrict the movement of goods, people and services, financial provisions, indirect taxation and Customs procedures at borders.

The adoption of the Cassis de Dijon Ruling

The Single European Act also seeks to establish common standards regarding:

- products
- health, safety regulations and environmental standards
- consumer law.

Agreed common standards coupled with the Cassis de Dijon Ruling had an immediate positive effect on the sale of British chocolate and German beer and cars. Now, no matter where a product is manufactured within the Community – provided it satisfies agreed environmental and consumer protection regulations – it can be sold anywhere in the EU. Thus it has become impossible to prohibit importation into another EU country (for example British lamb into France). Consumer choice is therefore increased and competition stimulated within the whole of the EU.

This, of course, does not prevent narrow sectional interests in each country from attempting to put up barriers to competitive goods – as in the case of the importation of British lamb into France – but at least the more extremist pressure groups do not have the protection of law for any obstructionist behaviour.

Competition

Free competition is seen as the hallmark of the single market. Much of the European Act is devoted to regulations designed to increase competition and prevent collusion between firms in respect of price fixing.

The movement of goods

Frontier controls delay the movement of goods and increase costs to all shipping and freight agencies. Vast amounts of paperwork needed to be reduced, while at the same time it was necessary to increase steps to:

- prevent smuggling
- comply with hygiene and agricultural regulations
- counter terrorism.

Well over 70% of the paperwork formerly required for frontier passage was eliminated by the use of a Single Administrative Document (SAD). Different rates of VAT in different member countries remain a problem. Two rates were originally proposed to be used throughout the Community – a standard rate at 14% and a lower rate (4%) on basic items such as food, domestic energy, public transport, books and periodicals – but this has not come about.

The abolition of many bureaucratic controls was aimed at reducing costs, the benefits being passed on to the Community in lower prices and hence increased competition with goods imported from outside the Community.

Community-wide procurement procedures for public utilities

Procurement refers to the process of bidding for public works contracts such as the building of highways, construction of dams, etc. It was envisaged that a single market would allow civil engineers in France, for example, to tender for such work across national boundaries, rather than be restricted to their own country. Such arrangements would have the advantages that:

- the costs of public utilities, transport and telecommunications would be reduced because competition would be increased via Community-wide competitive bidding
- cost savings could be passed on via tax reductions or in the form of reinvestment in the Community's infrastructure.

A free-market in financial services

The aim of the European Commission is to increase competition in the market for financial services in order to stimulate:

- a free flow of capital throughout the EU
- the sale of financial services (banking, mortgages, insurance) across the EU.

The right for financial agencies to set up in business in all member states is provided for. The advantages of these types of arrangement include:

- reduction in prices for financial services across the EU
- lower interest charges, stimulating higher manufacturing investment and a higher level of home ownership
- wider availability of credit at competitive rates of interest.

General advantages of a single market

To sum up, the essential aims of a single market are:

- to enable individuals and firms to exploit the weaknesses of competitor products and services throughout the Community and thus encourage high quality, at low prices
- to simplify Customs procedures and reduce paperwork, including the paperwork associated with VAT in Europe
- to facilitate the movement of capital and labour throughout the EU.

The effects of increased competition on the single market

Competition has come both from within the single market and from the trading blocs outside Europe. These areas are Japan, North America, the Pacific Basin (excluding Japan), other European competition and small business competition.

The impact of Japanese competition

Japanese competition was a major catalyst for the creation of a single market in Europe. Between 1975 and 1985, Japan displaced West Germany and the USA as leaders in world trade. Japanese companies operate on a global scale and dominate high-technology industries. They have fully integrated corporate strategies, and operate forward planning on a strategic scale; Japanese management thinks long term, rather than short term.

The legendary Japanese success is based on:

- the two managerial objectives of total company commitment to total quality management, coupled with high productivity and high quality products
- high gearing (using low-cost bank borrowing), thus reducing short-term pressures on working capital
- reinvestment of profits in research and development and new market initiatives
- the establishment of forward bases as 'springboards' into the high-technology markets of the future (for example South America, China and Europe).

This combination of high quality products and equally high quality marketing poses a unique threat to European companies.

North American competition

Most of the major Canadian and US companies already operate within the EU; many provide the training ground for the best European manpower. Unlike Japanese companies, they tend to go for quick returns on investment and their position in Europe suggests that they will seek to ally themselves with European companies, rather than compete with them.

Competition from the Pacific Basin (Korea, Taiwan, Singapore, Hong Kong)

This area also covers Indonesia, Thailand and Malaysia. Currently these countries' great competitive advantage is their supply of cheap labour. But they are also acquiring technology from Japan and favour the Japanese model of expansion. European companies with low levels of technology are under threat from this source of industrial production. Waiting in the wings are India and China with their vast resources of cheap labour and an in-place commercial elite.

European competition

A competitive edge will be gained by those countries in Europe dominated by large companies already operating on an international scale. The advantages of size (economies of scale) will force small companies to merge or collaborate in order to compete.

Small and medium-sized businesses

Many economists predicted that small firms would be wiped out by the dominant firms of the single market, but studies of the US economy suggest otherwise. Small enterprises are flexible and generate low costs – hence they are able to exploit niches in the market. Regionally based companies can supply specific regional needs and in this way can survive in the single market.

The overall effect of the single market can be summarised as follows:

1. The exit of some firms due to competitive pressures
2. Relocation of production to reap the benefits of low-cost market opportunities.
3. An increase in mergers, acquisitions, joint ventures, etc., to gain market advantages and reap the benefits of economies of scale.
4. The acquisition of European firms by Japanese and North American businesses.
5. Increased horizontal and vertical integration.

Legal considerations

This section will deal with certain aspects of the legal environment that affect the operation of business (see also Chapters 21, 22, 28 and 36). It will concentrate on five main areas, namely:

1. discrimination in the work place
2. Consumer Law
3. The Law of Contract
4. Company Law
5. Data Protection.

The Sex Discrimination Act 1975

This Act made it unlawful for any form of discrimination to be applied against women in respect of work, housing (including mortgages), education, recruitment, promotion and training.

In broad terms, such discrimination is defined as

unequal treatment of a person because of his or her sex. The Equal Pay Act 1970 entitled women to the same rate of pay as men if they do the same work under the same conditions. The terms of both Acts extend also to discrimination against women on grounds of marriage. Professions such as acting are exempt from the terms of the Act, if it can be proved that the sex of the person is 'a genuine occupational qualification'.

One of the most important sections of the Act applies to the provision of such services as banking, insurance and credit finance. The Act made it unlawful for financial institutions to discriminate against women in the granting of mortgages, insurance policies, loans or other forms of financial credit.

The Sex Discrimination Act also made it illegal to frame an advertisement for a job in a way which suggested discrimination against women.

Complaints

Complaints of discrimination are dealt with by the following:

- the county courts
- industrial tribunals, which deal specifically with complaints involving discrimination in relation to employment
- the Secretary of State, who is empowered to deal with complaints made against educational or training establishments
- the Equal Opportunities Commission, which deals with complaints of discriminatory advertising. The Commission conducts formal hearings which witnesses can be forced to attend. It advises people of their rights and helps them to prepare their cases for submission to the courts.

The Race Relations Act 1976

The 1976 Act replaced the Race Relations Acts of 1965 and 1968, which it repealed.

Terms of the Act

Broadly, the terms of the Act are similar to those of the Sex Discrimination Act. The Race Relations Act makes it illegal to discriminate in advertising for a job, selection, the terms of employment, promotion training and dismissal against a person because of his or her colour, race or creed, or ethnic or national origin. The employer can be held liable under the Act if his subordinates discriminate against an individual.

The Act abolished the former Race Relations Board and Community Relations Commission and established the Commission for Racial Equality.

Complaints

Complaints of discrimination may be made by the individual concerned, by any other person who may have witnessed discrimination, or by the Commission for Racial Equality, either to a county court, or to an industrial tribunal in the case of discrimination involving employment. Normally, complaints will first be dealt with by attempting to arbitrate and conciliate between the parties in the dispute, and only if this procedure fails will matters be put through the courts. If the employer is found guilty, the court may award damages, alter the terms of the contract of employment, or issue an injunction.

Exemptions

The Act does not apply if:

- The employer can prove that it is necessary to employ a person with special qualifications which are possessed by persons of a particular race or nationality, for example the ability to speak a foreign language perfectly (look at certain advertisements for jobs, for this is commonly used in the job description).
- The person is to be employed in a private household.
- The employee is working mainly outside Britain.
- Training is given to a particular racial group where that group had previously been *under-represented* in particular kinds of work.

Commission for racial equality code of practice

In August 1979, the Commission for Racial Equality issued a consultative draft entitled 'Code of Practice for the Elimination of Unlawful Discrimination and the Promotion of Opportunity in Employment'. The Code (which could be used in industrial tribunal cases) went further than an interpretation of employer action to comply with the Race Relations Act 1976: it also included actions to achieve fair employment opportunities.

The following are the most important elements of the code:

1. The main responsibilities of employers in recruitment, promotion, transfer, training, benefits and facilities to prevent direct and indirect racial discrimination.
2. Coordination of employer and trade union staff association efforts to foster equal opportunities at work.

3. The main responsibilities of employment agencies:
   - refusal to agree to racially discriminatory recruitment
   - instructions from employers; and
   - job applicants being given equal treatment by employment agency staff.

4. The relationship between good employment practice and equal opportunity.
   The code noted:

   - Selection criteria which are relevant to job requirements and carefully observed selection procedures not only help to ensure that individuals are appointed according to their suitability for the job and without regard to racial group; they are also part of good employment practice.
   - Monitoring and record-keeping of selection decisions, personnel practices and procedures regarding equal opportunities.
   - Identification of indirect discrimination.
   - Positive action and additional training for certain racial groups to compensate for previous discrimination

Consumer protection

The modern consumer requires legal protection for the following reasons:

1. The technological advances in production and marketing of goods and services produce very sophisticated products which the consumer can hardly be expected to understand fully at the moment of purchase.
2. Television and film advertising and modern sales techniques make the consumer vulnerable to high-pressure salesmanship.

Some companies (mail order firms) send goods through the post (books, records, etc.) which have not been solicited by the recipient. The receiver has no legal obligation to pay for such goods unless he intends to purchase or use them. The sender has the right to retrieve the goods within six months, (this is covered by the Unsolicited Goods and Services Act 1971) but the recipient has no legal obligation to return the goods at his or her expense. All of us are advised to read the 'small print' when joining such a club!

Statements of fact and opinion, sales promotion and advertising

'Statements of fact' have to be true. False statements of a factual nature about goods or services render the seller liable to prosecution and as such criminally liable. On the other hand, generalised statements expressing an opinion, or statements which by their very nature cannot be factually true (for example 'a most desirable residence', or 'the most delicious soup in the world') are allowed. It would, of course, be up to the court to decide what was a factual statement and what was not.

Misrepresentation

The buyer may claim damages for misrepresentation if the offending statement is part of the actual terms of the contract of sale. If the misrepresentation is decreed by the court not to be part of the essential contract, the buyer may claim damages if he can show that:

- The statement was fraudulent or intended to be fraudulent
- The statement was made by the seller without due care, and in a negligent manner.

Purpose for which the goods are bought; merchandisable quality

The various Sale of Goods Acts, require that the buyer satisfies himself as to the fitness of the goods purchased for the use to which they are to be put. The seller can be held liable if the goods prove unsatisfactory or if he attempts to sell faulty goods in the following circumstances. This has now been replaced by 'satisfactory quality' (see Sale of Goods Act 1994).

- The buyer has made clear the express purpose for which the goods are intended and the buyer has been sold goods manifestly unfit for that purpose. This reinforces the old notice of 'examine carefully before you buy'.
- The buyer relies upon the skill and judgement of the seller, and is compelled to do so by the terms of the sale or the complexity of the goods bought.

Exemption clauses

There are often clauses in a contract of sale which purport to excuse the seller from all liability. The Unfair Contract Terms Act is the main piece of legislation aimed at working the unfair exclusion of liability. The major part of the act applies to businesses which try to exclude their liabilities to consumers. These exclusions are deemed by the Act to be either void, or subject to a test of 'reasonableness'.

Goods not entitled to be sold

Goods may sometimes be sold unwittingly which have been stolen (unknown to the seller) or sold on whilst still subject to a hire-purchase agreement. In such circumstances, the buyer has the right to recover his money from the seller if the goods have to be returned, but he must not have been aware of their having been sold by someone not entitled to do so.

Sale by Hire Purchase (Consumer Credit Act 1974)

The resale of goods under a hire-purchase agreement which is still current at the time of sale is illegal. The seller has no right to sell them until the final instalment has been paid, and the original buyer, until then is their legal owner. The owner may retrieve, from a person who has innocently purchased them, goods still under a hire-purchase agreement if:

- the price of the goods is payable in instalments
- the terms of the original sale were that legal title to the goods passed on payment of the final instalment.

Important exceptions to this rule are motor cycles and vehicles bought in good faith by private persons for their own use. The hire purchase company in this instance has no right to reclaim the goods. Surrender of them would be ordered by the court if the vehicle had been purchased by a dealer in the trade, but not by a private individual.

Guarantee

The guarantee of fitness, etc., is a feature of the purchase of electrical goods, motor vehicles and consumer durables of all types. Generally, the courts have held that such a guarantee legally binds a manufacturer if the agreement was known to the purchaser before purchase, and is of such a nature as to confer benefit or detriment on the buyer. Any wording on the guarantee which tends to exclude the seller's obligations in law will not be upheld by the courts.

Hire purchase

The essential element of a hire-purchase transaction is that the original owner of the goods does not relinquish his ownership until the customer who has hired the goods has paid the final installment. There are three types of hire-purchase contract:

1. the true hire-purchase contract
2. a conditional sales agreement
3. a credit sales agreement.

In true hire-purchase, the retailer normally sells the goods to a finance company and the finance company becomes the legal owner of the goods. These are then hired by the finance company to the final customer over a given period of time for an agreed rent. At the end of the period the goods may be returned to the finance company or become the legal possession of the hirer on payment of the final instalment. Remember that in most cases you cannot sell on until you have paid in full.

The hirer has no right to sell the goods on hire purchase. Failure to pay may mean that the owner has to retrieve the goods by a court order.

Under a conditional sales agreement the goods are purchased over a specific number of instalments and, when condition of sale has been fulfilled, legal possession of the goods passes automatically into the hands of the customer. In a credit sales agreement the purchase price is paid in five or more instalments, and the buyer is the owner of the goods immediately. Thus the owner can sell the goods at any time and the seller has no right of legal repossession.

Like all legal issues, please read the small print very carefully.

Consumer credit

The Consumer Credit Act 1974 was designed to protect the rights of consumers, by establishing a new administrative system to control traders dealing in credit. The main provisions of the Act are set out below.

Director General of Fair Trading

Duties of the office include:

*   administering the licensing system set up by the Act
*   enforcing the terms of the Act
*   reviewing social and economic developments in the United Kingdom in relation to the Act and amending regulations in accordance with the evolution of credit finance
*   conducting inquiries regarding specific breaches of the terms of the Act.

Agreements covered

1. *Personal credit agreements.* These are defined as agreements between an individual (the debtor) and any other person (the creditor) by which the creditor provides the debtor with credit.
2. *Consumer credit agreement.* This is a personal

credit agreement for any amount less than £15,000.

3. *Running account credit and fixed sum credit.* This is an agreement made by a person with an individual (the hirer) for the hire of goods, which:
    *   is not a hire-purchase agreement
    *   lasts more than three months
    *   does not require the hirer to make payments exceeding £15,000.

Consumer credit agreements are exempt from the terms of the Act where the creditor is an insurance company, friendly society, charity, etc.

Licensing of credit and hire business

All consumer credit businesses and hire firms require a licence to carry on business but local authorities are exempt from obtaining such a licence.

A licence may be either:

1. A standard licence, which covers the activities of a named individual for a set period of time.
2. A group licence, which covers the activities of more than one person for an indefinite period.

An applicant must meet two provisions before the licence will be granted.

*   The applicant must prove he is fit to carry on a credit business (e.g. previous convictions might disqualify him).
*   The name of the business must not be misleading and must be clearly understood by all approaching it.

The Act gives the Director General of Fair Trading power to lay down specific regulations regarding the conduct of the business, for example the type of account books which must be kept.

If the Director refuses to grant a licence, he must state his reasons in writing to the applicants and invite them to resubmit the application. Final appeal is to the Secretary of State, who has the ultimate power to accept or reject a licence.

Seeking business – advertising and canvassing

General provisions

Part IV of the Act applies to any advertisement to provide credit or hire out goods of less than £15,000 in value to an individual. Advertisements must include specific information and ensure that this is brought to the attention of the general public. To provide false or misleading information is an offence. Not only the finance company but also the publisher of the advertisement is liable for such offences. You will notice that in newspapers they always stress you must read all details of advertisements thoroughly and be certain of the validity of the contents before entering into an agreement.

Canvassing

The Act particularly regulates the conduct of high-pressure salesmen soliciting business off trade premises – i.e. at the homes of private individuals. It is an offence to canvass debtor-creditor agreements off trade premises, or to persuade someone to sign a credit agreement during a visit to their home unless the visit has been requested in writing.

It is also an offence to:

- induce minors to borrow money or obtain goods on credit
- give persons unsolicited credit tokens.

Making an agreement

Form and content of agreement

The Secretary of State can regulate the form of credit agreements. The hirer must be aware of his rights and duties, the amount and rate of the total charge for credit, and the protection available to him under the Act.

Signing the agreement

Any Agreement between debtor and creditor falling within the scope of the Act is not properly executed unless:

- a document in the agreed form is signed by the parties to the agreement in the prescribed way
- the document contains all the terms of the agreement
- the document is fully legible.

The debtor/hirer must be given a period of consideration (seven days) so that he can think about the consequences of the financial obligations involved. During this period, the creditor is not entitled to approach the prospective debtor, except in response to a specific enquiry by him.

Copies of all unexecuted (i.e. unsigned) agreements and executed (signed) contracts must be sent to the debtor within seven days following the agreement.

Rights of cancellation

If the credit agreement includes rights of cancellation, these must be communicated in writing to the debtor – including how these rights may be executed. This information must be posted to the debtor within seven days of the agreement being signed.

Recovery of money

When a regulated agreement and its linked transactions are cancelled, any sum paid by the debtor/hirer in anticipation of the full transaction, including any charge for credit, is repayable. Goods must be returned on cancellation.

Where the whole or part of a loan has been received by the debtor before an agreement is cancelled, he must repay this credit. No interest is charged if he repays within a specified time.

Where a shop has requested a finance house to supply credit to a customer, the latter can take action against either the shop or the finance house under the Sale of Goods Act for the sale of faulty goods, if appropriate.

Default and termination

Default notices

Before one of the parties to a regulated agreement can claim compensation for default, a formal notice must be served on the offending party. This notice must:

- terminate the agreement from a specific date
- demand early payment of money owed
- warn of recovery action (in the case of goods hired)
- terminate other rights conferred by the agreement
- specify the nature of the alleged default, what action can be taken to remedy it, or the sum requested as compensation and the date by which such sum is to be paid.

If the defaulter complies with the terms of the default notice before the specified date, the contract continues as if no breach had occurred.

Repossession of protected hire-purchase goods

The creditor is *not* entitled to retake goods acquired by the debtor under a hire-purchase agreement if the debtor has paid one-third or more of the total price of the goods, except by a court order.

If the creditor recovers the goods in contravention of this regulation, the debtor is released from all obligations and is entitled to recover from the creditor all sums paid under the agreement.

The creditor is thus not within his rights if he enters premises to recover goods, except under the authority of a court order, nor may interest charges be increased on default by the debtor.

Early payment by the debtor

The debtor is entitled at any time, by giving notice to the creditor and paying off all outstanding debts, to make early payment and completely discharge his indebtedness. It is a duty of the creditor to give any information the debtor may require in order to effect early payment of the debt.

Modifications of existing agreements

Modifications may be made to the original credit agreement, but any variation is not deemed to have the force of law until notice of the changes has been sent to the debtor or hirer in the manner laid down by the Act.

Termination of agreements

The creditor is not entitled to terminate a regulated agreement for a specific duration, except by or after giving the debtor/hirer at least seven days' notice.

At any time before final termination of a regulated hire-purchase agreement, or regulated conditional sale, the debtor is entitled to give notice that he wishes to have the agreement ended. Debtors are still held accountable for any liabilities under the agreement which are outstanding before termination.

Collateral security

In some cases, debtors are required to operate collateral security (for example life assurance policies) for hired goods or credit facilities. The form and amount of such security must be expressed in writing in a prescribed manner.

The terms of the security arrangements must be brought to the attention of any third party providing the security. He must know the amount for which he will be held liable if the debtor defaults, the total sum paid under the agreement by the creditor and the cost of credit.

It is the duty of the creditor to give the person putting up security for a loan all possible information, so that he can assess the risks involved.

Extortionate terms

It is the task of the courts to examine and interpret agreements to determine whether the terms are extortionate. A credit agreement is extortionate if it requires payments which:

- in the opinion of the courts are grossly excessive
- otherwise grossly contravene normal commercial fair dealing.

The court will take into account the interest rates prevailing in society, and the circumstances of the debtor and the creditor.

Credit reference agencies

Credit reference agencies are now used extensively throughout business and commerce. They collect and disseminate information about individuals' financial standing and creditworthiness. The danger is that they can have access to essentially confidential information, keep it on computer file and pass it on without the knowledge or permission of the individual concerned, who may then be denied credit, perhaps unjustly or for reasons he does not know about and therefore cannot rectify.

In order to limit these abuses, the Consumer Credit Act 1974 provided that credit reference agencies must disclose filed information, when asked.

The law of contract

A contract is a legal agreement. Most business agreements centre on a 'contract' being made, but to be a formal, legally binding document the agreement must have the following features.

Offer and acceptance

To make an agreement legally valid one party must make an offer to perform or provide some specific function or to pay a particular price for a recognisable good or service. The other party to the agreement must unconditionally accept the offer. All terms of the offer must be accepted, neither party can be selective. When buying an item in a shop it is the purchaser who makes the offer to buy at a particular price. The price on an article is *not* an offer, but an *invitation to offer*. The retailer can accept or reject the purchaser's offer, which he normally accepts.

Consideration

This has to be something performed, given or suffered in return for benefits received. Both parties to the contract must show consideration. Money is the most common form of consideration, though it is perfectly acceptable and legal to exchange goods for goods and services for services.

Intention

Both parties to a contract must be prepared to show intention to create a legally binding agreement. It is assumed in business agreements that there is an intention to enter a legally binding relationship, unless it is formally stated that the agreement is 'binding in honour only'.

Capacity

The law tries to protect persons who might not be fit to enter a legally binding agreement. Such persons are those under 18 years of age (known as minors), those who are mentally disabled and those drunk at the time of signing the contract. All of these do not have the capacity to enter into a contract. With all but a few exceptions, e.g. an apprenticeship for a minor, a contract made by any of the above is void or voidable.

It is a fundamental rule of law that an unauthorised use of statutory power (*ultra vires*) is void and ineffective. This applies to companies, public corporations and nationalised industries and none of them may enter into contracts that are not authorised by their statutes, e.g. a company may only sell items stated in their Memorandum of Association.

Validity

Even if the contract meets the above criteria it may become invalid because of some other factors such as:

1. *Mistake.* People are not perfect; they do make mistakes. Error in a contract may make the agreement invalid. The most common error is mistaken identity and either of the parties can make the mistake. However, the rule does not cover carelessness; the mistake must be a genuine, and significant one, otherwise the rule of *caveat emptor*, i.e. let the buyer be aware, applies.
2. *Misrepresentation.* Some people do make false statements to try to induce an agreement. Under such legislation, such as a Trade Description Act 1968, makes misrepresentation a criminal offence. Any contract entered into as a result of misrepresentation can be voidable and the injured party can claim damages in civil action.
3. *Ubertimae fidei.* In most contracts it is important that all facts relevant to it are declared, otherwise the contract is voidable, e.g. in an insurance contract all previous illnesses must be declared, or the contract would be declared void.
4. *Unlawful intent.* Some contracts are not enforceable because they are not lawful. Illegal contracts are not valid, neither are lawful contracts that involve an unlawful act, e.g. a contract to commit a public nuisance. Some contracts are void by statute: that is they call for something to be performed that is against an Act of Parliament.

The law will not normally enforce a contract that was signed under pressure from the other party. Ignorance does not count, but a genuinely 'weaker' party must be protected. It is not always easy to determine 'undue influence', but Parliament usually tries to define those most at risk, e.g. unfair sums being charged for renting a property. An individual can ask for an independent rent assessment, and the findings should not affect the continuance of the contract.

Property law

As well as people, businesses are responsible for other assets. Companies may either own the land on which they operate, or they may lease the land. If they own the land, then it is considered to be 'freehold'. Some property is not bought outright, but is acquired via a mortgage, which is a long-term loan. Alas, failure to pay the instalments on the land may result in the property being claimed back by either the bank or the building society.

Agreements concerning the use of land may be subject to restrictions. These 'covenants' dictate what can or cannot be built on the land being leased, or in some cases bought freehold. An area of increasing concern is that of habitability. All reasonable precautions must be taken to protect people when they are on or near your property. Hence, the growth in signs warning you of a 'slippery surface' or of 'danger overhead work'. Visitors must react correctly to such warnings, and if necessary wear appropriate clothing, e.g. hard hats. A trespasser, however, has to take the property as he finds it. The law does not expect the occupier to safeguard a trespasser's interest. An occupier can sue a trespasser for damages or issue an injunction of restraint, or, with only due force, eject them from the property.

Non-physical property

There are a number of assets owned by a business that cannot be physically measured, these are known as *intangible assets*. Goodwill is one of these assets and occurs when a business is sold. Part of the purchase price includes the probability that part of the previous custom will continue to buy from the new management. As such those buying the business have to pay for the 'goodwill' as part of their bid price.

Trademarks and logos are another type of non-physical asset. They help customer recognition of products and outlets and can be registered and protected by law from others copying them. Just think of the selling power of the 'Coke' bottle.

Patents can also be registered and protected. They cover inventions. An investor (and these include corporate investors' inventions) applies to the Patents Office where experts examine the invention to ascertain its validity. When the validity is established the Crown grants the inventor a patent or monopoly rights. The purpose of this right is to encourage full disclosure of new products and processes by offering protection against 'pirating'. The originator can also maximise his revenue for a guaranteed period. Patents rights can be sold, or another party can be granted a licence which allows it to use the invention.

Copyright is similar to a patent, except that it does not have to be applied for. A composer or writer has a monopoly right for a guaranteed period. As with patents, copyright can be sold or assigned.

The Banking Act 1979

The day-to-day scrutiny of this sector is under the direct control of the Bank of England. The Bank's authority is held in the Bank of England Act of 1946. In addition to this, financial concerns are subject to various other *statutes*, namely the Moneylenders' Acts, the Protection of Depositor Acts, and the Consumer Credit Acts.

Why do we control banks?

- To enforce the control features needed to help the government influence the macro economic targets of its policies, e.g. inflation, unemployment, balance of payments.
- To control the financial institutions that emerged after the 1946 Act.
- To control the 'fringe' institutions, lest they be unstable.
- To monitor the overseas diversification of UK banks.
- To monitor the behaviour of overseas banks operating in the UK.
- EU regulations stipulate that banks must be licensed in order to operate within its boundaries.

Aims of the Act

- To prevent any bank or any other financial institution from accepting deposits from the general public without first obtaining authority to do so from the Bank of England.
- To issue specific criteria with which each finance house has to comply if such authority is to be received and retained.
- To provide the Bank of England with statutory authority to exercise these powers.
- To control the use of bank names and descriptions and limit them to recognised banks.
- To provide financial protection for depositors through the Depositors' Protection Scheme.

Institutions which are excluded

Some financial institutions are excluded from the terms of the Banking Act, mainly on the grounds that they are covered by existing legislation. They include building societies, insurance companies, the Girobank, the National Savings Bank, and the Trustee Savings Bank. There is now growing pressure to re-assess the scope of the Banking Act to include some of the above organisations.

Recognition

Those financial institutions seeking recognition and a licence must satisfy certain criteria set out in the Act. The minimum conditions are that the applicant must satisfy the Bank of England as to its solvency and the competence of its management. In addition, the institution must demonstrate that it provides the general public with a wide range of general or specialised banking services and that it has a *trustworthy* reputation in the financial community.

The five main services required are:
1. acceptance of deposits
2. granting of loans
3. provision of foreign currency
4. provision of bill finance and the handling of documents for foreign trade
5. provision of investment and corporation finance.

Solvency

Since 1979, new deposit takers need to have a minimum amount of capital and reserves before they can obtain recognition or a licence. The minimum figure is £250,000 for a licence and £5 million for a recognition as a bank. All established deposit takers simply have to prove that their resources are adequate for their existing business.

Deposit protection scheme

This is simply a cash fund to which all licensed banks contribute in order to protect the depositors, should one of the banks be unable to meet its obligations. The scope of the scheme as set out in the Act is rather modest compared with similar arrangements in the United States. In the UK, it is intended to protect only small depositors in a recognised institution, by limiting compensation from the fund to 75% of the first £10,000 of any one deposit. Thus, no depositor, however large, will receive more than £7,500. The aim is to protect the general public, but no deposit placed by a bank or licensed deposit taker is protected.

The Companies Act

The Companies Act 1985 is the main statute governing and regulating the promotion and conduct of companies, in both their internal and external relations. This Act also says that public limited companies must have their annual accounts audited by an independent firm of auditors and stipulates the type of information that must be disclosed.

Changing status – private to public company

Under the Companies Act 1985, a public company must be registered as such. For a private company to become public, a general meeting is called, at which special resolutions must be passed:

- resolving that the conversion from one legal form to another be made
- altering the Memorandum of Association, i.e. change of name and statement of being a public company
- making the necessary alterations in the Articles of Association.

Then the following documents are forwarded, with an application, in the prescribed form and signed by a director or secretary, to the Registrar of Companies:

- A printed copy of the Memorandum and Articles, altered as required.
- A copy of the auditors' written statement that they regard the sum of the company's assets to be not less than the aggregate figure for called-up share capital and undistributed reserves shown by the relevant Balance Sheet.
- An unqualified report by the auditors on the relevant balance sheet and a copy of the latter.
- A declaration that the special resolution changing the status has been passed, made in the prescribed form by a director or secretary.
- A declaration, as above, that there has been no major change in the finances of the company causing the net assets to be less than the aggregate figure comprising called-up share capital and undistributed reserves.
- A copy of a report, if applicable, regarding the value of any allotment made for other than cash:
  - between the balance sheet date and the passing of the special resolution and
  - during the six months prior to the allotment.

(This applies to full or part nominal payment or any premium.)

The share capital qualification of £50,000 must be met.

Directors' 'authority to allot'

Directors must have a specific authority from the company authorising issue of shares. The terms of the authority to allot must:

- contain the maximum amount of the relevant securities that may be allotted
- contain the expiry date of the authority, which must be a maximum of five years after the original authority was given, either by resolution or by being contained in the Articles.

The authority may be specific or in the form of a general authority leaving allotments to the discretion of the directors.

Pre-emption rights

Shareholders qualifying

New equity shares must be offered first to existing shareholders. Such pre-emption rights do not apply in the following cases:

1. Where shares allotted are not equity securities.
2. Where shares are not to be paid up fully in cash (cash includes foreign currency).
3. Where shares allotted under an employees' share scheme have been renounced or assigned.
4. Where the Memorandum or Articles of a private company are inconsistent with pre-emption rights.
5. Where the authority to allot so precludes. This could be a general or specific authority. Upon receipt of notice of a special resolution regarding such authority, the Registrar of Companies must publish the same in the Gazette.
6. Where a shareholder has waived his pre-emption rights.

'Equity securities' in this context refers to relevant shares, except bonus shares and subscribers' shares, and any rights to subscribe or convert to relevant shares.

Relevant shares are all the shares of a company except ones that have a limit as to the extent of receipt of distribution of dividend and capital, i.e. preference shares and others that are held for an employees' share scheme. Relevant shares may comprise more than one class.

A class of shares comprises all shares that have equal rights as far as voting and receipt of distribution are concerned.

Terms of the offer

1. Any offer is made to each person who holds relevant shares and must be on the same terms, or better, than the company proposes to apply to an offer to a third party.
2. The offer must be in writing and delivered in accordance with the provisions for serving of notice embodied in Table A (the model Articles of Association given in the 1985 Act). A copy of the offer in the Gazette will suffice for holders of share warrants and those without an address in the UK. Private companies can omit this requirement and the following one.
3. The offer period must be at least 21 days, during which time it may not be withdrawn and before the end of which no shares may be allotted unless each and every offer has been either accepted or refused.
4. The balance of a pre-emption offer to a specific class of shareholder which has been renounced must be made, again on a pre-emption basis, to the other classes holding relevant shares and relevant employee shares.
5. Non-cash payment may be made in certain circumstances. Payment in this way, by money's worth, includes goodwill and know-how. Excluded in money's worth, in the case of public companies, is an undertaking to perform a service or work, either for the company or for a third person.
6. Any non-cash payment must be valued by an independent person sufficiently qualified to be an auditor of the company.

Qualifications of secretary

Directors have a duty to ensure that the secretary of a public company is sufficiently qualified. He/she must fulfil one of the following requirements.

- Be secretary, assistant or deputy of the company on the appointed day.
- Prior to appointment as secretary, have been secretary of a public company for a minimum of three of the past five years.
- Be a member of one of the following professional bodies:
  - Institute of Chartered Accountants
  - Association of Certified Accountants
  - Institute of Chartered Secretaries and Administrators
  - Chartered Institute of Management Accountants
  - Chartered Institute of Public Finance and Accountancy

- Be qualified as a barrister, solicitor or advocate in the UK or be capable of working as a secretary, in the directors' opinion, through experience.

Insider dealings

Those who have been connected in some way with a company at any time during the six months prior to a deal, those who have been involved in a proposed takeover of the company, and others who have obtained information from either of the above groups, are prohibited from dealing in that company's securities. The knowledge necessary to be in breach of the rules must be 'price-sensitive' and unpublished. The 1985 Act covers the abuse of information obtained by position by Crown servants and off-market and Eurobond dealers.

Insider dealing is a criminal offence carrying a maximum penalty of two years' imprisonment and/or a fine.

Provisions for employees on winding-up

Under the 'Directors' duty to employees', provisions may be made for employees, ex-employees and employees of subsidiaries when a company ceases trading, totally or in part. Such provisions need not be in the best interest of the company. The ordinary resolution, to enact the provision, may be implemented by the liquidator.

Quorum

Two members present in person represent a quorum of any company if the Articles do not indicate otherwise.

Polls and oppressed members

1. The number of members present or by proxy who may demand a poll is two (previously it had been three).
2. The 1985 Act greatly increased the rights of members. Any member may apply for a petition if he considers:
   - that the way the company's affairs have been, or are being, handled is resulting in unfairness to him personally and/or some of the members
   - that any act proposed, taken or omitted by the company is against his and/or the other members' interests.

Resolutions

The 1985 Act introduced into Table A new

regulations giving validity to resolutions in writing signed by all the members entitled to vote at general meetings. Such resolutions are as effective as if passed at a properly convened meeting.

Class rights

The classes of shares held as shown on the balance sheet can be varied only with the written consent of 75% in nominal value of the issued shares of the class concerned, or the passing of an extraordinary resolution at a general meeting especially for holders of that class. Class rights may be set out in the Memorandum, but if no clause regarding variation exists in either the Memorandum or the Articles, the unanimous consent of all company members may vary the rights.

Company law and the European Union

The advantages to the UK business of our membership of the European Union (see Chapter 43) are normally agreed to be:

- the size of the market in which to sell domestically produced goods
- the lowering, and in some cases, eradication of tariff barriers (the single market came into existence in 1992) increases the flexibility of capital and labour to use freely around the EU
- the EU has a high proportion of high income earners, and as such represents a high technology market
- the UK can draw on the funds of the EU to help finance infrastructure projects.

In Europe company law differs considerably from one country to another. English law, for example, has forced full disclosure of information and public accountability. German and Dutch law, on the other hand, lay the emphasis on the responsibility of industry to society and insistence on a wide measure of worker participation – which it can be argued has contributed greatly to German industrial harmony. Full political as well as economic unity can be achieved only when company law in each of the member states is harmonised.

Evolution of a European company

Europe faces competition from the giant United States and Japanese multinational companies dealing in advanced technologies. Its response is to create similar enterprises. The European Union therefore intends to introduce a purely European type of company. Such a company will have the same status as any normal company in each member state. The company will be formed from two or more companies of different nationality whose main branches are in different states. Such a company will be registered with the European Court of Justice in Luxemburg. There will be a minimum capital requirement of 25,000 European units of account.

Benefits of adopting EU company law in the UK

1. Because parliamentary time is limited, company law is not often revised and therefore does not keep pace with changing industrial, economic and social realities.
2. The adoption of a common law for the whole of the EU would help British exports to the community.
3. A common law would help further the causes of European political and social integration.

Format and publication of accounts

The rules on the form and content of annual accounts are set out in the First Schedule of the Act, replacing Schedule 8 of the 1948 Act, as amended in 1967 (see Chapters 11, 12 and 13).

Certain types of business are exempt from the prescribed formats – mainly commercial and finance companies such as banks, and insurance and shipping companies.

Company accounts now have to be presented in one of the standard formats set out in the Companies Act (1989). Some items may be combined and shown in note form. The most important changes to format are as follows:

- Profit and Loss Accounts may either show both cost of sales and gross profit in a format most convenient for merchandising companies, or they may detail different types of cost peculiar to manufacturing enterprises (for example materials consumed).
- Debtors and creditors, as shown on the Balance Sheet, must be divided between amounts due in less than one year and in more than one year.
- Balance Sheets must show pensions and other similar provisions. Details must also be given (in note form) of pension commitments (and other obligations) for which the company has, as at the date of the balance sheet, made no provisions.
- Balance Sheet notes must provide details of the nature of any security given to a secured creditor. (Previous legislation required only details of the liability secured.)
- Loans made to employees to help them buy company shares must also be disclosed.

Full and abridged accounts

Where a company publishes full individual or group accounts, it must also publish the auditors' reports. Where a company publishes abridged accounts only, these must be accompanied by a statement saying:

- that they are not full accounts
- whether or not full accounts have been sent to the Registrar of Companies
- whether or not the auditor has made a report and whether this is an unqualified one.

Specific provisions for accounting disclosure

Balance Sheets must show information in one of two permitted formats; Profit and Loss Accounts must show information in one of four permitted formats. Once the company has decided on one of the formats, it must stick to it.

The following items must not be treated as assets:

- preliminary expenses
- expenses/commission on issues of shares or debentures
- costs of research and development.

In all cases, comparative figures for the previous financial year must be shown. Accounting principles must be consistent one year with another. Powers of 'setting off' are limited: assets or income items must not be set off against liabilities or expenditure.

Only profits actually realised at the date of the Balance Sheet may be included in the Profit and Loss Account. Liabilities or losses that have arisen or are likely to arise in the financial year or previous financial year must be taken into account. All income and charges relating to the financial year must be taken into account, regardless of their date of receipt or payment.

In the case of fixed assets having a limited economic life, the cost price must be shown and the assets systematically depreciated over their lives. Goodwill must be treated as an asset. It must be depreciated over its life and a note attached to the balance sheet stating the method of depreciation used, the period of life for the goodwill, and why this length of time has been chosen.

Other items of disclosure include:

- Details of indebtedness, repayments of loans, etc., on instalment plans exceeding five years.
- Turnover, by class of business.
- Guarantors.
- Particulars of staff employed, i.e. average number employed (by category of employee) wages and salaries, social security costs and pension costs.

Directors' report

Section 15 of the 1985 Act consolidated the 1967 Companies Act, requiring the auditors to check the consistency of Directors' Reports with the trends and information in the company accounts. Inconsistencies must be highlighted in the auditors' reports. Auditors must check that the Directors' Report contains a fair review of the development of the company and its subsidiaries during the financial year.

Under current legislation, the Directors' Report has to contain:

- The names of all persons who were directors of the company at the end of the financial year.
- Details of the main company activities during the year.
- Details of the company's subsidiaries.
- All relevant and significant changes which have occurred in the activities of the company and its subsidiaries during the current year.
- All details of changes in the company's fixed assets, together with details of stock and debenture interests.
- Details of all contracts made in which the firm's directors had a material interest, including the names of all parties to the contract, the nature of the contract, and the nature of the directors' interests in it.
- Generally, full information showing the financial interest of the directors in the company and its subsidiaries.

Additional information required by the 1985 Act includes:

- particulars of important events since the end of the year
- indications of likely future events
- activities in research and development.

The Directors' Report must also give details of their acquisition of the company's shares. Details which may now be given in note form appended to the Balance Sheet include the issue of debentures, analysis of profit and turnover by business or market, staff numbers and cost.

Directors' emoluments

Disclosure provisions in company accounts are as follows:

- All money received by directors, including former directors of a company, in respect of emoluments, pensions and compensation payments in respect of services to the company must be declared.
- Emoluments of the chairman must be declared,

unless his duties were performed wholly outside the United Kingdom.

- Emoluments of the highest paid directors must be declared, if these sums were greater than the chairman's emoluments and if the duties of the senior directors were wholly within the UK.
- The number of directors other than those working wholly abroad, who earned emoluments up to £50,000, between £5,000 and £10,000, and so on in bands of £10,000, must all be declared.
- The number of directors who have waived their emoluments, and the total amount so waived, must be declared.

Companies are entitled to ask for this information from the directors themselves, if it is not in the company's books of account, and auditors are required to note its absence from company records in their report.

Details of the emoluments of other senior employees working in the UK are also required.

Consolidated accounts need only show the above information for the directors and senior executives of holding companies.

Company shares

Purchase by a company of its own shares was declared unlawful as far back as 1887 (House of Lords – Trevor vs Whitworth). The Companies Act 1929 introduced the redeemable preference share. The 1981 Act legalised the provision that (with some exceptions) no limited company should acquire its own shares, whether by purchase, subscription or other means.

A company will not be able to purchase its own shares if, as a result of the purchase, there will no longer be any member of the company holding shares other than redeemable shares. A public company may redeem or purchase its own shares out of profits or the proceeds of a fresh issue provided:

- the company runs a capital redemption reserve fund to ensure maintenance of capital
- it fully declares its dealings.

Private companies are allowed to purchase their own shares out of capital if profits are insufficient to do this, provided the directors make a declaration certifying the company's solvency, and this is attached to the authors' report.

These regulations merely bring British companies into line with common practice in the USA and EU.

Complex rules have been evolved to cover an individual interest in company shares. These rules apply to public companies. Basically, an individual must notify a company when he has obtained a substantial interest in that company's voting shares. Any person owing 3% or more of the voting shares must notify the company, and any increase or decrease by 1% must also be notified. Disclosure also applies to individual shares as a joint venture.

Share premium account – mergers and reconstructions

Under the Companies Act 1985 companies have to introduce a share premium account whenever shares are issued at a premium.

Business names

When a business is conducted under a name other than the owner's, the Act requires disclosure of the following information:

- in a partnership the names of each partner
- the name of the individual owner (sole trader)
- for a company, its corporate name.

Each person named must also supply an address in the United Kingdom to which business correspondence and documents can be sent. All this information has to be displayed on the business premises.

The Act also prohibits the use of certain names (mainly names of existing companies and those likely to cause offence). The Registrar of Companies has to maintain an index of business names currently in use. If the Registrar feels that a name is undesirable or against the public interest, the company can be forced to change it.

It is difficult to see the real impact of these changes. First, they make it no easier for members of the public to register complaints with the real owners of a company. Secondly, the detailed clauses of the Act make it plain that, in this respect, the private sector is expected to police itself.

The Companies Act 1981 repealed the Registration of Business Names Act 1916. The Secretary of State has the power to order a company to change its name, and the Registrar of Companies also maintains a list of foreign companies operating in the United Kingdom.

Miscellaneous and supplementary provisions

1. *Treatment of development costs.* Such costs, shown as an asset, must be set off against profits and treated as a realised revenue loss.
2. *Directorships of companies (disqualification).*

Directors of companies which have become insolvent may not act as liquidators.

The Registrar of Companies now requires details of all directorships held within the last five years.

Grounds for disqualifying a person from managing a company's affairs were extended. The maximum period of disqualification is now 15 years.

Department of trade investigators

Inspectors from the DTI were given greater powers of investigation, and greater discretion as to when to circulate their findings.

Data Protection Act 1985

Current business law attempts to force companies and powerful corporations to disclose information; it also attempts to protect individuals from the undesirable consequences of advances in information technology and to protect individual privacy.

The Data Protection Act 1985 came into force in April 1986, and caused employers with personal information stored on computer files (the majority of companies) both to devise an organisation to deal with the implementation of the new Act and to work out agreed procedures to comply with its terms.

The new piece of legislation was in response to the proliferation and widespread communication of essentially private and often intimate information about people, without either their knowledge or consent, which has become a feature of societies linked by computer networks. Low priced, high powered computers can store and transmit vast amounts of information between companies and private computer users, entirely without the knowledge of the individual affected.

This trend has been accelerated by the growth in personal credit business and hence the need for firms to check on creditworthiness before they consent to grant loans. It is therefore the purpose of the Act to regulate and protect individuals from unwarranted and unlawful intrusions into their privacy by making it a legal requirement that all computer-stored information of a personal nature is known and can be checked by the individual concerned.

Main points of the legislation

The essential points of the new legislation are these:

1. The Act is aimed primarily at personnel records stored on computer file; manual information systems are not affected by the regulations.
2. The Act covers only 'personal data', which is defined as 'information which relates to a living individual who can be identified from that information or from other processes of the data user, including any expression of opinion about the individual'; hence records of job interviews, training assessments, the proceedings of promotion boards and disciplinary hearings are all covered by the Act if the information is on computer record.
3. The Act covers all the standard information usually found in the company's personnel records, such as:
    –   age and marital status
    –   salary
    –   union membership and other affiliations
    –   race, sex and religion
    –   performance appraisal.

The Act covers not only present employees of the company but former employees, and job applicants, and extends to companies who may provide computer bureau services for subsidiary companies.

Protection afforded by the Act

The Act places an obligation on companies and individual employees of the company:

*   to obtain and process personal data fairly and lawfully
*   to hold the data for a lawful purpose only
*   not to disclose that data for an unlawful purpose
*   not to hold data which is irrelevant or in excess
*   to ensure that data is accurate and kept up to date.

Individuals are entitled to:

*   be informed of any data user who holds personal data of which the individual is the subject
*   have access to any such data
*   have such data corrected or erased, where appropriate.

Appropriate security measures have to be taken against unauthorised access to, alteration, or disclosure of, personal data and against accidental loss or destruction of personal data.

Registration

These principles are enforced through a system of compulsory registration of data users and computer bureaux, supervised by the Data Protection Registrar. The Registrar is granted the power to refuse applications for registration on the grounds that the applicant is 'likely to contravene any of the data protection principles', and he has the power to close down all the data user's computer operations.

The unregistered processing of personal data is a criminal offence, punishable by an unlimited fine.

Civil action by the individual

Some of the new legal provisions, such as the right of subject access, are enforceable by the individual taking action in the normal courts. An individual employee who suffers damage as a result of data being inaccurate may bring a civil claim for compensation. The same possibility arises when an employee suffers damages as a result of the loss, or unauthorised destruction or disclosure, of personal information.

Action by firms

The individual firm now has to decide how much data and what type of information to store regarding its employees. The Registrar's guidance notes include:

- recruitment, recording work time
- the administration and payment of wages, salaries, pensions and other benefits, including a record of deductions
- employee assessment and training
- negotiation details and formal communications with employees
- manpower and career planning
- compliance with company policy
- health and safety matters
- data required to be gleaned by management for statutory returns.

Firms must also decide who in the organisation is to have overall responsibility for implementing the Act (this would probably devolve upon a data coordinator or data coordinating committee) and the methods to be adopted to inform their employees of their rights under this legislation.

Accuracy of data

Personal data must be accurate and kept up to date. Failure to meet this requirement could lead to a compensation claim under Section 22 of the Act and also a claim for rectification or erasure of the inaccurate information (Section 24). Much of the information supplied to management will have been given by the employees themselves, and they must be given an opportunity to check that such information has been entered accurately into the system. Here the onus for the accuracy of the information will rest largely with the employee. The employer can provide a print-out of information immediately it is entered into the system, or the information can be circulated to all staff at regular intervals. Whichever method is adopted, the information must be kept up to date.

Defence against inaccurate claims

Two statutory defences are possible against a charge of inaccuracy in the records:

1. that the source of the information (i.e. the employee) checked the accuracy at the time of entry into the system
2. that information supplied by a third party (for example a former employer, or credit agency) was not disputed by the individual concerned before entry into the computer system (an alternative form of this defence would be for the firm to show that it had taken all reasonable care in collecting and entering the information).

Subject access

Since November 1987, employees have had the right to see all information held about them on the firm's computer files. They also have the right to have inaccurate data corrected or erased and to claim compensation if they suffer loss or even distress as a result of an inaccurate statement.

The Act suggests that:

- Employees make a written request for access, which is to be met within 40 days.
- Firms may charge a fee before granting access.
- Firms can insist on proof of identification before granting access.

It is possible for a firm to refuse access to protect the identification of a third party (for example a job referee).

Formal written policies on data protection

Firms have to formulate written policies on data protection. These statements should cover:

- The information to be collected about employees, and the reasons for collecting it.
- The measures to be taken to protect employees' privacy and data security.
- The policy and procedure on subject access.
- The policy and procedure on external disclosure.
- Enforcement of the policy.

The social impact of new industrial processes

Resistance to change

Over the past few years, firms have been forced, by rising labour costs and the scientific advances made in automation, to introduce new technology on a vast scale into their manufacturing enterprises.

Opposition to the introduction of new technology is therefore found in industry changing from labour-intensive methods of production to capital intensive, low-cost methods of work.

The primary fear is that large sectors of the work force will be made redundant and lose their jobs, thus forfeiting not only pay, but also future security and status in the community. Old skills, often gained through long periods of apprenticeship, are made obsolete – sometimes quite quickly – by the introduction of new technology. It is not always possible for the firm to train unskilled or semi-skilled workers in new methods, even if these categories of workers would be willing to learn. Furthermore, worthwhile training schemes have been very sparse in Britain – many still mistrust the government's initiatives in this respect and there is a lack of labour mobility, particularly among older workers.

Even when it is possible to redeploy redundant labour, workers tend to fear such changes. Working groups will be split up and social relationships which often extend beyond work will be altered and possibly destroyed.

On the other hand, there are signs that as the older workers start to integrate, the acceptance of change becomes easier and response to it more objective and positive. This dimension of the problem will be discussed in some detail later, but a number of general points can be noted.

The hold of trade unions over their workers in blue-collar industries is beginning to break down. General public opinion appears not to favour militant union power.

Massive schemes of practical training as distinct from academic learning will have been introduced in schools and colleges and will, through the Training Commission, have practical on-going links with local industries. A further factor to consider is that change involves capital outlay. Labour redundancy is often decided by senior management in an atmosphere of secrecy (usually so that competitors are not aware of their rival's market opportunities) and without fully consulting trade union representatives. Secrecy is maintained and this can lead to tension.

The long wave theory of industrial decay and rejuvenation

Over recent years a number of economists and historians have attempted to provide a general explanation and a theoretical base for the fundamental change in our industrial and social structure. Three economists in particular (Joseph Schumpeter, Gerhard Mensch and Nicolai Kondratiev) have at various times throughout their writings suggested a general explanation based largely on historical evidence. In essence, these writers argue that what we experienced in the 1980s was essentially not new – it was in fact the type of change which accompanies all transitions from one type of predominant technology to a new technology, and has been repeated several times in the course of recent history.

It must also be remembered that the introduction of new technology benefits management and the company shareholders sooner than it benefits the workers. Indeed, in the short-run, those workers who remain after new technology has been introduced, while gaining job security and high wages, also often experience a period of psychological demoralisation because the old social relationships and status at work have been destroyed.

Traditional view of the impact of new technology

The traditional view is that the introduction of technology:

- invariably destroys jobs
- de-skills large sectors of the traditional work force.

Research into the impact of extensive new technology in the area of financial services challenges this view even when the computer can perform tasks 100 million times faster than human operators.

Precise impact of new technology

Researchers find that the precise impact of new technology will depend upon the nature of economic, social and organisational 'moderators', a moderator being defined as a process which prevents, or slows down, job losses or de-skilling in a particular industry or firm.

Economic moderators

Conventional wisdom suggests that the impact of new technology on employment depends upon the relative influence of two factors:

- The need to have specialised personnel to work the new technology.
- The loss of existing manpower.

But research indicates that far more important than these factors in deciding levels of a firm's or industry's employment use are:

- The ability of the new technology to create new products or services.
- The ability of the new technology to lower the costs of producing existing products or services.
- The contribution of the new technology in enhancing the appeal of products or services.

If the continued effect of the new technology is to stimulate consumer demand, jobs will not be lost.

The innovative cycle

Schumpeter explains the typical pattern of recession and slow recovery by making a distinction between 'invention' and 'innovation'. Each major downturn of the economic spiral appears to be marked by a proliferation of scientific discovery and invention – and this is true of all the four cycles of technology previously discussed. These inventions then lie dormant for a time and are commercially developed and applied only during the upward swing in the wave.

It is the wave of economic slump and renewal growth which Schumpeter argues provides the fundamental dynamic force of capitalist economies. As each wave of innovation progresses, the market for typical products of the predominant technology becomes saturated, leading to falling profits and rising unemployment.

Gerhard Mensch has taken the idea further. He argues that though inventions may occur at any time, the really significant ones for the development of new products, industries or new processes tend to occur over relatively short periods, one after another, and tend to have a 'knock-on' effect on each other. In the past, important inventions which quickly led to commercial innovation occurred in 1709 (iron smelting by the use of coke), 1825 (the steam locomotive), 1856 (the Bessemer process of steelmaking) and 1938 (nuclear fission of uranium). All occurred in the middle of depressions and were responsible for major uplifts in the economy some 10–20 years later. Something very similar has been happening during the past decade in biotechnology, genetic engineering, electronics and micropro-cessing.

How do firms meet social responsibilities?

The business activities of firms impinge on a number of groups, commonly referred to as the internal and external stake holders of the enterprise, which include:

- *Internal stake holders* – stock and debenture holders, managers, employees.
- *External stake holders* – customers, pressure groups (e.g. Friends of the Earth, Greenpeace), animal rights groups, the local community, etc.

Responsibilities to internal stake holders will usually be met by attention to long-term profit and increased market share objectives – the traditional objectives of business. Discharging responsibilities to the second group will tend to raise costs and hence reduce profit. This conflict will usually be resolved by compromise, formal systems of environmental and social policy analysis and contingency planning by the enterprise.

A firm might discharge its responsibilities to the local community and other groups by, for example, building a new factory on derelict land rather than on a 'greenfield' site and by taking special measures to limit air pollution. This decision might raise costs in the short run, but it avoids the hidden costs of local resident opposition (the hidden costs might include payment for a public enquiry, delay in construction, obstruction by local residents, damaging publicity in the press and on TV).

A firm may also have such responsibilities to customers, for example to produce goods which more than meet health and safety requirements. Here the extra cost involved can be recouped by featuring social responsibility messages in marketing and advertising campaigns which feature the extra safety measures. You will no doubt be familiar with many of the TV advertisements for new car models, which emphasise various improved safety devices. This is a relatively new feature of car industry marketing strategy. Note, too that this type of socially responsible policy is good long-term business – safety is important to a particular market segment and the size of that target group is growing.

Impact on policy planning

Many firms now consider it prudent to analyse the social impact of their corporate plans by studying such areas as health and safety, advertising, safety of products and environmentally sound products and processes. Social responsibilities can extend to providing local amenities such as sports centres and children's play areas. Alternatively they may involve the provision of cultural facilities. Sainsbury's has, for example, endowed the city of Norwich with an art gallery (the Sainsbury Centre for Visual Arts) sited at the University of East Anglia. Notice once again that the endowment advertises the name of the retail chain.

Social responsibility might also extend to the training of employees and the use of local suppliers.

Problems

The pursuit of such policies, no matter how worthy and socially desirable, does present difficulties, given the limited resources available to businesses. Trade-offs have to exist between what is good for society and what is good for the business. A firm might be able to manufacture ecologically sound products and packaging but at the expense of installing specialised machines and making workers redundant. Too much concern for social responsibility can lead to competitive disadvantage, particularly in international trade.

As we have already indicated, social responsibility programmes may increase costs; training local unemployed people can be more expensive than retraining existing workers or importing skilled labour. Location on a derelict site will be more expensive than building on a tailor-made site because of the expense of clearing and treating the site, the cost of providing staff amenities and improving communications.

Why meet social responsibilities?

It has already been noted that to meet social responsibilities raises costs; this may bring the Board of Directors into conflict with their shareholders, who want to maximise profits to earn dividends. It may also bring them into conflict with employees who want job security and higher wages.

Social responsibility can enhance the public image of a company and is often used for this purpose. At the very least firms may wish to avoid damaging publicity resulting from their own damage of the environment. Such policies could also improve industrial relations and their long-term sales, or the bases of their sales literature and advertising campaigns.

The social implications of business

Business and the environment

Managing the business so as to minimise damage to the environment is now of crucial importance, particularly for industries such as oil, chemicals and nuclear power. Failure to do so can have global effects, involve the firms within the industry in billions of pounds worth of compensation and cause permanent damage to customer relations and future sales. Also, do not forget the impact on the insurance markets of environmental catastrophes, such as oil spillage from inadequate sea tankers.

Many industries at risk from the consequences of environmental catastrophes have now begun to make detailed contingency plans on the basis of 'what if....', so they have a structure and response centre ready at hand if something unexpected occurs. These centres are now permanently manned by specialist staff trained to deal with the media, government and press.

The public concern given to environmental issues has forced business to take the issues seriously. Firms have also become aware of the need to react positively to the demands of 'green consumerism', i.e. demand from consumers for 'greener' products. Again note how a potential threat from the changing environment can be turned to an opportunity by responding to these changes. Firms can gain new market segments and market innovative products and packaging as part of their promotional effort.

Pollution as a world problem

The problems associated with the social costs of pollution cannot sensibly be discussed in terms of the UK alone. One country's waste is another country's pollution problem. Mercury dumped into the sea on the Pacific coast of the United States kills the fish population off the coast of Japan.

Ministers from all the European industrial nations have met to consider pollution problems in an international context and to establish areas of cooperation. The major problems currently worrying world statesmen are:

- an increasing amount of air pollution by chemical fumes
- an increase in pollution likely to be produced by the burning of coal
- the increase in tourist traffic, particularly as it affects congested areas such as the Mediterranean coast and the Adriatic coast
- the uncoordinated regulations of national legislation dealing with pollution, together with a lack of scientific information.

As industry expands and urbanisation spreads there is an increasing demand for fresh water (for domestic use, irrigation and industrial cooling). Levels of oxygen in rivers, lakes and reservoirs have tended to remain stable, but this is probably due to industrial recession, rather than the adoption of better waste disposal systems or of technologies which create the minimum pollution. Biological pollution of fresh water is therefore likely to rise as economic growth increases.

Metal and chemical pollution of water has increased (particularly from phosphate and nitrogen sources). This is due to the extensive use of fertilisers and washing detergents. The main effects of this type of pollution are the choking of waterways by fast growing weeds feeding on the chemicals, the proliferation of poisonous algae and the destruction of the fish population through lack of oxygen and sunlight. The quality of drinking water is also affected. Europe lacks widespread and practical control over this form of pollution.

Business ethics

Ethics can be defined as 'a code of morally correct behaviour relating to individuals, groups and professional conduct'. This code of behaviour suggests what a business should and should not do in particular circumstances. But a moral code has to be applied in particular circumstances by particular individuals, whose code of conduct has been fashioned by education, experience, upbringing, parental influence and peer group pressure. What is right or wrong will vary from one situation to another. A consideration of ethics in business will therefore raise a number of issues to which there is no absolute right answer. In each situation you must draw your own conclusions. What is required of you is to be able to state clearly both sides of an issue and to come to a conclusion with reasons to back that conclusion.

Ethical issues crop up in a variety of business situations. Examples include the sale of weapons to Iraq and the promotion and sale of tobacco products targeted at young women and consumers in the Third World, when most of the medical profession believes that such products cause premature death by cancer and heart disease.

The actions of a small minority of businesses are plainly criminal. Two examples include the fraud associated with the collapse of the Bank of Credit and Commercial International (BCCI). Over 120,000 account holders lost their deposits amounting to £250,000,000 in total. The Maxwell newspaper empire defrauded thousands of employees of their pensions.

Advertising ethics

Advertising has been criticised on ethical grounds for stimulating a desire for goods and services which many consumers cannot afford, do not really want, but purchase because of high pressure sale techniques (see Chapter 19). Many advertisements encourage people to keep buying goods which are addictive and harmful to health. Is it morally right that people on low incomes in times of high unemployment should be induced to buy on credit? Is it morally defensible that images of women should be used to sell cars or other commodities? Do not these images turn women themselves into objects?

Defenders of advertising point to the essential job of informing the public of new products; that advertising stimulates competition and therefore either reduces prices or at least keeps them stable. To these arguments could be added the fact that advertising stimulates mass consumption and therefore mass production, which maintains high levels of employment and a rising standard of living generally. It also encourages research and development.

Critics tend to attack advertising on ethical grounds, whereas business tends to counter with commercial arguments. Do commercial factors fully answer the accusation of a moral wrong?

Ethics are good for business

Dubious moral practice is bad for business in the long run; it is in the first place newsworthy, and bad publicity very quickly reaches every home via TV and newspapers. The overwhelming evidence is that businesses which practice dubious ethics will lose customers. Many firms recognise this and formulate their mission statement to include an ethical clause; they then go on to advertise and publicise the ethical conduct of the organisation, so helping to retain the market share of customer groups who are particularly ethically conscious.

Britain has been a more or less homogeneous society since the beginning of the eighteenth century. The truth of this generalisation can be gauged if you consider the diversity of religion, social class, political belief and racial composition which is apparent throughout France, Germany, Belgium and North America. This, of course, is not to argue that factors of diversity and division do not exist and in recent years have been growing steadily. The rise in immigrant population, ethnic discontent, the growth of regional poverty and unemployment among the young, the civil war in Northern Ireland – all are factors of potential conflict and even destruction in British national life. There are also deep economic and social divisions between North and South.

Changes in the distribution of population

The growth of new computer industries is slowly beginning to change the distribution of population. Recently the UK has experienced other major demographic changes associated with the decline of traditional industries in the old industrial centres (Liverpool, Birmingham and the North East) and a relative growth of light, small-scale industry, utilising new technology, located along the Thames Valley from London to Bristol and in East Anglia. The centre of the country has therefore tended to become depopulated, while population and business opportunity grow in the south and east of England.

A fairly recent development in modern Britain is an increasing tendency for populations to become more dispersed away from the central city area, spreading out into suburbs and spreading urban life as they move. This social factor has been accelerated by:

- car ownership
- the spread of public transport
- the spread of private property ownership
- the development of new towns, associated with new industries based on advanced technology, in many cases linked to universities of high technology.

The general consequences of this trend are:
- Growth of small scale capital-intensive industry outside the traditional areas of industrial and commercial activity.
- Increasing mobility of the relatively well-qualified middle class towards these new centres of work and economic opportunity.
- Decline of the areas being vacated in favour of new industrial locations.

General effects of social trends

The effects of these social trends upon the general life of the country can be summarised as follows:

- Continual growth of large-scale retail and wholesale outlets for goods and services, together with the growth of local community supermarkets.
- Continual expansion of the convenience foods and consumer durable goods market, particularly as the number of households in every socio-economic class owning fridges, washing machines, freezers, etc. is steadily increasing year by year.
- Those without cars (for example poorly paid manual workers, the aged and infirm) become more isolated and are unable to enjoy the amenities of the country.

- Pollution tends to increase.
- There are often conflicts between the requirements of people living in towns and the requirements of the car which they own.

A further feature of British society is the historical predominance of London politically, socially, administratively and culturally. The dominance of the capital city has tended to produce a national press and news service which overshadows local means of communication far more than is apparent in such countries as France and the United States. The spread of television reinforces this, just as it is increasing the influence of the city in most European countries.

In some important respects, recent economic and social developments have tended to weaken the traditional dominance of the centre and the south. These developments include:

1. Exploitation of North Sea oil and gas deposits, which, while they last, direct investment towards Scotland.
2. Growth of nationalist movements demanding more freedom from the central decision-making of Parliament, though this varies greatly in intensity and in the numbers of followers.
3. Influence of immigrants from Commonwealth countries, which has introduced a racial element into some areas of British life, particularly in communities where the social investment in terms of housing, education and amenities is inadequate to cope with overcrowding.

Governments are therefore faced with a dilemma; do they invest public money to bolster declining communities, or do they place investment in areas of new industry? Recently governments have tended to allow purely market forces to decide where public money should be invested, in the belief that long-term growth can come about only through new enterprise often based in new locations.

Rationalisation of agriculture

Another major feature of British society is the absence of an independent and isolated rural class of the type which has, until recently, wielded political and economic power in France, Germany and Italy.

The economic and social pattern

Employment and prosperity

In 1989, the total civilian labour force had reached 27.2 million. That there was an overall increase of

2.3 million between 1971 and 1987 is almost entirely attributable to an increase in the number of women entering the labour force.

The number of people employed in manufacturing fell sharply during the period 1989–91 and continues to fall at an accelerating rate as Britain's manufacturing base declines. Those employed in clerical, secretarial, sales and craft work remain relatively static. The numbers employed in managerial, entrepreneurial and professional work rose dramatically during the period 1987–91. Less than 2% are employed in agriculture and related occupations.

You will already have noted too the tendency for industrial societies to spend less on basic foodstuffs. Increase in expenditure over recent years in Britain has been on travel, housing, alcohol and recreation and entertainment, patterns of expenditure typical of societies enjoying a relatively high standard of living. Since 1972, the British people have also been willing to spend considerable sums of money on foreign foods and to spend more of their money on eating out.

Leisure trends

Almost the whole of the working population has enjoyed more free time than ever before. A steady fall in average working hours, down to 38.2 hours for male full-time employees by 1987, and increasing holiday entitlement (95% of full-time manual employees now get four weeks or more) have given people more time to spend at home and at leisure.

Despite the increase in incomes and an increase in leisure facilities, holidays are spent mainly at home or with a relative. Cheap holidays like camping and caravanning are also popular with a substantial proportion of the population. Since the 1960s, many people have tended to spend their holidays abroad, particularly in Spain.

Leisure pursuits in general are largely determined by age, sex, education and access to either a car or public transport. According to the general household survey, the three most important leisure activities apart from holidays, are watching television, going to the pub, and gardening.

Recent social surveys indicate that over 90% of all British households have a television. This medium of communication is therefore likely to remain the principal means of advertising and marketing goods and services.

Social attitudes

The structure of work

Advanced industrial societies such as Britain appear to be at a crossroads. Is our future to be determined by automated and computerised technology, or are we entering an age of rapid industrial decline, mass unemployment and inflation?

In Britain, most work is based on our industrial structure, whereby goods are mass produced by power-operated machines in factories. Industrialisation has led to the growth of cities, mass communication and a complex transport network.

Britain's industrialisation is capitalist based, i.e. each individual firm competes with others for a share of the market. The main stimulus to economic activity is therefore the ability to make a profit in the long run, which depends on the firm's ability to stimulate demand and to satisfy it. Buoyant demand and rising profits attract further investment. The system has a number of considerable advantages over a formal centralised economy:

- Resources are attracted to enterprises where they can grow.
- The variety of goods is vastly increased.
- Productivity is increased.
- Adjustments to the basic system allow a broad section of workers to participate, through investment schemes, in the general prosperity of the system.

The main drawbacks of the system are that enterprises which are desirable for other than economic grounds tend to be pushed into the background; and resources are not equally shared out in society – hence the problem of poverty and deprivation.

It is largely for these reasons that most Western societies have evolved a 'mixed economy', in which some areas of the economy belong to the government and others are individually owned. In addition, some are large corporations controlled by groups of managers on behalf of owners who may be foreign. The multinational Ford Motor Company, for example, is US owned. Its wage bill alone approaches the size of the Irish Republic's gross national product.

As we have already seen, primary production and secondary occupations are beginning to decline in importance in favour of service industries and this is a pattern of development typical of every advanced industrial nation.

The meaning of work

In our society, unlike primitive communities, work is a highly specialised activity marked off from other activities in time and space, i.e. work is undertaken for a specific period usually in a place away from the home.

Again, as we have seen, modern computer technology is beginning to change this pattern of activity, once so typical of a heavy industrial society.

Work is primarily a social activity and is essentially based on cooperation. When a person takes a job he adopts a particular work role, i.e. a social position to which are attached socially shared expectations. People quickly become attached to such roles as part of their self-identity and social status. Work is therefore a vital part of socialisation, the process by which the individual learns social norms, values and expected behaviour. It is for these reasons that to lose work or not to be able to gain an occupation is so traumatic for the individual concerned and also for those who know him, for they have no reference point to judge his conduct or behaviour; he is literally an outcast from a work-orientated society.

Nevertheless, it is a common observation that many people are highly dissatisfied with their jobs, particularly workers on modern assembly lines. The machines set the pace of work, and tasks are repetitive and require little skill. As we have already argued, the introduction of the computer and semi-automated system is beginning to reduce the monotony and the repetitive element of jobs in many areas of assembly line work.

A study commissioned by the Department of Employment and published in 1983 shows clearly how physical health can be impaired by repetitive work. The Stress Research Unit at Nottingham University looked at the way in which newcomers to routine jobs can be affected by setting up a simulated button-sorting production line. Apart from general changes in mood, and predictable effects like backache and neckache, the researchers found changes in blood glucose measures, saliva and heart activity.

There have been many attempts to make industrial work more satisfying:

- The 'cell' system of organising workers into small groups to carry out complex operations working as a team at their own pace and using a variety of machines is used in the Philips radio plant in Holland, but it is a costly change to make and it is questionable whether it is worth attempting as automotive systems become more flexible and versatile.
- Job rotation schemes mean people are trained for a variety of tasks; each group chooses its own leader and has amenities close to its work area. The central idea here is that the machines serve the people, not vice versa.
- The four-day week has been tried in the United

States, and experiments are being conducted in Britain, and other countries. Generally, workers seem more enthusiastic and hard working under this scheme, but it is not suited to some types of industrial work. Flexitime, where people work their own hours round a 'core day', has been far more successful in the UK. Nevertheless, as automation becomes more widespread, it ought to be possible to reduce hours of work and increase productivity at the same time.

The future of work

During the 1990s, the trend towards automation in manufacturing and service industries will gain momentum. Computers can control and coordinate the whole production process and much of the distribution. Only a few operatives are required to service and maintain such machines. The advantages are obvious:

- increased production
- greater leisure time
- the elimination of repetitive work.

Some of the technological changes already being introduced into advanced industrial societies include:

- Shopping by TV through the use of a bank account number fed through the computer telephone channels.
- People working from home rather than going to the office.
- Self-education by means of video-cassettes.
- Diagnosis of illness by the use of a computer rather than a doctor (already in operation in many large hospitals).

The impact of this type of revolution will be greatest in those areas where high levels of skill and training are normally required. On the other hand, jobs such as waitressing and cleaning are likely to be immune from the influence of the computer.

British Social Attitude survey

This is a survey of social attitudes is compiled each year. Some of the major results, comparing social attitudes in Britain with those in the United States, Australia and the EU countries, can be summarised as follows.

The social attitudes of the British conform more closely to social attitudes found in the EU, particularly to attitudes in West Germany, than to attitudes usually associated with the average American or Australian.

The desire in Britain to maintain important

elements of the welfare state, i.e. state education and the National Health Service, across a range of social classes, rather than to embrace a full-blown capitalist economy.

Effects of social change on markets and business decisions

It is of course impossible to predict with accuracy the effect of social change on business in general but the very broad effects would appear to be:

- An increase in emphasis on marketing and advertising of goods and services specially designed to attract the working woman; these are likely to be in the areas of convenience foods, consumer durables, banking, insurance and mortgage services.
- Increased real earnings, provided they are not hit by new tides of inflationary pressure, are likely to stimulate the demand for consumer goods, more foreign foods, leisure activities and holidays abroad. Sales of foodstuffs in general are likely to decrease as a percentage of the whole.
- The growth of automation will in the long run create new professions in the service sectors of the economy, which will increase demand for more sophisticated computer hardware and computer-based machines. In the short run there is likely to be very high structural unemployment and the further decline of old industrial areas until society can adapt to the new forms of technology.
- Severe economic imbalance between the North of England and the more prosperous South and Midlands is likely to continue.

Markets overseas

Social changes in Britain, which have also been a feature of other industrial nations, have altered significantly the pattern of Britain's overseas trade. Britain relies upon the importation by other countries of almost all its products: machinery, commercial vehicles, electronic apparatus of all kinds, chemicals and textiles.

Notice that most British exports are relatively sophisticated products of advanced industrial development, together with the products of the service sectors of the economy (banking, insurance and investment services). Most of Britain's trade, both import and export, is with the developed areas of the European Union, with oil and minerals forming the most important commodities of trade with the underdeveloped world.

Generally, in recent years there has been a slight downward trend in the importation of foodstuffs and primary raw materials and an increase of trade (both imports and exports) in manufactured goods and services. As with other advanced nations there has been a significant rise in recent years in the importation of semi-finished goods for re-export.

There has been a change in the pattern of British exports over recent years – the slowing down of exports to the developed areas of Europe and a very sharp increase in exports to the Arab nations. There are several reasons for this development:

1. The huge surplus earned by the Arab nations owing to their oil exports.
2. The determination on the part of Arab nations to develop their economies in preparation for the time when their oil supplies begin to decline and oil supplies in other parts of the world increase.

A further factor to upset present trade patterns will be the growing material expectations and reconstruction needs of Eastern Europe and Russia.

SUMMARY

Having studied this chapter, you should be able to:

▽ Describe the basic economic issues that concern business.

▽ Explain the impact of government legislation on business.

▽ Discuss all the legal requirements a business has to fulfil.

▽ Describe the impact of business decisions on individuals, society, the environment and the way the future evolves.

Questions and activities

Technical terms and glossary

In the section below you are given a series of technical terms and their meanings. They have been scrambled. You must match up the terms and the definitions. When you have them correctly paired, transfer them to your alphabetical vocabulary or glossary book.

You are also advised to transfer any definitions obtained during the exercises in the case studies into this glossary book.

Technical terms

1. A potential monopolist and liable for referral to MMC.
2. An important part of the Japanese business expansion.
3. De-industrialisation or reduction in industrial base.
4. Increased specialisation of labour.
5. Insider dealing.
6. A central condition of the Single European Act.

Definitions

A. Changes in the labour market whereby workers need to be capable of working more complicated technology.
B. A company which controls 25% or more of a specific market.
C. Decisions are now made by the majority and need not be unanimous.
D. The establishment of forward bases as spring boards into the high technology markets of the future.
E. The use of confidential information to enable an individual to purchase shares prior to a movement in their trading price.
F. The process of running down once prosperous industries and allowing other nations to provide the market that remains, regardless of its size.

Short answer questions

1. How might the business community help in raising the average standard of living of a country's citizens?
2. Why do governments promote balanced regional growth?

3. Outline why the numbers of people unemployed in EU countries continues to be historically high.
4. Explain why government considers it necessary to administer a competition policy.
5. In what ways should the business community gain from our entering the European single market?
6. Governments continue to offer consumers protection – why?
7. What are the main features of a legally binding contract?
8. Define:
   (a) goodwill
   (b) patents
   (c) copyright
   (d) trade marks
   (e) brands
9. Why was it thought necesary to pass the Data Protection Act 1984?
10. How do firms meet their social responsibilities?
11. Should business be concerned with 'green issues'?
12. In what ways are peoples attitudes to work altering?
13. Describe the ways in which life styles may differ in ten years time.

Data response questions

1. What would be the advantages to a UK based light engineering company of:
   (a) continued high levels of economic growth in Western Europe
   (b) increased standards offering in developing economies
   (c) upward movement in wage levels in Taiwan, South Korea and Malaysia?
2. Why might an adverse balance on the current account be beneficial to a domestic comapny heavily dependent on exports for sales revenue, and why might subsequent governemnt policy hinder profitability?
3. Explain and evaluate why you might consider setting-up a small charter airline from China to Liverpool (UK), the home of a number of large mail-order companies.

45

Coursework and projects in Business Studies

Preview

▼ A number of 'A' level syllabuses now offer a coursework or a project component. The opportunity to produce an 'external' piece of work may seem attractive, but they can be an option that causes problems.

▼ In this chapter we will try to unravel some of the difficulties encountered when coursework or projects appear on your syllabus (see Figure 45.1).

Board	Current options
London (ULEAC)	• 3 pieces of coursework of approximately 2,000 words in length (until 1997) then two pieces of 3,000 words • A project of 5,000 words (not after 1997)
Cambridge (UCLES)	Modular • a Research Assignment of at least 3,000 words Linear • a project of approximately 5,000 words
Associated Examination Board	Project, non compulsory 3000 + words (from 1998)

Note:

It is planned to provide four versions of assessment as from summer 1998. These will be:

Version   A – Non-modular without coursework

          B – Non-modular with coursework

          C – Modular without coursework

          D – Modular with coursework

***Figure 45.1** The Boards that offer coursework, projects or research assignments*

Coursework

These are 'untimed' pieces of work that can be completed at any time during your course of study. They are teacher assessed and then externally moderated. The aims of this type of work can be best summarised as:

- encouraging students to be aware of business through local studies
- allowing candidates to display evidence of careful observation and some originality
- providing an opportunity for the collection, selection and use of business information in ways which are appropriate to the chosen assignment
- promoting the demonstration of an awareness of a variety of solutions to business problems and the need to make reasoned statements and communicate these effectively.

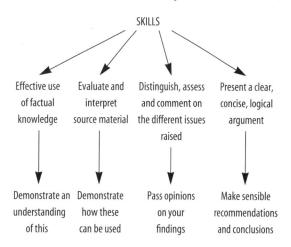

***Figure 45.2** The ingredients of a piece of coursework*

It is normal for the Examination Board to tell you what topics they expect analysed, you may then select what specific pieces of work you will attempt.

Length

It is expected that you will provide a piece of work, or pieces of work, that are at least 2000 words in length. The main issues to be covered are shown in Figure 45.2. If your coursework is to be marked out of 20 then the criteria used will be similar to this.

Mark

17–20 outstanding evidence of investigation, selection and interpretation of the subject matter, logically and carefully arranged

11–16 demonstration of good evidence of investigation, selection, etc.

5–10 some evidence of above

1–4 some evidence of positive achievement.

It is worth beginning from an awareness that examiners expect to see you perform better in coursework than in other components of your examination. What follows are based on our experience of reading other people's coursework.

1. Keep precisely to the topic being investigated.
2. Show clear evidence of having combined both field and desk research, and where possible relate your findings to relevant text book theory. This produces a pleasing degree of unity and cohesion.
3. Try not to be merely descriptive, but aim for an analytical piece of work.
4. Do not waste time and space including such inserts as Annual General Reports or transcripts of an interview. Once again you are supposed to analyse findings, and not merely report on the opinions of others.
5. Do not just pluck figures out of thin air, always support all your findings and calculations.

It is always pleasing to see a typed, bound and neatly presented piece of work, but remember that if you cannot provide such a document it does not matter. The Board examines your content, not your ability to produce documents.

Projects

The majority of these are suggested to be of at least 5000 words in length. A project affords you an opportunity to be adventurous and innovative. As such you are encouraged to aim for a blend of theory and practice that resolves an identifiable business problem.

Most Boards allow you to produce:

*   A project that embraces several relevant areas of the syllabus, so encouraging you to produce an interrelated piece of work.
*   A more specialised piece of work that concentrates on a narrower field within a discipline. This allows for greater emphasis on depth and precision of treatment.
*   A project concerned with a particular aspect.

You do not have to confine your research to a private company, as a public body, trades union or charity are also legitimate topics.

Presentation

You should produce a formal report, of approximately 5,000 words in length. Wherever possible you should use all methods of presentation available to you. All source material must be given a reference, but wherever possible you should use your own words. Try not to provide a large amount of printed material in support of your findings. It is seldom rewarded and costs large sums in postage!

Marking

If your project is to be marked out of 100 marks the scheme will be similar to what follows:

Assessment criteria

		Maximum marks
1.	Aims and Purposes of the project	10
2.	Application, terminology, convention, principles facts and appropriate technique	20
3.	Clarity of presentation, planning and logical sequence	20
4.	Analysis of information	20
5.	Content and comment	15
6.	Judgement and conclusions	15
	TOTAL	100

Some golden rules

*   Be careful of your choice of title. This greatly influences your ability to produce a tight and relevant piece of work.
*   If possible try to pose a question that provides a clear focus for the work, encourages the collection, processing and analysis of data and leads to a definite conclusion. Conversely, projects which centre on 'A Study of …' tend to be descriptive, lacking in focus and ultimately

inconclusive.

- Beware of topics that are only marginally business orientated in content, e.g. environmental issues. If you choose such a project you risk a low mark if the report is devoid of a business studies content.
- Some topics cannot be done justice in 5000 or even 10,000 words. It is advisable not to select such a title. Experience shows that the best projects are based on a single problem in a small business, or on a small unit of a larger business.
- Candidates do seem prone to select titles for which information is not available. The absence of relevant information leads to a descriptive, inconclusive and public relations dominated project.
- The best projects employ a number of techniques of business analysis, e.g. break even or payback. The use of such techniques where appropriate provides the route to a good mark.
- Background reading is very important. The best projects include a bibliography that goes beyond A Level texts, public relations materials, teachers' handouts and 'class notes'.
- Evaluation is often neglected in project writing.

You must try to pass a judgement about the validity or significance of the data you have produced.

- A good structure to follow is:
  - introduction: a clear, concise statement of the issue
  - a description of the business and its environment
  - the data from desk and/or field research underpinned by appropriate theory
  - analysis and evaluation of the data
  - conclusions and recommendations: this should be clear, concise and directly answer the questions posed in the introduction
  - bibliography
  - appendices - to be kept to a minimum

Essay techniques

Most syllabuses ask for essays or longer-styled responses. We introduce you to some guide essays: these are 'common themes' in business studies examinations. These guide answers are provided on page 500.

Appendix

Discount Table for Investment Appraisal

Present value of £1 received in the future

Years Hence	1%	2%	4%	6%	8%	10%	12%	13%	15%	16%	18%	20%	22%	24%	25%	26%	28%	30%	35%	40%	45%	50%
1	0.990	0.980	0.962	0.943	0.926	0.909	0.893	0.877	0.870	0.862	0.847	0.833	0.820	0.806	0.800	0.794	0.781	0.769	0.741	0.714	0.690	0.667
2	0.980	0.961	0.925	0.890	0.857	0.826	0.7978	0.769	0.756	0.743	0.718	0.694	0.672	0.650	0.640	0.630	0.610	0.592	0.549	0.510	0.476	0.444
3	0.971	0.942	0.889	0.840	0.794	0.751	0.712	0.675	0.658	0.641	0.609	0.579	0.551	0.524	0.512	0.500	0.477	0.455	0.406	0.364	0.328	0.296
4	0.961	0.924	0.855	0.792	0.735	0.683	0.636	0.592	0.572	0.552	0.516	0.482	0.451	0.423	0.410	0.397	0.373	0.350	0.301	0.260	0.226	0.198
5	0.951	0.906	0.822	0.747	0.681	0.621	0.567	0.519	0.497	0.476	0.437	0.402	0.370	0.341	0.328	0.315	0.291	0.269	0.223	0.186	0.156	0.132
6	0.942	0.888	0.790	0.705	0.630	0.564	0.507	0.456	0.432	0.410	0.370	0.335	0.303	0.275	0.262	0.250	0.227	0.207	0.165	0.133	0.108	0.088
7	0.933	0.871	0.760	0.665	0.583	0.513	0.452	0.400	0.376	0.354	0.314	0.279	0.249	0.222	0.210	0.198	0.178	0.159	0.122	0.095	0.074	0.059
8	0.923	0.853	0.731	0.627	0.540	0.467	0.404	0.351	0.327	0.305	0.266	0.233	0.204	0.179	0.168	0.157	0.139	0.123	0.091	0.068	0.051	0.039
9	0.914	0.837	0.703	0.592	0.500	0.424	0.361	0.308	0.284	0.263	0.225	0.194	0.167	0.144	0.134	0.125	0.108	0.094	0.067	0.048	0.035	0.026
10	0.905	0.820	0.676	0.558	0.463	0.386	0.322	0.270	0.247	0.227	0.191	0.162	0.137	0.116	0.107	0.099	0.085	0.073	0.050	0.035	0.024	0.017
11	0.896	0.804	0.650	0.527	0.429	0.350	0.287	0.237	0.215	0.195	0.162	0.135	0.112	0.094	0.086	0.079	0.066	0.056	0.037	0.025	0.017	0.012
12	0.887	0.788	0.625	0.497	0.397	0.319	0.257	0.208	0.187	0.168	0.137	0.112	0.092	0.076	0.069	0.062	0.052	0.043	0.027	0.018	0.012	0.008
13	0.879	0.773	0.601	0.469	0.368	0.290	0.229	0.182	0.163	0.145	0.116	0.093	0.075	0.061	0.055	0.050	0.040	0.033	0.020	0.013	0.008	0.005
14	0.870	0.758	0.577	0.442	0.340	0.263	0.205	0.160	0.141	0.125	0.099	0.078	0.062	0.049	0.044	0.039	0.032	0.025	0.015	0.009	0.006	0.003
15	0.861	0.743	0.555	0.417	0.315	0.239	0.183	0.140	0.123	0.108	0.084	0.065	0.051	0.040	0.035	0.031	0.025	0.020	0.011	0.006	0.004	0.002
16	0.853	0.728	0.534	0.394	0.292	0.218	0.163	0.123	0.107	0.093	0.071	0.054	0.042	0.032	0.028	0.025	0.019	0.015	0.008	0.005	0.003	0.002
17	0.844	0.714	0.513	0.371	0.270	0.198	0.146	0.108	0.093	0.080	0.060	0.045	0.034	0.026	0.023	0.020	0.015	0.012	0.006	0.003	0.002	0.001
18	0.836	0.700	0.494	0.350	0.250	0.180	0.130	0.095	0.081	0.069	0.051	0.038	0.028	0.021	0.018	0.016	0.012	0.009	0.005	0.002	0.001	0.001
19	0.828	0.686	0.475	0.331	0.232	0.164	0.116	0.083	0.070	0.060	0.043	0.031	0.023	0.017	0.014	0.012	0.009	0.007	0.003	0.002	0.001	
20	0.820	0.673	0.456	0.312	0.215	0.149	0.104	0.073	0.061	0.051	0.037	0.026	0.019	0.014	0.012	0.010	0.007	0.005	0.002	0.001	0.001	
21	0.811	0.660	0.439	0.294	0.199	0.135	0.093	0.064	0.053	0.044	0.031	0.022	0.015	0.011	0.009	0.008	0.006	0.004	0.002	0.001		
22	0.803	0.647	0.422	0.278	0.184	0.123	0.083	0.056	0.046	0.038	0.026	0.018	0.013	0.009	0.007	0.006	0.004	0.003	0.001	0.001		
23	0.795	0.634	0.406	0.262	0.170	0.112	0.074	0.049	0.040	0.033	0.022	0.015	0.010	0.007	0.006	0.005	0.003	0.002	0.001			
24	0.788	0.622	0.390	0.247	0.158	0.102	0.066	0.043	0.035	0.028	0.019	0.013	0.008	0.006	0.005	0.004	0.003	0.002	0.001			
25	0.780	0.610	0.375	0.233	0.146	0.092	0.059	0.038	0.030	0.024	0.016	0.010	0.007	0.005	0.004	0.003	0.002	0.001	0.001			
26	0.772	0.598	0.361	0.220	0.135	0.084	0.053	0.033	0.026	0.021	0.014	0.009	0.006	0.004	0.003	0.002	0.002	0.001				
27	0.764	0.586	0.347	0.207	0.125	0.076	0.047	0.029	0.023	0.018	0.011	0.007	0.005	0.003	0.002	0.002	0.001	0.001				
28	0.757	0.574	0.333	0.196	0.116	0.069	0.042	0.026	0.020	0.016	0.010	0.006	0.004	0.002	0.002	0.002	0.001	0.001				
29	0.749	0.563	0.321	0.185	0.107	0.063	0.037	0.022	0.017	0.014	0.008	0.005	0.003	0.002	0.002	0.001	0.001	0.001				
30	0.742	0.552	0.308	0.174	0.099	0.057	0.033	0.020	0.015	0.012	0.007	0.004	0.003	0.002	0.001	0.001	0.001					
40	0.672	0.453	0.208	0.097	0.046	0.022	0.011	0.005	0.004	0.003	0.001	0.001										

Answers

This section gives the answers for the 'mix and match' questions found at the end of the chapters.

Chapter 1
1 B; 2 K; 3 E; 4 G; 5 D; 6 H; 7 M; 8 A; 9 L; 10 F; 11 C; 12 I; 13 R; 14 O; 15 N; 16 J; 17 Q; 18 P

Chapter 2
1 E; 2 F; 3 H; 4 G; 5 N; 6 A; 7 M; 8 L; 9 C; 10 O; 11P; 12 I; 13 B; 14 D; 15 K; 16 J

Chapter 3
1 C; 2 I; 3 A; 4 L; 5 H; 6 E; 7 O; 8 N; 9B; 10 D; 11F; 12 J; 13 K; 14 G; 15 M

Chapter 4
1C; 2 D; 3 I; 4L; 5 K; 6 G; 7 A; 8 J; 9 F; 10 B; 11 H; 12 E

Chapter 5
1 G; 2 E; 3 I; 4 B; 5 O; 6 T; 7L; 8 N; 9 S; 10 R; 11 C; 12 J; 13 M; 14 P; 15 Q; 16 A; 17 K; 18 H; 19 F; 20 D

Chapter 7
1F; 2 P; 3 L; 4 M; 5B; 6 N; 7 T; 8 S; 9 H; 10 R; 11 Q; 12 J; 13 O; 14 K; 15 I, 16 E; 17 A; 18 G; 19 D; 20 C

Chapter 8
1 D; 2 H; 3 J; 4 I; 5 F; 6 G; 7 A; 8 E; 9 B; 10 C

Chapter 9
1 E; 2 I; 3 K; 4 N; 5 G; 6 O; 7 T; 8 J; 9 Q; 10 R; 11 L; 12 A; 13 D; 14 S; 15 H; 16 B; 17 P; 18 M; 19 F; 20 C

Chapter 10
1 B; 2 C; 3 F; 4 D; 5 J; 6 I; 7 A; 8 G; 9 H; 10 E

Chapter 11
1 C; 2 P; 3 H; 4 T; 5 K; 6 A; 7 Q; 8 L; 9 S; 10 E; 11 I; 12 B; 13 O; 14 J; 15 N; 16 F; 17 G; 18 R; 19 M; 20 D

Chapter 12
1 D; 2 F; 3 B; 4 H; 5 E; 6 A; 7 I; 8 L; 9 G; 10 K; 11 J; 12 C

Chapter 14
1 B; 2 F; 3 A; 4 J; 5 G; 6 C; 7 D; 8 I; 9 H; 10 E

Chapter 15
1 D; 2 I; 3 O; 4 B; 5 N; 6 H; 7 R; 8 K; 9 A; 10 G; 11 J; 12 T; 13 P; 14 E; 15 Q; 16 C; 17 S; 18 L; 19 M; 20 F

Chapter 16
1 D; 2 G; 3 M; 4 B; 5 J; 6 E; 7 I; 8 K 9 H; 10 A; 11 F; 12 L; 13 C; 14 N

Chapter 17
1 C; 2 F; 3 I; 4 A; 5 G; 6 H; 7 B; 8 E; 9 D; 10 J

Chapter 18
1 D; 2 I; 3 F; 4 M; 5 A; 6 J; 7 L; 8 E; 9 N; 10 B; 11 H; 12 K; 13 C; 14 G; 15 P; 16 R; 17 O; 18 Q

Chapter 19
1 B; 2 E; 3 I; 4 G; 5 L; 6 A; 7 F; 8 J; 9 C; 10 K; 11 H; 12 D

Chapter 20
1 D; 2 G; 3 I; 4 E; 5 B; 6 F; 7 J; 8 H; 9 A; 10 C

Chapter 21
1 F; 2 I; 3 B; 4 E; 5 H; 6 A; 7 J; 8 G; 9 D; 10 C

Chapter 23
1 D; 2 H; 3 A; 4 F; 5 I; 6 C; 7 E; 8 J; 9 B; 10 G

Chapter 24
1 B; 2 G; 3 C; 4 E; 5 I; 6 A; 7 F; 8 H; 9 J; 10 D

Chapter 25
1 D; 2 C; 3 E; 4 B; 5 A

Chapter 26
1 B; 2 D; 3 F; 4 A; 5 C; 6 E

Chapter 27
1 C; 2 A; 3 F; 4 D; 5 B; 6 E

Chapter 29
1 C; 2 A; 3 D; 4 E; 5 B

Chapter 30
1 B; 2 E; 3 C; 4 D; 5 A

Chapter 31
1 C; 2 D; 3 B; 4 E; 5 A; 6 I; 7 H; 8 K; 9 J; 10 G; 11 F; 12 L

Chapter 32
1 C; 2 I; 3 D; 4 J; 5 B; 6 E; 7 H; 8 F; 9 G; 10 A

Chapter 33
1 E; 2 D; 3 C; 4 B; 5 A

Chapter 34
1 B; 2 A; 3 D; 4 E; 5 C

Chapter 35
1 D; 2 B; 3 E; 4 A; 5 C

Chapter 36
1 G; 2 B; 3 F; 4 E; 5 C; 6 D; 7 A; 8 H

Chapter 37
1 B; 2 D; 3 E; 4 C; 5 A

Chapter 38
1 C; 2 B; 3 E; 4 A; 5 D

Chapter 39
1 B; 2 D; 3 E; 4 A; 5 C; 6 F

Chapter 40
1 D; 2 E; 3 B; 4 A; 5 C

Chapter 41
1 D; 2 A; 3 C; 4 E; 5 B

Chapter 42
1 C; 2 D; 3 A; 4 E; 5 B

Chapter 43
1 C; 2 D; 3 A; 4 E; 5 B

Chapter 44
1 B; 2 D; 3 F; 4 A; 5 E; 6 C

Short question answers

This section gives some sample answers to the short questions found at the end of each chapter.

Chapter 1: Business calculations – VAT

VAT is **added** to the price wanted/charged by the seller to fix the **ticket price**.

1. Firm's price + VAT = Ticket price

$$£350 + 25\% = ?$$
$$? = £350 \times 1.25$$
$$= £437.50$$

2. Firm's Price + VAT = Ticket price

$$? + 25\% = £550$$
$$? = £550/1.25 = £440$$

Therefore VAT paid = £110 = 20% of ticket price

5(i) Firm's price + VAT = Ticket price

$$? + 35\% = £600$$
$$? = £600/1.35 = £444.4$$

(ii) 444.4 + 18 ½% = ?

$$? = £444.4 \times 1.185$$
$$= £526.7 - \text{New ticket price}$$

8.

Firm	A	B
Production cost	£50	£55
Man mark-up	+ 20%	+ 20%
Selling price	£60	£66
+ VAT	+25%	+25%
Price to wholesalers	£75	£82.5
W. mark-up	+30%	+30%
Selling price	£97.5	£107.25
+ VAT	+25%	+25%
Price to retailer	£121.87	£134.06
R. mark-up	+50%	+50%
Selling price	£182.8	£201.09
+ VAT	+25%	+25%
Customer price	£228.51	£251.37

Difference £22.86 (Note: only £5 difference in production cost.)

Chapter 2: Data response question 2

(b) (i)

Year	1986	1987	Δ	%Δ
Annual sales	£2.2 bn	£3.1 bn	3.1 –2.2 = 0.9	0.9/2.2 x 100 = 41%
Units operated	12,500	15,000	15,000 – 12,500 = 2,500	2,500 ÷ 15,000 x 100 = 17%
Jobs	149,000	169,000	169,000 – 149,000 = 20,000	20,000 ÷ 169,000 x 100 = 12%

Chapter 4: Data response questions

1. **Maze Green Builders**
2. Cash flow

Cash Flow Forecast: Original Data (Units: £000s)

Month	J	F	M	A	M	J	J	A	S	O	N	D
Cash inflow (Sales)	100	100	100	300	300	400	400	300	300	200	200	100
Cash outflow (Build)												
Total Outflow	(40)	(90)	(90)	(90)	(90)	(90)	(90)	(90)	(90)	(90)	(90)	(90)
Net Cash flow	60	10	10	210	210	310	310	210	210	110	110	10
Bank Balance												
Opening Balance	(330)	(270)	(260)	(250)	(40)	170	480	790	1000	1210	1320	1430
Change	60	10	10	210	210	310	310	210	210	110	110	10
Closing Balance	(270)	(260)	(250)	(40)	170	480	790	1000	1210	1320	1430	1440

1. Profit = Sales – Cost of sales (irrespective of any credits given/taken).

Planned sales = 28 =	£2,800,000
Cost of sales: £60,000/house	(£1,680,000)
Gross profit	1,120,000
O/heads: £10,000 per month	(120,000)
Net profit	£1,000,000

3. Revised profits

Planned sales = 21 = £2,100,000	
Cost of sales	(1,260,000)
Gross profit	£840,000
O/heads	(120,000)
Net profit	£720,000

4. Revised cash flow: Assumption – Firm cannot adjust its building programme in the balance of the year

Month	J	A	S	O	N	D
Sales	200	200	100	100	100	100
Cash outflow	(90)	(90)	(90)	(90)	(90)	(90)
Net cash flow	110	110	10	10	10	10
Opening balance	480	590	700	710	720	730
Change	110	110	10	10	10	10
Closing balance	590	700	710	720	730	740

Note change in housing stock: Opening Stock (6) + Build (24) equals 30, minus sell (21) equals Closing Stock of 9 (cash tied up).

2. The main chance

(a) Profit = Sales – Cost of sales (ignoring credits)   Fixed: £5000 x 6   (£30,000)

Sales (A S inclusive)   1260   Net profit   £45,600 – Yes, it is profitable.

Prices £100/unit.

Therefore sales revenue   £126,000

Costs: Variable £40/unit   (£50,400)

                                  £75,600

	J	F	M	A	M	J	J	A	S	O	N	D
Sales (units)	100	120	140	160	180	200	220	240	260	280	300	320
Sales (Value: £'000s)	10	12	14	16	18	20	22	24	26	28	30	32
Cash received	-	-	-	10	12	14	16	18	20	22	24	26
Var. cost value (£'000S)	4	4.8	5.6	6.4	7.2	8	8.8	9.6	10.4	11.2	12	12.8
VC Paid	(5.6)	(6.4)	(7.2)	(8.0)	(8.8)	(9.6)	(10.4)	(11.2)	(12.0)	(12.8)	-	-
FC Paid	(5.0)	(5.0)	(5.0)	(5.0)	(5.0)	(5.0)	(5.0)	(5.0)	(5.0)	(5.0)	(5.0)	(5.0)
Total				(13.0)	(13.8)	(14.6)	(15.4)	(16.2)	(17.0)	(17.8)		
Net Cash Flow (£/000s)				(3.0)	(1.8)	(0.6)	0.6	1.8	3.0	4.2		
Bank account (£'000s)												
Opening balance		10		7		5.2		4.6		5.2		7.0
Change		(3.0)		(1.8)		(0.6)		0.6		1.8		3.0
Closing balance		7		5.2		4.6		5.2		7.0		10.0

(c) Sales: 1380 Revenue £138,000 (VCs £55,200) Gross profit £82,800 (Forecasts £30,000) Net profit £52,800 – an increase.

Cash flow chart	J	F	M	A	M	J	J	A	S	O	N
Sales (Units)	100	120	140	160	180	200	240	280	320	360	400
Cash received (£s)				10	12	14	16	18	20	24	28
VC paid (£'000s)				(8.0)	(9.6)	(11.2)	12.8	14.4	16.0)		
FC (£'000s)				(5.0)	(5.0)	(5.0)	(5.0)	(5.0)	(5.0)		
Total paid (£'000s)				(13.0)	(14.6)	(16.2)	(17.8)	(19.4)	(21.0)		
Net cash flow				(3.0)	(2.6)	(2.2)	(1.8)	(*1.4)	(1.0)		
Bank balance											
Opening balance		10		7.0		4.4		2.2		0.4	(1.0)
Change		(3.0)		(2.6)		(2.2)		(1.8)		(1.4)	(1.0)
Closing balance		7.0		4.4		2.2		0.4		(1.0)	(2.0)

But cash flow is worse. Overdraft seems to be just growing!

4. *CD plc and its accounts*

	A	M	J	J	A	S	O	N	D	J	F	M
Sales (Records-K)	200	250	300	350	400	500	500	4350	400	400	350	300
Sales value (£)m	2.4	3.0	3.6	4.2	4.8	6.0	6.0	5.4	4.8	4.8	4.2	3.6
Cash in (£m)				2.4	3.0	3.6	4.2	4.8	6.0	6.0	5.4	4.8
Production	250	250	350	400	450	500	500	600	600	450	450	450
Labour (£m) (+ S. Variables)	(1.25)	(1.25)	(1.75)	(2.0)	(2.25)	(2.5)	(2.5)	(3.0)	(3.0)	(2.25)	(2.25)	(2.25)
Mats	-	-	(0.88)	(0.88)	(1.23)	(1.40)	(1.58)	(1.75)	(1.75)	2.00)	(2.00)	(1.58)
Overheads		Tr	Tr	Tr	Tr	Tr	Tr	Tr	Tr	Tr	Tr	Tr
Royalty			-	-			(0.1)					
Cash out			(2.9)	(3.5)	(3.9)	(4.1)	(4.8)	(4.8)	(4.8)	(4.3)	(4.3)	(3.8)
Net cash flow			(0.5)	(0.5)	(0.3)	0.1	-	1.2	1.7	1.1	1.0

Answers

Chapter 7: Break-even calculation

DR1 P = 10/u VC = 6/u FC = 20,000/m
BEQ = 20,000/10-6 = 20,000/4 = 5,000u/m
DR2 P = 12 VC = 7 C = 50,000
BEQ = 50,000/12-7 = 50,000/5 = 10,000
Since CAP = 20,000 and Plan = 15,000
Margin of safety = 5,000 or 5,000/10,000 x 100% (50%)
Case Study 1
Key calculations:
DCs £20 FC £200,000 P = £30
BEQ = 200,000 ÷ 30-20 = 20,000 units.
1. Current Price: Sales 30,000 – M of S = 10,000 or 50%
2. P = 28 BEQ = 200,000 ÷ 8 = 25,000 units.
Sales 37,500 – M of S = 12,500 or 50%.
Profit: Current price (30,000 (3) – [(30,000) 20 + (200,000)]
900,000 – (600,000 + 200,000) = £200,000
Cut price (37,500) (28) – [(37,500) 20 + (200,000)]
1,050,000 – (750,000 + 250,000) = £100,000
No change, so must check other, non-financial factors.

Chapter 9: Case study and data response

1. %Δ Income = +10% Demand = +5%
   Income elasticity of demand = $\frac{+5\%}{+10\%}$ = 0.5

2. P1 250 Q1 30,000
   P2 300 Q2 18,000
   Q1-Q2/ Q1 = 20,000 - 18,000/ 20,000 = 2,000/ 20,000
   = 0.1
   P1–P2/ P1 = 250 - 300/ 250 = –50/ 250 = 1 5 = –0.2
   Price elasticity of demand = 0.1/ –0.2 = – 0.5

4. Cross price elasticity of CDs against price of players =
   %Δ Demand for CDs % Δ Price for players
   P1 = 250 P2 = 275
   P1–P2/ P1 = – 25/ 250 = – 0.1
   So % Δ Demand – 0.1 = 0.75
   Therefore % Δ Demand = + 0.075
   = + 7 1/2 %
   Sales were 150,000, New 161,250
   i.e. Increase of 11,250 units/month.

6. *Contribution statement*

Product	P Cases	D Cases	Fitted sheets	Total
Sales	100,000	120,000	70,000	290,000
VC's	75,000	102,000	52,500	
Contribution	25,000	18,000	17,500	60,500
			O/heads	47,100
			Profit (loss)	13,400

Analyse based on this. Cutting any line will not increase
profits since all make a positive contribution.

Chapter 10: Case Study 1

(a) Project: 04/007 Warrington Injection Moulder
Approved: 01/94   Review: 04/94
Part 1 Completed activities (Units: £'000s)

Cost centre	Budget	Actual	Variance
Section 1. Buildings and related services			
Buildings	15	18	+3
Related Services	25	22	–3
Sub-total	40	40	0

Section 2. Plant and equipment

Plant	250	260	+10
PVC's	10	8	–2
Utilities	50	60	+10
Instrumentation	30	25	–5
Mechanical Services	50	60	+10
Electrical Services	70	–	–
Sub-total	460	413	+23

Section 3. Installation and commissioning

Contractors	50
Co engineers	10
Travel and hotels	5
Sub total	65
Total	565
Contingencies	35
Grand total	600

Part 2 Incomplete activities

	Budge used	Actual variance	
Electrical services	40	50	+10
Contraction	30	50	+20
	70	100	+30

(b) Budget used	Variance	%
40 + 390 + 70		
500	+43	+8.6

% of budget: 83%
Expected outcome: £563 + 8.6% = £611,400
Full contingencies will be used.
Saving of £11,400 will keep budget at 600.
(Hard to achieve at this late stage.)

Chapter 12: Data response questions

1 a (i) Pre-tax profits were by 18.5% to £16m
   Therefore £16m is 118.5% of the previous profit.
   Therefore Profit for previous 6 months = £13.5m
   (Check: Increase = £2.5m
   = 2.5 13.5 x 100 = 18.5% - OK)
   a (ii) Sales were down 10.5% at £332.2m
   i.e. £332.2m is 89.5% of earlier level.
   therefore Sales were £371.2m
   (Check: 371.2 - 332.2 371.2 x 100 = 10.5?)
   a (iii) Profit/Sales ratio

Period (6 mth)	to 31st March	to 30 September
Profit	£13.5m	£16m
Sales	£371.2m	£332.2m
Ratio	3.6%	4.8%

'Good' improvement but need to have:
(i)   data for more periods.
(ii)   data for other firms in the same industry.
Actual levels seem low.

3. *Time Wire Ltd.*

	Was	Change	Plan
Sales Revenue (80,000 @ £20)	1,600,000	+ 20%	
(£19)	1,824,000		
DCs	(800,000)	+ 80% **	(960,000)
P O/heads	(300,000)		(300,000)
Gross profit	500,0000		564,000
M & S O/heads			
S. Persons Salaries	(80,000)	+ 14K	(94,000)
S. Admin	(40,000)	+ 14K	(54,000)
A + SP	(80,000	+ 20%	(96,000)

M Research	(20,000)		(20,000)
	(220,000)		(264,000)
Ad. O/heads	(100,000)	20%of GP	(112,800)
	(320,000)		(376,800)
Net profit	180,000		187,200
Net profit/sales	11.25%		10.26%

Chapter 18: Short answer questions

3. £1 = 2090 Lira = 323 Dr
   So 2090 L = 323 Dr
   2,090,000 L = 323,000 Dr
   1,000,000 L = $\frac{323,000}{2.09}$ Dr
   = 154,545 Drachmae

Chapter 19: Data response

2(b)

Year	Ad. Expenditure	Sales
1986	£2m	105 ml
1987	£2.5m	150 ml

Ad. Elasticity of demand = $\frac{\% \Delta \text{ Demand}}{\% \Delta \text{ Advertising}}$

% Δ Ad. = 0.5/2 = 25%
Ad. Elasticity = 43/25 = + 1.7

Chapter 23: Data response questions

		Output	Efficiency
1	Disc Inserter	10u/min	0.85
2	Label Setter	15	0.8
3	Overwrapper	12	0.75
4	Cartoner 10s	2 x 10 = 20	0.8
5	Bulk Packer - 12 x 10's	1 x 20 = 120	0.7
6	Transit wrapper	1 x 120 = 120	0.75
		(Based on Discs)	

(b) All units have to operate to get any output. This will
   happen for only (0.85 x 0.8 x 0.75 x 0.8 x 0.7 x 0.75),
   0.21 or 21% of the time.
   Rate is determined by the slowest stage – Disc Inserter.
   Therefore reliable long-term output = 10 x .21
   or 2.1 discs/min.
   or 1 bulk pack every 120/ 2.1 = 57.1 min.
(c) Try breaking the unit into 2, 3 or more stages with
   buffer stock areas between.

Chapter 24: Short answers
Data response questions
(a) Stock card

Date	Purchases	Sales	Stock	Av. Cost
1.1.92	50 @ £165	-	50	165
10.1.92	200 @ £143	-	250	
31.1.92	-	180 @ £175	70	
1.2.92	120 @ £170	-	190	
28.2.92	-	120 @ £215	70	
2.3.92	220 @ £210	-	290	
31.3.92	-	250 @ £230	40	
Total	590 @ ?	550 @ ?	590-550	
			40 check	

(Note the ability to set up check calculation columns or
rows.)

Av. Cost of Phones: 50 x 165 = 8,250
                  + 200 x 143 = 28,600
                  + 120 x 170 = 20,400
                  + 220 x 210 = 46,200
                  Σ 590 103,450
Av. cost = £175.34/phone.
FIFO cost = £230 LIFO = £165
Sales revenue: 180 x £175 = 31,500
             + 120 x £215 = 25,800
             + 250 x £230 = 57,500
                          114,800
Cost of sales = Opening stock + Purchases – Closing stock.
Opening stock = 0
Purchases = 103,450
Therefore cost of sales = £103,450 = Closing stock.
Closing stock = 40 phones.
Unit Value = FIFO =£230
LIFO =£165
AC =£175
Therefore cost of sales

	FIFO	LIFO	AV.
Purchases	103,450	103,450	103,450
Stock	9,200	6,600	7,000
Therefore cost of sales	94,250	96,850	96,450

Profit and loss account

	FIFO	LIFO	AC
SALES	£114,800	£114,800	
£114,800			
(Cost of sales)	94,250	96,850	96,450
Gross Profit	20,550	17,950	18,350
(Tax Liability	Maximum	Minimum	Average)

Chapter 27: Data response questions

1.

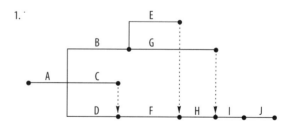

2.

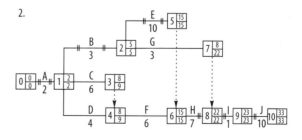

Critical path A – B – E – H – I – J

Sample essays and answers

To be of assistance to both teachers and students we have provided a set of guide answers to questions which are typical of the main issues that are examined by the Boards.

They are only guidelines. Where past examination questions have been used, the answers given represent our opinions and not necessarily those that would be used by the relevant Examination Board.

What are transnational corporations? What are their importance?

'An enterprise that owns and controls assets in various countries'. So, we have a clear 'focus' of ownership, but how much needs to be owned to have control? Is it 51%, or less?

Control may be exerted through – sub-contracting, franchising, licencing, joint-ventures, etc. The 'main' company may only have a relatively small head office staff, but it could operate on a world-wide basis, e.g. Laura Ashley. It may therefore be better to consider a TNC as 'a corporation that controls production in more than one country'.

Some analysts consider that TNCs have a larger impact on manufacturing output than pure statistics show. At present (early 90s) TNCs in UK control: 24% of UK manufacturing sales; 15% of total UK manufacturing employment.

It is therefore safe to say that TNCs are important in UK manufacturing and have a prominent position in the service industries.

Benefits: balance of payments, employment, technology.

Can you complain about TNCs in your economy if you want to export your own capital to other economies?

Against: How long does the employment last? Do they provide lasting exports? Are they so large that they can influence governments? Are they good payers? Do they provide good conditions for workers? How long will they stay before moving to another low-cost production country?

Other issues: dual sourcing = reduction in worker power; transfer pricing = keeps rewards low to sourcing country, and profits high to selling/production country.

Summary: What is a TNC? Can we accurately monitor/measure them? What benefits do they bring? What problems might they cause? Are they too big for national control?

How do exchange rates affect business?

External factors affect business decisions. Costs, competition and customers are the most important influence on business activity. Exchange rates influence costs of imports and exports global market for currencies.

E. rate – 'the price at which your own currency exchanges for that of others'

Different groups of people are interested in exchange rates. tourists – costs of holidays; speculators – profits/losses on 'gambles'; business – cost of imports, prices of exports.

When a business sells on credit it is taking a risk, this is centre on no payment, or a price that has lost all or a part of its profit since it was agreed.

Buys raw materials, components, part-finished goods or services from overseas → *A business* → Sells the same on international markets

The 'position' you hold in the overseas market and the 'proportion' of your output being exported will influence the affect of currency movements on your business.

The elasticity of demand for your product will also have an influence on its export competitiveness

Influences – interest rates; balance of payments; inflation; supply of money; political issues.

The value of a currency depends on the demand for and supply of it.

If your currency floats downwards, then you have to pay more to acquire foreign currency. If your currency floats upwards, then you have to pay less for foreign currency. This in turn affects the costs of imports and the price of exports.

Some mention of ERM. Global trading/trading blocks, a single currency, LIFFE.

Summary: Exchange rate is part of business environment and can effect a business that either imports or exports; it depends on the demand for and supply of the currency; elasticity of demand is an important part of this area of planning; some possible ideas have been put forward to control 'fluctuations'.

Why is effective communication in business important?

'Who says what by which means to whom to what effect'

Good communications = message received and understood, by all those affected by it.

This should allow the majority to accept the organisation they work in, for it all depends on their understanding and participation in the communication process.

Gaps do appear and these may be caused by barriers – poor vocabulary, technical terms, training/education of the individual, etc. These may show themselves via low morale, absenteeism, high labour turnover, and even strikes.

Vertical communications: (a) official chain of command via middle managers and supervisors; (b) via union officials; (c) grapevine.

Lateral communications: between groups at same level within hierachal organisations.

Poor communications routes can cause: information to go to wrong people; some people are by passed; information is destroyed; delays occur; people make assumptions, and these can be wrong; poor expression of message; the recipient can't understand the message; current knowledge is poorly used; secrecy = speculation; insufficient information – increased risk of disagreement; unwillingness to listen; tendency to evaluate and not listen.

Downward communication – Rigid structure, downward flows of communication (i.e. specific task direction, corporate goals, but can be prone to misinterpretation as too many layers for message to pass through).

Upward communication – Normally used to question, provide feedback, make complaints, but managers are less accustomed to receiving information, therefore flows in this direction may be subject to scrutiny and may have been 'lost'.

Vertical communication – Mainly used for task co-ordination, problem-solving, information sharing and conflict resolution. Some managers may fear a reduction in their authority. Such structures may create barriers as: 'patch defending'; tunnel vision/one department only exists! too little comm-unication with others outside the department; over-use of jargon; channels are selected on personal preference; some managers don't like sharing information; effective internal communication is taken for granted and is not managed.

Effective communication should: increase individual performance; improve understanding of company procedures; encourage employee participation; meet legal requirements; improve a sense of belonging amongst employees.

How do we achieve this? clarify before communi-cations; examine the purpose of the communication; think of where the message will be received; consult and plan before release of message; be aware of non-verbal content; make communication receiver-orientated; follow-up comunications; make your actions consistent with your words; listen to reactions; accept criterion and change if necessary.

Why do firms locate where they do?

'Classic' business studies dilemma for 'it all depends' (context-specific).

Location is an 'operational' issue, it always involves a risk and centres on a diverse set of variables (local, national and international).

Type of organisation	Principal location influences
Manufacturing	movement/transport of items from suppliers and to customers.
Supply	proximity to customers and the movement/transport of goods from suppliers.
Service	proximity to customers and/or at a pace that will be acceptable to customers.
Transport	proximity to customers e.g. easy access for starting point.

Location is in four Ps under Place. A firm must be in a competitive position if it manufactures, and at a convenient service delivery point if it's non-manufacturing.

Databases can be used to discover (a) geodemographic dispersal of customers; (b) concentration of customers

Costs of location have to be considered: (a) *fixed* – determined by nature of location e.g. rates; (b) *variable* – determined by accessibility, e.g. transport of raw materials.

Location may also be determined by geographic variation in: quantity, cost, quality of materials, labour, energy and services. A whole range of 'subjective' factors must be considered: local communities and their attitudes have an influence; the site must be examined for scope for growth; employees will be concerned about housing, education and recreation; location image can influence employees and customers; external economies of scale; crime in an area.

The location decision is a *key* part of business strategy.

Why are people the most important asset of an organisation?

Often the most expensive asset owned/managed by an enterprise is its staff.

Management has to aim to produce the most profitable output from this asset. They therefore must: plan, organise, direct and control: but as organisations become more complex these become more difficult to achieve.

People's behaviour is influenced by a number of factors; managers are involved via – selection/recruitment, utilising the asset (motivation), developing the asset (training), and maintaining the organisation (introducing change).

Selection – 'only as good as the people it selects'. different corporate cultures PE – fit, costs of failure/mistakes; procedures, tests; monitoring outcome; changes in social standards/traditions.

Motivation – money, activity, variety, temporal structure, social contacts, status and identity within society; application of technology.

Training – increase abilities; plan succession; flexibility; future planning; cost-effective.

Maintaining the organisation: manage change; corporate philosophies; new products; R & D; restructuring/downsizing; pooling resources; deve-loping skills; moving into new markets.

All of the above affect people, yet without their co-operation they will fail or under achieve.

Human Resource Development (HRD) is essential to individual companies and the country.

Off Balance Sheet items have considerable influence on corporate performance.

Ignore staff at a managers peril!

What is total quality management?

Useful to start from 'focusing on meeting the requirements of customers'.

So, we are aiming to produce a quality product or service that meets the purpose for which it has been purchased. Even this has problems in being applied to all customers, but certain essential features can be identified!

(i) How closely does the design/specification of the product/service meet the customer requirement?

(ii) How closely does the delivered product conform to the design?

Systems now aim for Zero Defects (ZD), which means less waste, easier stock management (JIT), the use of quality circles (QCs) and effective after-sales service.

Move away from statistical quality control, acceptance of some errors towards quality assurance and a process that does not produce mistakes.

Considerable influence of US and Japan through QCs and JIT. They have development systems that reduce defects to a few parts per million. This has boosted productivity, and widened margins, while keeping prices competitive.

Quality is everybody's business, no longer the sole responsibility of Quality Control Dept.; TQM = 'do unto others as you would have done unto you'. Quality has to permeate the entire organisation and not just the quality of supply to external customers.

TQM aim at **preventing** defects, not **detecting** them.

Concentrate on: design, delivery, and service.

TQM = documented quality management system; statistical tools and techniques; teamwork.

BS5750 and EU counterpart.

The financial pay off of TQM

TQM = Reduced costs = Increased profits.

Higher quality with constant prices = increased market share = higher profits.

Higher quality = better output, = price increases without eroding market share = higher profits.

Index